MW00783703

ENVIRONMENTAL SYSTEMS AND PROCESSES

ENVIRONMENTAL SYSTEMS AND PROCESSES
PRINCIPLES, MODELING, AND DESIGN

Walter J. Weber, Jr.

A JOHN WILEY & SONS, INC., PUBLICATION

New York • Chichester • Weinheim • Brisbane • Singapore • Toronto

For ordering and customer service, call 1-800-CALL-WILEY.

Library of Congress Cataloging-in-Publication Data:

Library of Congress Cataloging-in-Publication Data is available.
ISBN 0-471-40518-3

Printed in the United States of America.

10 9 8 7 6 5 4 3 2

. . . In the spirit of learning to fish . . .

आपोसमं, राहुल, भावनं भावेहि।
आपो मम, सत्था ।

Preface

The need for diligent stewardship of our environment has never been as clearly and compellingly documented as it is today. Fortunately, we are also better positioned than ever before to exercise such stewardship, at least in terms of relevant science and technology. This book is about that science and technology, and the manner of its use to preserve, sustain, and improve our environment and its ecosystems.

It would be a transpicuous understatement of fact to say that the environment is complex. It is, however, a matter of fact that environmental complexity relates more to innate scales and dimensions than to inherent concepts and principles. This premise serving as incentive, our approach in this book to understanding and explaining the environment and its myriad systems and processes is to: i) clearly enunciate concepts and related principles; ii) initiate analyses on scales at which the principles can be defined and applied rigorously; iii) use simple but accurate mathematical models to articulate those principles; and, iv) structure more elaborate models to integrate all relevant principles and thus facilitate their extension *comme ensemble* to the scale of any system or process of interest. There is an ancient Chinese proverb that says to give a man a fish will feed him for a day, but to teach him to fish will feed him for a lifetime. In this same spirit, I believe that anyone can solve *a* problem if given the correct algorithm, but it is the knowledge of how to use concepts and principles to construct correct algorithms that enables one to solve *any* problem.

While the relevant principles of science are straightforward, the multimedia character of the environment clouds their illustration and early understanding with further complexity. I have thus elected to use one principal medium for teaching and demonstrating these principles, and methods for extending them as needed in temporal and spatial scales. As artists generally select some specific medium (e.g., music, sculpture, painting, oils, watercolors) in which to express themselves, so scientists and engineers select some medium (e.g., medicine, biology, chemistry, engineering) within which to articulate concepts, principles, and their applications to particular systems. In part by fortune and in part by fancy, water is the environmental medium in which I have concentrated my professional exercise of principles, models, and designs. By logical choice, I select that medium to illustrate the art of environmental science and engineering in this text. If some defense of this selection is needed, I invoke Aristotle's attribution to Thales that, *the principle is water*, and Siddhartha Guatama's reflection that, *water is my teacher*. Be assured, however, that virtually every illustration of scientific principle and its application herein has one or more immediate parallels in every environmental medium. Irrespective of the medium or media in which environmental scientists and engineers focus their practice and practice their art, their works are based on the very same principles; said principles are indeed common to *all* foci of science and technology.

This book has its roots in undergraduate and graduate courses developed and taught at the University of Michigan. My hope is that it reaches out effectively to more than those personally taught and mentored in Ann Arbor. To some the material presented will be familiar, perhaps even second nature. To a larger audience it will be relatively new, and likely challenging. It is this audience for whom the book is written, for I believe the material it contains should ultimately *become second nature* to all environmental students and practitioners. Many of the most basic concepts presented in the text and their more obvious applications are introduced at Michigan in a sophomore-level environmental engineering and science course. Many students "stay the course" to concentrate further in environmental science and engineering studies, and these students are expected to master the content of the book by the time they are seniors. The book also serves as an introductory text for incoming graduate students, who are expected to develop a command of the material by the end of their first academic year in the program. We welcome opportunities to share experiences with any who may wish to use such approaches. My personal experience in teaching is that students rise to the levels at which they are meaningfully challenged, and I have found that the approaches developed herein work well.

The book is indexed somewhat uniquely to facilitate its integrated use across two or more courses. The index consists of six parts, four of which arrange subjects within the following topical groupings: i) an introduction to environmental systems and processes, ii) process energetics and equilibria, iii) process rates and mass transfer, and iv) system modeling and design. This allows identification of topical issues in the respective contexts of their applications. The examples developed for the text are specifically designed to be teaching tools rather than simple "plug and chug" exercises; they are therefore indexed separately in the fifth part of the index according to the principles, processes, and types of systems they involve. The sixth part is a more conventional subject index presenting selected key words and identifying pages in the text that contain related discussions, figures, tables, and/or examples.

The approach I have used to develop an understanding of and to explain environmental systems and the processes that drive them was outlined earlier. The principles are largely chemical and physical in nature, and the models used to describe them are modest in form but precise in detail. The designs advanced are predicated on accurate models of rigorous principles that control processes in the context of specific systems. Chemical and physical principles are extended to biological systems by presenting biological reactions as chemical reactions catalyzed by organisms for extraction of sustaining energy and generation of biomass. This is by no means meant to trivialize biological processes and phenomena, but simply to highlight relevant chemical principles.

All physical, chemical, and biological processes have two dominant characteristics by which they can be commonly identified and quantified. The first is the form and amount of energy available to make them occur, and the second is the speed or rate at which that energy is exercised to effect change. The latter of these common process features depends on many things. It depends upon the numbers (or masses) and the reactivities (or stabilities) of the "energy rich" and "energy poor" partners of a process, and on the pathways available to these partners for effecting their interaction in the context of a given system. In more pointed terms, all environmental processes depend upon: i) the availability of energy; ii) a means for that energy to be exercised in the time frame of interest; and, iii) a system of such spatial and physical characteristics that it allows the reactants to "communicate" for purposes of reaction. *These are the three tenets of environmental systems.* For successful descriptions and/or designs of such systems, these tenets must be: i) understood on the basis of fundamental principles; ii) represented rigorously in functional form; and, iii) integrated accurately with the functional forms of other pertinent governing principles in appropriate system models. For the complex systems with which we must deal ultimately in practice, empiricism and judgement are required to bridge gaps in absolute knowledge. It is therefore often necessary that we make assumptions in applying the above tenets. If we understand the functions and constraints embodied in the principles involved, our assumptions will be rational.

Environmental Systems and Processes is a derivative work, an offspring of *Process Dynamics in Environmental Systems*. The latter was a collaborative effort with a long-time friend and esteemed colleague, Professor Francis A. Di Giano of the University of North Carolina at Chapel Hill. Fran's keen insights and clear thinking are thus everywhere evident in this book, as they were in *Process Dynamics*. As is true for much of what I have written in my life, my students have left indelible marks on this book. Many have done so by challenging me to be as good as they expect me to be, and thus keeping me intellectually on my toes. Others have done so by patiently noting and helping me address glitches in various draft versions of the text. Particularly constructive efforts were made in these and other regards by Martin D. Johnson, Thomas M. Keinath II, Patrick B. Moore, and Andrew C. Woerner, all Michigan graduate students who worked with me at various times during the commission of this work. Marty Johnson and Mike Keinath provided input and feedback from beginning to end, while Pat Moore and Andy Woerner helped at the outset in developing a framework of appropriate subject coverage and level of approach. Susan De Zeeuw played the same invaluable role in the production of this book as she did in that of *Process Dynamics*, and Carrie Jankowski, a Michigan undergraduate at the time, provided Sue and I with able and creative assistance in the process. All of these individuals, and others not specifically mentioned, should feel a measure of "ownership" in this work.

Walter J. Weber, Jr.

Ann Arbor, Michigan

Contents

Chapter 1

Environmental Systems and Processes

Contents

1.0   CHAPTER OBJECTIVES

To develop an appreciation of the identifying features and important characteristics of environmental systems and processes that must be factored into their analysis, modeling, and design.

1.1   ENVIRONMENTAL PROCESSES

1.1.1   Processes and Systems

Engineers and scientists who deal with environmental systems are ultimately concerned with changes that result from processes occurring within them. It is thus logical to begin our discussion with the latter and then explore their roles in various types of systems of interest. Examples of such processes and their effects on environmental systems include: (1) acidification of rainfall by power plant emissions; (2) removal of gaseous sulfur oxides from power plant emissions by wet limestone scrubbing; (3) contamination of groundwater and subsurface soils by seepage from landfills; (4) removal of contaminants from water supplies by treatment with activated carbon; (5) consumption of dissolved oxygen by microbial degradation of organic matter in rivers and lakes; and, (6) reduction of the biochemical oxygen demand (BOD) of a wastewater by biological treatment prior to discharge to a receiving water. Each change in these examples is underlain by a specific process. Some processes take place in natural environmental systems while others occur in engineered systems.

Six different types of environmental systems are cited above, but they involve a total of only three fundamentally different processes; i.e., phase transfer (gas-liquid) and acid-base reactions in the first two examples, phase transfer (liquid-solid) reactions in the second two, and biological oxidation-reduction reactions in the last two examples. These three processes are operative in a large number of other types of systems as well. The point to be emphasized is that environmental systems are virtually limitless in number, but change is controlled by a relatively small number of fundamental processes.

The approaches we take to characterize and analyze processes are in most regards similar for natural and engineered systems. The underlying goal is to understand the cause of change in any system. Change in natural systems such as rivers or subsurface aquifers often occurs in an uncontrolled manner. Alternatively, change in engineered treatment systems is usually controlled to accomplish specific results. Each process is modified in extent and effect by the nature of the system in which it occurs. For example, microbial exertion of BOD takes place more rapidly and efficiently in a biological treatment plant than it does in a river because the plant is designed to support and enhance the process.

A number of processes common to a variety of environmental systems are identified and described in Table 1.1. For each process, examples are given

Table 1.1 Examples of Environmental Processes

Process	Engineered	Natural	Green-Tech
Absorption by Liquids	Aeration to provide dissolved oxygen in biological treatment systems (e.g., activated sludge systems).	Dissolution of atmospheric oxygen into lakes, streams, and estuaries.	Scrubbing and recovery of volatile compounds from process off-gas streams.
Adsorption by Solids	Removal of organic contaminants by activated carbon in water and wastewater treatment systems.	Adsorption of organic contaminants from groundwaters by soils and sediments.	Organic intermediate and product recovery by polymeric adsorbents.
Biochemical Transformation	Degradation of organic contaminants in biological treatment systems.	Biochemical oxygen demand (BOD) exertion in receiving waters.	Fermentation of waste biomass to produce fatty acid chemical and fuel stocks.
Chemical Transformation	Oxidation of organic compounds by ozone in contaminated surface or subsurface water supplies.	Oxidation of dissolved organic contaminants in surface waters by photochemically generated free radicals.	Utilization of chlorine dioxide for pulp and paper bleaching.
Chemical Precipitation	Removal of heavy metals and phosphates in wastewater treatment, and hardness ions (e.g., Ca^{2+} and Mg^{2+}) in water treatment.	Iron oxide deposition at wetted interfaces and deposition of calcium carbonates and magnesium silicates on submerged surfaces.	Removal of lead and other heavy metals from mine wastes using sulfate-reducing microorganism in anaerobic biocell filters.
Coagulation	Destabilization of suspended solids by inorganic coagulants or organic polyelectrolytes, in water and wastewater treatment.	Destabilization of colloids by natural salts in marine estuaries, or by natural biopolymers in fresh waters.	Destabilization of colloidal precipitates by organic polyelectrolytes in metal recovery and recycle processes.
Disinfection and Sterilization	Destruction or inactivation of pathogens using chemicals, heat, or shortwave irradiation.	Destruction or inactivation of organisms by naturally occurring chemical conditions, heat, or irradiation (e.g., sunlight).	Organism inactivation and growth suppression environmentally using benign reagents
Filtration	Removal of suspended solids from waters and wastes by deep-bed or septum filtration.	Deposition of bacteria and other colloid suspensions in subsurface systems.	Capture of aerosols in paint booth, coating, and plastics extrusion and casting operations.
Ion Exchange	Removal of metals from water and wastes by ion exchange; (e.g., softening, demineralization).	Multivalent cation uptake and retardation by soils.	Recovery of precious metals from inorganic process streams using ion selective exchange resins.
Membrane Separations	Desalination of brackish waters by reverse osmosis and electrodialysis.	Separation of dissolved oxygen from water by the gill membranes of fish.	Combustionless burning of hydrogen with oxygen in membrane fuel cells.
Thermal Transformation	Incineration of organic wastes.	Incineration of natural and man-made organic materials in volcanic eruptions and forest fires.	Molten-metal manufacturing of commercial products from heterogeneous organic wastes.
Volatilization	Stripping of taste and odor compounds from drinking waters, ammonia from wastes, and volatile organic contaminants from groundwaters.	Release of hydrogen sulfide from benthic deposits and overlying waters into the atmosphere.	Depressurization of spent supercritical CO_2 solvents and reaction media.

of a common engineered system application, a related phenomenon in natural environmental systems, and an example that is germane to the goal of environmentally friendly or benign industrial practices; i.e., "green-tech" systems. The examples given in Table 1.1, while focusing primarily on water quality transformations, generally occur in complex systems comprising multiple phases; i.e., gases, liquids and solids. As such, they are among the most complex of environmental processes. *Despite the inherent complexity of multi-phase environmental systems, however, need and practice have led in most instances to a substantial understanding of their dynamics, largely because the basic principles of process dynamics are common to all systems, and thus broadly applicable.*

1.1.2 Process Categories

Processes of interest in environmental systems can be divided into two principal categories, those affecting the transformation of particular constituents and those affecting their transport at either the macroscale (system scale) or the microscale (molecular scale). Transport processes at the macroscale include those affecting movement of constituents in the bulk of a system and across its boundaries. Transport processes at the microscale include small range diffusion processes that occur primarily at the interfaces between phases comprising a system. Microscale transport from one phase to another is generally referred to as mass transfer.

An example of a macroscale transport process is the flow of residual organic matter and associated BOD into a body of water in the effluent discharge from a wastewater treatment plant. The diffusion of atmospheric oxygen into the water body to accommodate the BOD introduced by the effluent discharge is an example of a microscale mass transfer process. Such mass transfer processes often control the rates at which system components contact and subsequently undergo reaction with one another. The nature of the reaction(s) underlying each process identified in Table 1.1 and the potential involvement of mass transfer (molecular scale) phenomena in controlling the reaction(s) are presented in Table 1.2. These topics are dealt with in detail in subsequent chapters.

It is evident from Table 1.2 that transformation processes of interest in environmental systems generally involve combined reaction and mass transfer considerations, irrespective of the systems in which they take place. This is the case whether the reaction processes are chemical, biochemical or physicochemical in nature. It is important to note that the system itself imposes important additional mass transport considerations at the larger scale; i.e., macroscale mass transport. Reaction and transport processes, which by themselves might be quite common in character, thus act in concert in any system to produce changes in composition that are for the most part unique to that system, each system being like a different symphony played by the same orchestra

Table 1.2 Reactions and Associated Mass Transfer Phenomena

Process	Nature of Reaction(s)	Mass Transfer
Absorption by Liquids	Gas/liquid mass transfer and dissolution of molecular oxygen.	Molecular diffusion of oxygen at air-water interfaces.
Adsorption by Solids	Interactions and accumulation of solutes at solid surfaces.	Interfacial and intraparticle diffusion of dissolved solutes.
Biochemical Transformation	Enzyme mediated transformations of chemical species by electron transfer.	Diffusion of substrates, nutrients, and metabolic products across microbial cell walls.
Chemical Transformation	Phase transformations of chemical species by electron transfer reactions.	Molecular diffusion of reacting species in quiescent systems and zones of stagnation.
Chemical Precipitation	Phase transformations of chemical species by coordination-partner exchange reactions.	Interfacial and intraparticle diffusion associated with crystallization and particle growth phenomena.
Coagulation	Modifications of particle surface and near surface chemistry to reduce particle-particle repulsions.	Molecular diffusion of dissolved species into particle double layers and to particle surfaces.
Disinfection and Sterilization	Enzyme inactivation, protein, denaturing, or cell lysis.	Mass or heat transfer across cell membranes.
Filtration	Particles or aggregate interception and accumulation at solid surfaces.	Microscopic particle transport and interfacial deposition.
Ion Exchange	Exchange of ions of like but unequal charge at charged surfaces.	Interfacial and intraparticle ion diffusion for porous ion exchange resins.
Membrane Separations	Selective separations of molecular species by microporous barriers.	Molecular diffusion across solid/water interfaces and within microporous membranes.
Thermal Transformation	Transformation of chemical species by electron transfer reactions at elevated temperatures in heterogeneous phase systems.	Gas-solid mass and heat transfer.
Volatilization	Phase transformations by volatilization at moderate (ambient) temperatures.	Molecular diffusion across phase interfaces.

1.1.3   Transformation Processes

Transformations in environmental systems have their bases in the reactions and interactions of chemical species with one another. All constituents of environmental systems are fundamentally chemicals, thus changes or transformations in them can be described in terms of chemical reactions. We should be careful here to differentiate between transformation processes, and the net changes that occur as a result of such processes in complex systems. Transformation processes are comprised by reactions, and in some cases by microscale mass transfer processes that control the rates of those reactions. Conversely, net changes in concentrations of reactants in systems involve additional (mass transport) considerations at the system scale, considerations that depend more on the system in which the reactions take place than on the reactions themselves. For example, the rates of most reactions are dependent on the masses (or concentrations) of the reacting substances. Therefore, if the concentrations of a reacting substance in various locations within an unstirred tank vary, the reaction rates in those locations will vary accordingly. Conversely, if stirring sufficient to completely mix the contents is introduced the concentrations and rates of reaction will be uniform throughout the tank. *These two different operational circumstances can yield much different rates of overall transformation.*

Chemical reaction phenomena adhere to a rigorous set of governing principles that establish a basis for quantification of environmental transformations. Certain of these principles derive from the thermodynamics and control the energetics of reactions. Some are involved in control of the intrinsic rates or kinetics of reactions, which are different than overall transformation rates if the latter are controlled by microscale mass transfer processes.

1.1.4   Transport Processes

Many processes of environmental interest involve transformations and mass transfer phenomena that occur at molecular or particle scales. *Molecular or particle scale transport processes are essentially processes within processes, fundamentally unaltered in character by the size and configuration of the system in which they occur. Conversely, the degree to which such processes operate to change the character of a system in which they occur is markedly dependent on their spatial (size and distance related) and temporal (time related at any spatial point) distributions (e.g., how they are distributed along a section of river or within a series of carbon adsorption beds). This dependence on scale relates to the fact that the influence of every one of these fundamental processes is dependent upon the masses of materials reacted or transferred. The distribution of these masses is, in turn, dependent on transport phenomena taking place at the system scale.*

To quantify environmental changes one must consider first the nature of fundamental processes involved and then interpret the way in which system properties influence the nature of those processes. Example 1.1 illustrates, in a qualitative and relatively intuitive way, how a process, in this example the oxidation of an organic compound by ozone, can be influenced by the physical characteristics of the system in which it takes place.

Example 1.1.   Oxidation of an Organic Compound by Ozone in Physically Different Systems I. (An illustration of the effects of system configuration and physical characteristics on process rates and efficiencies; phase and mixing effects.)

- *Situation.* Ozone and a moderately volatile organic compound are added in identical amounts to three sealed 1-L jars. The jars, or "systems," differ only in the following regards:

  System 1 contains ozone, the organic compound, and air;

  System 2 contains ozone, the organic compound, and water; and

  System 3 is the same as System 2, but there is a magnetic stirrer in the jar to mix its contents completely and continuously.

- *Question(s).* In which system will the organic compound be most rapidly oxidized by the ozone, and in which system will it be most slowly oxidized?

- *Assumption(s).* Assume that the organic compound and the ozone are both completely soluble in water. Assume also that the mechanism by which the molecules of these substances react with each other is the same whether they are in a gaseous state or a dissolved state. Assume also that the systems are all at the same temperature. These assumptions mean that any organic molecule that contacts any ozone molecule in any phase or system involved will react in exactly the same manner and at the same intrinsic reaction rate.

- *Logic and Answer(s).* Physical reality dictates that contact between molecules is required for a chemical reaction to occur. Molecules contained in a gas phase are free to move about rapidly under the influence of Brownian motion and thermal-gradient mixing, with little resistance to this motion being caused by other gas molecules. Water, on the other hand, is a dense matrix of molecules that presents a substantial resistance to Brownian motion and requires large thermal gradients to cause mixing of the water molecules and thus there are fewer contacts between dissolved molecules (i.e., water is much more viscous than air). The reaction will therefore take place much more rapidly in System 1 than in System 2. System 3 is physically mixed, enhancing molecular contacts and causing a greater number of contacts per unit time than will occur in System 2, which is otherwise identical. Nonetheless, the enforced mixing in System 3, regardless of how vigorous, cannot produce molecular collisions at a rate *as high as those occurring in unhindered movement of molecules in the gas phase. The rate of oxidation of the organic compound will thus be lowest in System 2.*

- *Key Point(s). Rates and extents of transformation and mass transfer processes that take place in a system are determined by the masses of materials being reacted or transferred, and the distribution of these masses is determined in turn by the nature of the system. Thus rates and extents of reaction, mass transport, mass transfer and therefore overall transformation are system specific.*

We thus distinguish between those elements of change that are rooted in reactions and mass transfer processes at the molecular level, and those that relate to the more macroscopic character and properties of the systems in which the processes take place. This distinction constitutes an overriding theme in our analyses of the process dynamics, modeling and design of environmental systems. We will pursue each aspect of process dynamics in detail, and persistently underscore the way in which they interact to motivate and control environmental change.

Let's first consider the similarities and differences between two broad categories of environmental systems, natural and engineered, and then address the temporal and spatial scales associated with those two categories of systems.

1.2   ENVIRONMENTAL SYSTEMS

1.2.1   Natural and Engineered

In natural systems we are concerned with understanding and describing changes in constituent concentrations and other quality parameters, while in engineered systems we are concerned with the selection of conditions required to effectively accomplish specific changes in concentrations and quality parameters. As illustrated in Tables 1.1 and 1.2, and depicted schematically in Figure 1.1, there are common aspects of concern for these two major categories of systems, and common ways in which those concerns are addressed.

Dissolved oxygen, for example, is a critical parameter for maintenance of desirable ecological conditions in natural aquatic systems as well as in engineered biological treatment systems, although the specific ecological conditions in the two systems are generally quite different. A typical process analysis for a natural aquatic system might involve measurement and characterization of the physical, chemical, and biological features of a lake or a section of a river to

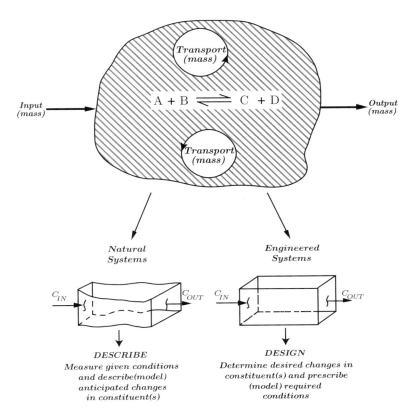

Figure 1.1 Transport and Transformation Processes

assess how a waste discharge containing a biologically degradable organic substance will change dissolved oxygen levels. This analysis would involve several of the individual processes listed in Table 1.1. In this case the analysis leads to a quantitative description, or model, of how dissolved oxygen varies temporally and spatially in that lake or section of a river.

An engineered-system counterpart might be a tank in which a biological or chemical treatment operation is used to reduce the oxygen-consuming properties of a waste prior to its discharge to a surface water. Any biological process by which the waste is treated in the tank may well be similar to that by which it consumes oxygen in the river or lake; i.e., by aerobic (oxygen using) microbially mediated transformation of organic matter. In this situation the same individual processes in Table 1.1 would be involved. Conversely, the waste may be chemically transformed using a highly reactive form of oxygen, such as ozone or hydrogen peroxide.

Process analysis and model development in the case of engineered systems focus on prescribing conditions required to ensure desired levels of microbial or chemical transformation of the organic waste. These considerations include: (1)

appropriate levels of oxygen, ozone, or hydrogen peroxide; (2) spatial factors (size and mixing); and, (3) temporal (holding or residence time) properties of the system.

While the objectives, information requirements, and expected results for natural and engineered systems are usually quite different, the underlying processes and principles of change are essentially the same. Similarly, the methods by which the processes are analyzed and described should be fundamentally the same. Successful approaches to system characterization, process analyses, and quantification of components and constituent changes must, in every instance, be based on the same principles and precepts of process dynamics.

1.2.2 Character and Scale

At the most elementary level we distinguish the character of a system on the basis of its scale. By character we mean the properties of a system and the nature of changes that occur within it. By scale we mean the size (spatial scale) of the system and the time (temporal scale) that together determine the boundaries within and over which the changes of interest occur. Figure 1.2 depicts a generalized multiphase

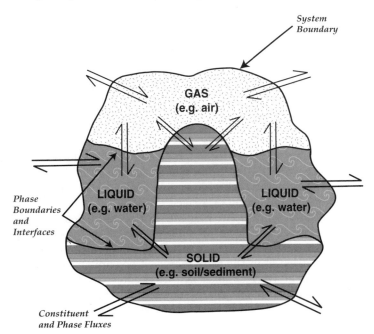

Figure 1.2 A Multi-Phase System

system of gaseous, liquid, and solid phases. In any particular application of process analysis we may be concerned with all three phases. Alternatively, we may be concerned with (or choose for simplification in some cases to limit our analysis to) considerations of changes within only one phase. Such single-phase characterizations can generally be accommodated by appropriate definition of system boundaries. *It is important to note, however, that the composition of each phase depicted in Figure 1.2 changes as a result of phase and constituent mass reductions and additions that may occur not only by reactions among constituents within the boundaries of phase, but also by movement of mass across its phase boundaries and accumulations or depletions within interfaces at those phase boundaries.*

The system shown in Figure 1.2 is schematic in terms of its components and configuration and unspecified in terms of its spatial scale. *As suggested in Figure 1.3, the environment is in fact a continuum of systems involving similar processes over a remarkable range of temporal and spatial scales.* The schematic given in Figure 1.2 might, in the context of Figure 1.3, be a representation of an extremely large megascale system, such as that comprising the lakes *Superior, Michigan, Huron, Erie* and *Ontario*; i.e., the *Great Lakes*. Here the gas phase would be the atmosphere, the aqueous phase

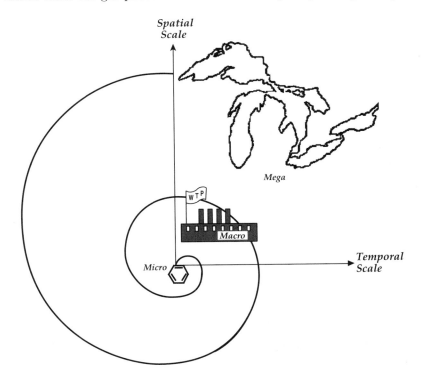

Figure 1.3 The Environmental Continuum

the hydrosphere, and the solid phase the lithosphere. We may be concerned in such a system with the long-term exchange of a dissolved constituent between the water column, the overlying atmosphere, and the underlying and suspended sediments. The boundaries and volumes of megascale systems are inherently difficult to describe. Significant changes in composition occur only over extended periods of time; typically, decades and centuries. Because megascale systems lack precise spatial and temporal detail, their descriptions warrant no more than correspondingly coarse quantification of the transport and transformation processes that take place at or within their boundaries.

The microscale counterpart of the megascale system example might be a sediment particle suspended in the nearshore waters of *Lake Michigan*. The local environment of that particle might well be comprised by the same components as those in Figure 1.2, with the particle itself being a complex "solid" phase suspended in the aqueous medium. The gas phase might consist of attached air bubbles generated by abiotic or biotic gas production within or on the surfaces of the particle, or by air entrapment or cavitation induced by wave action. This particle-scale system is subject to precise boundary quantification, and within it a variety of transformations might take place over short periods.

This text focuses primarily on systems that have time and space scales smaller than those of megascale systems. We will address macroscale systems having boundaries that are better defined than those of global systems, and that are commonly measured in fractions or multiples of meters. Transformations of interest in such macroscale systems occur within time periods ranging from tens of minutes to days in the case of most engineered operations to weeks and months for most natural systems. *Importantly, the behaviors of such macroscale systems are often markedly dependent on processes that occur within them at the microscale*.

A macroscale system in the context of Figure 1.3 might be comprised by an activated carbon absorber designed and engineered for removing traces of pesticides from *Lake Michigan* water in a water treatment plant (WTP) prior to distribution as a municipal water supply. In this case the scale of the carbon adsorber is on the order of meters, and the residence time of water within it on the order of minutes or hours. At the same time, this macroscale system is comprised by a multitude of particles of granular activated carbon of millimeter or micron scale. Like the particles suspended in the nearshore waters of *Lake Michigan*, each of these particles represents a microscale system wherein the pesticide interacts at the molecular level. We can thus further define, within each carbon particle, transport and reaction scales of microscopic and molecular levels, as suggested in Figure 1.4.

All systems are comprised by subsystems; megascale systems by macroscale systems, and macroscale systems by microscale systems. This is why many of the processes described in Table 1.1 can be influenced at the macroscopic scale by similar microscopic mass transfer phenomena. The most fundamental analysis of any system has its origins ultimately at the molecular level, and must provide that there is a continuity of principles derived from this scale to the full scale

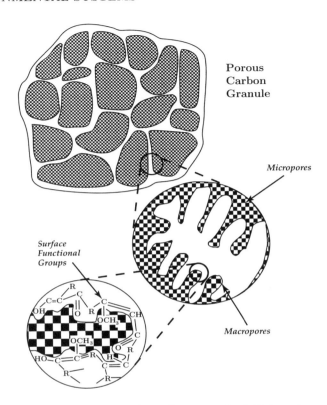

Figure 1.4 All Systems Are Composed of Subsystems

of the system. The description, analysis, or design of a megascale system or a macroscale system frequently involves characterization and quantification of processes at several levels of scale. The design of the activated carbon adsorber entails description of transport processes at both macroscale and microscale, as suggested schematically in Figure 1.5a . At the macroscale, bulk flow into and out of the adsorber carries organic matter to the external surfaces of the carbon particles. Once the organic matter reaches the external surfaces of the porous particles of activated carbon, it begins to diffuse into the pore structure and ultimately be adsorbed (reacted) on internal surfaces. In practice this second level of molecular or microscale mass transport frequently controls the overall rate of the process and residence time requirements for the adsorber. These same considerations are appropriate for the sorption of organic contaminants by soil and other aquifer material, and for the ultimate design of soil remediation operations such as vapor extraction of volatile organic contaminants (VOCs) from non-aqueous phase liquids (NAPLs), as depicted in Figure 1.5b.

Any analysis of a process for purposes of description or design must couple descriptions of phenomena at the appropriate microscale with those of phenomena at the macro or mega scales.

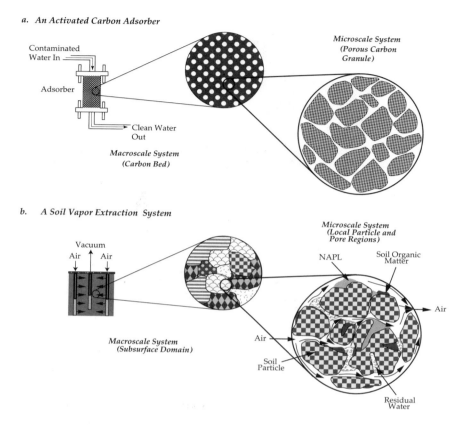

Figure 1.5 Integrated Macroscale and Microscale Systems

Many natural and engineered environmental systems involve multilevel scale and transport considerations similar to those described for the activated carbon adsorber. The necessity for these considerations often arises because more than one phase is involved. Therefore, interphase mass transfer, which implies microscale and molecular phenomena at phase interfaces, is involved. *It is essential that we appreciate the role of microscale process dynamics and understand how to incorporate information on processes at this scale in the characterization, analysis, interpretation, and design of environmental macroscale systems.*

Process characterization and analysis must be rigorous at all scales at which the gathering of data and development of information for process description are applied. For example, we can obtain accurate and detailed information about process reactions from small-scale laboratory observations, but only if the constraints of the systems in which such observations are made are accounted for and properly factored into the analysis of resulting data.

The effects of system size and configuration on mass transport and distribution must be properly recognized and separated from those aspects of a process that pertain to reactions only. The subsequent use of reaction rate data so obtained may then be applied to other systems of any scale or configuration as long as proper account is again made of the size, configuration, and properties of the system to which the information is applied. All of these considerations factor into what we refer to as spatial and temporal scaling.

Example 1.2 provides further illustration of how the physical characteristics of a system in which a process occurs can affect its rate and efficiency; in this case the size or scale of the system.

Example 1.2. Oxidation of an Organic Compound by Ozone in Physically Different Systems II. (An illustration of the effects of system configuration and physical characteristics on process rates and efficiencies; effects of system scale.)

- *Situation.* In Example 1.1 we considered the dependence of the rate at which a process occurs on different physical conditions in similarly sized systems. To now illustrate some of the points discussed above relative to scale, consider a fourth type of system, a series of three sealed reactor vessels, each filled half with air and half with water. The first is a 1-L jar, the second a 100-L carboy, and the third a 10,000-L tank. All three reactors are cylindrically shaped, and have the same ratio of cross sectional area to depth. In each there is a single 2-bladed rotating mixer blade located exactly in the middle of that volume of tank containing the water. The blades are the same size in each reactor, and all operate at the same number of revolutions per minute.

- *Question(s).* If the gas/liquid mass ratios for both the ozone and the organic compound are $2:1$ in each system at all times, and simultaneous reactions take place in both phases, will the overall rate of oxidation of the organic compound per unit volume of reactor be the same in each system?

- *Logic and Answer(s).* The rates of oxidation per unit volume of reactor will for several reasons not be the same in each system. First, all of the systems have the same energy input for mixing of the liquid phase; i.e., all blades are the same size and turn at the same rpm. The effectiveness of mixers of equal size and rotation rate in establishing completely mixed conditions will decrease with increasing size of the reactor, thus distributions of reacting masses will differ. Second, no purposeful mixing of the gas phase is provided in any of the reactors. Thus, as the volume of the gas phase in the series of three systems increases, the distances over which incidental mixing of that phase (caused by mixing of the liquid phase and the resulting shear at the water interface, by thermal gradients and by Brownian motion operate) increase, causing differences in the mixing conditions of the gas phase from reactor to reactor. Finally, the gas-phase reaction *will be more rapid than the liquid-phase reaction in each tank. Because both the ozone and organic compound are volatile, each will tend to move from the liquid phase to the gas phase as the latter is depleted to maintain the stipulated condition of a 2 : 1 molecular distribution of each reactant between the two phases. Movement of the molecules through the greater depths of liquid in the larger systems will mean a slower replenishment of molecules in the gas phase of the reactors. For these several reasons, the 1-L system will most closely approximate complete mixing; i.e., a homogeneous distribution of reacting masses. The large reactors, on the other hand, will deviate increasingly with size from complete mixing; i.e., will have increasingly different distributions of reacting masses, and thus different overall rates and extents of reaction per unit volume. As we move through our developments of process dynamics in this book, we will learn ways in which to quantify these differences.*

- *Key Point(s). Unless special steps are taken to ensure otherwise, mass distributions, and thus the rates and extents of transformation or mass transfer processes will vary as functions of system scale (i.e., reactor size).*

1.2.3   Components and Change

The components of environmental systems, like the properties of processes and changes that occur within them, are frequently categorized as physical, chemical, and biological. In the most elementary sense, however, all of these components are chemical. Examples common to the systems discussed above include: (1) inert particulate solids; (2) biochemically and chemically degradable organic substances, both dissolved and associated with particulate solids; (3) microbial organisms that use dissolved oxygen as the electron acceptor in oxidation of these chemicals; and, (4) other, more "activated" forms of oxygen, such as ozone or hydrogen peroxide, that do not require biological mediation. All of the above are comprised by chemicals. Inorganic particulates, for example, are largely mineral structures such as clays or sands, and organic solids and microbial organisms are highly structured arrangements of organic compounds.

More than 100 discrete chemical elements having different but well ordered combinations of neutrons and protons in the nuclei of their respective atoms and related numbers of electrons surrounding those nuclei have been identified. The ordered arrangement of these elements according to numbers of associated, positively charged elementary atomic particles (protons) is characterized in the *Periodic Chart*, or Periodic Arrangement of Chemical Elements, an abridged version of which is given in Figure 1.6.

The atomic number of an element on the periodic chart is equivalent to the number of protons in its nucleus. The "periodic law"

Group Number

Legend:

Atomic Number	Element Symbol
	Atomic Mass
	Other Oxidation State(s)

	IA	IIA	IIIA	IVA	VA	VIA	VIIA	← VIIIA →			IB	IIB	IIIB	IVB	VB	VIB	VIIB	VIIIB
Principal Oxidation State(s)	I	II	III	IV	V	VI	VII	II,III	II,III	→	I	II	III	IV	III,V	—	-I	0
1	1 H 1.008 NONE																	2 He 4.003 NONE
2	3 Li 6.939 NONE	4 Be 9.012 NONE											5 B 10.81 NONE	6 C 12.01 II,IV	7 N 14.01 II,IV-III	8 O 16.00 -II	9 F 19.00 NONE	10 Ne 20.18 NONE
3	11 Na 22.99 NONE	12 Mg 24.31 NONE											13 Al 26.98 NONE	14 Si 28.09 II,IV	15 P 30.97 IV,-III	16 S 32.06 II,IV,VI,-II	17 Cl 35.45 I,III,V,VII	18 Ar 39.95 NONE
4	19 K 39.10 NONE	20 Ca 40.08 NONE	21 Sc 44.96 NONE	22 Ti 47.90 III	23 V 50.94 II,III,IV	24 Cr 52.00 II,III	25 Mn 54.94 II,III,VI,VII	26 Fe 55.85 NONE	27 Co 58.93 NONE	28 Ni 58.71 III	29 Cu 63.54 II	30 Zn 65.37 NONE	31 Ga 69.72 NONE	32 Ge 72.59 II	33 As 74.92 -III	34 Se 78.96 IV,VI,-II	35 Br 79.91 IV	36 Kr 83.80 NONE
5	37 Rb 85.47 NONE	38 Sr 87.62 NONE	39 Y 88.91 NONE	40 Zr 91.22 NONE	41 Nb 92.91 III	42 Mo 95.94 II,III,IV,V	43 Tc (99) NONE	44 Ru 101.1 IV,V,VI,VIII	45 Rh 102.9 IV	46 Pd 106.4 IV	47 Ag 107.9 NONE	48 Cd 112.4 NONE	49 In 114.8 NONE	50 Sn 118.7 II	51 Sb 121.8 -III	52 Te 127.6 IV,VI,-II	53 I 126.9 I,V,VII	54 Xe 131.3 NONE
6	55 Cs 132.9 NONE	56 Ba 137.3 NONE	57 La 138.9 NONE	72 Hf 178.5 NONE	73 Ta 180.9 NONE	74 W 183.9 II,III,IV,V	75 Re 186.2 II,IV,VI,-I	76 Os 190.2 IV,V,VI,VIII	77 Ir 192.2 I,VI	78 Pt 195.1 IV	79 Au 197.0 III	80 Hg 200.6 I	81 Tl 204.4 I	82 Pb 207.2 II	83 Bi 209.0 NONE	84 Po (209) II,IV	85 At (210) I,III,V,VII	86 Rn (222) NONE
7	87 Fr (223) NONE	88 Ra (226) NONE	89 Ac (227) NONE															

Figure 1.6 Abridged* Periodic Chart or Arrangement of the Chemical Elements

* Above chart excludes lanthanide series (atomic numbers 58–71) and elements above atomic number 89.

of chemistry states that the physicochemical properties of the fundamental chemical elements are functionally related to their atomic numbers, and recur periodically when the elements are arranged in the orders of these numbers. In other words chemical science is not a matter of chance and/or rote memory, it is a matter of clear and readily applicable logic. Depending upon the balance or lack of balance between the number of electrons associated with any element at any time and its fixed number of protons, that element exists in an "oxidation state" that can be either stable or unstable as an atomic or molecular entity. The principal oxidation states (e.g., O, -I, II, etc.) identified in Figure 1.6 indicate the smaller or larger number of electrons than its fixed number of protons an element must have to become stable. The only elements that are naturally stable are those in Group VIIIB. To say that an element is stable is to say that it is in a favorable energy state with respect to its surroundings. If it is in an unfavorable energy state it will attempt to undergo some change in its electron structure to achieve a more stable state. This, however, will always require that it enter some reaction with another element to form mutually stable electron conditions. More will be said on this subject in Chapters 5 and 6, and elsewhere. *Suffice it now to say that, with more than 100 elements, each potentially having a variety of unstable electron states, virtually tens of thousands of different reactions among these unstable entities can occur in the environment to yield perhaps a million or more different combinations of chemical species, or environmental system constituents.*

It is evident from the principal oxidation states identified in Figure 1.6 that the elements that can most readily reach a stable state from their natural unstable state are those in groups I and VII. These elements, sodium and chlorine for example, can become and persist as essentially inactive species in the environment by respectively giving away or adding only one electron to become ions (i.e., Na^+ and Cl^-). Because elements in other groups must give away or add more than one electron to achieve a stable state, they are likely to be less "decisive" in their reaction behaviors, particularly if they can achieve transitory semi-stable states. This tendency is suggested by an element having one or more "other" oxidation states. In terms of environmental reactivity, the "hotspot" of the periodic table centers about carbon (C), nitrogen (N), oxygen (O), phosphorus (P), and hydrogen (H), these elements being among the most active in terms of forming large numbers of different and environmentally significant species. Can you deduce or at least speculate why this is the case?

Any constituent of a system that neither changes in composition nor causes change in any other component of the system may be considered environmentally stable, but we must distinguish important differences between chemical stability and environmental stability. The chloride ion, Cl^- is an example of a chemically and environmentally stable constituent of most natural waters and wastewaters. On the other hand, the parent element chlorine is both chemically and environmentally unstable. Chloride has eight electrons in its outer shell (same electron configuration as the inert gas argon) and thus remains virtually constant in concentration and has little or no effect on changes in the environmental quality of waters or wastes in treatment processes, other than those specifically designed for removal of dissolved salts. Changes in its concentration may signal other changes in composition, but do not result from actions of the chloride itself to modify water quality. Chlorine, having seven electrons in its outer shell and wanting to become more stable reacts readily with other constituents of waters and wastewaters to change their form and to undergo change itself, simply to add one more electron to become Cl^-. Like ozone and hydrogen peroxide, chlorine is a strong oxidant because of its high degree of instability and reactivity and is commonly employed for oxidation of inorganic and organic contaminants.

Because chlorine has oxidation states other than -I however (and particularly because those are positive oxidation states), certain chlorine-containing substances, such as polychlorinated biphenyls (PCBs), are not nearly as chemically unreactive and environmentally benign as the chloride ion. PCBs are chemically or thermodynamically stable in the sense that they do not readily undergo change in their chemical form under normal environmental conditions, but they can cause major changes in environmental quality by inducing toxic and carcinogenic reactions in living cells into which they find their way (i.e., if ingested by living organisms).

When present in water or wastewaters, environmentally reactive compounds are generally targeted for change, either by removal in phase separation processes such as precipitation, adsorption, or volatilization, or by transformation in some chemical or biochemical reaction process. The choice of the process depends on certain properties of the targeted compounds, their reactive tendencies, and their resultant susceptibility to specific separation or transformation phenomena. The reactor design should be one that maximizes the effectiveness of the process selected.

Ways in which reactor conditions can be designed to maximize the effectiveness of the process that we considered in Examples 1.1 and 1.2 are illustrated in Example 1.3.

Example 1.3. Oxidation of an Organic Compound by Ozone In Physically Different Systems III. (An illustration of the effects of system configuration and physical characteristics on process rates and efficiencies; system design to enhance process performance.)

- *Situation. A drinking water supply contains a volatile organic contaminant that can be destroyed effectively by ozone. The conditions surrounding this reaction are similar to those described in Examples 1.1 and 1.2.*

- *Question(s). Discuss several ways in which one might consider designing reactor conditions to maximize the effectiveness of the oxidation process.*

- *Logic and Answer(s).* We note that this reaction can be carried out more rapidly in the gas phase than in the liquid phase in the systems examined. This circumstance may be used to advantage in the design of a treatment system by carrying out the bulk of the transformation process in the gas phase. Specific considerations might include:

  1. ways in which to configure the system to maximize surface area and minimize water depth;

  2. mixing the water to facilitate movement of molecules to the liquid surface (gas-liquid interface);

  3. dispersing gas bubbles through the liquid to increase the gas-liquid interfacial area and reduce the liquid phase distances over which molecules have to move to reach the gas phase;

  4. collecting the gas phase continuously to keep the contaminant concentration in that phase low and thus increase the rate of its movement into the gas to maintain a $2:1$ distribution; and,

  5. compressing the collected gas to bring contaminant molecules into more immediate contact with one another to speed up the reaction rate per unit volume of gas phase.

  The problem posed in this example is a fairly common one for decontamination of groundwaters containing volatile compounds such as gasoline hydrocarbons and chlorinated solvents. The process may be restricted in some cases simply to "stripping" the organic contaminants from the water and dispersing them to the atmosphere, or to vapor phase adsorbers. Systems to accomplish this may involve bubbling air through the water, as indicated above, or more efficiently by allowing the water to drain over the surfaces of a loosely packed and highly porous tower of solid media while air is forced through the tower in the opposite direction; i.e., a countercurrent air stripper. In other cases the gas must be treated before release to destroy the organic contaminant, as in the example above. Because gases are compressible, concentrations of contaminants and reactants can be increased by increased pressure, and this is frequently done to provide higher reaction rates and smaller treatment systems.

- *Key Point(s). The fundamental factors and conditions that limit rates and extents of transformation and mass transfer processes must be understood in order to specify and design the most efficient type of reactor(s) to use for those processes. It is thus critical that we learn how to identify these factors and conditions.*

1.2.4 Measures of Quantity and Concentration

1.2.4.1 Extensive and Intensive Properties and Parameters

The properties of a system that characterize its inherent mass, energy or momentum relationships can be divided into two general categories, extensive and intensive. We assume for the purpose of this discussion that these properties do not vary spatially within the system (i.e., the system is completely mixed). *An extensive property is one whose magnitude depends on the size of the system or sample taken from the system (e.g. mass, volume, heat capacity, and calories). Conversely, an intensive property of a system does not depend on the size of the system or on that of any sample taken from it (e.g., temperature and pressure).*

The quantity of a substance (defined here as any matter of definite and recognizable composition and specific properties) may be expressed in terms of mass or weight, volume, or number of moles. Quantity is an absolute measure of the amount of a substance present in a system, and is thus an extensive property dependent upon the size of the system or sample. The term concentration expresses the quantity of a substance, i, present in a certain quantity of a particular phase, j. Concentration is thus a ratio of quantities that has a fixed value regardless of the system or sample size, and is thus an intensive property. In general, substance i and phase j may be any solid, liquid, or gas present in the system under study. Phase j often may represent a mixture of solids, liquids, or gases. For example, air pollution scientists are commonly concerned with the amounts of CO_2 (substance i, gas) or particulate matter (substance i, solids) present in air (phase j, a mixture of gases). In the field of water quality, we are often concerned with the amount of dissolved solids (substance i) present in water or wastewater (phase j). Many water or wastewater treatment operations involve the production and management of sludges, in which cases we are concerned with the amount of solid (substance i) present in the sludge (substance j, a mixture of water and solids). The selection of substance i and phase j will depend on the particular system of interest. For instance, if the sludge from a treatment operation is dewatered in preparation for landfilling, it may be more convenient to characterize the amount of water (substance i) in the sludge (phase j).

1.2.4.2 Expressions of Concentration

Based on methods for expressing quantities, the concentration of a substance may be expressed in terms of mass fractions, volume fractions, mole fractions, mass per unit volume, moles per unit volume, moles per unit mass, or equivalents (usually the number of electronic charges per ion times the number of moles of ions) per unit volume.

Mass fraction is a dimensionless concentration that expresses the mass of a particular substance per total system mass, and which may be expressed as a fraction $(0 - 1)$, *a percentage* $(0 - 100)$, *or as some other mass or weight ratio; e.g., parts per million (ppm), or parts per billion (ppb).* For example, if 2 kg of fine silt are mixed into 8 kg of water, the silt represents a solids concentration of 20% or 200,000 ppm. In most practical environmental situations, the amounts of solid (dissolved or suspended) present in aqueous phases do not appreciably change the densities of those phases. The total system mass is for all intents and purposes then equal to the mass of water (i.e., it remains essentially constant). For the case in which the density of the aqueous phase is equal to 1000 kilograms per cubic meter (kg/m^3, or $1 \ g/cm^3$), 1 ppm is the same as $0.001 \ kg/m^3$, or $1 \ mg/L$. In practice, therefore, we often see the ppm and mg/L units of concentration used interchangeably. Keep in mind that they are not equivalent units *a priori*; they may be used interchangeably only when the conditions outlined above apply.

Volume fraction is a dimensionless quantity that expresses the volume of substance per total system volume. For example, if 1 L of methanol is mixed with 3 L of water, the resulting volume fraction of methanol in the mixed solution is 25% and the volume fraction of water is 75% (assuming that total volume reduction upon mixing is negligible). In hydrology, soil moisture content is often expressed as a volume fraction $V_i/(V_i + V_j)$, where V_i and V_j are the water and solid volumes of a total wet soil sample, $V_T = V_i + V_j$.

Mole fraction is the thermodynamically most rigorous concentration unit, expressing the number of moles of a substance of interest per total number of moles of all components of a system. One mole (or mol) of any unit quantity (e.g., atoms, molecules or ions) of a substance is simply Avogadros number (6.022×10^{23}) of that unit quantity; i.e., a specific number of the most basic atomic or molecular units. Some elements naturally form molecules through electron sharing between two identical atoms. These molecules are for the most part gases, such as O_2 and Cl_2. In such cases, atomic weights of that element differ from their molecular weights. Expressed as a characteristic weight, 1 gram atomic weight (GAW) is the number of grams of weight represented by one mole or 6.022×10^{23} atoms of an element, whereas, gram molecular weight is that of 6.022×10^{23} of that element if it forms molecules with itself or of any compound combination of elements comprising a molecule (e.g., the GMW of O_2 is 32 and that of CO_2 is 44.01g). Molecular weight is represented here by the symbol $W_{g,mo}$. An object's weight is not the same as its mass. It is a measure of force given by mass times the gravitational acceleration constant, g (i.e., $W_g = M \times g$).

Because it is nearly impossible (or at least very expensive) to identify the individual species that comprise most environmental systems, the total number of moles in a system cannot in general be calculated exactly. For dilute aqueous solutions, however, the number of moles of water may be assumed to approximate closely the total number of moles in the system. Using this assumption, an approximate mole fraction may be computed.

Mass per unit volume is a common concentration unit expressing the mass of substance i per total system volume. For example, if 1 g of sucrose is added to a volumetric flask, which is then filled to the 1-L mark with water, the resulting concentration is 1 g per liter of sucrose solution, or 1000 mg/L. In general, the mass-per-volume concentration unit can be related to the mass fraction unit if the density of phase j (the sucrose solution) is known. The presence of the sucrose means that the volume of water added to the volumetric flask to reach the 1-L mark will be slightly less than 1 L, even though the sucrose dissolves. Thus the concentration of water in the sucrose solution is less than 1000 mg/L and the density of the resulting solution is greater than the density of pure water.

Moles per unit volume is concentration expressed as the number of moles of substance i present in a volume of phase j. The term molarity refers to the number of moles of substance i per liter of phase j. Thus, we could find the molarity of the sucrose solution in the example above by dividing the mass per volume concentration (g/L) by the gram molecular weight (g/mol) of sucrose (substance i). This computation would yield the number of moles of sucrose ($C_6H_{22}O_{11}$) per liter of sucrose solution. A 1-molar sucrose solution would be prepared by adding 1 mol of sucrose (342.3g) to a volumetric flask, and then filling the flask to the 1-L mark with solvent.

The molar concentration of dissolved species in dilute aqueous systems is often small. To facilitate working with these small numbers, it is convenient to define p-*notation*; a familiar example is pH. The notation pC_i is defined as the negative logarithm (base 10) of the molarity of substance i; thus, pH refers to the negative logarithm of the molar hydronium ion (hydrated proton, H_3O^+) concentration.

Moles per unit mass is a concentration expressing the number of moles of substance i per unit mass of phase j. When the mass of phase j is taken as 1 kg, the term molality is used (i.e., molality is the number of moles of solute per kilogram of solvent). In contrast to the molarity concentration unit, phase j is defined as the solvent used to make up the solution; thus phase j is not a mixture. To make up a 1-molal (1 m) sucrose solution, the volumetric flask would first be filled with 1 kg of water, then a mass of sucrose corresponding to 1 mol would be added to the flask. The final volume will be somewhat greater than 1 L. (Note that 1 L of water weighs 1 kg at 4°C).

Molality and molarity are not the same; a 1-molar sucrose solution refers to 1 mole of sucrose per liter of sucrose solution, while a 1-molal sucrose solution refers to 1 mole of sucrose per kg of solvent. The numerical difference between molar and molal measures differs by less than 1% in dilute aqueous solutions at 20°C. Molarity is more commonly used in practice because molality is not a convenient analytical concentration unit.

Equivalents per unit volume generally means the number of moles of charged units per unit volume. An equivalent is, in its most ordinary sense, one mole of electronic charges; i.e., one mole of Na$^+$ is one equivalent, two moles of Na$^+$ comprise two equivalents, one mole of Ca^{2+} two equivalents, etc.

The equivalent is a particularly useful unit for balancing plus and minus charges in a system to determine whether the requirement of electrical neutrality is satisfied (as it must be). There can be some confusion however when the use of this quantity is made to simplify calculations relating to chemical reactions that are not strictly electrostatic (i.e., that are not like $Na^+ + Cl^- \Leftrightarrow NaCl$ in character). In a general sense, if a reaction is expressed in terms of equivalents, the number of equivalents of each reacting species equals the number of equivalents of product. This leads then to specification of the quantities of the reactants and products involved in terms of their equivalent weights rather that their molar or molecular weights; therein lies the potential for confusion regarding the meaning of equivalent.

One equivalent weight, $W_{g,eq}$, of a substance per liter of solution defines the concentration unit of normality. Because equivalents are used in the context of specific chemical reactions, the definition of an equivalent weight depends on the reaction involved. In general, the equivalent weight of a substance is equal to its gram molecular weight ($W_{g,mo}$) divided by an integer factor that relates to a specific reaction. This may equal the charge of an ion in an ionic reaction, the number of protons or hydroxyl ions exchanged in an acid-base reaction, or the number of electrons transferred in an oxidation-reduction reaction. The same substance may therefore have up to three different equivalent weights.

Example 1.4. *Concentration Calculations Using the Equivalent Weight Concept. (An exercise in quantifying reactant and reaction product quantities; moles, equivalents, masses, and concentrations.)*

- **Situation.** *Phosphate is a limiting nutrient in many natural waters and must therefore be controlled in waste discharges to sensitive receiving waters. Phosphate can be precipitated with calcium, added as unslaked lime* $CaO(s)$, *according to the reaction*

$$3CaO(s) + H_2O + 2HPO_4^{-2} \Leftrightarrow Ca_3(PO_4)_2(s) + 4OH^-$$

  Adjustment of pH to ensure optimal precipitation can be accomplished by addition of caustic (NaOH) *or a mineral acid (e.g.,* H_2SO_4*).*

- **Question(s).** *What are the respective molarities and normalities of the reagents involved in this process?*

- **Logic and Answer(s).** *The equivalent charge concentration unit expresses the number of moles of charge units per liter of solution. The equivalent weight ($W_{g,e}$) is defined as the molecular weight ($W_{g,mo}$) divided by the ionic charge. GMW values can be calculated from the information given in Figure 1.6.*

  1. *For the lime-phosphate reaction, the equivalent weight of calcium in lime* $\left[\{Ca^{2+}\}\{O^{2-}\}\right](s)$ *is*

$$W_{g,eq} = \frac{W_{g,mo}}{2} = \frac{40.08 \ g/mol}{2 \ equivalents/mol} = 20.04 \frac{grams}{equivalent}$$

$$\text{1-Molar } \text{Ca}^{2+} = \frac{1 \; mol}{liter} = \frac{1 \; W_{g,mo}}{liter} = \frac{40.08 \; g}{liter}$$

$$\text{1-Molar } \text{CaO}(s) = (40.08) + (15.99) = 56.07 \; g/L$$

$$1 \; W_M \text{Ca}^{2+} = 2 \; moles \; of \; charge \; units$$

$$\text{1-Normal } \text{Ca}^{2+} = \frac{1 \; equivalent \; \text{Ca}^{2+}}{liter} = \frac{40.08 \; g}{2(liter)} = \frac{20.04 g}{liter}$$

$$\text{1-Normal } \text{CaO}(s) = \frac{56.07 g}{2(liter)} = \frac{28.04 g}{L}$$

2. *For the caustic reaction*

$$\text{NaOH} + \text{H}_3\text{O}^+ \Leftrightarrow \text{Na}^+ + 2\text{H}_2\text{O}$$

$$1 \; mol \; \text{NaOH} = 1 \; mol \; \text{Na}^+ = 1 \; mol \; of \; charge \; units$$

1-Molar NaOH = *1-Normal* NaOH = 22.99+15.99+1.01 = 39.99 g/L

3. *For the sulfuric acid reaction*

$$\text{H}_2\text{SO}_4 + 2\text{H}_2\text{O} \Leftrightarrow 2\text{H}_3\text{O}^+ + \text{SO}_4^{2-}$$

$$1 \; mol \; \text{H}_2\text{SO}_4 = 2 \; mol \; \text{H}_3\text{O}^+ = 2 \; mol \; of \; charge \; units$$

1-Molar H_2SO_4 = 2(1.01) + (32.06) + 4(15.99) = 98.04 \; g/L

$$\text{1-Normal } \text{H}_2\text{SO}_4 = \frac{98.04 \; g/l}{2 \; eq/mol} = 49.02 \; g/L$$

- *Key Point(s). One of the most fundamental characteristics of chemical substances is that they combine in specific molar ratios with each other in specific types of reactions. These molar ratios translate into specific equivalent weights that can be converted readily to masses and concentrations.*

1.3 CHAPTER SUMMARY

The overview presented in Chapter 1 provides an introduction to the identifying features and important characteristics of systems and processes that must be considered in the analysis and interpretation of environmental transformations. *The general nature of fundamental processes, the character of different types of environmental systems in which they occur, and the way in which these factors come together to influence the dynamics of processes and their effects on systems have been described. Appropriate considerations of such factors are prerequisite to the development of rigorous approaches for the analysis, characterization, modeling, and design of environmental processes and operations.* Having gained from this overview an appreciation of the important features of systems and processes, we turn now to considerations of how to better characterize and quantify these features in order to facilitate their incorporation in descriptive models of processes and systems.

Less by way of summary than postscript, you will find that most of the problem assignments at the end of this chapter are different in tone and character than the first three examples given in the text of the chapter. Like Example 1.4, the assigned problems focus mainly on calculations of quantities and units, while Examples 1.1 through 1.3 are more "thought provoking" in nature. This is by intent and purpose. It is important at this early point in the book and the beginning of our studies of environmental systems that we review and sharpen our skills in calculations relating to environmental parameters. This so that such calculations do not later present obstacles in the larger process of learning principles and concepts. The assigned problems for Chapter One therefore stress such calculations.

As noted in the Preface, however, the vast majority of the examples presented in this book are designed as learning exercises. Certain aspects of the first three "learning exercises" given in Examples 1.1 through 1.3 may not at this point be immediately obvious; don't worry about this. The examples are in fact designed to challenge your thinking, and to stimulate frequent asking of the question "why?" In other words, part of their intent is to peak your interest in reading further to satisfy your inherent desire to learn "why." If your natural acuity and academic ability have brought you this far, intellectual curiosity must certainly be one of your inherent characteristics; let's proceed on that basis.

1.4   CITATIONS AND SOURCES

W.J. Weber, Jr., and F.A. DiGiano, *Process Dynamics in Environmental Systems*, John Wiley & Sons, Inc., New York, 1996. PDES is the source of much of the material presented in Chapter 1. Chapter 1 of PDES presents a more extensive and in-depth introduction to environmental systems and processes, and a comprehensive bibliography of related references and suggested readings.

1.5   PROBLEM ASSIGNMENTS

1.1 Calculate the quantities (in grams) of the reagents per liter of solution required to make up the following solutions

(a) 0.4-Molar NaBr.

(b) 0.3-Molar $K_2Cr_2O_7$.

(c) 0.01-Molar $Fe(NH_4)_2(SO_4)_2$

Answers: (a) 41.16 g; (b) 88.26 g; (c) 2.84 g.

1.2 Given the following composition of dry air at sea level

Component	Mole Fraction %
O_2	20.95
N_2	78.09
Ar	0.93
CO_2	0.03

Assume that air is an ideal gas and that in the system of interest the atmospheric pressure is 1.0 atm and the temperature is 20°C. The ideal gas law is given by: $PV = nRT$, where $R = 8.21 \times 10^{-5} atm - m^3/mol - K$.

(a) Compute the density of the dry air at these conditions. Express your answer in g/m3.

(b) Determine the concentration of argon in air, expressed on a mass basis, in ppm.

Answers: (a) 1204 g/m³; (b) 12,791 ppm.

1.3 The pH of a popular soft drink is about 3.8, and the sucrose $(C_{12}H_{22}O_{11})$ concentration, C_{Su}, of this same drink is about 40,000 mg/L.

(a) Calculate the hydronium ion concentration $[H_3O^+]$ in mol/L.

(b) Determine $p[C_{Su}]$.

Answers: (a) 1.59 × 10⁻⁴ mol/L; (b) 0.93.

1.4 (a) Calculate the molarity of pure water at 20°C.

(b) Calculate the molarity of water in a 5.0-g/L NaCl solution at 20°C given that the mass of 1.0 L of this solution is 1000.2 g/L.

(c) Determine the percentage by which the molarity of pure water is decreased in the salt solution.

Answers: (a) 55.44 mol/L; (b) 55.29 mol/L; (c) 0.3%.

1.5 A wastewater treatment plant is located on a small river about two kilometers from the confluence of the river with a lake. The background concentration of sulfur in the river is 75 mg/l as SO_4^{2-}. The discharge from the plant represents 20% of the combined river flow immediately downstream. A water quality standard restricts total sulfur (S) at all points in the river to 150 mg per liter or less. Eighty five percent of the sulfur in the total discharge from the plant is in the form of SO_4^{2-} and fifteen percent is in the form of HS^-. a) What is the maximum allowable total S discharge from the plant that will not violate the stream standard? b) Is the distribution of S between the SO_4^{2-} and HS^- in the discharge likely to affect some water quality parameter in the river that is not directly related to total S? If so, what is that parameter and why is it affected?

1.6 It is desired to produce unslaked (unhydrated) lime (CaO) for use in a water-softening process from the combustion of a sludge containing calcium carbonate ($CaCO_3$). The sludge has the dry-basis weight composition of 80% $CaCO_3$ and 20% inert material. The reaction proceeds according to the equation

$$CaCO_3(s) \Leftrightarrow CO_2 + CaO(s)$$

Determine how many tons of $CaO(s)$ plus inert material will be produced from 100 tons of a wet sludge containing 40% water on a weight basis.

Answer: 38.9 tons

1.7 A water treatment plant that uses soda ash (Na_2CO_3) and unslaked lime in a lime-soda process for softening wishes to produce caustic soda for magnesium removal (as $Mg(OH)_2$) according to the reactions

$$CaO(s) + H_2O \Leftrightarrow Ca(OH)_2(s)$$

$$Mg^{2+} + 2HCO_3^- + Ca(OH)_2(s) \Leftrightarrow MgCO_3(s) + CaCO_3(s) + 2H_2O$$

$$Na_2CO_3 + Ca(OH)_2 \Leftrightarrow 2NaOH + CaCO_3(s)$$

(a) Identify the process(es) listed in Table 1.1 that are involved in this operation. Discuss the bases for your selections.

(b) Calculate how much NaOH can be obtained per short ton of Na_2CO_3.

Answer: (b) 1,510 lb per short ton (2000 lb), or 755 kg per metric ton.

1.8 The water treatment plant described in Problem 1.7 uses chlorine gas for disinfection. A municipal swimming pool requests that the plant provide 500 kg of sodium hypochlorite (NaClO) for its use, the hypochlorite ion (ClO^-) being a more stable form of active chlorine than Cl_2 gas. NaClO can be prepared as follows

$$Cl_2 + 2NaOH \Leftrightarrow 2Na^+ + Cl^- + NaClO + H_2O$$

Other forms of stable hypochlorite, such as $Ca(ClO)_2$, can be prepared in a similar manner.

(a) Determine how much Cl_2 will be required to produce 500 kg of NaClO, assuming 85% conversion efficiency.

(b) Reflect on Problem 1.7 and suggest an alternative disinfectant that can meet the requirement of the municipal pool operator for a stable disinfectant, yet be somewhat more compatible with the operating scheme at the water treatment plant.

(c) Specify what quantity of this alternative disinfectant would be required to have the same disinfection potential as the 500 kg of Na-ClO.

Answer: (a) 561 kg of Cl_2 *(g); (c) 481kg of* $Ca(OCl)_2$

1.9 A packed-tower stripping column (the packing is used to promote air-water mass transfer) is to be used as a pretreatment to remove ammonia from an industrial wastewater. The feed stream flow rate is 500,000 gallons per day (gpd), and has an NH_3 concentration of 500 mg $NH_3 - N/L$. The discharge permit allows a concentration of 100 mg $NH_3 - N/L$ in the effluent stream. Calculate how many moles of NH_3 must be stripped per day.

Answer: (a) 54,000 mol NH_3/day.

1.10 Complex phosphates are added to the boiler feed water of a steam power plant to control scaling of the steam boilers. Because of the high temperatures involved, the complex phosphates are hydrolyzed to orthophosphates. Analyses of the wastewater phosphorus content from the plant are tabulated below:

Phosphorus Species	Formula	Concentration
Trisodium Phosphate	Na_3PO_4	1 mg/l
Disodium Phosphate	Na_2HPO_4	0.25 mM
Monosodium Phosphate	NaH_2PO_4	0.3 ppm
Diammonium Phosphate	$(NH_4)_2HPO_4$	0.05% w/w

Determine the total phosphorus concentration of the wastewater as PO_4^{3-}.

Chapter 2

Process and System Characterization

Contents

2.0 CHAPTER OBJECTIVES

To learn how to quantify information about the important and identifying features of environmental processes and systems, and how to employ descriptive mathematical models to organize that information in ways that allow its use for system analysis, design and performance predictions.

2.1 INTRODUCTION

There are a number of ways in which physical systems and the processes that take place within them can be described. The most quantitative of these are precise mathematical descriptions that fully capture appropriate system properties (e.g., shape, size, mass) and dynamics (e.g., flow rates, chemical reaction rates, mixing conditions).

The most important properties of a system are its energy, mass, and momentum, and its most important dynamics relate to changes in these three fundamental properties. To understand this is to grasp the most basic tenet of system and process modeling. Each extensive property of a system is fully definable once the boundaries that contain the system are defined. Moreover, changes in the properties of concern follow well known laws of physics and chemistry, laws that can be written in terms of accurate mathematical expressions.

Our primary focus in terms of extensive system properties is mass, usually the mass of an impurity or contaminant, and the ways and rates of its change in a specific system. We shall see, however, that all three extensive system properties are interrelated, and generally coupled.

2.2 SYSTEM CHARACTERIZATION

In Chapter 3 we will begin to develop rigorous mass and material-balance based approaches to system characterization and modeling. Those approaches will then be extended throughout the text to the analysis and design of systems involving increasingly more complex transport and transformation phenomena. Before embarking on that challenging journey, however, let's warm up with some mental calisthenics by considering a relatively simple environmental system and several sets of different circumstances that lend themselves to intuitive and common sense approaches to material-balance based "modeling." With subsequent due mind to, and diligent practice of, some basic ground rules to be learned along the way, we will discover that the analysis of even the most complex of environmental system yields eventually to the same intuition and common sense we apply to our warm-up exercise.

2.2.1   Intuition and Common Sense

Figure 2.1 presents a schematic representation of a system of two lakes having various inflows and outflows. Two of the outflows, Q_B from *LAKE I* and Q_E from *LAKE II*, are unknown. Lets try to determine the magnitudes of Q_B and Q_E from the information presented in the figure.

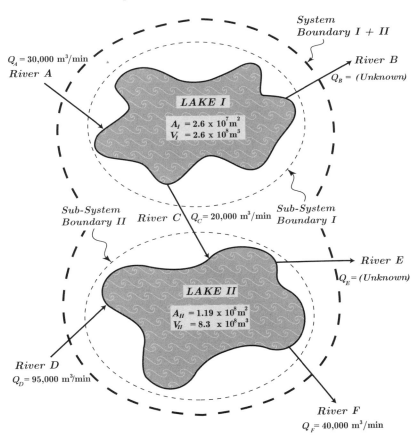

Figure 2.1 An Environmental System Comprising Two Lakes and Six Rivers

In this case we are interested in balancing the mass of water, knowing only four of six flow rates. We see that the respective volumes of the lakes are constant, so there is no net water accumulation in either of them. The first thing we must do in order to balance the flows around the system is to define boundaries.

2.2.2   Defining Boundaries

We might logically start by defining a boundary that encompasses the entire system, as illustrated in Figure 2.1 (i.e., *System Boundary I + II*). The flow balance for this boundary condition is

$$Q_A + Q_D = Q_B + Q_E + Q_F \qquad (2.1)$$

Equation 2.1 states simply that the total flow into the system of two lakes *via Rivers A* and *D* is equal to the total flow out *via Rivers B, E*, and *F*. This is a condition defined by the fact (either a confirmed observation or a reasonable assumption) that the volumes of the lakes in the system are constant over time; ***this temporally-stable condition is termed the condition of steady-state***. If this condition is not observed or assumed the flow balance equation becomes a complex function of time; i.e.,

$$(Q_A + Q_D) - (Q_B + Q_E + Q_F) = \frac{d(V_I + V_{II})}{dt} \qquad (2.2)$$

an equation that cannot be solved with the information given.

In fact, the balance given in Equation 2.1 cannot be solved with the information given, even if the simplification of a steady-state condition is justifiable. That is, we have one equation but two unknown quantities (Q_B and Q_E). ***We must redefine our boundary conditions in a manner that will yield a solvable balance equation.*** The sensible alternative approach is to define a sub-system boundary around *LAKE I* only (i.e., *Sub-System Boundary I*), in which case we can write

$$
\boxed{\begin{array}{ll} \textbf{\textit{Steady-State}} & \\ \textbf{\textit{LAKE I}} & \qquad Q_A - Q_B - Q_C = 0 \\ \textbf{\textit{Flow Balance}} & \end{array}} \qquad (2.3)
$$

and, knowing both Q_A and Q_C we can calculate

$$Q_B = (30,000 \text{ m}^3/\text{min} - 20,000 \text{ m}^3/\text{min}) = 10,000 \text{ m}^3/\text{min}$$

Using the same sub-system boundary definition approach for *LAKE II* (i.e., *Sub-System Boundary II*), we write the balance equation

$$
\boxed{\begin{array}{ll} \textbf{\textit{Steady-State}} & \\ \textbf{\textit{LAKE II}} & \qquad Q_C + Q_D - Q_E - Q_F = 0 \\ \textbf{\textit{Flow Balance}} & \end{array}} \qquad (2.4)
$$

substituting the known values of Q_C, Q_D and Q_F yields

$$Q_E = 75,000 \text{ m}^3/\text{min}$$

The above exercise seems a simple balance of volumetric flows of water, and Equations 2.3 and 2.4 are indeed given as volumetric flow balance equations. *There are, however no continuity relationships that relate to volumetric flows of anything in a general sense. What allows us to write Equations 2.1, 2.3, and 2.4 as they are is that the mass concentration of water in water is constant and equal to its density ρ_W.*

2.2.3 Water Mass Balances

What we have actually balanced above without explicitly saying so is mass flows, pursuant to the principle of mass continuity; i.e., for *Sub-System I* the water mass balance is

$$\boxed{\begin{array}{l} \textit{Steady-State} \\ \textbf{\textit{LAKE I}} \qquad Q_A\rho_W + Q_B\rho_W - Q_C\rho_W = 0 \\ \textit{Mass Balance} \end{array}} \qquad (2.5)$$

which, upon dividing both sides of the balance equation by the constant ρ_W, yields Equation 2.1. The balance for *Sub-System II* is obtained in the same way.

By way of an interim recap, the three key factors that enabled us to intuitively balance the mass of water as we have done were: (1) we assumed that the system involved incurred no change in its properties (i.e., by setting the right-hand side of all equations to zero we stipulated a steady-state condition for the system); (2) by dividing the system into two Sub-Systems we allowed ourselves to choose boundaries that reduced the complexity of the balance equation; and, (3) the water concentration was constant in time and uniform throughout the systems (i.e., our problem was reduced to a boundary-value problem).

As our system conditions become more complex, so must the mass balance equations we use to model the system. Let's complicate our problem (system) somewhat by acknowledging that evaporation may be a player in the water balance for the system; i.e., *we introduce a sink term (net evaporative outflow) that has a time-variable (i.e., rate) characteristic.* Applying a maximum evaporation rate of $r = 0.5$ cm/day, the system parameters we have now to deal with are:

1. boundaries, same as before;

2. water is the component being mass balanced, same as before;

3. water mass transport, $QC_W = Q\rho_W$ (C = water mass concentration and ρ_W = water density), same as before;

4. no transformation, water remaining in system remains water (i.e., same as before); and,

5. new sink term(s), evaporation $rAC_W = E_V \rho_W$ where A is the surface area of a lake and E_V is the volume of water evaporated per day.

The new balance equation for *Sub-System I* is then

$$Q_A \rho_W - Q_B \rho_W - Q_C \rho_W - E_{V,I} \rho_W = 0 \qquad (2.6)$$

and that for *Sub-System II* is

$$Q_C \rho_W + Q_D \rho_W - Q_E \rho_W - Q_F \rho_W - E_{V,II} \rho_W = 0 \qquad (2.7)$$

Rounding flows to the nearest pre-decimal number we calculate $E_{V,I}$ as

$$E_{V,I} = rA_I = (0.5 \text{ cm/day})(2.6 \times 10^7 \text{m}^2)(0.01 \text{ m/cm})(\text{day}/1440 \text{ min})$$

$$E_{V,I} = 90 \text{ m}^3/\text{min}$$

Then, from the *Sub-System I* balance condition in Equation 2.6 for constant ρ_W we write

$$Q_B = Q_A - Q_C - E_{V,I} = 30,000 \text{ m}^3/\text{min} - 20,000 \text{ m}^3/\text{min} - 90 \text{ m}^3/\text{min}$$

$$Q_B = 9910 \text{ m}^3/\text{min}$$

Next, again rounding, we calculate $E_{V,II}$ as

$$E_{V,II} = (0.5 \text{ cm/day})(1.19 \times 10^8 \text{ m}^2)(0.01 \text{ m/cm})(\text{day}/1440 \text{ min})$$

$$E_{V,II} = 413 \text{ m}^3/\text{min}$$

From the *Sub-System II* balance condition in Equation 2.7, for constant ρ_W we write

$$Q_E = (Q_C + Q_D - Q_F) - E_{V,II} = 75,000 \text{ m}^3/\text{min} - 413 \text{ m}^3/\text{min}$$

$$Q_E \approx 74,600 \text{ m}^3/\text{min}$$

2.2.4   Constituent Mass Balances

As an additional complication, lets consider a component other than water. To simplify the consideration, lets make it a conservative (i.e., not transformed) component such as chloride (which, because it is conservative, is commonly employed as a tracer to determine "system flow behavior" and the validity of assumptions related thereto). We now have the following system parameters to consider:

1. boundaries, same as before;

2. chloride (Cl^-) is now the component being mass balanced;

3. chloride mass transport, QC_{Cl}, is a function of both Q and the distribution of chloride (C_{Cl}) within Q (i.e., a function of the degree of mixing of chloride throughout the rivers and lakes);

4. no transformation, Cl^- is conservative;

5. Cl^- is not evaporated, thus the evaporation sink term is not included; and

6. it is given that $C_{A,Cl} = 40$ mg/l and $C_{D,Cl} = 60$ mg/l.

Then, for the *Sub-System I* balance condition we write

$$Q_A C_{A,Cl} - Q_B C_{B,Cl} - Q_C C_{C,Cl} - r_I A_I C_{EVAP\ I,Cl} = 0 \qquad (2.8)$$

With the assumptions that $C_{C,Cl} = C_{B,Cl}$ (complete mixing of the contents of *LAKE I*) and $C_{EVAP\ I,Cl} = 0$ (no Cl^- in evaporating water vapor), simplification and solution of Equation 2.8 yields

$$C_{B,Cl} = C_{C,Cl} = (Q_A/(Q_B + Q_C))C_{A,Cl} = \frac{(30,000\ \text{m}^3/\text{min})(40\ \text{mg/L})}{(9,910\ \text{m}^3/\text{min} + 20,000\ \text{m}^3/\text{min})}$$

$$C_{B,Cl} = C_{C,Cl} = 40.1\ \text{mg/L}$$

The *Sub-System II* balance condition can be written as

$$Q_C C_{C,Cl} + Q_D C_{D,Cl} - Q_E C_{E,Cl} - Q_F C_{F,Cl} - r_{II} A_{II} C_{EVAP\ II,Cl} = 0 \quad (2.9)$$

Again with the assumptions that $C_{E,Cl} = C_{F,Cl}$ (complete mixing of the contents of *LAKE II*) and $C_{EVAP\ II,Cl} = 0$ (no Cl^- in evaporating water vapor), simplification and solution yields

$$C_{E,Cl} = C_{F,Cl} = (Q_C C_{C,Cl} + Q_D C_{D,Cl})/(Q_E + Q_F)$$

$$= \frac{[(20,000\ \text{m}^3/\text{min})(40.1\ \text{mg/L}) + (95,000\ \text{m}^3/\text{min})(60\ \text{mg/L})]}{(74,587\ \text{m}^3/\text{min} + 40,000\ \text{m}^3/\text{min})}$$

$$C_{E,Cl} = C_{F,Cl} = 56.7\ \text{mg/L}$$

In reviewing the constructs of these intuitive "models", note and contemplate these several important points: (1) proper selection of boundaries can simplify solutions by reducing the number of unknowns; (2) a separate and perhaps somewhat different material balance equation must be written for each component of interest; (3) all transport and transformation processes should be first identified in physical context, and then translated into equations; (4) any and all assumptions you are making should be identified, stated explicitly, and analyzed for merit; and, (5) balance equations should be developed in terms of general variables first, checked for dimensional consistency, and then quantified with numerical parameter values having appropriate units.

Assigned Problem 2.8 is something of a "capstone" exercise relating to the two-lake system presented in Figure 2.1 and discussed above. Another layer of complication is added in this problem by considering the balance of a reactive (non-conservative) contaminant.

2.3 PROCESS CHARACTERIZATION

2.3.1 Transformation Processes

If, as noted in Section 1.1.3 of Chapter 1, all components of a system are in the most elementary sense comprised by chemical substances, then all changes in the composition of that system must also, in the most elementary sense, involve the change or transformation of one chemical form to another. Microbial degradations of organic substances, for example, involve transformations of chemical substances that serve as fuel or food sources for microbes to other chemicals that are released as waste products. The microbes produce yet other special types of chemicals, termed enzymes, that carry out these microbially mediated (biochemical) reactions.

Chemical reactions by which transformations occur can be broadly categorized as either homogeneous or heterogeneous, depending upon the number of phases they involve. As stressed earlier, environmental systems are typically heterogeneous; i.e., they usually involve more than one phase. Transformation reactions that occur within them, however, are not necessarily heterogeneous.

A macroscale elaboration of the three-phase system depicted in Figure 1.2 is given in Figure 2.2. This is a system from which water is drawn continuously for use and into which used water is discharged continuously. The boundaries of such a system are defined by particular circumstances, such as the need to consider a specific reach of a river, or by specification of the size and configuration of a holding tank or treatment unit. Generalized cocurrent mass fluxes of water and other constituents into and out of the system are indicated by the bold arrows, and the specific fluxes and reactions of several generic constituents, A, B, C, and D, by the single-headed arrows. In this example the particular chemical species of interest undergo transformations that change their state within the aqueous phase. These transformations involve reaction of species A with species B to form species C and D. The species involved can also change their distributions among the three phases of the system. Species A might well represent dissolved oxygen in a river system or activated sludge basin, or ozone in a pretreatment unit of a water treatment plant, and species B an organic compound. Certain of the transformations of species A and B that occur along pathways 1 through 10 in this system are homogeneous, while others are heterogeneous. Species A and reaction product C, which may, for example, represent oxygen

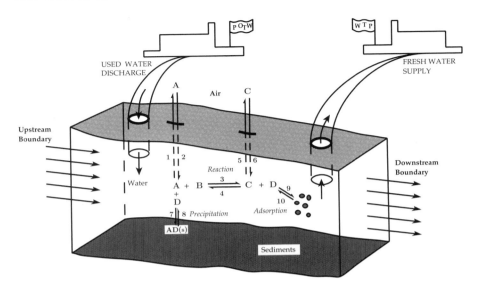

Figure 2.2 A Natural Environmental Macroscale System

and carbon dioxide respectively, are transformed from dissolved states in the water phase to gaseous states in the air phase along reaction pathways 1 and 5; A and C may be retransformed to dissolved states, respectively, along reaction pathways 2 and 6. Reactions 1, 2, 5, and 6 are heterogeneous, involving two different phases and two correspondingly different states of species A and C. Reactions 7 and 8 are also heterogeneous because they involve the reaction of product D with A to form a precipitate, a separate solid phase, and the re-dissolution of this solid phase. Similarly, reactions 9 and 10 are heterogeneous because they involve interfacial sorption and desorption reactions of reaction product D with suspended solids, such as clays or other sediments. In contrast, reactions 3 and 4 are homogeneous reactions because they involve changes only in the aqueous-phase states of the species involved.

2.3.1.1 Homogeneous Reactions

Homogeneous reactions are governed by relationships requiring that certain entropy, enthalpy, and energy balances be obeyed among the components or species participating in transformation processes that occur within a single phase. These relationships yield characteristic thermodynamic properties and corresponding equilibrium constants. Although having fundamentally the same origin for such different classes of transformations as acid-base reactions, oxidative-reduction reactions, and complex formation reactions, these equilibrium constants are commonly given somewhat different names, such as acidity constants, electrochemical potentials, and stability constants, respectively.

The most fundamental governing conditions or relationships for homogeneous reactions are the rules of stoichiometry, which derive from the fact that every chemical transformation involves a discrete amount of energy and, because energy and mass are inextricably related in classical thermodynamics, a discrete amount of mass of each reacting substance.

Consider, for instance, the reaction of species A with species B to yield species C and D in Figure 2.2

$$A + B \Leftrightarrow C + D \qquad (2.10)$$

This reaction can be written more generally as

$$
\boxed{
\begin{array}{ll}
\textbf{\textit{Reaction}} & \\
\textbf{\textit{Stoichiometry}} & \gamma_A A + \gamma_B B \Leftrightarrow \gamma_C C + \gamma_D D
\end{array}
} \qquad (2.11)
$$

where the coefficients γ_A and γ_B define the respective quantities of the reacting substances, A and B, required to form the quantities γ_C and γ_D of products, C and D, respectively. These coefficients are termed stoichiometric coefficients.

As generalized in Equation 2.11, the stoichiometric coefficients in any specific reaction may very well be different than one and different from one another, but they always have fixed integer values. This relates to the fact that each chemical unit of each reacting substance possesses a well defined characteristic potential or available energy for reaction, and that each reaction requires a fixed amount of energy to occur. The stoichiometric coefficients prescribe the respective numbers of units (e.g., molecules or moles) of each chemical substance required to accomplish a specific change in a specific reacting substance to form a specific product.

With each unit of change there is an associated transfer of a discrete amount of energy, either produced by a reaction that is spontaneous, or required as input to induce a non-spontaneous reaction. *The amount of associated energy either produced spontaneously or required to make a specific reaction occur is termed the free energy change, ΔG_r, of that reaction.* The free energy change has a characteristic and prescribed value that relates to the number of chemical units involved in the reaction, which in turn, because each unit of a chemical substance has a well defined mass, relates to the masses of the reacting substances. The incremental change in the concentration, ΔC, of a substance to be expected in a transformation process is thus a function of $\phi \Delta G_r$, or, in the limit,

$$
\boxed{
\begin{array}{l}
\textbf{\textit{Relationship Between Energy and Reaction Extent}} \\[4pt]
(dC) = \phi(dG_r) = \phi(Constituent\ Mass)
\end{array}
} \qquad (2.12)
$$

The relationships given in Equations 2.11 and 2.12 form the building blocks for structured approaches to process characterization and analysis. Every process involves a change in chemical constituents, and a specific amount of energy is involved for each set of reactants and products. For example, in biochemical and physicochemical oxidations, a given amount of a particular organic chemical requires a specific amount of dissolved oxygen or other chemical oxidant (e.g., ozone, hydrogen peroxide, or chlorine) to be transformed ultimately into a specific amount of non-oxygen-consuming product; that is, to be "mineralized" to a stable inorganic form of carbon (e.g., CO_2).

Example 2.1 provides some simple illustrations of the practical significance of the stoichiometric coefficients defined in Equation 2.11 and of the reaction energy concepts discussed above.

Example 2.1.   Calculations of Reactant and Product Quantities Using the Laws of Chemical Stoichiometry. (An example of a practical application of a straightforward chemical principle.)

- *Situation. The operating board of a water softening plant in which soda ash (Na_2CO_3) and unslaked lime (CaO) are used to precipitate calcium hardness (Ca^{2+}) as calcium carbonate $CaCO_3$ is considering recovery of the lime for reuse by calcining (heating) the limestone sludge, which is 90% pure $CaCO_3$; i.e., by the reaction*

$$CaCO_3 + heat \Leftrightarrow CaO + CO_2$$

- *Question(s). (a) How much lime can be recovered per unit weight of sludge produced? (b) The soda ash purchased by the plant is of commercial grade. You are requested to determine whether a particular shipment meets the minimum purity specifications of 90% Na_2CO_3.*

- *Logic and Answer(s).*

  1. *The molecular weights of $CaCO_3$ and CaO can be determined to be 100 and 56.1 g/mol, respectively (see Figure 1.6 for atomic weights of individual elements). By a molar balance, 1 mol of $CaCO_3$ (100 g) yields 1 mol of CaO (56.1 g) plus one mol of CO_2 (44.0 g). The maximum amount (i.e., at 100% efficiency) of CaO to be recovered per 100 kg of limestone sludge is then*

$$(100 \ kg \ limestone) \left(\frac{0.9 \ kg \ CaCO_3}{kg \ limestone} \right) \left(\frac{56.1 \ kg \ CaO}{100 \ kg \ CaCO_3} \right) = 50.5 \ kg$$

  2. *The purity of the Na_2CO_3 shipment can be determined by carrying out a reaction of known stoichiometry. For example, the soda ash*

can be reacted with $CaCl_2$ *and the amount of the resulting precipitate determined (i.e., a gravimetric analysis). The reaction involved is*

$$Na_2CO_3 + CaCl_2 \Leftrightarrow CaCO_3 + 2NaCl$$

Suppose 6.0 g of the soda ash is reacted with a solution of $CaCl_2$ *and the amount of* $CaCO_3$ *precipitated, after filtration and drying, is determined to be 5.1 g. Assume that this precipitate does not contain any significant amount of impurities. The number of moles (remember, reaction stoichiometry is based on molar quantities) of* $CaCO_3$ *formed is determined to be*

$$[CaCO_3](s) = 0.051 \; mol = 51 \times 10^{-3} \; mol = 51 \; mmol$$

Then, since the stoichiometric coefficients for $NaCO_3$ *and* $CaCO_3$ *are the same (i.e., 1)*

$$[Na_2CO_3](s) = [CaCO_3](s) = 51 \times 10^{-3} \; mol$$

The molecular weight of Na_2CO_3 *is 106.0 g* Na_2CO_3/mol. *The mass of pure* Na_2CO_3 *in the sample assayed can then be determined*

$$[Na_2CO_3](s) = 51 \times 10^{-3} \; mol \times (106.0g/mol) = 5.4g$$

and the percentage Na_2CO_3 *purity of the commercial grade soda ash calculated*

$$\% \; purity = 90.1\%$$

The shipment is acceptable.

- **Key Point(s). The laws of stoichiometry specify that molecules and atoms of different chemical species combine in well defined ratios and multiples. This allows us to write quantitative reaction expressions that have both theoretical justification and great practical utility.**

2.3.1.2   Heterogeneous Reactions

The chemical relationships governing the heterogeneous reactions of species are different than those for homogeneous reactions, but they also have their fundamental origins in chemical thermodynamics. Reactions 1, 2, 5, and 6, in Figure 2.2 for example, adhere to a general proportional relationship between concentrations in each of two phases. *This relationship, known as Henry's law, characterizes the equilibrium state of phase partitioning for species between dilute aqueous solutions and air and gas phases; namely*

$$\boxed{\text{Henry's Law} \qquad P = \mathcal{K}_H C} \tag{2.13}$$

where P is the concentration of a substance in the gas phase, expressed in terms of its pressure (e.g., atmospheres) and C is the molar concentration (e.g., moles per cubic meter) of the substance in the aqueous phase. The constant of proportionality $\mathcal{K}_H$, in Equation 2.13, Henry's constant, defines the relative preference of a substance for air and water at a point of thermodynamic stability (i.e., the condition of equilibrium). Thus, for components A and C in reactions 1, 2, 5, and 6 in Figure 2.2

$$P_A = \mathcal{K}_{H,A} C_A \tag{2.14}$$
$$P_C = \mathcal{K}_{H,C} C_C \tag{2.15}$$

Every chemical species has a specific and well-known Henry's constant to characterize its tendency to escape from dilute aqueous solutions into air. Oxygen, for example, has a relatively high Henry's constant. Thus it is abundant in the atmosphere, but found in only relatively low concentrations in water. Carbon dioxide, on the other hand, has a low Henry's constant, preferring more to partition from gas phase into water. Table 2.1 provides a listing of Henry's constants for a number of inorganic gases of common interest for environmental systems.

Table 2.1 Henry's Constants for Inorganic Gases

	$\mathcal{K}_H[(atm - m^3)/(mol)] \times 10^3$			
Gas	10°C	15°C	20°C	25°C
Carbon dioxide (CO_2)	18.7	22.0	25.6	29.5
Carbon monoxide (CO)	796	880	965	1,044
Chlorine (Cl_2)	8.8	10.7	13.3	16
Hydrogen (H_2)	1,145	1,190	1,229	1,273
Hydrogen sulfide (H_2S)	6.6	7.6	8.7	9.8
Nitric oxide (NO)	392	436	475	517
Nitrogen (N_2)	1,202	1,328	1,447	1,557
Nitrous oxide (N_2O)	25.4	29.9	35.6	40.5
Oxygen (O_2)	589	655	722	788
Ozone (O_3)	44.6	51.8	67.7	82.3
Sulfur dioxide (SO_2)	0.43	0.49	0.62	0.72

Calculated from constants and solubility data in Perry *et al.*, (1963).

An illustration of how Henry's constant can be determined and applied is given in Example 2.2. Further discussion and applications of Henry's law are given in Chapter 12.

Example 2.2.   Determination of a Henry's Law Constant. (An illustration of the physical significance of thermodynamic "property" constants.)

- **Situation.** An experimental determination and application of Henry's constant.

- **Question(s).** (a) Devise an experiment to measure Henry's constant for oxygen in water in contact with air at $20°C$ and 1 atm pressure; (b) Determine how much oxygen will be dissolved in water at $20°C$ if pure oxygen gas is bubbled through the water until it is saturated.

- **Logic and Answer(s).**

  (a) Henry's constant is a constant of proportionality relating to the distribution of a gas between a dilute aqueous phase and a gaseous phase at equilibrium. The concentration of oxygen in air, expressed as a dimensionless partial pressure, p_{O_2}, is 0.21; that is, air is comprised by 21% oxygen on a molar basis. If we bubble a large amount of air through a liter of water until it is saturated with the air, the amount of oxygen dissolved in the water at this condition of equilibrium is dictated by Henry's law (Equation 2.13). If this amount of oxygen is measured, Henry's constant can be calculated.

  1. For example, if the aqueous phase oxygen concentration is measured and found to be 9.3 mg/L, and the density of water is taken as 1.0 g/cm^3, the mass ratio of oxygen in the water is

  $$X_{O_2, H_2O} = 9.3 \times 10^{-6} g/g$$

  2. Given that 1 mol of gas occupies 24.05 L of volume at 1 atm pressure according to the ideal gas law $(V = n\mathcal{R}T/P$ and $\mathcal{R} = 8.21 \times 10^{-5} atm - m^3/mol\text{-}K)$, and that the density of air at $20°C$ (293 K) is 1.2 g/L, the mass ratio of oxygen in the air is

  $$X_{O_2, Air} = \frac{p_{O_2}(32 \ g \ O_2/mol)}{24.05(L/mol)(1.2 \ g/L)}$$
  $$= \frac{0.21(32 \ g \ O_2/mol)}{24.05(L/mol)(1.2 \ g/L)} = 0.233 \ g/g$$

  3. Henry's constant in nondimensional form is then

  $$\mathcal{K}_H^\circ = \frac{0.233}{9.3 \times 10^{-6}} \left(\frac{g \ O_2/g \ air}{g \ O_2/g \ water} \right) \times \frac{1.2 \times 10^3 g/m^3 \ air}{0.998 \times 10^6 g/m^3 \ water}$$
  $$= 30.12 \frac{mol \ O_2/m^3 \ air}{mol \ O_2/m^3 \ water}$$

  or, in units of atm-m^3/mole

  $$\mathcal{K}_H = \mathcal{K}_H^\circ \mathcal{R}T = 30.12 \times 8.21 \times 10^{-5} \times 293 = 0.725 \ atm - m^3/mol$$

4. *It will be noted that this value for $\mathcal{K}_H$ is close to that given for oxygen in Table 2.1.*

(b) If pure oxygen is used to saturate the water, the dissolved oxygen concentration can then be determined from the Henry's constant calculated above as follows

1. *From Henry's Law (e.g., Equation 2.13)*

$$P_{O_2} = \mathcal{K}_H C_{O_2}$$

2. *For pure oxygen, $P_{O_2} = 1$ atm, thus*

$$C_{O_2} = \frac{P_{O_2}}{\mathcal{K}_H} = -\frac{1.0\ atm}{0.725\ atm - m^3/mol}$$

$$C_{O_2} = 1.38\ mol/m^3 = \frac{1.38\ mol(32\ g/mol)}{m^3}$$

$$C_{O_2} = 44.1\ g/m^3 = 44.1\ mg/L$$

- ***Key Point(s). The tendency of chemical species to distribute themselves between water and air can be expressed in terms of their respective values of Henry's constant, a thermodynamic measure of this particular property of chemical species that can be determined experimentally, and values for which are readily available in standard references.***

Relationships similar to Henry's law exist for the distribution or partitioning of chemical species from water into organic liquids, solids, or biological life forms; their precipitation from solution to form solid phases; and their adsorption onto solid surfaces. The relative tendencies of species to undergo phase transformations are characterized by a set of corresponding thermodynamic constants. Prime examples of such constants are the solubility limit, C_S, and the solubility constant, $\mathcal{K}_S$; vapor pressure, P^v; the octanol-water partitioning coefficient $\mathcal{K}_{OW}$; the bio-concentration factor, $\mathcal{K}_B$; and the Freundlich adsorption coefficients, $\mathcal{K}_F$ and $\mathfrak{n}$.

Table 2.2 presents a list of different types of phase transformation constants for a series of organic compounds of environmental concern. Although it is not expected that the exact physical significance of each of these constants is obvious to the reader at this point, there are certain intuitive relationships and trends that become evident by even cursory examination of their ranked values. Examination reveals, for example, distinct trends in the expected environmental behavior of the compounds listed. To illustrate these trends, compare the two aromatic hydrocarbons, benzene and ethylbenzene, and note from their respective values of C_S, P^v, $\mathcal{K}_{OW}$, $\mathcal{K}_F$, and $\mathcal{K}_B$ the consistently greater tendency for benzene to accumulate in aqueous phases.

Table 2.2 Properties and Constants for Organic Contaminants

COMPOUND	C_S mg/L	P^v atm $\times 10^3$	$\mathcal{K}_H$ $\dfrac{atm-m^3}{mol} \times 10^3$	$log\mathcal{K}_{OW}$	$\mathcal{K}_F$	ℓ	$log\mathcal{K}_B$
Benzene	1,770	125.7	5.49	2.13	0.5	0.46	1.11
Toluene	534	37.6	6.66	2.73	1.2	0.47	1.62
Ethylbenzene	160	12.6	7.94	3.15	1.6	0.39	1.98
o-Xylene	175	8.68	5.27	3.12	1.1	0.47	1.95
Chlorobenzene	472	15.6	3.71	2.84	1.8	0.40	1.71
1,4-Dichlorobenzene	145	1.55	1.95	3.38	3.2	0.41	2.17
1,2,4-Trichlorobenzene	40.6	0.6	2.75	4.26	6.2	0.44	2.92
Nitrobenzene	1900	0.2	0.024	1.85	4.0	0.39	0.87
Lindane	7.3	0.0004	0.00043	3.72	3.2	0.35	2.46

Source: Adapted from Weber et al. (1987).
   All values at 25° C except $\mathcal{K}_F$, ℓ, and $\mathcal{K}_B$, which were determined at room temperature.
[a] Freundlich coefficients for Equation 13.11 ($q_e = \mathcal{K}_F C_e^{\ell}$).
   Determined for Hydrodarco C activated carbon for $q_e = \mu g/mg$ and $C_e = \mu g/L$.
[b] From empirical correlation $\log \mathcal{K}_B = 0.85 \log \mathcal{K}_{OW} - 0.70$.

The consistency of the trends in different types of constants noted above is not surprising. They are in fact to be expected because most of these constants are thermodynamically based, and thus interrelated in one way or another. In subsequent considerations of the thermodynamic properties of transformations reactions in Chapters 5, 6 and 12 we elaborate more fully on various thermodynamic constants and their interpretation and significance as measures of the environmental tendencies of different chemical and biochemical species.

2.3.1.3   Reaction Rates

A second fundamental element of processes upon which we ultimately structure our approach to their characterization and analysis lies in the fact that reaction rate, r, just as reaction energy, is functionally dependent upon the numbers of reacting units and the masses of reacting substances; i.e.,

$$\textbf{\textit{Relationship Between Energy and Reaction Rate}}$$
$$r = \frac{dC}{dt} = \phi(dG_r) = \phi(Constituent\ Mass) \qquad (2.16)$$

This relationship has its origins in the law of mass action, or mass law, which states that rates of reactions are *proportional* to the masses of the reacting substances. For a specific reaction, therefore, rate will increase with the available free energy. This does not, however, imply that the relative rates of distinctly different reactions can be related to their respective free energies because the coefficients of proportionality may vary from reaction to reaction.

In the case of simple elementary (one-step) homogeneous phase reactions the coefficients of proportionality are related directly to the stoichiometric coefficients; i.e., to γ_A through γ_D in the reaction illustrated in Equation 2.11. In reactions that involve oxidation of organic matter, the rate of consumption of oxygen or other chemical oxidant is proportional to the concentrations (or masses) of the organic matter and of the oxidant. *Regardless of whether these reactions between organic matter and oxygen occur in a river or engineered treatment system, the energy requirements are exactly the same. The rate of conversion of organic matter in the treatment system, however, can be more readily manipulated by varying the masses of the reactants to reduce required reaction times and sizes of reactor systems.*

Knowledge of the rate-dependence of reactions on process parameters is essential for describing process dynamics. This information also provides insight into how processes may be optimized and reactor sizes and costs minimized. *In complex nonelementary reactions and in heterogeneous systems the dependencies of reaction rates on the numbers of reacting units are generally different than the dependencies of chemical energy, although they often increase and decrease in similar directions among reacting constituents.* These rate dependencies must be quantified in process characterization and analysis, often experimentally. Reaction rates frequently depend on more than simple molecular or elementary reaction kinetics. They often involve complex phenomena, such as microtransport processes, related to the characteristics of the systems in which the reactions occur. These characteristics must also therefore be identified and quantified in process analysis.

2.3.2 Transport Processes

A complete description and quantification of compositional changes in a system must account for changes related to transport processes. These include: (1) changes related to the movement of components into or out of the system; (2) distributions of components within its boundaries, and, (3) distribution of components across and within the boundaries of sub-systems comprising the overall system. Movements of components across and within system boundaries affect and are affected by a number of different processes categorized earlier as macroscale and microscale transport processes. Macroscale transport processes occur at the scale of the system or reactor, whereas those that are microscale occur at the scale of subcomponents (e.g., suspended particles, phase interfaces, etc.).

Transport processes occur as the result of specific driving forces. In essence, these driving forces are spatial energy gradients. In the case of the macroscale transport of a constant-density fluid between two hydraulically connected tanks, for example, the driving force may be as simple as the difference in the free-surface elevations of water in the tanks. This position gradient or elevation head causes the fluid to flow from the tank having the higher free-surface elevation to the one of lower free-surface elevation. Alternately, a density gradient induced by a difference in temperature or in the concentration of a dissolved salt in a single quiescent tank at a fixed elevation will cause fluid elements to move from one point in the tank to another, often called natural convection. Pressure gradients in systems having no free surfaces (e.g., flowing in filled pipes) exert the same influence on the movement of a fluid and thus on the macroscale transport of substances dissolved or suspended in that fluid.

Physical or mechanical macroscopic transport phenomena may in many instances dominate overall process performance. It is essential to include them in the analysis of any chemical, biochemical or physicochemical process. Reaction models alone, no matter how relevant and well understood they may be, are not adequate in and of themselves for description of anticipated process behavior in a system or for explanation of observed behavior. The same reaction occurring in two different systems (or reactors) of different configuration will probably produce different extents of conversion. This is true because reactor configuration influences fluid mixing patterns and thus influences local concentrations of reactants. This point was illustrated qualitatively in Example 1.2 in Chapter 1. We define movement of dissolved and suspended material which occurs as the result of bulk fluid movement as advective transport in our discussions of macroscopic transport processes in Chapter 4.

Even in the absence of bulk fluid motion, dissolved and suspended matter may migrate under the influence of spatial energy gradients that relate to other system properties. Most common among such transport processes are those that occur as a result of spatial gradients in concentration. These processes generally involve much lower rates (velocities) of migration than do advective processes and thus involve much smaller spatial scales and distances. They are for this reason termed microscale processes. The purest form (smallest scale) of microscale mass transport is molecular diffusion, or diffusive transport. We will learn in Chapter 4 that there is another important form of transport, referred to as dispersive transport, which derives from spatial gradients in momentum, and which thus lies intermediate between advective and diffusive transport in both scale and mechanism.

There are many environmental systems in which both microscale and macroscale transport phenomena must be considered; a number of examples of processes involving microscale mass transport (mass transfer) as a factor in transformation reaction rates were given in Table 1.2 in Chapter 1. Such systems generally involve separations of components among phases, or reaction phenomena that require molecular-level transport of species to reactive components contained within, or at the surfaces of, another phase. The activated carbon system depicted in Figure 1.5a and discussed in our consideration of system scales is, for example, a system in which both macroscopic and microscopic transport must be characterized and quantified, the first in the context and scale of the reactor, and the second in the context and scale of the reaction. The system process model must then interface appropriate characterizations of macroscopic and microscopic transport and reaction phenomena to ensure process continuity.

Briefly stated, spatial gradients in energy are associated with all transport phenomena, and different types of transport are caused by spatial gradients in different forms of energy. *Elevation, pressure, and density differences represent gradients in mechanical energy, while concentration differences represent chemical energy gradients. Similarly, spatial differences in electrical potential can cause fluid or solute transport as a result of electrical energy gradients.*

Spatial energy gradients are rarely singular in environmental systems. Net transport is most commonly determined by some combination of different types of energy gradients. In fact, transport induced by one type of energy gradient may produce other types of energy gradients and thus different (additional) types of transport. Transport of mass, like transformation of mass, occurs as a direct result of the exercise of available energy. Energy exists in a variety of forms; chemical energy, electrical energy, mechanical energy, and thermal energy are common examples. Several different forms of energy may be associated with any environmental system at any time. In fact, most environmental systems involve all of the above four forms of energy. As the nature of a system changes, so do the quantities and forms of available energies. It is, in fact, appropriate to say that changes that occur in the quantities and forms of a system's energy result in changes in the nature of that system.

Each form of energy can vary with both distance and time, thus yielding spatial and temporal energy gradients within and between systems. The laws of thermodynamics dictate that these gradients in energy must eventually dissipate themselves. For example, consider the three different conditions depicted in Figure 2.3 for two vessels containing a fixed total quantity of water. The vessels are situated on a level table and connected at their bottoms with a tube and a valve that can be opened to allow the water to flow from one to the other. The energy gradient represented by the differences in the height of water between the two vessels for the initial condition and for the transient condition, multiplied by the gravitational force associated with the mass of water in the respective differential volumes, will cause a net flow of water mass from vessel A to vessel B until the gradient in gravitational energy is dissipated and the water elevations in vessels A and B are the same; i.e., until equilibrium is reached.

Note that the initial condition represented in part a of Figure 2.3 involves two isolated systems, thus the energy gradient is a potential energy gradient. It is only when the systems are interconnected to allow mass transport that this potential energy is realized. Thus, since energy is associated with mass, mass will naturally redistribute itself

*within a system to reduce and eventually eliminate energy gradients,
at which time the system will have no net energy, and all net transport
of mass will cease.*

a. *Initial Condition (t = 0)*

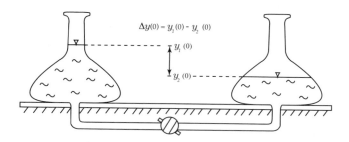

b. *Transient Condition (t = t)*

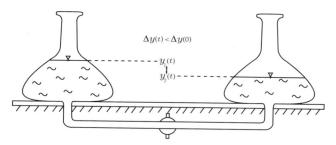

c. *Equilibrium Condition (t = ∞)*

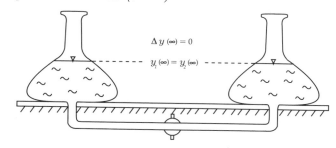

Figure 2.3 Energy Gradient Driven Transport of Mass and Energy

Energy can manifest itself in a number of forms, thus potentially yielding
several "coupled" gradients in time and space. Consider, for example, Figure
2.4 depicting two fluid elements in a two-dimensional (x, y) spatial domain. A
fluid element, initially at position $A(x_A, y_A)$ in the domain, moves over time to
the spatial position $B(x_B, y_B)$, while the element that initially occupied that
position moves on to another point in the (x, y) spatial domain.

Fluid mass is transported in this system in a third dimension, the tempo-

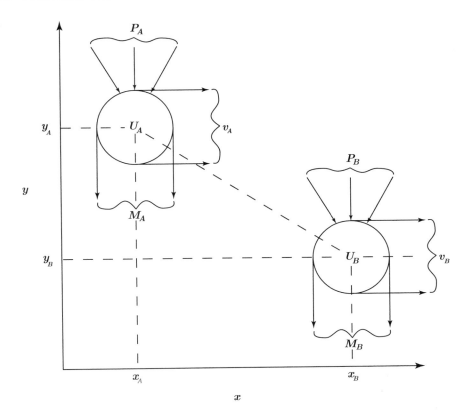

Figure 2.4 Fluid Elements Subject to Mechanical Energy Gradients in a Two-Dimensional Spatial Domain

ral or time dimension, now because these are several coupled and interactive mechanical energy gradients attempting to drive the system to equilibrium, the final condition in which all energy gradients have been dissipated. The several coupled forms of mechanical energy per unit of element mass, e_m, are

potential energy = (e_m)gravitational = $y(\mathcal{G})$

kinetic energy = (e_m)velocity = $v^2/2$

internal energy = (e_m)internal = U

pressure energy = (e_m)pressure = P/ρ

where $\mathcal{G}$ is the gravitational constant (L^2t^{-1}), v is the element's advective velocity in the x direction (Lt^{-1}), U is the internal energy of the element (ML^2t^{-2}), and P is the pressure acting on it (ML^{-2}).

Thus, the total energy per unit mass of fluid element is

$$\boxed{\textbf{\textit{Fluid Energy Per Unit Mass}} \qquad (e_m)_T = y\mathcal{G} + \frac{v^2}{2} + U + \frac{P}{\rho}} \qquad (2.17)$$

$$(e_m)_{T,A} = y_A\mathcal{G} + \frac{v_A^2}{2} + U_A + \frac{P_A}{\rho} \qquad (2.18)$$

and at position B is

$$(e_m)_{T,B} = y_B\mathcal{G} + \frac{v_B^2}{2} + U_B + \frac{P_B}{\rho} \qquad (2.19)$$

and the total energy gradient is

$$\boxed{\textbf{\textit{Energy Gradient}} \qquad (e_m)_{T,A} - (e_m)_{T,B}} \qquad (2.20)$$

The condition of equilibrium dictates that

$$\frac{\partial (e_m)_{T,A}}{\partial x} = \frac{(\partial e_m)_{T,A}}{\partial t} = \frac{(\partial e_m)_{T,B}}{\partial x} = \frac{(\partial e_m)_{T,B}}{\partial t} = 0 \qquad (2.21)$$

There is a condition short of equilibrium which requires only that *the time derivatives* of the energy gradients be zero; i.e., relative to Figure 2.4.

$$\frac{\partial \left[(e_m)_{T,A} - (e_m)_{T,B} \right]}{\partial t} = 0 \qquad (2.22)$$

but

$$\frac{\partial \left[(e_m)_A - (e_m)_B \right]}{\partial x} \neq 0 \qquad (2.23)$$

The condition expressed by Equation 2.23 is the steady-state condition. This is a condition in which various energy gradients cause mass flow or transport but the coupled energy gradients are balanced at all times (i.e., $y(\mathcal{G})$, $v^2/2$, U, and P/ρ).

Regardless of the specific energy gradient(s) and primary and secondary process(es) involved, all transport phenomena can be grouped into one of three major categories; advective, dispersive, diffusive. These phenomena can be quantified in terms of relatively simple conceptual models that are developed in Chapter 4 and used extensively throughout the book as a basis for characterizing and describing the transport aspects of process dynamics. They form the basis for interpreting complex transport and separation phenomena that occur in natural systems and for designing engineered systems to perform desired transport and separation functions.

2.3.3 Intuition and More Common Sense

We have in the two preceding sections of this chapter discussed some of the most fundamental aspects of environmental process and system dynamics; i.e., transformation and transport processes. Various combinations of processes of these two types act in concert to change the state of a given environmental system to some other state having different properties. We as engineers and scientists must come to understand the nature of the processes sufficiently well to quantify them in the form of descriptive models. Such models comprise the basis for predicting the behavior of a system and for prescribing measures to ensure that environmentally harmful processes are curtailed and environmentally beneficial processes are promoted whenever and wherever feasible.

The bottom line for all transformation and transport processes with which we deal is energy; more specifically the availability of sufficient energy, in the appropriate form, to either make a process happen or to arrest it, whichever of the two is our objective in a given circumstance. In this context, we should reflect further on some intuitive aspects of energy and processes, and some common sense facts that can be put to immediate use in helping us understand the interrelationships between these two important elements of environmental systems. The logical starting point is to examine how the natural energies of systems affect and effect some of their most apparent behaviors.

Part a of Figure 2.5 illustrates a hypothetical energy state of an elementary hypothetical system comprised by five molecules of substance AB occupying a given volume. This system may undergo a variety of changes from the tight molecular arrangement and relatively small system volume depicted in part a of Figure 2.5. Each molecule of AB in this system exists at a characteristic natural energy level (we will learn more about this in later chapters). The system energy density (i.e., the energy per unit volume) is high because the molecules are closely grouped in the configuration or state shown in part a. There is more energy available in this state than needed to cause the system to seek a lower energy state by undergoing some type of change. One possible change is for the molecules to simply move (i.e., undergo spontaneous transport) away from each other to create a larger system volume, V_2, in which new state they do not collide with each other as frequently and as energetically as in the original state. Such a natural change would lead to the reduced energy state depicted in part b of Figure 2.5. In this state the system has the same molecular composition and the the same total energy, but now in a larger volume (i.e., a lower energy density). This change occurs strictly by spontaneous molecular transport (i.e., no transformation). It is a change of state that is in some ways analogous to that undergone by a balloon filled with gas in a system of high ambient pressure expanding when the ambient pressure of the system is lowered until it reaches a mechanical equilibrium with its surrounding environment.

An alternative spontaneous change in response to an excess system energy is illustrated schematically in part b of Figure 2.5. In this case the volume of

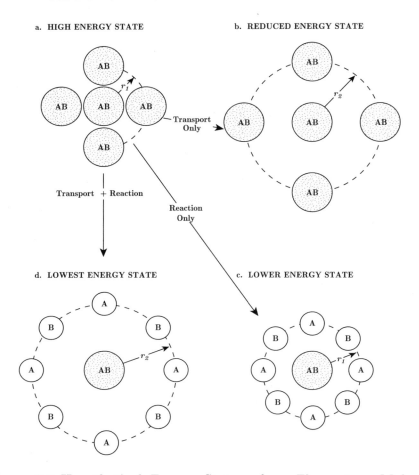

Figure 2.5 Hypothetical Energy States of an Elementary Molecular System

the system is constrained in some way (i.e., the balloon is placed in a tight mesh bag before the ambient pressure of the system is lowered), and the excess energies associated with the molecules of AB now cause them to split into their respective atoms, A and B (i.e., AB $\Leftrightarrow$ A + B). Energy is consumed in this process until there is no longer enough to effect further reaction, at which condition we have an internal chemical equilibrium corresponding to the energy state depicted in part c of Figure 2.5. Because the energy changes associated with spontaneous molecular transformations are generally greater than those associated with spontaneous molecular transport, the system depicted here will likely be in a lower energy state than the reduced state depicted in part b of the figure.

It should be intuitive at this point that the lowest relative energy state, and thus the most stable condition for this particular system, will result if both transformation and transport processes occur, as depicted in part d of Figure 2.5.

Some common sense "take home" observations that can serve us well are:

- *latent (potential) chemical energy is a characteristic property of every molecular entity (e.g., each molecule, ion, or mole of a substance);*

- *the total latent internal chemical energy of a system comprised by particular numbers of one or more molecular entities is the sum of the chemical energy of each times the respective number of each present in the system;*

- *the internal energy density (i.e., energy per unit volume) of a system determines its energy state;*

- *the energy state of a system is thus defined by its energy "concentration", which in turn is defined in terms of the respective concentrations of its molecular entities (e.g., molecules, ions, or moles per unit volume);*

- *the energy state of a system is thus proportional to the mass density or mass concentration (e.g., grams per unit volume) of its constituents;*

- *the energy state of a system can undergo spontaneous change to some lower energy state by the movement of its components in a way that causes a lowering of molecular mass concentration, or by transformation of these components to molecular entities having lower characteristic latent chemical energies;*

- *the spontaneous transport of a molecular entity between two points is thus directly proportional to its difference in concentration between those points (i.e., to its spatial concentration gradient, or in the x dimension, dC/dx);*

- *if the molecular entity is restrained from movement within or across the boundaries of a system, then its transformation from one form to another over a given time period is directly proportional to the difference in its temporal concentration over that period (i.e., to its average concentration gradient, dC/dt).*

2.3.4 Processes and Reactors

Thinking about systems? Think reactors! Transport and reactions of constituents take place within the three-dimensional space of environmental systems. We refer to these space volumes as reactors, regardless of whether they are described by highly irregular geometry (typical of natural systems) or by regular geometry (typical of engineered systems). Characterizations of transport phenomena depend on reactor scale, configuration, and boundary conditions, all of which are embodied by the term reactor dynamics.

Assume, for example, that the space volume of the reactor system depicted in Figure 2.2 represents a 20-km river stretch within which we are concerned with changes in the concentration of dissolved oxygen in the water. This reactor system thus includes the overlying atmosphere and underlying sediments of that section of the river, and all other associated inputs and outputs that contain dissolved oxygen or materials that can effect changes in dissolved oxygen. If, on the other hand, the issue is treatment of an oxygen-demanding waste discharge to the river, the space volume and the reactor itself reduce to a smaller, less complex, better defined, and more controllable scale. The space volume of the reactor reduces further in size and the reactor in both size and structure if we are interested in conducting a laboratory or pilot-scale test to assess the feasibility of using a particular process to change the oxygen-demanding character of the waste. Differences in temporal and spatial scales, configurations and boundaries, and conditions of mass distribution within and across reactor system boundaries can cause significant differences in the extent and rates at which processes will occur among those systems. This is true even if the basic processes and constituents of the systems are similar.

Primary factors determining how mass is distributed in a system can be subdivided into two categories: the ways in which mass enters and leaves the system across its boundaries; and, the ways in which mass is mixed within the system boundaries. These are both primarily transport considerations, although they eventually dictate the "efficiency" of a transformation reaction in a given process operation. It is possible, for example, in engineered systems to cause flows of constituents across the systems, and mixing of constituents within them, which will effect much higher efficiencies (greater extent, higher rate) of contaminant conversion than might occur by the same fundamental reaction(s) in natural river systems.

The major difference between natural systems and engineered reactors is that in the latter we select and control temporal and spatial scale, boundaries, and conditions of mass distribution within and across system boundaries. Engineered reactors lend themselves well to description, design, and control to achieve specific process behavior and accomplish specific treatment results. Different types of processes require different reactor configurations and conditions of operation to achieve optimal behavior and cost-effective results. Reactor behavior and design considerations comprise a major aspect of process analysis, and reactor engineering thus comprises a major focus of this text.

The levels of detail that are possible or practical in the characterization of processes vary greatly with the complexity of the reactions and the systems in which they take place. Reaction complexity is determined by reaction molecularities and by the number of components (species and phases) involved. System complexity is determined by temporal and spatial scales, boundary conditions, and initial conditions.

2.4 CHAPTER SUMMARY

Chapter 2 has built upon the introduction to important and identifying features of environmental systems and processes presented in Chapter 1. Our discussion has focused on ways in which the general nature of fundamental processes, and the character of different types of environmental systems in which they occur can be described and quantified in intuitive and common sense ways to formulate elementary process and system models. *From this discussion a recognition of three core elements of process and system analysis has emerged. In review of the chapter you should be able to identify these core elements as: (1) the availability of sufficient specific energy in a system to effect a particular chemical or biochemical transformation reaction; (2) the rate at which the specific energy can drive the reaction and the relevance of rate to the temporal scale of the process and system analysis; and, (3) the configuration, boundary conditions, and physical dynamics of the system (i.e., reactor) in which the transformation reaction occurs.* We use the foundation laid here to develop more detailed considerations of process dynamics and more rigorous characterizations of environmental systems in Chapter 3.

2.5 CITATIONS AND SOURCES

R.H. Perry, C.H. Chilton, and S.D. Kirkpatrick, *Chemical Engineers Handbook*, 4th Edition, Section 14, McGraw-Hill Book Company, New York, 1984. (Table 2.1)

W.J. Weber, Jr., B.E. Jones and L.E. Katz, "Fate of Toxic Organic Compounds in Activated Sludge and Integrated PAC Systems," *Water Science and Technology*, *19*, 471-482, 1987. (Table 2.2)

W.J. Weber, Jr., and F.A. DiGiano, *Process Dynamics in Environmental Systems*, John Wiley & Sons, Inc., New York, 1996. PDES is the source of most of the material presented in Chapter 2. Chapters 1 and 2 of PDES present more extensive and in-depth discussions of methods for quantitative analysis and characterization of environmental processes and systems, as well as comprehensive bibliographies of related references and suggested readings.

2.6 PROBLEM ASSIGNMENTS

2.1 The solubility of a gas in water can be expressed in terms of its gas-phase partial pressure by Henry's law. From Table 2.1 we note that Henry's constant for oxygen is 722×10^{-3} atm $-$ m^3/mol at 20°C. The pressure of a gas in a mixture of gases is given by $P = X_g P_T$, where X_g is the mole fraction of the gas in the atmosphere. For an atmospheric pressure (P_T) of 1.0 atm, calculate the solubility of oxygen in water at 20°C expressed on a mass per unit volume basis, mg/L.

Answers: 9.33 mg/L (or for $r_w = 1.0$ g/cm³, 9.33 ppm.)

2.2 The solubility of nitrogen gas at 20°C is $C_{S,N2} = 19$ mg/L.

(a) Calculate the maximum molar and mass concentrations of N_2 in water equilibrated with air.

(b) Discuss whether the Pacific Ocean is in equilibrium with the overlying atmosphere with respect to N_2. Describe how you arrived at your answer and why your answer makes sense in terms of the systems involved.

Answer: (a) 0.54 ×10⁻³ mol/L, or 15.2 mg/L.

2.3 The ammonia stripping column in Problem 1.9 must be analyzed to determine if an air standard of 10 ppm (*volume* per *volume*) can be met. The least amount of air that can be used in the stripping process is that which yields equilibrium between the air and liquid phase as the air leaves the air-water contacting device. If the packed-tower is operated in countercurrent fashion, the ammonia in the exiting air is equilibrated with that in the *incoming* water; if operated in cocurrent fashion, ammonia in the exiting air is equilibrated with that in the exiting water. The Henry's constant for ammonia at 20°C is 1.37×10^{-5} atm $-$ m³/mol.

(a) Compare the minimum airflow rates for countercurrent and cocurrent operation to determine if either mode meets the air standard for ammonia.

(b) Discuss what can be done if neither of the stripper operations described meet the air standard.

2.4 Based on the properties of the organic chemicals given in Table 2.2, identify which of the four compounds benzene, chlorobenzene, nitrobenzene, and o-xylene is the most: a) soluble in water, b) soluble in organic liquids, and c) volatile. Referring to the properties of solubility and vapor pressure only, rank these four chemicals in terms of decreasing values of Henry's constant. Explain the logic behind your ranking of $\mathcal{K}_H$ values and then check Table 2.2 for the accuracy of your ranking.

Answers: a) nitrobenzene, b) xylene, c) benzene.

2.5 A 10-mg quantity of phenanthrene (MW = 178) is added to a 1-L flask containing 500 mL of air and 500 mL of water. Predict the aqueous phase equilibrium concentration of phenanthrene at 25° C if the values for this compound for the first four properties and constants listed in Table 2.2 are: $C_S = 1.1$ mg/L, $P^v = 1.6 \times 10^{-7}$ atm, $\mathcal{K}_H = 4.0 \times 10^{-5}$ atm $-$ m³/mol, and $log\mathcal{K}_{OW} = 4.52$.

2.6 A tightly closed 1-L flask initially containing 7.4 g of liquid n-decane (MW = 142 g/mol), an amount that occupies a volume of 10 mL ($\rho = 0.74$ g/mL), is left undisturbed for ten weeks on a shelf at $25°$ C. What quantity of n-decane would you expect to find remaining in its liquid form after this period? Show your calculations and state your assumptions. Pertinent property data for n-decane at $25°$ C are: $C_S = 0.015$ mg/L, $P^v = 1.74 \times 10^{-3}$ atm, $\mathcal{K}_H = 6.9$ atm $-$ m^3/mol, and $log\ \mathcal{K}_{OW} = 6.25$.

2.7 Empirical correlations among different types of phase transformation properties are often used in process analysis. Using the properties and constants for organic compounds presented in Table 2.2, plot Henry's constant for each compound against its respective C_S, P^v, and $\mathcal{K}_{OW}$ values. Identify trends, if any, and attempt to find correlations based on regression analyses of your data. Discuss the goodness of your fitting parameters in light of your results (*Hint:* looking up the molecular structure of the compounds may help in this regard). Using the same approach, plot Henry's constant for each compound against C_S/P^v. Compare any trend(s) you observe with the results from Problem 2.4.

2.8 Consider for the scenario described below the potential contamination by lead of a raw drinking water drawn from one of the rivers in the lake system presented schematically in Figure 2.1.

A large underground clay-lined waste pit at a former industrial site is located alongside *River A*, near its confluence with *LAKE I*. The existence of this pit has been known for some time, but no seepage has ever been found. After a recent Richter-Scale three earth tremor, however, a waste plume from the pit has been discovered, the major contaminant in the stream being lead (Pb^{2+}). Following the onset of the relatively steady new seepage from the pit, dissolved Pb^{2+} concentrations averaging 100 μmol/l are found in *River A* immediately above its discharge to *LAKE I*.

A community located along *River F* just down stream from *LAKE II* draws its public water supply from that river. The community has a relatively simple water treatment plant that has no provision for removal of dissolved Pb^{2+}. The drinking water standard for lead is 15 μg/l. Determine whether the water supply to the community will exceed this standard if there is no remediation of the pit seepage.

The Pb^{2+} undergoes a precipitation reaction of the form

$$Pb^{2+} + 2OH^- \Leftrightarrow Pb(OH)_2(s) \downarrow$$

at a rate given by $r = k[Pb^{2+}][OH^-]^2$, where $k = 5.0 \times 10^7$ $(1/mol)^2 (min^{-1})$. The lakes are well buffered at pH $= 8.3$.

Answer: The lead concentration in River F will reach an eventual level of approximately 0.54 mg/l, more than thirty fold greater than the standard.

2.9 The sole sources of water and chloride (Cl^-) to a lake are three rivers: A, B and C. The flow rate of water in *River A* is 300 gpm and in *River B* is 550 gpm. *River C* flows into the lake, but the flow rate is unknown. The flow out of the lake is by *River D* only. The concentration of chloride in *River A* is 50 mg/l. The chloride concentrations in *Rivers B* and C are the same. The concentration of chloride in the lake is 75 mg/l. If the detention time in the lake is 2.5 years and the volume is 2400×10^6 gallons, find the following:

(a) The flow rate of *River C* in gpm;

(b) The concentration of chloride in *River C* in mg/l.

2.10 Wastewater from the steam power plant operation described in Problem 1.10 in Chapter 1 is discharged first to cooling ponds and then to a river. The 10-year 7-day low flow in the river is 25 ft^3/sec (cfs), the average stream velocity is 100 ft/min, and the wastewater discharge averages 100 gallons per minute (gpm).

A phosphate stream standard of 0.1 mg/l has been established to control eutrophication in a downstream impoundment used for recreation. The background phosphate concentration is 0.05 mg/l (upstream of the discharge). As a consultant representing the steam power plant, you are asked to

(a) Determine the degree of treatment (% removal in PO_4) of the wastewater discharge necessary to meet the State regulations assuming the maximum allowable industrial discharge;

(b) Compute the expected phosphate flux in the stream below the confluence of the discharge (assume complete mixing);

(c) If the discharge plume only spreads to one half of the stream cross-sectional area, calculate the expected phosphate flux in the plume below the confluence of the discharge;

(d) Calculate the annual phosphate loading into the downstream impoundment; and,

(e) Determine the percentage of the annual phosphate loading to the impoundment contributed by the industry.

Chapter 3

Process and System Modeling

Contents

3.0   CHAPTER OBJECTIVES

To identify ways in which the transformation and transport pro-
cesses identified in Chapter 1 and described qualitatively in Chap-
ter 2 interact to cause changes in environmental systems, and to
learn means to develop rigorous mathematical equations with which
to describe these interactions and models with which to quantitatively
characterize natural systems and design engineered systems.

3.1   A RATIONAL APPROACH

System characterizations and designs generally involve some analog or model
of the system(s) of interest. Physical models that capture the essential features
of a full scale system on a smaller and more manageable scale are useful in
some circumstances, but the most flexible, cost effective, and rational approach
is more commonly the use of a mathematical rather than physical analog. The
development and application of mathematically based models to describe the
components, composition, and related transport and transformation processes
of any environmental system involves a sequence of procedures that will be
developed and elaborated on throughout this chapter.

The equations used to structure mathematical models for environ-
mental systems must meet certain criteria. First and foremost, the
transport and transformation processes involved must interact in a
manner that satisfies the fundamental principles of thermodynamics
and continuity, and this must be reflected in the equations comprising
such models. These principles dictate that any change in a system
must be such that the energy, mass, and momentum of that system
are conserved, although each may change in form.

When the changes that occur within a system involve transformation of one
or more of its constituents, the overriding continuity relationships are driven by
changes in the number of units (e.g., molecules or moles) of specific chemical
species. Each unit has a well-defined weight (e.g., molecular or molar weight) or
mass. Although the numbers of units of individual species comprising a system
are changed by a transformation process, the summed mass of those species
must at any time remain constant if the system is closed, that is, if no mass
enters or leaves the system in the course of the transformation. This is inherent
in the stoichiometric relationship given in Equation 2.11 in Chapter 2. Equation
2.11 relates only to transformation reactions in closed systems. As suggested
in Figures 1.1, 1.2, 2.1 and 2.2, most environmental systems are open systems;
that is, they involve transport of mass across their boundaries. We are able
to characterize the net effects of these transport and transformation processes
only if we can fully account for the changes in the molecular units or masses
of individual species and can balance those factors that add units or masses of
components with those that decrease them. Such balances may be stated in
terms of either molecular units or mass, and referred to as either material or

mass balances. The term material balance is more general because transport and reaction phenomena occur in units of chemical entities (i.e., molecules, atoms, ions or moles) that are often not expressed as masses, and that are further usually given in terms of concentration, an intensive (e.g., per unit volume) quantity.

3.2 MATERIAL BALANCE EQUATIONS

Material balance equations (MBEs) comprise the basic framework for mathematical modeling of physical systems. They are the logical starting point for integrating the three core elements of process and system analysis (energetics, rates and reactor dynamics) into a quantitative description of process and system dynamics. To reiterate for emphasis, the three core elements of process and system analysis are: (1) energy availability for constituent transformation(s); (2) rate(s) of energy utilization; and (3) the configuration and physical dynamics of the system (reactor) of interest.

3.2.1 Control Volumes and Material Balances

The MBE for a constituent within a reactor accounts for changes in the composition and concentration of that constituent which occur by both transport of materials across the reactor boundaries and reactions or processes that take place within the reactor. The material relationships associated with these phenomena translate, for specific systems, to mass relationships by virtue of stoichiometry and molecular structure (mass). Fluid balances can be best described in terms of mass; i.e., mass of water, mass of air, etc. In this text we use primarily the more general term, material balance.

The control volume approach employed in fluid mechanics to derive the continuity equations for fluid mass, momentum and energy is applicable also for any component dissolved or suspended in a fluid. *The general "word equation" for the balance of a substance, i, within any control volume is given as*

$$
\boxed{
\begin{array}{l}
\textbf{\textit{WORD FORM OF THE}} \\
\textbf{\textit{MATERIAL BALANCE EQUATION}} \\[1em]
\begin{array}{lclcl}
\textit{Rate of} & & \textit{Rate of} & & \textit{Rate of} \\
\textit{change} & & \textit{flow of i} & & \textit{reaction} \\
\textit{of i in} & = & \textit{through} & \pm & \textit{of i in} \\
\textit{a control} & & \textit{the control} & & \textit{the control} \\
\textit{volume} & & \textit{volume} & & \textit{volume}
\end{array}
\end{array}
}
\qquad (3.1)
$$

The word-form MBE given in Equation 3.1 can be expressed in terms of the mass of a substance, but it should be kept in mind that re-

action stoichiometry is based on molar relationships. The conversion from one form to another is straightforward for discrete chemical entities, but may become problematic when lumped parameter measures of concentration are used; e.g., Biochemical Oxygen Demand (BOD), Chemical Oxygen Demand (COD) and Total Organic Carbon (TOC).

3.2.2   Point and Integral Forms

The most fundamental mathematical elaboration of the MBE given in Equation 3.1 is developed by application of the principles of continuum mechanics to a general control volume, V; more specifically to a differential element of that control volume, dV. The differential element is fundamentally a point form representation of the control volume; that is, the control volume reduced to an infinitely small scale. The point form is considered to be the largest truly homogeneous form of the control volume, a necessary, although not completely sufficient condition for application of continuum theory. A detailed discussion of this approach to development of material balance equations is given in Chapter 2 of PDES.

A somewhat more intuitive approach, often referred to as the shell balance approach, may be made by considering a material balance on a finite volume. Consider, for example, Figure 3.1. Suppose that the volume represented is sealed in the x, y and x, z planes, so that mass flux, $N(\text{ML}^{-2}\text{t}^{-1})$, of a component occurs only across the finite element area $\Delta A_{yz} = \Delta y \Delta z$ in a direction perpendicular to the y, z plane, as in Figure 3.1; i.e., a one-dimensional flux. The discrete elemental control volume, ΔV, in this figure has the finite dimensions $\Delta x = x_2 - x_1, \Delta y = y_2 - y_1$, and $\Delta z = z_2 - z_1$.

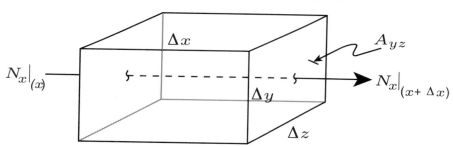

Figure 3.1 One-Dimensional Flux Through a Control Volume

Assuming that A_{yz} and ΔV are constant, we can write a single-component material balance for the finite volume, ΔV, from Equation 3.1

$$\begin{bmatrix} Mass\ change \\ within\ \Delta V \end{bmatrix} = [Mass\ in] - [Mass\ out] + \begin{bmatrix} Mass\ change \\ due\ to\ reaction \end{bmatrix} \quad (3.2)$$

or, in mathematical terms

$$(N\mid_x - N\mid_{x+\Delta x})\, A_{yz}\Delta t + r\Delta V\Delta t = (C\mid_{t+\Delta t} - C\mid_t)\,\Delta V \quad (3.3)$$

where the respective terms have the units

$$(ML^{-2}t^{-1})(L^2)(t) + (ML^{-3}t^{-1})(L^3)(t) = (ML^{-3})(L^3)$$

Equation 3.3 can be divided through by A_{yz}, Δt, and Δx, to yield the finite-volume form of the material balance equation

$$\left[\frac{N\mid_x - N\mid_{x+\Delta x}}{\Delta x} \right] + r = \left[\frac{C\mid_{t+\Delta t} - C\mid_t}{\Delta t} \right] \tag{3.4}$$

where $\Delta V = A_{yz}\Delta x$. *To develop the point-form of the material continuity equation we now let the finite volume, ΔV, and the time increment, Δt, each shrink to zero. Note that in Equation 3.4 the expressions in brackets have forms resembling those in the definition of the derivative of any function, $\phi(u)$, namely*

$$\frac{d\phi(u)}{d(u)} = \lim_{\Delta u \to 0} \left[\frac{\phi(u + \Delta u) - \phi(u)}{\Delta u} \right] \tag{3.5}$$

Taking the limits of Equation 3.4 as Δx and $\Delta t \to 0$ thus yields

$$\boxed{\begin{array}{l} \textbf{\textit{One-Dimensional}} \\ \textbf{\textit{Point Form of}} \qquad -\dfrac{\partial N}{\partial x} + r = \dfrac{\partial C}{\partial t} \\ \textbf{\textit{The MBE}} \end{array}} \tag{3.6}$$

We shall see shortly that the shell balance approach can be used similarly to develop point-form material balance equations for one-dimensional radial transport in spherical and cylindrical coordinates.

The shell balance approach used to develop the one-dimensional point form of the mass continuity equation (Equation 3.6) can be extended to development of continuity equations that address multi-dimensional transport phenomena. Consider, for example, the control element shown in Figure 3.2. If flux is assumed to occur normal to each of the three planes of this discrete element, we can write the corresponding material balance equation as

$$\left[N_x\mid_{(x)} - N_x\mid_{(x+\Delta x)} \right] \Delta y \Delta z + \left[N_y\mid_{(y)} - N_y\mid_{(y+\Delta y)} \right] \Delta x \Delta z +$$
$$\left[N_z\mid_{(z)} - N_z\mid_{(z+\Delta z)} \right] \Delta x \Delta y + r \Delta x \Delta y \Delta z = \frac{\Delta C}{\Delta t}(\Delta x \Delta y \Delta z) \tag{3.7}$$

The point form of the continuity equation derives immediately by dividing both sides by the volume $(\Delta x \Delta y \Delta z)$ of the discrete element, and taking the limit as this volume approaches zero; i.e., as $\Delta x \to 0$, $\Delta y \to 0$, and $\Delta z \to 0$

$$\boxed{\begin{array}{l} \textbf{\textit{Three-Dimensional}} \\ \textbf{\textit{Point Form of}} \qquad -\left[\dfrac{\partial N_x}{\partial x} + \dfrac{\partial N_y}{\partial y} + \dfrac{\partial N_z}{\partial z} \right] + r = \dfrac{\partial C}{\partial t} \\ \textbf{\textit{The MBE}} \end{array}} \tag{3.8}$$

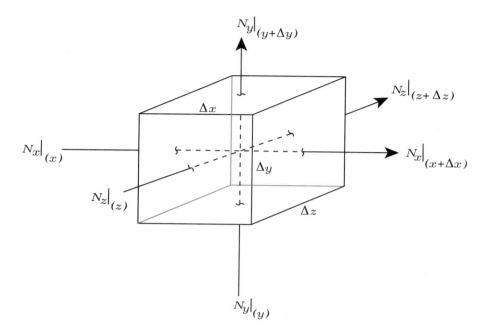

Figure 3.2 Three-Dimensional Flux Through a Control Volume

A complementary view of the MBE is given when the word form of Equation 3.1 is expressed in a somewhat different mathematical form referred to as the integral form of the MBE. For the general case in which the net molar rate of input to an irregular three-dimensional differential control volume occurs over all surfaces it would be necessary to perform a surface integration of the *scalar product* of $(N \cdot n_v)$, where N is now the flux vector and n_v the inward directed vector normal to dA (see PDES for full development).

A one-dimensional version of the integral form of the MBE, can also be developed from the control volume given in Figure 3.1. For the specific case given in Figure 3.1 in which the net molar rate of input occurs only across the interfaces A_{yz} at $x = 0$ and $x = \Delta x$, the surface integral reduces to

$$\begin{matrix} \textbf{\textit{Net molar rate of input}} \\ \textbf{\textit{to} } V_C \end{matrix} = - \int\limits_{S_c} N dA \qquad (3.9)$$

The molar rate of chemical reaction in the material balance is defined as the time rate of change in the concentration of the substance of interest in the control volume, V_C, due to reaction alone. However, the reaction rate, r, usually depends on concentration, and concentration can vary within the control volume. The most general form of the MBE therefore accounts for a reaction rate which varies with space in the control volume such that

$$\text{\textit{Rate of chemical reaction within } } V_C = \int_{V_C} r\,dV \qquad (3.10)$$

Finally, the net rate of accumulation of mass (expressed in moles) in the control volume is obtained from the change in mass of the component of interest over an increment of time, $\Delta t = t_2 - t_1$, such that

$$\text{\textit{Rate of accumulation within } } V_C = \frac{\int_{V_C} C\,dV\,|_{t=t_2} - \int_{V_C} C\,dV\,|_{t=t_1}}{\Delta t} \qquad (3.11)$$

At steady state, the above term is zero. Replacing the word description of the material balance given in Equation 3.1 with Equations 3.9, 3.10, and 3.11, and taking the limit as Δt approaches zero gives the integral form of the MBE; i.e.,

$$\boxed{\text{\textit{Integral Form of The MBE}} \qquad -\int_{S_C} N\,dA + \int_{V_C} r\,dV = \frac{\partial}{\partial t}\int_{V_C} C\,dV} \qquad (3.12)$$

As we will discuss further in our considerations of transport processes in Chapter 4, the integral form of the continuity equation for the mass of a component in a fluid is useful conceptually because it is analogous to those for the mass, energy, and momentum of the fluid itself. It is valid for any arbitrary control volume and is not dependent on the operative form of either the mass transport or reaction rate expressions. It further accommodates variations in flux with control surface area and therefore conveniently describes the dynamics of such natural systems as lakes and groundwaters, where flux may vary with surface area selected for the control volume. Total system or reactor descriptions and quantifications require superposition of appropriate reaction processes on transport processes. In other words, we must develop equations that simultaneously describe not only bulk transport by fluid flow but also any pertinent chemical reactions. Both types of processes involve rather complicated dynamics.

3.2.3 Configurational Alternatives

3.2.3.1 Dominant One-Dimensional Transport

The three-dimensional point form of the MBE given in Equation 3.8 is a rigorous representation of the most fundamental basis for description of natural systems and design of engineered reactors. This form of the continuity equation requires integration to determine concentration patterns as functions of distance and time. Its application as written is often problematic in environmental systems because of their complexities and associated deficiencies in system data and details. Approximations are thus frequently employed where warranted to simplify the mathematical treatment of three dimensional systems. For example, for situations in which flux occurs dominantly in only one direction (e.g., in the x dimension, normal to the y, z plane), the terms $\partial N_y/\partial_y$ and $\partial N_z/\partial_z$ may be neglected in Equation 3.8, essentially reducing it to Equation 3.6 to obtain a much more readily solved approximation. This approach is illustrated in Example 3.1, in which the behavior of a complex reactor system is approximated by a simplified one-dimensional form of its material balance relationship.

Example 3.1. Treatment of an Industrial Waste Using an Anaerobic Biological Reactor. (Development of a steady-state material balance equation and a process model.)

- ***Situation.*** *An anaerobic biological reactor (a high-density biofilm device) has been selected over an aerobic biological reactor for treatment of an industrial waste containing a high concentration of a volatile organic chemical (VOC). Because the wastewater does not contact air in anaerobic treatment, there is no opportunity for volatilization of the organic chemical in the biological treatment step. The VOC is not completely biodegraded during treatment, and some residual thus remains.*

- ***Question(s).*** *Develop the steady-state material balance relationship and process model to describe the loss of the residual VOC as the treated wastewater passes from the biological treatment unit through a long, narrow open channel to a polishing lagoon before discharge to a river.*

- ***Logic and Answer(s).***

  1. *We will assume that the flow in the channel is essentially one-dimensional (x) along its length such that the flux of the VOC is can be defined by*

  $$N = \frac{QC_x}{A} = v_x C_x$$

  where Q is the flow rate; A is the cross-sectional area of the channel filled with water; and v_x is the velocity in the direction of the channel length. The concentration of the volatile component is a function of position, x, along the channel, and changes due to losses to the air as the water travels as a "slug" down the channel; thus the point form of a material balance expression is appropriate.

  2. *Volatilization is a transport process that occurs at the interface between the air and water. It represents a rate of loss of VOC from the water to air as given by*

  $$r_v = -k_f(a_s^\circ)_R(C_x - C_s)$$

  where r_v is the rate of volatilization ($M/L^{-3}t^{-1}$); k_f is the mass transfer coefficient (Lt^{-1}); $(a_s^\circ)_R$ is the surface area available for *mass transfer per unit volume of the "reactor"* (L^{-1}); *and C_S is the concentration of the VOC that is predicted by Henry's law to exist in the water when equilibrium is reached with the atmosphere. Because the VOC transferred to the air above the channel is being greatly diluted, the partial pressure of the VOC is very close to zero and thus by Henry's law, C_S must also be close to zero (see related discussion in Chapter 2).*

3. *Steady-state is a reasonable assumption if the VOC concentration entering the channel and the wastewater flow rate remain the same for all time. The point form of the material balance is obtained either by writing a shell balance over a distance x of the channel (see Example 3.2 for an illustration) or by writing directly an expression for the change in flux over a differential element, dx. The latter approach being illustrated below*

$$-dN A + \boldsymbol{r}_v A dx = 0$$

Dividing through by $A dx$, the volume of the differential element, gives

$$-\frac{dN}{dx} + \boldsymbol{r}_v = 0$$

4. *Substituting for the flux (step 1) in the x direction and the volatilization rate (step 2) provides the final form of the material balance*

$$-v_x \frac{dC}{dx} + k_f (a_s^\circ)_R (C_S - C) = 0$$

or given that $C_S = 0$,

$$-v_x \frac{dC}{dx} - k_f (a_s^\circ)_R C = 0$$

5. *A process model is obtained by separation of variables and integration*

$$\frac{C_x}{C_o} = \exp\left[\frac{-k_f (a_s^\circ)_R x}{v_x}\right]$$

where C_o is the concentration of VOC entering the channel $(x = 0)$.

- *Key Point(s). In this example we bring together some of the intuitive and common sense approaches to modeling learned in Chapter 2 with some of the more sophisticated mathematical descriptions learned in this chapter. Most specifically, we follow the recommendation made in Section 2.2.4 in Chapter 2, that "all transport and transformation processes should be identified in words first and then translated into equations."*

3.2.3.2   Radial Transport in Spheres and Cylinders

In some instances we must apply material balances for transport and reaction in spheres (e.g., adsorbent or ion exchange particles) and cylinders (e.g., reactive surfaces on tubular membranes or pipe walls). Three-dimensional point forms of the continuity equation for spherical and cylindrical geometries are derived by spatial transformation of flux gradients from rectangular to either spherical or cylindrical coordinates by use of vector mathematics. Details of these transformations are beyond the scope of this text.

Simpler, one-dimensional forms result when flux is normal to the surface (i.e., radially directed). We can use the same type of shell-balance approach we learned earlier in this chapter to develop these relationships. For spherical coordinates, and for radial transport only we can write from Equation 3.2 an expression analogous to that given for rectangular coordinates in Equation 3.3

$$\left(N\mid_r - N\mid_{r+\Delta r}\right)4\pi r^2 + \boldsymbol{r}\left(4\pi r^2 \Delta r\right) = \frac{\partial(C \cdot 4\pi r^2 \Delta r)}{\partial t} \tag{3.13}$$

where r is the radial coordinate originating at the core of the sphere, $4\pi r^2$ is the surface area of a sphere of radius r, normal to the radial flux, and Δr is the incremental transport distance along r. Dividing Equation 3.13 through by $4\pi r^2 \Delta r$ and taking the limit as $\Delta r \to 0$ then gives

$$\boxed{\begin{array}{ll} \textit{\textbf{Radial Transport}} & \\ \textit{\textbf{and Reaction}} & \quad -\dfrac{1}{r^2}\dfrac{\partial}{\partial r}(r^2 N_r) + \boldsymbol{r} = \dfrac{\partial C}{\partial t} \\ \textit{\textbf{in a Sphere}} & \end{array}} \tag{3.14}$$

It is possible to use a steady-state approximation for radial diffusion without reaction in spherical and cylindrical coordinates in certain situations. Radial diffusive flux through a sphere is described by Fick's law. According to Equation 3.14, the steady-state diffusive flux at any specific radial position of interest, r_1, is related to that at any general value of the position variable, r, by

$$\boxed{\begin{array}{ll} \textit{\textbf{Radial Diffusion}} & \\ \textit{\textbf{Flux in a}} & \quad (N)_{r_1} = \left(\dfrac{r}{r_1}\right)^2 (N_r)_r = -\left(\dfrac{r}{r_1}\right)^2 \mathcal{D}_l \dfrac{dC}{dr} \\ \textit{\textbf{Sphere}} & \end{array}} \tag{3.15}$$

If concentrations are specified at the two specific radial positions r_1 and r_2, the flux at r_1 can be obtained by integration of Equation 3.15.

For radial transport only in cylindrical coordinates and assuming a unit length along the axis of the cylinder

$$\left(N_r\mid_r - N_r\mid_{r+\Delta r}\right)2\pi r + \boldsymbol{r}(2\pi r \Delta r) = \frac{\partial(C \cdot 2\pi r \Delta r)}{\partial t} \tag{3.16}$$

where r is the radial coordinate originating at the axis of the cylinder, $2\pi r$ is the surface area of a unit length of cylinder normal to the radial flux, and Δr is the incremental distance along r. Dividing Equation 3.16 through by $2\pi r \Delta r$ and taking the limit as $\Delta r \to 0$ gives

$$\boxed{\textbf{\textit{Radial Transport and Reaction in a Cylinder}} \quad -\frac{1}{r}\frac{\partial}{\partial r}(rN_r) + \boldsymbol{r} = \frac{\partial C}{\partial t}} \tag{3.17}$$

Radial diffusive transport without reaction in cylindrical coordinates (see Example 3.2) can be analyzed using the same steady-state approximation as we used for spherical coordinates. Beginning with Equation 3.17, we obtain

$$\boxed{\textbf{\textit{Radial Diffusion Flux in a Cylinder}} \quad (N_r)_{r_1} = \frac{r}{r_1}(N_r)_r = -\frac{r}{r_1}\mathcal{D}_l\frac{dC}{dr}} \tag{3.18}$$

3.2.3.3   Two-Dimensional Transport in Cylinders

The shell balance is a useful intuitive approach for describing axial flux along the length (x) of a hollow cylinder (e.g., a pipe or a fiber membrane) of radius, R, coupled with radial transport through the wall, as illustrated in Figure 3.3. For this situation we can write

$$(N_x\,|_x - N_x\,|_{x+\Delta x})\,\pi R^2 + \boldsymbol{r}(\pi R^2 \Delta x) - N_r\,|_R \cdot 2\pi R \Delta x$$
$$= \frac{\partial(C \cdot \pi R^2 \Delta x)}{\partial t} \tag{3.19}$$

Dividing through by $\pi R^2 \Delta x$ and letting $\Delta x \to 0$ gives

$$\boxed{\textbf{\textit{Axial and Radial Transport and Reaction in a Cylindrical Pipe}} \quad -\frac{\partial N_x}{\partial x} + \boldsymbol{r} - \frac{2}{R}N_r\,|_R = \frac{\partial C}{\partial t}} \tag{3.20}$$

Equation 3.18 can be applied in Equation 3.20, where an expression is needed for radial flux at the inner edge of a pipe or membrane wall $(r_1 = R)$. The concentration at the inner edge is the same as that throughout the internal cross section at location x. If a steady-state concentration is specified at the outer edge, it is possible to integrate Equation 3.18 and obtain a simple expression for $N_r\,|_R$.

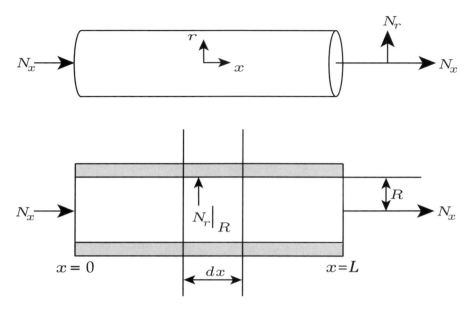

*Figure 3.3 One-Dimensional Axial Transport and Reaction in a
Plastic Pipe with Radial Transport Through the Pipe Walls*

*Typically, the axial flux, N_x, in the above equation is determined
by macrotransport processes through the reactor whereas the radial
flux, N_r is determined by microtransport processes across an interface (e.g., diffusion through the thickness of a pipe wall).* As written,
Equation 3.20 expresses the loss of material from a pipe due to radial transport outward. An illustration of the use of Equation 3.20 in modified form is
presented in Example 3.2.

---

*Example 3.2. Contamination of a Buried Irrigation Pipe by Gaso-
line Leaked from Underground Storage Tanks. (An illustration of
combined axial and radial contaminant transport in a cylindrical system.)*

- *Situation.* Leakage of gasoline from underground storage tanks has contaminated the groundwater in the vicinity of a submerged plastic pipe that
  carries irrigation water to the fields. Various components of gasoline are
  known to "soften" plastic pipe material such that it becomes permeable.
  Among the major components of gasoline is toluene.

- *Question(s).* Develop a material balance-based model to predict the
  toluene concentration in the irrigation line after it passes through the region of contaminated soil.

- **Logic and Answer(s).**

  1. *The first step in analysis is to develop a definition sketch in order to visualize the components needed in the material balance. (The reader is asked to do this as an exercise)*

  2. *The diffusive flux of toluene is inward through the pipe wall and there is no subsequent reaction. Steady state is a reasonable assumption if the toluene concentration surrounding the pipe wall is large and is not depleted significantly by diffusion into the pipe. Thus, for this situation, a modified version of Equation 3.20 can be written as*

$$-\frac{\partial N_x}{\partial x} + \frac{2}{R_I} N_{r,R_I} = 0$$

  3. *The advective flux of toluene in the direction of pipe flow is defined as the mass of toluene carried along by the flow rate, Q, of water per unit area of the pipe normal to the flow (flux = mass/area-time)*

$$N_x = \frac{QC_x}{\pi R_I^2} = v_x C_x$$

  where v_x is the velocity of water in the pipe (see Chapter 4).

  4. *The diffusive flux normal to the pipe wall is governed by Fick's first law of diffusion (see Chapters 4 and 13)*

$$N_r = -\mathcal{D}_m \frac{dC_r}{dr}$$

  where $\mathcal{D}_m$ is the diffusivity of toluene through the pipe material, i.e., the characteristic constant of proportionality between the concentration gradient and the flux. The material balance for diffusive flux through a differential element of the pipe wall of unit length is

$$(N_r \mid_r - N_r \mid_{r+\Delta r}) 2\pi r = \frac{\partial C_r}{\partial t} 2\pi r \Delta r$$

  Dividing through by the control volume $2\pi r \Delta r$ and letting $\Delta r \to 0$ gives

$$-\frac{1}{r}\frac{\partial}{\partial r}(rN_r) = \frac{\partial C_r}{\partial t}$$

  5. *Because the concentration of toluene outside the pipe wall, C_O is assumed constant, the diffusive flux at any location along the pipe wall, x, must be at steady state ($\partial C_r/\partial t = 0$) and the product, rN_r, must accordingly be a constant. This simplification together with Fick's law allows the diffusive flux at $r = R_I$ to be expressed in terms of diffusive flux at $r = R_O$ as*

$$N_{r,R_I} = -\frac{\mathcal{D}_m(C_I - C_O)}{R_I \ln(R_I/R_O)}$$

6. *Substituting the advective flux expression (step 3) and the diffusive flux expression (step 5) with the proper sign to account for flux into the pipe, the material balance for toluene in the pipe (step 2) leads to*

$$-v_x \frac{dC_x}{dx} - \frac{2\mathcal{D}_m}{R_I \ln(R_O/R_I)}(C_x - C_O) = 0$$

An implicit assumption is that concentration in the radial direction at the inside edge of the pipe wall (C_I) *is equal to the concentration everywhere in the cross-section of the pipe at a particular location,* x. *The solution to this differential equation is easily obtained by separation of variables*

$$\frac{C_x}{C_O} = 1 - \exp(-Kx/v_x)$$

where

$$K = \frac{2\mathcal{D}_m}{R_I \ln(R_O/R_I)}$$

- **Key Point(s).** *The dynamics of a seemingly complex environmental problem are reduced to a reasonably simple descriptive mathematical model by using common sense assumptions to combine submodels for two transport processes operating in two different spatial dimensions.*

3.3 FRAMES OF REFERENCE

The word form of the MBE (Equation 3.1) expresses rates of change in the contents and components of any system in terms of associated rates of input and output to, and rates of reaction within, that system. We must, therefore, eventually learn how to describe both types of rates in appropriate mathematical form(s). This is not a simple task because rates of reaction and rates of transport of reacting substances are affected by many factors that vary from one system to another. The specific forms appropriate for expressing both types of rates in any given circumstance are thus specific to that circumstance; i.e., reaction and transport rates are system specific. In this context we reiterate with emphasis a point made in Section 2.3.4 of the previous chapter; to wit, if you're thinking about systems, think reactors!

We will soon begin to develop rational bases for writing such rate equations and placing them in the construct of specific systems. These exercises will be predicated on certain immutable laws of physics and chemistry that dictate the forms of reaction and mass transfer rate expressions that are appropriate for specific types of systems and conditions. As we go forward, however, it will be helpful for us to have some simple points of reference regarding certain elementary cases of reaction rates, transport rates, and system (i.e., reactor) configurations.

3.3.1 Reactions, Processes, and Microscale Transport

Many of the reactions that characterize environmental processes can be expressed as what are termed "first-order" reactions. Simply stated, a first-order reaction proceeds at a rate, r, that is directly proportional to the concentration of the reacting substance; i.e.

$$\textbf{\textit{First-Order Reaction Rate}} \qquad \frac{dC}{dt} = r = kC \qquad (3.21)$$

where k is a constant of proportionality termed a rate coefficient.

Mass transport, a second prime characteristic of environmental process and system dynamics, can proceed at two distinctly different scales; i.e., microscopic and macroscopic scales. Mass transport at the microscale, because it usually occurs at the interfaces of two phases across which transfer of a substance takes place, is commonly referred to as mass transfer. Rates of simple one-dimensional microscale mass transfer processes in homogeneous fluids or solids are expressed in terms of Fick's first law of diffusion

$$\textbf{\textit{Fick's First Law of Diffusion}} \qquad N_x = \mathcal{D}_l \frac{dC}{dx} \qquad (3.22)$$

in which N_x is the flux $(ML^{-2}t^{-1})$ across a plane of elemental thickness dx, and $\mathcal{D}_l$ is the free liquid diffusion coefficient if the medium of the plane is water (appropriate values of $\mathcal{D}_g$ and $\mathcal{D}_s$ would apply for gaseous and solid media, respectively). Diffusive transport across the plane is thus directly proportional to the spatial gradient in concentration across the plane. If the diffusion involves mass transfer from one phase to another across an interfacial boundary or film of thickness $dx = \delta$, Equation 3.22 can be written as

$$\textbf{\textit{Diffusional Mass Transfer}} \qquad N_x = k_f(C_\delta - C) \qquad (3.23)$$

where $k_f = \mathcal{D}_l/\delta$ is the film mass transfer coefficient. Note that the dimensions of k_f are the same as those of velocity (Lt^{-1}), in essence stating that diffusive mass flux is given by the product of a molecular velocity and a linear concentration driving force (energy difference).

The similarity between Equation 3.21 and Equations 3.22 and 3.23 should come as no surprise, given our earlier discussion in Section 2.3.3 about the energy states of environmental systems and their associated tendencies (and rates) for undergoing change to achieve more stable lower energy states. We concluded in that discussion that changes by transformation in a system of fixed volume occur directly in proportion to temporal gradients in concentration, while system changes caused by transport are in direct proportion to spatial gradients in concentration. Such direct proportionalities are referred to as linear or first-order relationships. To put this in context, consider a simple plot of y calculated as a specific function of x in rectangular coordinates. If the trace of the function is flat (i.e., has no slope) then y is said to be independent of x; (i.e., y is a constant and its order of dependence on x is zero). If the trace is linear, the slope is constant and the variable y is said to have a first-order dependence on x (i.e., $y = \pm ax$). If the trace is non-linear, then the dependence of one variable on the other is either higher or lower than first order (i.e., $y = \pm ax^n$ where $n \neq 0$ or 1).

Our comparison of the forms of equations describing frame of reference transformation and transport processes, two categories of processes that are quite different from a phenomenological perspective, reveals that they are each motivated in fundamentally the same way by the same related system properties; i.e., by gradients in energy/mass/concentration. As a consequence, both categories of processes can often be described by models having similar mathematical forms.

3.3.2   Macroscale Transport and Reactors

The rate of change of a substance within a control volume also includes macroscale mass transfer into and out of that control volume. A control volume can be defined in many ways, depending upon the system to be described. If, for example, the contents of the system are completely mixed, then the control volume becomes the system itself. Conversely, if there are spatial concentration gradients within the system, the control volume must be a much smaller part of the system, a part that can be considered to have homogeneous content.

If a reacting system having spatially homogeneous contents and a fixed volume, V_R, has no flow across its boundaries, as depicted schematically in Figure 3.4a, then dC/dt for that system is a time variable quantity that is precisely equal to the rate of reaction. In other words, the system is a completely mixed batch reactor (CMBR), and the material balance relationship is written as in Equation 3.24.

$$\begin{array}{ll} \textbf{MBE} & \\ \textbf{for a} & V_R \left(\dfrac{dC}{dt}\right)_{reactor} = \pm V_R \left(\dfrac{dC}{dt}\right)_{reaction} \\ \textbf{CMBR} & \end{array} \qquad (3.24)$$

a. No-Flow Ideal CMBR Configuration and Behavior

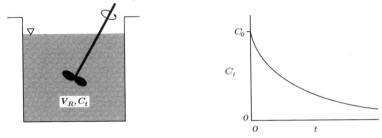

b. Flow-Through Ideal CMFR Configuration and Behavior

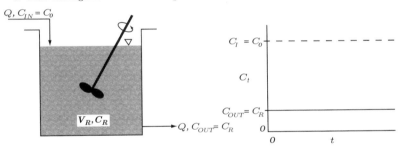

c. One-Dimensional Steady-State Ideal PFR Configuration

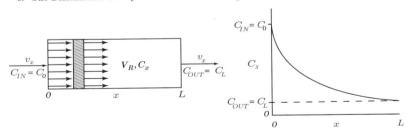

Figure 3.4 Frame of Reference Reactor Systems

If the system with homogeneous contents and fixed-volume V_R has flow into it (Q_{IN}) and flow out of it (Q_{OUT}), as shown in Figure 3.4b, for which the system is termed a completely mixed flow reactor

(CMFR), then

$$V_R \left(\frac{dC}{dt} \right)_{reactor} = QC_{IN} - QC_{OUT} \pm V_R \left(\frac{dC}{dt} \right)_{reaction} \qquad (3.25)$$

or, since $(dC/dt)_{reaction} = r$ *(Equation 2.16, Chapter 2),*

$$
\boxed{
\begin{array}{ll}
\textbf{MBE} \\
\textbf{for a} \qquad V_R \left(\frac{dC}{dt} \right)_{reactor} = QC_{IN} - QC_{OUT} \pm rV_R \\
\textbf{CMFR}
\end{array}
} \qquad (3.26)
$$

If there is no net change in the system contents, the left hand term in Equation 3.26 is zero and, for this **steady-state condition** we can write

$$
\boxed{
\begin{array}{ll}
\textbf{Steady-State} \\
\textbf{MBE for a} \qquad QC_{IN} - QC_{OUT} \pm rV_R = 0 \\
\textbf{CMFR}
\end{array}
} \qquad (3.27)
$$

In this material balance, the "net molar rate in" is equal to $QC_{IN} - QC_{OUT}$ where Q is the steady uniform flow rate through the volume, V_R. Because point forms of the MBE (e.g., Equations 3.6 and 3.8) describe reactor conditions at one point in space and time, they are expressed in terms of moles or mass per unit volume per unit time. On the other hand, integral forms of the MBE (e.g., Equation 3.12) express reactor conditions within specific control volumes and are therefore expressed in terms of moles or mass per unit time. It is evident that the point forms of the MBE obtain as the volume of a discrete element approaches that of a differential element (i.e., as $\Delta V \rightarrow dV$). Differential forms of the continuity equation develop directly from balances on the differential element itself, whereas the discrete control volume approach (or shell balance approach) involves development of the corresponding differential continuity equation by taking the limits of a finite difference relationship.

For clarity and simplicity of equation development, we generally use the differential element (e.g., dx, dV, dC, dt, etc.) approach in this book. The finite difference notation (e.g., $\Delta x = x_2 - x_1, \Delta V = V_2 - V_1, \Delta C = C_2 - C_1, \Delta t = t_2 - t_1,$ etc.) is reserved for situations in which discrete differences in quantities are represented.

Example 3.3 provides an illustration of the differences and interrelationships between the reaction and transport elements of Equation 3.1.

Example 3.3. The Partial Chemical Oxidation of a Biologically Persistent Organic Waste to "Soften" it for Subsequent Biological Oxidation. (An illustration of the important interplay between the reaction and mass transport elements of the MBE, and a simple example of process integration.)

- **Situation.** *A simple reactor system in which a highly concentrated hydrogen peroxide (H_2O_2) solution is fed to an aqueous waste containing a non-volatile and biologically resistant organic compound that is used to partially oxidize the organic compound in the waste prior to its discharge to a biological treatment process. The waste water is introduced at one end of the tank and withdrawn at the other at a flow rate of Q. The contents of the tank are kept completely mixed by a mechanical mixer.*

- **Question(s).** *Develop a material balance relationship for the original organic compound for this system. Assume that the rate of oxidation of the organic compound is directly proportional to its concentration.*

- **Logic and Answer(s).** *Equation 3.1 can be written for the organic compound as detailed below*

  · *rate of input of organic compound = QC_{IN};*

  · *rate of output of organic compound = QC_{OUT}; and,*

  · *rate of chemical oxidation of organic compound = $r_{ox} = (k_{ox})_{ps}C_{OUT}$ (What condition justifies this statement?).*

  Note that the control volume in this particular example is the entire reactor volume and thus the expressions for mass rates of input and output are given respectively by the products of the volumetric flow rate and the concentrations of the organic compound at the tank entrance and exit. The resulting material balance on the compound is then

  $$QC_{IN} - QC_{OUT} + r_{ox}V_R = V_R \frac{dC_{OUT}}{dt}$$

  or, for steady-state operation,

  $$QC_{IN} - QC_{OUT} - (k_{ox})_{ps}C_{OUT}V_R = 0$$

- **Key Point(s). The word description of the MBE given in Equation 3.1 readily translates into a mathematical form. Note, however, that the particular form may vary with subtle differences in the type of system in which the process is embodied. For example, could we write the rate of oxidation as $(k_{ox})_{ps}C_{OUT}$ if the contents of the tank were not stirred?**

Finally by way of frames of reference, consider the exact opposite of the flow system having completely mixed contents, as depicted in Figure 3.4c. If the flow into and out of the system is one-dimensional in x over a flow length L, then any reaction occurring in the system will lead to a different concentration of the reacting substance of every point x in the system. It is now no longer possible to describe the system as a control volume if we impose on the control volume the requirement of a completely mixed condition. The control volume must therefore represent only a small fraction of length, Δx, along the flow length of the system. Now what must be considered to define the difference in concentration in the system between point $x = 0$ and point $x = L$ is the balance between the rate of movement of our minisystem of length Δx as it moves from $x = 0$ to $x = L$.

Application of Equation 3.1 to this type of elementary system, which is referred to as a plug flow reactor (PFR), yields the MBE

$$\boxed{\begin{array}{ll} \textbf{\textit{MBE}} \\ \textbf{\textit{for a}} & \dfrac{dC}{dt} = -v_x \dfrac{dC}{dx} + \boldsymbol{r} \\ \textbf{\textit{PFR}} \end{array}} \tag{3.28}$$

where v_x is the velocity of the control volume along the length of the system. Equation 3.28 is written as a partial differential equation because C varies both spatially and temporally. If the rate of change due to transport is exactly the same as the rate of change due to reaction, the steady-state form of the PFR material balance equation is given by

$$\boxed{\begin{array}{ll} \textbf{\textit{Steady-State}} \\ \textbf{\textit{MBE for a}} & \displaystyle\int_0^L \dfrac{dx}{v_x} = \dfrac{L}{v_x} = \dfrac{V_R}{Q} = \displaystyle\int_{C_{IN}}^{C_{OUT}} \dfrac{dC}{\boldsymbol{r}} \\ \textbf{\textit{PFR}} \end{array}} \tag{3.29}$$

Real systems can (and usually do) vary in behavior from the ideal and very simple "limiting-case" systems described by the CMBR, CMFR and PFR material balance relationships given in Equations 3.24 through 3.29 above. So too will real system reaction and mass transfer rates vary from the simple forms given respectively in Equation 3.21 and Equations 3.22 and 3.23. Nonetheless, armed with these simple relationships we are now in a better position to both better understand their origins in basic physics and chemistry and better appreciate how we can develop more general basic relationships that can similarly be "adapted" to specific systems as we have adapted the relationships discussed above by system-specific assumptions that are rooted in an understanding of principles.

3.4 PRINCIPLES, PLATFORMS, PROTOCOLS, AND PHILOSOPHY

3.4.1 Types and Levels of Analysis

Equation 3.1, the general description of the MBE, is the basic platform for rigorous deterministic modeling of environmental processes and systems. The proper articulation of this equation in a mathematical form that captures the essential and identifying features of the physical system to be modeled is the first and most important step in process analysis and system modeling. Mathematical elaborations of this relationship vary from one model to another, depending upon the nature and level of information known about the system (model structure and input) and the nature and level of information desired from the modeling effort (output requirements). In this text we consider many different applications of process analysis based on the general material balance principle and the development of specific types of process models. In certain situations, the nature of reactor operation, the choice of scale, or the specification of temporal or spatial limits on a model drives one or more of the terms in Equation 3.1 to zero, as we have seen for example for assumptions of steady-state conditions. We will also encounter a variety of reaction rate expressions and reactor geometries.

3.4.2 Models Based on Material Balance Equations

The most sophisticated environmental models are usually comprised by one or more MBEs, written in the form of differential equations describing the change of one system variable as a function of another, the latter most commonly being either time or distance. This level of modeling requires a thorough conceptual knowledge of processes operating within a system, as well as a sufficient data base upon which to evaluate all of the equations involved in the model structure. A data base may be very useful to determine model parameters for use in MBE-based models; many well-determined empirical correlations have been developed and these are often appropriate for various practice/applications. If this level of knowledge and data is available and incorporated in an MBE based model, that model should be versatile with respect to the examination of a variety of conditions, and its output or predictions can be expected to be accurate and precise.

Based largely on our discussions to this point, we can articulate a general protocol for application of material balance relationships to the modeling of any environmental process or system. At a minimum, such a protocol requires:

- *identification of the purpose and goals of the modeling effort;*

- *visualization of the system and its components;*

  - *develop system representation,*

- *assign notation,*
- *categorize variables as input, operating parameters, or output,*
- *list underlying and simplifying assumptions,*
- *refine system representation;*

- *development of equations of state;*

  - *identify unit or control volume,*
  - *write material balances in differential forms,*
  - *rearrange and take limits to convert to differential forms;*

- *evaluation of system parameters;*

  - *develop and list correlations,*
  - *substitute where appropriate;*

- *stipulation of boundary and/or initial conditions;*

  - *develop and list;*

- *conversion of state equations to dimensionless forms;*

- *solution of equations;*

  - *analytical solutions,*
  - *numerical solutions;*

- *calibration with a robust data set;*

- *performance of parameter sensitivity analyses;*

- *verification with second robust data set for different conditions; and, finally,*

- *application for prediction and design.*

Once the overall purpose and goals of the modeling effort have been established, the system and its components can be visualized and pictured. Notation is assigned and underlying and simplifying assumptions are noted. The material conservation equation is written for the appropriate control volume and converted to differential form. Equations defining model parameters are identified and substituted where appropriate. The essential boundary and initial conditions are then determined and listed.

The working equations are often most conveniently represented in dimensionless form, particularly if the ultimate solution technique (algorithm) is numerical. If analytical solutions are employed, this conversion may be deferred until after the solution equation is derived. We will demonstrate in numerous examples in this text that the conversion of systems of differential equations describing complex processes to dimensionless form generalizes those equations, and extends their utility to broader ranges of application.

Finally, the equations must be solved in the appropriate manner. Throughout the entire modeling process, the available data base influences model development, form and detail. Ultimately, the model results feed back into the sampled and available data, indicating where efforts regarding future experiments and data collection should be directed.

One of the major factors in the successful application of material balance based models such as those presented in Section 3.2 is to select the correct conditions for which a model should be solved. Of particular import are the initial and boundary conditions of the problem and system to be modeled.

3.4.3 Initial and Boundary Conditions

A key consideration in applying the foregoing material balance relationships is the specification of appropriate conditions existing at system boundaries and at initial points in time from which system behavior is evaluated. The equations we have developed to describe material balances are differential equations in certain specified dependent variables. Applications of any differential equation in dependent variables require that the variables satisfy the differential equation throughout some domain of their corresponding independent variables, and at the boundaries of the domain. Initial and boundary conditions are selected to reflect physical phenomena and assumptions within a system and along its interfaces with surrounding environments.

Initial conditions (ICs) involve specification of state variables, such as concentration and temperature, at time $t = 0$ for all points in the system. This specification implies a knowledge of the initial value of spatial derivatives (e.g., dC/dx) as well.

A boundary condition (BC) specifies conditions at a particular boundary of the domain which must be satisfied by the dependent variable, say u, while an initial condition (IC) specifies the value of u throughout the domain such that the initial value of that variable is defined by

$$u_o = \phi(x, y, z) \tag{3.30}$$

Boundary conditions involve specification of state variables along the system boundaries for all times considered. Boundary conditions include the absolute value of the variable as well as spatial derivatives when necessary. The number of spatial derivatives required corresponds to one less than the order of the material balance equation. For example, if the model equation is second order (i.e., including d^2C/dx^2), then boundary values for C and dC/dx are necessary.

Equilibrium requirements for concentrations at an interface (e.g., Henry's law at an air-water interface) generally lead to specifications of boundary value concentrations. Conservation requirements for material fluxes at interfaces generally lead to specification of spatial derivatives. The appropriate conservation equations are similar to the general material balance relationship given in Equation 3.1, having the form

---

Boundary Condition Conservation Equation

Rate of		**Rate of**			**Accumulation**	
Flux to	$-$	**Flux from**	$=$		**Rate at**	(3.31)
Boundary		**Boundary**			**Boundary**	

When mass transport is by diffusion, the driving force for transport between two points in space is a function of the difference (gradient) in concentration of the diffusing species between those two points. This leads to a boundary condition involving the first derivative of concentration. System geometry and the location of inputs and sinks may also define boundary conditions.

There are three different boundary conditions which apply to most environmental systems, namely:

- *the Type 1, or Dirichlet condition;*

- *the Type 2, or Neumann condition; and,*

- *the Type 3, or Robin condition.*

For the *Type 1* condition the value of the unknown function, u, is specified at the boundary, either as a constant or as a function of time. The specification of a constant value for u at the boundary generally implies a steady-state condition for the dependent variable at that spatial location. Let us reconsider, for example, the PFR system shown schematically in Figure 3.4c. Suppose that an oxidation reaction occurs between a strong oxidant and organic matter. The reaction rate may be considered as first-order with respect to the organic matter concentration if the oxidant has been added in excess and is not depleted. Flow through the reactor follows steady "plug-flow" behavior at constant velocity v_x along one primary dimension, x. The initial concentration of organic matter is C_o and it decreases along the length of the reactor as shown in Figure 3.4c, at a rate proportional to the residual concentration C; i.e., $r = \phi(C)$. If there is no change in the inlet concentration, flow rate or temperature, the reaction rate should not change. Thus the concentration pattern along the length of the reactor should be constant with time, so the system is said to be at steady state; i.e., $(\partial C/\partial t)_x = 0$. Beginning with Equation 3.6 and substituting $v_x C$ for N, the material balance for this reactor reduces to

$$-v_x \frac{dC}{dx} + r = 0 \qquad (3.32)$$

The *Type 1* condition is the appropriate boundary condition for this case. Thus, specifying the value of C at the boundary as

$$C = C_o \text{ @ } x = 0 \tag{3.33}$$

If r is given by a first-order reaction, such as kC, the solution of the differential equation describing the concentration profile along the reactor is

$$C = C_o e^{-kx/v_x} \tag{3.34}$$

The *Type 2* condition involves specification of the value of the derivative of the function u normal to the domain boundary. A typical application of this type of BC is the "no flux" boundary. For the one-dimensional PFR shown in Figure 3.4c we have

$$\frac{dC}{dx} = 0 \text{ @ } x = L \tag{3.35}$$

Finally, the *Type 3* condition characterizes values of $hu + du/dn_v$ at the boundaries, where h may be a constant or a function of corresponding independent variables. In transport problems, a *Type 3* BC is typically invoked to specify values of boundary flux attributable to macroscopic transport phenomena. The *Type 3* BC is appropriate to use, for example, to describe the inlet condition for the reactor system pictured in Figure 3.5, where it is assumed that macrotransport upgradient of (before) $x = 0$ occurs by advection only whereas macrotransport downgradient of $x = 0$ occurs by a combination of advection and internal mixing (see Equation 3.37 below).

Internal mixing causes dispersion (see discussion in Chapter 4) of fluid elements along the x axis so that some move faster than the average velocity, v_x, and some move more slowly, the distribution of differential velocities being approximately Gaussian, or normal. Such deviations from plug-flow can be characterized in terms of a "dispersion" coefficient, $\mathcal{D}_d(\text{L}^2\text{t}^{-1})$, and, as we shall demonstrate in Chapter 4 (Equation 4.25), the flux N, then given by the sum of $v_x C - \mathcal{D}_d dC/dx$. The material balance relationship for operation of this system at steady-state then, from substitution into Equation 3.6, has the form

$$-v_x \frac{\partial C}{\partial x} + \mathcal{D}_d \frac{\partial^2 C}{\partial x^2} + r = 0 \tag{3.36}$$

Complete mixing of the zone above $x = 0$ is assumed so that the source can be treated as constant; i.e., no spatial gradient develops in the saturated sump above $x = 0$. The stipulation of mass conservation across the inlet of this reactor requires no mixing precisely at $x = 0$, yielding a *Type 3* boundary condition; i.e.,

$$\left[v_x C - \mathcal{D}_d \frac{\partial C}{\partial x} \right]_{x=0} = v_x C_o \tag{3.37}$$

Equation 3.36 is the steady-state version of what is often referred to as the one-dimensional advection-dispersion-reaction (ADR) transport model. The ADR model is commonly employed for description of contaminant behavior in engineered reactors in which flow is specifically controlled to occur in essentially only one direction. It is also frequently employed empirically for descriptions of natural systems, such as rivers and certain subsurface flow domains, in which cases it often provides reasonably close approximations to

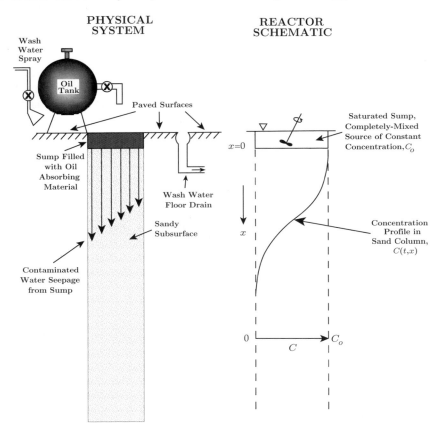

Figure 3.5 Modeling Constant-Source Contamination of a Semi-Infinite Domain with Dispersion Along the Axis of Flow

conditions that would otherwise require complex, and potentially unnecessary, modeling detail. Criteria and assumptions invoked in the use of simplified models to describe complex systems are discussed in more detail in the ensuing section of this Chapter.

Because the solution of the material balance equation for a reactor system is a function of the boundary conditions specified, we must in practice be careful to choose boundary conditions which match the physical problem(s) being modeled. If boundary conditions are not correct physically, the mathematical solutions generated by descriptive and design models may very well also be incorrect. The impact of boundary conditions in mathematical solutions is illustrated in Example 3.4; two totally different solutions of the material balance model are presented for the system for two different boundary conditions, only one of which is correct.

Example 3.4. Subsurface Vertical Migration of Oil Leaked from an Above Ground Storage Tank. (A complex contamination scenario involving the visualization of a simplified transport model and selection of appropriate conditions for its solution.)

- **Situation.** *An environmental contamination event and its equivalent one-dimensional "semi-infinite" reactor are pictured in Figure 3.5. In this situation the absorbent material filling the sump beneath the tank spigot completely captures and retains the small amount of oil spilled during filling and withdrawal operations of the tank. The area is washed down frequently, and some of this wash water is collected and held in the sump, draining from it into the underlying soil column at a slow but essentially constant velocity (v_x) and contaminant saturation level (i.e., $C_0 = C_S$).*

- **Question(s).** *Specify the appropriate model equations and boundary conditions for describing this situation.*

- **Logic and Answer(s).** *For this example we cannot assume steady-state because the concentration profile of the contaminant is changing in space and time. Thus the right hand term in Equation 3.36 is not zero*

$$-v_x \frac{\partial C}{\partial x} + \mathcal{D}_d \frac{\partial^2 C}{\partial x^2} + \boldsymbol{r} = \frac{\partial C}{\partial t}$$

The reaction rate term, $\boldsymbol{r}$, is assumed to be zero. If the reactor is free of solute at the beginning of the simulation, the initial $C(x,t)$ condition is given by

$$C(x,0) = 0$$

For the inlet BC a Type 3 condition identical to that given by Equation 3.37 would apply, while for the outlet BC a Type 2 condition is appropriate, so that

$$\frac{\partial C}{\partial x} = 0 \text{ as } x \to \infty, \text{ all } t$$

Solution of the unsteady-state form of Equation 3.36 for these initial and boundary conditions yields (Gershon and Nir, 1969)

$$\frac{C_x}{C_s} = \frac{1}{2} erfc \left[\frac{x - v_x t}{2(\mathcal{D}_d t)^{0.5}} \right] - \frac{1}{2} \exp\left(\frac{v_x x}{\mathcal{D}_d} \right) erfc \left\{ \left(\frac{x + v_x t}{2(\mathcal{D}_d t)^{0.5}} \right) \left(1 + \frac{v_x(x + v_x t)}{\mathcal{D}_d} \right) \right\}$$

$$+ \left[v_x \left(\frac{t}{\pi \mathcal{D}_d} \right)^{0.5} \right] \exp \left[\frac{v_x x}{\mathcal{D}_d} - \frac{1}{2} \left(\frac{x + v_x t}{(\mathcal{D}_d t)^{0.5}} \right)^2 \right]$$

Detailed discussion of the error function, erf(z), and complimentary error function compliment, erfc(z), of a variable, z, is provided in Chapter 8 of PDES. What is important to note here is that an entirely different solution to the unsteady state version of Equation 3.36 is obtained if a different inlet BC is chosen; in other words, the solution to the material balance equation for a particular system is a function of the chosen bound conditions. If, for example, a Type 1 BC is chosen, so that $C(0,t) = C_0 = C_S$, the solution for Equation 3.36 becomes

$$\frac{C_x}{C_x} = \frac{1}{2} erfc\left[\frac{x - v_x t}{2(\mathcal{D}_d t)^{0.5}}\right] + \frac{1}{2} \exp\left(\frac{v_x x}{\mathcal{D}_d}\right) erfc\left[\frac{x + v_x t}{2(\mathcal{D}_d t)^{0.5}}\right]$$

For this problem, the Type 1 boundary condition is clearly not correct because it does not conserve mass across the reactor inlet.

- **Key Point(s). Accuracy in the modeling of complex environmental systems is not guaranteed by selection of the appropriate form of an MBE. Subsequent definition of the appropriate initial and boundary conditions for solution of the MBE is just as critical for accurate representation of the physical system.**

3.4.4   Alternative Modeling Approaches

Our general preference for deterministic models based on the material balance equation ascribes to the fact that this equation is firmly rooted in physical concepts and readily derived from a consideration of basic mass transport and reaction phenomena. Moreover, appropriate solution techniques, both analytical and numerical, are fully developed and readily available.

Not all mathematical models that are based on material balance relationships, however, lead inexorably to a set of differential equations. In particular, one can develop probabilistic models in which the material balance relationship is satisfied by the requirement that probabilities associated with different system states must sum to one. The method of solution generally involves integration over a probability domain to determine expected values, such as first moments (means), and other statistically related moments (e.g., second moments, or variances) of the desired output.

Some environmental systems are not sufficiently well defined to warrant the deterministic levels of model sophistication discussed to this point. In other instances the level of information or prediction required may be no more than approximations or estimates, for which mathematical elegance is neither necessary nor cost effective. Material balance equations written in terms of descriptive relationships, predicated on empirical observations or statistical correlations are often sufficient in such instances.

Probabilistic models may require additional, restrictive assumptions related to system processes, but often lead to simplification of solution procedures. A serious drawback of such models is that there is less generality in their output, providing, for example, only means and variances rather than entire time histories of the parameters of interest. In certain situations, however, this may be the only output the analyst requires.

The above discussion suggests that when environmental processes are too complex for adequate representation of exact material balance relationships it may be both necessary and sufficient to fall back upon empirical or statistical correlations as a basis for modeling. Empirical equations and nomagraphs have a long history of use in water and waste treatment practice. Relationships between process performance (e.g., pollutant removal) and the flow rates at which unit processes are operated, for example, are commonly developed from pilot-plant experiments. This practice is to be distinguished from the use of empirical correlations to determine model parameters for a material-balance-based model.

Statistical regressions which relate water quality at a water supply inlet to upland rainfall, industrial activity, and land use, provide another example. These models are often simpler to develop and easier to apply than rigorous material balance models. In some circumstances, their predictive capabilities may equal or exceed those of a material balance model. This is particularly the case when data required to address the full complexity of the more rigorous model(s) are lacking. Because such models are not rooted in physical principles and processes, however, they have definite drawbacks. They are more likely to yield inaccurate results outside their range of calibration because of conceptual misrepresentation. In addition, many of the insights gained by developing and applying material balance models (e.g., exposition of transport paths, delineation of source effects, sensitivity to model parameters, etc.). - are not realized when an empirically derived equation is used for modeling purposes. As such, the statistical-empirical model may be viewed as an approach of last resort. There remain, however, a number of applications for which this last resort is necessary and appropriate.

Each of the modeling steps itemized in Section 3.4.2 should be performed from the perspective of maximizing their respective relationships to the goals and constraints of the overall modeling effort. It is always possible to build great complexity into a mathematical model. Such complexity, however, may be counter-productive if the level of detail in the model exceeds that required in the decision-making process which depends upon interpretation of the model results. The modeler must be certain, even in cases where additional complexity is useful, that the additional data requirements necessitated by a more complex model can be justified. Inevitably, a balanced approach which considers the model complexity, the data requirements, the accuracy of the results, the intended use of the results, and, of course, the cost of its development and application, must be established.

3.4.5   Evaluation Criteria

Any set of system boundaries, processes, assumptions and equations used to structure a model for an environmental system should be evaluated according to three criteria:

- *the level of detail established should be consistent with the intended use of the model;*

- *acceptably accurate field measurements should be obtainable at the level of detail established by the model; and,*

- *system processes must be understood and quantifiable at the level of data established.*

To illustrate the first criterion, consider the engineering of a system to upgrade the performance of a municipal water treatment plant to meet standards for taste and odor. Suppose that taste and odor are generated intermittently by organic substances during periods of algal activity in a lake which serves as the raw water source. Let us further suppose that the taste and odor causing compounds can be readily treated by addition of a slurry of powdered activated carbon to the rapid-mix chamber of the coagulation unit of the plant, on an as-needed-basis. The adsorption process to be engineered is thus one of relatively straightforward design and inherent flexibility. In this case the model required to engineer and design the adsorption system to produce acceptable estimates of cost and predictions of performance can be relatively simple in both structure and function. The dosages of powdered carbon needed under worst conditions can be readily measured and projected with reasonable accuracy given the seasonal occurrence of taste and odor; moreover, dosages can be changed periodically as needed. In addition, the reactor systems are already in place to affect treatment; i.e., the rapid mix basin, the coagulation and flocculation units, the sedimentation basins, and the final filters. Their performance is well known. Finally, the unlikely worst-case situation is failure of the planned adsorption system, the outcome of which is temporarily irate consumers who object to the taste or odor of the water.

Consider the contrasting situation in which a lake is found to contain organic pesticides during certain times of the year, and, as a result of runoff from surrounding streets and paved lots, is subject periodically to transient contamination by aromatic gasoline components and combustion products (e.g., benzene, toluene, xylene, and selected polynuclear aromatic hydrocarbons). The carbon adsorption system required to protect the public from these potentially toxic and carcinogenic chemical contaminants must be much more sophisticated, and more rigorously designed and operated than for control of occasional taste and odor problems. To achieve more effective treatment, carbon adsorption contactors may be installed following the filtration step in the plant. Continuous protection is required and thus, these contactors will be a regular on-line unit operation. Both frequency of appearance and concentration of pesticides and other contaminants may not be easily predicted. The presence of many contaminants will result in competition for adsorption sites and potentially the displacement of weakly adsorbed components. Because the adsorption system will be continuously in operation and have stringent performance requirements, carbon replacement and regeneration will be frequent, and these needs and costs must be accurately predicted.

A failure of the adsorption system in treating organic contaminants such as pesticides and gasoline components for any reason in the situation described above could lead to serious degradation not only of the palatability of the product water, but of its potability as well. Some redundancy must therefore be built into the system as a contingency against such failure. This system would require more careful consideration of an appropriate model for process engineering and design than would a system to handle occasional taste and odor problems. In addition, the data required to properly calibrate and verify that model must correspondingly be more detailed and more accurate.

The second criterion for model structure is that acceptably accurate field measurements should be obtainable at the level of detail established by the model. We are often forced to use a simpler analysis than that demanded by the intended use of a model because of the lack of sufficient and appropriate data. For instance, there would be little value in developing a multi-dimensional model to predict speciation, concentration and behavior of each organic substance contributing to taste and odor removed by carbon adsorption if we neither have, nor can make, detailed measurements of such parameters on a regular basis.

Typically, an engineer or scientist in charge of a project to design a treatment process must make decisions on the allocation of project resources between modeling and sampling. The ability to gather data may also be limited by fundamental considerations. We noted in Figure 1.4 in Chapter 1, for example, that the transport of a toxic substance within the pore structure of an activated carbon granule is of concern in the design of adsorption systems. There are, however, inherent limitations associated with making direct measurements at the microscopic scale. We are thus forced to rely on data collected from experimental systems containing fairly large populations of carbon particles, and to attempt extrapolation of these data to behavior at the single-particle scale. Other measurement limitations at a fundamental level are associated with investigations of highly complex but not readily characterized systems, such as heterogeneous subsurface environments, or unstable systems in which individual chemical species change in a rapid and non-measurable manner.

Finally, the third criterion for model development requires that system processes be understood and quantifiable at the level of data established. It is not uncommon in the modeling of environmental systems to encounter "frontiers" of available knowledge regarding complex transport and transformation process. We may be forced to rely upon obvious simplifications of complex phenomena simply because we do not understand the processes involved sufficiently to incorporate more detail in a model. A model developed to predict the frequency and concentrations of gasoline components present in the influent to the water treatment plant of our second example might have to utilize empirical relationships to describe surface runoff and lake mixing conditions. Runoff and mixing may be very important in determining the time of appearance and the concentrations of various components at the water intake crib. However, empirical relationships would ignore known differences in the uptake of the individual components by suspended solids in the runoff and in the lake. Unfortunately, the information required to quantify these differences for all of expected components and to specify how the distributions of these components change in time is lacking.

3.4.6 Philosophical Approach

The modeling of an environmental system and its associated processes involves reduction of related mass transport and transformation or separation processes to a logical system of mathematical analogs. The system of equations comprising the model is then resolved, calibrated with appropriate data pertaining to the physical system, verified on a prototype basis with data other than that employed for calibration, and used for the descriptions, predictions, or other design applications for which it was devised.

The respective roles and interactions of physical systems and mathematical analogs in the modeling process are presented schematically in Figure 3.6. *A physical system is generally first visualized or conceptualized in terms of its constituent components, compartments, and processes. Each one of these components is then represented by an appropriate description equation or set of equations. The modeling process brings these descriptive equations together into a system of equations comprising the mathematical analog of the physical system. Adjustment and tuning of this system model is done by calibrating it to one or more sets of data from laboratory or controlled field measurements. The calibrated model is used to design a prototype system or experiment. The latter is employed to collect an independent set of data from a field application, which, if it conforms to model predictions, serves to validate the model.*

For large natural environmental systems such as lakes or rivers, and for complex existing engineered systems such as water or wastewater treatment plants, the system and the prototype depicted in Figure 3.6 are usually one and the same. It is seldom possible, or necessary, to construct a representative physical prototype for such systems. Instead, the calibration data and verification data are generally collected from field measurements of the physical system at different times and under different conditions.

A much different circumstance exists if the physical system is a component treatment unit of a pollution control facility that is to be designed and constructed. In such situations there is usually an opportunity to build a pilot-scale prototype based on laboratory bench-scale studies. The pilot unit is then operated under particular and closely controlled sets of conditions. The design model can be calibrated with data from the independent bench-scale studies and verified rigorously with data developed in the pilot-scale study. In this regard, pilot-scale investigations can provide important information for full-scale design. In fact, the most effective use of pilot-plant investigations is as a means for intermediate verification of design models, rather than for collection of fundamental information and data.

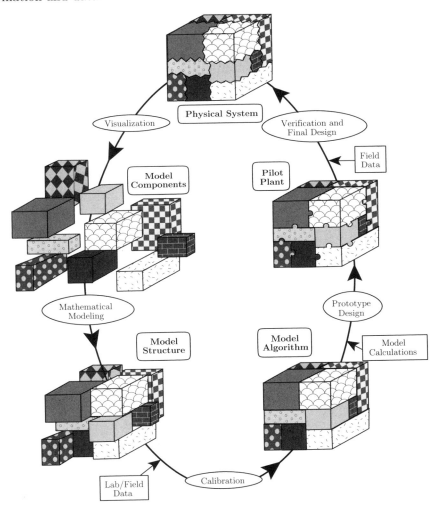

Figure 3.6 Physical Systems and Mathematical Analogs in Process and System Modeling

Both the mathematical model and the pilot-scale prototype are valuable conceptual and operational tools for environmental scientists and engineers. Too frequently, however, these tools are misused in specific applications. *The value of a mathematical model is constrained by the degree to which it reliably accounts for the physical characteristics, transport pro-*

cesses, and transformation processes comprising a particular system; in other words, by how accurately it describes, or captures, the physical system. If a model is over-simplified or incorrectly structured, or if calibrated to one system and indiscriminately applied to another without appropriate modification and revalidation, it may be more detrimental than beneficial to the ultimate objectives of the modeling process.

The best approach to environmental system description and process design is to integrate properly the use of mathematical models and prototype studies. Proper integration can be accomplished by first structuring mathematical models on the basis of sound process concepts and principles. Appropriate data for initial model calibration can then be obtained from bench-scale experiments. Because of their ease of operation, relatively low cost, small sample requirements, and easily characterized conditions, bench-scale experiments afford examination of a large number and broad range of pertinent variables. Prototype pilot or field studies, on the other hand, are usually lengthy, costly, and require elaborate equipment and large sample volumes. Thus, they seldom permit extensive investigation of the full scope and range of significant variables. Moreover, the transport dynamics of full-scale natural systems and of the types and sizes of reactors commonly used in pilot-scale systems may not be particularly well defined. Without well-defined dynamics it is difficult, if not impossible, to use such systems to characterize sufficiently the roles of pertinent system variables relative to transformation processes.

Once a mathematical model is calibrated with experimental bench-scale data, it can be used to design a pilot-scale system and to predict, *a priori*, the performance of that system for a given matrix of conditions. If the experimental results of the pilot-study confirm the model predictions, the model is verified for the range of conditions examined. If the experimental results deviate only marginally from predictions, the model can be recalibrated or tuned with these data and tested on another set of pilot-system data for a different matrix of system conditions (e.g., concentrations, flow rates, pH, etc.).

To restate for emphasis, the pilot or prototype system investigation is best used to tune and verify a mathematical model, not for its structure or calibration. The amount of tuning required will depend upon the complexity of the system. In an ideal situation, a verified design model will be calibrated with data obtained independently of the prototype system, and thus be more of a predictive tool than simply a simulator of observed data.

In addition to facilitating the description of natural environmental systems and the design and optimization of engineered systems, well structured and verified models can be used to evaluate responses to changes in selected variables; that is, for sensitivity analyses. For engineered systems, such models can further be used as interpretive elements in feed-forward and feed-back control systems. Modeling for purposes of control is particularly useful for processes subject to non-steady-state (time-variable) operating conditions.

3.5 CHAPTER SUMMARY

In Chapter 3 we have defined how the core elements of process analysis can be integrated and interpreted to characterize systems and processes. The most rigorous means for accomplishing core element integration and interpretation is provided by the principles of continuity; specifically, by mass continuity or material balance relationships. These relationships have been shown to incorporate both the transport and transformation aspects of process dynamics. We have learned, in a qualitative way, how to express transport and transformation relationships and how to incorporate them into material balance equations. To fully exploit the potential of the material balance approach to process analysis and design, however, we must delve in greater detail into the character and forms of both transport processes and reaction processes. We turn now to a closer examination of the former class of process in Chapter 4.

3.6 CITATIONS AND SOURCES

N.D. Gershon, and A. Nir "Effects of Boundary Conditions of Models on Tracer Distribution in Flow Through Porous Mediums," *Water Resources Research,* 5(4), 830-839, 1969. (Example 3.4)

W.J. Weber, Jr., and F.A. DiGiano, *Process Dynamics in Environmental Systems*, John Wiley & Sons, Inc., New York, 1996. PDES is the source of most of the material presented in Chapter 3. Chapter 2 of PDES provides more extensive in-depth coverage of MBEs and their use in the modeling of a broader range of environmental systems and conditions.

3.7 PROBLEM ASSIGNMENTS

3.1 A reactor is to be designed in which the oxidation of cyanide (CN^-) to cyanate (CNO^-) is to occur by the following reaction

$$\frac{1}{2}O_2 + CN^- \Leftrightarrow CNO^-$$

The reactor is to be a tank that is vigorously stirred so that its contents are completely mixed, and into and out of which there is a constant flow of waste and treated effluent, respectively. The feed stream flow rate is 100,000 gal/day, and contains 15,000 mg/L CN^-. The desired reactor effluent concentration is 10 mg/L CN^-. Assume that oxygen is in excess and that the reaction is directly proportional to the cyanide concentration, with a rate constant of k = 1 sec-1. Determine the volume of reactor required to achieve the desired treatment objective. (Hint: See Example 3.2)

Answer: 1,735 *gallons.*

3.2 Repeat Problem 3.1 for a reactor comprised by a long tubular chamber (e.g., a large diameter pipe) through which flow passes laminarly and there is no fluid mixing. Explain any differences you determine in the volume requirements from those calculated in Problem 3.1.

Answer: 8.46 gallons.

3.3 A water storage tank in a distribution system is filled at a rate of 300 m^3/h. The chlorine concentration of the water entering the tank from the treatment plant is 6 mg/L. Chlorine reactions with organic and inorganic constituents are first order with respect to chlorine and the average rate constant is 0.004 h^{-1}. Find the chlorine concentrations at :

(a) the end of filling the storage tank if the volume at the beginning of the fill period is 2000 m^3;

(b) the end of the next storage period of 10 h (assume no withdrawal; and,

(c) as a function of time during withdrawal from the storage tank if the rate of withdrawal is 500 m^3/h.

Answers: (a) 4.46 mg/L; (b) 4.28 mg/L.

3.4 A process used to treat a specific chemical waste is packaged in prefabricated reactor modules of fixed volume. The performance of each reactor module is close to that of an ideal CMFR. The reaction is first order and the existing treatment facility, which consists of one such module, achieves 90% removal. By how much can the volumetric treatment capacity be increased and still achieve 90% removal if a second unit is installed: (a) in parallel to the first unit; (b) in series with the first unit?

3.5 A CMFR has a hydraulic residence time of 10 min. The steady-state feed concentration increases by tenfold from 10 to 100 mg/L.

(a) What is the anticipated increase in effluent concentration if the reaction in the CMFR is first order with a rate constant of 0.1 min^{-1}?

(b) What is the anticipated increase in effluent concentration if the reaction is second order with a rate constant of 0.1 L/mg-min? Discuss the difference between these results.

3.6 A fluid containing a radioactive element having a very short half-life of 20 h is passed through two CMFRs in series. If the flow rate is 100 L/h and the volume of each reactor 40,000 L, what is the decay in activity?

3.7 Polynuclear aromatic hydrocarbons (PAHs) are common environmental contaminants. These compounds, consisting of three or more benzene rings interlinked in various arrangements, may originate in the atmosphere from two major processes: (1) evaporation during heating of PAH-containing matter; (2) formation by pyrolysis or incomplete combustion.

Phenanthrene is a PAH consisting of three benzene rings that typically enters the atmosphere through fuel emissions.

Consider a lake contaminated with trace amounts of phenanthrene. The lake has a volume of 50,000 cubic meters and a mean depth of 2 meters. The inflow and outflow to the lake are equal, at 500 gallons per minute. The temperature of the lake is 20°C. Phenanthrene enters the lake from several sources. Inflow stream(s) each have a phenanthrene concentration of 0.1 mg/L. As a result of emissions, there is an atmospheric flux of phenanthrene into the lake at a rate of 10 mg/(m²/day). In addition, phenanthrene leaches into the lake from a nearby coal-tar waste pit site at an essentially constant rate of 100 g/day. Assume that this source has negligible water flow with respect to concentration, with a rate constant $k = 0.01$ per day at 20°C. [Note: The reaction rate term in you material balance equation will be in the form: $rV = -.01CV$ (day^{-1}), with V in m³ and C in g/m³]. Assume that the lake is completely mixed.

(a) Using a material balance approach, determine the steady state concentration of phenanthrene in the lake.

(b) Develop an analytical expression describing the temporal response of the lake following the termination of all phenanthrene loadings at time $t = 0$.

(c) From the $C(t)$ expression in part (b), determine the concentration of phenanthrene in the lake 10 days after termination of the loadings.

3.8 Years of pesticide manufacturing have resulted in contamination of Turkey Creek, pictured in the sketch given below, with a common pesticide precursor, pyridine. Recently, the RBM Corporation (RBMC) has begun to manufacture a new type of self-cleaning auto-glass using titanium dioxide (TiO₂) dust, a catalyst that can destroy organic material when exposed to sunlight. In their haste to market this new product, RBMC begins its manufacture before they have completed the reengineering of their wastewater treatment facilities required for removal of residual TiO₂. The RBMC effluent discharges into Twelve Mile Creek, also pictured in the sketch below.

The aqueous oxidation of pyridine is catalyzed by TiO₂ dust and light according to the reaction scheme

$$\text{Pyridine} + O_2 \xrightarrow[\text{TiO}_2]{h\nu} \text{Various Oxidation Products}$$

The TiO₂ is not destroyed in the reaction since it is a catalytic agent. For this problem, the rate of pyridine oxidation can be modeled as a pseudo-first order ($r = -kC_{\text{pyridine}}$) reaction.

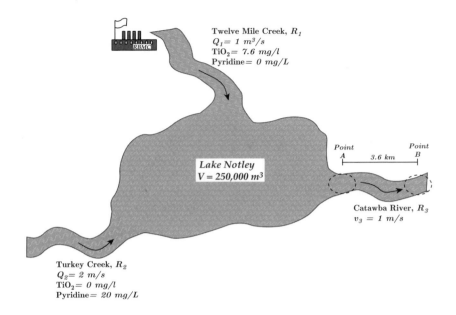

(a) The concentration if pyridine exiting Lake Notley at Point A is 5.61 mg/L. Determine the value of the rate constant, k (in min^{-1}), for the reaction.

(b) Using the value of k calculated in part a, calculate the concentration of pyridine in the Catawba River (R_3) at Point B.

(c) If the Catawba River were modeled using the ADR equation with a dispersion coefficient ($\mathcal{D}_d$) of 50 m^2/s, what would be the concentration of TiO$_2$ at point B?

(d) Discuss qualitatively how the concentration or pyridine would differ at point B with dispersion coefficients $\mathcal{D}_d$ of 0 m^2/s, 5 m^2/s, and 50 m^2/s.

Assume that: (1) the creeks and river can be modeled as PFRs and the lake as a CMFR; (2) oxygen is present at an approximately uniform concentration within the system; (3) the day/night issue can be ignored (assume light is present at all times); and (4) the system is at steady state.

3.9 An activated sludge system is used to treat a municipal wastewater. In this system microbes utilized oxygen to oxidize (degrade) organic matter in a CMFR. The system is aerated and mixed using several large bubble diffusers. Additional mixing is provided by a mechanical stirrer. At steady state the influent to the reactor contains 200 mg/l of BOD, a measure of the concentration of biologically degradable organic matter, and 1 mg/l of dissolved oxygen (DO). The reactor effluent contains 20 mg/l BOD and 7 mg/l of DO. You are given the following additional information:

V = reactor volume = 12,000 L

Hydraulic residence time = 6 hours

C_S = saturation concentration of oxygen (DO) in water = 8.5 mg/l

r = rate of oxygen consumption by microbes with in reactor = 0.5 mg/L/min

Due to an operator error, both the fluid pumps and the aeration system are turned off suddenly (but the mechanical stirrer remains operational). If the microbes in the reactor cannot survive at DO concentrations below 2 mg/l, how much time will elapse before they die? State any assumptions you make that are critical to your approach to the problem.

3.10 A well-mixed reactor is being used to treat a hazardous waste chemically. Catalytic reagent A is delivered to the inlet of the reactor by a chemical feed pump. This pump is supposed to maintain a concentration of 25 mg/L of A in the wastewater stream as it enters the reactor. Being a catalyst, this chemical is not depleted within the reactor but merely facilitates the reaction. The treatment process can operate effectively as long as the concentration of the catalyst does not drop below 15 mg/L. Operation proceeds at steady state until, suddenly, the feed pump malfunctions and begins to deliver a concentration of 10 mg/L of A at the inlet to the reactor instead of 25 mg/L.

Determine how much time the operators have before the treatment process becomes ineffective.

Volume, V_R, of the reactor = 400 m^3

Flow rate, Q, of process water = 200 m^3/h

NB: The flow of the feed pump delivering the chemical is negligible relative to the wastewater flow.

Chapter 4

Fluid Flow and Mass Transport

Contents

4.0 CHAPTER OBJECTIVES

To learn the underlying fundamentals of, and practical methods for developing, models to describe the movement of fluids in which substances are dissolved or dispersed, and thus the associated transport of these substances in environmental systems.

4.1 TRANSPORT PROCESSES

Changes in the concentrations of substances in environmental systems can be caused independently by either transport or reaction processes, or, more commonly, by the concurrent action of both processes. Transport processes are divided into two broad categories; macroscale processes, the subject of this chapter, and microscale processes, to be briefly described here and discussed in more detail in Chapters 13 and 14. Figure 4.1 presents a two-dimensional schematic

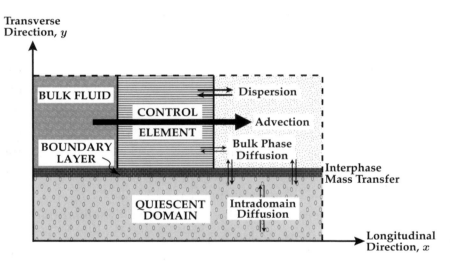

Figure 4.1 Mass Transport and Mass Transfer Processes

illustration of several of the major individual processes comprising these two categories of transport phenomena. The fluid element in this illustration contains a constituent, either dissolved or in stable suspension, that is moved principally by: (1) macroscale processes in the x and y directions in the bulk fluid; (2) microscale processes in the y direction at the boundary between the element and a quiescent domain (e.g., a non-flowing viscous fluid or a sediment); and (3) microscale processes in the x and y directions within the quiescent domain. The relative magnitudes of the several bulk-phase transport processes for typical flow conditions are suggested by the widths of the corresponding arrows.

4.1.1 Macroscale

Macroscale transport operates at the reactor or system scale, and is comprised principally by the processes of advection and dispersion. There is a third form of transport that also operates at the reaction or system scale, and that can thus also be considered a macroscale process. However, the effects of this process, bulk-phase diffusion, are usually negligible with respect to those of advection and dispersion.

Advective transport involves the cocurrent bulk movement of a constituent substance as a direct result of the movement of the fluid element(s) in which it is contained; that is, substance mass is carried along with fluid mass in the principal direction of flow. This type of transport is characterized directly by the bulk flow conditions of the system involved, most importantly bulk flow velocity.

Dispersive transport can result from several different physical phenomena operating at several different scales, and thus can be described by several different names. The dispersion represented in Figure 4.1 involves the movement of a constituent substance as a result of the macroscopic exchange of momentum between fluid elements in a turbulent flow field; this is termed turbulent or eddy dispersion. Other types of dispersion include Taylor dispersion and hydrodynamic (or mechanical) dispersion. All three types of dispersion are described by mathematical relationships having identical form, as is bulk-phase diffusion.

Transport by turbulent or eddy dispersion is significant in large channels, rivers, streams, and lakes. Dispersion of this type results from velocity fluctuations created by fluid turbulence acting across large advection-dominated flow fields. These velocity fluctuations lead to momentum and mass exchanges among fluid elements. The ensemble averages of the velocity fluctuations are distributed in an essentially normal or Gaussian manner, and the momentum and mass exchanges are therefore similarly distributed.

Bulk-phase diffusion, like turbulent or eddy dispersion, functions in concert with advective transport, and for this reason only is classified as a macroscale process. Diffusion differs mechanistically from dispersion in that it is molecularly driven rather than fluid-element driven. It is described for steady-state conditions by Fick's first law, a relationship that specifies solute flux to be proportional to a spatial gradient in solute concentration. This relationship derives from an assumption that the movement of molecules under the influence of Brownian forces in a quiescent space is essentially random, and that the distribution of forces acting on the molecules is normal, or Gaussian. Net random movement of the molecules between two points separated by a distance Δx will thus occur only if there is a net concentration difference, ΔC, between those two point; i.e., a spatial gradient in concentration, $\Delta C/\Delta x \rightarrow dC/dx$.

We noted above that velocity fluctuations and fluid element movements in turbulent flow fields are also normally distributed phenomena. It is therefore not surprising that in Chapter 3 we observed that dispersion is also proportional to a spatial gradient in solute concentration. The relationships for transport of dissolved substances by molecular diffusion and turbulent or eddy dispersion are therefore of the same functional form (i.e., the flux of the solute in one dimension along a path of length dx is in both cases given by $N \propto dC/dx$).

While we make note of the fact that molecular diffusion and turbulent dispersion have identical mathematical forms, which means that their coefficients of proportionality may be treated as additive in any transport model, we also emphasize that these two different processes have different roles and exert remarkably different effects in environmental systems. Most importantly, the coefficients of proportionality (i.e., diffusion and dispersion coefficients) relating fluxes to spatial concentration gradients generally differ by several orders of magnitude. The terms diffusion and dispersion should thus not be used casually, and certainly not interchangeably.

Taylor dispersion, which is not pictured in Figure 4.1, occurs in laminar flow in pipes and narrow channels, flow characterized by parabolic distributions of velocities resulting from the action of fluid drag forces at boundary surfaces (i.e., different rates of movement of fluid elements along parallel flow paths). These parabolic velocity distributions in turn result in parabolic-like distributions of solute concentration fronts in the axial (longitudinal) direction, creating concentration gradients in the radial (transverse) direction (i.e., normal to the principal flow direction). Diffusion of solute in the transverse direction thus occurs as bulk laminar flow proceeds in the longitudinal direction. *Taylor dispersion coefficients are unique in two regards; (1) they are inverse functions of the free liquid molecular diffusion coefficient of a solute, and (2) they can be calculated explicitly from known properties of the flow field and the diffusion coefficient.*

The third type of dispersion, termed hydrodynamic or mechanical dispersion, is a process of considerable importance in flow through porous media (e.g., in sand or carbon filters and in groundwater systems). It is in some cases similar to Taylor dispersion, occurring as it often does in small pores and fissures in fractured rock. At a somewhat larger scale, hydrodynamic dispersion may result from irregular disruptions of flow around obstacles such as sand, carbon grains, or soil aggregates. The irregularly varied flow paths that result lead to varied flow velocities, which like velocity fluctuations in large-scale turbulent flow fields are normally (Gaussian) distributed over large transport scales. The resulting distributed flow paths and velocities lead in turn to distributed solute concentration fronts, and thus to solute fluxes in directions normal to irregular flow paths. *Hydrodynamic or mechanical dispersion coefficients for large transport scales generally: (1) are several orders of magnitude larger than turbulent or eddy dispersion coefficients; (2) are highly system specific, and (3) must be measured experimentally for each individual system in question.*

We can say as a general rule that virtually all solute spreading effects in totally quiescent fluid domains result from molecular dif-

fusion, while solute spreading effects in any system that involves advective flow, either laminar or turbulent, are caused by dispersion. If advective flow is turbulent, the dispersion can be referred to as eddy dispersion, whereas spreading effects in advective flow fields that are macroscopically laminar are attributable to hydrodynamic or mechanical dispersion.

Eddy dispersion transport and bulk-phase diffusion are both pictured in Figure 4.1 as acting only in the x direction, an intentionally simplistic representation. Dispersion and bulk diffusion phenomena can and generally do occur in three dimensions. Moreover, the extent of dispersion taking place in each direction is often unequal. For example, temperature stratification of fluid in the y direction can result in density gradients that can cause turbulence (and thus dispersion) to be different in this direction than that in the x direction.

4.1.2 Microscale

Reactions in environmental systems, particularly multiphase systems, are often controlled by transport processes that occur at the molecular or near-molecular scale; i.e., the reaction scale. These processes, largely driven by gradients in concentration, are termed microscale mass transport or mass transfer processes. These are depicted in Figure 4.1 as interphase mass transfer and intradomain (within a quiescent domain) diffusion. Interphase mass transfer involves microscale transport across a relatively thin resistance boundary or interface separating two phases; in the example above, across the hydrodynamic boundary layer between a moving fluid and a quiescent domain. Diffusion is the only means of transport through this "semi-rigid" boundary. *Interphase mass transfer must be treated differently than simple molecular diffusion, however, because the length of the diffusion path is generally: (1) dependent upon the characteristics of the macrotransport processes and phases/domains involved; and (2) not measurable.*

As illustrated in Figure 4.1, molecular diffusion may become important again after a substance has been transported across the interface and enters a second quiescent domain. This domain may be comprised by a homogeneous liquid or solid, or by a porous nonhomogeneous medium (e.g., a matrix of solid and fluid volumes). *This transport process is referred to as intradomain diffusion. It may occur directly through the substance comprising a homogeneous domain or along solid surfaces (surface diffusion) or within the fluid contained in the pore spaces of a heterogeneous domain (pore diffusion).*

Each of the four mass transport mechanisms discussed above has a unique mathematical representation as a flux term, N, in the one-dimensional point form of the continuity equation developed in Chapter 3; i.e., Equation 3.6

$$-\frac{\partial N}{\partial x} + r = \frac{\partial C}{\partial t} \qquad (3.6)$$

One critical step in the modeling of process dynamics is the expression of Equation 3.6 in a form that can be integrated to provide information on the spatial and temporal variations of the concentration of a substance. This requires specification of appropriate mathematical expressions for both transport and transformation processes, the latter being represented in Equation 3.6 by the reaction rate term, r.

4.1.3 Transport Modeling

In the remainder of this chapter we develop characterizations of fluid flow and macrotransport processes employing principles of mass, energy and momentum conservation. While we focus on macroscale processes, the relationships (mass, energy and momentum balances) used for describing fluid flow and constituent transport (material balances) within flowing fluids are derived at a point in space (i.e., they are the point forms of the balance equations). To appreciate this blending of macro- and microscale concepts, consider briefly the flux term in the point form of the continuity equation given by Equation 3.6. This equation, although it represents transport and reaction processes occurring in a microscopic fluid control volume (i.e., a point in space), is a required starting point for description of macrotransport movements of constituents in fluids. Because macroscale flux is produced principally by advection and dispersion, velocity and dispersivity are usually averaged over some length scale. This perspective is essential for subsequent developments of mass and momentum balances on fluids in which constituents are transported.

In other words, we write point forms of mass and momentum balances so we can describe fluid velocity and pressure in a space continuum. For practical computations, however, it ultimately becomes necessary to average these velocities and pressures over some finite scale that is consistent with the particular macrotransport processes being described.

4.2 ADVECTIVE MASS TRANSPORT

In Section 4.1.1 we defined advective transport as the cocurrent bulk movement of a constituent substance contained in a fluid element (i.e., a dissolved or suspended substance) as a direct result of the bulk flow movement of the fluid element itself. The corresponding flux in the direction of bulk flow is then given by

$$\boxed{\begin{array}{l} \textbf{\textit{Advection}} \\ \textbf{\textit{Flux of}} \qquad N_{x,a} = v_x C \\ \textbf{\textit{Constituent}} \end{array}} \qquad (4.1)$$

where v_x is the velocity of fluid flow in the x direction and C is the concentration of the constituent of interest. It will be helpful in the *ensuing discussion to consider fluid velocity as a volumetric fluid flux, the dimensions of which are volume $(L)^3$ of fluid per unit area (L^{-2}) per unit time (t^{-1}); i.e., Lt^{-1}. Thus, the advective molar flux $N_{x,a}$ (moles $\cdot$ area^{-1} $\cdot$ time^{-1}) of a constituent contained in a given element of fluid is the product of fluid flux and the concentration of the substance within that element.*

4.2.1 Flow Characterization

The character of fluid flow, and thus of cocurrent advective transport of a dissolved or suspended constituent, varies widely from a system of one size and configuration to another. Flow may, for example, be laminar or turbulent, steady or unsteady, and uniform or nonuniform, and thus so may be the advective transport of the constituent in question. Laminar flow, as the name implies, involves the transport of fluid elements within discrete parallel laminae along smooth flow paths. The greater the viscosity of the fluid and the lower the velocity at which it moves, the greater the tendency for flow to be laminar. Such flow eventually becomes unstable as (1) viscosity decreases, (2) velocity increases, and/or (3) the dimensions and scale of the flow field increase. When this occurs, individual fluid elements comprising the flow move in irregular pathways, with a resulting irregular transfer of mass and momentum between fluid elements and between different coordinate points in the system. From the fluid-flow perspective, this causes a larger and more rapid proportional conversion of the inherent mechanical energy, or "head," of a system to thermal energy, or frictional "head loss," than occurs under conditions of laminar flow, a significant consideration for process design and operation. *This is reflected in the familiar fluid mechanics axiom that rate of head loss (energy dissipation) varies linearly with fluid velocity for laminar flow and roughly as the square of velocity for turbulent flow.*

Most natural water systems and treatment operations involve turbulent flow conditions and, therefore, irregular patterns of advective mass transport. Irrespective of whether flow is laminar or turbulent, however, Newton's laws of motion holds for every fluid element at every time, and the integrity of appropriate continuity relationships must be maintained. As discussed in more detail in ensuing sections, certain assumptions and approximations can be made in the engineering of real systems to facilitate characterization and modeling of mass transport phenomena in the presence of turbulent flow fields at both macroscopic and microscopic scales.

The terms steady and unsteady flow relate to the temporal variability of advective velocity and other flow conditions at any coordinate point in a system, while uniform and nonuniform flow address the spatial variability of flow conditions. Steady flow exists when all pertinent flow conditions at any point in the flow field are constant over time, and flow is unsteady when such conditions vary with time. These qualifications relate to both the magnitude and direction of the advective velocity, v. Thus, in terms of time, t, and an arbi-

trary space variable, ζ, the specifications for flow conditions in one
dimension are

$$
\begin{array}{ll}
\textbf{\textit{Flow Condition Specifications}} & \\
\textbf{\textit{Steady}} & \dfrac{\partial v}{\partial t} = 0 \\
\textbf{\textit{Unsteady}} & \dfrac{\partial v}{\partial t} \neq 0 \\
\textbf{\textit{Uniform}} & \dfrac{\partial v}{\partial \zeta} = 0 \\
\textbf{\textit{Nonuniform}} & \dfrac{\partial v}{\partial \zeta} \neq 0
\end{array}
$$

(4.2)

(4.3)

(4.4)

(4.5)

The definition of steady flow given by Equation 4.2 must be generalized to
accommodate the irregular movement of fluid elements in turbulent advective
flow fields. In this case it is necessary to consider the time variability of the
temporal mean velocity in each dimension; for example

$$
v_{x,t} = \frac{\displaystyle\int_{t_1}^{t_2} v_x \, dt}{\displaystyle\int_{t_1}^{t_2} dt}
\tag{4.6}
$$

For turbulent conditions then, steady flow implies that $\partial v_{x,t}/\partial t = 0$.

4.2.2   Conservation of Mass, Energy, and Momentum

Fluid motion (kinematics) is governed by the laws of conservation of mass,
energy and momentum. This motion determines the advective mass transport
of a constituent substance by cocurrent flow both within the bulk of the fluid
and in the boundary layer between the fluid and a surface. **With regard to the
latter, the law of conservation of momentum is particularly important
for understanding the nature of boundary layers and interphase mass
transport. For these reasons, we will undertake a brief review of fluid
kinematics.**

The control volume concept is the cornerstone of fluid kinematic analysis.
This concept was introduced in Chapter 3 to develop a mass or material balance
for a component within a fluid and, subsequently, the differential and integral
forms of the mass continuity equation. Continuity equations for mass, energy
and momentum of the fluid itself can be derived similarly. **The Lagrangian
perspective for describing fluid movement characterizes the motion
of a fluid by tracking individual fluid particles as they move through
time and space. In contrast, the Eulerian perspective selects a control**

volume to fix a position in space at which to account for fluid passing through it. The differences between these two perspectives or approaches are illustrated in Example 4.1.

Example 4.1. Model Development for Setting Ocean Outfall Discharge Standards. (An elaboration on the importance of understanding modeling objectives in establishing model perspectives.)

- **Situation.** *Treated wastewater is discharged to the ocean through a submerged outfall located several kilometers offshore. The outfall consists of a series of diffusers that direct the discharge horizontally. New effluent standards that include consideration of aquatic toxicity are to be set. The responsible regulatory agency in this case has experience with setting standards for discharges to rivers but not to oceans. For river discharges, a "mixing zone" (i.e., a volumetric segment of the river) is allowed in determining the extent of "instantaneous" dilution of the wastewater that occurs upon its discharge to the river. Standards are set based on a specified percent survival of a test organism after selecting a worst-case dilution factor based on historical stream (river) flow data (e.g., the consecutive 7 days of low flow occurring once in 10 years, or 7Q10). The discharge of wastewater into the ocean presents an entirely different hydrodynamic situation.*

- **Question(s).** *What factors should be considered in an analysis of the mixing and dilution of an ocean discharge designed to set aquatic toxicity standards?*

- **Logic and Answer(s).**

  1. *Both the Eulerian and Lagrangian control volume perspectives are important when analyzing the potential aquatic toxicity of a discharge plume rising to the ocean surface, as illustrated below.*

  2. *The size and shape of the plume depicted above depends on the initial velocity and density of the jet (advective flow), flow induced by ocean currents, and macroscale turbulence (dispersion) that causes mixing of the wastewater with the ocean water. At any vertical distance, the concentration (C) of potential toxicants in the plume decreases from the centerline due to dispersion, in the general fashion shown by the inset graph.*

  3. *The Eulerian perspective involves selection of a control volume fixed in space. This viewpoint is important, for example, for analysis of the exposure of stationary crustaceans to the wastewater discharge. If the concentration of potential toxicants in the discharge is constant with time, crustaceans that remain near the discharge point are constantly exposed to a relatively fixed concentration.*

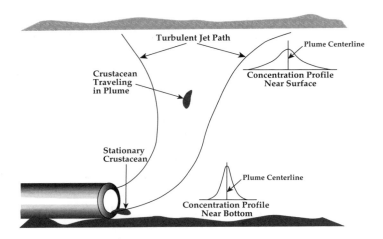

4. In contrast, the Lagrangian perspective is important for assessing the exposure of traveling crustaceans to toxicants because such organisms travel with the plume, and thus experience decreasing concentrations of toxicants with time of travel to the surface. Accordingly, a toxicity standard for fixed crustaceans requires determination of the initial dilution of wastewater with ocean water and an emphasis on long-term chronic exposure, whereas a toxicity standard for traveling crustaceans requires devising a short-term toxicity test (i.e., an acute toxicity test) that simulates the change in dilution of the wastewater over the time of rise of the plume.

5. Mathematical models to describe rising plumes clearly must incorporate mass and momentum balances on the fluid to represent these two diverse circumstances. These fundamentals are discussed next.

- **Key Point(s). An understanding of all problem perspectives to be addressed in the development of a contaminant transport model may be as important as an understanding of the transport mechanisms involved.**

Consider the macroscopic control volume shown in Figure 4.2. In the most general of terms, we are interested in developing balance equations for three properties of a fluid; i.e., its mass, its energy, and its momentum. **These are extensive properties because they are each additive; i.e., the addition of two volume elements of fluid containing the same amounts of mass, energy or momentum doubles the amounts of these quantities in the resulting volume of fluid. By contrast intensive properties are not additive and do not vary with the size or volume of a system.** For example, fluid density expresses the mass of fluid per unit volume of fluid, and

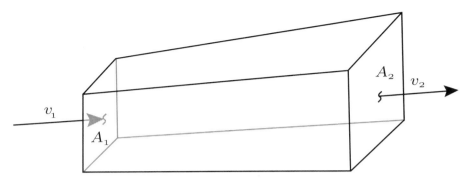

Figure 4.2 One-dimensional Flow through a System Control Volume

is thus independent of the amount of fluid involved. The addition of two volume elements of the same fluid having the same temperature increases the resulting volume of fluid but does not change its density. Temperature and pressure are similarly intensive, while heat and mass are extensive. Extensive and intensive properties apply equally well to any substance within a fluid. The number of moles of a substance dissolved in a fluid system is an extensive property of that system, whereas its concentration (moles per volume of fluid) is an intensive property.

A generalized conservation or balance equation for any extensive property (*e-prop*) of a system can be written in terms of its control volume (*c-vol*) behavior as

$$
\begin{array}{c}
\textbf{\textit{Extensive Property Balance Equation}} \\[6pt]
\begin{bmatrix} \textit{Rate of} \\ \textit{system} \\ \textit{e-prop} \\ \textit{change} \end{bmatrix}
=
\begin{bmatrix} \textit{Rate of} \\ \textit{c-vol} \\ \textit{e-prop} \\ \textit{gain} \end{bmatrix}
+
\begin{bmatrix} \textit{Rate of} \\ \textit{c-vol} \\ \textit{e-prop} \\ \textit{output} \end{bmatrix}
-
\begin{bmatrix} \textit{Rate of} \\ \textit{c-vol} \\ \textit{e-prop} \\ \textit{input} \end{bmatrix}
\end{array}
\qquad (4.7)
$$

This is, in essence, a word statement of the Reynolds transport theorem. We reiterate for emphasis that the left-hand side of Equation 4.7 represents the change in an extensive property for the entire system in question, which includes the control volume and its surroundings. The left hand term is zero if the extensive property in question is mass; this because by definition the mass of a fluid cannot change within the system that contains the control volume. If the extensive property is energy, however, the first law of thermodynamics requires that we account for the change between heat addition from the surroundings of the control volume and work done by the control volume on its surroundings. Similarly, if the extensive property is momentum, Newton's second law of motion requires that we account for its time rate of change, which is equal to the external forces acting on the control volume.

The rate of accumulation and net rate of output of mass, energy or momentum, given respectively by the first term and by the sum of the second and third terms on the right-hand side of Equation 4.7, can each be expressed as the product of a set of extensive and intensive properties of the control volume. If V_c is the control volume, S_c the control surface normal to the velocity of the fluid, and the flow is one-dimensional as shown in Figure 4.2, then the extensive property in the first term on the right-hand side of Equation 4.7 is the differential volume, dV, and the sum of the second and third terms is the product of the volumetric flux of fluid. Thus, with respect to Figure 4.2, we can write the Reynolds transport theorem as

$$
\begin{array}{c}
\textbf{\textit{Reynolds Transport Theorem}} \\[2mm]
\left[\dfrac{\partial(extensive\ property)}{\partial t} \right]_{system} = \\[4mm]
\dfrac{\partial}{\partial t} \int_{V_c} \left(\begin{array}{c} intensive \\ property \end{array} \right) dV + \int_{S_c} \left(\begin{array}{c} intensive \\ property \end{array} \right) v_x dA
\end{array}
\tag{4.8}
$$

The intensive property in the fluid mass balance (continuity equation) is ρ, the fluid density (mass/volume), that in the energy balance is $e_m\rho$, where e_m is the energy per unit mass; and, that in the momentum balance is ρv, where v can be thought of as momentum per unit mass of fluid.

We can similarly describe the MBE presented in Chapter 3 for any constituent substance within a fluid in terms of extensive and intensive properties. The integral form of the MBE as given by Equation 3.12 expresses the change in the mass of a component of interest per unit time (i.e., a time rate of change of an extensive property). The corresponding intensive property for the two terms on the right hand side of Equation 4.8 is thus the concentration of the component of interest. After rearrangement, the integral form of Equation 3.12 for the time rate of change of solute mass in a system for the flow circumstance depicted in Figure 4.2 is

$$
\frac{\partial(mass)}{\partial t} = \frac{\partial}{\partial t} \int_{V_c} C dV + \int_{S_c} C v_x dA
\tag{4.9}
$$

Close inspection of this relationship reveals that the term on the left represents the time rate of change of solute mass within the system, which must in turn be attributed to some type of chemical or biochemical transformation reaction. This equation has the same form as the generic statement of the Reynolds transport theorem for the mass, energy and momentum of the fluid in which the substance is transported. *Accounting for transformation of a substance by reaction is therefore analogous to accounting for a change of energy in a system due to external work or a change in momentum caused by external forces.*

4.2.3 Fluid Mass Balance

To describe one-dimensional transport of fluid along velocity streamlines normal to the control surface areas in Figure 4.2, Equation 4.8 is written in terms of the intensive property of fluid density, ρ, as

$$\text{Fluid MBE} \quad \frac{\partial}{\partial t}\int_{V_c}\rho dV + \int_{S_c}\rho v dA = 0 \tag{4.10}$$

For steady flow, the first term on the right-hand side must be zero, giving

$$\text{Steady Flow Fluid MBE} \quad \int_{S_c}\rho v dA = 0 \tag{4.11}$$

This is a formal statement of the mass continuity equation for steady flow. If we analyze the mass flow of water through a control volume under isothermal conditions, mass density is constant because water is an incompressible fluid. Further, if uniform flow exists over the cross section, Equation 4.11 yields the well-known flow continuity equation for constant mass density

$$\text{Constant Density Flow Continuity} \quad v_{x,1}dA_1 = v_{x,2}dA_2 = constant \tag{4.12}$$

4.2.4 Energy and Momentum Balances

Mathematical balances for fluid energy and momentum can be developed from the generalized word-form balance for an extensive property given in Equation 4.7 in a manner similar to that we used to develop a fluid mass balance, as illustrated in PDES. As done in PDES, mathematical expressions for fluid energy and fluid momentum balances can be developed, in a manner similar to that we used to develop a mathematical expression specific to fluid mass balances from Equation 4.7. *It is noteworthy that the coupling of an energy balance developed in this manner with the assumptions of steady, incompressible, and isothermal flow for an ideal fluid (nonviscous, or inviscid) yields the important Bernoulli equation, an expression of* *the energy per unit mass of fluid, e_m, as a summation of kinetic, potential and internal energies*

$$\boxed{\textbf{Bernoulli}\atop\textbf{Equation} \qquad e_m = \frac{v^2}{2} + \mathcal{G}y + U} \qquad (4.13)$$

where y is the distance above an arbitrary datum, $\mathcal{G}$ is the acceleration of gravity and U is the internal energy.

The reader is asked in assigned problem 4.1 to compare Equation 4.13 to those developed intuitively in Chapter 2 (Equations 2.17 and 2.18) and to comment on similarities and differences. In reference to the control volume depicted in Figure 4.2, mass enters only at section 1 and leaves only at section 2. Thus the surface integral reduces to

$$\left(\frac{v_x^2}{2} + \mathcal{G}y + U + \frac{P}{\rho} \right)(\rho v_x A) = \text{constant} \qquad (4.14)$$

The internal energy, U, in the Bernoulli equation is constant if there is no heat transfer, no shear work and isothermal flow. If steady flow (i.e., $\rho v_x, A = $ constant) is assumed, the Bernoulli equation for these conditions takes the form

$$\boxed{\textbf{Bernoulli Equation}\atop\textbf{for Steady Isothermal}\atop\textbf{Flow With No Shear} \qquad \frac{v_x^2}{2\mathcal{G}} + y + \frac{P}{\rho\mathcal{G}} = constant} \qquad (4.15)$$

where $\rho\mathcal{G}$ is the specific weight (W_g) of the fluid. The first term describes the kinetic energy head attributable to any velocity differential (the velocity head); the second represents the energyhead relating to differences in elevation of the fluid mass across the element (the static or elevation head), and the last term is the energy head contribution of any pressure differential across the element (the pressure head). Bernoulli's equation thus states that total mechanical energy remains constant along any flow streamline, although the forms in which this energy exists may change.

Water is a viscous fluid, and its flow causes shear stresses that convert mechanical energy to thermal energy. This thermal energy is rarely reconverted to mechanical energy, and thus represents unavailable or lost energy. Equation 4.15 can be modified to reflect the magnitude of this loss between any two points along the flow path. Consider, for example, coordinate points 1 and 2 in a one-dimensional advective flow field. The mechanical energy balance for a given element of water moving from point 1 to point 2 is then

$$E_1 = E_2 + h_l \qquad (4.16)$$

where E is available energy and h_l is the loss of energy, or head loss, between points 1 and 2. Combining Equations 4.15 and 4.16 gives

$$\boxed{\begin{array}{l} \textbf{\textit{Bernoulli Equation}} \\ \textbf{\textit{for Shear-Flow Loss}} \qquad y_1 + \dfrac{P_1}{\mathcal{G}} + \dfrac{v_{x,1}^2}{2\mathcal{G}} = y_2 + \dfrac{P_2}{\mathcal{G}} + \dfrac{v_{x,2}^2}{2\mathcal{G}} + h_l \\ \textbf{\textit{of Available Energy}} \end{array}} \qquad (4.17)$$

The important Bernoulli equation derives from application of the Reynolds Transport Theorem to energy balances. An equally important but less familiar relationship that derives from application of the Reynolds Theorem to momentum balances is the Navier-Stokes equation, which for the incompressible fluids such as water can be written in three-dimensional form as

$$\boxed{\begin{array}{l} \textbf{\textit{Navier-Stokes}} \qquad \rho\dfrac{\partial v}{\partial t} = \rho\mathcal{G} - \nabla P + \mu_v \nabla^2 v \\ \textbf{\textit{Equation}} \end{array}} \qquad (4.18)$$

where μ_v is absolute viscosity, $\mathcal{G}$ is a gravity vector, and P is a pressure vector. This equation can be solved together with the continuity equation and boundary conditions to find velocity and pressure as a function of time and space in natural and engineered water systems. The resulting system of equations is nonlinear, and exact solutions are thus limited to a few special situations (e.g., steady and uniform flow in one or two dimensions so that the acceleration term on the left-hand side of Equation 4.18 can be set equal to zero). *There are, however, many practical situations in which simplifying assumptions are reasonable and for which very important working relationships can be developed from the Navier-Stokes equation. For example the Hagen-Poisseuille equation for laminar-flow pressure drops in pipes and the Darcy equation for flow through porous media derive from the momentum balance given by Equation 4.18 (see PDES for development of these relationships).*

Because turbulent stress forces are inherently included in momentum flux terms, the Navier-Stokes equation applies also for turbulent flow fields. An application for analysis of steady, three-dimensional incompressible flow in two differently baffled tanks is shown in Figure 4.3. If the space within these tanks is discretized, or divided into meshes, to facilitate use of a finite-element numerical solution, the velocity fields obtained by solution of the Navier-Stokes equations for the two differently baffled systems reveal distinct differences. Baffle System A exhibits more uniform velocity fields than baffle System B, and, therefore, far less mixing of the flow. Less mixing implies a greater tendency for plug-like flow behavior and less fluid dispersion. Figure 4.3 shows how this difference is reflected in different transport behavior for dissolved components of the fluid.

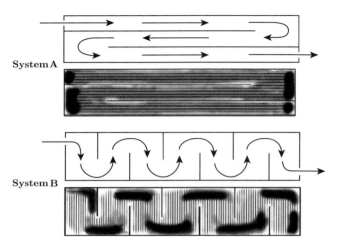

a.   Baffle Configurations and Predicted Velocity Fields

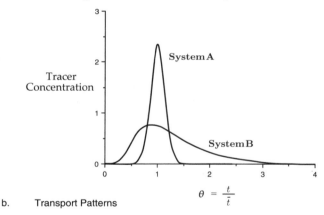

b.   Transport Patterns

Figure 4.3 Baffle Configurations and Transport Patterns

The curves shown here result if a slug of dye is injected instantaneously at the inlet of each system and its concentration at the outlet measured with time. We note that for baffle System A the dye undergoes much less spread in time and arrives at the outlet at a point in time very close to that of the hydraulic detention time, $\bar{t}$ of the tank; i.e., the elapsed time for advective transport without dispersion.

For inviscid fluids, the last term in the Navier-Stokes equation is zero, and Equation 4.18 becomes the Euler equation

$$\boxed{\boxed{\begin{array}{ll} \textit{Euler} & \rho\dfrac{\partial v}{\partial t} = \rho\boldsymbol{\mathcal{G}} - \nabla\boldsymbol{P} \\ \textit{Equation} & \end{array}}} \qquad (4.19)$$

It can be shown that the form of the Bernoulli equation given in Equation 4.15 represents an integration of the Euler equation along a streamline in a steady incompressible flow field.

Both the energy balance and the Euler equation (a special case of the momentum balance) describe advective transport of fluid elements and associated components under the assumed conditions of an ideal fluid and frictionless flow. In certain instances, as in the Bernoulli equation for shear-flow loss of available energy given in Equation 4.17, friction effects and losses are considered but not related directly to the flow characteristics of real fluids. The principal difference between ideal and real fluids is that the latter exhibit the property of viscosity. *The Navier-Stokes equation and the Bernoulli equation make clear the important relationships among viscosity, stress and energy loss. The Navier-Stokes equation (Equation 4.18) derives from a momentum balance that includes shear stress caused by viscosity, while the common form of the Bernoulli equation (Equation 4.15) derives from an energy balance on an inviscid fluid for which internal energy (U) remains constant.* The extension of Bernoulli's equation to a viscid fluid (Equation 4.17) implies that internal energy is no longer constant (i.e., shear stress converts available mechanical energy to unavailable thermal energy).

4.2.5 Dimensionless Transport Numbers

Several characteristic dimensionless groupings of variables that provide powerful tools for flow characterization develop from the Reynolds Transport Theorem, the Reynolds number being one of these. An appreciation of the origin of the Reynolds number from an analysis of momentum exchange in the Navier-Stokes equation makes it clear why this is so. Momentum exchange occurs along a continuum from laminar to turbulent flow. Laminar flow involves only molecular interchange of momentum. Tendencies for instability and turbulence are damped by viscous shear forces, which resist relative motion of fluid elements in parallel flow laminae. Conversely, turbulent flow involves erratic movement of fluid elements, with significant transverse exchange of momentum among them. *We have seen that the Navier-Stokes equation provides a complete mathematical description of flow dynamics. It was Reynolds, however, who showed experimentally that geometrically similar flow systems are dynamically similar if they also exhibit the same relative significance of shear stresses resulting from turbulence and from viscosity (i.e., the same ratio of these shear stresses). Reynolds modified the Navier-Stokes equation to include turbulent flow by representing both velocity and pressure as the sum of two terms, an average value term plus a fluctuating-value term, to produce a time-averaged velocity and pressure in the Navier-Stokes equations. For many practical applications, characteristic flow dynamics lie somewhere between those of discretely laminar and discretely turbulent flow. These conditions produce irregular patterns of transport of constituent masses.*

Dedimensionalization of the Navier-Stokes equation leads to isolation of several dimensionless parameters having distinct physical meanings. For example, dividing Equation 4.18 by the density ρ introduces the kinematic viscosity $(\nu_v = \mu_v/\rho)$ and changes the overall dimensions of both sides of the Navier-Stokes equation to Lt^{-2}. The equation can then be dedimensionalized by selecting a characteristic velocity, v_c, and a characteristic length, L_c, both of which by definition are system specific; i.e., they are "characteristic" of the system to which they apply. For example, v_c may be defined as the bulk velocity or as the shear velocity at a boundary. Similarly, L_c may be defined as the diameter of a cylinder, the diameter of a sphere, or the length along a flat surface. Substitution of the dimensionless parameters above into Equation 4.18 gives

$$\boxed{\begin{array}{l} \textbf{\textit{Dedimensionalized}} \\ \textbf{\textit{Navier-Stokes}} \\ \textbf{\textit{Equation}} \end{array} \qquad \frac{\partial v^\circ}{\partial t} = -\nabla P + \frac{\nu_v}{v_c L_c}\nabla(v^\circ)} \qquad (4.20)$$

where the "degree" superscript indicates a dimensionless variable comprised by one or more dimensionless groupings of subvariables. Importantly, for example, the dimensionless Reynolds number appears in the dimensionless pressure term, P, as

$$\boxed{\begin{array}{l} \textbf{\textit{Reynolds}} \\ \textbf{\textit{Number}} \end{array} \qquad \mathcal{N}_{\mathrm{Re}} = \frac{inertial\ force}{viscous\ force} = \frac{L_c v_c}{\nu_v}} \qquad (4.21)$$

Two other dimensionless parameters are included in p°, namely the Froude number

$$\boxed{\begin{array}{l} \textbf{\textit{Froude}} \\ \textbf{\textit{Number}} \end{array} \qquad \mathcal{N}_{\mathrm{Fr}} = \frac{inertial\ force}{gravity\ force} = \frac{v_c^2}{g L_c}} \qquad (4.22)$$

and the Euler number

$$\boxed{\begin{array}{l} \textbf{\textit{Euler}} \\ \textbf{\textit{Number}} \end{array} \qquad \mathcal{N}_{\mathrm{Eu}} = \frac{pressure\ force}{inertial\ force} = \frac{P}{\rho v_c^2}} \qquad (4.23)$$

The Froude and Euler numbers are defined by statement of the boundary conditions needed to solve the Navier-Stokes equation, and are particularly important in situations where free surface effects on flow must be considered. The explicit appearance of the Reynolds number in the Navier-Stokes equation emphasizes its importance in determining temporal and spatial distributions of velocity and pressure.

The Reynolds number is arguably the most important dimensionless group in fluid mechanics. The larger the Reynolds number, the more will the general character of flow be determined by turbulence. The absolute value at which viscous effects become less significant than turbulent effects depends entirely upon the characteristic properties of the fluid and the characteristic geometry of the system in which flow takes place. For flow in pipes, a value of $\mathcal{N}_{Re} \approx 2,000$ usually defines the point above which flow is no longer discretely laminar. Flow in such systems is usually considered discretely turbulent above $\mathcal{N}_{Re} \approx 4,000$.

The potential importance of the Froude number in environmental systems is not to be overlooked. A useful illustration is provided by the notion of specific energy in open channel flow. The specific energy head, h_{se}, is defined by letting the datum in the steady isothermal flow Bernoulli equation (Equation 4.15) be the bottom of the channel, so that the water depth is $y = H_D$, and $h_{se} = v^2/2g + H_D$. The Bernoulli and continuity of flow $(Q = Av = H_D Z_W v)$ equations for a channel of width Z_W are solved together for a constant discharge per unit width, Q/Z_W. The resulting relationship between h_{se} and H_D shows a minimum in specific energy at a depth referred to as the critical depth, $H_{D,c}$. Two alternate depths (one higher and the other lower than the critical depth) are possible at all other specific energies. After setting the derivative, dh_{se}/dH_D, to zero at critical depth, the Froude number (with characteristic length being the depth) is obtained and its value is 1. A Froude number value of $\mathcal{N}_{Fr} > 1$ defines supercritical flow (i.e., high inertial flow that occurs when $H_D < H_{D,c}$). Flow at the same specific energy but at the alternate depth, $H_D > H_{D,c}$, is characterized as subcritical because $\mathcal{N}_{Fr} < 1$. Channel transitions that produce hydraulic jumps give vivid practical meaning to the Froude number. Flow is supercritical (high inertia) and changes to subcritical as a result of a sudden and large rise in a channel bottom that causes a large decrease in specific energy. It has been shown experimentally that the extent of turbulence downstream of a hydraulic jump increases as the Froude number upstream increases.

Much use is made of the Reynolds and Froude numbers and other dimensionless parameters in the development of physical hydraulic models of large systems (e.g., rivers and harbors) to facilitate application of experimental data from models to prototype systems. The first requirement for dynamic similarity or similitude is that the model and prototype systems in question have geometric similitude (i.e., equal ratios of corresponding dimensions). Second, corresponding ratios of forces in the model and prototype must be equal. For example, any combination of length, velocity and kinematic viscosity which gives the same Reynolds number will have the same flow characteristics if viscous forces dominate over gravity and pressure forces.

Dynamic similitude is a critical concept in aerodynamic and hydrodynamic design problems (e.g., the hull shape of a ship having the least fluid drag). It is also vitally important in the physical design of bench- and pilot-scale models for environmental treatment processes and small-scale simulations of natural surface and subsurface systems. In these applications it is essential to account not only for dynamic similitude but process similitude as well. In most systems of interest in process engineering, viscosity forces dominate over gravity and pressure forces, such that similarities in the Froude and Euler numbers are not as important when developing a physical model as are similarities in the Reynolds number. The Froude number, however, can be important if forces at free surfaces are significant (e.g., wave action). It may not always be easy to achieve similitude in both the Reynolds and Froude number, as illustrated in Example 4.2.

Example 4.2. Use of a Physical Model to Lay a Foundation for the Design of a Lagoon Treatment System. (An exercise in the application of similitude relationships for physical systems of different scale.)

- ***Situation.*** *A lagoon treatment system is used to process wastewater from a particleboard fabrication facility. It is important to remove fine particles in the lagoon to comply with effluent limitations on suspended solids. The lagoon is subject to significant wind action. The physical and chemical processes governing particle settling are difficult to predict with a mathematical model, especially in such a complex hydrodynamic setting. In view of this, a decision is made to construct a small-scale physical hydraulic model of the essentially rectangular lagoon to obtain experimental information on the settling process.*

- ***Question(s).*** *What considerations must be involved in the design of the hydraulic scale model to ensure reasonable simulation of the settling characteristics of the full-scale lagoon?*

- ***Logic and Answer(s).***

  1. *Dynamic similarity or similitude is important because fluid flow directly affects the trajectory of particles. If wave action is important, dynamic similitude requires that we consider both free surface forces ($\mathcal{N}_{Fr}$) and viscous forces ($\mathcal{N}_{Re}$).*

  2. *The characteristic length of the lagoon is L_{actual}. The characteristic length of the scale model is $L_{model} = R_L L_{actual}$, where R_L is the scaling factor ($R_L \ll 1$). The widths of the lagoon and scale model are $Z_{W,actual}$ and $Z_{W,model}$, respectively. Equating the Froude numbers (Equation 4.22) for the model and the actual lagoon we obtain*

$$(v_c)_{model} = R_L^{0.5}(v_c)_{actual}$$

and, using the relationship above to equate the respective Reynolds numbers (Equation 4.21) while equating the Froude numbers

$$(v_c)_{model} = R_L^{1.5}(v_c)_{actual}$$

3. *Because $R_L << 1$, fluid velocity and viscosity must be decreased for the small-scale tests, the latter from one to two orders of magnitude. Although it is not difficult to decrease velocity, it is impossible to decrease viscosity by the amount needed, even by using another fluid. Even were it possible to decrease viscosity, it would be further necessary, according to Stokes law, to employ smaller particles and/or particles of much lower density in the scale model than are present in the actual lagoon system in order to simulate settling velocity properly. The effects of the free surface forces on the settling of particles thus cannot be easily determined.*

4. *While hydraulic similarity is important, the resulting scale model must also be appropriate in terms of reasonably simulating the settling process operative in the full-scale lagoon. As a beginning point, we examine factors governing settling under ideal hydraulic conditions (advective transport along parallel laminar streamlines in a fluid of uniform density). For discrete particles it is known that particle removal increases as the ratio of flow rate to surface area of the tank (the so-called overflow rate) decreases; for flocculant particles, removal increases with increasing depth, and thus with detention time [see, for example, Weber (1972)]. The scale model should, therefore, reproduce the overflow rates and detention times associated with the actual lagoon.*

5. *Suppose that $R_L = 0.1$, and we wish to maintain similitude only with respect to the Reynolds number. According to the first equation in step 2, the velocity in the scale model is $0.1 v_{actual}$. If we also wish to maintain geometric similarity, the model flow rate is*

$$Q_{model} = 0.1 v_{actual}(0.1 Z_{W,actual})(0.1 H_{actual}) = 0.001 Q_{actual}$$

where H_{actual} is the depth of wastewater in the lagoon. The hydraulic residence time (HRT) in the scale model is thus

$$(HRT)_{model} = \frac{0.001}{0.0032}(HRT)_{actual} = 0.31(HRT)_{actual}$$

The model overflow rate would be

$$\frac{0.0032\, Q_{actual}}{(0.1\, Z_{W,actual})(0.1\, L_{actual})} = 0.32(overflow\ rate)_{actual}$$

The result is a shorter HRT, which may or may not compensate for the smaller value of overflow rate in determining the settling efficiency. Thus, the geometric and Reynolds number similitude conditions required to achieve a reasonable hydraulic model lead to a scale model that may not simulate the removal of particles properly if both detention time and overflow rate are important.

6. *An alternative is to keep the respective overflow rates and Reynolds numbers of the two systems equal. If*

$$Z_{W,model} = 0.1(Z_{W,actual}) \text{ and } L_{model} = 0.1(L_{actual})$$

then equal overflow rate means $Q_{model} = 0.01(Q_{actual})$. *To obtain equal values for the Reynolds number requires that*

$$\frac{0.01 Q_{actual}}{(0.1 \ Z_{W,actual})(0.1 \ v_{actual}})$$

$$H_{D,model} = H_{D,actual}$$

7. *If Froude number similitude were the goal, and the viscosity of the test scale system could not be changed, then Reynolds number similarity could not be achieved; that is,*

$$(\mathcal{N}_{Re})_{model} = \frac{R_L^{0.5} \ (v_c)_{model} \ L_{model}}{(v_c)_{actual}} = 0.032(\mathcal{N}_{Re})_{actual}$$

In addition, the HRT would be $0.1 \ L_{actual}/0.32 \ v_{actual}$, *or* 0.31 *times the actual value. A lower Reynolds number in the model would mean less turbulence and more effective settling, whereas the shorter detention time would mean less effective settling. It is more likely that the effect of shorter detention time would more than offset that of smaller Reynolds number, leading to an underestimate of the extent of settling.*

- ***Key Point(s). The effects of geometry, inlet and outlet structures, density currents, wind action, and other factors make the hydrodynamics of settling tanks complex. Recirculation zones, dead zones and scouring introduced by such factors all impact the settling of particles. There is thus no single mathematical model for settling tanks that has gained wide acceptance. As seen here, correct physical models are also difficult to construct, owing to difficulties in achieving dynamic similitude while satisfying the geometry needed to simulate accurately the settling processes occurring in full-scale systems.***

4.3   DISPERSIVE MASS TRANSPORT

4.3.1   Dispersion Mechanisms and Effects

Bulk flow in large tanks and open water systems is more likely to be turbulent than laminar. We noted in Section 4.1.1 that in such cases complex fluid motions involving irregular velocity fluctuations (eddies) transport elements of fluid in an irregular manner. We noted also that dispersive mass transport may occur even when flow is laminar at the macroscale, a circumstance commonly encountered for flow through packed beds of filter media or adsorbents and around soil particles and aggregates in subsurface systems. Losses of energy in a fluid as it encounters obstructions cause flow velocities to decrease near surfaces. In cases of flow path disruptions by regular surfaces in small channels or pores, this causes parabolic distributions of velocities (e.g., Taylor dispersion). In cases of sharp and irregular flow-path disruptions by irregular obstacles, microscale eddies form.

Regardless of the mechanism(s) involved or whether the bulk flow is laminar or turbulent, the net effect of dispersion is to cause a spreading of fluid elements about the average advective velocity vector in a manner consistent with the distribution of local velocity vectors within the flow profile. This spreading effect is depicted schematically in Figure 4.4 for periodic and instantaneous injections of a dye into a microscale cluster of fluid elements moving along the centerline of flow through a pipe of macroscale diameter and length.

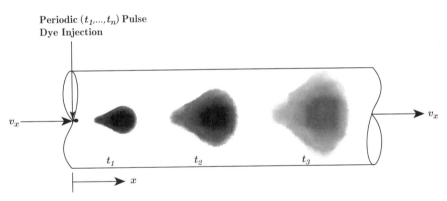

Figure 4.4 Constituent Spreading by Dispersion in an Advective Flow Field

4.3.2 Dispersion Coefficients and Numbers

Mathematical development of each specific form of dispersion is beyond the scope of this text, but they are readily available to the interested reader in a number of sources, including PDES. *In the large majority of transport modeling applications in natural and engineered environmental systems we treat the multiple forms of dispersion in a quasi empirical way. In other words, we experimentally measure them for the specific systems we are modeling.* As noted earlier, dispersion like molecular diffusion is largely a random process, regardless of its origins or causes. We can therefore use a functional expression having the same form as Fick's law to describe it; i.e., a linear relationship that expresses concentration changes over time as directly proportional to spatial concentration gradients. In this case, the proportionality "constant" is referred to simply as a dispersion coefficient, $\mathcal{D}_d$. The flux contribution of dispersion in a one-dimensional transport situation is thus given by

$$
\boxed{\begin{array}{l}
\textbf{\textit{Constituent}} \\
\textbf{\textit{Dispersion}} \qquad N_{x,d} = -\mathcal{D}_d \dfrac{dC}{dx} \\
\textbf{\textit{Flux}}
\end{array}}
\qquad (4.24)
$$

Unlike free liquid diffusion, the coefficient for which can be estimated from the molecular characteristics of a component and the viscosity and temperature of the fluid, depends on flow conditions and upon the scale at which fluid mixing is measured. *The dispersion coefficient is therefore necessarily system specific. As such, it generally cannot be extrapolated from one system to another, or predicted with confidence by any general model or correlation not specifically structured for and calibrated to the system in question.*

In most systems of practical concern, macroscale transport of components occurs principally by some combination of advection and dispersion. That is, the components of a fluid are carried along by bulk flow while also being dispersed by momentum exchange of fluid elements due to turbulence. In the fixed-coordinate system depicted in Figure 4.1, the total molar flux in the x direction is the sum of the advective flux and dispersive flux, or

$$
\boxed{\begin{array}{l}
\textbf{\textit{Total}} \\
\textbf{\textit{Constituent}} \qquad N_x = N_{x,a} + N_{x,d} = v_x C - \mathcal{D}_d \dfrac{dC}{dx} \\
\textbf{\textit{Flux}}
\end{array}}
\qquad (4.25)
$$

In natural systems, dispersion occurs in two and three dimensions. In such cases, dispersion coefficients generally do not have the same value in each direction. Even if the medium is isotropic (i.e., has the same dispersive properties in each direction in space), the fact that there is a principal direction to bulk flow means that more dispersion is created in that direction (longitudinal dispersion) than in directions normal to the flow (transverse dispersion). A simple example of directional differences in dispersion for an isotropic medium is evident in the spreading of a wastewater discharge plume in a river.

If a medium has different diffusion properties in different directions, it is said to be anisotropic. For example, lakes stratify vertically due to development of thermoclines, and this limits vertical dispersion. Dispersion in subsurface systems is even more complex because of three-dimensional heterogeneity (e.g., different shapes, sizes and orientations of soil grains, and the layering of different soil types). The dispersive flux in each of three dimensions is therefore influenced by the concentration gradients of solutes and dispersion coefficients in the other two dimensions. In subsurface systems, groundwater may even flow along tilted beds such that the local direction of transport is along the bedding planes while the global direction is along the horizontal. *Given the obvious complexities of most natural systems, $\mathcal{D}_d$ is generally acknowledged to be, and treated as, a strictly empirical hydrodynamic dispersion coefficient.*

To describe systems in which change occurs as a result of reaction as well as both forms of transport, the advection-dispersion-reaction (ADR) equation is written by substitution of the total flux equation (Equation 4.25) into the one-dimensional point form of the material balance (Equation 3.6). The one-dimensional form of the resulting equation is

$$
\boxed{
\begin{array}{ll}
\textbf{\textit{ADR}} \\
\textbf{\textit{Equation}}
\end{array}
\qquad
-v_x \frac{\partial C}{\partial x} + \mathcal{D}_d \frac{\partial^2 C}{\partial x^2} + \boldsymbol{r} = \frac{\partial C}{\partial t}
}
\qquad (4.26)
$$

a steady-state form of which was developed in Chapter 3 (Equation 3.36) in our discussion of *Type 3* boundary conditions. Equation 4.26 allows spatial and temporal determination of the concentration of components in systems involving advective and dispersive transport coupled with homogeneous reactions. *By dedimensionalizing the ADR equation, we can isolate a dimensionless dispersion number*

$$
\boxed{
\begin{array}{ll}
\textbf{\textit{Dispersion}} \\
\textbf{\textit{Number}}
\end{array}
\qquad
\mathcal{N}_d = \frac{\mathcal{D}_d}{v_x L}
}
\qquad (4.27)
$$

in which L is the characteristic length in the x direction. The dispersion number is important in reactor engineering and for description of mass transport in natural systems. The larger $\mathcal{N}_d$, the more significant is dispersion in macroscale transport phenomena. Example 4.3 demonstrates an application of the ADR equation for a condition of steady state.

Example 4.3. Transport and Die-Off of Bacteria Released in a Wastewater Effluent Discharge to a River System. (An illustration of the use of models to forecast potential contamination events, and of the role of dispersion in transport phenomena in natural aquatic environments.)

- *Situation. The outfall from a municipal wastewater treatment plant is located on a river 10 km above a bathing beach. A plant malfunction causes the coliform bacteria count in the river to rise almost instantaneously to 325 cells per 100 mL. The velocity of the river is 10 km per day and the dispersion coefficient is 100 km² per day. The die-off rate of bacteria is first order with respect to bacteria count, with a rate constant of k = 0.5/day. The bathing standard is ≤200 cells per 100 mL.*

- **Question(s).** *Will the bathing standard be violated at the beach?*

- **Logic and Answer(s).**

  1. *The ADR equation (Equation 4.26) can be applied to this analysis.*
  2. *The reaction rate term in the ADR equation is in this case*

  $$r = -kC = -0.5C$$

  3. *Steady-state conditions can be assumed to exist if the river flow and bacteria count at the discharge point are reasonably constant in time. The equation to be solved is then*

  $$\mathcal{D}_d \frac{d^2C}{dx^2} - v_x \frac{dC}{dx} - kC = 0$$

  4. *It is shown in Chapter 9 of PDES that integration of this expression with appropriate initial and boundary conditions yields*

  $$\frac{C}{C_{IN}} = \frac{4\beta_D \exp\left(0.5 v_x L/\mathcal{D}_d\right)}{(1 + \beta_D)^2 \exp\left(0.5\beta_D v_x L \mathcal{D}_d\right) - (1 - \beta_D)^2 \exp\left(-0.5\beta_D v_x L/\mathcal{D}_d\right)}$$

  $$\beta_D = \left(1 + 4\frac{kL}{v_x}\frac{\mathcal{D}_d}{v_x L}\right)^{0.5}$$

  where C_{IN} is the concentration of bacteria in the river at the outfall. The value of the dispersion number (Equation 4.27) that applies to this case is $\mathcal{N}_d = 1.0$. The resulting fractional concentration is 0.645. Thus the value of C at the beach is $(0.645)(325) = 210$ cells per mL, which violates the standard.

  5. *To examine the relative contribution of dispersion to bacterial transport to the beach, we can calculate a value of C for which dispersion is ignored entirely. The ADR equation given in step 3 then reduces to*

  $$-v_x \frac{dC}{dx} - kC = 0$$

  which can readily be solved by separation of variables to give

  $$\frac{C}{C_{IN}} = \exp\left(\frac{-kx}{v_x}\right)$$

  The fractional concentration at $x = 10$ km without dispersion would be 0.606. This would yield a value of C at the beach of $(0.606)(325) = 197$ cells per mL; i.e., the standard would not be violated were it not for the effects of dispersion.

Dispersion results in more elements of the fluid reaching the bathing area in a given period of time than would be true if transport were by advection only. The fractional concentration ratio given by the relationship presented in Step 4 therefore increases because less time is available for die-off of bacteria.

- *Key Point(s). While engineered systems can often be configured to minimize the influence of dispersion on primary reactor transport processes, natural systems almost always involve complex patterns of dispersion. It is important to take dispersion effects into account in modeling efforts, at least with respect to analysis of model sensitivity to expected levels of dispersion. As we see in this example, to not do so might very well lead to erroneous conclusions.*

4.4 CHAPTER SUMMARY

The transport of component mass through a fluid system may involve a variety of processes, including: (1) advection, (2) dispersion, (3) bulk-phase molecular diffusion, (4) intradomain diffusion, and, (5) interfacial or interdomain mass transfer. The discussion in this chapter has focused on the macroscale processes of advection and dispersion. The nature of fluid flow is in these cases determined by mass, energy, and momentum balances that lead to well-known equations developed by Bernoulli and Navier-Stokes, and equally well-known dimensionless parameters, such as the Reynolds and Froude numbers. These equations and dimensionless numbers have great utility for analyzing flows in engineered reactors, rivers, lakes, oceans, and subsurface systems.

Under purely laminar flow conditions, components are transported advectively at the velocities of fluid elements comprising the flow streamlines. Environmental systems more commonly involve some degree of turbulence at various scales, such that the macroscale component of transport becomes a complex process that cannot be quantified in terms of fluid velocity alone. Whether in the form of large-scale eddies in bulk fluids or small-scale disturbances to flow patterns caused by fluid shear near solid surfaces, turbulence produces dispersive transport.

The dispersion coefficient is an essential tool for estimating macroscale transport in practical situations. In particular, the dispersion number, an important dimensionless group that incorporates the dispersion coefficient, provides a means for quantifying the relative importance of dispersive and advective macroscale processes in engineered and natural systems. It is intuitive that the dispersion number and the Reynolds number should be closely related. The Reynolds number quantifies turbulence, and we have seen that turbulence is a factor that can significantly influence dispersion. The connection between these two dimensionless parameter groups will be explored further in Chapter 11.

4.5 CITATIONS AND SOURCES

Bishop, M.M., J.M. Morgan, B. Cornwell and D.K. Jamison, 1993, "Improving the Disinfection Detention Time of a Water Treatment Plant Clearwell," *Journal of the American Water Works Association, 85* (3), 68-75. (Problem 4.4)

Weber, W.J., Jr. and F.A. DiGiano, 1996, *Process Dynamics in Environmental Systems*, John Wiley & Sons, Inc., New York. The source of most of the material presented in Chapter 4, Chapter 3 of PDES provides an expanded coverage of mass transport phenomena and guidance with respect to related source materials.

4.6 PROBLEM ASSIGNMENTS

4.1 Compare Equation 4.13 to Equations 2.17 and 2.18 in Chapter 2. Comment on similarities and differences.

4.2 The tank shown below is initially filled with an industrial solvent.

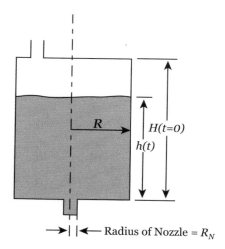

In ordinary operation, the nozzle at the bottom of the tank is opened and closed electronically. A malfunction results in the nozzle remaining open. Derive an expression to predict the time for the tank to empty if the exit nozzle velocity is $v_N = (2\mathcal{G}h)^{0.5}$. [*Hint:* The beginning point is an energy balance assuming that atmospheric pressure exists at the top of the fluid and at the exit point of the fluid.]

$$Answer:\ t = \left(\frac{R}{R_N}\right)^2 \left(\frac{2H}{\mathcal{G}}\right)^{0.5}$$

4.3 Use the information given in Example 4.3 to make a plot of the dependence of the residual bacterial cell count at the bathing beach on the dispersion number (ranging from 0.01 to 0.1). Repeat this plot for a die-off rate of 1.0 per day instead of 0.5 per day. Discuss these results relative to those for an assumption of complete mixing.

4.4 Bishop et al. (1993) used physical models to simulate flow patterns in full-scale disinfection clearwells. In light of Example 4.2, review their paper and explain their approach to scaling and the evidence they present to show that similitude was achieved. Discuss whether the bacteria kill would necessarily have been the same as that expected for the full-scale system if both a disinfectant and bacteria had been introduced in the influent to the model clearwell and the bacteria remaining in the effluent measured.

4.5 A highly treated industrial wastewater from a small manufacturing process is injected into a well (30-cm diameter) which fully penetrates a 4-m-thick confined aquifer. The recharge pumping rate is 200 m^3/day. If 50 μg/L of a solvent is present in the injected wastewater and the solvent is degraded in the subsurface by microbial action in a first-order rate process ($k = 0.2$ per day), find the solvent concentration at a radial distance of 10 m from the injection well. Assume steady-state conditions and that transport is dominated by one-dimensional radial advection. The aquifer porosity, ε_d, is 0.2. [*Hint:* See Chapter 3 for a description of material balances in the radial direction. The radial seepage velocity is the pumping rate divided by the cross-sectional area of the confined aquifer (accounting for porosity) normal to the radial direction of flow and is therefore a function of radius.]

Answer: 7.6 mg/L.

4.6 A large stream flows into and out of a temperature stratified lake at 3.04 m^3/sec. The lake has a 39 $10^6 m^3$ epilimnion (the warmer surface water) and a 14 $10^6 m^3$ hypolimnion (the colder, deeper water). The lake is 5.25 m deep and has nearly vertical sides so that the areas of the surface, the interface between the epilimnion, and the bottom can be taken as essentially the same. At time $t = 0$ the phosphorous concentration of the stream jumps from 0 ug/L to 48 ug/L. Phosphorous is assumed to have a settling velocity of 0.05 m/day in the epilimnion and 0.0 m/day in the hypolimnion. The streamflow passes through the epilimnion only.

(a) Construct a mass balance equation describing the steady-state phosphorous flux from the epilimnion into the hypolimnion. Calculate the steady-state flux.

(b) Construct a mass balance equation describing the concentration of phosphorous in the epilimnion as a function of time starting at $t = 0$.

(c) Construct a mass balance equation describing the concentration of phosphorous in the hypolimnion as a function of time (for this problem ignore complications that would arise due to the limited solubility of phosphorous, etc.) starting at $t = 0$.

Hints: The settling velocity is a component of a flux, which can be converted into a form you can use. Match the units of the terms in your mass balance to reveal how to use this information in your mass balance equation.

Use a table of integrals from a calculus text; the integrals are not especially difficult if you do so.

4.7 Fluid flow rates can be measured using an orifice-plate meter. The device is comprised by a circular disk having a central orifice of cross sectional area A_0. This disk is inserted between, and held in fixed position by the flanges of, two sections of a pipe having equal cross sectional areas A_1, as illustrated schematically below. Pressure drop across the orifice is correlated with stream velocity.

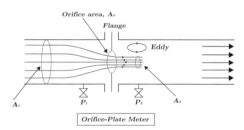

(a) Apply the Bernoulli equation to develop an expression for the volumetric flow rate, Q.

(b) Discuss potential problems associated with application of the Bernoulli equation downstream of the orifice.

4.8 At steady state the Navier-Stokes equation for flow in the x direction becomes

$$v_x \frac{\partial v_x}{\partial x} + v_y \frac{\partial v_x}{\partial y} + v_z \frac{\partial v_x}{\partial z} = g_x - \frac{1}{\rho} \frac{\partial \rho}{\partial x} + \frac{\mu_v}{\rho} \left(\frac{\partial^2 v_x}{\partial x^2} + \frac{\partial^2 v_x}{\partial y^2} \frac{\partial^2 v_x}{\partial z^2} \right)$$

(a) Show that this equation leads directly to the Froude, Reynolds, and Euler numbers. *Hint:* define a characteristic unit for each parameter in the equation; e.g., v_x, v_y, $v_z \sim v_c$.

(b) These three dimensionless parameters govern the dynamic similarity of fluid flow. Suggest some situations when similarity analysis might be independent of $\mathcal{N}_{Re}$ and $\mathcal{N}_{Fr}$; i.e., is dependent only on the Euler number.

4.9 Chicago's Shedd Aquarium uses ozonation to disinfect the water that flows through the marine habitats. Proper disinfection requires that a minimum ozone concentration of 3.0 mg/L remain at the end of the process. In order to meet the demands of animal caretakers that suggest that the concentration of ozone within the tanks be no more than 0.1 mg/L, the ozone in treated water is allowed to decompose in a plug flow reactor before use.

Ozone decay occurs by the following reaction:

$$2O_3 \Leftrightarrow 3O_2$$

where $r = 0.041\ C_{O_3}(\text{min}^{-1})$

(a) Given a reactor of length L, develop an analytical expression for the velocity of ozonated water through the reactor. Assume steady state operation.

(b) Consider a nonideal reactor system (with dispersion). If the ozone generator fails, causing an instantaneous decrease in the O_3 concentration ($C_{O_3} = 0$ mg/L) and a dramatic increase in the O_2 concentration entering the PFDR, will ozone-free water arrive at the end of the reactor before or after we would expect it to under ideal conditions (PFR)? Explain your answer mathematically.

4.10 Head loss across a hydraulic jump is given by the Bernoulli equation for shear flow loss

$$y_1 + \frac{v_1^2}{2g} = y_2 + \frac{v_2^2}{2g} + h_l$$

(a) Show that the dimensionless head loss, h_l/y_1, is given by

$$\frac{h_l}{y_1} = 1 - \frac{y_2}{y_1} + \frac{\mathcal{N}_{Fr,1}}{2}\left[1 - \left(\frac{y_1}{y_2}\right)^2\right]$$

where $\mathcal{N}_{Fr,1}$ is the upstream Froude number.

(b) A horizontal stream with a depth of 1 m travels at a velocity of 4.2 m/s. The stream is forced to undergo a hydraulic jump. Calculate the downstream depth and head loss.

Chapter 5

Elementary Process Equilibria

Contents

5.0   CHAPTER OBJECTIVES

To learn to identify common energy flows associated with different transformation reactions in single-phase environmental systems, and to establish a link between energy availability for reactions and the characteristic equilibrium states they attain when that energy is fully expended and reaches a net value of zero.

5.1   CONCEPTS

In earlier chapters we related environmental process dynamics to changes in constituents that occur because of transport and transformation or reaction processes. Having completed our characterization of macroscale processes responsible for mass transport in Chapter 4, we turn now to characterizing reaction processes. In Chapters 5 and 6 we deal most specifically with relationships associated with a particular state of such processes; i.e., the equilibrium state. Our focus is chemical reactions. Although these reactions may in some cases be biologically mediated, their chemical components and the interactive energies that drive them toward the equilibrium state are fundamentally the same as if there was no biological mediation. The energy relationships discussed in Chapters 5 and 6 are for single-phase systems. In Chapter 12 energy and associated equilibrium relationships are extended to multi-phase systems, wherein the focus of interest is the distribution of chemical species between the aqueous phase and other liquid, gas and solid phases.

Regardless of whether we deal with transformation reactions in single-phase or multi-phase systems, certain well defined intrinsic thermodynamic relationships among chemical species ultimately govern the extent of transformation that is energetically possible in a reaction. These energy relationships are rooted principally in equilibrium concepts, however, and therefore do not necessarily determine rates of transformation. The corresponding reaction rate relationships (i.e., kinetics) for single-phase systems are discussed in Chapters 7 and 8. Reactions at interfaces cause depletion or accumulation of species at phase boundaries in multiphase systems, and species are therefore transferred from one phase to another. Reaction phenomena in systems thus cannot be considered alone, but rather must be addressed in conjunction with phase transfer processes.

A thermodynamic rationale for describing any system begins with examination of the chemical properties of its principal components. The characteristics of these components lead inherently to transformation, accumulation, and separation reactions that must be identified. Finally, the reactions must be quantified with respect to appropriate energy balances and thermodynamic properties of each particular system.

5.2 WATER AND THE AQUEOUS PHASE

5.2.1 Process Roles

Single-phase reactions of interest to water quality scientists and engineers generally take place in dilute aqueous systems. Maximum levels of contaminants in natural waters and water supplies seldom exceed several milligrams per liter (mg/L), and in wastewaters normally not more than a few hundred mg/L. Even the concentrations of residual precipitates and sludges are rarely greater than 10,000 to 30,000 mg/L or about 1 to 3% by weight. Water is clearly the principal component of aqueous systems, being commonly present in concentrations several orders of magnitude larger than the concentrations of other reacting species.

The dominant concentration of water in aqueous environmental systems has a number of implications for water quality processes. In single-phase systems, water is likely to control the behavior of dissolved substances, and to participate in or mediate their reactions with each other. In multi-phase systems, the properties and characteristics of water will determine the extent to which other chemical species will remain dissolved in the aqueous phase, volatilize to a gas phase, or precipitate to form solid phases. Most solid phases with which water comes into contact are comprised by chemical structures exhibiting reactivity at their phase boundaries, or surfaces. As a result, water is likely to affect surface phenomena as significantly as it does dissolved-phase processes. Water may be actively involved in the reactions of other components in aqueous phases. Its mass concentration will not generally change significantly, however, because it is present in such large excess with respect to any other species. Its solution-phase reactivity thus cannot generally be assessed in terms of changes in its mass or concentration.

5.2.2 Constituent Character Behaviors

The properties of aqueous environmental systems can be attributed largely to the properties of pure water, the constituent atoms of which are hydrogen and oxygen. The reactivity and energy relationships of chemical species relate to the structure and form of the atoms that comprise them, a circumstance not unique to water. What is different about water is the uniqueness of its constituents, hydrogen and oxygen. In a rudimentary sense, the atoms of chemical elements owe their reactivity to particular numbers and arrangements of neutrons, protons, and, most importantly, electrons. Atoms of all elements other than hydrogen, the smallest atom, have at least one neutron and at least one stable shell of electrons surrounding its nucleus. The hydrogen atom has neither. Helium, an inert substance and the second smallest atom, has the capacity of its innermost, or K, shell filled by two electrons. This would be the stable or "inert" electron configuration for hydrogen as well. The fact that the hydrogen atom does not have an enclosing shell of electrons like helium makes it particularly reactive in combining with other atoms to "surround" its single proton with two electrons to satisfy its electron capacity. The proton can no more exist as a stable entity than can the electron, or the neutron. To achieve the stability imparted by a complete enclosing electron shell, the hydrogen atom shares its single electron, often with a number of other atoms simultaneously. The bond that it forms with other elements to "complete" its K shell is termed the hydrogen bond.

All elements are energetically inclined to undergo reactions that cause them to move from one electron configuration and associated energy state to another more stable electron configuration and lower energy state until the most stable and lowest energy state is reached. The two-electron configuration of helium is the most stable state for the five elements having the lowest atomic numbers. The most stable state for carbon and elements of higher atomic number is characterized by an outer shell containing eight electrons. This gives the same electron configuration as that of the inert gas that is closest to the element in total electron number and structure, and therefore closest to it in the periodic table. *The periodic table is an arrangement of elements according to the number of protons contained in their nucleus and the number of electrons contained in their surrounding shells, and thus characterizes their inherent stability and reactivity.*

Figure 1.6 in Chapter 1 presented an abridged periodic arrangement of selected chemical elements of particular environmental interest. There are sixteen "groups" in the periodic table (IA through VIII). Except for the VIIIA group, the numeral in each group designation signifies that number of electrons present in the outermost shell that will yield an atomic balance (equal number) of protons and electrons. The only atoms that are stable under these conditions, however, are the "inert gases" in group VIII, each of which achieves its atomic balance of electrons and protons with eight electrons in its outer shell. As we noted above, chemical elements have a tendency to undergo reaction continually until they achieve a stable electron configuration; that electron configuration is then identical to that of the next higher or next lower inert gas. In the third row, for example, Na and Mg become stable by divesting one and two electrons, respectively, to form the same electron configuration as Ne, their next lower inert gas; Cl on the other hand, finds it easier to add one electron to form the same electron configuration as Ar, its next higher inert gas.

The existence of eight electrons in any shell of an atom does not mean that the electron capacity of that shell has been reached, simply that a stable configuration has been achieved. Shells further from the nucleus of an atom may begin to fill when the next innermost shell contains eight electrons. The order of filling relates to the relative stability of electrons in different orbitals within different shells. Because inner shells may still have capacities for additional electrons, reactions other than those involving outer shell, or valence, electrons are possible; these reactions, referred to as coordinate-covalent or complexation reactions, will be discussed later.

The other primary component of water, oxygen, is also highly reactive. Its reactions comprise the primary mechanisms by which energy is derived from other substances; for example, the respiration of living cells and the combustion of fuels. As an atom, oxygen is deficient with respect to the number (eight) of electrons required in its outermost shell to impart thermodynamic stability. The oxygen atom thus enters reactions with other elements to attain a more stable electron configuration.

In combination to form water, hydrogen and oxygen share electrons through hydrogen bonding. Each oxygen atom has six electrons in its outer shell and requires two additional electrons to configure its electron structure like that of neon. Each hydrogen atom has one electron and requires one more to assume the electron structure of helium. Thus, the smallest conceivable molecular structure for water would be comprised by two atoms of hydrogen and one atom of oxygen, with intermixed shells of orbiting electrons. The geometric configuration of this molecule is asymmetric, resulting in an asymmetric distribution of electrons, or negative charges. Thus, although water has no net electrical charge, its molecules are polar, which makes water compatible with other polar and charged (ionic) chemical species and incompatible with nonpolar and uncharged (nonionic) species. Water is thus an excellent solvent for salts or ions (e.g., Na^+, K^+, Cl^-, and SO_4^{2-}), a fair solvent for polar molecules (e.g., CO_2, NH_3, CH_3Cl, and C_6H_5OH) and a poor solvent for nonpolar molecules (e.g., N_2, CH_4, C_6H_6, and C_6H_{14}).

5.2.3   Structure and Properties

Although the smallest molecular structure for a water molecule is two hydrogen atoms and one oxygen atom, the strong tendency of the hydrogen atom to share electrons generally results in its bonding with several other oxygen atoms simultaneously. The structure of water is thus more that of a large loosely knit polymer than a discrete molecule; that is, $(H_2O)_n$ rather than H_2O. This imparts some interesting properties to water, for example, its density. It is one of the few compounds for which the solid state (ice) is less dense than the liquid state. Ice is less dense because its molecular structure is more organized than water (i.e., there is a regular orientation between the hydrogen and oxygen atoms). Water is also one of the few liquids for which flow does not involve the sliding of molecules past each other. The flow of water requires a breakage and reformation of hydrogen bonds; this has relevance with respect to the viscosity of water.

Water is a good solvent for ionic species because it has a high dielectric constant, $\mathcal{K}_D$. The dielectric constant is a measure of the capacity of a fluid to neutralize attractive or repulsive forces between charged units dissolved or dispersed therein, as depicted schematically in Figure 5.1. Coulomb's law states that

$$F_C = \frac{1}{\mathcal{K}_D} \frac{z_1^{\circ} z_2^{\circ}}{L^2} \tag{5.1}$$

where $F_C(MLt^{-2})$ is the net Coulombic (electrostatic) force between two units (e.g., ions or colloids) of electronic charge z_1° and z_2° separated by a distance

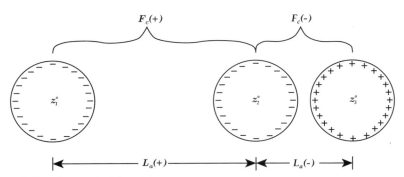

a. Low dielectric constant (eg air).

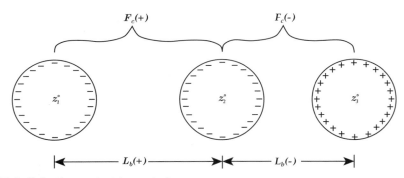

b. High dielectic constant (eg water).

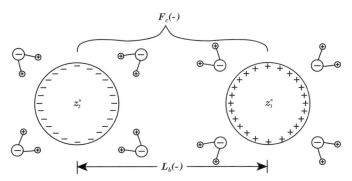

c. Insulating role of adjacent layers of water molecules.

Figure 5.1 Schematic Characterization of Electrostatic Forces,
Separation Distances, and the Effects of Water

L. Figure 5.1 illustrates schematically and qualitatively the relative separation distances between charge units for a fixed value of the Coulombic force F_C. If the charge units are somehow fixed in space, the separation distance L remains constant and F_C is essentially a latent or potential force. If the charge units are free to move in response to the force, however, then the separation distance will increase for a repulsion force [(+)(+) or (-)(-) = (+)] or decrease for an attraction force [(+)(-) or (-)(+) = (-)] until $F_C \to 0$. Conversely, if an external force (e.g., a mechanical force such as fluid shear) is applied to the charge units so that they are moved relative to one another, then the Coulombic force between them will change accordingly. This is an important concept in the coagulation and flocculation of charged colloidal particles in engineered and natural systems.

A comparison of parts a and b of Figure 5.1 reveals that water, because of its much higher dielectric constant, has a significantly larger effect on Coulombic forces than does air, allowing closer approaches for units of the same charge $[L_b(+) < L_a(+)]$ and causing further separation of units of opposite charge $[L_b(-) > L_a(-)]$. As shown in Figure 5.1c, this is mechanistically attributable to orientation of polar water molecules about charged units. The negative poles of the adjacent layers (water layers closest to the charged units) of molecules comprising the multimolecular associations of surrounding water are able to orient around positively charged units and the positive poles of these associations around negatively charged units, forming cages that effectively insulate positive units from negative units, thus maintaining these units in a dissolved or dispersed state. When the charge units are ions of opposite charge, such as sodium (Na^+) and chloride (Cl^-), this causes normally solid salts such as NaCl to dissolve readily in water. Although pure water itself is a poor conductor of electricity, aqueous solutions usually have high conductivity. The reason is that water acts as a universal solvent for charged species, and is thus seldom free of dissolved ionic impurities.

Heat capacity, $Q_H^\circ (ML^2t^{-2}T^{-1}$ per mole or unit mass), is another property that is significantly influenced by the unique structure of water. The total energy required to break all of the hydrogen bonds involved in a multimolecular association of water is large; this accounts for its high boiling and melting points relative to other liquids. The heat of melting or fusion $Q_{H,m}(ML^2t^{-2}$ per mole or unit mass), of ice is 334.7 Joules (J) per gram at $0°C$. The heat of vaporization, $Q_{H,v}$ of water is 2.26 kJ per gram at $100°C$, which translates to 40.6 kJ (9.7 kcal or 38.5 BTU) per mole. Its average specific heat capacity, Q_H°, is 1.00 cal/g-K(4.184 J/g-K) and deviations from this between the freezing and boiling points average less than 1%. This translates to approximately 75.4 J (18 cal or 0.07 BTU) per mole per degree Kelvin. Thus, simply to raise the temperature of 1 liter of water from $20°C$ to $25°C$ requires an energy input of nearly 20 BTU. For a flow of 3785 m^3 of water per day (1 million gallons per day, or 1 mgd), for example, raising the temperature from $2°C$ to $25°C$ would require approximately 76×10^6 BTU or 22.3 MW-h/day. Distillation at this same flow would require a daily energy input approaching 9.3×10^9 BTU or 2725 MW-h. Increasing or decreasing the temperature of water to facilitate or accelerate a particular treatment process is clearly energy and cost intensive.

Consequently, two of the most straightforward and seemingly obvious means for purifying water, distillation and freezing, are usually cost prohibitive, at least when configured as direct single-stage operations, as illustrated for distillation in Example 5.1.

Example 5.1. Single-Stage Direct Distillation of Sea Water to Produce Drinking Water. (Calculations of fuel requirements and desalinized water produced in a simple sea water distillation process.)

- **Situation.** *A small water distillation plant is to be built for a remote coastal outpost located on a shallow marine bay and having no access to fresh water. It is planned that ethylene will be used as fuel for the plant.*

- **Question(s).** *Assuming 90% efficiency, how much sea water at 20° C can be converted to steam at 100° C by each cubic meter of C_2H_4 gas burned?*

- **Logic and Answer(s).** *The combustion of ethylene involves the following reaction*

$$C_2H_4(g) + 3O_2(g) \Leftrightarrow 2CO_2(g) + 2H_2O(l)$$

1. *We first determine from information that is readily available in standard handbooks that the combustion of ethylene yields a heat output of 1410 kJ/mol (e.g., Table 6.1, and enthalpy balances to be introduced later in Chapter 6).*

2. *We know from elementary physics that 1 mol of gas occupies a volume of 22.4 L at standard temperature and pressure (STP) (i.e., 1 atm and 0° C). Thus, the number of moles of C_2H_4 in one cubic meter is*

$$\frac{1,000 \ L/m^3}{22.4 \ L/mol} = 44.6 \ mol/m^3$$

3. *The heat available in the combustion of 1.0 m^3 of C_2H_4 is then*

$$(44.6 \ mol/m^3)(1,410 \ kJ/mol) = 6.3 \times 104 \ kJ/m^3$$

The useful heat is 90% of this, or

$$(0.90)(6.3 \times 10^4 kJ/m^3) = 5.7 \times 10^4 kJ/m^3$$

4. *The overall process involves raising the water from its ambient temperature to 100° C and then vaporizing it. Assuming that the average water temperature at the shallow bay intake is 20° C, we have*

$H_2O(l, \ 20°C) \Leftrightarrow H_2O(l, \ 100°C)$
heat required $= (4.184 \ kJ/kg \ °K)(80° K) = 334.7 \ kJ/kg$
$H_2O(l, 100°C) \Leftrightarrow H_2O(g, 100°C)$

> *heat required* $= 2,259 \; kJ/kg$
>
> *The total heat requirement is therefore 2594 kJ/kg.*
>
> 5. *The mass of water converted is equal to the amount of heat available divided by the heat requirement per kilogram, or the amount of* H_2O *produced per cubic meter of* C_2H_4
>
> $$\frac{5.7 \times 10^4 kJ}{2,594 kJ/kg} = 21.97 kg$$

- *Key Point(s). While direct distillation can be highly effective for all types of water purification, it is shown above to produce only 22 L, or 0.022 m^3 of water per cubic meter of ethylene burned. This is obviously an energy-intensive process, and thus not particularly cost effective under most conditions.*

5.3   CHEMICAL STRUCTURE AND REACTIVITY

5.3.1   Electrons and Oxidation States

We have referred to the thermodynamic periodicity of elements and to the role of electron structure in determining the reactivity of chemical species. In the simplest sense, the reactivity of a substance defines the tendency for its atoms to attain the thermodynamically stable electron configuration of the nearest inert gas. Stability can be reached by giving up, taking on, or sharing electrons. The fact that atoms and molecules are electron-active forms the basis for transformation processes in aquatic systems.

Some elements behave in a very direct and predictable fashion to form a limited number of discrete species and/or combinations. Other elements must undergo more extensive and more complex changes to approach thermodynamic stability. Elemental carbon, C, which exists in its simplest form as graphite, has four electrons in its outer shell. This element commonly attempts to achieve the stable electron configuration of neon by sharing its electrons with other atoms. It is easier to share four electrons than to give them away in order to approach the electron configuration of helium, or to strip other species of four electrons. *There are many atoms with which carbon can share one or more of its four electrons to achieve at least a quasi- or metastable electron configuration and energy state, as evidenced by the large number and wide diversity of natural and synthetic organic (carbon-based) compounds that exist.*

Atoms that either completely give up or take on electrons are electronically imbalanced with respect to the number of protons in the nucleus and the total number of electrons surrounding the nucleus. They therefore exhibit a charge, and are termed ions. Atoms that share electrons with other atoms to form molecules or compounds may or may not impart a charge to the resulting species. For example, the chlorine atom, Cl, can take on an electron to form the chloride ion, Cl^-, or share electrons with another chlorine atom to form the uncharged chlorine molecule, Cl_2. Alternatively, it may share its electron with a hydrogen atom to form an uncharged compound, HCl. Electrons are actually shared in pairs, either with each atom contributing one electron per pair or with one atom contributing both electrons to each shared pair.

An electronically balanced atom, an atom in its elemental state, has an oxidation state of zero. Its oxidation state increases by one for every electron it gives up, and decreases by one for every electron it takes on. The sharing of electrons can lead to intermediate oxidation states. For convenience in such cases, however, the more electronegative of two species sharing one or more pairs of electrons is usually considered to have its oxidation state decreased, while that of the more electropositive is increased. For example, the hydrogen atom in HCl is generally considered to be in a unit positive (I) oxidation state, and the chlorine atom in a unit negative (-I) state. Oxidation state is an important property of elements with respect to their reactivity, particularly for complex species and in substitutive oxidation/reduction reactions; e.g., substitution of Cl(I) for H(I), as in the chlorination of ammonia to form chloramines.

Figure 1.6 reveals that the principal oxidation state of an element (excepting those in groups VIIIA and VB through VIIIB) has the same numerical value as its corresponding group number. These elements have a clear preference to give up that number of electrons to form the electron configuration of the next lowest inert gas. The group VB elements have the same tendency, but can also achieve a semi-stable oxidation state by divesting three electrons. The group VIIB elements all achieve a stable oxidation state by assuming the electron configuration of the next higher inert gas. Lastly, as seen by the other oxidation states listed in their respective boxes, all but oxygen of the environmentally significant elements of group VIIB are highly ambivalent about their oxidation states and electron configurations. You will also note, again from the "other oxidation state" information, that the environmentally significant members of group VB exhibit the same tendency toward oxidation state ambivalence.

5.3.2   Reactivity and Reactions

Atoms that have either given up or taken on an electron to gain greater stability as ions will in further reactions tend to combine with other ions of opposite charge. That is, they will be attracted by the electrostatic or Coulombic forces defined by Equation 5.1. The sodium ion, Na^+, which is in an oxidation state of (I), is strongly attracted, for example, to the chloride ion, Cl^-, which is in an oxidation state of (-I); the result is formation of sodium chloride according to the reaction

$$Na^+ + Cl^- \Leftrightarrow \{Na^+Cl^-\} = NaCl \tag{5.2}$$

The immediate right hand side of Equation 5.2 is written in a form that emphasizes the attractive force between these ions as being clearly electrostatic. This is then the nature of the bond between the two, and as such each substance retains its original electron configuration in the resulting combination or compound (in this case a "salt"). This type of bond is termed electrovalent. Conversely, when the hydrogen atom reacts with the chlorine atom to form hydrochloric acid, HCl, the two atoms are bonded by sharing a pair of electrons. This type of bond is termed either covalent or coordinate covalent, depending upon the origin(s) of the shared electrons. The true oxidation states of the hydrogen and chlorine atoms in HCl are intermediate between (I) and (-I), whereas those for Na^+ and Cl^- in NaCl are clearly (I) and (-I), respectively.

Remarkable differences in chemical reactivity are imparted to combinations of atoms by virtue of the manner of their bonding. The electrovalently bonded salt, NaCl, exhibits totally different reactivity than does the hydrogen-bonded mineral acid, HCl. A similar difference can be noted between the electrovalently bonded sodium salt, NaOH, of the hydroxide ion, and hydrogen-bonded water, HOH. As a general rule, electrovalently bonded compounds have high melting and boiling points and high solubility in water. Conversely, covalently bonded compounds, in which each partner sharing a pair of electrons provides one electron, generally exhibit low melting and boiling points and are less soluble in water.

Electrovalent reactions between oppositely charged ions can also involve ions of different oxidation states, as illustrated below

$$\textbf{\textit{An Electrovalent Reaction}}$$
$$Mg^{2+} + 2Cl^- \Leftrightarrow \{Mg^{2+}(Cl^-)_2\} = MgCl_2 \tag{5.3}$$

Examples of predominantly covalent reactions and products are

$$\textbf{\textit{Covalent Reactions}}$$
$$\textbf{\textit{and Electron Pair Sharing}}$$
$$C + O_2 \Leftrightarrow \{O = C = O\} = CO_2(g) \tag{5.4}$$

$$C + 2H_2 \Leftrightarrow \left\{ H - \overset{\displaystyle H}{\underset{\displaystyle H}{\overset{|}{\underset{|}{C}}}} - H \right\} = CH_4(g) \tag{5.5}$$

where each dash (bond) between atoms represents one pair of shared electrons. Equations 5.4 and 5.5 imply that the atoms constituting the oxygen (O=O) and hydrogen (H-H) molecules, respectively, are themselves sharing electrons. This is typical of the way in which the atoms of a substance combine to form molecules. Other examples include Br_2, Cl_2, and N_2.

The third type of bonding arrangement, coordinate or coordinate-covalent bonding, is similar in its eventual form to covalent bonding in that two atoms share one or more pairs of electrons. In contrast to covalent bonding, however, one of the two atoms involved in the sharing of an electron pair contributes both of the electrons to the partnership. That is, one atom is a donor of an electron pair and the other is an electron-pair acceptor. The number of pairs of electrons brought to or accepted by a species in such bonding is termed the coordination number of that species. The properties of compounds that result from such bonding arrangements are usually intermediate to those of electrovalent and covalent compounds. Examples of coordinate covalent reactions, including the unique case of hydrogen bonding, are given in Equations 5.6 through 5.9

Coordinate Covalent Reactions and Electron Pair Sharing

$$\{H_2O\} + H^+ \Leftrightarrow \left\{ \begin{array}{c} H \\ | \\ H - O - H \end{array} \right\}^+ = H_3O^+ \tag{5.6}$$

$$NH_3 + H^+ \Leftrightarrow \left\{ \begin{array}{c} H \\ | \\ H - N - H \\ | \\ H \end{array} \right\}^+ = NH_4^+ \tag{5.7}$$

$$Fe^{2+} + 4H_2O \Leftrightarrow \left\{ \begin{array}{c} H_2O \\ | \\ H_2O - Fe - OH_2 \\ | \\ H_2O \end{array} \right\} = Fe^{2+}(aq) \tag{5.8}$$

$$Cd^{2+}_{(aq)} + 3OH^- \Leftrightarrow \left\{ \begin{array}{c} OH \\ | \\ HO - Cd - OH_2 \\ | \\ OH \end{array} \right\}^- + 3H_2O \tag{5.9}$$

The resulting species are termed complexes or, as in cases such as those illustrated in Equations 5.6 through 5.9, complex ions. The electron-pair acceptors are termed the central ions of the resulting complexes, and the electron-pair donating species (e.g., OH^- and H_2O) are ligands. The hydrogen ion, or proton, is unique because it accepts only one pair of electrons and, as noted in Equations 5.6 and 5.7, cannot be considered the central ion of the water and ammonium ion complexes. Although the reactions given in Equations 5.6 and 5.7 both qualify as complexation reactions, they are often more specifically referred to as protolysis reactions because of the involvement of the proton.

Equations 5.6 and 5.7 represent only half-reactions in that, as mentioned earlier, free protons do not exist in nature. Thus, these half-reactions must be coupled with other half-reactions in which protons are released. For example, rearranging and combining the reactions in these two equations yields

$$NH_3 + H_3O^+ \Leftrightarrow NH_4^+ + H_2O \qquad (5.10)$$

The cadmium and iron ions in Equations 5.8 and 5.9 have eight electrons in their outer shells and thus satisfy the stable electron configuration of the closest inert gases. Moreover, the product of the reaction given by Equation 5.9 has the same charge characteristics as the central ion because the ligand, H_2O, has no net charge. The product of the reaction given by Equation 5.8 also bears a net charge equal to the sum of the electronic charges of the reactants. These observations point to the fact that the outer electron sphere configurations of the two metal ions are not changed in these reactions as they are in simple covalent bonding. In these instances, as for most reactions between heavy metal ions and other species of environmental interest, the electron pairs are shared within inner electron spheres. Although the inner spheres may already contain eight electrons, they can accommodate still more. The metal ion retains its outer-shell configuration, and thus its oxidation state, in such reactions.

Example 5.2 illustrates how the oxidation states of elements vary as they interact with one another to form different compounds and complex ions. The example also shows how oxidation states can be determined based on the composition of a compound or complex ion.

Example 5.2. Calculation of the Oxidation States of Atoms in Compounds. (An illustration of the underlying basis of reaction stoichiometry.)

- ***Situation.*** *It is often helpful when assessing the stability of various chemical compounds to know the oxidation states in which the atoms comprising those compounds exist.*

- ***Question(s).*** *Determine the oxidation states of the atoms of the following compounds of sulfur: (1) Na_2SO_4; (2) $FeSO_4$; (3) H_2SO_4; (4) H_2SO_3; (5) H_2S.*

- ***Logic and Answer(s).*** *Certain of the atoms involved in these compounds are known to have only one stable oxidation state. These include H(I), Na(I), and O(−II). We can assume that these atoms have achieved their respective stable states in the compounds listed. We know that these compounds are uncharged, so that the net sum of the negative and positive oxidation states of the atoms or ions comprising them must be zero. The oxidation states on the remaining atom sulfur, a group VIB element and therefore somewhat ambivalent (and thus flexible) about its oxidation states, may then be calculated as follows*

1. *The sum of the* $Na(I)$ *oxidation states* $= 2 \times 1 = 2$. *The sum of the* $O(-II)$ *oxidation states* $= 4 \times (-2) = -8$. *The sum of the sulfur atom oxidation states must be equal and opposite in sign to the sum of the* $Na(I)$ *and* $O(-II)$ *oxidation states. Thus, the single atom of sulfur must exist as* $S(VI)$ *in* Na_2SO_4. *The sulfate group,* SO_4^{2-}, *in this compound exists as a complex ion in which the sulfur and oxygen atoms are held together by four coordinate covalent bonds. This is similar to the* H_3O^+, NH_4^+, $Fe^{2+}(aq)$, *and* $[Cd(OH)_3]^2$ *complex ions illustrated in Equations 5.6 through 5.9. These are stable species involving one atom of known stable oxidation state; i.e.,* $O(-II)$, $N(-III)$, $Fe(II)$, *and* $Cd(II)$, *respectively.*

2. *The sulfate group in* $FeSO_4$, *like that in* Na_2SO_4 *is a complex ion. This* SO_4^{2-} *complex ion bears a net negative charge of two, which in the compound* $FeSO_4$ *must be balanced by an equal positive charge on the iron, indicating that the iron exists as* $Fe(II)$ *in the compound.*

3. *Using the same logic as in parts 1 and 2, the atoms comprising* H_2SO_4 *exist in the following oxidation states:* $H(I), S(VI), O(-II)$.

4. *The sum of the* $H(I)$ *oxidation states* $= 2 \times 1 = 2$. *The sum of the* $O(-II)$ *oxidation states* $= 3 \times (-2) = -6$. *The sulfur atom in* H_2SO_3 *must therefore exist as* $S(IV)$.

5. *The sum of the* $H(I)$ *oxidation states* $= 2 \times 1 = 2$. *The sulfur atom in* H_2S *must therefore exist as* $S(-II)$.

• *Key Point(s).* **This exercise in oxidation state determinations illustrates an important reason why certain chemical species combine with each other in very well ordered combinations of atoms or molecules; i.e., it illustrates the underlying basis of reaction stoichiometry.**

5.3.3   Some Important Types of Reactions

Acid-base reactions are highly significant for aqueous environmental systems. Not only do they play a major role in governing the chemical and biochemical balance and stability of natural aquatic ecosystems, but they participate in and mediate most chemical and biochemical transformations in natural systems and in engineered water quality control processes. Table 5.1 presents several such processes to illustrate their respective acid-base characteristics. The first reaction shown in Table 5.1 involves the first of several ligand exchanges that can occur when aluminum, a multivalent metal ion, dissolves in water. Aluminum has a coordination number of six; i.e., it can form six coordinate covalent bonds with various ligands. The exchange of one type of dominant ligand (H_2O) for another (OH^-) is in essence an acid-base or protolysis reaction. Such ligand

Table 5.1 Proton Transfer Reactions in Environmental Processes

Process	Reaction	pH Effect
Coagulation	Protolysis of Metal-Ion Coagulants	Decrease
	$\{Al(H_2O)_6\}^{3+} + H_2O \Leftrightarrow \{Al(H_2O)_5(OH^-)\}^{2+} + H_3O^+$	
Softening	Precipitation of Calcium Hardness	Decrease
	$Ca^{2+} + HCO_3^- + OH^- \Leftrightarrow CaCO_3(s) + H_2O$	
Recarbonation	Dissolution of Carbon Dioxide	Decrease
	$CO_2(g) + 2H_2O \Leftrightarrow HCO_3^- + H_3O^+$	
Aerobic Biological Processes	Biochemical Mineralization of Organic Matter	Decrease
	$C_6H_{12}O_6 + 6O_2 \Rightarrow 6CO_2 + 6H_2O$	
	Biochemical Nitrification of Ammonia	Decrease
	$NH_3 + 2O_2 \Rightarrow NO_3^- + H_3O^+$	
Anaerobic Biological Processes	Biochemical Oxidation and Nitrate Reduction	Increase
	$5C_6H_{12}O_6 + 24NO_3^- + 24H_3O^+ \Rightarrow 30CO_2 + 12N_2 + 66H_2O$	
	Biochemical Oxidation and Sulfate Reduction	Increase
	$C_6H_{12}O_6 + 3SO_4^{2-} + 3H_3O^+ \Rightarrow 6CO_2 + 3HS^- + 9H_2O$	
	Biochemical Oxidation and Methane Fermentation	Decrease
	$C_6H_{12}O_6 + 3CO_2 \Rightarrow 3CH_4 + 6CO_2$	
Odor Reduction and Corrosion Control	Biochemical Oxidation of Sulfide	Decrease
	$HS^- + 2O_2 + H_2O \Rightarrow SO_4^{2-} + H_3O^+$	
	Chemical Oxidation of Sulfide	Increase
	$HS^- + H_2O_2 + H_3O^+ \Rightarrow S + 3H_2O$	
Oxygen Production in Lakes and Oxidation Ponds	Photosynthesis by Algae and Other Aquatic Plants	Increase
	$6CO_2 + 6H_2O \Rightarrow C_6H_{12}O_6 + 6O_2$	

exchange reactions are common to many multivalent metal ions, as illustrated in Table 5.2.

The pH of an aqueous solution, which is an expression of the negative logarithm of the hydronium ion (H_3O^+) concentration, exerts such a large effect on reactions which occur in water that it can be thought of as a master variable, or control variable, and the concentrations of most other chemical species as response variables. The importance of pH is detailed in entire texts and courses in aquatic chemistry devoted to its description as the master variable in proton exchange (i.e., acid-base, complexation and precipitation reactions) and electron exchange (i.e., oxidation-reduction reactions).

While this chapter focuses primarily on homogeneous systems, we would be remiss not to mention one of the most closely related and well-recognized examples of the transition of proton transfer reactions from homogeneous to het-

Table 5.2 First Protolysis Constants for Hydrated Metal Ions

Metal Species		pK_a
Tin	Sn^{2+}	1.7
Iron III	Fe^{3+}	2.2
Mercury	Hg^{2+}	2.5
Chromium	Cr^{3+}	2.9
Aluminum	Al^{3+}	5.0
Lead	Pb^{2+}	6.7
Cadmium	Cd^{2+}	7.6
Copper	Cu^{2+}	7.9
Iron II	Fe^{2+}	8.3
Zinc	Zn^{2+}	9.6
Manganese	Mn^{2+}	10.6
Nickel	Ni^{2+}	10.6
Magnesium	Mg^{2+}	11.4
Cobalt	Co^{2+}	12.2
Chromium	Cr^{2+}	12.5
Calcium	Ca^{2+}	12.7
Strontium	Sr^{2+}	13.2
Barium	Ba^{2+}	13.4

General Reaction for Metal M

$$\{M(H_2O)_m\}^{n+} + H_2O \Leftrightarrow \{M(H_2O)_{m-1}(OH^-)\}^{(n-1)+} + H_3O^+$$

$$K_a = \frac{\left[\{M(H_2O)_{m-1}(OH^-)\}^{(n-1)+}\right][H_3O^+]}{\left[\{M(H_2O)_m\}^{n+}\right]} \quad ; \quad pK_a = -\log K_a$$

N.B.: The general reaction scheme presented above includes water molecules as metal ion and proton coordination partners. For ease of notation and conservation of space, these coordination partners are not included in the tabular list of hydrated (aq) metal ions. Thus, for example, $Fe^{2+} = Fe^{2+}_{(aq)} = \{Fe(H_2O)_4\}^{2+}$, etc. This abbreviated notation will be used in most subsequent tables and figures in this book except where full notation is used for particular emphasis (e.g., Table 5.3). *Sources of numerical values:* Freiser and Fernando (1963), and Smith and Martell (1976).

erogeneous systems in aquatic environments; i.e., the carbonate system. This system, which includes $CO_2(g)$ in the gas (air) phase, $H_2CO_3(aq)$, HCO_3^-, and CO_3^{2-} dissolved in aqueous phase, and $CaCO_3(s)$ as the precipitated solid phase, is frequently the dominant inorganic acid-base system in fresh waters. The system is important because: (1) $CaCO_3$ is one of the most abundant mineral phases in the earth's outer geosphere (crust) and commonly exposed to its hydrosphere; (2) carbon dioxide is one of the most reactive gases in the earth's atmosphere and universally in contact with its hydrosphere; (3) bicarbonate is one of the most widely distributed dissolved species in the waters of the earth and largely responsible for regulating much of its natural chemistry and biochemistry; and (4) Ca^{2+} is the major contributor to the hardness of most water supplies. We will briefly consider the heterogeneous aspects of this system, aspects that markedly affect such engineered processes as water softening, neutralization, and the use of lime (e.g., CaO) for metal precipitation and coagulation. The primary reactions involved in this three-phase open environmental system are pictured schematically in Figure 5.2. The water column or aqueous

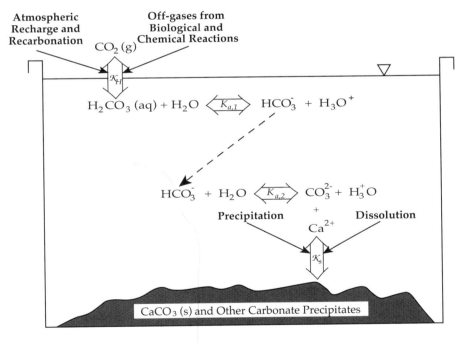

Figure 5.2 Phase Exchange Reactions of Carbonate Species

phase transformations for the system are

$$H_2CO_3(aq) + H_2O \Leftrightarrow HCO_3^- + H_3O^+ \, , K_{a,1} \qquad (5.11)$$

and

$$HCO_3^- + H_2O \Leftrightarrow CO_3^{2-} + H_3O^+ \, , \ K_{a,2} \qquad (5.12)$$

To quantify these relations properly, appropriate account must be taken of the parallel interphase reactions

$$CO_2(g) + H_2O \Leftrightarrow H_2CO_3(aq) \ , \ \mathcal{K}_H \tag{5.13}$$

and

$$Ca^{2+} + CO_3^{2-} \Leftrightarrow CaCO_3(s) \ , \ \mathcal{K}_S \tag{5.14}$$

The effects of these interphase reactions are to either increase or decrease the total concentration of calcium and carbonate species dissolved in the water, as shown in Figure 5.2. In turn, different concentrations and distributions of carbonate species are produced. ***Carbonate system reactions therefore govern and impact the water quality parameters of both hardness (e.g., Ca^{2+}) and alkalinity (e.g., HCO_3^- and CO_3^{2-}).***

Similar considerations apply to the interactions of other metal ion species with acid-base-reactive ligands. Table 5.3 identifies solid phases and associated solubility constants and process considerations for a broad range of environmentally significant metals. As discussed above, the insoluble states of the metals shown in Table 5.3 are actually intermediate states in different ligand exchange reactions of these metals. Several ligand exchange reactions that do not lead to solid precipitates are shown in Table 5.4. The information given in Tables 5.3 and 5.4 can be combined to determine solubility relationships between solid phases and various intermediate coordination species, as illustrated in Example 5.3.

Example 5.3. Calculation of Equilibrium Constants for Reactions from Information Regarding Different but Related Reactions. (An example of the interrelationships of reaction energies among reacting species.)

- ***Situation.*** *We wish to determine the solubility of* Fe(II) *as a function of pH in an aqueous carbonate system, but have information on the solubility constants for only* Fe^{2+} *with respect to* $Fe(OH)_2(s)$ *and* $FeCO_3(s)$.

- ***Question(s).*** *Calculate solubility constants for the* $\{Fe(OH)\}^+$ *species of soluble iron with respect to each of the two solid phases involved: (a) ferrous hydroxide and (b) ferrous carbonate.*

- ***Logic and Answer(s).*** *We can apply thermodynamic principles to this heterogeneous system by calculating the solubility product for complexed species such as* $\{Fe(OH)\}^+$ *from the primary solubility constants for* Fe^{2+} *with respect to the two solid phases and the complex formation constants for* Fe^{2+} *with respect to* $\{Fe(OH)\}^+$.

  1. From Table 5.3

$$Fe(OH)_2(s) \Leftrightarrow Fe^{2+} + 2OH^- \qquad \mathcal{K}_S = 10^{-15.1}$$

Table 5.3 Solubility Relationships for Hydrated Metal Ions

Precipitate	Application	Hydrated (H_2O-Complexed) Metal Ion	Exchanging Ligand	pK_S (@ 25°C)
$Al(OH)_3$	Coagulation	$\{Al(H_2O)_6\}^{3+}$	OH^-	33.5
$AlPO_4$	Phosphate Removal	$\{Al(H_2O)_6\}^{3+}$	PO_4^{3-}	20.6
$CaCO_3$	Softening; Corrosion	$\{Ca(H_2O)_4\}^{2+}$	CO_3^{2-}	8.2
CaF_2	Fluoridation and Defluoridation	$\{Ca(H_2O)_4\}^{2+}$	F^-	10.3
$Ca(OH)_2$	Softening	$\{Ca(H_2O)_4\}^{2+}$	OH^-	5.2
$Ca_3(PO_4)_2$	Softening; Phosphate Cycle and Removal	$\{Ca(H_2O)_4\}^{2+}$	PO_4^{3-}	28.7
$Ca_5(PO_4)_3(OH)$	Phosphate Cycle and Removal	$\{Ca(H_2O)_4\}^{2+}$	$PO_4^{3-} + OH^-$	55.6
$CaHPO_4$	Phosphate Cycle and Removal	$\{Ca(H_2O)_4\}^{2+}$	HPO_4^{2-}	6.6
$CaSO_4$	Hardness; Scale Formation	$\{Ca(H_2O)_4\}^{2+}$	SO_4^{2-}	4.6
$Cu(OH)_2$	Algae Control	$\{Cu(H_2O)_4\}^{2+}$	OH^-	19.4
$Fe(OH)_2$	Corrosion; Iron Cycle and Removal	$\{Fe(H_2O)_4\}^{2+}$	OH^-	15.1
$FeCO_3$	Iron Cycle	$\{Fe(H_2O)_4\}^{2+}$	CO_3^{2-}	10.7
FeS	Anaerobic Corrosion	$\{Fe(H_2O)_4\}^{2+}$	S^{2-}	18.1
$Fe(OH)_3$	Coagulation; Iron Cycle and Removal	$\{Fe(H_2O)_6\}^{3+}$	OH^-	38.8
$FePO_4$	Phosphate Cycle and Removal	$\{Fe(H_2O)_6\}^{3+}$	PO_4^{3-}	26.4
$MgCO_3$	Hardness	$\{Mg(H_2O)_4\}^{2+}$	CO_3^{2-}	7.5
$MgCO_3 \cdot 3H_2O$	Hardness	$\{Mg(H_2O)_4\}^{2+}$	CO_3^{2-}	4.7
MgF_2	Defluoridation	$\{Mg(H_2O)_4\}^{2+}$	F^-	8.2
$Mg(OH)_2$	Softening	$\{Mg(H_2O)_4\}^{2+}$	OH^-	11.1
$MnCO_3$	Manganese Cycle	$\{Mg(H_2O)_4\}^{2+}$	CO_3^{2-}	9.3
$Mn(OH)_2$	Demanganization	$\{Mg(H_2O)_4\}^{2+}$	OH^-	12.8
$Pb(OH)_2$	Lead Dissolution; Corrosion	$\{Pb(H_2O)_4\}^{2+}$	OH^-	10.9
SiO_2	Amorphous Silica	$\{Si(IV)\}$	$O(-II)$	2.7
$Zn(OH)_2$	Corrosion	$\{Zn(H_2O)_4\}^{2+}$	OH^-	17.2

Source: Numerical values from Freiser and Fernando (1963), and Smith and Martell (1976).

From Table 5.4

$$Fe^{2+} + OH^- \Leftrightarrow \{Fe(OH)\}^+ \qquad K_f = 10^{5.7}$$

Summing these equations yields the solubility constant for $\{Fe(OH)\}^+$
with respect to the $Fe(OH)_2(s)$ *solid phase*

$$Fe(OH)_2(s) \Leftrightarrow \{Fe(OH)\}^+ + OH^- \qquad \mathcal{K}_S = 10^{-9.4}$$

2. *From Table 5.3*

$$FeCO_3(s) \Leftrightarrow Fe^{2+} + CO_3^{2-} \qquad \mathcal{K}_S = 10^{-10.7}$$

From Table 5.4

$$Fe^{2+} + OH^- \Leftrightarrow \{Fe(OH)\}^+ \qquad \mathcal{K}_f = 10^{5.7}$$

Summing these two equations yields the solubility constant for
$\{Fe(OH)\}^+$ *with respect to the* $FeCO_3(s)$ *solid phase*

$$FeCO_3(s) + OH^- \Leftrightarrow \{Fe(OH)\}^+ + CO_3^{2-} \qquad \mathcal{K}_S = 10^{-5}$$

- **Key Point(s). *The rigorous interrelationships of reaction energetics allow us to calculate equilibrium constants for reactions
  from information regarding different but related reactions; i.e.,
  from an appropriate number of reactions involving one or more
  of the same chemical species for which the reaction energies are
  unknown.***

Table 5.4 Formation Constants for Metal-Hydroxo Complexes

Reaction			$p\mathcal{K}_f$ (at 25°C)
$Al^{3+} + OH^-$	$\Leftrightarrow$	$\{Al(OH)\}^{2+}$	-9.0
$2Al(OH)^{2+}$	$\Leftrightarrow$	$\{Al_2(OH)_2\}^{4+}$	-3.0
$Al(OH)_3(s) + OH^-$	$\Leftrightarrow$	$\{Al(OH)_4\}^-$	-5.0
$Fe^{3+} + OH^-$	$\Leftrightarrow$	$\{Fe(OH)\}^{2+}$	-11.8
$Fe(OH)^{2+} + OH^-$	$\Leftrightarrow$	$\{Fe(OH)_2\}^+$	-9.4
$2Fe(OH)^{2+}$	$\Leftrightarrow$	$\{Fe_2(OH)_2\}^{4+}$	-1.5
$Fe(OH)_3(s) + OH^-$	$\Leftrightarrow$	$\{Fe(OH)_4\}^-$	+5.0
$Ca^{2+} + OH^-$	$\Leftrightarrow$	$\{Ca(OH)\}^+$	-1.3
$Mg^{2+} + OH^-$	$\Leftrightarrow$	$\{Mg(OH)\}^+$	-2.6
$Fe^{2+} + OH^-$	$\Leftrightarrow$	$\{Fe(OH)\}^+$	-5.7

Source: Numerical values from Freiser and Fernando (1963) and Smith and
Martell (1976).

5.4 CHEMICAL STATES AND PROCESS STABILITY

5.4.1 Stability

According to the concepts of electron structure and chemical reactivity, all atoms exist in a state of instability until they have achieved an electron configuration corresponding to that of either the next lower or next higher inert gas in the periodic table. The degree of instability is relative; that is, any particular electron configuration in which an atom can exist may be a more or less stable state than another. Instability relates conceptually to differences in thermodynamic potential, or energy, between states, and operationally to the presence or absence of a facilitating mechanism for moving from one state to another. Figure 5.3 presents an analogy between chemical and gravitational states and stability. Like the block in Figure 5.3, an atom can be temporarily stable, or metastable, until such time as it has an opportunity, through facilitating reactions, to move to a lower energy or more stable state.

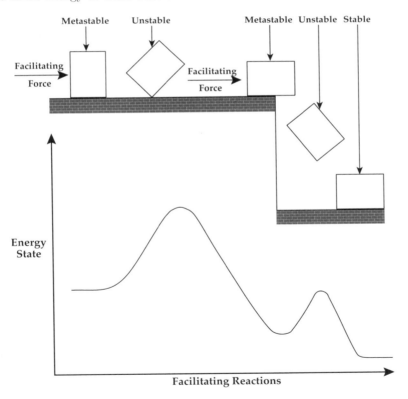

Figure 5.3 A Mechanical Analogy to Chemical States and Stability

The energy levels of the various states of an atom are defined by its nuclear and electron structure. The facility with which it can move from one state to another is dependent upon the reactions in which it can participate in a given system, that is, the availability of partners with which it can either exchange or share electrons. In a larger sense, the same is true of each chemical component of a given system, and thus of the entire system. Environmental systems can therefore exist in various states of relative chemical stability, and various facilitating reactions can convert them from one state to another.

A reaction takes place when chemical species undergo transformation to different energy states, either by chemical change within a phase or by transfer to another phase. This may occur exergonically or endergonically, that is, with energy being either released or consumed in the reaction(s). The analogy given in Figure 5.3 depicts changes from higher energy levels to lower levels, thus releasing energy to the system in which those changes occur. Conversely, if energy is input to the system, it is possible to force the reactions in the reverse direction and induce conversion of species from lower-energy states to higher states. To reverse the direction would involve lifting the block in Figure 5.3 from the floor and standing it upright on the table.

5.4.2   Types of Change

Any change that occurs in the chemical composition of a system may be classified as one of three different types; namely, a natural change, an unnatural change, or a reversible change. A natural change, as the name implies, results from a reaction that brings the system closer to the equilibrium state; that is, moves it toward maximum stability. Conversely, an unnatural change is caused by a reaction that drives the system further from the equilibrium state and toward decreased stability. Unnatural changes are not spontaneous, and must therefore be driven by an external energy input.

The galvanic cell of the lead-lead oxide (**Pb-PbO$_2$**)*battery pictured in Figure 5.4 tends by spontaneous chemical reaction to an equilibrium state of maximum stability, with a discharge of electrical energy occurring during this natural change. Recharging the battery with an external electrical energy source represents an unnatural change for which the energy input forces the chemical system of the battery away from its equilibrium state.* Reversible changes represent a limiting case between natural and unnatural processes. Reversible changes involve the continuous passage of a system in either direction through a series of equilibrium states.

The energy output or input associated with a change in a system may take the form of chemical energy, mechanical energy, thermal energy, or electrical energy. The inherent energy release from the chemical reactions, which take place between the components of a lead ($Pb - PbO_2$) storage battery like that pictured in Figure 5.4, for example, is manifest as electrical energy generated by the flow of electrons between chemical species comprising the battery.

The battery produces an electrical energy until such time as its chemical components achieve more stable (lower) energy states. At this point the bat-

Electrochemical Cell

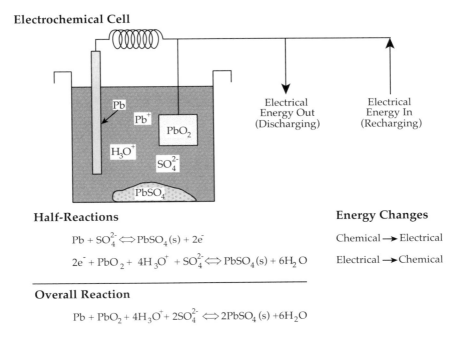

Half-Reactions

$$Pb + SO_4^{2-} \Longleftrightarrow PbSO_4(s) + 2e^-$$

$$2e^- + PbO_2 + 4H_3O^+ + SO_4^{2-} \Longleftrightarrow PbSO_4(s) + 6H_2O$$

Energy Changes

Chemical $\longrightarrow$ Electrical

Electrical $\longrightarrow$ Chemical

Overall Reaction

$$Pb + PbO_2 + 4H_3O^+ + 2SO_4^{2-} \Longleftrightarrow 2PbSO_4(s) + 6H_2O$$

Figure 5.4 An Electrochemical Cell

tery has reached a condition of chemical equilibrium, and it becomes necessary to "recharge" it by input of electrical energy, which functions to reconvert the chemical components to higher (less stable) energy states. This recharging process involves reversing the chemical reaction. The reversible character of most strictly chemical reactions is indicated by the double arrows between the reactants and products depicted in Figure 5.4 and in preceding equations in this chapter. Certain electron transfer reactions, such as the combustion or biological degradation of an organic compound, are not directly reversible, as indicated by the "one-way" arrows in Table 5.1.

5.4.3 Equilibrium and Steady States

Any closed chemical system or system for which changes in composition result only from internal reactions will, if it is in a state other than equilibrium, undergo reaction and internal change until it reaches equilibrium. Consider, for example, a sealed tank full of organically contaminated wastewater to which a strong chemical oxidant has been added just before it was sealed. Upon addition of the oxidant, the system is displaced from whatever chemical equilibrium it may previously have attained. So displaced, the contents of that system will continue to react with each other, the organic matter being oxidized and the oxidant reduced, until a new equilibrium state is achieved.

In open systems composition may be changed continuously by addition and/or subtraction of components as well as by internal reactions. An example equivalent to that for the closed system might be a tank into which the contaminated waste and oxidant solutions are continually added and an effluent continually withdrawn. In this type of system the condition of fixed composition in the tank represents a steady state rather than an equilibrium, a distinction sometimes obscured by improper use of the two terms interchangeably in the description of environmental systems. Steady state and equilibrium are clearly different situations. Failure to distinguish them properly can result in confusion and misinterpretation of system information and behavior.

The reactions occurring in a system (reactor) are not necessarily at thermodynamic equilibrium for any given steady-state condition; they may, in fact, be very far removed from equilibrium. Because of a balanced input of reactants and output of products, however, the system is poised in a condition for which no net change in its composition is realized from the ongoing internal reactions. In the context of the material balance statement given in Equation 3.1, the net rate of change of the composition of the contents of a reactor is zero at steady state; that is, the right hand term of Equation 3.1 is zero.

5.5 CHAPTER SUMMARY

Thermodynamic feasibility is a fundamental requirement for any change to occur in any constituent of any environmental system, regardless of the specific nature of the transformation (i.e., acid-base, coordination, electron exchange, precipitation, or other reaction) or the phases involved (i.e., air, water, sediment, soil, or other solid phase). An assessment of the thermodynamic feasibility of any such change translates into a determination of whether the balance of energies associated with the masses of potential reactants in a system is such that there is net energy available to drive the system in the direction of that change. Because energy is related to mass, the ratios of the masses of potential products and reactants, expressed in the terms of equilibrium constants in a manner dictated by reaction stoichiometry and the law of mass action, provide means for assessment of whether any particular system is in its natural equilibrium state (i.e., will undergo no change) or will be driven by the energies associated with its constituent mass distribution to move toward equilibrium (i.e., undergo change).

We have also shown that mass law equilibrium constants vary somewhat in form for different types of reactions. Thus, for example, certain reactions of hydronium and hydroxide ions with various metal ions may act principally to change the pH of a water, while others may act principally to precipitate the metal. While similar chemistry is involved, the equilibrium constants (the acid-base and solubility constants, respectively) of these two arbitrary "classes" of reactions have slightly different forms.

We have seen that water, which covers approximately two-thirds of the surface of Earth, is a remarkable chemical. Because water functions as a "universal solvent" for virtually all gases, solids, and other liquids that exist on Earth, its properties and reactions are extremely important with respect to environmental systems and change. Indeed, the very form into which mankind has evolved is related to water, its chemistry, and to its geobiochemical dynamics, and we are therefore very sensitive to its composition. There is thus no question about why we must be concerned with significant changes in its composition.

In Chapter 6 we will develop more rigorous relationships between various types of equilibrium constants by more closely examining their underlying and common roots in chemical thermodynamics.

5.6 CITATIONS AND SOURCES

Freiser, H. and Q. Fernando, 1963, *Ionic Equilibria in Analytical Chemistry*, John Wiley & Sons Inc., New York. (Tables 5.2, 5.3 and 5.4).

Smith, R. M. and A. E. Martell, 1976, *Critical Stability Constants*, Plenum Press, New York. (Tables 5.2, 5.3 and 5.4).

Weber, W.J., Jr., and F.A. DiGiano, 1996, *Process Dynamics of Environmental Systems,* John Wiley & Sons, Inc., New York. General source of all material presented. Chapter 5 of PDES expands on and extends Chapter 5 of this text, and identifies additional related readings.

5.7 PROBLEM ASSIGNMENTS

5.1 The pH of an acid mine drainage through which hydrogen sulfide bubbles continuously is measured and found to have a value of pH 3.7. Estimate the concentration of S^{2-} in this water.

Answer: $23 \times 10^{-15} mol/L$.

5.2 The acid mine drainage of Problem 5.1 is found to contain 56 mg/L of Fe(II). How much more Fe(II) might be able to dissolve in this water before FeS precipitates?

Answer: 16.6 *mg/L*.

5.3 The free copper ion concentration of a $Cu(NO_3)_2$ waste is to be reduced to a maximum level of 0.6×10^{-2} ng/L by complexation with ammonia. The complex formation constant for $\{Cu(NH_3)_4\}^{2+}$ is $pK_f = -11.7$. Neglecting the amount of copper in complexes containing fewer than four ammonia groups per central ion, calculate the amount of ammonia to be added if the original concentration of $Cu(NO_3)_2$ is 188 mg/L.

Answer: 6.54 *g/L*.

5.4 Determine the amount of NH_4Cl that must be added to a solution containing 170 mg of ammonia and 24.3 mg of Mg(II) per liter to repress the reaction

$$NH_3 + H_2O \Leftrightarrow NH_4^+ + OH^-$$

sufficiently to prevent $Mg(OH)_2$ from precipitating. The pK_a of ammonia is 9.3.

Answer: 66.8 mg/L.

5.5 Calculate $[Cd^{2+}]$ in 1 L of solution prepared by dissolving 10^{-3} mol of $Cd(NO_3)_2$ and 1.5 mol of NH_3. The overall dissociation constant for the $[Cd(NH_3)_4]^{2+}$ complex is 1.8×10^{-7}. Neglect complexes containing fewer than four ammonia ligands.

Answer: $3.6 \times 10^{-11} mol/L$.

5.6 Determine the concentration of free Cd^{2+} in a 5.0-mM solution of $CdCl_2$ if the first formation constant $pK_{f,1}$ for chloride complexation of Cd^{2+} is -2.0 and the second complexation step is neglected.

Answer: 315 mg/L.

5.7 A 1660-mg quantity of dry KI is added to a 1-L solution containing 28 mg of Cd(II). If the first and second formation constants for complexation of Cd^{2+} by I- are given by $pK_{f,1}$ = -2.28 and $pK_{f,2}$ = -1.64, determine the percentages of Cd(II) present as Cd^{2+}, CdI^+, and CdI_2 at equilibrium.

Answers: 27%, 51%, 22%, respectively.

5.8 Calculate the aqueous solubilities of Ni(II) in the presence of $Ni(OH)_2(s)$ and of $NiCO_3(s)$ at pH 8. The system is open to air. Which solid phase allows a higher dissolved-phase concentration of Ni(II)?

5.9 A stream passes through a region rich in dolomite, $CaMg(CO_3)_2(s)$. If the Mg^{2+} concentration in the stream is 30 mg/L and the pH is 7.8, what is the concentration of calcium ion? Assume that the calcium is not involved in any other significant reactions.

$$CaMg(CO_3)_2(s) = Ca^{2+} + Mg^{2+} + 2CO_3^{2-} \; ; \; p\mathcal{K}_S(25°C) = 17.9$$

5.10 A 0.5-L sample of wastewater having a phosphate concentration of 750 mg-P/L is to be treated with $FeCl_2$ in a bench-scale feasibility test for phosphate removal. Assuming that all of the $FeCl_2$ added fully dissociates, how much should be added to the sample to produce a final phosphate concentration of 5 mg/L?

Chapter 6

Process Energy Relationships

Contents

6.0   CHAPTER OBJECTIVES

To conceptualize and quantify the tendencies of reactions to seek stable equilibrium conditions in terms of reactant and product distributions, and to understand the roots and logic of these reaction characteristics as they are set forth in chemical thermodynamics.

6.1   THERMODYNAMIC LAWS AND FUNCTIONS

6.1.1   Fundamental Laws

The science underlying classical thermodynamics is structured upon four fundamental laws. Three of these, the zeroth, first, and second laws of thermodynamics, are of particular interest for developing an understanding of the energetics of environmental processes and systems.

The zeroth and first laws, respectively, specify criteria for thermal energy and total energy conditions relating to the equilibrium state of a process or system. The zeroth law states that there is no heat flow among the components of systems in thermal equilibrium. The first law extends the concept to total energy, recognizing that heat is only one form of energy. This law further requires the conservation of energy, regardless of the form in which it may exist. That is, heat energy may be converted to chemical energy, electrical energy, mechanical energy, and so on, but it can be neither created nor destroyed.

The second law of thermodynamics, which is less intuitive than the first two, is particularly important in considerations of environmental processes. This law delineates the concept that when energy is changed from one form to another, it may not be possible subsequently to change all of it back to its original form (i.e., part of the change is irreversible). As a result, systems can attain what is termed a disordered state, a state that is at or close to the most probable and natural (and thus eventual) state of stability for that system. The extent of irreversibility associated with a change to a disordered state depends on temperature and is reflected by the increase in temperature that occurs as a system changes states. Entropy can be thought of as a measure of the extent of disorder in a system. While the total energy of a system remains constant as it is converted from one form to another, entropy may remain constant or increase with each change in the form of energy. It remains constant for any completely reversible change in the form of energy, but it increases for any irreversible change. There may be local decreases in entropy within certain components of a system, but these will be offset by other larger local increases to yield a net increase in entropy.

Entropy is an important concept for energy conversions involving the transformation of chemical species. This concept provides the basis for interrelationships between chemical mass or concentration and chemical potential, activity, and fugacity. We will demonstrate that chemical potential, activity and fugacity are themselves closely interrelated and that, in many ways, they are similarly descriptive of the state of particular components within a system. The logical point of beginning for these developments is in the characteristic state functions defined in classical thermodynamics.

6.1.2 Characteristic Functions

The five fundamental thermodynamic functions of systems are

- *enthalpy = H*

- *Gibbs free energy = G*

- *Helmholtz free energy = I*

- *internal energy = U*

- *entropy = S*

the first four of which have the dimensions ML^2t^{-2}, and the last of which has the dimensions of the first four per degree Kelvin, $(ML^2t^{-2}T^{-1})$. These functions are termed state functions because changes that occur in them depend only on the initial and final states of a system (i.e., they are independent of the pathways by which change occurs).

The thermodynamic state functions are useful for assessing the overall heats and energies associated with complex multipath environmental processes. They are extensive characteristics of a system, which means that they are dependent upon the magnitude or size of the system, and they are interrelated in the following ways

---

Basic State Functions

$$H = U + PV \qquad (6.1)$$
$$G = H - TS \qquad (6.2)$$
$$I = U - TS \qquad (6.3)$$

---

where V is the volume of a system (L^3), P its pressure ($ML^{-1}t^{-2}$), and T its absolute temperature (K). Like the five characteristic functions, volume is extensive, whereas P and T are independent of the magnitude or size of a system and thus intensive variables or properties. The terms PV and TS are commonly referred to as the work and entropy gain functions, respectively.

Equations 6.1 through 6.3 are termed "basic" state function relationships because they are predicated on systems of constant composition. That is, they ignore the energy implications of chemical reactions. We will return to this issue shortly, but for the moment let's bring the present subject to closure.

For single-component systems, or for systems comprised by mixtures of components having constant composition, the net change in the internal energy of a system as it moves from one state to another is given by the difference between the entropy gained and the work done in the change. This statement is tantamount to a combination of the first and second laws of thermodynamics. If the change is isothermal (constant temperature) and isobaric (constant pressure), we can combine Equations 6.1 and 6.2 and differentiate the work function (PV) and the entropy gain or heat function (TS) with respect to the changing extensive quantities to obtain

$$dU = TdS - PdV \qquad (6.4)$$

Equation 6.4 is often referred to as the "First Law" equation, but this is not exactly true. The First Law states only that the sum of the heat change, TdS, and work change (PdV) to the system is independent of the path of the change, regardless of whether the change is reversible or irreversible. The negative sign in front of the work change term relates to the convention that heat is positive when added to a system from its surroundings but work is positive when it leaves a system to enter its surroundings.

Changes in the other characteristic functions with respect to changes in the intensive variables of pressure and temperature can be similarly developed from Equations 6.1 through 6.4, yielding

> ### Differential State Functions
> $$dH = TdS + VdP \qquad (6.5)$$
> $$dG = -SdT + VdP \qquad (6.6)$$
> $$dI = -SdT - PdV \qquad (6.7)$$

The foregoing relationships among characteristic functions are particularly useful for evaluation of heat or energy changes associated with the transformation of a system from one state to another. Because they were obtained from characteristic state functions, values of dH, dG and dA do not depend on the pathway(s) along which a system is transformed from one state to another. As such, they lend themselves to ready quantification and referencing to some baseline state.

Let's now return to an extremely important thermodynamic consideration for environmental systems; i.e., the effects of reactions or transformations that change the chemical compositions of systems.

6.1.3   Free Energy Concepts

The free energy of a reaction is the energy available for that reaction at any particular state of a system, and its minimum value (zero) is reached when the system is in its equilibrium state. We can use Equation 6.2 to define free energy in most simple terms for *a single chemical substance as the difference between the enthalpic and entropic state functions for that substance. To describe reaction or transformation processes in a system, however, the sum of the associated chemical potential terms, μ_i for each reacting and product species, i, must be added to the basic Gibbs equation given by in Equation 6.2. Thus, for a closed system undergoing reaction, the differential change in free energy is given by*

$$\text{Gibbs Equation for Reacting Systems} \qquad dG = VdP - SdT + \Sigma\mu_i dn_i \qquad (6.8)$$

The chemical potential of a substance or species is essentially its partial molar free energy contribution to the reaction, and is given by

$$\text{Chemical Potential} \qquad \mu_i = \mu_i^{\circ} + \mathcal{R}T \ln a_i \qquad (6.9)$$

where μ_i° is the standard state value of the chemical potential of species i, a_i is its chemical activity (which is related to its concentration) and the other terms are as defined previously. For the standard state, $a_i^{\circ} = 1$.

The change in the free energy of a system undergoing reaction is thus the sum not only of its heat (SdT) and work (VdP) functions, but also of a chemical function $(\Sigma\mu_i dn_i)$. We note that, like the other energy component functions, the chemical function is also the product of a characteristic intensive variable, μ_i, and a related extensive variable, n_i.

6.1.4 Reaction Free Energy Change

By convention, the free-energy change associated with a specific reaction is the difference between the free-energy changes of its products and its reactants

$$\text{Reaction Free Energy Change} \qquad \Delta G_r = \Sigma(\Delta G)_{products} - \Sigma(\Delta G)_{reactants} \qquad (6.10)$$

For a reaction in a state of equilibrium, ΔG_r must be zero. In other words, the energy available to drive the reaction to the right $[\Sigma(\Delta G)_{reactants}]$ is precisely equal to the energy available to drive it to the left $[\Sigma(\Delta G)_{products}]$. If ΔG_r has a negative value, then $\Sigma(\Delta G)_{reactants} > \Sigma(\Delta G)_{products}$ and the reaction is driven to the right (forward direction) with a net accumulation of product and a net disappearance of reactants. This type of reaction is said to be thermodynamically spontaneous. Conversely, if dG_r has a positive value, then $\Sigma(dG)_{reactants} < \Sigma(dG)_{products}$ and the reaction is driven to the left (reverse direction) with a net disappearance of product and a net accumulation of reactants. Figure 6.1 is a schematic representation of the variation of free energy with extent of reaction, where extent of reaction represents the fraction of a given reactant converted to a corresponding product.

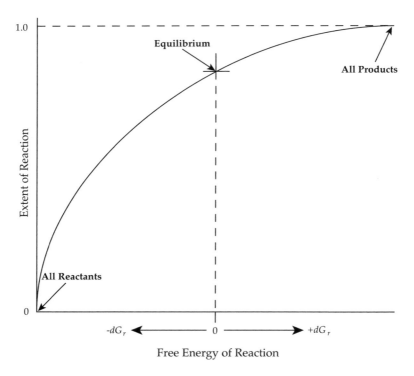

Figure 6.1 Variation of Free Energy with Extent of Reaction

6.1.5   Reference State Free Energies

Reference values for free energy and enthalpy for a specified standard state are given in Table 6.1. The values in this table are free energies and enthalpies associated with the formation of chemical species from their elements. These parameters are denoted by ΔG_f° and ΔH_f°, reflecting that they represent a finite quantity (Δ) associated with the formation (subscript f) of a finite number of moles (one) of a substance from its elements at a standard state condition (superscript $\circ$). The need for a standard-state reference condition for various characteristic thermodynamic functions is inherent in any practical application of the foregoing energy concepts.

Table 6.1 Thermodynamic Properties of Selected Chemical Species

Substance	State[a]	ΔH_f° kJ/mol	ΔG_f° kJ/mol	Substance	State[a]	ΔH_f° kJ/mol	ΔG_f° kJ/mol
Ca^{2+}	aq	-542.7	-553.1	Cs^+	aq	-261.9	-296.0
$CaCO_3$				Fe^{2+}	aq	-87.9	-84.9
(calcite)	c	-1207.1	-1128.8	Fe^{3+}	aq	-47.7	-10.6
CaO	c	-635.5	-604.2	$\{Fe(OH)\}^{2+}$	aq		-233.9
$Ca(OH)_2$	aq	-1002.9	-867.8	$\{Fe(OH)_2\}^+$	aq		-444.3
CO	g	-110.5	-137.2	$Fe(OH)_3$	c		-694.5
CO_2	g	-393.7	-394.6	Fe_2O_3			
	aq	-413.0	-386.2	(hematite)	c	-822.2	-741.0
CO_3^{2-}	aq	-676.1	-528.0	H_2	g	0.0	0.0
HCO_3^-	aq	-691.2	-587.0	H_2O	lq	-285.8	-237.2
H_2CO_3	aq	-698.7	-623.4	H_3O^+	aq	-285.8	-237.2
CH_4	g	-74.9	-50.6	H_2O_2	aq	-191.2	-131.8
C_2H_4	g	52.3	68.2	I_2	aq		16.3
C_2H_6	g	-84.5	-33.1	$HI(I^-)$	aq	-56.1	-51.9
C_3H_8	g	-103.8	-23.4	I_3^-	aq	-55.9	-51.5
$C_4H_{10}(n)^6$	g	-124.7	-15.9	Mg^{2+}	aq	-461.9	-456.1
$C_5H_{12}(n)^6$	g	-146.4	-8.4	$Mg(OH)_2$	c	-924.7	-833.9
C_6H_6				Mn^{2+}	aq	-218.8	-223.4
(benzene)	g	82.8	129.7	MnO_4^-	aq		-449.4
$C_6H_{14}(n)^6$	g	-167.4	0.4	MnO_4^{2-}	aq		-503.8
C_8H_{10}				$Mn(OH)_2$	ppt		-614.6
(ethylbenzene)	g	29.7	130.5	$MnCO_3$	ppt		-813.0
$C_8H_{18}(n)^6$	g	-208.4	17.2	NH_3	aq	-80.8	-26.8
$C_{10}H_{22}(n)^6$	g	-249.8	34.3	NH_4^+	aq	-132.6	-79.5
CH_2O	g	-115.9	-110.0	NO_2	g	33.9	51.9
CH_3OH	g	-201.3	-161.9	$HNO_3(NO_3^-)$	aq	-206.7	-110.5
	lq	-238.5	-166.1	O_2	g	0.0	0.0
CH_3Cl	g	-82.0	-58.6	O_2	aq	—	16.5
CH_2Cl_2	g	-87.9	-58.6	O_3	g	142.3	163.6
	lq	-117.2	-63.2	OH^-	aq	-230.1.	-157.3
$CHCl_3$	g	-100.4	-66.9	Rb^+	aq	-248.5	-283.0
	lq	-131.8	-71.5	Rn	g	0.0	0.0
CN^-	aq	151.0	165.7	H_2S	aq	-39.3	-27.2
CNO^-	aq	-140.2	-98.7	S^{2-}	aq	32.6	8.6
HCN	aq	105.4	112.1	HS^-	aq	-17.6	12.6
$HCNO$	aq	-146.9	-120.9	$H_2SO_4(SO_4^{2-})$	aq	-907.5	-741.8
Cl_2	g	0.0	0.0	Sn^+	aq	-10.0	-24.3
Cl^-	aq	-167.4	-131.4				
ClO_2	g	103.3	123.4				
	aq		11.3				
$HClO$	aq	-118.0	-79.9				

Source: Numerical values calculated from values given in National Bureau of Standards (1952).
[a] *aq*, Aqueous; *g*, gaseous; *c*, crystalline; *lq*, liquid; *ppt*, precipitate.

Before examining the reference and actual states of systems further, however, we consider several of the functions cited earlier that relate the chemical mass or concentration of a species in a system to its thermodynamic properties and behavior.

Example 6.1 reinforces the practical use of thermodynamic calculations to interpret observed environmental processes, and indicates how the thermodynamic conditions required to accomplish a desired, or engineered, transformation can be determined.

Example 6.1. Estimation of the Release or Absorption of Energy in Simple Acid-Base Reactions. (An elementary application of enthalpy calculations for chemical reactions.)

- ***Situation.*** *Energy is either released or absorbed even in simple dissolution or acid-base reactions. This energy frequently takes the form of heat energy, or enthalpy. Such heat releases or absorptions may be important in certain types of natural systems and engineered treatment systems. Consider, for example, the use of a strong base to neutralize an acidic industrial waste containing hydrogen cyanide. Cyanide (CN^-) and its conjugate acid (HCN) are common constituents of a number of different types of industrial wastes, such as metal processing and plating wastes.*

- ***Question(s).*** *How much heat is either liberated or absorbed in the protolysis of 1 mol of HCN in water? Measurements in the laboratory show that the heat liberated on neutralization of HCN by NaOH under standard-state conditions is 12.1 kJ/mol.*

- ***Logic and Answer(s).*** *The most fundamental neutralization reaction for aqueous systems is that involving protolysis of the hydronium ion by the hydroxide ion to yield water*

$$H_3O^+ + OH^- \Leftrightarrow 2H_2O$$

  1. *The following reference-state enthalpy values for the components of this reaction are obtained from Table 6.1*

$$\Delta H_f^\circ = -285.8 \ kJ/mol \ for \ H_2O \ and \ H_3O^+$$

  and

$$\Delta H_f^\circ = -230.1 \ kJ/mol \ for \ (OH^-)$$

  Thus, because enthalpy is an extensive (additive) property of a system or reaction, the above ion protolysis reaction has an enthalpy value of

$$\Delta H_r^\circ = 2(-285.8) - (-285.8) - (-230.1) = -55.7 \ kJ$$

2. The neutralization of HCN by NaOH in aqueous solutions may be thought of as the sum of two processes, protolysis of HCN and neutralization of H_3O^+ with OH^-. NaOH is a strong base that dissociates completely when added to water. Thus, the amount of OH^- added by addition of NaOH is equivalent to the latter on a molar basis. The following reactions and associated heat releases or absorptions may then be summed

$$\begin{array}{ll}
HCN + H_2O \Leftrightarrow H_3O^+ + CN^- & \Delta H^\circ_{r,1} \\
H_3O^+ + OH^- \Leftrightarrow 2H_2O & \Delta H^\circ_{r,2} = -55.7 \ kJ \\
\hline
HCN + OH^- \Leftrightarrow H_2O + CN^- & \Delta H^\circ_{r,T} = [\Delta H_{r,1^\circ} + (55.7)] \ kJ
\end{array}$$

3. The enthalpy, $\Delta H^\circ_{r,T}$, for the overall reaction has been measured experimentally as $-12.1 \ kJ$ (negative because heat is liberated on neutralization). Thus, applying the principle of additivity to the extensive enthalpy relationships for the individual reactions, the enthalpy for deprotonation of HCN in water under standard-state conditions is

$$\Delta H^\circ_{r,1} = \Delta H^\circ_{r,T} - (-55.7) = (-12.1) - (-55.7) = 43.6 \ kJ/mol$$

4. Because this value is positive, the protolysis reaction is endothermic and thus enhanced by increased temperature.

- **Key Point(s). The overall energy flow associated with any reaction (i.e., the amount of energy yielded by or required for the occurrence of the reaction) can be determined for standard state conditions by additions/subtractions of readily available standard state energies of formation for the individual products and reactants involved.**

An illustration of how standard-state reference values for the free energies of formation of different species can be used in an assessment of their inter-reaction tendencies is given in Example 6.2. This is a useful approach to a "first-cut" evaluation of process feasibility.

Example 6.2. Assessment of the Feasibility of Using a Strong Oxidant to Oxidize an Environmentally Stable Ionic Species to Produce an Effective Disinfectant for Water Treatment. (An illustration of the use of reactant and product free energies to calculate reaction free energy and associated thermodynamic feasibility.)

- **Situation.** *Consideration is being given to the potential use of iodine (as I_3^-) to provide continuous disinfection of a public swimming pool. Unlike chlorine, iodine does not react with ammonia to cause eye-irritating trihaloamines. For this reason it is sometimes preferred to chlorine, although it is more expensive. One major problem with this disinfectant is that it cannot be obtained easily as either a pure gas (as can Cl_2) or a solid (as can $Ca(OCl)_2$), and it degenerates with time in aqueous solutions. It therefore cannot be stored for significant periods of time.*

- **Question(s).** *What is the feasibility of oxidizing iodide ($I-$) to iodine by hydrogen peroxide (H_2O_2) in slightly acidic aqueous solution to provide I_3^- on a continuous basis? Both I_3^- and H_2O_2 are effective disinfectants. I_3^- provides residual protection and is thus effective for a longer period than H_2O_2.*

- **Logic and Answer(s).** *The reaction corresponding to the proposed process is*

$$3I^- + H_2O_2 + 2H_3O^+ \Leftrightarrow I_3^- + 4H_2O$$

  1. *In this analysis of feasibility we will consider the reaction only from a thermodynamic point of view, to illustrate the application of free energy of formation values.*

  2. *From Equation 6.10, and considering for the present only standard-state conditions*

$$\Delta G_r^\circ = \Sigma \Delta G_{f,products}^\circ - \Sigma \Delta G_{f,reactants}^\circ$$

  3. *From Table 6.1*

Component	$\Delta G_f^\circ, kJ/mol$
I^-	−51.9
H_2O_2	−131.8
H_3O^+	−237.2
I_3^-	−51.5
H_2O	−237.2

  4. *Then*

$$\Delta G_r^\circ = [(-51.5 + 4(-237.2)] - [3(-51.9) + (-131.8) + 2(-237.2)]$$

$$= [-1,000.4] - [-761.9] = -238.5 \ kJ$$

  5. *The thermodynamics of the proposed process are thus favorable for it to proceed as written, at least for standard state conditions. We will shortly see how to extend the analysis to other than standard-state conditions.*

- **Key Point(s).** **Readily available thermodynamic data enable us to do rapid first-cut analyses of whether sufficient energy to** *drive any given reaction is available if all reactants and products have unit activity and other standard state conditions apply; i.e., whether the reaction is spontaneous at conditions of standard state.*

6.1.6   Biologically Mediated Reactions

The free-energy concepts discussed above apply to the transformation of a chemical species to some other form, regardless of the means by which the transformation occurs. A particular organic compound, for example, may be oxidized chemically at room temperature with oxygen to form carbon dioxide, combusted to CO_2 in an oxygen atmosphere in a furnace, or metabolized by aerobic microorganisms to yield CO_2. The reaction rates are markedly different in these several cases, but the total amount of energy released by the reaction of that compound with oxygen will be exactly the same regardless of the means by which the reaction is facilitated.

Table 6.2 presents a summary of selected biologically mediated chemical reactions and associated free-energy values for dilute aqueous systems at pH $= 7$. These reactions illustrate the point that the fundamental energetics of all reactions are determined by chemical thermodynamics. The reactions are stoichiometrically normalized to a one-electron transfer basis; thus the values for ΔG_r are given in units of kilocalories per electron equivalent. A "generic" biooxidation reaction for an organic compound having a general composition defined by the stoichiometric formation coefficients a, b, c, and d is as follows

$$
\begin{aligned}
&\textit{Generic} && C_aH_bO_cN_d + (2a - c)H_2O \Rightarrow aCO_2 + dNH_4^+ \\
&\textit{Bio-oxidation} && \\
&\textit{Reaction} && +(4a + b - 2c - 4d)H^+ + (4a + b - 2c - 3d)e^-
\end{aligned}
\tag{6.11}
$$

Microorganisms mediate such reactions to derive energy from them, but they cannot alter inherent energy balances. The organic reactions given in Table 6.2 are all oxidation (electron donor) half-reactions, and the corresponding standard-state free energies are the amounts of energy associated with each mole of electrons released or "donated" by a half reaction. Conversely, the reactions for the electron acceptors are written as reduction half-reactions. The overall free energy for a given biological transformation can be obtained simply by summing the appropriate half reactions. The energy derived from aerobic and anaerobic oxidation of a substrate will be different because the electron acceptor half-reactions are not the same. The difference can be substantial, as illustrated in Example 6.3.

Table 6.2 Biologically   Mediated   Half-Reactions   and   Associated Aqueous-Phase Free Energies of Reaction

Half-Reaction	$\Delta G_r(aq)$, kJ/equiv.
Organic (Electron Donor) Oxidations	
Carbohydrate (cellulose, starch, sugars)	
$\frac{1}{4}CH_2O + \frac{1}{4}H_2O \Rightarrow \frac{1}{4}CO_2 + H^+ + e^-$	-41.8
Methanol	
$\frac{1}{6}CH_3OH + \frac{1}{6}H_2O \Rightarrow \frac{1}{6}CO_2 + H^+ + e^-$	-37.7
Protein (amino acids, proteins, nitrogenous organics)	
$\frac{1}{66}C_{16}H_{24}O_5N_4 + \frac{27}{66}H_2O \Rightarrow \frac{8}{33}CO_2 + \frac{2}{33}NH_4 + \frac{31}{33}H^+ + e^-$	-32.2
Domestic Wastewater	
$\frac{1}{5}C_{10}H_{19}O_3N + \frac{9}{25}H_2O \Rightarrow \frac{9}{50}CO_2 + \frac{1}{50}NH_4 + \frac{1}{50}HCO_3^- + H^+ + e^-$	-31.8
Ethanol	
$\frac{1}{12}CH_3CH_2OH + \frac{1}{4}H_2O \Rightarrow \frac{1}{6}CO_2 + H^+ + e^-$	-31.8
Benzoate	
$\frac{1}{30}C_6H_5COO^- + \frac{13}{20}H_2O \Rightarrow \frac{1}{5}CO_2 + \frac{1}{30}HCO_3^- + H^+ + e^-$	-28.9
Acetate	
$\frac{1}{8}CH_3COO^- + \frac{3}{8}H_2O \Rightarrow \frac{1}{8}CO_2 + \frac{1}{8}HCO_3^- + H^+ + e^-$	-27.6
Grease (fats and oils)	
$\frac{1}{46}C_8H_{16}O + \frac{15}{46}H_2O \Rightarrow \frac{4}{23}CO_2 + H^+ + e^-$	-27.6
Inorganic (Electron Acceptor) Reductions	
Oxygen	
$\frac{1}{4}O_2 + H^+ + e^- \Leftrightarrow \frac{1}{2}H_2O$	-78.2
Nitrate	
$\frac{1}{5}NO_3^- + \frac{6}{5}H^+ + e^- \Leftrightarrow \frac{1}{10}N_4 + \frac{3}{5}H_2O$	-71.6
Carbon Dioxide	
$\frac{1}{8}CO_2 + H^+ + e^- \Leftrightarrow \frac{1}{8}CH_4 + \frac{1}{4}H_2O$	+24.3
Sulfate	
$\frac{1}{8}SO_4^{2-} + \frac{19}{16}H^+ + e^- \Leftrightarrow \frac{1}{16}H_2S + \frac{1}{16}HS^- + \frac{1}{2}H_2O$	+21.3

N.B. The reactions in this table are written for a one-electron exchange. The term $\Delta G_r(aq)$ is thus expressed as the amount of free energy (kJ) exchanged per electron equivalent rather than per mole reacted. The notation (aq) further defines the value for neutral aqueous solutions; i.e., pH = 7. Although not specifically stated in the source from which these $\Delta G_r(aq)$ values were calculated (Christenson and McCarty, 1975), a reference given in that source suggests that they are based upon a temperature of 25°C.

Example 6.3. Determination of the Thermodynamic Feasibility of a Biological Waste Treatment Process. (An illustration of the applicability of chemical thermodynamics to biological reactions.)

- ***Situation.*** *A caustic waste stream from a food processing operation contains simple sugars and starches. The waste is to be treated biologically after neutralization with sulfuric acid.*

- ***Question(s).*** *Which type of biological treatment process would be energetically favorable, an aerobic process or an anaerobic process?*

- ***Logic and Answer(s).*** *A logical first approach to this question would be to compare the relative amounts of energy to be derived from the biological transformation of a simple carbohydrate under aerobic conditions using oxygen as an electron acceptor, and under anaerobic conditions using sulfate as an electron acceptor.*

  1. *From Table 6.2 we determine half-reaction free energies and calculate overall reaction free energies for aerobic and anaerobic conditions*

Reaction	$\Delta G_r(aq), \text{kJ/eq}$
Oxidation Half-Reaction	
$\frac{1}{4}CH_2O + \frac{1}{4}H_2O \Rightarrow \frac{1}{4}CO_2 + H^+ + e^-$	-41.8
Reduction Half-Reaction	
$\frac{1}{4}O_2 + H^+ + e^- \Leftrightarrow \frac{1}{2}H_2O$	-78.2
Overall Reaction	
$\frac{1}{4}CH_2O + \frac{1}{4}O_2 \Rightarrow \frac{1}{4}CO_2 + \frac{1}{4}H_2O$	-120.0

  2. *Anaerobic*

Reaction	$\Delta G_r(aq).\text{kJ/eq}$
Oxidation Half-Reaction	
$\frac{1}{4}CH_2O + \frac{1}{4}H_2O \Rightarrow \frac{1}{4}CO_2 + H^+ + e^-$	-41.8
Reduction Half-Reaction	
$\frac{1}{8}SO_4^{2-} + \frac{9}{8}H^+ + e^- \Leftrightarrow \frac{1}{8}HS^- + \frac{1}{2}H_2O$	$+21.3$
Overall Reaction	
$\frac{1}{4}CH_2O + \frac{1}{8}SO_4^{2-} + \frac{1}{8}H^+ \Rightarrow \frac{1}{4}CO_2 + \frac{1}{8}HS^- + \frac{1}{4}H_2O$	-20.5

  3. *It is evident that a greater amount of energy can be derived from oxidation of the organic material using oxygen as an electron acceptor. The analysis further tells us that even in the presence of the sulfate resulting from neutralization of the waste with sulfuric acid, thermodynamics dictate that noxious hydrogen sulfide will not be produced by microbial degradation of organic wastes as long as aerobic conditions prevail.*

- **Key Point(s).** *Even complex biologically mediated reactions adhere to the well defined laws of chemical energetics, and are subject to the same types of straightforward analyses of energy flow.*

Table 6.2 and Example 6.3 provide an opportunity to reinforce the caution expressed earlier about overinterpretation of thermodynamic spontaneity. A reaction may indeed be thermodynamically spontaneous but its rate very slow. Only in those cases for which equilibrium is readily obtained, as in elementary electron transfer reactions, does a favorable standard free energy (or electrode potential) indicate that the reaction will in fact occur within a relevant period of observation. Most oxidations involving organic reactions occur under nonequilibrium conditions, and in such instances thermodynamic favorability does not guarantee that a reaction will occur within a particular time period.

We will learn in Chapter 7 that the most significant factor governing rates of reactions is activation energy. Activation energy can be viewed as an energy barrier to potential reactivity. It is an energy level that must be achieved over and above the initial energy level of a substance in order for a reaction to occur. The greater the energy barrier, the smaller will be the fraction of molecules in a system possessing sufficient "excess" energy, and the slower will be the reaction. This point is illustrated vividly by the coexistence of organic matter and atmospheric oxygen in the face of obviously favorable free energies for its oxidation, as typified by the values given in Table 6.2. Activation energy serves in this instance as a fortuitous natural barrier (more accurately, retardant) to the destruction of organic life, sustaining a metastable organic world.

The activation energy barrier is reaction-path dependent, whereas free energy is not. Thus, if an alternative pathway of lower activation energy can be found, an otherwise slow reaction can be speeded up, perhaps so much as to transform a temporally metastable system into a reactive system. There are a number of chemical and biochemical substances that can provide alternate pathways, particularly for electron exchange reactions. These substances are termed catalysis. Enzymes comprise one of the major classes of chemical catalysts. These materials are the substances that allow microbes to accomplish reactions having favorable free energies but otherwise very slow reaction rates, such as those illustrated in Table 6.2.

6.2 THERMODYNAMICS AND REACTIVITY

6.2.1 Reaction Energies and System Composition

Consider the general reaction scheme

$$\boxed{\textbf{\textit{General Reaction Scheme}} \quad \gamma_A A + \gamma_B B + \gamma_C C + \cdots \Leftrightarrow \cdots + \gamma_X X + \gamma_Y Y + \gamma_Z Z} \quad (6.12)$$

where γ_A represents the number of units of substance A involved in the reaction, γ_B the corresponding number of units of substance B, and so on. The units involved may be molecules, moles, or any other molecular multiple. As discussed in Chapter 2 relative to Equation 2.11, the parameter γ_i is termed the stoichiometric coefficient for component i, and as also noted there the basis of reaction stoichiometry lies in the fact that the ratios of γ_i for the components of a reaction are fixed and well defined.

From Equation 6.8 we note that change in the Gibbs free energy of a system at constant temperature and pressure will be given by

$$dG_r \mid_{T,P} = \sum_i \mu_i dn_i \quad (6.13)$$

and that the condition for thermodynamic equilibrium in a closed system is

$$dG_r = \sum_i \mu_i dn_i = 0 \quad (6.14)$$

For any particular degree of advance, ν of a reaction the term dn_i in Equations 6.13 and 6.14 can be replaced by $\gamma_i d\nu$, where ν is the same for all components of the reaction; i.e., $d\nu = dn_i/\gamma_i$. For each finite degree of advance of a reaction (i.e., for $d\nu = 1$), the change in the number of moles, Δn_i, of species i is then equal to the stoichiometric coefficient, γ_i for that species. Thus, again for constant temperature and pressure, a finite free-energy change for a reaction can be written

$$\Delta G_r = \sum \mu_i \gamma_i \quad (6.15)$$

A similar expression can be written for the standard state

$$\Delta G_r^\circ = \sum \mu_i^\circ \gamma_i \quad (6.16)$$

The finite free-energy change associated with the progression of a specific reaction, from a nonequilibrium or non-standard-state condition to an equilibrium or standard state condition is given by ΔG_r. This energy can be related to the changing ratio of reactants and products of that reaction in a given system at constant temperature and pressure. First, by substituting Equation 6.9 for μ_i in Equation 6.15 we obtain

$$\Delta G_r = \sum \left(\mu_i^\circ + \mathcal{R}T(\ln a_i) \right) \gamma_i \qquad (6.17)$$

which upon rearrangement yields

$$\Delta G_r = \sum \mu_i^\circ \gamma_i + \mathcal{R}T \sum \gamma_i \ln a_i \qquad (6.18)$$

$$\Delta G_r = \Delta G_r^\circ + \mathcal{R}T \sum \gamma_i \ln a_i \qquad (6.19)$$

$$\Delta G_r = \Delta G_r^\circ + \mathcal{R}T \prod \ln(a_i)^{\gamma_i} \qquad (6.20)$$

For the general reaction scheme described by Equation 6.12 we can now write

$$\boxed{\textbf{\textit{Reaction Free Energy}} \qquad \Delta G_r = \Delta G_r^\circ + \mathcal{R}T \ln \frac{(a_X)^{\gamma_X} (a_Y)^{\gamma_Y} (a_Z)^{\gamma_Z}}{(a_A)^{\gamma_A} (a_B)^{\gamma_B} (a_C)^{\gamma_C}}} \qquad (6.21)$$

The product-reactant ratio in the last term on the right-hand side of Equation 6.21 is termed the reaction quotient, Q_r

$$\boxed{\textbf{\textit{Reaction Quotient}} \qquad Q_r = \frac{(a_X)^{\gamma_X} (a_Y)^{\gamma_Y} (a_Z)^{\gamma_Z}}{(a_A)^{\gamma_A} (a_B)^{\gamma_B} (a_C)^{\gamma_C}}} \qquad (6.22)$$

6.2.2   Reaction Energies and Equilibrium Constants

Thermodynamic relationships such as those developed above are usually incorporated in some operational parameter to facilitate their application. For example, as a reaction approaches equilibrium (i.e., as $\Delta G_r \rightarrow 0$ in Equation 6.21) the value of the reaction quotient given in Equation 6.22 approaches a constant value, such that

$$\mathcal{R}T(\ln Q_r)_{Equilibrium} = -\Delta G_r^\circ \qquad (6.23)$$

The particular value of Q_r attained at equilibrium under a stipulated set of standard conditions is constant for any reaction. Thus, from Equation 6.23 the equilibrium constants is referred to as the equilibrium constant for that reaction and is defined as

$$\boxed{\textbf{\textit{Equilibrium Constant}} \qquad K = exp\left(\frac{-\Delta G_r^\circ}{\mathcal{R}T} \right)} \qquad (6.24)$$

The equilibrium constant was discussed in several contexts in Chapter 5. Many types of equilibrium constants are possible, depending on the fundamental nature of the reaction and on whether it is homogeneous or heterogeneous. Relevant examples are acidity constants, complex formation constants, solubility constants, Henry's constants, partitioning coefficients, and Freundlich isotherm constants. Equation 6.21 can then be modified to define the relationship between reaction free energy and the equilibrium constant as

Reaction Free Energy and the Equilibrium Constant	$$\Delta G_r = \Delta G_r^{\circ} + \mathcal{R}T \ln Q_r = \mathcal{R}T \ln \frac{Q_r}{K}$$	(6.25)

The standard-state free energy change of a reaction can thus be determined by direct computation using a reaction-specific equation and tabulated standard-state molar free-energy values for the reactants and products. Alternatively, it can be determined from experimentally established values for the equilibrium constant, using Equation 6.23. In the absence of experimental data, the equilibrium constant can be calculated from the free energy values given in Tables 6.1 and 6.2. Uses of standard-state free energy values to calculate equilibrium constants and to assess non-standard-state reaction feasibility are illustrated in Example 6.4.

Example 6.4. Controlling pH to Facilitate the Oxidation of Cyanide by Chlorine to Produce an Environmentally Acceptable Product. (The role of background solution conditions in determining thermodynamic reaction feasibility.)

- **Situation.** *An industrial plant that produces a 26,000-mg/L cyanide waste plans to treat this material by oxidizing it to cyanate by alkaline chlorination (pH > 10.5), and then to create appropriate conditions for the cyanate to undergo acid hydrolysis to yield carbonic acid and ammonium ion. The reactions are to be carried out at the ambient temperature of the waste, 25° C.*

- **Question(s).** *From the perspective of thermodynamics, determine to what pH the cyanate solution resulting from alkaline chlorination must be lowered to reduce the final cyanate concentration to 0.5 $\mu g/L$ by hydrolysis.*

- **Logic and Answer(s).** *Alkaline oxidation of cyanide proceeds by the reaction*

$$CN^- + OCl^- \Leftrightarrow CNO^- + Cl^-$$

The pH is then reduced to cause acid hydrolysis of the cyanate to the hydronium ion and carbonic acid

$$CNO^- + 2H_3O^+ \Leftrightarrow NH_4^+ + H_2CO_3$$

1. *Convert weight concentrations to molar concentrations. The molecular weight of* CN^- *is 26 g and that of* CNO^- *is 42 g (see Figure 1.6). Thus, 26,000 mg/l of* CN^- *is 1 mol/L, and* $< 0.5\ \mu g/l$ *of* CNO^- *is essentially* 10^{-8} *mol/L.*

2. *The following free energy of formation values given below can be obtained from Table 6.1*

Species	ΔG_f°, kJ/mol
CNO^-	-98.7
H_3O^+	-237.2
NH_4^+	-79.5
H_2CO_3	-623.4

3. *From Equation 6.25*
$$\Delta G_r = \Delta G_r^\circ + RT \ln Q_r$$
$$\Delta G_r^\circ = \sigma \Delta G_{f,products}^\circ - \sigma \Delta G_{f,reactants}^\circ$$
$$= [-623.4 + (-79.5)] - [-98.7 + 2(-237.2)] = -129.8\ kJ/mol$$

4. *At equilibrium,* $\Delta G_r = 0$ *and* $-\Delta G_r^\circ = -(-129.8) = RT \ln K = 5.7 \log K$

$$\log K = 129.8/5.7 = 22.8 \qquad K = 10^{22.8} = \frac{[NH_4^+][H_2CO_3]}{[CNO^-][H_3O^+]^2}$$

$$[H_3O^+]^2 = \frac{[NH_4^+][H_2CO_3]}{[CNO^-]K}$$

5. *The final pH will determine the distribution between* $[H_2CO_3]$ *and* $[HCO_3^-]$. *For this example, we assume that the contributions of* $[HCO_3^-]$ *to the hydrolysis of* CNO^- *are the same as those of* $[H_2CO_3]$.

6. *We want* $[CNO^-] = 10^{-8}$ *mol/L and have* $[NH_4^+] = [H_2CO_3] = 1$ *mol/L. Thus,*

$$[H_3O^+]^2 = \frac{1}{[10^{-8}][10^{22.8}]} = \frac{1}{10^{14.8}} = 10^{-14.8}$$

$$[H_3O^+]^2 = 10^{-14.8}$$

$$[H_3O^+] = 10^{-7.4}$$

7. *To ensure sufficient hydrolysis, the pH of the cyanate solution must therefore be reduced to pH = 7.4.*

- *Key Point(s). Reaction feasibility frequently depends on the pH of a water because the hydronium ion is so highly reactive that it is often involved in the stoichiometry of aqueous phase reactions. The thermodynamic relationships inherent in all reactions allow us to determine required values of such control variables for a reaction to be energetically feasible.*

6.2.3 Reaction Energies and Electrode Potentials

For oxidation-reduction reactions the free energy and the equilibrium constant can be related to a corresponding parameter commonly associated with electron transfer processes, the standard-state electrode potential, E_H°

$$\mathcal{R}T \ln K = n_e \mathcal{F} E_H^\circ = -\Delta G_r^\circ \qquad (6.26)$$

where n_e is the number of electrochemical equivalents/mol of reactant, and $\mathcal{F}$ is the Faraday constant (96,485 C/mol; 96.485 kJ or 23.060 kcal per electron-volt). To illustrate the significance of the parameter E_H°, the electrochemical cell depicted in Figure 5.4 in Chapter 5 is reproduced in Figure 6.2 along with corresponding energy flow and quantification of relationships given in terms of this parameter.

Substitution of the relationships given in Equation 6.26 into the Gibbs free-energy relationship (Equation 6.21) yields the Nernst equation

$$\boxed{\textbf{The Nernst Equation} \qquad E_H = E_H^\circ + \frac{\mathcal{R}T}{n_e \mathcal{F}} \ln \frac{(a_X)^{\gamma_X}(a_Y)^{\gamma_Y}(a_Z)^{\gamma_Z}}{(a_A)^{\gamma_A}(a_B)^{\gamma_B}(a_C)^{\gamma_C}}} \qquad (6.27)$$

Values of E_H° for redox reactions, are readily available in chemical and chemical engineering reference and handbooks. Examples for reactions of common environmental interest are given in Table 6.3. Standard-state free-energy changes for oxidation-reduction reactions can be computed directly from the standard electrode potential using Equation 6.26. For E_H°, in volts and ΔG_r° in kJ/eq, Equation 6.26 reduces to

$$\Delta G_r^\circ = -96.485 n_e E_H^\circ \qquad (6.28)$$

Different sign conventions are used for electrode or redox potentials in different scientific literature. The convention used in this text is one adopted by the International Union for Pure and Applied Chemistry (IUPAC), in which all half- reactions are written as reductions, with an E_H° sign corresponding to the sign of log K for the reduction reaction.

Table 6.3 Standard Electrode Potentials for Selected Inorganic Species

Reduction Half-Reaction			E_H° volts
$Ag^+ + e$	$\Leftrightarrow$	Ag	0.80
$As + 3H^+ + 3e^-$	$\Leftrightarrow$	AsH_3	-0.54
$Cd^{2+} + 2e^-$	$\Leftrightarrow$	Cd	-0.40
$Cl_2(g) + 2e$	$\Leftrightarrow$	$2Cl^-$	1.36
$ClO_2 + H^+ + e$	$\Leftrightarrow$	$HClO_2$	1.27
$Co^{2+} + 2e$	$\Leftrightarrow$	Co	-0.28
$Cr^{3+} + 3e^-$	$\Leftrightarrow$	Cr	-0.74
$Cr^{6+} + 3e$	$\Leftrightarrow$	Cr^{3+}	1.10
$Cu^{2+} + 2e^-$	$\Leftrightarrow$	Cu	0.34
$F_2 + 2e^-$	$\Leftrightarrow$	$2F^-$	2.87
$Fe^{2+} + 2e^-$	$\Leftrightarrow$	Fe	-0.41
$Fe^{3+} + e$	$\Leftrightarrow$	Fe^{2+}	0.77
$2H^+ + 2e^-$	$\Leftrightarrow$	H_2	0.00
$H_2O_2 + 2H^+ + 2e^-$	$\Leftrightarrow$	$2H_2O$	1.78
$Hg^{2+} + 2e^-$	$\Leftrightarrow$	Hg	0.85
$I_2 + 2e^-$	$\Leftrightarrow$	$2I^-$	0.54
$Mn^{2+} + 2e^-$	$\Leftrightarrow$	Mn	-1.03
$Mn^{3+} + e^-$	$\Leftrightarrow$	Mn^{2+}	1.51
$N_2O + 2H^+ + 2e^-$	$\Leftrightarrow$	$N_2 + H_2O$	1.77
$Ni^{2+} + 2e^-$	$\Leftrightarrow$	Ni	-0.23
$2NO + 2H^+ + 2e^-$	$\Leftrightarrow$	$N_2O + H_2O$	1.59
$HNO_2 + H^+ + e^-$	$\Leftrightarrow$	$NO + H_2O$	0.99
$NO_3^- + 3H^+ + 2e^-$	$\Leftrightarrow$	$HNO_2 + H_2O$	0.94
$O_2 + 4H^+ + 4e^-$	$\Leftrightarrow$	$2H_2O$	1.23
$O_3 + 2H^+ + 2e^-$	$\Leftrightarrow$	$O_2 + H_2O$	2.07
$Pb^{2+} + 2e^-$	$\Leftrightarrow$	Pb	-0.13
$S + 2e^-$	$\Leftrightarrow$	S^{2-}	-0.51
$Se + 2e^-$	$\Leftrightarrow$	Se^{2-}	-0.78
$Sn^{2+} + 2e^-$	$\Leftrightarrow$	Sn	-0.14
	$\Leftrightarrow$		
$Zn^{2+} + 2e^-$	$\Leftrightarrow$	Zn	-0.76

Source of numerical values: Handbook of Chemistry and Physics (1982)

N.B.: E_H° values are given with respect to the Standard Hydrogen Electrode at 25°C.

Electrochemical Cell

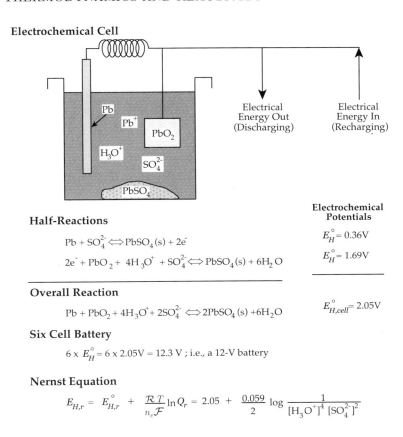

Half-Reactions

$$Pb + SO_4^{2-} \Longleftrightarrow PbSO_4(s) + 2e^-$$

$$2e^- + PbO_2 + 4H_3O^+ + SO_4^{2-} \Longleftrightarrow PbSO_4(s) + 6H_2O$$

Electrochemical Potentials

$$E_H^\circ = 0.36V$$

$$E_H^\circ = 1.69V$$

Overall Reaction

$$Pb + PbO_2 + 4H_3O^+ + 2SO_4^{2-} \Longleftrightarrow 2PbSO_4(s) + 6H_2O$$

$$E_{H,cell}^\circ = 2.05V$$

Six Cell Battery

$$6 \times E_H^\circ = 6 \times 2.05V = 12.3 \text{ V ; i.e., a 12-V battery}$$

Nernst Equation

$$E_{H,r} = E_{H,r}^\circ + \frac{RT}{n_e\mathcal{F}}\ln Q_r = 2.05 + \frac{0.059}{2}\log\frac{1}{[H_3O^+]^4 [SO_4^{2-}]^2}$$

Figure 6.2 Energy Flow in an Electrochemical Cell

6.2.4   Reaction Feasibility

The thermodynamic relationships and functions developed above are useful for preliminary evaluation of the feasibility of reactions involved in proposed treatment processes, and for interpretation of observed transformations in natural and engineered systems. They can be employed also to determine the amount of energy required to either cause a desirable reaction that otherwise would not be feasible or to prevent an undesirable reaction that might otherwise proceed. Such energy inputs can be thermal, mechanical, electrical, or chemical in nature.

All the equations above include temperature as a variable; thus the potential role of thermal energy is clear. Mechanical energy inputs are primarily useful for reactions that respond to pressure or volume changes. Homogeneous reactions of this type include all gas-phase processes and such processes as reverse osmosis in the aqueous phase. Pressure-responsive heterogeneous reactions include virtually all reactions involving gas-liquid, gas-solid and gas-liquid-solid systems. Equations 6.26 through 6.28 illustrate the relationships between chemical and electrical energy for redox reactions such as chemical oxidation and electrochemical corrosion. Chemical alterations of the free energy of a system and of its electrochemical potential can be made by adding or withdrawing quantities of reactants and/or products, as illustrated in Figure 5.4 of Chapter 5. The importance of reactant and product activity is evident from Equations 6.17 through 6.21 and Equation 6.27.

The potential for manipulating the energy balances of reactions by input or withdrawal of chemical energy is a valuable asset in process design and operation. For example, as suggested by the types of reaction examples given in Table 5.1 of Chapter 5 and by Example 6.4, the hydronium ion, $a_{H_3O^+}$, appears in the reaction quotient Q_r in Equations 6.21, and 6.27 for many reactions in aquatic environmental systems. Changes in pH thus effectively change the energy state of the system; this was illustrated in Example 6.4. Even when the hydronium ion is not involved, it may still be possible to reduce the magnitude of the activity or concentration of one of the products of a particular reaction by involving that product in a secondary reaction, thus preventing a continual decline in energy and reactivity as equilibrium is approached. For example, a metal cation formed as a product in the primary reaction of a process can be removed by precipitation in a secondary reaction with an added anion. Removal of a product will decrease the magnitude of the reaction quotient for the primary reaction (see Equation 6.22), and thus maintain a favorable free-energy or electrochemical potential for that reaction.

The discussion above is designed to encourage use of thermodynamic data and relationships to interpret and modify process dynamics. As always, however, appropriate caution must be taken in reaching conclusions when the information is limited to this singular aspect of process dynamics (i.e., equilibrium considerations).

6.2.5 Enthalpy and the Temperature Dependence of Equilibrium

The free energy of a system and the equilibrium constant defining the distribution of its species are both functions of enthalpy. The connection between free energy and enthalpy is explicitly stated in Equation 6.2, and that between enthalpy and the equilibrium constant, K, is explicitly stated through its relationship to dG_r (Equation 6.24). Enthalpy data for chemical species, like data for free energy and standard redox potentials, are readily available in a number of reference books. Enthalpy is an extensive variable, and subject to the same type of treatment given free energy. Several important formal relationships among enthalpy, free energy, and the equilibrium constant are illustrated below.

Differentiation of the Gibbs free energy relationship given in Equation 6.6

with respect to temperature at constant pressure yields

$$\left(\frac{\partial G}{\partial T}\right)_P = -S \tag{6.29}$$

Integration of Equation 6.29 requires knowledge of S as a function of temperature, T. While this relationship can be established, it is at best a tedious process. An alternative approach can also be arrived at by combining Equation 6.29 with Equation 6.2. We can write a relationship termed the Gibbs-Helmholtz equation to describe the variation of dG_r with temperature in a specific reaction

$$\boxed{\textbf{Gibbs-Helmholtz Equation} \qquad \left(\frac{\partial (dG_r)}{\partial T}\right)_P = -dS_r = \frac{dG_r - dH_r}{T}} \tag{6.30}$$

Equation 6.30, the Gibbs-Helmholtz equation, allows us to determine dH_r from knowledge of dG_r. We can show that

$$\frac{\partial}{\partial T}\left(\frac{dG_r}{T}\right) = \frac{1}{T}\frac{\partial (dG_r)}{\partial T} + \frac{dG_r}{T^2} \tag{6.31}$$

The first term in the right-hand side of Equation 6.31 can be replaced with Equation 6.30 to give an alternative form of the Gibbs-Helmholtz equation

$$\left[\frac{\partial}{\partial T}\left(\frac{dG_r}{T}\right)\right]_P = \frac{-dH_r}{T^2} \tag{6.32}$$

With the aid of differential calculus (i.e., $d \int T^{-2} dT = -dT^{-1}$) Equation 6.32 can be rewritten

$$\left[\frac{\partial (dG_r/T)}{\partial (1/T)}\right]_P = dH_r \tag{6.33}$$

The van't Hoff equation, which expresses the dependence of the equilibrium constant or temperature, follows directly from Equation 6.33 after replacing dG_r/T from Equation 6.24 with $-\mathcal{R}\ln K$

$$\boxed{\begin{array}{c} \textbf{\textit{van't Hoff Equation}} \\[2mm] \dfrac{d\ln K}{d(1/T)} = \dfrac{-dH_r}{\mathcal{R}} \qquad (6.34) \\[4mm] \textit{or,} \\[2mm] \left(\dfrac{d\ln K}{dT}\right)_P = \dfrac{dH_r}{\mathcal{R}T^2} \qquad (6.35) \end{array}}$$

According to Equation 6.34, a plot of $\ln K$ vs T^{-1} should yield a straight line with a slope of $-dH_r/\mathcal{R}$, as illustrated in Figure 6.3; more correctly, this slope is $-\Delta H_r/\mathcal{R}$ because it involves a finite temperature difference. The plot in Figure 6.2 is for a reaction that is endothermic (i.e., the equilibrium constant increases with increasing temperature). The slope is negative, so the enthalpy is positive. Thus, we see that endothermic reactions have positive enthalpy and, by extension, exothermic reactions have negative enthalpy.

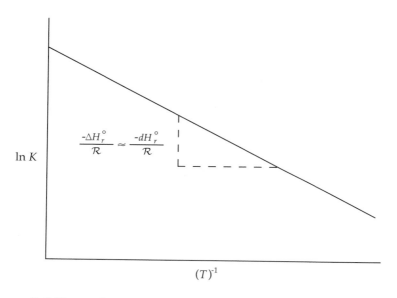

Figure 6.3 *Dependence of the Equilibrium Constant on Absolute Temperature for an Endothermic Reaction*

If ΔH_r° is assumed constant over a relatively narrow temperature range, Equation 6.35 can be integrated at two temperatures, T_1 and T_2, and the constant of integration taken as the same for both temperatures to give, in terms of common logarithms

$$\boxed{\begin{array}{l} \textit{\textbf{Estimation of}} \\ \textit{\textbf{K Values}} \\ \textit{\textbf{Over Narrow}} \\ \textit{\textbf{ΔT Ranges}} \end{array} \qquad \log \frac{K_2}{K_1} = \frac{\Delta H_r^\circ}{2.3\mathcal{R}} \frac{T_2 - T_1}{T_1 T_2}} \qquad (6.36)$$

Equation 6.36 facilities another important use of the enthalpy concept; i.e., for calculation of an equilibrium constant for a reaction at some temperature given knowledge of the standard-state molar enthalpy, ΔH_r°, and K at another temperature. The value of ΔH_r° can be found by applying the same concepts employed to calculate the standard-state free energy of a reaction, now using tables of standard-state partial molar enthalpy values, such as Table 6.1.

Applications of the enthalpy relationships to other characteristic thermodynamic functions of reactions are several fold. The most obvious is for calculation of the temperature dependence of equilibrium constants, thereby eliminating the need to measure K at all temperatures of interest. The temperature dependence of equilibrium constants is, of course, very important in process engineering because it provides information about reaction feasibility, at least from an equilibrium point of view.

An additional use of enthalpy relationships is for interpretation of the mechanistic character of complex reaction processes from experimental measurements of their equilibrium properties. Equation 6.35 relates enthalpy to the ratio of equilibrium constants at different temperatures. This ratio can be replaced by a ratio of values for any measurable equilibrium property (e.g., extent of reaction, or sorption capacity) which is directly proportional to K, as long as the proportionality is temperature independent. Experimental measurements of such a property for a system at several values of temperature thus allows calculation of an enthalpy value for the primary reaction of that system.

Enthalpy values are characteristic of reaction mechanisms and frequently permit more rigorous process analysis than otherwise possible in complex systems. This type of analysis can suggest appropriate variables which should be controlled to enhance or retard primary reaction(s). For example, the biological metabolism of an organic substrate may proceed by several different mechanisms, all of which have different characteristic enthalpy values. An appropriate equilibrium property, perhaps simply the concentration of a reaction product may be used to determine the operative mechanism by way of an estimation of enthalpy from Equation 6.36. Once the enthalpy is calculated, it may be possible to alter system conditions to achieve greater contaminant metabolism.

6.3 CHAPTER SUMMARY

We have invoked the laws of chemical thermodynamics in a fairly elementary and straightforward way in Chapter 6 to explain and rigorously quantify the tendencies for reactions to occur and the equilibrium states and associated reactant and product distributions to which net energies in excess of zero (equilibrium) drive them.

Examples have been presented to emphasize that thermodynamic calculations are practical in the assessment of the extent of change. Standard free energies, enthalpies and entropies are available for a wide array of chemical formations involved in reactions of concern in environmental systems. The outcomes of analyses of these properties are equilibrium constants, associated knowledge of the free energies involved in change, and the dependence of these energies dependence on temperature. Equilibrium constants based on these thermodynamic constants can be determined for many common reactions (e.g., acid-base, precipitation and complexation reactions).

Another important outcome of the thermodynamic perspective presented in this chapter is the recognition that proton and electron transfer reactions, two of the most common reaction phenomena operative in environmental systems, are interrelated (e.g., the Gibbs and Nernst equations). The most vivid example is the dependence of oxidation-reduction reactions and related precipitation reactions on pH. This is particularly important in aquatic systems because pH is the master variable, a variable that gives each natural water its unique reaction environment, especially when reactions with anthropogenic agents must be assessed.

Despite the extensiveness of thermodynamic data and the appeal of associated concepts, it would be misleading to suggest that the feasibility of any reaction of environmental interest can be assessed singularly on the basis of thermodynamic information. In Chapter 7 we will begin to learn how to quantify reaction rates, and their significance for environmental systems. First, thermodynamic feasibility does not ensure that a reaction or process will occur at a sufficiently rapid rate as to be important in the time scale for which a given environmental system is designed or evaluated. Further by way of limitations on thermodynamic analyses alone, there remain innumerable reactions of anthropogenic chemicals with each other and with constituents of natural systems for which such calculations have not been made. As discussed in Chapter 5 of PDES, linear free energy relationships, a form of structure-activity relationship, may hold promise for the future as an approach for overcoming limitations in experimental thermodynamic data, a particularly critical problem with respect to microbially mediated chemical transformation processes.

As will become clearer in Chapter 7, rate relationships are heavily dependent upon making accurate experimental measurements, an effort that is both costly and time consuming. It thus makes good sense to invest first in the analysis of the thermodynamic predispositions of reactions and processes whenever possible. Such analysis can usually help determine whether rate relationships are in fact needed, and how the associated data should be collected.

6.4   CITATIONS AND SOURCES

Christenson, D. R. and P. L. McCarty, 1975, "Multi-Process Biological Treatment Model," *Journal of the Water Pollution Control Federation*, 47, 11. (Table 6.2).

Handbook of Chemistry and Physics, 1982, 62nd Edition, CRC Press, Boca Raton, FL. (Table 6.1).

National Bureau of Standards, 1952, *Selected Values of Chemical Thermodynamic Properties*, Circular 500, U.S. Government Printing Office, Washington DC. (Table 6.1)

Weber, W.J., Jr. and F.A. DiGiano, 1996, *Process Dynamics of Environmental Systems,* John Wiley & Sons, Inc., New York. General source of all material presented. Chapter 5 of PDES expands on and extends Chapter 6 of this text, and identifies additional related readings.

6.5 PROBLEM ASSIGNMENTS

6.1 A 0.2-g quantity of platinum is immersed in 1 g of water in a 50-g glass beaker. Calculate the energies required to heat each of these materials from 15°C to 65°C, given that the specific heat capacities for glass and platinum are 0.84 J/g - K and 0.134 J/g -K, respectively.

Answers: Water, 209 J; platinum, 1.34 J; beaker, 2100 J.

6.2 Methane is to be used as fuel in a heater in an industrial process for raising the temperature of an aqueous dye bath solution from 15°C to 95°C. The heat of combustion of methane is 891 kJ/mol. Assuming that 50% of the heat is useful, determine how many kilograms of dye bath can be heated to specification by burning 200 L of methane, CH_4, measured at S.T.P.

Answer: 11.9 kg.

6.3 The dye bath of Problem 6.2 is at a temperature of 50°C after use. To render it more amenable to biological treatment, its temperature is to be lowered by addition of waste ice from a refrigerated storage operation. Estimate the resulting temperature of the waste stream if the ice (0°C) is added on a 1:9 weight basis.

Answer: 37° C.

6.4 Ten cubic meters of water stored in an uninsulated outdoor water feed tank for a steam generation plant has frozen during a 2-week plant shutdown. A preheater in this tank will be used to convert the ice to water at50°C, which will then be processed to steam. Determine the total heat required to change the ice at 0°C to steam at 100°C.

Answer: 301×107 kJ.

6.5 The quick lime produced in a recalcination operation is to be slaked to hydrated lime before use, according to the reaction

$$CaO(s) + H_2O(l) \Leftrightarrow Ca(OH)_2(s)$$

Determine the amount of heat associated with this reaction and indicate whether heat is evolved or required as input.

Answer: $\Delta H_r^\circ = -65.3$ kJ. The negative value indicates that the reaction is exothermic (i.e., heat is evolved).

6.6 Data obtained from experimental measurements of the amounts of heat evolved or absorbed on the combustion of compounds can be used to determine standard enthalpy values for formation of these compounds. If the heat liberated on complete combustion of 1 mol of CH_4 gas to $CO_2(g)$ and $H_2O(l)$ is 890 kJ and that for combustion of 1 g of starch, $(C_6H_{10}O_5)_n$, into $CO_2(g)$ and $H_2O(l)$ is 17.5 kJ, determine the standard-state enthalpy of formation of 1 mol of $CH_4(g)$ and 1 g of starch.

Answers: $H^\circ_{r,CH_4} = -75$ kJ/mol; $\Delta H^\circ_{r,starch} = -5.88$ kJ/g.

6.7 A shallow ponded area at a strip mine in a semiarid region is in equilibrium with underlying gypsum, $CaSO_4(s)$, deposits. An organic pollutant, formaldehyde (CH_2O) is discharged to the pond. Biodegradation of this pollutant may occur by an anaerobic reaction in which sulfate is used as an electron acceptor

$$SO_4^{2-} + 2CH_2O + 2H^+ \Leftrightarrow H_2S(g) + 2CO_2(g) + H_2O$$

or, if sufficient oxygen is present, by the following aerobic reaction

$$O_2(aq) + CH_2O \Leftrightarrow CO_2(g) + H_2O$$

with $\Delta G^\circ_r = $ -538.7 kJ/mol. A partial analysis of the system indicates the following

$$[Ca^{2+}] = 500 \text{ mg/L} \quad O_2(aq) = 5 \text{ mg/L}$$
$$p_{H_2S} = 10^{-2.0} \text{ atm} \quad [CH_2O] = 10^{-6}M$$
$$p_{CO_2} = 10^{-3.5} \text{ atm} \quad pH = 7$$

Determine whether either or both of these reactions are thermodynamically feasible under the stipulated conditions.

Answers: $\Delta G_R(aerobic) = -502.7$ kJ/mol
$\Delta G_R(anaerobic) = -242$ kJ/mol

6.8 Hypochlorous acid, a weak acid, is a much stronger disinfecting agent than its conjugate base, the hypochlorite ion. The pK_a for HOCl is 7.52 at 25°C. If 2.0×10^{-4} moles of hypochlorous acid is added to buffered (pH 8.0) water at 25°C, what is the equilibrium concentration of the HOCl species?

$$HOCl + H_2O = OCl^- + H_3O^+$$

6.9 If the equilibrium constant for an oxidation reaction at 25°C is twice as large as it is at 0°C, what is the enthalpy of the reaction at standard state?

6.10 A metal-plating plant attempts to reduce hexavalent chromium, $Cr_2O_7^{2-}$, to the trivalent form, Cr^{3+}, using ferrous ion, Fe^{2+}. The stoichiometry of the overall reaction is given by

$$Cr_2O_7^{2-} + 14H^+ + 5Fe^{2+} \Leftrightarrow 2Cr^{3+} + 6Fe^{3+} + 7H_2O$$

$$\Delta H^\circ_r = 776 \text{ kcal/mol}$$

$$pK = -57.0 \text{ at } 25°C$$

Given the information below, determine whether reduction of the hexavalent chromium by this means is thermodynamically feasible. Plating bath water temperature = 40°C, pH = 6.0, $[Cr_2O_7^{2-}] = 0.8 \times 10^{-4}M$, $[Cr^{3+}] = 3.0 \times 10^{-7}M$, $[Fe^{2+}] = 0.8 \times 10^{-4}M$, and $[Fe^{3+}] = 0.8 \times 10^{-8}M$.

Chapter 7

Elementary Process Rates

Contents

7.0   CHAPTER OBJECTIVES

To learn how to determine, interpret, and model rates at which reactions and processes occur in order to describe and predict species distributions as functions of time independently of the reactor or system in which they occur.

7.1   CONCEPTS

7.1.1   Terms and Conditions

In our discussion of reaction rates we differentiate between homogeneous and heterogeneous reactions, and in this chapter focus on the former. We further differentiate between reversible and irreversible changes. In general terms, a reversible reaction is one that proceeds toward a final state in which there exists a well-defined distribution of reactant and product species, all being present in measurable quantities. Conversely, an irreversible reaction is one in which a stoichiometric combination of reactants leads to their essentially complete conversion to products. These general definitions are not rigorous.

According to the definition of equilibrium, all reactions are, in principle, reversible. There are, however, numerous chemical reactions for which the extent of change in the reverse direction is so small that it cannot be detected experimentally over the period of observation or concern. For practical purposes such reactions may be treated as irreversible. When applicable, the assumption of irreversibility greatly facilitates interpretation and representation of reaction rates in environmental processes and systems.

7.1.2   Measurements

Reaction rates and reaction rate constants are generally determined from measurements of C_A, C_B, and time, t. Completely mixed reaction vessels having no inflow or outflow are usually used to collect rate data. As discussed in Chapter 3, this type of system is referred to as a completely mixed batch reactor (CMBR). The explicit statement of conditions embodied by the term CMBR must be carefully considered; namely, it is a closed system of homogeneous content.

It is absolutely essential in the measurement of rate data for reaction characterization and rate coefficient determination that the explicit conditions of the mathematical model used to describe reactor behavior be in fact met in the experimental system employed. As discussed earlier in Chapter 3 (Section 3.3.2) there is no inflow or outflow of reactant for a CMBR, and the contents of the reactor can be considered homogeneous because they are completely mixed. The material balance equation thus reduces to

$$V \left(\frac{dC}{dt} \right)_{reactor} = \pm V \left(\frac{dC}{dt} \right)_{reaction} \qquad (3.24)$$

The important message in Equation 3.24 for this discussion is that data collected from a true CMBR experiment reflect not only the reactor behavior, but define the reaction rate as well.

7.1.3 Mass Law Relationships

The law of mass action states that the rate of an elementary homogeneous chemical reaction is directly proportional to the product of the masses of the reacting species. The term elementary refers to a reaction that proceeds directly as written, with no intermediate steps. The term homogeneous means that all reactants and products exist in the same physical state (e.g., dissolved) in the same phase. The term elementary as applied to description of reactions in this context is more rigorous than it is in its application to description of processes in the title of this chapter, in which case it means only relatively simple or uncomplicated processes.

For example, the stoichiometric equation for an irreversible and homogeneous elementary reaction between two chemical species, A and B, to form a new compound, AB, is written

$$A + B \Rightarrow AB \qquad (7.1)$$

The law of mass action stipulates that the rates of disappearance of A and B and production of AB for this condition should be given by

$$\boxed{\text{Law of Mass Action} \qquad r_{AB} = -r_A = -r_B = k[A][B] = kC_A C_B} \qquad (7.2)$$

where k is a constant of proportionality termed the rate constant, and $[A] = C_A$ and $[B] = C_B$ represent the molar concentrations (more rigorously, activities) of A and B, respectively, at any time, t. Mass concentrations can be substituted for $[A]$ and $[B]$ with a resulting change in the units and magnitude of the rate coefficient. The basic relationships expressed in Equation 7.2 and ensuing mass law rate expressions are, however, predicated on molecular, and thus molar, proportionalities. The importance of this concept to our interpretations of reaction orders will be illustrated shortly.

For the reaction illustrated in Equation 7.1 we can write from the law of mass action expression given in Equation 7.2 the following rate equation

$$\left(\frac{dC_{AB}}{dt} \right)_{reaction} = \left(\frac{dC_{AB}}{dt} \right)_{CMBR} = r_{AB} = kC_A C_B \qquad (7.3)$$

Mass conservation considerations allow the concentrations C_A and C_B in Equation 7.3 to be expressed in terms of their initial values, $C_{A,0}$ and $C_{B,0}$, less the concentration of product formed, or reactant reacted (C_R).

If $C_{AB,0} = C_{R,0} = 0$, introduction of these concentration parameters to Equation 7.3 yields

$$\left(\frac{dC_{AB}}{dt}\right)_{reactor} = \frac{dC_R}{dt} = kC_AC_B = k(C_{A,0} - C_R)(C_{B,0} - C_R) \qquad (7.4)$$

or, for the special case when $C_{A,0} = C_{B,0} = C_0$

$$\frac{dC_R}{dt} = k(C_0 - C_R)^2 \qquad (7.5)$$

Integration of Equation 7.4 yields

$$kt = \frac{1}{C_{A,0} - C_{B,0}} \ln \frac{C_{B,0}(C_{A,0} - C_R)}{C_{A,0}(C_{B,0} - C_R)} \qquad (7.6)$$

while the integrated form of Equation 7.5 is

$$kt = \frac{C_R}{C_0(C_0 - C_R)} \qquad (7.7)$$

It is possible, in principle, to use the law of mass action to develop an appropriate rate equation for any chemical reaction in the manner in which Equations 7.6 and 7.7 were obtained, as long as the reactions are elementary and homogeneous as specified and defined above.

7.1.4   Monomolecular Reactions

For many simple irreversible reactions the rates of change in the reactant and product concentrations are directly proportional to the molecular concentration of only one reactant. For example, consider the decomposition of a single chemical substance, such as the common environmental oxidant hydrogen peroxide

$$\boxed{\begin{array}{ll} \textbf{\textit{A Monomolecular}} & H_2O_2 \Rightarrow H_2O + \dfrac{1}{2}O_2 \\ \textbf{\textit{Reaction}} & \end{array}} \qquad (7.8)$$

Equation 7.8 describes what is termed a monomolecular reaction because it involves only one reactant molecule. The rate of disappearance of peroxide according to the stoichiometry given in Equation 7.8 may be written

$$-r = kC = k(C_{A,0} - C_R) \qquad (7.9)$$

The reactant concentration for a monomolecular reaction in a perfectly mixed closed system is then found by integrating the expression

$$\boxed{\begin{array}{ll} \textit{Monomolecular} & \dfrac{dC}{dt} = -kC \\ \textit{Rate Equation} & \end{array}} \qquad (7.10)$$

We observe after integration of Equation 7.10 that a monomolecular reaction is characterized by an exponential decrease in reactant concentration with time, i.e.

$$\frac{C}{C_0} = e^{-kt} \qquad (7.11)$$

We can replace C with $(C_0 - C_R)$ in Equation 7.10 to express the rate of change in the concentration of reactant that has reacted

$$\frac{dC_R}{dt} = k(C_0 - C_R) \qquad (7.12)$$

Integration of Equation 7.12 yields

$$kt = \ln \frac{C_0}{C_0 - C_R} \qquad (7.13)$$

The fraction, ϕ_R°, of peroxide reacted in time t is

$$\phi_R^\circ = \frac{C_R}{C_0} \qquad (7.14)$$

Equation 7.13 can then be expressed as

$$k = \frac{-\ln(1 - \phi_R^\circ)}{t} \qquad (7.15)$$

Thus, for a monomolecular reaction, a fixed fraction of the amount of material present at the start of the reaction is reacted for each fixed unit of time thereafter. The time required for a given fraction to react is referred to as a corresponding fractional reaction time. For a 50% reaction of a monomolecularly reacting substance, for example, this time is referred to as its 0.5-fractional reaction time, or more simply, its half life.

The decomposition of hydrogen peroxide shown in Equation 7.8 illustrates also how rates of disappearance of reactants and appearance of products relate to stoichiometry. According to the stoichiometry shown in Equation 7.8, the rate of disappearance of hydrogen peroxide is related to the rate of production of molecular oxygen by

$$-r_{H_2O_2} = 2r_{O_2} \qquad (7.16)$$

and, because $-r_{H_2O_2} = kC_{H_2O_2}$ and $r_{O_2} = k'C_A$, it follows that $k = 2k'$.

7.1.5   Reaction Orders

A monomolecular reaction is dependent on the concentration of only one reacting species, and is thus said to be a first-order reaction. Pursuant to the law of mass action, the general expression for the rate of an elementary multimolecular reaction involving components A, B, C and D may be written

$$\textit{\textbf{r}}_{A,B,C,D} = k(C_A)^{\gamma A}(C_B)^{\gamma B}(C_C)^{\gamma C}(C_D)^{\gamma D} \qquad (7.17)$$

| General Mass Law Rate Equation |

This reaction is said to have an overall order of $n = (\gamma_A + \gamma_B + \gamma_C + \gamma_D)$; it is nth-order overall, γ_A order in C_A, γ_B order in C_B, and so on. The order of a reaction with respect to each reactant corresponds to the stoichiometric coefficient, γ, of that reactant only if the reaction is elementary.

Stated another way, for elementary reactions, and for elementary reactions only, the mechanism of reaction is expressed by the number of molecules involved. Corresponding to our prior use of the term monomolecular to describe H_2O_2 decomposition, the order of the reaction is also the molecularity of the reaction. For nonelementary reactions, however, the reaction order may be significantly different from that suggested by the stoichiometry.

The elementary irreversible reaction

$$2A \xrightarrow{k} B + C \qquad (7.18)$$

has a molecularity of two, and the rate of this reaction is thus second order

$$-\textit{\textbf{r}}_A = k(C_A)^2 \qquad (7.19)$$

The stoichiometry of the reaction given in Equation 7.18 is preserved if it is written as

$$A \xrightarrow{k} \frac{1}{2}B + \frac{1}{2}C \qquad (7.20)$$

Equation 7.20 does not express the proper molecularity however, and thus does not represent the mechanism of the elementary reaction. In this case the bimolecular reaction might mistakenly be interpreted as monomolecular.

Further examples of the relationship of reaction order to molecularity for elementary reactions are provided by Equations 7.4, 7.5, and 7.10. Equations 7.4 and 7.5 are rate equations for an elementary reaction that is second-order overall. Equation 7.4 is applicable to an elementary reaction that is first order with respect to each of two reactants, whereas Equation 7.5 is additionally applicable to a reaction which is second order with respect to one reactant. Application of the latter equation to a reaction that is first order with respect to each of two reactants is, as specified in its introduction, limited to the case where the initial concentrations of each are identical. Equation 7.10 is a rate expression for an elementary reaction that is first order.

Reaction order must be an integer value for elementary reactions because the mechanism of reaction necessarily involves a discrete number of molecules or multiples (e.g., mols) thereof. On the other hand, the order of reaction can be fractional if the reaction is nonelementary. Non-integer reaction orders complex reactions and processes may result either from the use of experimental rate data to devise an empirical rate expression, or from a characterization of the overall mechanism of a nonelementary reaction by analysis of the kinetics of each intermediate elementary reaction comprising the overall process.

We will illustrate shortly that there are also many nonelementary reactions for which the reaction rate expression is not of the multiplicative form given by Equation 7.17. In these instances, an observed or apparent order of reaction developed from experimental rate data will not likely reflect the molecularity or stoichiometry of the reaction in a precise manner.

Rate equations expressing zero-order, first-order and second-order dependence of rate on concentrations are of most practical interest for physicochemical and biological reactions in environmental systems. For nonelementary reactions, higher degrees of molecularity are probably involved. In many cases, however, the overall process occurs by way of a number of elementary reaction steps which are of first or second order in their dependence on reactant concentration. When these reaction steps are sequential, the appropriate rate expression is determined by the slowest single step; the rate-limiting step. Thus many reactions that are described by complicated stoichiometric equations may require only relatively simple expressions for description of their reaction rates.

The final test for reaction order must be experimental. A given set of experimental data that fits an assumed rate expression does not, however, prove that the actual molecularity of the reaction is given by the assumed rate expression. The only conclusion is that the data are consistent with that rate expression within the limits of observation.

The law of mass action hypothesis that stoichiometric coefficients characterize molecularity, and thus that they may be used as shown in Equation 7.17, is valid only if a reaction is elementary, and if its stoichiometry represents its entire reaction scheme.

Regardless of whether a reaction is elementary or nonelementary, however, the law of mass action is always valid when relating the position of equilibrium for a reversible reaction to the point at which the forward (F) and reverse (R) reaction rates are equal. For example, if the reaction given in Equation 7.1 is reversible and generalized in terms of stoichiometric coefficients, such that

$$\gamma_A A + \gamma_B B \underset{k_R}{\overset{k_F}{\rightleftharpoons}} \gamma_{AB} AB \qquad (7.21)$$

then, at equilibrium

$$r_{Forward} = k_F C_A C_B = r_{Reverse} = k_R C_{AB} \qquad (7.22)$$

and, expressing concentrations rigorously in terms of activities

> **Mass Law Rate Equilibrium Constant Relationship**
>
> $$\frac{(C_{AB})^{\gamma_{AB}}}{(C_A)^{\gamma_A}(C_B)^{\gamma_B}} \approx \frac{(a_{AB})^{\gamma_{AB}}}{(a_A)^{\gamma_A}(a_B)^{\gamma_B}} = \frac{k_F}{k_R} = (Q_r)_{Equilibrium} = K$$

$$(7.23)$$

where K is the mass law equilibrium constant. We will make further use of this aspect of the law of mass action in Chapter 8.

7.1.6   Nonelementary Reactions

Nonelementary reactions are those in which the stoichiometry represents only the net result of a reaction, and not its complete molecular scheme. In other words, nonelementary reactions involve one or more steps in which intermediate products that are not specifically identified in the stoichiometry of the reaction form and then disappear. Each intermediate step is an elementary reaction for which the kinetics are described rigorously by the law of mass action. The kinetics of the overall reaction then follow from analysis of the kinetics of each intermediate step.

Suppose that Equation 7.1 is not representative of an elementary reaction but represents instead the overall stoichiometry for a reaction that leads to formation of AB through an intermediate step involving the transformation of A to some short- lived species, A*. The overall reaction now has two rate steps

> **A Nonelementary Reaction**
>
> $$A \underset{k_2}{\overset{k_1}{\rightleftharpoons}} A^* \qquad (7.24)$$
>
> $$A^* + B \overset{k_3}{\rightleftharpoons} AB \qquad (7.25)$$

Two different approaches can be used to obtain rate expressions for the reaction scheme shown in Equations 7.24 and 7.25; these are the stationary-state approximation (see PDES for further details) and the rate-controlling step approach to be discussed in Chapter 8.

Stoichiometry does not allow us to predict rates of nonelementary reactions directly. However, we can initiate the analysis of any reaction of interest by assuming that it is elementary and using its stoichiometry to postulate a rate model. This model can then be tested against the experimental rate data to determine whether or not the assumption is reasonable. If the data do not agree with the model, the reaction is probably more complicated than the overall stoichiometry suggests (i.e., it is probably nonelementary).

If we determine by the above means that a given reaction is nonelementary, there are two alternative pathways along which to proceed for further analysis: (1) postulate intermediate reactions that lead to alternative rate expressions; or, (2) fit an empirical rate model to the data without attempting to characterize the reaction mechanisms. In many instances the reaction may be too complex to unravel the reaction pathway, leaving only an empirical approach practical. The inherent limitations of empirical rate models must, however, be recognized. Most importantly, such models should not be applied outside the range of reaction conditions for which they have been formulated and experimentally calibrated.

The aqueous phase reactions of hypochlorous acid (HOCL) with natural organic matter (NOM) to form trihalomethanes (THMs) illustrate a situation in which, because so much uncertainty exists about the fundamental mechanisms of such reactions, empirical overall reaction rate modeling has been used in lieu of reaction pathway models. In such instances, a relatively simplistic equation is used to describe the overall reaction

$$\gamma_i(\text{HOCL}) + \gamma_j(\text{NOM}) = \gamma_k(\text{THMs}) + \text{other products} \qquad (7.26)$$

A balanced stoichiometric relationship for the reaction given in Equation 7.26 cannot be written because NOM represents a collection of molecular structures and molecular weights that are for the most part unknown. Moreover, the reactivity of each NOM constituent to chlorine is not well understood. Additionally, not all of the products may be identified, nor are the influences of reaction conditions such as pH and the presence of other halides (e.g., bromide) completely understood. Chlorination in the presence of bromide can lead, for example, to formation of bromoform. Accurate characterization of intermediate reactions is virtually impossible in such cases, yet a reliable rate relationship is needed for engineering practice. The only answer in such cases lies in the development of an empirical rate model of the type illustrated in Example 7.1.

Example 7.1. Development of a Rate Model for Trihalomethane Production During Disinfection of a Water Supply. (An exercise in structuring an empirical rate expression to characterize a complex process involving unknown mechanisms and stoichiometry.)

- *Situation. A large regional water supply network employs a number of different raw water sources. To facilitate development of a uniform policy with respect to control of chlorine doses to minimize THM formation, the regional engineer has asked you, his laboratory director, to conduct a series of studies designed to develop an appropriate model for THM formation rates.*

- **Question(s).** *Design an experimental approach to the development of an appropriate empirical rate model for this situation.*

- **Logic and Answer(s).**

  1. *Rates of trihalomethane formation are dependent on a variety of natural water conditions as well as on the dosage of chlorine applied. The first step in this development will thus be to perform a series of rate experiments with samples of each of the different natural waters involved.*

  2. *Ambient temperature, pH, nonpurgeable organic carbon (NPOC) concentration and bromide concentration are different for the waters to be tested, so there must be some common denominator for the experiments. For example, the chlorine to NPOC ratio can be fixed to a given value for a series of baseline experiments in which TTHMs are measured with time for the different ambient conditions.*

  3. *Additional experiments in which one parameter is varied while holding the others constant at the ambient condition should be conducted for each natural water.*

  4. *Simple and multiple nonlinear regressions can then be performed to analyze the resulting data. One approach might utilize transformation of the independent and dependent variables into logarithmic forms followed by a multiple linear regression. Another might involve development of a nonlinear model without log transformation. A model of the former type is presented for illustration purposes*

  $$TTHM = \gamma_1 (UVA \cdot TOC)^{\gamma_2} (\text{Cl}_2)^{\gamma_3} (t)^{\gamma_4} (T)^{\gamma_5} (\text{pH} - 2.6)^{\gamma_6} (\text{Br}^- + 1)^{\gamma_7}$$

  where TTHM is total trihalomethane [i.e., the sum of the concentrations (mg/L) of chloroform, bromodichloromethane, dibromochloromethane and bromoform]; UVA · TOC is the product of the ultraviolet light absorbance (UVA, cm^{-1}) at 254 nm and total organic carbon (TOC) concentration (mg/L), these both serving as surrogate measures of NOM; Cl_2 is the applied chlorine dose (mg/L); t is the reaction time (hours); T is temperature ($^\circ C$); and Br^- is the bromide concentration (mg/L). This model also implies that TTHMs are not formed if pH < 2.6, an experimental, not theoretical, conclusion.

  5. *The values of γ_1 through γ_7 can then be determined by best fit of the pooled data after excluding results where no chlorine residual existed at the end of some specified time period, a practical problem in such rate analysis where the stoichiometric amount of chlorine needed is unknown.*

- *Key Point(s). Complex environmental processes often allow only empirical characterization and modeling of reaction rates. Such modeling approaches must be subjected to sensitivity analyses to determine the level of accuracy required regarding information on the magnitude of specific dependent variables, and then subjected to verification using external data sets [For a related application of the particular correlation given above, see Amy, et al. (1987)].*

7.2 FIRST-ORDER RATE EQUATIONS

First-order rate equations are widely applicable for description of a number of different types of environmental reactions. In addition to true monomolecular reactions, like those of radioactive decay and other self-decomposition reactions (e.g., Equation 7.8), mathematical expressions of the first-order type are often found useful for empirical descriptions of:

- *multimolecular reactions in which the concentrations of all but one of the reactants remains essentially constant;*

- *complex processes, such as unsaturated microbial growth and disinfection, for which overall reaction rates may be represented approximately by a first-order equation; and,*

- *certain purely physical processes, such as the mass transfer processes associated with the dissolution of solids and gases in water, which follow this general mathematical form (e.g., compare Equations 3.21 and 3.23).*

A reaction in which the concentrations of all but one of the reactants are so large that they change very little over the course of the reaction is termed pseudo-first order. Consider, for example, the case of the base-catalyzed hydrolysis of 1,1,2,2 per(tetra)chloroethane to trichloroethane

$$C_2H_2Cl_4 + 2H_2O \rightarrow C_2HCl_3 + H_3O^+ + Cl^- \tag{7.27}$$

In dilute aqueous solution the concentration of H_2O remains substantially constant at 55.6 mol/L; consequently, the rate of hydrolysis for this bimolecular reaction is sensitive only to, and therefore essentially dependent only upon, the concentration of the perchloroethane.

One of the most familiar empirical applications of the first-order rate equation to complex processes in water quality analysis is for description of rates of exertion of biochemical oxygen demand (BOD). Microbial oxygen utilization

during oxidation of substrates comprised by mixtures of carbonaceous and ni-
trogenous organic compounds is a highly complex process. Recognizing this,
and further being unable to characterize lumped parameters such as BOD in
terms of molar concentration units, we use mass units for expressing associated
rate relationships. The differential and integrated forms of the first-order BOD
equation are generally written as

BOD Rate Equations

$$r = \frac{dC_{R,\infty}}{dt} = k(C_{R,\infty} - C_R) \tag{7.28}$$

and

$$C_R = C_{R,\infty}(1 - e^{-kt}) = C_{R,\infty}(1 - 10^{-0.4343kt}) \tag{7.29}$$

---

respectively, where C_R is the cumulative amount of BOD that has been exerted
at any time, and $C_{R,\infty}$ is the "ultimate" (usually assumed to be exerted within
approximately five days; i.e., the "5-day") carbonaceous (first-stage) BOD. In
chemical reactions, $C_{R,\infty}$ would correspond to the initial concentration of a
measurable reactant, and thus be a known quantity. In the BOD test, however,
the ultimate BOD cannot be measured at the outset of the experiment, but
must instead be determined along with the rate constant, k. For such situations,
analysis of rate data by multiple nonlinear regression techniques is required to
search optimal values for two unknown parameters (i.e., two-parameter search
routines).

Another situation in which simple first-order expressions are used empirically
to describe complex biochemical processes is evident is in the differential and
integrated forms of Chick's law for die-off of bacteria

Chick's Law Rate Equations

$$r = \frac{dC_N}{dt} = -kC_N \tag{7.30}$$

and

$$\ln \frac{C_{N,0}}{C_N} = kt; \; \log \frac{C_{N,0}}{C_N} = 0.4343kt \tag{7.31}$$

---

where C_N is the number of organisms per unit volume remaining at any time
and $C_{N,0}$ is the original number. This first-order expression is often used to
describe the rate of kill of bacteria by disinfectants, but it is valid for such
use only if the disinfectant is present in excess concentration. In most water

treatment applications a disinfectant is not in excess, so the rate expression must also include the disinfectant concentrations raised to same order, which adds more empiricism.

The first-order expression is useful also for empirically describing certain purely physical processes, particularly mass transfer processes, under conditions of perfect mixing. Consider, for example, the dissolution of a solid with surface area A° in a volume V_R of water in a CMBR; if the equilibrium saturation concentration (aqueous solubility) is C_S and the concentration at any time is designated as C, then the rate of accumulation of C in solution is given by the material balance equation

$$
\boxed{
\begin{array}{c}
\textit{\textbf{Solids Dissolution Rate Equation}} \\[2mm]
r = \dfrac{dC}{dt} = k_f \dfrac{A^\circ}{V_R}(C_S - C) = k_f(a_s^\circ)_R(C_S - C)
\end{array}
}
\qquad (7.32)
$$

where k_f is the mass transfer coefficient and $(a_s^\circ)_R$ the specific surface area per volume of reactor; i.e., a rate expression that is first order in C.

Applications of first-order expressions for empirical description of certain rate processes (biochemical, chemical or physical) may require more than one parameter to be determined experimentally. The dissolution rate of a solid is one such situation, as illustrated in Example 7.2.

Example 7.2. Development of a Rate Model to Describe the Dissolution of Phenanthrene into Water. (An example of the use of a simple pseudo first-order rate model to characterize a complex two-phase phenomenon.)

- *Situation.* Polynuclear aromatic hydrocarbons (PAHs) are hydrophobic compounds having generally very low water solubilities. Like PCBs, these compounds are therefore commonly found associated with solids (e.g., soils, suspended solids, sludges), and their biodegradation thus potentially limited by their rates of desorption and dissolution. An experiment is devised to measure the rate of dissolution of phenanthrene, a representative PAH. Solid crystals of phenanthrene of known surface area are placed in a flask and shaken. The data for dissolved concentration of phenanthrene with time are provided below [data from Grimberg et al. (1995)]

Time (min)	Concentration (μg/L)
0	0
21.5	235
56.5	508
169.5	950
299.5	1069
4298.5	1152

- **Question(s).** *Postulate a rate expression to describe phenanthrene solubilization and to obtain the solubility limit.*

- **Logic and Answer(s).**

  1. *The flask in which phenanthrene solubilization is measured can be considered a CMBR. One model for the rate of solubilization is given in Equation 7.32, for which mass transfer is postulated as a pseudo-first-order reaction*

  $$\frac{dC}{dt} = k_f (a_s^\circ)_R (C_S - C)$$

  where C is the concentration of phenanthrene in solution, C_S is its solubility limit, k_f is a mass transfer rate coefficient, and $(a_s^\circ)_R$ is the specific surface area of phenanthrene per unit volume of reactor.

  2. *The specific surface area of the phenanthrene, is known to be 0.09 cm^{-1} initially. Although $(a_s^\circ)_R$ decreases with time, the solubility of phenanthrene is so small that this change can be considered insignificant over the period of observation. Equation 7.32 can then be rearranged and integrated over time and concentration to yield*

  $$C = C_S \left(1 - e^{k_f (a_s^\circ)_R t}\right)$$

  3. *Both k_f and C_S are unknown. Nonlinear regression analysis is therefore used as shown below to obtain values of $C_S = 1.14$ mg/L and $k_f = 0.12$ cm/min for these parameters.*

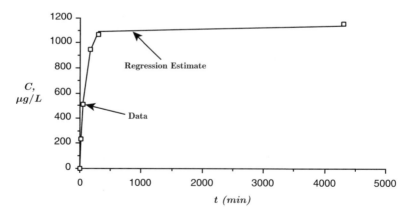

- **Key Point(s).** *This is another example of the utility of simple rate expressions for describing complex reactions and processes. In this case a first-order equation works well because it has the same linear-gradient form as a mass transfer expression.*

7.3 ANALYSIS OF REACTION RATES

7.3.1 Data

The suitability of any empirical rate expression for describing a particular reaction can be ascertained only by collecting and analyzing experimental rate data, as illustrated in Example 7.2. However, the proper rate model may not always be as simple to specify as it was in that example. In general, it is necessary as a first step to assess carefully all available information about the reactants and products. Not all reactants or products may be known, and this presents a problem at the outset of rate data analysis and modeling.

Rate expressions reported in the literature for reactions of interest should be verified before being used for the specific conditions and system of applications interest. Each environmental system contains a unique mix of dissolved and particulate chemical species that might affect the rate of a specific type of reaction, either by altering the rate constant or even the reaction mechanism.

Rate data are usually collected in CMBR systems operated at bench scale. The study of certain reactions may in some cases, however, require more sophisticated experimental designs. For example, a reaction may depend strongly on temperature and light, in which case these parameters must be carefully controlled. Heterogeneous reactions also require special consideration with respect to the intensity of mixing between reacting phases.

The reasons for selecting CMBRs whenever possible are two fold. First, the volume of sample required can be minimized, and a larger number of measurements formed. Second, regardless of how simple any experimental system appears, the interpretation of rate data involves several assumptions. The conditions associated with these assumptions must be satisfied in the experiment in order to make the interpretation valid. Such assumptions are explicitly clear if a system functions truly as a completely mixed batch reactor (i.e., closed, so the volume of its contents can be assumed to be constant if the sizes of samples are correspondingly small, and completely mixed, so the contents are homogeneous). If these conditions are not met, the relationships given in Equation 3.24 are not valid for interpretation of the data collected.

For those cases in which rate experiments can be conducted in CMBRs data collection is reasonably straightforward. As noted, sample requirements are minimal because the systems are closed. The reactor itself may be as simple as a flask that is shaken or stirred continuously in a manner that ensures complete mixing of its contents. Samples are then withdrawn at specific time intervals to allow measurement of residual concentrations of reactants or products. The ensuing discussion focuses on interpretation and modeling of experimental rate data collected in CMBRs. A rate expression can be readily obtained from such data using either integral or differential analysis. Several special methods for development of rate data will also be considered; these are referred to commonly as the half-life method, the method of excess, and the initial-rate method.

7.3.2   Integral Method of Analysis

This method of analysis uses the integrated form of an appropriate reaction rate expression to characterize observed data regarding the concentration of reactant remaining, or product generated, with time. The general material balance relationship for a CMBR of volume V_R is written from Equation 3.24 as

$$V_R \frac{dC}{dt} = r V_R \tag{7.33}$$

where r is the reaction rate and C is the concentration of the species of interest. Except for a zero-order reaction, r depends on the concentration of the reacting species, and possibly on the concentration of other species as well.

The most common approach to analysis of rate data is to assume a particular rate expression and determine whether the data are fit adequately by that expression. To illustrate application of the integral analysis approach, assume that a particular reaction depends on the concentration of only the ith species, ignoring the possibility of a more complex reaction in which other components may be involved. We can further assume that k is constant if experimental conditions (e.g., temperature and pH) are held constant. For these assumed conditions, $r = k\phi(C)$, and Equation 7.33 can be integrated by separation of variables to yield

$$\boxed{\textbf{\textit{General Integral}} \atop \textbf{\textit{Method Equation}} \qquad \int_{C_0}^{C} \frac{dC}{\phi(C)} = k \int_0^t dt = kt} \tag{7.34}$$

where C_0 is the initial concentration. Experimental values of C at each value of t are used to calculate the value of the integral on the left-hand side of Equation 7.34. If the proper rate expression has been selected for $\phi(C)$, a plot of this integral against time should yield a straight line, the slope of which yields the rate constant, k. A plot of this type is illustrated in Figure 7.1.

To demonstrate use of the integral method for testing the fits of several common rate models to experimental rate data, assume first that the rate of disappearance of a reactant is first order. In this case Equation 7.34 becomes

$$\boxed{\begin{array}{c} \textbf{\textit{First-Order Integral Method Equations}} \\[2mm] kt = - \int_{C_0}^{C} \frac{dC}{C} = \ln \frac{C_0}{C} \qquad (7.35) \\[2mm] \textbf{\textit{and}} \\[2mm] \ln C = \ln C_0 - kt \qquad (7.36) \end{array}}$$

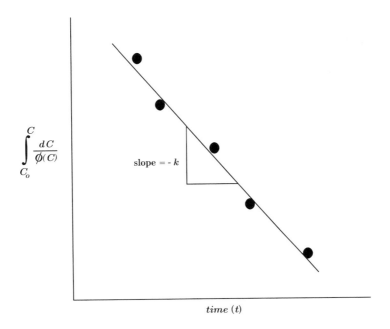

Figure 7.1 Integral Method of Rate Data Analysis

You will note from Equation 7.35 that this is precisely the approach used for data analysis in Example 7.2. If a plot of $\ln C$ (or $\log C$) versus t for a given set of experimental data is found within experimental error to be linear, the order of the reaction may be taken as unity, and the rate constant may be calculated directly from the slope, $-k$, of the resulting trace. A plot of this type is illustrated in Figure 7.2 for the decomposition of ozone in buffered aqueous solutions of different carbonate concentration. In this example, the rate constant decreases with increasing carbonate concentration because carbonate serves as a scavenger for hydroxyl radicals, which would otherwise promote ozone decomposition.

    The first-order rate model may also be tested in terms of the amount reacted, $C_R = (C_0 - C)$, rather than C. Substitution of C_R for C in Equation 7.36 gives an expression that is identical in form to Equation 7.13

$$\boxed{\begin{array}{ll} \textit{\textbf{Alternative Equation}} \\ \textit{\textbf{for First-Order}} & kt = \ln \dfrac{C_0}{C_0 - C_R} \\ \textit{\textbf{Integral Method}} \end{array}} \qquad (7.13)$$

and a plot of $\ln (C_0 - C_R)$ or $\log (C_0 - C_R)$ versus t should therefore be linear. This approach is particularly useful for analysis of BOD reaction rates, in that BOD is a measure of the amount reacted, and $C_0(C_{R,\infty})$ is an unknown quantity. Another example of a common circumstance in which Equation 7.13 can be put to good use is in the determination of rates of reaction of chlorine with

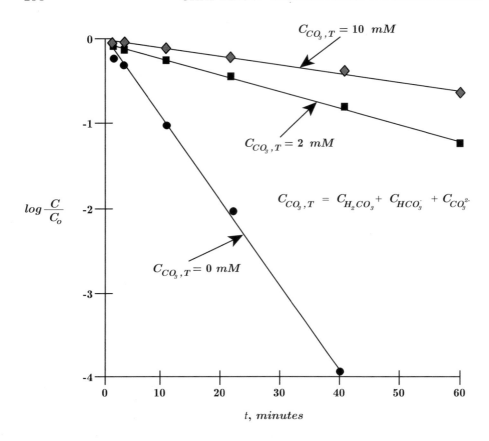

Figure 7.2 Statistical Best Fits (Solid Lines) of First-Order Rate
Equation to Experimental Data for Decomposition of
Ozone in Buffered Solutions (pH 7) of Different Carbon-
ate Concentration. (Adapted from Hull et al., 1992)

organic compounds during its use as a disinfectant. In such cases it may be
easier to measure a chlorinated product of a chlorine-substitution reaction than
its unchlorinated precursor. Suppose that A reacts to form B. The rate of
formation of B is then given by

$$r_B = kC_A \qquad (7.37)$$

and application of the material balance relationship yields

$$\frac{dC_B}{dt} = kC_A \qquad (7.38)$$

If the stoichiometry of the reaction specifies that 1 mole of B is formed for every
mole of A reacted, then C_A can be replaced by $C_{A,0} - C_B$. Equation 7.38 can

then be integrated to give

$$kt = -\ln \frac{C_{A,0} - C_B}{C_{A,0}} \tag{7.39}$$

or

$$\ln(C_{A,0} - C_B) = \ln C_{A,0} - kt \tag{7.40}$$

Because $C_A = C_{A,0} - C_B$ this equation is identical to Equation 7.36. We have shown therefore that the rate of formation of B is the same as the rate of disappearance of A. This must, in fact, be true to satisfy the stoichiometric relationship between A and B specified above for this particular reaction. Different stoichiometric relationships will yield correspondingly different relationships between the two rates. We can test the suitability of the first-order rate expression to describe the data by plotting $\ln(C_{A,0} - C_B)$ with time; the result should be a straight line with slope equal to the rate constant, k.

The rate expression for an elementary second-order reaction rate involving A and B was given in Equation 7.2. This can likewise be substituted into Equation 7.34 and integrated to reveal a linear relationship between C^{-1} and t similar to that given in Equation 7.7 for the case of two reactants having the same initial concentration. Equation 7.7 is equally applicable to a reaction that is second order with respect to the concentration of one reactant rather than first order with respect to each of two reactants. For testing of data in which we postulate the rate of disappearance of one reactant as second order, it is convenient to express Equation 7.7 in the form

$$kt = \frac{C_R}{C_0(C_0 - C_R)} \frac{C_0 - C}{C_0 C} = \frac{1}{C} - \frac{1}{C_0} \tag{7.41}$$

Accordingly, the experimental data should be linearized by plotting C^{-1} versus t, and the slope of this plot yields the value of the rate constant, k. Figure 7.3 is an illustration of such a plot.

Example 7.3 illustrates an application of the second-order model when the rate of a complex reaction can be treated as first order in each of two principal components. The reaction is in this case the chlorination of a specific organic compound formed in the pretreatment of water with ozone. The example also illustrates a somewhat different spin that can be put on the use of data for the amount of a substance reacted.

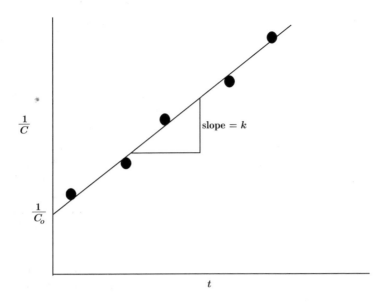

Figure 7.3 *Linearization of a Rate Equation for a Reaction That Is Second-Order with Respect to One Reactant*

Example 7.3. Reaction of Chlorine Added to Ensure a Disinfection Residual with Oxidation Products Produced During Primary Disinfection with Ozone. (An application of second-order rate equation to describe a complex process.)

- ***Situation.*** *Ozone enjoys widespread use as a disinfectant and oxidant in drinking water treatment. Because ozone decomposes rapidly, however, it is generally necessary to add a secondary disinfectant, such as chlorine, to ensure that the water has residual disinfection potential after it leaves a treatment plant. Health concerns have been raised about some of the by-products formed when ozone reacts with natural organic matter; more specifically, about the potential further reactions of these by-products with chlorine added for residual protection. As director of laboratories for the regional water supply system discussed in Example 7.1, you conduct a series of tests which show that chlorine can react with acetaldehyde (AcA) produced by ozonation to form other disinfection by-products, pursuant to the general reaction scheme*

$$\gamma Cl_2 + A \rightarrow \text{ products}$$

You suspect that the reaction pathway may involve an oxidation step followed by a series of chlorine substitution reactions leading to trichloroacetaldehyde (TCAcA), which would consume three moles of free chlorine *per mole of acetaldehyde (i.e., $\gamma = 3$). A CMBR rate experiment with acetaldehyde in excess shows, however, that the reaction is first order in chlorine, which suggests that it is probably nonelementary (if it were elementary, the reaction should be third order with respect to chlorine, given the presumed stoichiometry for trichloroacetaldehyde formation). Another experiment is designed so that the initial concentrations of chlorine and acetaldehyde are in the stoichiometric ratio of 3 to 1. Measurements of free chlorine residual FCR (i.e., not combined with products of acetaldehyde chlorination) with time are given below (data from McKnight and Reckow, 1992).*

Time (h)	FCR Concentration (mg/L)
0.1	3.6
13	3.3
29	2.7
59	2.4
72	2.1

- **Question(s).** *From the CMBR rate data provided, investigate the possibility of the reaction between chlorine and acetaldehyde being first order in each reactant and therefore second order overall.*

- **Logic and Answer(s).** *Assume from the hypothesis of trichloroacetaldehyde formation that*

$$3Cl_2 + A \rightarrow TCAcA$$

1. *Letting C_R be the moles of chlorine reacted per liter, we postulate that*

$$\frac{dC_R}{dt} = k \left(C_{Cl_2,0} - C_R \right) \left(C_{A,0} - C_R/3 \right)$$

The CMBR experiment was initiated with

$$C_{Cl_2,0} = 3C_{A,0}$$

so that

$$\frac{dC_R}{dt} = \frac{k}{3} \left(C_{Cl_2,0} - C_R \right) \left(C_{Cl_2,0} - C_R \right)$$

2. *We note that $C_R = C_{Cl_2,0} - C_{Cl_2}$ where C_{Cl_2} is the free chlorine residual remaining at time, t. Thus the rate expression above can be written in the simpler form*

$$-\frac{dC_{FCR}}{dt} = k' C_{FCR}^2$$

where $k' = k/3$. The rate data are now in a suitable form for testing by the integral method

$$\int_{C_{FCR,0}}^{C_{FCR}} \frac{dC_{FCR}}{C_{FCR}^2} = -k' \int_0^t dt$$

which yields

$$k't = C_{FCR}^{-1} - C_{FCR,0}^{-1}$$

As shown below, a plot of the reciprocal of C_{FCR} against time yields a straight line for which the slope determines the rate constant, $k' = k/3$.

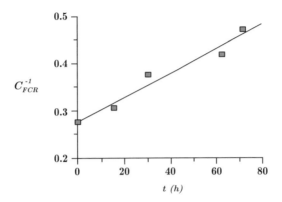

- **Key Point(s).** *The chlorosubstitution of background organic matter is in this case not as complex as that described in Example 7.1 because of the conversion of the organics by ozone pretreatment to a dominant end product. The approach to modeling can therefore in this case be somewhat less empirical in nature.*

The integral method applies equally well even when the assumed rate expression cannot be integrated analytically. In this instance, the right-hand side of Equation 7.34 can be integrated numerically from C_0 to any experimental value of C at time t.

Rate expressions and integrated material balance equations for forward reactions of different order with respect to one reactant in CMBR are summarized in Table 7.1. The first entry in this table is a zero-order reaction (i.e., a reaction in which the rate of change is independent of the concentration of the reactant). A zero-order reaction is unique in that the reaction rate is given simply by the rate constant, which in turn is given simply by the concentration reacted, C_R, over a given time $(ML^{-3}t^{-1})$. For other reaction orders, the dimensions of the rate constant vary and it is easy to show that they generalize to (concentration)$^{1-n}$ per unit time $[(ML^{-3})^{1-n}t^{-1}]$. The rate constant is dependent on the particular combination of reactants and products (reacted material C_R) and of course on the chemical nature of the reactants themselves, but it is independent of the initial concentration of reactant (to prove this, substitute $C_0 = C + C_R$ in the

Table 7.1 Rate Relationships for Reactions of Different Order with Respect to One Reactant

Reaction Order, n	Forward Reaction Rate, r	Rate Constant, k
0	k	C_R/t
0.5	$kC^{0.5} = k(C_0 - C_R)^{0.5}$	$\dfrac{2}{t}\left[C_0^{0.5} - (C_0 - C_R)^{0.5}\right]$
1	$kC = k(C_0 - C_R)$	$\dfrac{1}{t}\ln\dfrac{C_0}{C_0 - C_R}$
2	$kC^2 = k(C_0 - C_R)^2$	$\dfrac{C_R}{C_0 t(C_0 - C_R)}$
3	$kC^3 = k(C_0 - C_R)^3$	$\dfrac{2C_0 C_R - C_R^2}{2C_0^2 t(C_0 - C_R)^2}$

rate constant relationships given in Table 7.1). The rate constant also depends on temperature, as discussed in Chapter 8.

7.3.3 Differential Method of Analysis

The differential method of analysis involves approximating reaction rates from experimental measurements of changes in concentration over small increments in time. This method is especially convenient for complex rate expressions for which the integral method is cumbersome because numerical integration must be used, or where a rapid screening tool for a rate expression is sought. Values for the reaction rate, r, which is given by dC/dt (or dC_R/dt), can be determined for different stages of a reaction as the slopes or tangents of a plot of C (or C_R) versus t. This procedure is depicted in Figure 7.4a. The amount and quality of the rate data are critical to a close estimate of dC/dt by $\Delta C/\Delta t$.

If the reaction rate expression is of the general form, $r = \phi(k, C)$ and k is a constant for the experimental conditions, then the differential method gives

$$\frac{\Delta C}{\Delta t} \cong \frac{dC}{dt} = k\phi(C) \tag{7.42}$$

The values for $\Delta C/\Delta t$ (or $\Delta C_R/\Delta t$) are then plotted versus $\phi(C)$ to determine the validity of the rate model proposed. A first-order expression is confirmed if, as shown in Figure 7.4b, $\Delta C/\Delta t$ (or $\Delta C_R/\Delta t$) plots linearly against C. The slope of this plot is equal to the first-order rate constant, k. Several useful

a. Analysis of CMBR Rate Data

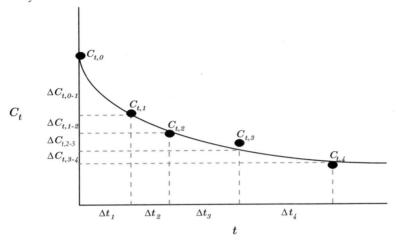

b. Confirmation of First-Order Reaction Rate and Evaluation of Rate Coefficient

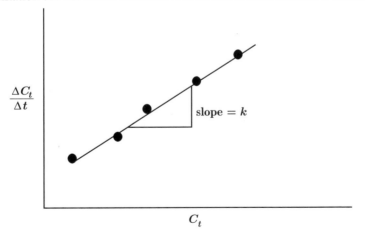

Figure 7.4 Differential Method for Rate Data Analysis

applications of this method will be illustrated in subsequent sections of this chapter.

7.3.4 Alternative Experimental Methods

7.3.4.1 Initial-Rate Method

The initial-rate method is an experimental variation on the differential rate method of analysis. The objective is to estimate the reaction rate that occurs at the initial concentration in the reaction vessel. Data to test the proposed rate expression are obtained by measuring the initial reaction rate in a series of experiments at different initial concentrations. This is equivalent to measuring the rate at various stages of reaction in a single experiment. The data are described by

$$\begin{array}{|c|c|} \hline \textit{Initial} & \left(\dfrac{\Delta C}{\Delta t}\right)_0 \cong \left(\dfrac{dC}{dt}\right)_0 = k\phi(C_0) \\ \textit{Rate Method} & \\ \hline \end{array} \qquad (7.43)$$

where $(\Delta C/\Delta t)_0$ is the experimental approximation of the initial-rate; the expression is otherwise identical to Equation 7.42.

An inherent assumption associated with using the initial-rate method is that ΔC is small enough to let $C = C_0$ over the entire period, Δt. An alternative form of this method involves measurement of the initial-rate of product formation instead of reactant consumption. As long as the reaction stoichiometry is known, product analysis may be preferred if the product is initially present in low concentration relative to the reactant. A significant change in concentration can thus be measured, in contrast to measurement of a small change in the much larger concentration of reactant.

7.3.4.2 Half-Life Method.

As the name implies, the half-life method involves experimental determination of a rate expression by analysis of the time required to decrease the reactant concentration by 50%. This method is applicable to any reaction of the general form

$$-r_A = kC^n \qquad (7.44)$$

The time to obtain a 50% reduction in C_o is given by the integral method as

$$k \int_0^{t_{0.5}} dt = - \int_{C_0}^{0.5C_0} \frac{dC}{C^n} \qquad (7.45)$$

Upon integration we obtain for n = 1

$$
\boxed{
\begin{array}{l}
\textbf{First-Order} \\
\textbf{Reaction} \\
\textbf{Half Life}
\end{array}
\quad
t_{0.5} = \frac{\ln 2}{k}
}
\tag{7.46}
$$

We conclude from Equation 7.46 that for a first-order reaction rate $(n = 1)$, the time required for the initial concentration to decrease by 50% is (1) independent of the initial concentration, and (2) a constant multiple of the first-order rate constant, k. The rate constant for such a reaction can thus be expressed in terms of its corresponding half-life. This is an important characteristic of first-order reactions. In other words, the time for the concentration to fall from C_0 to $0.5C_0$ is the same as the time for the concentration to fall from $0.5C_0$ to $0.25C_0$, and so on. The decay of a radioisotope is an example of this type of exponential process rate.

As shown in Equation 7.47, the half-life for an nth-order reaction in which $n \neq 1$ depends on the initial concentration.

$$
\boxed{
\begin{array}{l}
\textbf{nth Order } (n \neq 1) \\
\textbf{Reaction} \\
\textbf{Half Life}
\end{array}
\quad
\ln t_{0.5} = \ln \left[\frac{2^{n-1} - 1}{(n-1)k} \right] + (1 - n) \ln C_0
}
\tag{7.47}
$$

To test the suitability of this method for description of the rate data for any particular system, we need to conduct a series of half-life experiments in which the initial concentration is varied. If the resulting data are suitably described by this form of rate expression, a plot of $\ln t_{0.5}$ against $\ln C_0$ will be linear with a slope of $(1-n)$, as illustrated in Figure 7.5. Although we cannot use Equation 7.47 to test a first-order reaction, the same series of experiments will produce a slope of zero because the half-life is independent of initial concentration.

7.3.4.3 Method of Excess.

This experimental technique is designed and used to simplify the analysis of rates for reactions that involve two or more reactants. The concentrations of all but one reactant in the test reactor are maintained far in excess of stoichiometric requirements, and thus remain approximately constant over the course of the reaction. If the reaction rate expression is of the form

$$
r_B = -kC_A^n C_B^m
\tag{7.48}
$$

and A is present in excess, then

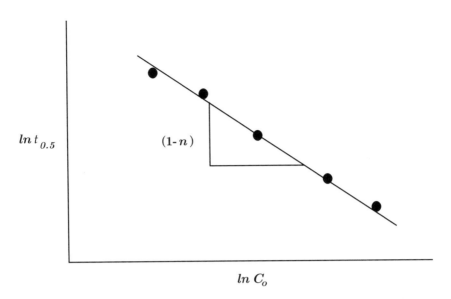

Figure 7.5 Half-Life Method for Evaluation of Reaction Rate Order

---

Method of Excess

$$\mathbf{r}_B = -k_{obs}C_B^m \qquad (7.49)$$

where

$$(7.50)$$

$$k_{obs} = k\left(C_A^n\right)_{Excess}$$

In other words, the effect of A on the reaction rate is accounted for in the observed reaction rate coefficient in the method of excess, and the reaction rate is pseudo m^{th} order with respect to B. The order of reaction with respect to B can be determined using either the integral method or the differential method of rate analysis described in Section 7.3. The dependency of rate on C_A in Equation 7.50 can be determined by conducting a series of experiments in which C_A is varied but always kept far in excess of the required stoichiometric amount. The intrinsic rate constant, k, and the order of the reaction with respect to A can be determined from the logarithmic transform of Equation 7.50

Intrinsic Rate Coefficient $\qquad \ln k = \ln k_{obs} - n \ln C_A \qquad (7.51)$

A plot of $\ln k_{obs}$ against $\ln C_A$ should produce a straight line from which both

n and k can be estimated.

The method of excess is most appropriate for development of initial-rate data because the reactant(s) which are added in excess remain so over the duration of the experiment. However, if more than initial-rate data are used, either the integral or differential methods of analysis can be applied as long as the reactant remains in excess throughout the time of data collection.

Example 7.4 provides a practical illustration of how the method of excess can be incorporated in an overall rate assessment and model development for a complex reaction scheme.

Example 7.4. Determination of a Reaction Rate Model for a New Synthesizing Reagent in a Chemical Production Plant. (An example of how an experimental technique can be used to develop more informative rate data.)

- **Situation.** *A new synthesizing reagent, A, is being considered as a means to minimize waste generation in the production of an organic chemical. Pilot tests of the synthesis have shown that A also slowly reacts with an impurity, I, in the chemical stock feed to form a side product, P, that may require an additional waste treatment step. No information is available on the stoichiometry of the reaction. Two series of laboratory flasks with stir bars were used to measure concentrations of P with time. In Series 1, the initial concentration of I was kept the same and the initial concentration of A was varied. In Series 2, the reverse was true. The concentrations of both I and A did not change significantly during the first 12 h of either test series, but trace amounts of P were detected and measured accurately. The data are given below.*

Rate Data for Series 1 $C_{I,0} = 2.0$ mmol/L		Rate Data for Series 2 $C_{A,0} = 240$ mmol/L	
C_P formed in first 12 hours, mmol/L$\times 10^3$	C_A added initially, mmol/L	C_P formed in first 12 hours, mmol/L$\times 10^3$	C_I added initially mmol/L$\times 10^3$
11.0	64.2	330	2500
40.9	139	250	1920
95.0	210	164	1360
138.0	263	109	1000
106.0	204	54.6	450

- **Question(s).** *Use the rate data to determine reaction orders with respect to the reactant and the impurity as well as the intrinsic rate constant.*

- **Logic and Answer(s).**

1. *With no information available on stoichiometry, a general rate model of the following form must be tested*

$$\frac{dC_P}{dt} = kC_I^n C_A^m$$

2. *The stirred laboratory flasks were sealed and well mixed and thus may be considered to have behaved as CMBRs. Because the concentrations of I and A did not decrease significantly during the 12-h test, the initial-rate method of analysis is appropriate for this very slow reaction. Thus, the rate of product formation is*

$$\frac{\Delta C_P}{12} \simeq \frac{dC_P}{dt}$$

3. *If the proposed rate model is valid, the data from series 1 should plot linearly according to*

$$\ln\left(\frac{\Delta C_P}{\Delta t}\right) = \ln(k_{obs})_1 + m \ln C_{A,0}$$

where

$$(k_{obs})_1 = kC_{I,0}^n$$

4. *The graph below shows a linear plot with a slope of $m = 1.85$. Given the small amount of data, an integral order of 2 for the reaction with respect to A is assumed. The intercept value gives*

$$(k_{obs})_1 = e^{-14.7} = 4.13 \times 10^{-7}$$

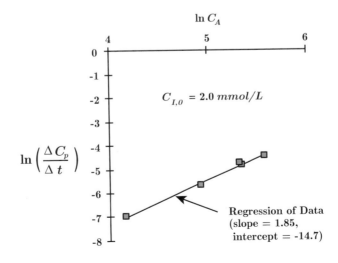

5. *The proposed rate model can also be tested to determine the order of the reaction with respect to I from the data in series 2*

$$\ln\left(\frac{\Delta C_P}{\Delta t}\right)_1 = \ln(k_{obs})_2 + n\ln(C_{I,0})_1$$

where

$$(k_{obs})_2 = kC_{A,0}^m$$

6. *The resulting fit to the model is shown below.*

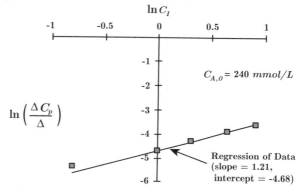

The slope of the plot is $n = 1.2$, *which suggests an integer first-order dependency on I. The intercept value then gives*

$$(k_{obs})_2 = e^{-4.68} = 9.28 \times 10^{-3} h^{-1}$$

7. *The intrinsic rate constant, k, should be the same for the data obtained in both series.*

$$k\mid_{series\ 1} = \frac{(k_{obs})_2}{C_{I,0}} = \frac{4.13 \times 10^{-7}}{2.0} = 2.07 \times 10^{-7} L^2(mol^2 - h)^{-1}$$

$$k\mid_{series\ 2} = \frac{(k_{obs})_1}{C_{A,0}^2} = \frac{9.28 \times 10^{-3}}{[240]^2} = 1.61 \times 10^{-7} L^2(mol^2 - h)^{-1}$$

Values of the intrinsic rate constant are thus similar for both series. In summary, then, the following rate relationship is suggested

$$\frac{dC_P}{dt} = kC_I C_A^2$$

- **Key Point(s).** **Given that the data are limited and that the agreement with the assumed elementary reaction is not exact, more rate data should be obtained before accepting the rate relationship determined above. To add further validity, series 1 could be repeated with a different $C_{I,0}$ and series 2 with a different $C_{A,0}$. These data would yield different values of k_{obs} in proportion to the values of $C_{I,0}$ and $C_{A,0}$ that were used.**

7.3.5 Precautions

The suitability of any rate expression for description of a particular set of data is determined by assessing the degree to which it captures the $C - t$ trend of that data. For example, a first-order rate expression is tested in the integral method by plotting $\ln C_0/C$ versus t and a second-order expression by plotting C^{-1} versus t. A given rate expression is a good candidate for use if the data are successfully fit when plotted according to the normalized version of that rate expression, and within the limits of experimental error, each combination of C and t within the set is accounted for by the calculated value for k. An alternative to the graphical approach is to perform either a linear or a nonlinear (or both) regression of the data and statistically evaluate goodness of fit.

After selecting a rate expression and determining a coefficient from the initial data for the same temperature but for a different initial concentration, C_O should be obtained. A test of the rate expression for the new data should then be carried out and a second value for k obtained. If the second value of k is essentially the same as that calculated from the first set of experimental data (again within limits of experimental error), the rate expression is probably applicable for description of the particular chemical reaction and conditions under consideration. The larger the number of such iterative tests the more extensive of course will be the evaluation of applicability.

Experimental errors in rate data will often introduce some uncertainty in the selection of an appropriate rate expression. To judge whether the data conform to the linearized form of a particular rate expression, it is important to distinguish between experimental error and systematic error. When data are tightly but randomly scattered about the linear trace given by a normalized rate expression, experimental error is likely, but if the data consistently diverge from a linear trace as time increases, systematic error due to an inappropriate choice of rate model is suggested.

When a given set of data are only approximately normalized by the linear form of a rate model, alternative expressions should be tested to determine whether better agreement can be obtained. Rate models corresponding to simple elementary reactions (typically first or second order) are the logical first choices for testing. However, we also must recognize that nonelementary reactions are possible, in which case trial-and-error evaluations of alternative rate expressions may be necessary.

7.4 CHAPTER SUMMARY

Significant challenges are presented in the application of rate relationships to transformations in environmental systems because: (1) not all reactants may be known, so that chemicals must be lumped into surrogate or group parameters; (2) reaction pathways may be complex and poorly understood, so that empirical rate expressions are needed; (3) many reactions (some unknown) may occur simultaneously, so that only an overall rate can be expressed with confidence; and (4) reactions of interest may occur either too fast or too slow to allow convenient measurement, so that rate experiments must be designed carefully.

The rate expressions developed in Chapter 7 and the experimental methods described for their determination have been illustrated using reactions of interest in dilute aqueous solutions. However, the same principles employed can be extended to other important environmental conditions. Reactions in concentrated aqueous solutions (where concentration is adjusted for activity) and nonaqueous solutions (including air and organic solvents) can be analyzed similarly. Experimentally determined rate relationships have been emphasized because this is state of the art for complex environmental systems. Rate expressions and rate constants reported in the literature for reactions that are similar, but not necessarily the same, are often useful starting points for the design of such experimental determinations.

7.5   CITATIONS AND SOURCES

Amy, G.L., P.A. Chadik, and Z.K. Chowdury, 1987, "Developing Models for Predicting Trihalomethane Formation Potential and Kinetics," *Journal of the American Water Works Association, 79* (7), 89-97. (Example 7.1)

Grimberg, S.J., M.D. Aitken, and W.T. Stringfellow, 1994, "The Influence of a Surfactant on the Rate of Phenanthrene Mass Transfer into Water," *Water Science and Technology 30(7)*, 23-30. (Example 7.2)

Hull, C.S., P.C. Singer, K. Saravan, K., and C.T. Miller, 1992, "Ozone Mass Transfer and Reaction: Completely Mixed Systems," *Proceedings of the 1992 American Water Works Association Annual Conference*, Vancouver, British Columbia, pp. 457-465 (Figure 7.2 and Problem 7.2).

McKnight, A. and D.A. Reckhow, 1992, "Reactions of Ozonation Byproducts with Chlorine and Chloramines," *Proceedings of the 1992 American Water Works Association Annual Conference*, Vancouver, British Columbia, pp. 399-409. (Example 7.3)

Snider, E.H. and F.C. Alley, 1979, "Kinetics of the Chlorination of Biphenyl under Conditions of Waste Treatment Processes," *Environmental Science and Technology, 13*, 1244-1248. (Problem 7.3)

Weber, W.J., Jr. and F.A. DiGiano, 1996, *Process Dynamics in Environmental Systems*, John Wiley & Sons, Inc., New York. General source of all material presented in Chapter 7. Chapter 7 of PDES, which is also the source of the material covered in Chapter 8, provides additional details not presented in either Chapters 7 or 8 of this book, particularly on complex reaction rates.

7.6 PROBLEM ASSIGNMENTS

7.1 The following reaction is carried out in a 10-L aqueous solution in a stirred tank

$$A + B \Rightarrow AB$$

At the outset of the reaction the reagents A and B are added to the reactor in equal 1-mole quantities. After 10 minutes the concentration of AB in the reactor is measured as 5 mmol/L. Determine an appropriate rate constant. State all assumptions made in arriving at your answer.

7.2 The oxidation of Fe(II) by oxygen is carried out in a solution buffered at pH 7.0 and in contact with an airstream that contains an essentially constant partial pressure of oxygen (and, therefore, an essentially constant dissolved oxygen concentration) at 20°C. The following data are collected

Time (min)	Fe(II) $\times 10^5 M$
0	3.3
5	2.1
10	1.3
15	0.82
20	0.59
25	0.32

The reaction is postulated to be first order each with respect to Fe(II) and p_{O_3} and second order with respect to OH^-. Verify the first-order dependency on Fe(II) and determine the rate constant.

7.3 Disinfection of anthrax spores in a CMBR yields the data

Time (min)	Number of Survivors
0	400
100	100
200	18
300	3
410	1

Assuming a first-order dependency on number of survivors, find the corresponding rate constant.

7.4 A radioactive waste contains 2 curies (Ci) of ^{60}Co per liter and 2 mCi of ^{45}Ca per liter. The waste can be discharged only if its total activity does not exceed 20 μCi/L. If the half-life of ^{60}Co is 10.7 min and that of ^{45}Ca is 152 days, determine how long the waste must be stored before it can be discharged.

Answer: 1010 d.

7.5 Given the elementary and reversible reaction shown below, develop an equation to support your discussion of why the net (forward) rate of the reaction might be enhanced by either adding reactant(s) or by removing the products of the reaction as they are formed. Clearly state all assumptions involved in your work.

$$A + B \underset{k_2}{\overset{k_1}{\rightleftharpoons}} C + D$$

7.6 Ozone decomposes in water according to the reaction

$$2O_3 \Rightarrow 3O_2$$

measurements residual ozone concentration, C_{O_3}, in an aqueous solution of pH 9 as a function of time in a CMBR and in the absence of any constituent which may be oxidized yield the data set

Time (sec)	$C_{O_3} mg/L$
0	2.00
30	1.50
60	1.05
90	0.82
120	0.57

It is thought that the rate of ozone decomposition is nonelementary (i.e., that the decomposition proceeds through a series of intermediate steps). Use the data set given and the integral method of analysis to determine the effective order of the reaction and the value of the associated rate coefficient.

7.7 Rates of ozone decomposition are retarded by carbonate ions, which act as hydroxyl radical scavengers. Three sets of batch data collected at pH 7.0 with the same carbonate concentration (0.01 molar total carbonate species) and three different initial ozone concentrations are given below (Hull et al., 1992). Also shown is one set of data without addition of carbonate. Verify the order of the rate of decomposition determined in Problem 7.5 and determine the effect of the carbonate on the rate coefficient.

Time (min)	C_{O_3}, mg/L — For $CO_{3,T} = 0.01$ mol/L			For $CO_{3,T} = 0$
0	0.3	1.0	3.0	3.0
1	0.28	0.98	2.71	2.24
3	0.27	0.89	2.63	1.99
10	0.23	0.80	2.11	1.12
20	0.20	0.70	1.98	0.46
40	0.16	0.53	1.40	0.06
60		0.36	0.90	

7.8 Use the differential method, the data set given in Problem 7.5, the data set in Problem 7.7 for $C_{CO_{3,T}} = 0.01$mol/L, and an initial ($t = 0$) value of $C_{O_3} = 1.0$mg/L to verify the reaction rate order and the effect of carbonate. Compare your results with those obtained using the integral rate analysis.

7.9 Biphenyl (BP) is used as a dye carrier in the textile industry and is thus potentially present in wastewaters from such facilities. The discharge of such wastewater to a publicly owned treatment facility where chlorine is used for odor control could allow for reaction with BP to form *o*-chlorobiphenyl (OCBP). Snider and Alley (1979) studied the kinetics of chlorination of BP and proposed that the formation of OCBP is given by

$$\frac{dC_{OCBP}}{dt} = kC_{BP}C_{HOCL}^2$$

where HOCl is undissociated hypochlorous acid and all concentrations are on a molar basis. The protolysis constant for HOCl is given by

$$K_a = \frac{C_{H^+}C_{OCl^-}}{C_{HOCl}} = 3.66 \times 10^{-8}$$

The rate of formation of OCBP, and the initial-rate method was therefore used for verification of reaction order. The initial-rate is calculated by measuring the C_{OCBP} after 12 h. Verify the rate relationship and show that the rate constant, k, is about the same in each data set.

Molecular weights (g/mol): BP = 154 ; OCBP = 188.5; HOCl = 52.5

C_{BP}, mg/L	$C_{(HOCl)_T}$, mg/L	pH	C_{OCBP}, µg/L after 12 h
3770	17.9	7.0	1.2
″	38.5	″	5.7
″	54.7	″	11.0
″	74.7	″	23.0
″	90.5	″	34.3
3400	247	6.78	222
2720	″	″	163
2040	″	″	122
1360	″	″	83.4
680	″	″	42.5
3590	304	7.06	187
″	″	7.47	92.0
″	″	8.04	18.4
″	″	8.31	7.4
″	″	9.17	3.4

7.10 A steel industry waste stream referred to as a "pickling liquor" generally contains very high concentrations of ferrous iron [Fe(II)]. The iron is typically removed by oxidizing it to [Fe(III)], and precipitating it as ferric hydroxide. The process involves the reactions

$$\frac{1}{4}O_2 + Fe^{2+} + H^+ \Leftrightarrow Fe^{3+} + \frac{1}{2}H_2O$$

$$Fe^{3+} + 3OH^- \Leftrightarrow Fe(OH)_3(s) \downarrow$$

The rate constant, k_2, for the second reaction is much larger than that for the first, k_1.

(a) Develop a rate expression for the overall treatment process, being sure to define the resultant $k_{overall}$ in terms of the given variables and appropriate units.

(b) An experiment in a CMBR is conducted to determine the reaction rate coefficient for the expression you've developed in part (a). The concentration of Fe^{2+} in the reactor is observed to decrease over time from an initial value of $[Fe^{2+}]_0 = 20$ mg/L to a final value of $[Fe^{2+}] = 10$ mg/L 45 minutes later. If the initial O_2 concentration of the water in the reactor was 8 mg/L, what is the final O_2 concentration at 45 min? Can you obtain a reaction rate coefficient from this data set using one or more of the various methods presented in this Chapter? If so, explain how; if not, explain why.

(c) If your answer to the last question in part (b) is no, describe some alternative method of analysis and/or experimental design to verify the overall rate expression developed in part (a) and to determine the value of the reaction rate coefficient.

Chapter 8

Complex Process Rates

Contents

8.0   CHAPTER OBJECTIVES

To extend the fundamental reaction rate concepts learned in Chapter 7 to the interpretation and modeling of some complex reaction schemes frequently encountered in environmental processes and systems.

8.1   COMPLEX REACTION RATES

8.1.1   Sequential Reactions

Complex environmental processes often proceed through a number of consecutive reaction stages or steps. For example, the formation of a product, C, from a reactant, A, may involve the formation of an intermediate species, B. A reaction sequence of this type can be represented by the scheme

$$
\boxed{\quad \textbf{\textit{Sequential}} \qquad \\ \textbf{\textit{Reaction}} \qquad A \overset{r_1}{\Longrightarrow} B \overset{r_2}{\Longrightarrow} C \\ \textbf{\textit{Scheme}} \qquad\quad} \tag{8.1}
$$

where r_1 represents the rate of formation of the intermediate B from the reactant A, and r_2 the rate of the formation of the final product C from the intermediate B. The temporal distributions of species for a reaction scheme of this type are depicted in Figure 8.1. The successive chlorination of ammonia (NH_3) to form monochloramine and dichloramine is an example of such a reaction sequence, as is the oxidation of cyanide (CN^-) to cyanate (CNO^-) by chlorine followed by acid hydrolysis of the cyanate to ammonia.

In that many environmental reactions are either first order or can be approximated as such, we will focus our discussion of sequential reaction rates on series of first-order rate expressions. For a series of sequential first-order reactions in a CMBR, the time rate of decrease of the reactant A is expressed as

$$
r_1 = \frac{dC_A}{dt} = -k_1 C_A \tag{8.2}
$$

and the rate of increase of the product C as

$$
r_2 = \frac{dC_C}{dt} = k_2 C_B \tag{8.3}
$$

The rate of change of the concentration of the intermediate B depends on the net difference between the two reaction rates; i.e.,

$$
r_1 - r_2 = \frac{dC_B}{dt} = k_1 C_A - k_2 C_B \tag{8.4}
$$

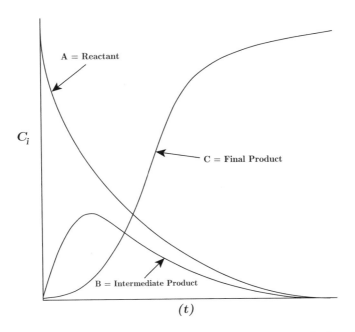

Figure 8.1 Species Distribution in a Series of First-Order Reactions

The concentration of the reactant steadily decreases with time, whereas the concentration of final product steadily increases. The concentration of the intermediate, conversely, increases steadily to some maximum value, after which it steadily decreases.

Upon integration, Equations 8.2 through 8.4 can be written respectively in terms of the initial concentration of the reactant A, as follows

> ### Reactant and Product Concentrations in a First-Order Reaction Sequence
>
> $$C_A = C_{A,o}e^{-k_1 t}$$
>
> $$\quad (8.5)$$
>
> $$C_B = \frac{k_1 C_{A,o}}{k_2 - k_1}[e^{-k_1 t} - e^{-k_2 t}]$$
>
> $$\quad (8.6)$$
>
> $$C_C = C_{A,o}\left[1 + \frac{k_1 e^{-k_2 t}}{k_2 - k_1} - \frac{k_2 e^{-k_1 t}}{k_2 - k_1}\right]$$
>
> $$\quad (8.7)$$

Consecutive reaction schemes are very common in environmental processes and systems. Fortunately, we are frequently able to approximate the rates for such overall reaction schemes in terms of the slowest in the series; i.e., the "rate limiting step" approach. It is *not uncommon for one of the steps in a consecutive series to be significantly slower than any of the others. Under such conditions, the overall reaction rate is controlled essentially by the rate of that slowest step, which then becomes rate limiting. For example, if the rate r_1 of the reaction given in Equation 8.1 is much slower than the rate r_2, then $k_1 \ll k_2$ and Equation 8.7 may be closely approximated by*

$$\boxed{\begin{array}{l} \textit{\textbf{Approximation}} \\ \textit{\textbf{of Equation 8.7}} \quad C_C \approx C_{A,o}(1 - e^{-k_1 t}) \\ \textit{\textbf{for }} k_1 \ll k_2 \end{array}} \qquad (8.8)$$

This approach is often extended beyond consecutive reactions to processes that involve reaction and transport (particularly microscale) steps in series. We will discuss these cases further in Chapters 14-16.

8.1.2   Parallel Reactions

A number of reactive species may in any environmental process be involved in two or more reaction schemes concurrently. Chlorine and ozone, for example, can simultaneously oxidize inorganic and organic compounds while also causing disinfection of microorganisms, and chlorine can simultaneously react with ammonia and phenol to form chloramines and chlorophenols. In other words, a reactant A might undergo two or more parallel and unrelated reactions to form multiple products, such as B and C in the essentially irreversible reaction scheme

$$\boxed{\begin{array}{c} \textit{\textbf{Parallel Reaction Scheme}} \\[2ex] A \xrightarrow{\ r_1\ } B \\[2ex] A \xrightarrow{\ r_2\ } C \end{array}}$$
$$(8.9)$$
$$(8.10)$$

The overall rate of disappearance of reactant A is for this case given by the sum of the rates r_1 and r_2, or

$$-\frac{dC_A}{dt} = r_1 + r_2 \qquad (8.11)$$

If the reactions given in Equations 8.9 and 8.10 are both first order with respect to C_A, then Equation 8.11 may be written

---

Parallel First-Order Reaction Rate

$$\frac{-dC_A}{dt} = k_1C_A + k_2C_A = (k_1 + k_2)C_A$$

(8.12)

The overall reaction is thus first order with respect to C_A, with the effective rate constant given by the sum of the rate constants for the individual first-order reactions. This is true regardless of the number of parallel first-order reactions involved.

The general form of Equation 8.12 is in fact not limited to first order reactions. It holds for all parallel schemes of reactions having the same order. That is, as long as the parallel reactions are of common order, the overall rate constant for disappearance of the reactant(s) is always determined by adding together the individual rate constants. Accordingly, for the elementary parallel reactions

$$aA + bB \xrightarrow{\; r_1 \;} C \tag{8.13}$$

$$aA + bB \xrightarrow{\; r_2 \;} D \tag{8.14}$$

$$aA + bB \xrightarrow{\; r_3 \;} E \tag{8.15}$$

*the overall rate of disappearance of reactant **A** is given by*

$$-\frac{dC_A}{dt} = r_1 + r_2 + r_3 \tag{8.16}$$

and, if the reaction orders are in each case defined by the stoichiometric coefficients a and b

---

Parallel Common-Order Reaction Rate

$$\frac{-dC_A}{dt} = k_1C_A^aC_B^b + k_2C_A^aC_B^b + k_3C_A^aC_B^b = (k_1 + k_2 + k_3)C_A^aC_B^b$$

(8.17)

If the parallel reactions are not of the same order, the overall rate of change of the reactant of interest can still be written in terms of the sum of the rates of the individual reactions as in Equation 8.16, but the individual coefficients cannot be aggregated in the manner shown in Equations 8.12 and 8.17.

8.1.3 Reversible Reactions

We have to this point assumed that reaction schemes are essentially irreversible. In so doing we have not necessarily assumed true thermodynamic irreversibility. Rather, we have simply assumed that the state of the reaction under consideration is far removed from the state of thermodynamic equilibrium. The assumption is generally valid for the initial stages of most reactions and is especially so for reactions in which the equilibrium state favors a very high product to reactant ratio; i.e., when the equilibrium constant for the reaction is large.

In some environmental processes and systems a reaction may not be sufficiently far removed from equilibrium to justify an assumption of irreversibility, and in such cases we cannot neglect the rates of reverse reactions. This is particularly true when high relative concentrations of reactants remain at the final position of equilibrium; i.e., for reactions having relatively small equilibrium constants. Indeed, as any reversible reaction proceeds toward an equilibrium state the rate at which product species revert to reactant species becomes more and more significant. As the rate of the reverse reaction becomes appreciable, it has the net effect of decreasing the observed or net rate of reaction in the forward direction. For such cases it is necessary to employ an expression that takes account of reaction rates in both forward and reverse directions.

The development of rate expressions for reversible reactions lies beyond the scope of this text. The reader should consult PDES for full discussions of such rate expressions. The purpose of this section of Chapter 8 is simply to caution that the rate relationships presented here are applicable only for situations in which the assumption of irreversibility is valid, and to alert the reader to general types of applications in which the assumption is not valid.

8.1.4 Reaction Rates and Thermodynamics

Although the equilibrium constant of a reaction is based on thermodynamic principles (e.g., Equation 6.24, $K = exp(-\Delta G_r/\mathcal{R}T)$), it also defines the ratio of the forward and reverse rate constants associated with a Law of Mass Action (Mass Law) characterization of reaction rate orders (i.e., reaction orders given by the stoichiometric coefficients of the reaction). This "kinetic" interpretation of the equilibrium constant is intuitive for elementary reactions as demonstrated for the reversible elementary reaction given in Equation 7.21 of Chapter 7. It is not necessarily intuitive for nonelementary reactions, although we stated in Section 7.1.2 of Chapter 7 that it is valid for such reactions as well. If we can in fact apply mass law relationships between the energies and rates of reactions to nonelementary processes we can use thermodynamic information to provide valuable insight into certain kinetic aspects of a system that otherwise may not be feasible or easy to measure experimentally. It therefore behooves us to convince ourselves that this is so.

The nonelementary reaction scheme presented in Section 7.1.3 of Chapter 7 will be used here to demonstrate the validity of the mass law relationship between kinetics and thermodynamics for such reactions. In that instance, two irreversible elementary reaction steps (Equations 7.24 and 7.25) were combined to yield a nonelementary scheme. The more general situation in which both steps are reversible will be analyzed here. We begin with Equation 7.24

$$\text{A} \underset{k_2}{\overset{k_1}{\rightleftharpoons}} \text{A}^* \tag{7.24}$$

and, a modified (i.e., reversible) version of Equation 7.25

$$\text{A}^* + \text{B} \underset{k_4}{\overset{k_3}{\rightleftharpoons}} \text{AB} \tag{8.18}$$

The condition of equilibrium for each elementary reaction can be expressed as

$$K_{1-2} = \frac{C_{A^*}}{C_A} = \frac{k_1}{k_2} \quad \text{and} \quad K_{3-4} = \frac{C_{AB}}{C_{A^*}C_B} = \frac{k_3}{k_4} \tag{8.19}$$

Pursuant to the treatment discussed in Chapter 5 for the addition of reactions (e.g., Example 5.3) we obtain the equilibrium constant for the overall reaction by multiplying the equilibrium constants for each of the summed reactions

$$K_{1-4} = K_{1-2} \cdot K_{3-4} = \frac{C_{AB}}{C_A C_B} = \frac{k_3}{k_4} \frac{k_1}{k_2} \tag{8.20}$$

The equilibrium constant defined by Equation 8.20 can now be compared to that derived from kinetic considerations.

Irrespective of the nature of the forward and reverse reaction rate expressions, these may be equated for the condition of thermodynamic equilibrium, for equilibrium is defined (Chapter 6) as the state for which the net reaction velocity, r_{net}, is zero ($r_{net} = r_f - r_r = 0$). At equilibrium the net rate of change of each component is zero because the concentration of each component remains constant.

The law of mass action also applies at equilibrium, so that

$$r_{A^*} = 0 = k_1 C_A - k_2 C_{A^*} - k_3 C_{A^*} C_B + k_4 C_{AB} \tag{8.21}$$

$$r_A = 0 = -k_1 C_A + k_2 C_{A^*} \tag{8.22}$$

Equation 8.21 can be rearranged to solve for C_{A^*}, yielding

$$C_{A^*} = \frac{k_1 C_A + k_4 C_{AB}}{k_2 + k_3 C_B} \tag{8.23}$$

and then substituted into Equation 8.22 to obtain

$$\frac{C_{AB}}{C_A C_B} = \frac{k_3}{k_4} \frac{k_1}{k_2} = K_{1-4} \tag{8.24}$$

Equation 8.24 is identical to Equation 8.20, proving that the equilibrium constant for a nonelementary reaction is defined by the ratio of the products of the rate coefficients associated with each step in the reaction scheme. Thus, for the condition or state of equilibrium, the equilibrium constant, K, is given by the ratio of the forward and reverse rate coefficients, regardless of the forms of the rate equations.

Examination of Equations 8.20 and 8.24 further reveals that the ratio of the forward and reverse reaction rates for a complex reaction can be directly related to the overall free energy for that reaction. This relationship becomes evident on substitution of the following terms for the reaction rate constants in Equation 8.20

$$k_1 = \frac{r_1}{C_A} \; ; \; k_2 = \frac{r_2}{C_{A^*}} \; ; \; k_3 = \frac{r_3}{C_A \cdot C_B} \; ; \; \text{and,} \; k_4 = \frac{r_4}{C_{AB}} \qquad (8.25)$$

Thus we have

$$K = \left(\frac{r_3}{C_{A^*} C_B}\right) \left(\frac{r_1}{C_A}\right) \left(\frac{C_{AB}}{r_4}\right) \left(\frac{C_{A^*}}{r_2}\right) \qquad (8.26)$$

$$K = \left(\frac{r_3 r_1}{r_4 r_2}\right) \left(\frac{C_{AB}}{C_A C_B}\right) = \left(\frac{r_3 r_1}{r_3 r_2}\right) Q_r \qquad (8.27)$$

Substitution of Equation 8.27 into Equation 6.25 then yields

$$dG_r \mid_{T,P} = \mathcal{R}T \ln \frac{Q_r}{K} = \mathcal{R}T \ln \left(\frac{r_4 r_2}{r_3 r_1}\right) \qquad (8.28)$$

or, more generally

$$dG_r \mid_{T,P} = \mathcal{R}T \ln \left(\frac{r_R}{r_F}\right)_{overall} \qquad (8.29)$$

We may thus conclude that the equilibrium mass law relationships between reaction kinetics and reaction thermodynamics apply to the nonelementary reaction scheme given by combining Equations 7.24 and 8.18 above. They are, in fact, general and applicable to all nonelementary reactions. We observe also that, although the net overall reaction rate is zero at equilibrium, the individual rates of reaction in the forward and reverse directions may be large. Indeed, the magnitude of the equilibrium reaction rate is a measure of the degree of reversibility of a reaction; the higher that rate, the higher the degree of reversibility.

8.1.5   Modified First-Order Expressions

Nonelementary reaction schemes similar to those discussed above are frequently encountered in environmental processes and systems. While it is sometimes possible in such cases to determine appropriate rate expressions by careful analyses of pathways for reactions conducted in well controlled laboratory experiments, there are many instances in which the information required for such rigorous treatment is not available. This is especially true if the data to be interpreted has been collected under field conditions that constrain the analysis and render sophisticated interpretation neither possible nor warranted.

It is a reality of nature that many very complex processes that occur in the environment, and in living systems in general, exhibit rate behaviors that reasonably approximate those of first-order phenomena, and the first-order rate equation is therefore frequently employed empirically to represent such behaviors. This is in fact often the only approach possible when data are limited and difficult to obtain. The first-order approximation is appropriate and valid as long as interpretations and generalizations are constrained accordingly.

It is commonly observed that first-order expressions applied in an empirical way to environmental processes and systems provide a good fit of observed data only over limited ranges, and that adjustments in rate parameter values are required to fit other ranges of the data. Gradual deviations of data trends from apparent first-order behavior are suggestive of nonelementary reactions having rates of progression that gradually either decrease or increase with time. Biochemical transformations of organic substrates often manifest this type of rate behavior.

A reaction rate that appears initially to be of the first order but which then is observed to decrease with time is said to be retarded, while one that increases with time is termed accelerative. The effect of such behavior on the fitting of a first-order rate expression is either to decrease or increase the apparent (measured) value of the rate "constant," k, with increased period of experimental observation. It is possible to accommodate gradual deviations of retarded and accelerative reaction rates in an empirical way by incorporating "sliding" factors in the elementary first-order rate equation.

In some cases good approximations to extended data sets can be made if the first-order equation is modified by dividing the rate constant by a factor that increases with increasing time for purposes of modeling retarded reaction rates. By doing so, and by writing the CMBR material balance equation in terms of the concentration of reactant that has reacted, we obtain the expression

$$
\boxed{
\begin{array}{c}
\textit{Differential Form of Retarded} \\
\textit{First-Order Rate Equation} \\[2mm]
\dfrac{dC_R}{dt} = \dfrac{k}{1 + \alpha_r t}(C_0 - C_R)
\end{array}
}
\tag{8.30}
$$

where α_r is a reaction-characteristic coefficient. Integration of Equation 8.30 yields

$$
\frac{k}{\alpha_r} \ln \frac{1}{1 + \alpha_r t} = \ln \frac{C_0 - C_R}{C_0}
\tag{8.31}
$$

or

> ### Integrated Form of Retarded
> ### First-Order Rate Equation
>
> $$C_R = C_0[1 - (1 + \alpha_r t)^{-k/\alpha_r}]$$

(8.32)

Introduction of α_r requires determination of an additional unknown, which can be done using nonlinear regression analysis and a two-parameter search routine to find the best fit of the experimental data.

An accelerative reaction is one for which rate appears to increase spontaneously as time progresses. An acceleration in rate is usually effected by the action of one of the products of the reaction. If that product is not changed or transformed in its reaction-accelerating role, the reaction can properly be termed autocatalytic. When reaction rates become dependent on the concentration(s) of product(s) formed as well as on the concentration(s) of reactant(s), the first-order expression may be modified to yield the differential form of the accelerative first order rate equation

> ### Differential Form of Accelerative
> ### First- Order Rate Equation
>
> $$\frac{dC_R}{dt} = k_1(C_0 - C_R) + k_2(C_0 - C_R)C_R$$

(8.33)

The first term on the right-hand side of Equation 8.33 is an elementary first-order equation. The second term expresses the rate acceleration factor as the product of a second rate constant, the remaining concentration of reactant, and the amount reacted or concentration of product formed. This term increases geometrically with time to a maximum value of $0.25\, C_0^2 k_2$, and decreases thereafter. The acceleration causes an increase in the forward rate of reaction that is especially noticeable if $k_2 >> k_1$. However, the subsequent pattern of decrease of reaction rate from its maximum value will not be precisely the reverse of its pattern of approach to this maximum. The integrated form of Equation 8.33 is

> ### Integrated Form of Accelerative
> ### First-Order Rate Equation
>
> $$(k_1 + k_2 C_0)t = \ln \frac{C_0(k_2 C_R + k_1)}{k_1(C_0 - C_R)} = \ln \frac{C_0[k_2(C_0 - C_t) + k_1]}{k_1 C_t}$$

(8.34)

where C_t is the concentration of reactant remaining at time t. This equation is used for describing rate data which follow the general S-shaped pattern illustrated by the solid line in Figure 8.2.

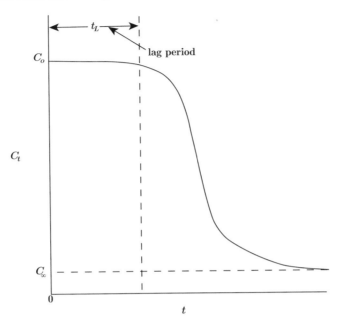

Figure 8.2 Lag-Period Approximation of Accelerative First-Order Rate Behavior

It is often convenient and permissible to approximate accelerating rate behavior by neglecting the initial portion of the S- curve and considering the remainder as an elementary first-order reaction having a delayed starting point, as indicated by the vertical dashed line in Figure 8.2. This approximation amounts to introducing a lag period in the first-order rate expression. If t_L is designated as the value of t at the end of the lag period (as noted in Figure 8.2) and $t \geq t_L$, then the first-order rate expression may be written as

$$
\begin{array}{|c|}
\hline
\textit{Lag-Period Approximation of Accelerative} \\
\textit{First-Order Rate Behavior} \\
\\
k(t - t_L) = \ln \dfrac{C_0}{C_0 - C_R} \\
\hline
\end{array}
$$

(8.35)

or

$$C_t = C_0 - C_R = C_0 e^{-k(t-t_L)}$$

(8.36)

If the lag period, t_L, is constant for a given reaction, e^{kt_L} is also constant. Equation 8.36 may thus be written in terms of a reaction specific rate coefficient, β_r, such that

$$C_t = C_0(e^{kt_L})e^{-kt} = C_0\beta_r e^{-kt} \qquad (8.37)$$

As for the case of the retardant reaction, k, β_r, and, if necessary, C_0, of Equation 8.37 may be solved for using a nonlinear regression technique and a multiparameter search routine for data analysis.

8.2 TEMPERATURE AND ACTIVATION ENERGY

Analysis of the temperature dependence of reaction rate data can provide information necessary for process modeling and design. It may also be useful for interpretation of reaction mechanisms and identification of rate-limiting conditions in complex processes.

8.2.1 Arrhenius Equation

Chemical reaction rates generally (although not always) increase monotonically with increasing temperature, in a manner similar to that illustrated in Figure 8.3. Rates that follow the behavior shown in Figure 8.3 can be described by the Arrhenius equation. Expressed

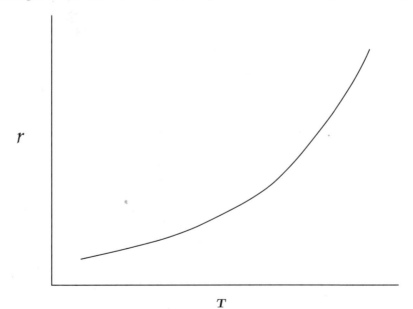

Figure 8.3 Dependence of Reaction Rate on Temperature

in differential form, this equation is

$$\boxed{\begin{array}{ll} \textit{The Arrhenius} & \dfrac{d\ln k}{dT} = \dfrac{E_a}{\mathcal{R}T^2} \\ \textit{Equation} & \end{array}} \tag{8.38}$$

where k is the reaction rate coefficient, E_a the energy of activation, $\mathcal{R}$ the universal gas constant, and T the absolute temperature.

Equation 8.38 has the same form as the van't Hoff equation (Equations 6.34 and 6.35) for expression of the variation of the equilibrium constant, K, with temperature. In the Arrhenius equation, the activation energy, E_a, replaces the standard-state reaction enthalpy term, dH_r°, of the van't Hoff equation. As will be discussed shortly (Section 8.2.3), the Arrhenius equation and activation energy can be justified by an analysis of the probability that a molecular collision will result in a chemical reaction between colliding molecules.

8.2.2 Activation Energy

The activation energy, generally expressed in units of calories or joules per mole, has characteristic values for particular types of reactions and is thus useful for identification of individual reaction steps that control overall rates in complex processes. The magnitude of the activation energy for a complex reaction involving several stages or steps is commonly determined by the slowest step. Thus, its evaluation for complicated processes can provide indication of the nature of rate-limiting reaction steps. For complex biological processes, for example, values for E_a of 70, 67, 50, and 33 kJ/mol commonly correspond, respectively, to rate-limiting reactions involving: (1) oxidative dehydrogenation; (2) oxidative reactions catalyzed by iron; (3) OH-catalyzed oxidative reactions; and, (4) oxidative hydrolysis.

Given the similar forms of the Arrhenius and van't Hoff equations, experimental determinations of E_a can be made from values of k measured at different temperatures in exactly the same manner illustrated in Figure 6.3 of Chapter 6 for determination of enthalpy from measured values of the equilibrium constant at different temperatures.

Activation energy is a direct determinant of reaction rate; the larger is E_a, the slower is the reaction. For simple homogeneous gas-phase reactions, the energy of activation is directly proportional to the strength of the bond that must be broken during the rate-determining step of a reaction. Air-phase oxidations of volatile organic compounds by oxygen tend to be sluggish, for example, because the breaking of oxygen-oxygen bonds requires a relatively high energy. Other energetic factors (e.g., solvation energy) may strongly contribute to the energy of activation for reactions in solution, even for homogeneous reactions.

Integration of Equation 8.38 yields the indefinite integral

$$\ln k = \ln \kappa_1 - \frac{E_a}{\mathcal{R}T} \tag{8.39}$$

where κ_1 is a constant of integration and all other terms are as defined previously. A form that both illustrates the exponential dependence of the rate constant on the absolute temperature and assigns a physical significance to κ_1, namely $\kappa_1 = A_f$, a collision frequency factor, is

$$\boxed{\begin{array}{ll} \textbf{\textit{Integrated Form}} & \\ \textbf{\textit{of the}} & k = A_f e^{-E_a/\mathcal{R}T} \\ \textbf{\textit{Arrhenius Equation}} & \end{array}} \tag{8.40}$$

The relationship above provides further insight to reaction rate mechanisms and a basis for a conceptual definition of activation energy. Reactions between molecules can occur only when they are in contact with one another (recall Example 1.1). Reaction rates should thus be expected to relate to the frequency of contacts between molecules of reacting species, which in turn relates to the kinetic energies of these molecules. The number of such molecular contacts is extremely large in most systems, values of A_f typically being on the order of 10^{15} L/mol-s for a gas at 1 atm pressure, for example. If collisions were all that were required for reactions to occur, nearly all reactions would take place at practically instantaneous rates. The fact that most chemical reactions proceed at finite and measurable rates suggests that only a fraction of the collisions that occur lead directly to reaction; these are termed reactive collisions.

8.2.3   Reactive Collisions

A reactive collision is one that involves molecules possessing an energy of sufficient magnitude to permit reaction to occur. Only a fraction of the molecules in any particular system possess sufficient energy to accomplish a reactive collision. Such molecules are said to be in a reactive or activated state, and the energy required to achieve this state is termed the activation energy. Activation energy is not to be confused with the equilibrium energy states of reactants and products. The differences are illustrated graphically in Figure 8.4 for both exothermic (ΔH_r negative) and endothermic (ΔH_r positive) reactions of the form

$$\mathrm{A} + \mathrm{BC} \Longleftrightarrow \mathrm{AB} + \mathrm{C} \tag{8.41}$$

Enthalpy, rather than free energy, is used as a measure of the thermodynamic potential in Figure 8.4 because of the similar relationships of ΔH_r and E_a to temperature. As shown in this figure, E_a is a potential energy barrier that must be overcome for a particular reaction to occur, whether the reaction is thermodynamically favorable or unfavorable. The higher the magnitude of this

a. Exothermic Reaction

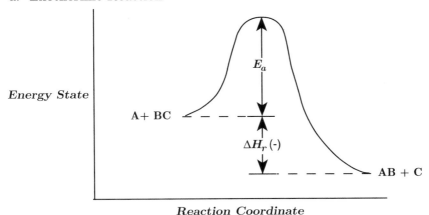

b. Endothermic Reaction

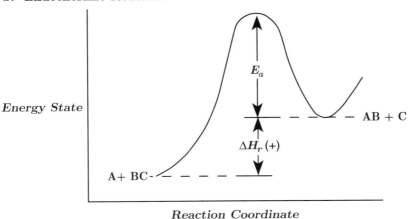

Figure 8.4 Energy States and the Activation Energy Barrier

barrier, the slower is the reaction rate, because the lower is the fraction of molecules in a system possessing an energy E_a in excess of the average energy of the system.

Probability analysis reveals that the fraction of molecules possessing an energy in excess of a value E_a is given by $e^{-E_a/RT}$, as illustrated by the shaded area in the Gaussian or normal distribution curve shown in Figure 8.5.

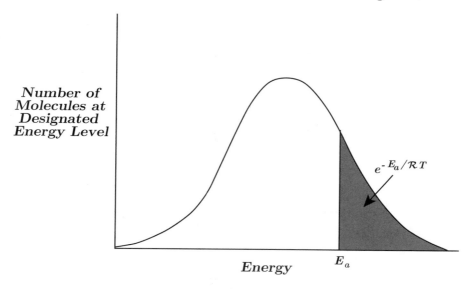

Figure 8.5 Energy Distribution Curve

The total number of reactive collisions in a system is then given by the product of the number of collisions per unit time, A_f, and the number of molecules of energy level E_a or greater; that is

$$reactive\ collision\ frequency = A_f e^{-E_a/RT} \qquad (8.42)$$

Equation 8.42 is identical in form to the integrated Arrhenius equation (Equation 8.40). This means that the rate coefficient for a reaction is directly a measure of the number of reactive collisions per unit time. The law of mass action is thus essentially a statement to the effect that the rate of a reaction is equal to a reactive collision frequency "coefficient" times the product of the numbers of molecules per unit volume (i.e., concentrations) undergoing potentially reactive collisions. For monomolecular reactions (e.g., Equation 7.10) the term A_f represents the probability that an activated molecule will undergo decomposition (reaction) before it loses its energy of activation to some other molecule.

One fundamental shortcoming of the collision theory for description of reaction mechanisms is that it assumes that no entropy change occurs for reversible reactions at temperatures other than absolute zero. This shortcoming can be seen in interpreting the equilibrium constant (and its associated thermodynamic properties) as the ratio of the rate constants for the forward and reverse reaction rates. We first write the Arrhenius expressions for the forward and reverse components of a reversible reaction such as that given by Equation 8.41

$$(k)_F = A_{f,F} e^{-E_{a,F}/\mathcal{R}T} \tag{8.43}$$

$$(k)_R = A_{f,R} e^{-E_{a,R}/\mathcal{R}T} \tag{8.44}$$

and the equilibrium constant, K, is then

$$K = \frac{(k)_F}{(k)_R} = \frac{A_{f,F}}{A_{f,R}} e^{-(E_{a,F}-E_{a,R})\mathcal{R}T} \tag{8.45}$$

It is reasonable to assume that the frequency factors for the forward and reverse reactions must be nearly the same, and that the ratio $A_{f,F}/A_{f,R}$ must therefore be approximately equal to one. We observe that Equation 8.45 has the form of a van't Hoff equation for which the enthalpy difference between the products and the reactants is given by the difference between the forward and reverse activation energies, $(E_{a,F} - E_{a,R})$,. This can be true, however, only for absolute zero temperature or for a reaction involving no entropy change. Such reasoning leads us to conclude that the experimental activation energy calculated from Equation 8.40 is to some extent variable with temperature, and that the frequency factor, A_f, therefore involves an entropy term.

Without knowing the value of A_f, the activation energy for a particular reaction can be calculated directly from measured values of the rate constant at two or more different temperatures assuming that A_f remains constant over the range of temperatures in question. For temperatures T_1 and T_2 we can from Equation 8.40 write

$$
\boxed{\;\textbf{\textit{Activation Energy Estimation}}\qquad \ln \frac{(k)_1}{(k)_2} = \frac{E_a(T_1 - T_2)}{\mathcal{R}T_1 T_2}\;}
\tag{8.46}
$$

A plot of ln k versus $1/T$ will thus give a straight line with a slope of $E_a/\mathcal{R}$. As noted earlier, this procedure is analogous to that presented in Chapter 6 for evaluation of $\Delta H°$. Written in terms of base-10 logarithms, Equation 8.46 is

$$\log \frac{(k)_1}{(k)_2} = \frac{0.4343\ E_a(T_1 - T_2)}{\mathcal{R}T_1 T_2} \tag{8.47}$$

8.2.4 Temperature-Rate Approximations

For situations in which temperature varies over a relatively narrow range (10 degrees or so), as is often the case in natural waters and in treatment processes, the term $0.4343E_a/\mathcal{R}T_1T_2$ in Equation 8.47 remains reasonably constant, and can be approximated by the constant β^A, so that

$$\log \frac{(k)_1}{(k)_2} \cong \beta^A(T_1 - T_2) \tag{8.48}$$

where T_1 and T_2 may now be expressed in degrees Celcius rather than Kelvin because the difference (ΔT) is the same in both cases. The antilog of this equation is

$$\boxed{\textbf{\textit{Temperature-Rate}} \quad \frac{(k)_1}{(k)_2} \cong 10^{\beta^A(T_1 - T_2)} \cong \beta_T^{(T_1 - T_2)}} \tag{8.49}$$
$$\textbf{\textit{Approximation}}$$

where $\beta_T = 10^{\beta^\circ}$. *Equation 8.49 is widely employed in the water quality field for characterizing the temperature dependence of the rate constant. For example, commonly quoted values of β_T are 1.047 for biochemical reactions and 1.024 for gas transfer. In essence, β_T is used instead of E_a to designate the temperature coefficient. However, β_T is not truly constant but is dependent upon the two temperatures over which it is evaluated. The activation energy is thus a more rigorous parameter with which to characterize the temperature dependence of a chemical or biochemical reaction.*

A common empirical rule is that reaction rates increase by a factor of 2 to 3 for each 10-degree rise. This rule applies, however, only if E_a is in the range of those measured for typical rate-limiting biological reactions (33 to 70 kJ/mol) discussed earlier and the temperature is the common range of environmental systems (0 to 30°C, or 273 to 303°K).

An illustration of alternative ways in which to project reaction rates for temperatures other than those at which rates have been measured is provided in Example 8.1. An assessment of potential error associated with one of the approaches is made, and other cautions regarding projections beyond conditions tested are given.

Example 8.1. Estimating Yield Increases Associated With the Operation of A Biochemical Process at Elevated Temperatures. (A comparison of projections based on activation energy and on temperature-rate approximations).

- *Situation. Commercial demand for a rhamnolipid biosurfactant product of a biochemical production operation has increased sharply over the past few years. You are in charge of a biotech facility in which this production process is currently conducted at 10°C. Increasing the operating temperature should increase rate of production. You are asked by management to estimate the increase in yield that might be expected if the operating temperature is increased by a factor of four.*

- **Questions(s).** *Compare estimates made using activation energy analysis and the temperature-rate approximation method.*

- **Logic and Answer(s).**

  1. *Rate coefficients for the apparent first-order reaction associated with this process have been made at $5° C$ and $10° C$, for which temperatures the values have been determined to be $k_1 = 0.15$ per day and $k_2 = 0.19$ per day, respectively.*

  2. *Equation 8.49 gives the temperature-rate approximation expression as*
  $$\frac{k_1}{k_2} \cong 10^{\beta^A (T_1 - T_2)} \cong \beta_T^{(T_1 - T_2)}$$

  3. *Rearranging and solving for β^A and β_T yields*
  $$\beta^A = \frac{log\,(k_1/k_2)}{T_1 - T_2} = 0.020532/°C$$
  $$\beta_T = 10^{\beta^A} = 1.0484$$

     over the temperature range if $5°C - 10°C$. Note that β_T is often reported with no units, while in fact it has units of inverse temperature.

  4. *As discussed earlier in this Section (8.2.4), β_T is only approximately constant over a small temperature range, while activation energy, E_a, at least it is theoretically independent of temperature. We can thus calculate E_a and use this value to calculate a new β_T for the temperature range $5° C$ to $40° C$.*

  5. *From the development of the temperature-rate approximation in the text we know that*
  $$\beta^A = \frac{0.4343 E_a}{R T_1 T_2}$$

     Rearranging and solving for E_a
  $$E_a = \frac{R T_1 T_2 \beta^A}{0.4343}$$
  $$E_a = \frac{(8.314)(278)(283)(0.020532)}{0.4343} = 30923\,\frac{J}{mol} \approx 31\,\frac{kJ}{mol}$$

  6. *We can now calculate β_T for the expanded temperature range as follows*
  $$\beta^A = \frac{0.4343 E_a}{R T_1 T_2} = \frac{(0.4343)(30923)}{(8.314)(278)(313)} = 0.018564/°C$$
  $$\beta_T = 10^{\beta°} = 1.0437$$

     Note that this new β_T value is smaller than the original β_T value, 1.0484.

7. *Again utilizing Equation 8.49, we can calculate the rate constant at*
   $40°C$ *with* β_T *values obtained by both methods.*

$$\beta_T = 1.0437 \rightarrow k(40°C) = 0.67 \ day^{-1}$$

$$\beta_T = 1.0484 \rightarrow k(40°C) = 0.78 \ day^{-1}$$

Thus, the potential error associated with using the temperature-rate
approximation to extrapolate the original β_T *value to* $40°C$ *is about*
15%.

- *Key Point(s).* **In temperature dependence calculations for re-**
  action rates the approximation factor β_T **is only approximately**
  constant, even over narrow temperature ranges. Extrapolations
  to temperatures outside a given data set is generally not advised.
  There is another point to be made in this case; namely, that one
  must consider all aspects of a process when projecting behavior
  for conditions not experimentally confirmed. Simple extrapola-
  tions to temperatures outside of measured ranges of operation
  are particularly risky for biochemical reactions because of the
  varied effects of temperature on microbial metabolism. Temper-
  ature affects different bacterial strains differently, and in some
  cases $40°C$ **may be high enough to alter cellular protein confor-**
  mation, which might completely shut down a biologically facili-
  tated (enzymatic) reaction.

8.3 CATALYSIS

A catalyst is defined in most simple terms as a substance that accel-
erates a chemical reaction while itself remaining unchanged in form
and concentration by the reaction. The accelerating action of a cat-
alyst is termed catalysis.

The way in which a catalyst functions is to alter the rate at which a reaction
approaches its normal position of thermodynamic equilibrium. A catalyst does
not have the ability either to initiate a reaction or to change the magnitude
of an equilibrium constant. Because a catalyst does not alter the equilibrium
constant, it follows that the rate of the reverse reaction must be affected to the
same extent by a catalyst as is the rate of the forward reaction.

A catalyst must thus alter the rate of a chemical reaction by pro-
viding an alternate pathway along which that reaction may approach
equilibrium; i.e., as illustrated schematically in Figure 8.6, a pathway
having a lower activation energy. In Section 8.2.2 we noted that a
lower activation energy translates into a greater fraction of the total

number of molecules in a system having an equal or greater energy level, and thus the reaction rate is greater. This point was illustrated graphically in Figure 8.5. We note in Figure 8.6 that the catalyst has no effect on the equilibrium thermodynamics of the system, which are determined only by the relative energy levels of the reactants and products.

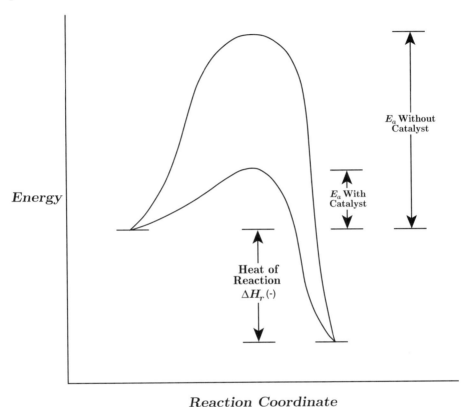

Figure 8.6 Activation Energy and Catalysis for Exothermic Reactions

8.3.1   Homogeneous

In homogeneous catalysis, a reaction proceeds through one or more parallel and/or sequential stages or steps, to provide a pathway of lower resistance than the direct pathway suggested by the reaction stoichiometry. This is illustrated below for the following general reaction scheme

$$A + B \Leftrightarrow AB \tag{8.50}$$

Although the thermodynamics for formation of AB from the two reactants according to the stoichiometry depicted in Equation 8.50 may be favorable, the direct one-step reaction may involve an energy of activation sufficiently high to slow the reaction to only an imperceptible rate. If an appropriate catalyst, C^*, is added, the reaction may proceed more rapidly through an alternate two-step pathway such as

$$Step\ 1: \ A + C^* \Longleftrightarrow AC^* \tag{8.51}$$

$$Step\ 2: \ AC^* + B \Longleftrightarrow AB + C^* \tag{8.52}$$

Summation of Equations 8.51 and 8.52 gives the same results as Equation 8.50. Thus the thermodynamic position of equilibrium remains unaltered even though a more favorable rate mechanism has been introduced by way of the intermediate AC* compound or complex.

Various transition metal ions and coordination compounds serve as important homogeneous catalysts. Complexes of cobalt, palladium, platinum, rhodium, ruthenium, and other metals play important roles in various electron-transfer, hydration, hydrogenation, oxidation, and polymerization reactions of many organic substances. The catalytic versatility of the relatively stable, yet highly reactive transition metal complexes can be attributed in large part to their reactivity patterns being similar to those of the principal intermediates of organic reactions, such as free radicals, carbenes, and carbanions. This similar behavior results from the nature of the transition metal ions with respect to electron configuration and coordination state.

8.3.2   Heterogeneous

Heterogeneous catalysis commonly involves presorption of reactant species at the surfaces of a solid catalyst, followed by formation of surface intermediates, completion of the overall reaction scheme, and desorption of the product(s). Except for a few unusual reactions, presorption by van der Waals or strictly physical forces does not suffice for heterogeneous catalysis. Instead, it is generally necessary for at least one reactant to be chemically adsorbed on the surface of the catalyst. The differences between physical and chemical adsorption are discussed in Chapter 13.

Complex reactions generally proceed by various series and parallel combinations of more simple reactions. Heterogeneous catalysts provide reactive surface sites that enhance the speed of a reaction by introducing new elementary intermediate steps, which in turn allow more rapid combination of reactant species. Although catalysts remain chemically unchanged after participation in a reaction, heterogeneous catalysts may undergo physical change. For example, the surfaces of smooth platinum, a catalyst commonly used for chemical oxidation reactions, are often found to be roughened during the course of an oxidation reaction. A change in surface characteristics suggests participation in the reaction and subsequent regeneration. Activated carbon is often thought of as a heterogeneous catalyst for the oxidation reactions of chlorine, monochloramine, and ozone, which are observed to be reduced rapidly at carbon surfaces. It is also well known, however, that these reduction reactions are accompanied by the accumulation of surface oxides, which eventually prevent efficient reduction of the oxidants. This is termed catalyst deactivation or poisoning.

The precise nature of the reactive surface sites of a particular catalyst is rarely well known. Indeed, even for smooth metal catalysts there is some controversy as to whether all surface atoms possess the same catalytic reactivity, or whether reactivity is associated only with certain surface ridge atoms, dislocations, or point defects (i.e., distributed reactivity), as discussed for adsorption in Chapter 6 of PDES. Fortunately, the development of descriptive mechanisms for heterogeneous catalysis has been able to proceed without complete knowledge of the precise character and distribution of catalytic surface sites. Various aspects of heterogeneous catalytic processes are discussed in several chapters (e.g., 7-12) of PDES.

Example 8.2 illustrates how we can approach the development of rate models for complex heterogeneous processes. A step type of analysis with appropriate assumptions incorporated along the way is used to facilitate the development.

Example 8.2. Catalytic Oxidation of Cyanide by Oxygen on the Surfaces of Activated Carbon. (Formulation of a rate model for a heterogeneous catalytic reaction.)

- **Situation.** *Cyanide is a common constituent of a variety of wastes emanating from metal plating, steel, and petroleum operations. The catalytic oxidation of cyanide using oxygen as oxidant and activated carbon as a catalyst has been examined (e.g., Corapcioglu and Weber, 1982) as a potential alternative to the process of alkaline oxidation with chlorine discussed in Example 6.4.*

- **Question(s).** *You are considering application of this process and wish to develop a rate law to express the overall oxidation reaction sequence in terms of only rate constants, equilibrium constants, and measurable aqueous phase concentrations of reactant and product.*

- **Logic and Answer(s).**

    1. *The first step in the heterogeneous catalysis reaction involves adsorption of the cyanide to surface sites on the activated carbon. The adsorbed cyanide is oxidized to cyanate by surface reaction with oxygen. The cyanate in turn desorbs to solution where it undergoes acid hydrolysis to carbon dioxide and ammonia.*

    2. *The overall oxidation reaction can be represented by the following four steps*

(a) $\mathrm{CN^-} + \mathrm{S^*} \underset{k_{R,1}}{\overset{k_{F,1}}{\rightleftharpoons}} \mathrm{S^*CN^-}$

(b) $\mathrm{S^*CN^-} + \frac{1}{2}\mathrm{O_2} \underset{k_{R,2}}{\overset{k_{F,2}}{\rightleftharpoons}} \mathrm{CNO^-} + \mathrm{S^*}$

(c) $\mathrm{S^*CNO^-} \underset{k_{R,3}}{\overset{k_{F,3}}{\rightleftharpoons}} \mathrm{CNO^-} + \mathrm{S^*}$

(d) $\mathrm{CNO^-} + 2\mathrm{H_3O^+} \underset{k_{R,4}}{\overset{k_{F,4}}{\rightleftharpoons}} \mathrm{CO_2} + \mathrm{NH_4^+} + \mathrm{H_2O}$

where S* represents an activated carbon adsorption site and S*CN⁻ and S*CNO⁻ represent sorbed CN⁻ and CNO⁻, respectively.

3. *Assume that the rate limiting step is the desorption of* $\mathrm{CNO^-}$, *and that reaction rates are not limited by reactant or product diffusion to or from sorption sites. How can we ultimately determine whether or not our assumptions are valid?*

4. *The overall reaction for oxidation of cyanide is*

$$\mathrm{CN^-} + \frac{1}{2}\mathrm{O_2} + 2\mathrm{H_3O^+} \rightleftharpoons \mathrm{CO_2} + \mathrm{NH_4^+} + \mathrm{H_2O}$$

Thus, we wish to develop a reaction rate law including concentrations of these initial and final species and reaction rate and equilibrium constants. Assume that each of the four steps can be described by an elementary reaction rate expression.

5. *First, we write a rate expression for the reaction given in step (a) above*

$$r_1 = k_{F,1} C_{CN} C_{S^*} - k_{R,1} C_{S^*CN}$$

$$r_1 = k_{F,1} \left(C_{CN} C_{S^*} - \frac{C_{S^*CN}}{K_1} \right)$$

$$\text{where } K_1 = \frac{k_{F,1}}{k_{R,1}}$$

6. *The rate expression for the reaction in step (b) is*

$$r_2 = k_{F,2} C_{S^*CN} C_{O_2}^{0.5} - k_2 C_{S^*CNO}$$

$$r_2 = k_{F,2} \left(C_{S^*CN} C_{O_2}^{0.5} - \frac{C_{S^*CNO}}{K_2} \right)$$

$$\text{where } K_2 = \frac{k_{F,2}}{k_{R,2}}$$

7. *The rate expression for the reaction in step (c) is*

$$r_3 = k_{F,3}C_{S^*CNO} - k_{R,3}C_{CNO}C_{S^*}$$

$$r_3 = k_{F,3}\left(C_{S^*CNO} - \frac{C_{CNO}C_{S^*}}{K_3}\right)$$

where $K_3 = \dfrac{k_{F,3}}{k_{R,3}}$

8. *The rate expression for the reaction in step (d) is*

$$r_4 = k_{F,4}C_{CNO}C_{H_3O}^2 - k'_{R,4}C_{CO_2}C_{NH_4}$$

where $k'_{R,4} = k_{R,4}C_{H_2O}$

$$r_4 = k_{F,4}\left(C_{CNO}C_{H_3O}^2 - \frac{C_{CO_2}C_{NH_4}}{K_4}\right)$$

where $K_4 = \dfrac{k_{F,4}}{k'_{R,4}}$

9. *Assuming that reaction 3 (cyanate desorption) is the rate limiting step, propose the following simplifying assumptions*

$$k_{F,1},\ k_{F,2},\ k_{F,4} \gg k_{F,3}$$

At steady state, all four reactions proceed at the same rate, dictated by the rate limiting step.

$$r_1 = r_2 = r_3 = r_4$$

$$\frac{r_1}{k_{F,1}} \approx 0,\ \frac{r_2}{k_{F,2}} \approx 0,\ \frac{r_4}{k_{F,4}} \approx 0$$

10. *Because we want to express r_3 in terms of only measurable aqueous concentrations and reaction constants, we need to develop expressions in these terms for the following three concentrations*

$$C_{S^*CNO},\ C_{CNO},\ C_{S^*}$$

If $\dfrac{r_1}{k_{F,1}} \approx 0$, *then* $C_{CN}C_{S^*} = \dfrac{C_{S^*CN}}{K_1}$, *and* $C_{S^*CN} = K_1 C_{CN}C_{S^*}$

If $\dfrac{r_2}{k_{F,2}} \approx 0$, *then* $C_{S^*CN}C_{O_2}^{0.5} = \dfrac{C_{S^*CNO}}{K_2}$, *and* $C_{S^*CNO} = K_2 C_{S^*CN}C_{O_2}^{0.5}$

If $\dfrac{r_4}{k_{F,4}} \approx 0$, *then* $C_{CNO}C_{H_3O}^2 = \dfrac{C_{CO_2}C_{NH_4}}{K_4}$, *and* $C_{CNO} = \dfrac{C_{CO_2}C_{NH_4}}{K_4 C_{H_3O}^2}$

11. *In order to express C_{S^*} in terms of measurable quantities, we must perform a total mass balance on carbon sorption sites*

$$C_T = C_{S^*} + C_{S^*CN} + C_{S^*CNO}$$

where C_T = total concentration of activated carbon sorption sites either actively catalyzing the reaction or available to catalyze the reaction. However, it should be noted that the total number of sites available for surface reaction will change over time if the activated carbon is continually adsorbing other pollutants from a waste stream. We are assuming here that either (1), the carbon is adsorbing other pollutants at a negligible rate compared to oxidation of cyanide, or (2), the fraction of "spent" carbon over time can be defined. This mass balance leads us to

$$C_T = C_{S^*} + K_1 C_{CN} C_{S^*} + K_1 K_2 C_{CN} C_{S^*} C_{O_2}^{0.5}$$

Rearranging,

$$C_{S^*} = \frac{C_T}{1 + K_1 C_{CN} + K_1 K_2 C_{CN} C_{O_2}^{0.5}}$$

12. *Finally, substituting into reaction 3 for C_{S^*CNO}, C_{CNO}, and C_{S^*}*

$$r_3 = \frac{k_{F,3} C_T \left[K_1 K_2 C_{CN} C_{O_2}^{0.5} - C_{CO_2} C_{NH_4} (K_3 K_4 C_{H_3O}^2)^{-1} \right]}{1 + K_1 C_{CN} - K_1 K_2 C_{CN} C_{O_2}^{0.5}}$$

- *Key Point(s). Heterogeneous catalytic reactions involve complex kinetics, but a step-by-approach and carefully chosen simplifying assumptions make the development of rate models manageable. In such situations we must ultimately determine whether or not our assumptions are valid. To assess whether the above rate equation does in fact describe the kinetics of cyanide oxidation, and thus whether or not desorption of cyanate is rate limiting, we can try to fit it to reaction rate data for various related concentrations of CN^-, O_2, H_3O^+, CO_2, and NH_4^+, all of which are measurable. A nonlinear regression statistical software package can be used to determine coefficients that best fit the model to the data. If the model does not fit the data for any coefficient values, this expression is not suitable for describing the overall reaction rate, and we should proceed with an alternative rate equation development by assuming that one of the other three reaction steps is rate limiting.*

8.4 BIOLOGICAL CATALYSIS

Microbes are capable of carrying out a wide range of organic oxidation reactions using various ultimate electron acceptors (e.g., oxygen, nitrate, carbon dioxide, sulfate). As illustrated in Chapter 6 (Table 6.2 and related discussion), free energy calculations show these reactions to be thermodynamically favorable. However, without enzymatic catalysts to provide alternative pathways of lower activation energy, such reactions would be so slow that the reactants would appear for practical purposes to be stable.

Our previous discussions of the role of organometallic compounds such as vitamin B_{12} in reductive dehalogenation reactions and of biologically produced superoxide in radical generation and organic oxidations stresses the close link between abiotic and biotic transformation reactions. In those instances, metals and organometals were shown not only to be important catalysts but also to be present within the enzyme structures of common microbes.

8.4.1 Enzymes

Enzymes are chemical compounds produced by microbial synthesis. They are most commonly conjugated proteins, or combinations of large protein molecules and some other small organic molecules. The small prosthetic group is referred to as the coenzyme, while the protein molecule itself is termed the apoenzyme. Enzymes far exceed any known synthetic catalysts in their ability to accelerate chemical reactions, but they are also highly specific in their respective roles as catalysts. The enzyme urease, for example, catalyzes the hydrolysis of urea, $(NH_2)_2CO$, in concentrations as low as 1 mg of enzyme per liter but does not detectably alter the rate of hydrolysis of a substituted molecule such as methyl urea, $(NH_2)(CH_3NH)CO$. These specific biocatalysts, although produced by living cells, are often capable of functioning effectively outside of the cell; that is, cell-free filtrates containing enzymes can act as catalytic solutions in many instances.

The importance of enzyme-catalyzed reactions in both natural and engineered systems cannot be overstated. They underlie all anaerobic and aerobic processes used to biostabilize organic matter in wastewater treatment and all biostabilization that occurs spontaneously or is induced (e.g., in situ bioremediation) in the natural environment. As more is learned about enzymatic reactions, new ways are being devised to take advantage of their specificity and speed for treatment of hazardous organic chemicals. For example, many fungi and plants possess peroxidase enzymes, which have been shown to be effective in mediating the oxidation of resistant aromatic structures by hydrogen peroxide.

The molecular diameters of enzymes range from approximately 100 angstroms to about 1000 angstroms, thus falling somewhere between the boundaries used to differentiate between homogeneous and heterogeneous catalysts;

they are thus often referred to as microheterogeneous catalysts. Theoretical interpretation of the mechanism of enzyme catalysis can be based with about equal justification on either the formation of an intermediate compound between an enzyme and substrate (i.e., a homogeneous reaction) or the adsorption of the substrate at the surface of the enzyme (i.e., a heterogeneous reaction). Most developments pursue the formation of an intermediate compound, so this has been chosen for our further examination of enzyme kinetics and rate expressions.

The importance of enzyme reactions in biological treatment of water and wastewater is more than ample reason by itself to explore the conceptual basis of their associated rate expressions. Another reason, however, is that rate expressions of mathematical forms similar to those developed for enzyme reactions can be used as well to describe many complex physicochemical reactions and processes which occur in environmental systems.

8.4.2   Michaelis-Menten Model

The general scheme for depiction of an enzyme reaction is

$$\textbf{General Enzymatic Reaction Scheme} \qquad \text{E} + \text{S} \Leftrightarrow \text{ES} \Leftrightarrow \text{(I)}_n \Leftrightarrow \text{EP} \Leftrightarrow \text{P} + \text{E} \qquad (8.53)$$

where the enzyme, E, and substrate, S, interact to form an enzyme-substrate complex, ES. Chemical transformation of the enzyme-substrate complex, possibly over a number of intermediate steps, $(I)_n$, ultimately leads to an enzyme-bound product, EP, which in turn dissociates to yield free product, P, and enzyme.

The most common simplification of Equation 8.53 is referred to as the Michaelis-Menten model

$$\textbf{Michaelis-Menten Reaction Scheme} \qquad \text{E} + \text{S} \underset{k_2}{\overset{k_1}{\Longleftrightarrow}} \text{ES} \overset{k_3}{\Longrightarrow} \text{P} + \text{E} \qquad (8.54)$$

The catalytic nature of this nonelementary two-step reaction is indicated by the fact the enzyme is conserved. The assumptions associated with developments that follow from Equation 8.54 are: (1) the substrate is reversibly associated with the enzyme in the ES complex; (2) the transformation of the ES complex into the free product and enzyme is rate limiting; and, (3) the reverse reaction between free product and enzyme is negligible during the initial course of the reaction. With these assumptions, two basic relationships may be set forth. First, the rate of increase of product concentration (C_{PR}) and decrease of substrate concentration (C_{SU}) are both functions of the concentration of the enzyme-substrate complex, C_{ES}; that is

$$\frac{dC_{PR}}{dt} = \frac{-dC_{SU}}{dt} = k_3 C_{ES} \qquad (8.55)$$

Second, the conservation of mass relationship can be applied to the enzyme, such that

$$C_{EN,0} = C_{EN} + C_{ES} \tag{8.56}$$

where $C_{EN,o}$ is the concentration of enzyme present at the start of the reaction.

If the further assumption is made that the ES complex attains a steady-state concentration immediately after a brief transient initial period, we may write

$$\frac{dC_{ES}}{dt} = k_1 C_{EN} C_{SU} - k_2 C_{ES} - k_3 C_{ES} = 0 \tag{8.57}$$

The forward step in Equation 8.57 involving formation of the enzyme-substrate complex from the free enzyme and substrate has the general form of a second-order reaction, whereas both the reverse reaction and that for the formation of free product and enzyme from the enzyme-substrate complex have the general forms of first-order reactions. The assumption of a steady-state value for enzyme-substrate complex concentration is akin to an assumption that the first-order dissociation of the complex to free product and enzyme is rate controlling. This assumption is appropriate only for an extent of reaction $(C_{SU,0} - C_{SU}) > C_{ES}$ when $C_{SU} >> C_{EN,0}$ or $C_{ES} << C_{EN,0}$. Solving Equation 8.57 for the steady-state concentration of enzyme-substrate complex gives

$$C_{ES} = \frac{k_1 C_{SU} C_{EN}}{k_2 + k_3} = \frac{k_1 C_{SU} C_{EN,0}}{k_1 C_{SU} + k_2 + k_3} \tag{8.58}$$

Combining this relationship with Equation 8.55 then leads to an expression for the time-rate of decrease of substrate

$$\frac{-dC_{SU}}{dt} = \frac{dC_{PR}}{dt} = k_3 C_{ES} = \frac{k_3 k_1 C_{SU} C_{EN,0}}{k_1 C_{SU} + k_2 + k_3} \tag{8.59}$$

The overall combination of rate constants given by $(k_2 + k_3)/k_1$ is termed the Michaelis constant, $\mathcal{K}_M$. Equation 8.59 may then be written

$$\frac{-dC_{SU}}{dt} = \frac{k_3 C_{SU} C_{EN,0}}{\mathcal{K}_M + C_{SU}} \tag{8.60}$$

The Michaelis constant is a measure of enzyme-substrate affinity. That is, $\mathcal{K}_M$ is nearly equal to the dissociation constant (k_2/k_1) for an enzyme-substrate complex when the concentration of ES is in equilibrium with the concentrations of E and S, [i.e., $k_2 >> k_3$ (see Equation 8.54)]. This is another way of stating that the rate-controlling step is conversion of the enzyme-substrate complex to enzyme and product as given by Equation 8.55.

The concentration of the enzyme in Equation 8.60 generally may be considered to remain constant. Thus, the rate of the reaction will depend only upon the concentration of the substrate. The effect of substrate concentration on the rate of the reaction for a constant enzyme concentration is illustrated in Figure 8.7.

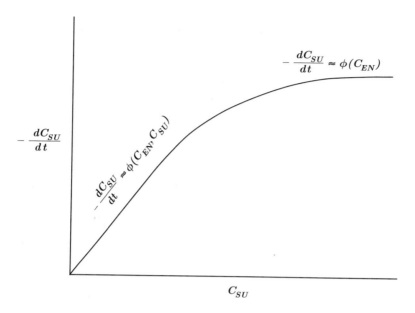

Figure 8.7 Michaelis-Menten Reaction Rate Model Trace

At low substrate concentrations, the rate of substrate depletion is approximately first order with respect to substrate, whereas at high levels, the rate approaches zero order. A zero-order rate is explained by saturation of the enzyme with substrate such that $C_{EN,0} = C_{ES}$. It follows from Equation 8.60 that the maximum rate, r_{max}, must equal $k_3 C_{EN,0}$. Therefore, we can replace $C_{EN,0}$ in Equation 8.60 to arrive at the final form of the Michaelis-Menten equation

$$\begin{array}{l}\textbf{\textit{Michaelis-Menten}} \\ \textbf{\textit{Substrate Utilization}} \\ \textbf{\textit{Rate Equation}}\end{array} \qquad \frac{dC_{PR}}{dt} = \frac{-dC_{SU}}{dt} = r = \frac{r_{max} C_{SU}}{\mathcal{K}_M + C_{SU}} \qquad (8.61)$$

The Monod model for biological process engineering uses an equation of the same form as Equation 8.61 for description of microbial growth rate and rate of substrate utilization as function of substrate concentration. The Monod model is a useful empirical approach which, although it does not describe each of the steps enzyme-substrate steps involved in biodegradation, does have a fundamental origin.

The constants, $\mathcal{K}_M$ and r_{max}, of the Michaelis-Menten equation provide a way to characterize each enzyme system. Their values can be obtained from experiments in which the initial-rate of product formation, dC_{PR}/dt, is determined for a number of different initial substrate concentrations (see Section 7.3.2.1 of Chapter 7). The constants in Equation 8.61 can be obtained either by using commonly available computer software to perform a multiple, nonlinear regression or by taking the reciprocal of both sides of Equation 8.61 to give the following linear expression

$$-\frac{1}{dC_{SU}/dt} = \frac{1}{\boldsymbol{r}_{max}} + \left(\frac{\mathcal{K}_M}{\boldsymbol{r}_{max}}\right)\frac{1}{C_{SU}} \tag{8.62}$$

A plot of $(-dC_{SU}/dt)^{-1}$ versus C_{SU}^{-1} will give a linear trace with an intercept on the $(-dC_{SU}/dt)^{-1}$ axis of $1/\boldsymbol{r}_{max}$ and a slope of $\mathcal{K}_M/\boldsymbol{r}_{max}$. An illustration of this linearized form of the Michaelis-Menten equation (sometimes referred to as a Lineweaver-Burk plot) is given in Figure 8.8. Although a multiple, nonlinear regression will provide a more accurate determination of the appropriate constants, the linearization procedure is convenient and gives an intuitive sense of whether the data conform to the model. Further discussions of enzyme catalyzed reactions are given in PDES.

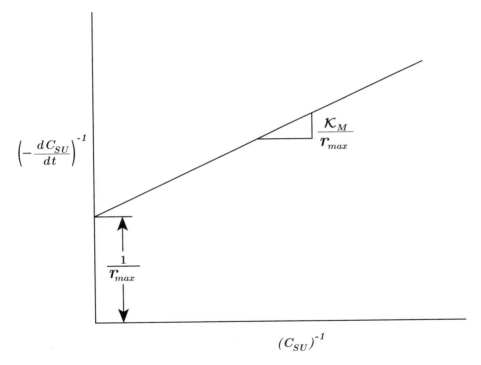

Figure 8.8 Linearized Form of Michaelis-Menten Equation

8.4.3   Monod Model

Based largely on empirical observations reportedly made without benefit of the Michaelis-Menten developments, Monod subsequently advanced a microbial growth model having essentially the same mathematical form as Equation

8.61; i.e.,

$$
\boxed{
\begin{array}{ll}
\textbf{\textit{Monod}} & \\
\textbf{\textit{Microbial Growth}} \quad & \dfrac{dC_{BM}}{dt} = r_{BM} = \dfrac{r_{BM,max}C_{SU}}{\mathcal{K}_{BM} + C_{SU}} \\
\textbf{\textit{Rate Equation}} &
\end{array}
} \qquad (8.63)
$$

where C_{BM} is the biomass concentration, r_{BM} the rate of biomass growth, $r_{BM,max}$ the maximum rate that r_{BM} will attain under substrate "saturation" conditions, and $\mathcal{K}_{BM}$ the value of C_{SU} at which $r_{BM} = 0.5\, r_{BM,max}$; $\mathcal{K}_{BM}$ is thus often referred to as the "half-saturation" constant.

The Monod model suggests that growth rate is related directly to the concentration of some limiting substrate; this is indeed the central concept underlying that model. The distinction between the Monod biomass growth model and the enzyme kinetics model of Michaelis and Menten is significant. The former is predicated on an assumption that growth is controlled (limited) by availability of the particular substrate of interest. This implies that the substrate under consideration is present in sufficient concentration and is sufficiently bioavailable to dominate and support independently the cell production observed in a given system. Unfortunately, because they have identical mathematical forms, the fitting of experimental data by the enzymatic and biomass growth models provides no particular insight to which of the respective conditions actually apply in a given system. The Monod model is a useful model for appropriate conditions. It does not, however, develop from the same enzyme-substrate step analysis used by Michaelis and Menten, and the two models should not be treated as either one in the same or as directly equivalent.

The common roots of different biokinetic models and their relative suitability for description of different types and different ranges of biological process data are illustrated in Example 8.3.

Example 8.3.   Design of a Bioreactor for Treatment of a By-Product Stream in a Pharmaceuticals Plant.   (Determination of a rate model for interpretation of CMBR biomineralization data).

- **Situation.** *An organic by-product stream of a chemical processing operation contains* [14]*C-labeled benzoate. This* [14]*C-labeled compound is to be removed prior to discharge of the stream to a collection system in which radioactive materials are not permitted. The compound cannot be removed effectively by adsorption because of the presence of competing sorbates, nor is membrane treatment a viable alternative. The compound can, however, be biologically mineralized to* [14]CO_2*, which can then be removed by air stripping.*

- **Question(s).** *Select a rate model that best describes the mineralization process and is thus suitable for subsequent incorporation in a bioreactor design model.*

• **Logic and Answers.**

1. *The logical starting point for description of biological substrate utilization rates is the Michaelis-Menten relationship given in Equation 8.61*

$$-\frac{dC_{SU}}{dt} = \frac{r_{max}C_{SU}}{K_M + C_{SU}}$$

2. *The rate sets presented below were determined in two separate experiments conducted in CMBRs having markedly different initial substrate concentrations but the same initial biomass concentration (2000 mg/l). This data is presented below.*

Data Set #1 $C_{SU,0} = 0.32\ \mu g/ml$ ^{14}C Benzoate		Data Set #2 $C_{SU,0} = 32\ \mu g/ml$ ^{14}C Benzoate	
time (hr)	Concentration (DPM/ml)	time (hr)	Concentration (DPM/ml)
0	1300	0.5	1250
0.2	1150	1.1	1200
0.4	870	1.3	1180
0.5	760	1.8	1180
0.7	625	2	1180
0.85	530	2.3	1150
1	400	2.8	1100
1.1	400	3	1080
1.3	380	3.3	1080
1.5	300	3.5	1070
1.7	350	3.75	990
1.85	280	4	1010
2	310	4.5	940
2.25	350	4.75	840
2.5	320	5	810
2.75	340	5.5	730
3	240	6	510

3. *The Michaelis-Menten rate equation was developed with the assumption that enzyme concentration remains constant over time, and is thus limited to describing biodegradation of substrates by nongrowing populations of microorganisms. If a bacterial population is growing in the presence of excess substrate and nutrients, however, the cells may very well reproduce by binary fission, and cell population will thus increase logarithmically. In this case the Michaelis-Menten equation may no longer accurately describe substrate utilization rates.*

4. *Simkins and Alexander (1984) have presented a rate model for substrate utilization during logarithmic cell growth based on a limiting*

form of the Monod equation (Equation 8.63) having the form

$$\frac{dC_{SU}}{dt} = r_{BM,max}(C_{SU,0} + C_{MB,0} - C_{SU})$$

where $C_{SU,0}$ is the initial substrate concentration and $C_{BM,0}$, representing biomass concentration, is a product of cell population density and a yield factor for conversion of substrate mass to cell mass.

5. *We will examine both the exponential growth model and the Michaelis-Menten model to assess their suitability for description of the above substrate utilization rate data. To facilitate use of the latter model we will assume a $\mathcal{K}_M$ value of 0.5 mg/l developed in earlier experiments with the same substrate and bioculture.*

6. *If substrate utilization rate data can best be described by the Michaelis-Menten equation, then a plot of the corresponding data such as that given in Figure 8.8 should approximate a straight trace. If, on the other hand, the rate data is best described by the logarithmic model, then a plot of $-dC_{SU}/dt$ versus C_{SU} should yield a straight line. Both data sets are plotted by each of the methods in the graphs below*

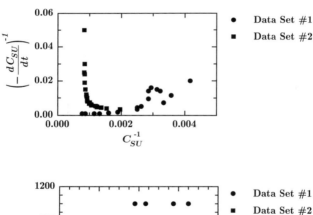

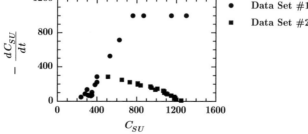

7. *Data Set #1 is better described by the Michaelis-Menten model and Data Set #2 by the model for substrate utilization with logarithmic cell growth. This result makes sense, comparing the initial reaction*

conditions to the assumptions involved in developing the two rate expressions. For Data Set #1, $C_{BM,O} >> C_{SU,O}$, while for Data Set #2, $C_{SU,0} >> \mathcal{K}_M$.

- *Key Point(s). The Michaelis-Menten model assumes that enzyme concentration is constant throughout the course of the reaction, so if the biomass is actively growing while degrading the substrate, an alternative rate model must be employed. Linearization of rate expressions and the graphing of experimental data accordingly is a useful method for investigating the validity of a proposed rate model.*

8.5 CHAPTER SUMMARY

Contemporary approaches to environmental process engineering and system analysis, modeling and design demand the use of appropriate rate relationships for development of rigorous material-balance-based models. In Chapter 7 we identified several challenges in the application of rate relationships to transformations in environmental systems. In this chapter we have introduced modeling tools that help us address certain complex phenomena in relatively simple and successful ways despite the lack of elaborate molecular-level information.

As in Chapter 7, experimental determinations of rate relationships have been emphasized because this is the state of the art for complex environmental systems. Rate expressions and coefficients reported in the literature for reactions that are similar are often useful starting points for such experimental efforts.

As our field continues to advance, however, we will necessarily have to refine our means for dealing with increasingly complex and incompletely defined problems in a practical manner. Even now, for example, waste minimization in the chemical synthesis industry requires knowledge of rates at which environmentally regulated chemicals may be produced in side reactions with trace contaminants of the feedstock or with industrial catalysts. Heretofore such reactions have often been ignored or considered unimportant because concentrations of unwanted by-products were thought to be insignificant.

In another contemporary arena, thermal processing to destroy or immobilize hazardous wastes requires that the role of temperature and pressure on reaction kinetics and production rates of unwanted by-products be quantified. The general rule that reaction rate doubles for a $10°C$ rise in temperature is not applicable in such cases because of the nature of the oxidation reactions and the temperature ranges involved. This is the case for example, for super critical water oxidations, in which temperatures exceed $374°$ and pressures are greater than 218 atm. It is also true in the cases of thermal desorption and subcritical water extractions for removal of contaminants from soils, sediments, and other solid matrices. As a final example, more refined knowledge of catalyzed reactions (both biotic and abiotic) that offer potential for transformation of hazardous chemicals is essential to developing improved means for destruction of such materials, and for remediation of sites contaminated by them.

For all of the processes cited above, as well as for others not specifically identified, associated rate relationships are certain to be more complex than those given by the relatively simple models discussed here. Nevertheless we should consider what we have learned about reaction rates to be a good foundation. In particular, we should pay careful attention to assumptions made in formulating rate expressions, and the related implications of these assumptions for the accurate representation of complex processes.

8.6   CITATIONS AND SOURCES

Corapcioglu, O. and W.J. Weber, Jr., 1982, "Catalytic Oxidation of Cyanides in Metal Plating Wastes," *Proceedings of the 36th Industrial Wastes Conference* (Purdue University), Section 11, p 500-508, *Ann Arbor Science Publishers, Inc.* Example 8.2)

Simkins, S.M. Alexander, 1984, "Models for Mineralization Kinetics with the Variables of Substrate Concentration and Population Density," *Applied Environmental Microbiology, 47,* 1299-1306. (Example 8.3)

Weber, W.J., Jr. and F.A. DiGiano, 1996, *Process Dynamics in Environmental Systems,* John Wiley & Sons, Inc., New York. General source of all material presented. More advanced approaches to complex process and system rate characterization and modeling are presented in Chapters 7 and 8 of PDES for homogeneous and heterogeneous systems respectively.

8.7   PROBLEM ASSIGNMENTS

8.1 Nitrification is a fairly slow biochemical reaction in which ammonia is converted to nitrite by one genus of microorganism (e.g.; *Nitrosomonas*) and to nitrate by another genus (e.g; *Nitrobacter*)

$$NH_4 \rightarrow NO_2^- \Rightarrow NO_3^-$$

If ammonia is present in a surface water, there is the potential for nitrification in the water distribution system; nitrate formation is of concern because of health risks to infants. A batch kinetic study is undertaken to determine how fast nitrification occurs under worst-case conditions. A large number of cells of *Nitrosomonas* is added to a CMBR containing 0.5 mM solution of NH_4^+ (9 mg/L); solution chemistry and temperature are similar to that of the drinking water. A first-order formation of nitrite is observed with a rate constant of 10^{-4}min^{-1}. A second experiment is conducted in which large cell numbers of both *Nitrosomonas* and *Nitrobacter* are added to the CMBR containing a 0.5 mM solution of NH_4^+ and nitrate concentration (mM) is measured with the following results:

Time min $\times 10^{-3}$	$C_{NO_3}^-$ mM	Time min $\times 10^{-3}$	$C_{NO_3}^-$ mM
0	0	7	0.16
1	0.01	8	0.19
2	0.02	9	0.21
3	0.05	10	0.24
4	0.07	12	0.28
5	0.10	14	0.32
6	0.13	18	0.38

Use this information to: (a) determine the rate constant for first-order conversion of nitrite to nitrate; (b) investigate the sensitivity of results to the choice of rate constants for both nitrite and nitrate formation; and, (c) draw a conclusion about which step is rate controlling.

Answer: (a) $k= 3 \times 10^{-4} min^{-1}$.

8.2 Manganese oxidation by oxygen occurs in the following sequence of elementary reactions

$$Mn^{2+} + O_2 \xrightarrow{k_1} MnO_2(s)$$

$$Mn^{2+} + MnO_2(s) \xrightarrow{k_2} \{Mn^{2+} \cdot MnO_2(s)\}$$

$$\{Mn^{2+} \cdot MnO_2(s)\} + O_2 \xrightarrow{k_3} 2MnO_2(s)$$

where $\{Mn^{2+} \cdot MnO_2(s)\}$ represents a short-lived intermediate product. Derive expressions for the rate of disappearance of Mn^{2+} and the rate of appearance of MnO_2 when O_2 is in excess.

Answers:

$$-\frac{dC_{Mn^{2+}}}{dt} = k_{ps}C_{Mn^{2+}} + k_2 C_{Mn^{2+}} C_{MnO_2(s)}$$

$$\frac{dC_{MnO_2(s)}}{dt} = k_{ps}C_{Mn^{2+}} + k_2 C_{Mn^{2+}} \left\{(C_{Mn^{2+}})(C_{MnO_2(s)})\right\}$$

where a pseudo-first order rate constant, k_{ps}, is given by

$$k_{ps} = k_1 C_{O_2}$$

8.3 In Problem 7.6 of Chapter 7 we analyzed data for the rate of ozone decomposition to oxygen in water, determined an appropriate rate equation, and calculated a corresponding rate coefficient.

Another set of experiments is conducted to measure the rate of ozone consumption by methanol oxidation. The reaction of ozone with methanol is thought to be elementary. In analyzing the results of this set of experiments it is necessary to consider the parallel reactions

$$O_3 + CH_3OH \xrightarrow{k_1} \text{products}$$

$$2O_3 \xrightarrow{k_2} 3O_2$$

The experiments were conducted with excess amounts of methanol so that the methanol concentration, C_{Me}, could be considered constant during collection of the rate data. Three runs were made with different methanol concentrations to verify that the reaction was, in fact, first order with respect to methanol and second order overall. The experimental data are tabulated below for each run.

Run 1: $C_{Me} = 1.25 \times 10^{-4}$ mol/L

Time (sec)	C_{O_3}, mg/L
0	3.00
6	2.64
18	1.80
30	1.38

Run 2: $C_{Me} = 3.125 \times 10^{-4}$ mol/L

Time (sec)	C_{O_3}, mg/L
0	3.00
6	2.16
18	1.32
30	0.60

Run 3: $C_{Me} = 1.25 \times 10^{-3}$ mg/L

Time (sec)	C_{O_3}, mg/L
0	3.00
6	1.05
18	0.18
30	0.03

Determine the order of the ozone oxidation of methanol and calculate the associated rate constants.

8.4 Show for an accelerative reaction the amount of reactant remaining as a function of time for assumed values of k_1, k_2 and C_o. Illustrate the effects of variations in k_1 and k_2 on the "lag period" of a first-order approximation of the accelerative behavior.

8.5 The nocturnal chirping rate of crickets has been reported to increase with temperature according to the relationship:

$$(\text{number of chirps in 15 seconds}) + 40 = (\text{temperature, } °F)$$

Assuming that chirping rate is a direct measure of metabolic rate, determine the cricket activation energy corresponding to a temperature range of 60 to 80°F. Discuss the magnitude of this activation energy in the context of typical rate-limiting steps in biochemical reactions.

8.6 The rate constant, k, for a second-order reaction between substances A and B is 0.135 L/mol-s at 69.4°C and 3.70 L/mol-s at 81.2°C. Determine the rate constant for the reaction at 55.0°C.

8.7 A low-volume blowdown from a batch pharmaceutical operation involving phenol polymerization via enzyme catalysis is treated with chlorine for enzyme deactivation prior to discharge to a municipal wastewater treatment plant. The deactivation process is carried out in a reactor operated on a fill-and-draw basis, with Cl_2 being bubbled through the blowdown after the reactor is filled and prior to subsequent draw down. The chlorine coincidentally reacts with residual phenol in the reactor to form mono-, di-, and tri-substituted products; i.e.,

$$C_6H_5OH + HOCl \xrightarrow{k_1} C_6H_4ClOH + H_2O$$

$$C_6H_4ClOH + HOCl \xrightarrow{k_2} C_6H_3Cl_2OH + H_2O$$

$$C_6H_3Cl_2OH + HOCl \xrightarrow{k_3} C_6H_2Cl_3OH + H_2O$$

Develop an appropriate rate of formation equation for each of the three substituted phenols, and an approach for describing the change in the concentration of any one of these in terms of the concentration of any other.

8.8 Consider a homogeneous catalysis reaction

$$A + B^* \underset{k_2}{\overset{k_1}{\rightleftharpoons}} AB^* \implies C + B^*$$

in which the catalyst B^* also undergoes reversible complexation by the intermediate product AB^* to form AB_2^*.

(a) Develop an expression for the net rate of product (C) generation as a function of the reactant (A) concentration.

(b) Construct comparative plots of product (C) generation rate as a function of reactant (A) concentration for the above case, and for a case in which the complexation reaction between A and AB^* does not occur.

8.9 Peroxidase, an enzyme isolated from white rot fungus, is proposed to enhance the peroxide oxidation of phenol. A Michaelis-Menten rate relationship is postulated for the case of peroxide being present in large excess

$$-r_A = \frac{k_3 C_{Ph} C_{EN,o}}{K_M + C_{Ph}}$$

The initial enzyme concentration, $C_{EN,o}$, in a CMBR experiment designed to test the rate relationship is 0.01 mmol/L, and the initial phenol concentration, $C_{Ph,o}$, is 1 mmol/L. The resulting rate data are tabulated below.

Time (h)	C_{Ph}, (mmol/L)
1	0.84
2	0.68
3	0.53
4	0.38
5	0.27
6	0.16
7	0.09
8	0.04
9	0.018
10	0.006

Determine whether these data can be fit reasonably by the Michaelis-Menten model and if so, evaluate the rate constants.

Answers: $k_3 = 13.2\ h^{-1}$ and $K_M = 0.063\ mmol/L$.

8.10 Enzymes are known to deactivate naturally with time; alternatively, they may be deactivated by other components in a solution. An enzymatic process is being considered for treatment of an industrial high-strength phenolic waste. The waste is generated in small volumes and the concentrations of phenols are so high that conventional biological treatment is impossible due to substrate inhibition. The enzymatic system requires, however, that hydrogen peroxide be added to promote hydroxyl free radicals but hydrogen peroxide also causes deactivation of the enzyme. A set of four rate tests were conducted to measure the rate of enzyme deactivation by hydrogen peroxide (in the absence of phenols). In each test, the starting concentration of enzyme was $1\mu M$ and the hydrogen peroxide

(H_2O_2) was added in excess at four different concentrations. The fractional remaining activity of the enzyme was measured with time to give the data listed below.

Time(min)	100 μm	500 μm	1000 μm	2000 μm
	\multicolumn{4}{c}{[H_2O_2] in Excess in Each Test}
0	1.00	1.00	1.00	1.00
10	0.90	0.84	0.79	0.70
20	0.82	0.70	0.63	0.50
30	0.74	0.58	0.50	0.35
40	0.67	0.49	0.40	0.25
50	0.61	0.41	0.32	0.17
60	0.55	0.34	0.25	0.12
80	0.45	0.24	0.16	0.06

Determine the rate constant and the order of the deactivation reaction with respect to enzyme and hydrogen peroxide concentrations.

Chapter 9

Ideal System Modeling and Design

Contents

9.0   CHAPTER OBJECTIVES

To develop familiarity with performance equations and facility with models for the design of simple reactors exhibiting discretely different ideal flow conditions, with a strong emphasis on developing an appreciation of the utility and limitations of such models.

9.1   INTRODUCTION

We will here focus on full development of the characteristics, behaviors, and descriptive models for the three "frame of reference" ideal reactors introduced briefly in Chapter 3. Subsequently, in Chapters 10, 11 and 16, we will explore different variants of these three ideal reactor configurations and their related behaviors.

Reactor principles are used routinely in the field of chemical engineering to describe a broad range of industrial transformation processes involving gases, liquids, and solids. These same principles can be applied for description of the behavior of natural systems and to the design of engineered systems. *There are, however, several important distinctions between the conditions under which reactors for specific product or by-product recovery and recycle processes operate in the chemical industry and in those associated with most environmental systems. Foremost, the precise composition of environmental "feedstocks," such as raw water supplies and wastewater streams, is rarely known. For example, such surrogate lumped measures of constituent concentrations as BOD, TOC, and conductivity must often be used in place of specific chemical entities in reaction rate expressions, thereby immediately introducing empiricism. In contrast, reactor design in the chemical industry generally deals with the conversion of well-characterized chemical feed stocks to well-known products.*

Not only are the specific compositions of environmental systems largely unknown, they are also commonly variable, which is true as well for rates of flow. Temporal variabilities complicate process descriptions by necessitating consideration of reactor performance under nonsteady-state conditions. Such circumstances must be fully understood in order to recognize the proper application of process performance models in environmental systems.

9.2   REACTOR CONCEPTS

9.2.1   Definition

A reactor is defined here as any device in which an incoming constituent undergoes chemical (or biochemical) transformation, phase transformation, or phase separation. A constituent is defined again in its broadest sense to include soluble, colloidal, and particulate substances. The material balance relationship described in word form in Equation 3.1 and elaborated mathematically in point form in Equations 3.6 and 3.8 and integral form in Equation 3.12 is the starting point for analysis of reactor performance. Mathematical expressions appropriate for each specific type of reactor system must then be developed for the input, output, and reaction terms in these equations. The input and output (i.e., mass transport) terms must accommodate mass continuity through the reactor and account for advection and dispersion processes within the bulk fluid(s) therein. These macroscale fluid transport processes were discussed in Chapter 4. The reaction rate term for homogeneous-phase reactions may be any of the rate expressions discussed in Chapters 7 and 8. Heterogeneous-phase reactions, on the other hand, such as those to be described in Chapters 14 and 15 require consideration not only of macroscale transport with the bulk fluid but also microscale transport between and within other phases contained in the reactor. Descriptions of such microscale mass transfer processes are incorporated in the reaction rate expression term of the material balance equation when they control overall process rate, as they so often do in environmental systems.

Given the broad definition of a constituent with which we have begun, it is necessary to analyze each term of the material balance relationship carefully to ensure its appropriate use. Strictly speaking, for example, the principles of chemical kinetics described in Chapter 7 are intended to apply only to atoms and molecules in homogeneous phases. However, as touched upon briefly in several places in Chapter 8, and expanded upon in Chapters 14 and 15, rates of interaction of particulate constituents and rates of particle capture by collectors are often described by rate expressions developed in a fashion analogous to that employed for molecular reactions. Many reactors employed in environmental systems are in fact designed to provide principally for phase transfer or phase separation processes rather than for chemical transformation processes. The reaction rate term in the material balance equation is in such cases replaced by an interphase mass transfer term. The objective of broadening the definition of a reactor is to provide a unified approach to process design and system description.

9.2.2 Flow and Residence Times

The pattern of flow through a reactor determines the residence time of fluid elements within that reactor, and thus the time available for transformations and separations to occur. At one particular extreme or limiting condition of ideal reactor behavior, all fluid elements spend the same time in the system, and mass transport occurs by advection only. This condition is termed plug flow. At the other extreme, a reactor is uniformly mixed, a condition producing an infinite extent of dispersion. This condition is referred to as completely mixed, a condition for which the residence time of fluid elements within the reactor varies conceptually from zero to infinity.

In practice, ill-described intermediate fluid mixing patterns are frequently encountered, with mass transport occurring by a combination of dispersion and advection somewhere between the two extreme conditions. ***These flow patterns are referred to as nonideal. If the precise nature of the nonideal flow pattern is not known, the residence time distribution must be estimated from experimental measurements. These measurements are then interpreted in the context of an ideal model for nonideal flow (i.e., a model having specific hypothesized advection and dispersion characteristics).*** The fact that experimental data on flow patterns must be obtained before the extent of transformation or separation can be calculated complicates prediction of reactor performance under nonideal flow conditions.

9.2.3   Frame of Reference Reactors

Ideal reactor models represent approximations to reality. In particular, assumptions about concentration gradients and mixing patterns allow simplification of the dependence of reaction rates on spatial position within a reactor volume. The assumptions are critical in model formulations, and the restrictions they impose must be recognized in model applications. Three of the four most common classifications of ideal reactors are those identified in our brief "frame of reference" introduction in Chapter 3; i.e., the completely mixed batch reactor (CMBR), the completely mixed flow reactor (CMFR), and the plug flow reactor (PFR). The fourth type of "ideal" reactor model is the advection-dispersion model used to mimic the observed nonideal behaviors of arbitrary flow systems, referred to as the plug flow with dispersion reactor (PFDR) model. The PFDR model provides a quantitative approach for describing nonideal flow patterns to facilitate prediction of reactor performance. Our discussion in this chapter focuses on the first three types of ideal reactor models. The PFDR model is discussed in Chapter 11.

For ease and control, continuous flow reactors are often designed to operate at or near steady-state conditions, allowing the accumulation term in the material balance relationship to be treated as essentially zero. There are many environmental reactor applications in which unsteady-state conditions exist, however. It is common practice in such applications to employ equalization basins at the headworks of facilities for the smoothing of unsteady flow and concentration conditions in order to accommodate steady-state design and operation of subsequent treatment units. For the most part, this book focuses on steady-state conditions, or conditions that may be so approximated. Unsteady-state conditions and related reactor design principles and analysis approaches are treated in depth in PDES.

9.3 IDEAL REACTORS

9.3.1 Completely Mixed Batch Reactors

As illustrated in Figure 9.1, a CMBR has no inflow or outflow. Thus, as a reaction proceeds, the composition and the relative distribution of reactants and products change with time. The term completely mixed stipulates that no spatial concentration, density, or thermal gradients exist. A CMBR is well suited for bench-scale experimental studies of reaction rates (see Chapters 7 and 8). Moreover, it can be applied effectively for treatment of small quantities of materials, particularly materials that are relatively expensive, toxic, or otherwise hazardous to deal with in flow-through reactors.

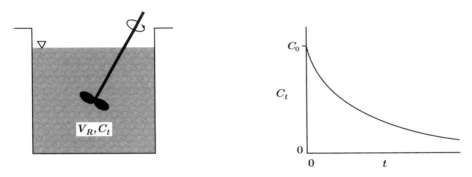

Figure 9.1 Completely Mixed Batch Reactor Schematics

Vigorous mixing is employed in CMBRs to ensure that the concentrations of reactants and products are uniform and that reaction rates are therefore the same everywhere within the reactor volume. The material balance relationship (MBE) for an ideal CMBR thus reduces to

$$\boxed{\begin{array}{l} \textbf{\textit{MBE}} \\ \textbf{\textit{for a}} \\ \textbf{\textit{CMBR}} \end{array} \qquad r V_R = V_R \frac{dC}{dt}} \qquad (9.1)$$

As written, this MBE incorporates the implicit assumption that the reactor volume (volume of fluid in the reactor), V_R, remains constant. In Chapter 10 we deal with certain cases of time-variable volumes, specifically those relating to reactions that take place during the filling of a reactor. This mode of operation is sometimes referred to as semibatch, an operation frequently associated with sequencing batch reactors (SBRs). More complicated cases of time-variable volumes and other transient conditions are dealt with in various chapters of PDES.

Recognizing that r is generally a function of concentration, Equation 9.1

can be written

$$\int_0^t dt = \int_{C_0}^{C_t} \frac{dC}{r}$$

(9.2)

The equation resulting from integration of Equation 9.2 can be used to determine the reaction time interval (RTI) or "holding time" required for the concentration of a substance undergoing reaction at a rate r to change from C_0 to C_t in a CMBR; i.e.,

$$\boxed{\begin{array}{ll} \textbf{\textit{RTI for}} & \\ \textbf{\textit{a CMBR}} & t_R = \displaystyle\int_{C_0}^{C_t} \frac{dC}{r} \end{array}}$$

(9.3)

For a reaction in which concentration decreases with time, r is negative. When there is production or generation of the reactant of interest, r is positive. Example 9.1 illustrates an application of the foregoing relationship to the selection of an appropriate RTI for a specified level of treatment of a waste of known composition and known reaction characteristics in a CMBR.

Example 9.1. Periodic Point-of-Generation Batch Enzyme Pretreatment of a Bioresistant Organic Waste. (Determination of the required RTI for periodic enzyme pretreatment of an organic waste product in a CMBR.)

- *Situation. An enzyme treatment process is to operate offline on batches of an industrial wastewater that contains 50 μM of an aromatic substrate (SU). The enzyme (EN) involved accomplishes partial oxidation (ring opening), making the substrate amenable to further degradation in the plant's main biotreatment system. Bench-scale studies have shown that the initial enzyme concentration decreases with time due to thermal deactivation in a process described by the rate relationship*

$$C_{EN} = C_{EN,0}e^{-kt}$$

The Michaelis-Menten rate relationship applies in the following modified form to account for the loss of enzyme with time

$$-r = \frac{r_{max}e^{-kt}C_{SU}}{\mathcal{K}_M + C_{SU}}$$

where $r_{max} = 10 \ \mu M/min, \mathcal{K}_M = 20 \ \mu M,$ and $k = 0.1 \ min^{-1}$.

- *Question(s). Determine the RTI required for 80% removal of the substrate in the CMBR.*

- *Logic and Answer(s).*

1. *The material balance for a CMBR is given by Equation 9.1, and the reaction rate term derives directly from the reactor design equation*

$$-\boldsymbol{r} = \frac{dC_{SU}}{dt}$$

2. *Substitution of the modified Michaelis-Menten expression for $\boldsymbol{r}$, followed by separation of variables, gives*

$$\frac{\mathcal{K}_M + C_{SU}}{C_{SU}} dC_{SU} = -\boldsymbol{r}_{max} e^{-kt} dt$$

This equation can be integrated analytically to yield

$$\left. (\mathcal{K}_M \ln C_{SU} + C_{SU}) \right|_{C_{SU,0}}^{C_{SU,t}} = \left. \frac{\boldsymbol{r}_{max}}{k} e^{-kt} \right|_0^t$$

3. *An expression for the RTI needed for treatment is obtained by rearrangement*

$$t_R = \frac{-\ln\left[(k\mathcal{K}_M/\boldsymbol{r}_{max})\left[\ln(C_{SU,t}/C_{SU,0})\right] + (k/\boldsymbol{r}_{max})(C_{SU,t} - C_{SU,0}) + 1\right]}{k}$$

4. *Substitution of the numerical values given for the respective rate constants and the initial and final substrate concentrations yields*

$$t_R = \frac{-\ln\left[(2/10)[\ln(10/50)] + (0.1/10)(10 - 50) + 1\right]}{0.1} = 12.8 \text{ min}$$

- *Key Point(s). The determination of required residence times and associated reactor volumes for reactors of well defined flow characteristics is straightforward, regardless of the complexity of the reaction rate relationship(s) involved. The reader is encouraged, however, to explore the sensitivity of treatment time to input data and associated model parameterization. In cases of complex rate expressions, such as that of the Michaelis-Menten model, errors in rate expression parameters can be critical.*

The above analysis applies to reactors operated at constant volume. This is the typical condition under which bench-scale experiments are conducted to determine the form of the rate expression for $\boldsymbol{r}$, as discussed in Chapter 7. Constant-volume CMBR design equations may also be appropriate for certain treatment applications wherein sporadically generated waste streams are collected over time, and the reactants necessary to convert the contaminants added only when a specific fixed volume of waste is accumulated.

9.3.2   Completely Mixed Flow Reactors

The CMFR configuration is illustrated schematically in Figure 9.2. In contrast to CMBRs, CMFRs involve continuous flows of feed and product water. As noted earlier, the CMFR designation describes the explicit physical conditions required by the associated ideal reactor model; namely, a flow-through reactor, the contents of which are completely mixed. *Two noteworthy features of reactors that behave like CMFRs are rapid dilution of influent reactants, and smoothing of time-variable input concentrations.*

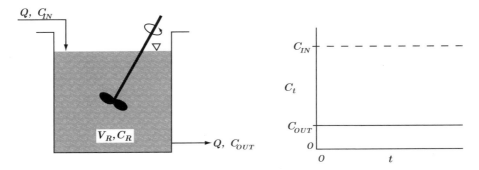

Figure 9.2 Completely Mixed Flow Reactor Schematics

Many process reactors closely approximate the behavior of ideal CMFRs. Two common examples are the rapid-mix tanks used to introduce chemicals in coagulation processes and the aeration tanks of completely mixed activated-sludge biological treatment processes. The features of CMBRs cited above are important considerations in applications of these reactors. The rapid-mix operations associated with the initial stages of coagulation processes are critical because the chemical behaviors of coagulants depend markedly on their concentrations and on solution pH, neither of which conditions can be allowed to fluctuate because of incomplete mixing. Moreover, chemical dosing must be paced with incoming particle concentrations, and thus be quickly reactive to concentration changes. The same considerations are important for reactor systems used in biological treatment processes. Sudden changes in substrate concentrations and chemical compositions, or the sudden appearance of toxicants, can adversely affect biochemical reactions, and therefore process performance. Although the primary application of CMFRs is for full-scale treatment processes, the configuration is useful also for bench-scale experiments designed to evaluate the rates of certain types of processes, particularly biological processes, as discussed in Section 9.4.2.

Under normal operating conditions the flow rates entering and leaving the the CMFR illustrated in Figure 9.2 are equal, and the volume in the reactor is thus constant. *As for the CMBR, the CMFR is perfectly mixed, and the concentration, C_R, thus uniform throughout the volume; moreover, for the condition of complete mixing, C_R must be equal to the* *exit concentration, C_{OUT}. It follows that the reaction rate, r, is also uniform through the reactor and, as important, controlled by the effluent concentration $[r = \phi(C_R) = \phi(C_{OUT})]$. The material balance equation is written*

$$\boxed{\begin{array}{ll} \textbf{MBE for} & V_R\dfrac{dC_{OUT}}{dt} = QC_{IN} - QC_{OUT} + rV_R \\ \textbf{a CMFR} & \end{array}} \qquad (9.4)$$

The first two terms on the right-hand side of Equation 9.4 are the molar or mass flow rates of component entering and exiting the reactor, respectively, and the difference between them is the net mass or molar flow rate into the reactor.

Designs of CMFRs for use in engineered systems are most commonly based on given influent conditions, fixed effluent objectives, and steady performance; i.e., steady-state operation. For this condition the rate of accumulation is zero, and Equation 9.4 becomes

$$\boxed{\begin{array}{ll} \textbf{Steady-State} & \\ \textbf{MBE for} & V_R\dfrac{dC_{OUT}}{dt} = 0 = QC_{IN} - QC_{OUT} + rV_R \\ \textbf{a CMFR} & \end{array}} \qquad (9.5)$$

The steady-state value of the exit concentration, C_{OUT}, is conveniently expressed in terms of its ratio with respect to the influent concentration, C_{IN}, or

$$\frac{C_{OUT}}{C_{IN}} = 1 + r\frac{V_R}{QC_{IN}} \qquad (9.6)$$

The reactor volume required to give the desired exit concentration is then given by

$$V_R = -\frac{Q}{r}\left(C_{IN} - C_{OUT}\right) \qquad (9.7)$$

Equation 9.7 can be divided by Q to obtain the mean hydraulic residence time (HRT) or space time, $\bar{t}$, required under steady-state conditions to accomplish a desired reduction in concentration across a CMFR; i.e.

$$\boxed{\begin{array}{ll} \textbf{Steady-State} & \\ \textbf{Design HRT} & \bar{t} = \dfrac{V_R}{Q} = -\dfrac{1}{r}\left(C_{IN} - C_{OUT}\right) = \dfrac{-\Delta C}{r} \\ \textbf{for a CMFR} & \end{array}} \qquad (9.8)$$

It will be shown later that $\bar{t}$ is also equal to the mean value of the residence times of fluid elements (and thus reacting components) in a CMFR.

Once the rate relationship for a particular reaction is known, a more specific design equation can be written. For example, if a given component undergoes a first-order reaction, $r = -kC_{OUT}$, Equation 9.8 becomes

$$\bar{t} = \frac{1}{k}[(C_{IN}/C_{OUT}) - 1] \qquad (9.9)$$

We note from Equation 9.9 that for a fixed influent concentration the HRT needed to achieve a given exit concentration increases as the rate constant decreases, and for a given rate constant, increases as the designed effluent concentration decreases. These intuitive effects are illustrated in Example 9.2 for an empirically derived half-order reaction involving the oxidation of color bodies by ozone in a raw water supply source.

Example 9.2.   Assessment of Reactor Capacity Requirements to Meet an Effluent Objective in Ozone-Sparged Flow-Through Tanks. (An exercise in selecting a reactor model, evaluating an empirical rate model, and evaluating a proposed treatment scheme.)

- **Situation.** *Field-scale tests are conducted to determine the effectiveness of ozone in oxidizing color-producing compounds in a water treatment operation. Ozone is sparged into a tank having an HRT of 10 min. The color units entering and leaving the ozone contactor are measured in three separate tests with the results shown below.*

Test Number	Color Units In	Color Units Out
1	8	1.9
2	15	4.8
3	22	8.0

These levels of removal are deemed unsatisfactory. The color entering the treatment plant typically averages about 10 Color Units, and the design goal is to achieve a product water of 1 Color Unit.

- **Question(s).** *It is proposed to add another ozone contactor in parallel to the original tank and split the flow evenly between them to lengthen hydraulic residence time and obtain greater color removal. The following empirical rate expression is assumed to best describe the process*

$$r = -kC^{0.5}$$

where C is a lumped-parameter measure of the concentration of color-causing compounds expressed in terms of intensity as Color Units. Determine whether the proposed scheme will meet the treatment objective.

- **Logic and Answer(s).**

1. *The ozone contactor is assumed to behave as a CMFR.*

2. *Before removal can be predicted at HRTs longer than those provided by the original tank, it is necessary to verify the assumed rate expression using the data provided and to obtain an appropriate rate constant.*

3. *The material balance for a CMFR operated at steady state (Equation 9.5) is*

$$QC_{IN} - QC_{OUT} + rV_R = 0$$

4. *After substitution of the proposed empirical rate expression, this material balance equation can be rearranged to determine the rate constant for each of the three tests*

$$k = \frac{C_{IN} - C_{OUT}}{\bar{t}C_{OUT}^{0.5}}$$

As shown below, the three values of k are reasonably close, suggesting that the proposed empirical rate expression is valid.

Test Number	$k(Color\ Units)^{0.5}/min$
1	0.44
2	0.47
3	0.50

5. *The new HRT will be 20 min if a parallel ozone contactor of the same size as the original tank is employed. The CMFR design equation can be used to solve for C_{OUT} with the new $\bar{t}$ or, alternatively, the $\bar{t}$ needed to reach the new treatment objective of 1 color unit can be determined to evaluate whether it is greater or less than 20 min. Using an average k value of 0.47 $(Color\ Units)^{0.5}/min$ the latter approach gives*

$$\bar{t} = \frac{C_{IN} - C_{OUT}}{kC_{OUT}^{0.5}} = \frac{10 - 1}{0.47(1)^{0.5}} = 19.1 \text{ min}$$

6. *As long as $C_{IN} \leq 10$ Color Units the proposed parallel reactor scheme therefore provides a hydraulic residence time which is just sufficient to achieve the treatment objective. However, the evident variability around the average value for C_{IN} suggests that the treatment objective frequently will not be met unless a longer HRT is used.*

- **Key Point(s).** **Your evaluation in this case must be predicated on an assumed ideal reactor model, an empirical rate expression and a limited amount of observed data. About which of these three issues do you feel least comfortable with respect to selecting the required HRT? What would you recommend?**

9.3.3   Plug Flow Reactors

A PFR, often referred to somewhat inappropriately as a tubular reactor, is pictured schematically in Figure 9.3. Flow in an ideal PFR is assumed to be such that fluid velocity is uniform across any cross section orthogonal to the axial flow. Elements of fluid are assumed to proceed through the reactor in an orderly and uniform manner, such that each differential (dx) orthogonal element or plug of fluid is transported along the reactor length remaining completely mixed within itself but not intermixing with adjacent elements. *The time spent by each fluid element in a PFR is thus is the same. It is important to recognize that laminar flow in a tubular reactor does not produce a PFR condition because velocity is parabolically distributed rather than uniform across the cross section, just as it is for flow in circular pipes. The residence times of individual fluid elements in such nonideal reactors are therefore not equal.*

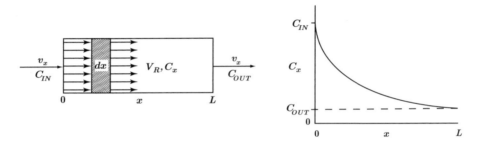

Figure 9.3 Plug-Flow Reactor Schematics

As shown in Figure 9.3, concentrations of nonconservative reactants and products vary continually along the length of a PFR because reaction time is proportional to reactor length. Rates for all reactions other than zero-order depend on concentration, and r thus varies along the length of the reactor. Because r is not constant over length in a PFR, the integral form of the material balance that is used for the CMFR does not apply. Instead, the material balance relationship is written for a differential volume element (dV_R) sufficiently small that reaction rate can be assumed uniform across the element. As noted in Chapter 3, this yields what is essentially the point form of the MBE for a PFR given in Equation 3.28, namely

$$\frac{dC}{dt} = -v_x\frac{dC}{dx} + r \tag{3.28}$$

Equation 3.28 can be simplified for steady-state conditions to

$$-v_x\frac{dC}{dx} + r = 0 \tag{9.10}$$

The variables may then be separated and the equation integrated over the length, L, of the reactor to yield

$$\int_0^L \frac{1}{v_x}\,dx = \int_{C_{IN}}^{C_{OUT}} \frac{dC}{r} \tag{9.11}$$

or, in terms of a steady-state design HRT,

$$\boxed{\textbf{\textit{Steady-State Design HRT for a PFR}} \quad \bar{t} = \frac{L}{v_x} = \int_{C_{IN}}^{C_{OUT}} \frac{dC}{r}} \tag{9.12}$$

Note that the term $\bar{t}$ in Equation 9.12 is the travel time or residence time of each fluid element in the reactor. Example 9.3 provides an illustration of the analysis of process behavior in reactors having the flow properties of ideal PFRs.

Example 9.3. Design of a Heated-Pipe High Temperature Hydrolysis Process for a Cyanide By-Product Stream in a Pharmaceutical Plant. (A comparison of alternative reactor sizes and temperature conditions assuming ideal PFR behavior.)

- **Situation.** *Cyanide is used in the production of intermediates in the pharmaceutical industry. A small resulting waste stream containing an organic cyanide, R-CN, is to be treated by a high-temperature hydrolysis process involving the reaction*

$$\mathrm{R - CN} + 2\mathrm{H_2O} \Rightarrow \mathrm{NH_3} + \mathrm{R{-}\underset{\underset{\mathrm{OH}}{|}}{C}{=}0}$$

The reaction has been studied at temperatures between 170 and 250° C and found to be first order with respect to R-CN concentration. The activation energy is 46 kJ/mol and the rate constant at 170° C is 8 h^{-1} (Midler et al., 1992). The goal of treatment is to reduce R-CN from 2000 mg/L to less than 5 mg/L.

- **Question(s).** *A convenient means for carrying out hydrolysis reactions of this type is in heated pipes. Compare the lengths of heated pipe required at temperatures of 170° and 250° C if the flow rate is 30 L/min and the inside pipe diameter is 15.2 cm (6 in.).*

Logic and Answer(s).

1. *The pipeline reactor can be assumed to behave as a PFR and the general process design equation written from Equation 9.12 as*

$$\bar{t} = \int_{C_{IN}}^{C_{OUT}} \frac{dC}{r}$$

2. *The specific process design equation for a first-order cyanide destruction rate is*

$$\bar{t} = \int_{C_{IN}}^{C_{OUT}} \frac{dC}{-kC} = \frac{\ln(C_{IN}/C_{OUT})}{k}$$

$$\bar{t}(h) = \frac{\ln(2000/5)}{k} = 6k^{-1}$$

3. *The rate constant (k_2) at $250° C$ is obtained from the activation energy and the rate constant (k_1) at $170° C$ as follows*

$$\ln \frac{k_2}{k_1} = \frac{E_a(T_2 - T_1)}{RT_1 T_2}$$

$$k_2 = k_1 \exp \left[\frac{46\text{x}10^3(523 - 443)}{8.314(523)(443)} \right] = 54 h^{-1}$$

4. *Once the HRT is calculated, the length of the pipeline, L, is determined from*

$$L = \frac{Q\bar{t}}{\pi d^2/4} = \frac{30(10^3)(60)(4)\bar{t}}{\pi(15.2)^2(100)} \ meters$$

5. *A summary of the two alternative designs is presented below. As expected, increasing the temperature increases reaction rate and greatly reduces the length of pipe required to meet the treatment objective.*

Temperature (°C)	$k(h^{-1})$	$\bar{t}(h)$	$L(m)$
170	8	0.75	74.4
250	54	0.11	10.9

- *Key Point(s).* **Many process designs involve trade-offs between reactor size and adjustment of conditions (e.g. temperature, pH, etc.) favoring reaction rates. These in turn generally involve, and in fact may be motivated by, associated trade-offs between capital costs (reactor size) and operating costs (alteration of reaction conditions).**

9.3.4   Comparison of Reactor Performances

A comparison of performance predictions for different reactor configurations offers valuable insights into important reactor engineering concepts. Inspection and comparison of Equation 9.3 for a CMBR and Equation 9.12 for a PFR, for example, reveals that the same *residence time is needed for each to achieve a given extent of reaction; i.e., the same fractional conversion. The relationship between these two types of reactors can be appreciated if we picture each cross sectional element of fluid entering a PFR as an independent and infinitesimally thin CMBR that travels down the length of the reactor with the bulk flow velocity, so that its residence time in the PFR is $\bar{t}$.*

HRT design equations for the two principal types of ideal flow through reactors, CMFRs and PFRs, operated at steady-state conditions are given in Equations 9.8 and 9.12, respectively. Substitution of appropriate rate expressions for reactions of zero-, first-, second-, and nth-order for r in these equations leads to the design relationships given in Table 9.1. More detailed discussion of relative CMFR and PFR behaviors under varying conditions is given in PDES, including evaluations based on fractional conversions of influent substances.

Table 9.1 *Hydraulic Residence Time Requirements for Reactions of Different Order in CMFRs and PFRs*

Reaction Order	HRT Required to Obtain a Specified Fractional Conversion (C_{OUT}/C_{IN})	
	t_{CMFR}	$\bar{t}_{PFR}$
0	$\dfrac{(C_{IN} - C_{OUT})}{k}$	$\dfrac{(C_{IN} - C_{OUT})}{k}$
1	$\dfrac{(C_{IN}/C_{OUT}) - 1}{k}$	$\dfrac{\ln(C_{IN}/C_{OUT})}{k}$
$n(n \neq 1)$	$\dfrac{(C_{IN}/C_{OUT}) - 1}{kC_{OUT}^{n-1}}$	$\dfrac{(C_{IN}/C_{OUT})^{n-1} - 1}{k(n-1)(C_{IN})^{n-1}}$

Example 9.4 provides a comparison of the HRTs required in reactor systems of different configuration to obtain a given level of removal of a contaminant from a waste stream by a process controlled by a first-order reaction.

Example 9.4. Selection of a Flow-Through Reactor Configuration for a Contaminant Removal Process. (An illustration of the dependence of reactor size on reactor configuration and reaction rate expression.)

- *Situation. A biocide contained in a process waste stream in a pesticide production plant is detoxified by partial chemical oxidation with hydrogen peroxide in a pretreatment step prior to discharge to a municipal sewer system. The reaction is first-order with a rate coefficient, k.*

- **Question(s).** *Compare the respective HRTs needed to achieve 95% removal of the biocide in a CMFR and in a PFR.*

- **Logic and Answer(s).**

  1. *The HRT design equation for a CMFR is*

  $$\bar{t} = \frac{(C_{IN}/C_{OUT}) - 1}{k}$$

  which, when $C_{OUT}/C_{IN} = 0.05$, gives $\bar{t} = 19k^{-1}$.

  2. *The corresponding design equation for a PFR is*

  $$\bar{t} = \frac{\ln(C_{IN}/C_{OUT})}{k}$$

  which reduces to $\bar{t} = 3k^{-1}$ for $C_{OUT}/C_{IN} = 0.05$.

  3. *The results, summarized below, show the clear residence time advantages of the ideal PFR over the ideal CMFR configuration for similar performance requirements.*

Reactor Configuration	HRT
CMFR	$\bar{t} = 19k^{-1}$
PFR	$\bar{t} = 3k^{-1}$

- **Key Point(s).** *The residence time requirements for an ideal PFR are always smaller than those for an ideal CMFR for any reaction order greater than zero. The difference in size and HRT requirements will increase with increasing reaction order. Why is this so?*

9.4   REACTION RATE MEASUREMENTS IN CMFRs

9.4.1   Concepts

The methods for determining reaction rate expressions given in Chapters 7 and 8 were all based on measurement of data in CMBRs. An alternative approach is to use CMFRs operated at steady state. The usual process control variables are C_{IN} and $\bar{t}$, while C_{OUT} is the measured response variable. The CMFR is experimentally more complex than a CMBR. It requires a feed tank and a system to regulate flow. The reactor must be monitored to verify that steady state is maintained, and several experiments must be conducted for testing a rate expression to obtain a range of C_{OUT} values spanning the desired concentration range. *The CMFR, however, may provide more reliable rate information because it better simulates the flow reactor environments in which treatment processes are most likely to take place at full scale.*

The relationship between reaction rate, process control variables, and the measured response variable is given by rearrangement of Equation 9.8

$$-r = \frac{C_{IN} - C_{OUT}}{\bar{t}} \tag{9.13}$$

Several experiments using different values of C_{IN} and $\bar{t}$ will result in a range of observations of C_{OUT}, from which r may be calculated using Equation 9.13. The objective is to test the rate data to determine a reaction rate expression of the general form

$$r = \phi(C_{OUT}) \tag{9.14}$$

9.4.2   Applications

Zero- and first-order rate relationships can be determined from arithmetic plots of r against C_{OUT}, as shown in Figure 9.4. The reaction rate is zero order if r is independent of C_{OUT} and the rate constant, k, is simply the value of r. A first-order reaction is indicated if r increases linearly with C_{OUT} (i.e., $r = -kC_{OUT}$), and k is obtained from the slope of the graph. A reaction rate higher than first order is indicated if r increases more than proportionally with C_{OUT}.

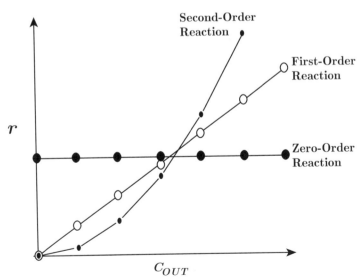

Figure 9.4 Determination of Reaction Orders from Rate Measurements in CMFRs

Reactions having rate relationships other than zero and first order can also be verified for alternative formulations. The second-order rate expression is given by

$$\boldsymbol{r} = -kC^2 \tag{9.15}$$

for which a plot of $\boldsymbol{r}$ versus $(C_{OUT})^2$ data yields a straight line. If no initial insights into reaction order are available, the more general rate expression

$$\boldsymbol{r} = -kC^n \tag{9.16}$$

can be postulated, and the values of k and n determined by a logarithmic transformation of the data to give

$$-\ln \boldsymbol{r} = \ln k + n \ln C_{OUT} \tag{9.17}$$

The method of excess described in Section 7.3.2.3 of Chapter 7 for reaction rates that are dependent on the activities or concentrations of two chemical species can also be applied to CMFR data. For example, suppose that

$$\boldsymbol{r}_l = -kC_i{}^n C_j{}^m \tag{9.18}$$

and $C_{j,IN} \gg C_{i,IN}$ so that $C_{j,R} \approx C_{j,IN}$. The resulting logarithmic transformation of the rate data for different $C_{i,IN}$ for different $\bar{t}$ values for the CMFR is

$$-\ln \boldsymbol{r} = \ln k_{obs} + n \ln C_{i,OUT} \tag{9.19}$$

where $k_{obs} = kC_{j,OUT}^m$. Thus the order of the reaction, n, with respect to component i is the slope of the $\ln \boldsymbol{r}_i$ versus $\ln C_{i,OUT}$ plot. The experiment can be repeated with component i in excess to determine the order of the reaction, m, with respect to component j, and k follows from determination of k_{obs}.

The advantages of CMFRs over CMBRs for rate analysis are perhaps most evident in their applications to biological oxidation reactions (e.g., rate relationships like those of the Michaelis-Menten enzymatic and Monod biogrowth models). A CMFR approximates the metabolic process environment of biological treatment operations better than does a CMBR because it operates at steady state; in such applications, the CMFR is commonly referred to as a chemostat. For the unsteady-state conditions existing in a CMBR, metabolic processes tend to shift as substrate concentrations change with time, and microbial growth rates change accordingly. Such shifts in biomass activity in turn influence the results of rate experiments and measurements.

The Michaelis-Menten rate expression given in Chapter 8 for an enzyme reaction is

$$\frac{dC_{PR}}{dt} = \frac{-dC_{SU}}{dt} = \boldsymbol{r} = \frac{\boldsymbol{r}_{max}C_{SU}}{\mathcal{K}_M + C_{SU}} \tag{8.61}$$

which, in terms of C_{SU}, can be rearranged for the case at hand as

$$\frac{1}{\boldsymbol{r}} = \frac{\mathcal{K}_M}{\boldsymbol{r}_{max}} \left(\frac{1}{C_{SU}}\right)_{OUT} + \frac{1}{\boldsymbol{r}_{max}} \tag{9.20}$$

Rate data adhering to this relationship will yield a linear trace when plotted as $1/r_{max}$ versus $1/(C_{SU})_{OUT}$ for a series of CMFR experiments in which $(C_{SU})_{IN}$ or $\bar{t}$ is systematically varied.

As discussed in Chapter 7 the foregoing method for testing the suitability of various rate expressions by plotting observed data according to their respective linearized forms is not necessary; i.e., nonlinear regression methods can be used instead. Linearization techniques do however allow a quick assessment of whether a proposed rate expression has sufficient promise to merit further testing by more exacting methods.

9.5 CHAPTER SUMMARY

Material balance, macroscale transport, and chemical reaction rate principles developed in previous chapters have been brought together in Chapter 9 to describe the performance of reactors of different "ideal" configuration and flow characteristics. We have seen that the extent of reaction that occurs in a flow-through reactor of given reaction volume is critically dependent upon the manner in which the flow does in fact move through that volume, and therefore upon the physical configuration of that reactor. A reactor may be a device in an engineered treatment system or simply a volume segment in a natural system. Complete mixing and no intermixing of fluid elements provide the CMFR and PFR "frame of reference" boundaries of reactor behavior. They define, respectively the minimum and maximum extents of reaction possible for any specified entrance condition, volume configuration, and exit condition.

9.6 CITATIONS AND SOURCES

Leuking, A.D., W. Huang, S.B. Soderstrom-Schwarz, M. Kim and W.J. Weber, Jr., 2000, "Relationship of Soil Organic Matter Characteristics to Organic Contaminant Sequestration and Bioavailability," *Journal of Environmental Quality, 29*, 317-323. (Problem 9.8)

Midler, M., Jr., C.M. Bagner, A.S. Wildman, and E.S. Venkataramani, 1992, "Destruction of Cyanides by Alkaline Hydrolysis in a Pipeline Reactor," *Environmental Process. 11*(4), 251-255. (Example 9.4)

Weber, W.J., Jr., and F.A. DiGiano, 1996, *Process Dynamics in Environmental Systems*, John Wiley & Sons, Inc., New York. (PDES is the source of most of the material presented in Chapter 9. Chapter 9 of PDES covers and expands upon the material presented in Chapter 9 of this text. It also identifies additional related background reading sources).

Wilber, G.G., and G.F. Parkin, 1995, "Kinetics of Alachor and Atrazine Biotransformations under Various Electron Acceptor Conditions," *Environmental Toxicology and Chemistry, 14*(2), 237-244. (Problem 9.4)

9.7   PROBLEM ASSIGNMENTS

9.1 A "slop" tank in an oil refinery is used to collect various intermittent aqueous flows containing tank bottom residues, floor and pad wash downs, reactor blow downs, organic lab wastes, and rejected product streams. When the tank is filled, mixers are activated and its contents are vigorously mixed. While mixing continues, a strong oxidant is added in excess to reduce the TOC of the tank contents to less than 100 mg/L. The tank contents are then discharged to a central biological treatment facility. The oxidation process is known to be first-order in TOC, with an empirically correlated rate coefficient of $k = 2.5 \times 10^{-3}(\text{TOC})_0$ per day. For a starting concentration of 12,500 mg TOC/L, determine the minimum reaction time interval required to meet the pretreatment objective. Comment on why in this type of situation k might in fact be found to correlate with the initial TOC concentration.

9.2 Chlorine is to be used to oxidize ammonia in the effluent from a physico-chemical waste treatment plant according to the overall stoichiometry

$$2\text{NH}_3 + 3\text{HOCl} \Longleftrightarrow \text{N}_2 + 3\text{Cl}^- + 3\text{H}_3\text{O}^+$$

Effluent quality standards require that 90% removal of ammonia be maintained in the oxidation process. Assuming that the dosages of chlorine to be applied will be sufficient to reduce the rate dependency of the reaction to first order with respect to ammonia, determine the relative sizes of a single CMFR oxidation basin and a PFR oxidation channel required to accomplish the stated degree of treatment.

9.3 An open discharge channel having a length of 200 ft is to be designed to serve the additional purpose of providing contact for disinfection of the effluent from a wastewater treatment plant. The channel must provide sufficient contact time for 99% kill of *E. coli* under maximum flow conditions of 10 cfs. CMBR reactor tests in the laboratory show that 99.9% destruction of *E. coli* is accomplished in 30 min with the 10 mg/L design dose of chlorine.

(a) The rate of destruction of microorganisms can be expressed by the first-order relationship referred to as Chick's law

$$-\frac{dC_N^\circ}{dt} = kC_N^\circ$$

Determine the value of k using the laboratory results.

(b) For the given flow conditions, the contact channel can be treated as an ideal plug-flow reactor and the reaction as first order. Determine what the cross-sectional area of the channel must be to ensure adequate contact time for the required disinfection level.

9.4 A river has been contaminated with approximately $150\mu g/L$ of atrazine. It has been proposed to pass part of the river through a marsh in which the atrazine would be degraded by microorganisms. The degradation of atrazine follows the rate equation

$$-r_{antrazine} = kC_{BM}C$$

where k is the rate constant, C_{BM} is the biomass concentration, and C is the atrazine concentration. The marsh is rectangular and the flow of the water through it can be modeled as plug flow. The rate constant is experimentally determined to be 2×10^5 L/mg volatile suspended solids (VSS)/hr under steady state conditions at a biomass concentration of 60 mg VSS/L. In order to meet environmental standards, the concentration of atrazine exiting the marsh must be less than $3\mu g/L$. The entering flow rate is $2m^3/hr$.

(a) Determine the marsh volume necessary to meet the environmental standards. If the average depth of the marsh is 0.25 m and the width is 100 m, is the necessary length reasonable?

(b) If the entering flow rate increases to $3m^3/hr$ during a high precipitation event, what will be the expected exit concentration of atrazine? What would you recommend doing to prevent this concentration from being too high? What variables other than flow rate might cause a high exit concentration of atrazine?

9.5 A CMFR has an HRT of 10 min. The steady-state feed concentration increases by tenfold from 10 to 100 mg/L.

(a) What is the anticipated increase in effluent concentration if the reaction in the CMFR is first order with a rate constant of 0.1 min^{-1}?

(b) What is the anticipated increase in effluent concentration if the reaction is second order with a rate constant of 0.1 L/mg-min? Discuss the difference between these results.

9.6 The following empirical rate expression is found to describe the oxidation of aqueous phase iron Fe(II) to Fe(III) by dissolved molecular oxygen

$$-\frac{d[\text{Fe(II)}]}{dt} = k[\text{Fe(II)}]p_{O_2}[\text{OH}^-]^2$$

where $k = 8.0 \times 10^{13} L^2/mol^2$-min and p_{O_2} is the oxygen partial pressure. If a groundwater that is strongly buffered at pH = 6.5 contains 1.0 mg/L of dissolved Fe(II), how long must be the detention time of an aeration process designed to saturate the water with air to provide sufficient Fe(II) oxidation to insoluble Fe(III) to meet the EPA National Secondary Drinking Water Regulation of 0.3 mg/L? State your assumptions and justify your choice of a reactor type for this situation.

9.7 A CMBR is to provide for disinfection of a well water at a small, remote
military installation. The water residence time in the reactor must be
sufficient to reduce Giardia cysts to 0.001 of their original concentration.
The rate of disinfection is given by

$$\frac{dC_N}{dt} = -k_d C_{HOCl} C_N$$

where C_N is the number concentration (number/L) of *Giardia* and the
concentration of the disinfectant, C_{HOCl}, is in mg/L. In a laboratory-
scale CMBR, 2 mg/L of HOCl was added to distilled water containing
Giardia cysts (no inorganic species present) and the fraction *Giardia* concentration remaining $(C_N/C_{N,0})$ after 30 min 2 as 0.027. Although HOCl
remained constant in this test, it will not be constant in the field-scale
CMBR because simultaneous oxidation reactions occur that involve inorganic constituents (primarily H_2S, Fe, and Mn) in the well water. The
rate expression for these reactions is given by

$$\frac{dC_{HOCl}}{dt} = -k_{ox} C_{HOCl} \left(\sum_i^n C_i \right)$$

where the summation term refers to all reduced inorganic species that can
be oxidized. In another laboratory-scale CMBR, 2 mg/L of HOCl was
added to the well water to be disinfected and 50% of the HOCl disappeared
after 20 min; the concentrations of the reduced inorganic species did not
decrease substantially due to their presence in excess of the chlorine added.
Assume that all HOCl depletion is due to inorganic oxidation reactions
and that inorganic species remain in excess.

(a) How much time is required to achieve the treatment goal in the proposed CMBR is the starting HOCl concentration is 5 mg/L?

(b) What is the chlorine residual concentration after this disinfection
time?

(c) How much time would be required to achieve the same cyst removal
if the inorganic species could be eliminated before adding the disinfectant?

Answers: (a) 46 min; (b) 1 mg/L; (c) 23 min.

9.8 A biological CMFR operation is to be developed to treat phenanthrene
contaminated groundwater. A pilot scale chemostat is used to determine
the phenanthrene degradation rate at different residence times by varying
the entering flow rate. The results are tabulated below.

Run Number	C_{OUT} $\mu g/L$	$-r_{phenanthrene}$ $\mu g/L/day$
1	800	56566
2	700	52622
3	600	48146
4	500	43022
5	400	37101
6	300	30178
7	200	21976
8	100	12106
9	50	6377
10	10	1333
11	5	670

(a) Determine the values for the Michaelis-Menten parameters, r_{max} and $\mathcal{K}_M$.

(b) What volume CMFR is required to treat $5m^3/hr$ of contaminated water with an initial phenanthrene concentration of $800\mu g/L$ if the desired effluent concentration is $50\mu g/L$?

9.9 Chlorine is to be used to oxidize ammonia in the effluent from a waste treatment plant according to the overall stoichiometry

$$2NH_3 + 3HOCl \Longrightarrow N_2 + 3Cl^- + 3H_3O$$

Effluent quality standards require that 90% removal of ammonia be maintained. Assume that dosages of chlorine to be provided will be sufficient to reduce the rate dependency of the reaction to first order with respect to ammonia.

(a) Determine the relative sizes of a CMFR oxidation basin and a PFR oxidation channel required to accomplish the stated degree of treatment.

(b) Determine the sizes of one CMFR required to accomplish 50% removal followed by another one to provide the remaining 40% removal. What do you observe about the total size of the system relative to the reactor sizes determined in part (a)? Explain your observations.

9.10 Two reactors of equal volume but different configurations are available for use for a second-order chemical oxidation process. One, Reactor A, is a round tank and the other, Reactor B, is a long cylindrical pipe. which of the following systems using both reactors would result in the highest treatment efficiency? clearly state all assumptions involved in your analysis.

(a) Reactor A followed by Reactor B

(b) Reactor B followed by Reactor A

(c) Reactors A and B in parallel with half the feed going into each and the exit streams from each being combined.

Chapter 10

Hybrid System Modeling and Design

Contents

10.0   CHAPTER OBJECTIVES

To investigate ways in which ideal reactors can be reconfigured to better serve process and operational objectives.

10.1   INTRODUCTION

Various modifications can be made to the completely mixed batch, completely mixed flow and plug flow ideal reactors described in Chapter 9 to provide alternative configurations designed to best address specific types of natural and engineered environmental systems. These modifications can lead to intermittent flow reactors, reactors in series, and various flow and solids recycle schemes involving virtually any type of "standard" reactor component.

10.2   SEQUENCING BATCH REACTORS

10.2.1   Concept

A sequencing batch reactor (SBR) is an intermittent-flow operational variation on the CMBR that allows for continuous treatment of a process stream while providing the flexibility of adjusting treatment time to accommodate different feed conditions or reaction environments. A schematic representation of the three principal operating stages of an SBR is presented in Figure 10.1. The first reactor shown in Figure 10.1 depicts the SBR in the fill stage, during which reactions may or may not occur simultaneously, the second the SBR in the reaction stage at constant volume, and the third illustrates the drawdown stage, in preparation for either an idle stage or another fill stage.

Three parallel SBRs with alternating operation in the three respective stages depicted in Figure 10.1 can thus theoretically provide for essentially continuous treatment of a water or waste stream. Adjustments to the time spent in each stage can be made by using more than three reactors and by providing for flexibility in the fill and drawdown volumes.

The SBR has its greatest utility for streams of heterogeneous character requiring combinations of treatment by species transformation and phase separation. For example, the settleability of biomass in waste treatment may vary due to a number of factors that are difficult to control. In conventional continuous-flow operation, periods of slow settling in a secondary clarifier may lead to biomass carryover in the effluent, thus potentially compromising treatment objectives. In the SBR configuration this problem can be overcome by delaying the onset of the drawdown period (now a decanting period), or by extending this period sufficiently to ensure the desired degree of solids settling and separation.

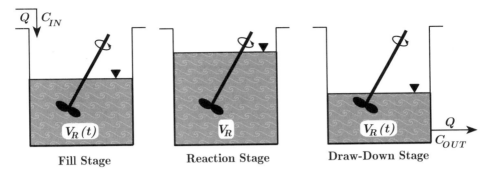

Figure 10.1 Operating Stages of a Sequencing Batch Reactor

10.2.2   Process Design Options

Process designs for SBRs begin with the writing of material balances for both fill and reaction stages. The material balance during the fill stage must account for the molar or mass rate of entry of a reactant, the resultant increase in volume of the reactor with time, and any reaction that occurs during the filling process. If filling involves an influent of constant composition and occurs at a steady (constant) rate, then we can write

$$
\begin{array}{l}
\textbf{\textit{Constant-Rate}} \\
\textbf{\textit{Fill-Stage MBE}} \qquad QC_{IN} + rV_R(t) = \dfrac{dCV_R(t)}{dt} \\
\textbf{\textit{for an SBR}}
\end{array}
\tag{10.1}
$$

The term Q in Equation 10.1 is the steady flow rate during filling, C_{IN} is the concentration of the substance of interest in the influent, $V_R(t)$ is the volume of liquid in the reactor at any time during the fill stage, r is the rate of reaction that takes place during filling, and C is the corresponding concentration within the volume V_R. The volume of liquid in the reactor during the fill stage is

$$
V_R(t) = Qt + V_R(0)
\tag{10.2}
$$

where t is time measured from the beginning of the fill operation and $V_R(0)$ is the volume of liquid initially in the reactor (i.e., at $t = 0$). Substitution of Equation 10.2 into Equation 10.1 followed by differentiation of the right-hand side yields

$$
QC_{IN} + r[Qt + V_R(0)] = [Qt + V_R(0)]\dfrac{dC}{dt} + QC
\tag{10.3}
$$

Analytical solutions to Equation 10.3 are possible for zero and first-order rate relationships, but higher-order expressions require numerical solution techniques. A convenient form of solution for first-order rate equations is obtained by writing Equation 10.1 in terms of the cumulative mole or mass quantities $[M(t) = CV_R(t)]$ of reactant in the SBR at any time rather than in terms of concentration. For a first-order reaction, substitution of $r = -kC$ gives

$$Q_{M,IN} - kM(t) = \frac{dM(t)}{dt} \tag{10.4}$$

where $Q_{M,IN} = QC_{IN}$ is the mass rate of reactant addition to the reactor during the fill stage. Separation of variables and integration of Equation 10.4 yields

$$\int_{M(0)}^{M(t)} \frac{dM(t)}{Q_{M,IN} = kM(t)} = \int_0^t dt \tag{10.5}$$

where $M(0)$ is the mass of reactant present in the reactor at the start of the fill stage (e.g., the mass in the residual volume left from the previous cycle at $t = 0$). Integration of Equation 10.5 gives

$$\ln \frac{Q_{M,IN} - kM(t)}{Q_{M,IN} - kM(0)} = -kt \tag{10.6}$$

or

$$M(t) = \frac{Q_{M,IN}}{k}(1 - e^{-kt}) + M(0)e^{-kt} \tag{10.7}$$

The final form of the solution in terms of reactant concentration is

Fill-Stage MBE for a First-Order Reaction	$C = \dfrac{C_{IN}}{(t + t_0)k} - \left[\dfrac{C_{IN}}{t_0 k} - C(0)\right]\dfrac{t_0}{t_0 + t}e^{-kt}$	(10.8)

where $t_0 = V_R(0)/Q$ and $C(0)$ is the initial concentration of reactant in the volume present in the reactor at the beginning of the fill stage. Figure 10.2 illustrates a sample solution for Equation 10.8. The concentration increases at the beginning of the fill period because the rate at which mass enters is greater than that at which it can be eliminated by the first-order reaction. The concentration reaches a maximum and then declines as residence time and volume increase.

A major objective of any process design is to determine the total residence time required to achieve a desired final concentration. Equation 10.8 provides the relationship between concentration in the reactor and fill time, t, for a given ratio of the initial volume, $V_R(0)$, to fill rate, Q. The fill rate is determined by the waste generation rate, and the fill time by the maximum volume selected for the reactor, the latter usually being constrained by certain economic and/or operational considerations.

In most instances, reactions that occur during the fill stage will not by themselves be sufficient to achieve the desired reduction in feed

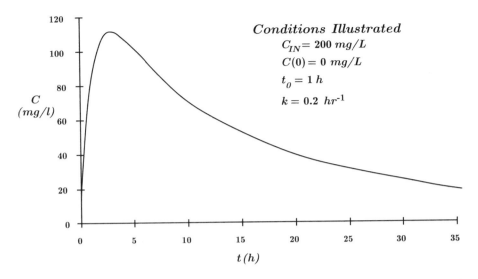

Figure 10.2 Fill-Stage Performance Characteristics of a Sequencing Batch Reactor for a First-Order Reaction

concentration, thus requiring that additional time be provided in the constant-volume reaction stage. The time required in this stage is calculated using the CMBR reaction time interval (RTI) relationship given in Equation 9.3, the limits of integration being from C_{FILLED}, the concentration at the end of the fill stage, to $C_{REACTED}$, the desired final concentration at the end of the reaction stage, and the corresponding (RTI) for the reaction stage being t_R. For a first-order reaction, this time is given by

$$\boxed{\text{Reaction-Stage RTI for a First-Order Reaction} \qquad t_R = -\frac{1}{k}\ln\frac{C_{REACTED}}{C_{FILLED}}} \qquad (10.9)$$

Various combinations of fill and reaction times can be employed to achieve a given effluent concentration. To approach an essentially continuous overall operation with a system of parallel reactors, short fill times and long RTIs require a larger number of reactors than long fill times and short RTIs.

10.3 CMFRs IN SERIES

CMFRs may be connected in series in treatment operations to the benefit that only the reaction rate in the last reactor in the series is *controlled by the final effluent concentration. Such series arrangements thereby increase overall process efficiency and thus reduce total CMFR volumes and detentions time needed to meet target effluent concentrations.*

A typical series arrangement of identical CMFRs in which the exit concentration of one reactor is the feed concentration of the next reactor in the series is illustrated schematically in Figure 10.3.

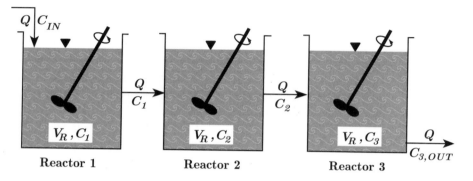

Figure 10.3 Identical CMFRs in Series

At steady state, the normalized effluent concentration for the nth reactor in a series of n identical reactors is

$$\frac{C_{n,OUT}}{C_{IN}} = \frac{C_1}{C_{IN}}\frac{C_2}{C_1}\ldots\ldots\frac{C_{n,OUT}}{C_{n-1}} \tag{10.10}$$

which can be determined by iterative solution of Equation 9.9, beginning with the first reactor in series.

10.3.1   Design Relationships

The steady-state design equation for identical CMFRs in series for a first-order reaction is obtained by substituting a rearrangement of Equation 9.9 in terms of C_{OUT}/C_{IN} into Equation 10.10 to yield

$$\boxed{\begin{array}{ll} \textit{MBE for a First} \\ \textit{Order Reaction} \\ \textit{in a Series of} \\ \textit{n CMFRs} \end{array} \quad \frac{C_{n,OUT}}{C_{IN}} = \left(\frac{1}{1+k\bar{t}}\right)^n} \tag{10.11}$$

Taking the nth root of both sides of Equation 10.11 provides the complementary design equation expressed in terms of the hydraulic resi-

dence time, $\bar{t}$, for each of the series of n identical CMFRs

$$\boxed{\begin{array}{ll} \textbf{\textit{HRT for Each}} \\ \textbf{\textit{of n CMFRs}} & \bar{t} = \frac{1}{k}[(C_{IN}/C_{n,OUT})^{1/n} - 1] \\ \textbf{\textit{in Series}} \end{array}} \qquad (10.12)$$

The total series HRT, $n\bar{t}$, required for a first-order reaction to achieve a given fractional concentration in the exit stream is

$$\boxed{\begin{array}{ll} \textbf{\textit{Total HRT for n}} \\ \textbf{\textit{Identical CMFRs}} & n(\bar{t}) = \frac{n}{k}[(C_{IN}/C_{n,OUT})^{1/n} - 1] \\ \textbf{\textit{in Series}} \end{array}} \qquad (10.13)$$

in which $\bar{t}$ has the same value for each identical reactor in a series of n.

In Example 9.4 we compared the residence time requirements of single CMFR and single PFR systems for achieving a specific level of treatment in a process involving a first-order reaction. Example 10.1 extends this comparison to CMFRs in series. Example 10.2 then illustrates how to approach situations in which the mean residence times of the reactors in a series of CMFRs may vary from one reactor to another.

Example 10.1. Assessment of Reactor-In-Series Configurations for Use in a Chemical Oxidation Process. (A comparison of HRTs with those of single CMFR and single PFR configurations and an illustration of the effect of the number of reactors involved in such series configurations.)

- *Situation. As in Example 9.4 in Chapter 9, a biocide in a pesticide plant waste stream is partially oxidized with hydrogen peroxide in a pretreatment step designed to detoxify the waste prior to its discharge to a municipal sewer system. The first-order reaction has a rate constant, k.*

- *Question(s). Compare the relative HRT required to achieve 95% removal of this contaminant in an in-line series of three CMFRs with the results obtained in Example 9.4 for a single CMFR and a single PFR.*

- *Logic and Answer(s).*

  1. The design equation for CMFRs in series given in Equation 10.13 is

  $$n(\bar{t}) = \frac{n}{k}[(C_{IN}/C_{n,OUT})^{1/n} - 1]$$

which, when $C_{OUT}/C_{IN} = 0.05$, gives $\bar{t} = 19k^{-1}$ and for $n = 3$ gives

$$(\bar{t})_{total} = 5.14k^{-1}$$

and for $n = 6$ gives

$$(\bar{t})_{total} = 3.89k^{-1}$$

2. *The results obtained here and those in Example 9.4 are summarized below, showing the advantage of CMFRs in series over a single CMFR, and that of a PFR over both CMFRs in series and a single CMFR.*

Reactor Configuration	HRT
CMFR	$\bar{t} = 19k^{-1}$
Three CMFRs in series (total $\bar{t}$)	$\bar{t} = 5.14k^{-1}$
Six CMFRs in Series (total $\bar{t}$	$\bar{t} = 3.89k^{-1}$
PFR	$\bar{t} = 3k^{-1}$

- **Key Point(s).** **The CMFR-in-series model gives results intermediate between the models for single CMFRs and single PFRs. We note, however, that as the number of CMFRs in series increases, the results more closely approach those for a single PFR. What result do you expect intuitively as $n \to \infty$?**

Example 10.2. Fecal Coliform Reduction in a Series of Waste Treatment Lagoons. (A CMFRs-in-series analysis of residence times required to meet discharge standards by natural coliform die-off.)

- **Situation.** *Two completely mixed lagoons are connected in series to provide wastewater treatment for a small community. The HRT for the first lagoon is 10 days and that for the second is 5 days. Along with BOD removal, these lagoons achieve significant reduction of fecal coliform organisms through natural die-off. The die-off rate is considered to be first order in character. Rate constants reported from a number of different lagoon systems, however, suggest that die-off rate may depend also on hydraulic residence time, $\bar{t}$ (days), as shown by the empirical formulation below*

$$k = 0.2\bar{t} - 0.3$$

- **Question(s).** *An estimate of the fecal coliform die-off is needed to determine whether or not a new regulatory discharge standard of 99.9% reduction of coliforms can be met without adding a specific disinfection process to the treatment system. In the event the standard cannot be met in the existing system, it is of interest to explore the possibility of increasing the percent reduction by adding a third lagoon in series.*

- *Logic and Answer(s).*

  1. *The general process design model for two CMFRs in series is given by Equation 10.10 as*

  $$\frac{C_{2,OUT}}{C_{IN}} = \frac{C_1}{C_{IN}} \frac{C_{2,OUT}}{C_1}$$

  2. *Equation 10.11 cannot be used to solve this problem because neither the HRT nor the first-order rate constant are the same for the two CMFRs. Instead, the solution proceeds by determining the product of the fractional reduction in fecal coliform in each CMFR*

  $$\frac{C_{2,OUT}}{C_{IN}} = \left[\frac{1}{1 + k_1 \bar{t}_1}\right]\left[\frac{1}{1 + k_2 \bar{t}_2}\right]$$

  3. *From the relationship provided between the rate constant and the hydraulic detention time, the values if k_1 and k_2 are 1.7 and 0.7 day^{-1}, respectively. The fraction of fecal coliforms remaining is*

  $$\frac{C_{2,OUT}}{C_{IN}} = \left[\frac{1}{1 + (1.7)(10)}\right]\left[\frac{1}{1 + (0.7)(5)}\right] = 0.0123$$

  and the percent reduction is $(1 - 0.0123) \times 100 = 98.77\%$, which is less than the requirement of 99.9% $(C_{OUT}/C_{IN} = 0.001)$.

  4. *The effect of adding a third lagoon to bring the total reduction to 99.9% can be expressed by*

  $$\frac{C_{3,OUT}}{C_{IN}} = \left[\frac{C_2}{C_{IN}}\right]\left[\frac{C_{3,OUT}}{C_2}\right] = 0.001$$

  The fraction of fecal coliforms remaining through treatment in the third lagoon would then be

  $$\frac{C_{3,OUT}}{C_2} = 0.001 \left(\frac{1}{0.0123}\right) = 0.081 \text{ or } 8.1\%$$

  5. *The numerical value of the product of the reaction rate coefficient k and the HRT required in the third lagoon to achieve this level of treatment can be found from Equation 9.9 describing the performance of a CMFR with a first-order reaction rate*

  $$k\bar{t} = \frac{C_2}{C_{3,OUT}} - 1 = 11.35$$

  The quadratic equation resulting from substitution of $k = 0.2\bar{t} - 0.3$ into this relationship can then be solved for $\bar{t}_3$ to give

  $$\bar{t}_3 = \frac{0.3 + [(0.3)^2 + 4(0.2)(11.35)]^{0.5}}{2(0.2)} = 8.3 \text{ days}$$

> *6. To evaluate fully the two alternative methods for meeting the new fecal coliform standard, the cost of constructing the third lagoon would need to be compared to the cost of adding appropriate disinfection facilities.*

- *Key Point(s). Relatively simple models can be used to analyze complex systems if the assumptions underlying those models are valid for the system to which the models are applied. In this case the assumption of identical CMFRs in series implied by Equations 10.11, 10.12, and 10.13 is not valid, but a modified approach can be taken to circumvent this problem.*

10.4   REACTORS WITH RECYCLE

10.4.1   Recycle Objectives

Recycle reactors offer advantages over other reactor configurations in a number of different circumstances, particularly those involving both fluid and solid phases. Reactors with recycle equalization are commonly used to approximate steady-state conditions in batch-type bench-scale studies of fluid-solid mass transfer rates or fluid-solid reaction rates. Direct recycle of either fluids or solids is commonly employed in continuous-flow reactors to improve treatment performance.

Recycling of the fluid phase produces performance characteristics between those of ideal PFRs and CMFRs, much as do CMFRs in series. In certain cases, such as for attached growth FBR bioreactors, effluent recycling helps to dilute feed concentrations to prevent overloading. Similarly, recycling of solids is used to increase reactive mass concentrations and rates of reaction in CMFR and PFR processes such as chemical precipitation, adsorption by powdered forms of activated carbon, and suspended-growth biotreatment processes.

10.4.2   Recycle Equalization

Reactors with recycle equalization are generally combinations of small CMFR or PFR reaction systems with large completely mixed tanks in which concentration equalization rather than reaction occurs. We designate these as completely mixed equalization tank (CMET) recycle reactors.

CMET recycle reactors are commonly referred to simply as batch-recycle reactors, in which context the term "batch" is a relative term; that is, the large size of the completely mixed equalization tank in a recycle loop relative to the small size of the recycle flow to and from a small associated CMFR or PFR. It is this important feature, however, that makes it possible to treat the entire system as essentially a

CMBR. While the CMET-recycle concept can accommodate virtually any reactor configuration, its greatest advantage accrues to its use in conjunction with an FBR, for reasons discussed below.

A typical PFR/CMET-recycle scheme in which the reaction section is a small fixed-bed reactor (FBR) containing a reactive solid phase is illustrated in Figure 10.4. The return flow from the FBR shown in Figure 10.4 passes into

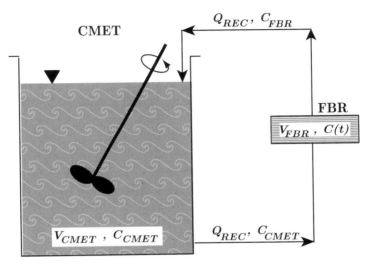

Figure 10.4 A PFR with Recycle to a CMF Equalization Tank

a large CMET in which its concentration is smoothed by dilution; this flow is then recycled to the FBR. The most common objective of this type of experimental design is to provide differential reactor operation in the FBR section of the system. That is, the recycle rate and the relative sizes of the FBR and CMET components of the system are selected to make the residence time of each pass through the FBR section short enough that only a small (differential) concentration change occurs due to either mass transfer or reaction. The concentration in the CMET thus changes only very slowly for a given reaction volume and rate. Alternatively, the concentration in the reservoir can regularly be adjusted to maintain an essentially constant value, either continuously or in frequent incremental fashion. By such adjustment, the rate process in the FBR may be considered approximately constant, just as for a CMFR operated at steady state.

In either mode of rate data collection (i.e., either with a slowly decreasing concentration or with incremental additions that maintain an essentially constant concentration), reaction rates can be determined much more easily than they can be by attempting to measure small differences in concentration across the reactive PFR section. This type of chemostat provides an especially attractive way to study rates of fast, fluid-solid phase processes. The material balance around the entire FBR/CMET recycle system pictured in Figure 10.4 is

$$\int_0^{V_{FBR}} r \, dV_{FBR} = V_{FBR} \frac{dC_{FBR}}{dt} + V_{CMET} \frac{dC_{CMET}}{dt} \qquad (10.14)$$

If a true differential reactor condition applies (i.e., a " Δ-FBR" condition), $C_{FBR} \approx C_{CMET}$ and the rate, r, is essentially constant throughout the volume, V_{FBR}. With these assumptions, Equation 10.14 simplifies to

$$\boxed{\begin{array}{c} \textbf{\textit{Overall Reaction Rate for a}} \\ \textbf{\textit{Δ-FBR/CMET Recycle Reactor}} \\[6pt] r = \dfrac{V_{TOTAL}}{V_{FBR}} \left[\dfrac{dC_{CMET}}{dt} \right] \approx \dfrac{V_{CMET}}{V_{FBR}} \left[\dfrac{dC_{MET}}{dt} \right] \end{array}} \qquad (10.15)$$

where $V_{TOTAL} = V_{FBR} + V_{CMET}$ and $V_{CMET} >> V_{FBR}$. The reaction rate can in this case be estimated by determining the instantaneous slope of a plot of C_{CMET} versus time data. Analysis of the dependency of reaction rate on concentration follows the same procedure as for other reactor configurations. Inspection of Equation 10.15 shows that the effect of V_{CMET} is to accumulate and thereby "integrate" a differential change in concentration across V_{FBR} over longer time periods to measure more accurately the reaction rate in the $\Delta - FBR$.

For the design of a Δ-FBR/CMET recycle reactor we must determine a reasonable value for V_{CMET}, large enough to satisfy the Δ-FBR condition but small enough to allow meaningful measurements of ΔC_{CMET} in reasonable increments of time, Δt. If V_{CMET} is too large, the Δt required for measurable ΔC_{CMET} values may be unreasonably long. In the extreme, this increment may even exceed the time required for completion of the reaction in the FBR.

The establishment of a differential-reactor operating condition must in fact be determined by a material balance around the FBR component rather than around the entire system. Allowing at any instance of time a finite difference between the concentrations in the two system components, we can write

$$Q_{REC} (C_{CMET} - C_{FBR}) + \int_0^{V_{FBR}} r \, dV_{FBR} = V_{FBR} \frac{dC_{FBR}}{dt} \qquad (10.16)$$

where Q_{REC} is the recycle flow rate and C_{FBR} is the exit concentration from the differential reactor. Substitution of the integral from Equation 10.14 gives

$$C_{CMET} - C_{FBR} = -\frac{V_{CMET}}{Q_{REC}} \left[\frac{dC_{CMET}}{dt} \right] \qquad (10.17)$$

The differential-reactor condition assumed in writing Equation 10.15 must apply as well to Equation 10.17. Thus dC_{CMET}/dt may be replaced by Equation 10.15 to obtain a Δ-FBR/CMET design equation

$$
\boxed{\begin{array}{l} \textbf{Δ-FBR /CMET} \\ \textbf{Recycle Reactor} \\ \textbf{Design Equation} \end{array} \quad C_{CMET} - C_{FBR} = -\frac{V_{CMET}}{Q_{REC}}\left[\frac{V_{FBR}}{V_{TOTAL}}\right]r} \qquad (10.18)
$$

Inspection of Equation 10.18 shows that, for an FBR reaction in which concentration decreases, $C_{CMET} \rightarrow C_{FBR}$ as the recycle flow rate increases and as the FBR volume decreases. The validity of an assumption of differential reactor operation depends upon what is determinable and acceptable in the magnitude of difference in concentrations between the reactor components. The more accurate are our measurements of concentration, the closer we can design for the $\Delta - FBR/CMET$ condition. We must, however, make an initial estimate of r to select the volumes of the two system components to be used for measuring r. Experimental iterations may then be required to meet a desired value of $C_{CMET} - C_{FBR}$.

10.4.3 PFRs with Flow Recycle

Our development of recycle reactor design equations begins with a steady-state analysis of the performance of a PFR with fluid-phase recycle, as illustrated in Figure 10.5.

The one-dimensional steady-state point form of the material balance relationship for a PFR was given earlier in Equation 9.10.

$$
-v_x\frac{dC}{dx} + r = 0 \qquad (9.10)
$$

In this instance, the flux of a specific constituent is defined by

$$
v_x = \frac{Q_{IN} + Q_{REC}}{A_N} \qquad (10.19)
$$

where Q_{IN} is the flow rate of the feed stream to the reactor, Q_{REC} the effluent recycle flow rate, and A_N the cross-sectional area of the reactor normal to the incoming flow. The steady-state mass balance equation for this condition is

$$
\int_{C_{MIX}}^{C_{OUT}} \frac{dC}{r} = \frac{1}{Q_{IN} + Q_{REC}} \int_0^L A_N dx = \frac{V_R}{Q_{IN} + Q_{REC}} \qquad (10.20)
$$

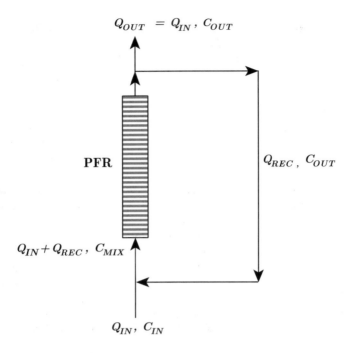

Figure 10.5 A PFR with Flow Recycle

where C_{MIX} is the concentration after blending the feed and recycle streams and V_R is the volume of the reactor. The recycle ratio, the ratio of recycle flow to influent flow, is usually defined as

$$R_Q = \frac{Q_{REC}}{Q_{IN}} \qquad (10.21)$$

A steady-state HRT design equation for a PFR with flow recycle is obtained by substituting Equation 10.21 and $\bar{t} = V_R/Q_{IN}$ into Equation 10.20 to yield

$$
\boxed{
\begin{array}{l}
\textbf{Steady-State} \\
\textbf{Design HRT} \\
\textbf{for a PFR} \\
\textbf{with Flow Recycle}
\end{array}
\quad
\bar{t} = (1 + R_Q) \int\limits_{C_{MIX}}^{C_{OUT}} \frac{dC}{r}
}
\qquad (10.22)
$$

As evident by comparing Equation 10.22 with Equation 9.12 for a simple PFR, flow recycle directly increases the required HRT. The extent to which it does so cannot be determined directly from Equation 10.22, however, until the value of C_{MIX} is calculated. The concentration of the blended feed and recycle flow, C_{MIX}, is necessarily *less than the feed concentration, C_{IN} and the value of the integral is therefore smaller than that for a similar PFR operated without recycle.*

The blend concentration C_{MIX} is given by the following mass balance

$$(Q_{IN} + Q_{REC})C_{MIX} = Q_{IN}C_{IN} + Q_{REC}C_{OUT} \qquad (10.23)$$

$$C_{MIX} = \frac{C_{IN} + R_Q C_{OUT}}{1 + R_Q} \qquad (10.24)$$

As recycle increases, C_{MIX} decreases, and the concentration change across the reactor becomes smaller. At very high recycle rates, the reaction rate becomes nearly constant throughout the reactor. Equation 10.22 may then be written as

$$\bar{t} = (1 + R_Q)\frac{C_{OUT} - C_{MIX}}{r} \qquad (10.25)$$

After substitution for C_{MIX} from Equation 10.24, this expression reduces to the steady-state design equation for a simple CMFR given in Equation 9.8

$$\boxed{\begin{array}{ll} \textbf{\textit{Steady-State}} & \\ \textbf{\textit{Design HRT}} & \bar{t} = -\frac{1}{r}(C_{IN} - C_{OUT}) = \frac{-\Delta C}{r} \\ \textbf{\textit{for a CMFR}} & \end{array}} \qquad (9.8)$$

The above analysis supports an intuitive conclusion; that is, a continuous-flow recycle reactor is identical to a PFR when $R_Q = 0$, and to a CMFR when R_Q approaches infinity. Between these extremes, the detention times required for recycle reactors are intermediate to those of PFRs and CMFRs, as was shown earlier to be the case as well for CMFRs in series.

An application of Equation 10.22 for the design of a PFR with recycle is given in Example 10.3, and the results compared to those obtained in Example 9.4 for single CMFRs and PFRs, and in Example 10.1 for CMFRs in series. The comparison illustrates the design flexibility afforded by different reactor configurations and arrangements.

Example 10.3. Assessment of a PFR with Flow Recycle for Use in a Chemical Oxidation Process. (A comparison of HRTs for two recycle ratios with those for single CMFR, single PFR, and CMFRs-in-series configurations.)

- *Situation. As in Examples 9.4 and 10.1, a biocide contained in a process waste stream in a pesticide production plant is detoxified by partial chemical oxidation with hydrogen peroxide in a pretreatment step prior to discharge to a municipal sewer system. The reaction is first-order with a rate constant, k.*

- **Question(s).** *Compare the HRTs for recycle reactors with $R_Q = 1$ and $R_Q = 3$ to those calculated in Examples 9.4 and 10.1 for a single CMFR, three and six CMFRs in series, and a single PFR.*

- **Logic and Answer(s).**

  1. The design equation for a first-order reaction follows from Equation 10.22

$$\bar{t} = (1 + R_Q) \int_{C_{MIX}}^{C_{OUT}} \frac{dC}{r} = (1 + R_Q)\frac{-\ln(C_{OUT}/C_{MIX})}{k}$$

  2. C_{MIX}/C_{IN} is given by dividing both sides of Equation 10.24 by C_{IN}

$$\frac{C_{MIX}}{C_{IN}} = \frac{1 + R_Q(C_{OUT}/C_{IN})}{1 + R_Q}$$

  3. For $C_{OUT}/C_{IN} = 0.05$, the values of C_{MIX}/C_{IN} (from Equation 10.24), C_{OUT}/C_{MIX} [which is given by $(C_{OUT}/C_{IN}) \times (C_{IN}/C_{MIX})$], and $\bar{t}$ (from Equation 10.22) are presented below. Note by comparison with the findings of Examples 9.4 and 10.1 that the $\bar{t}$ values are intermediate between a single $PFR(3k^{-1})$ and a single $CMFR(19k^{-1})$; a recycle ratio of 1 corresponds roughly to three CMFRs in series.

R_Q	C_{MIX}/C_{IN}	C_{OUT}/C_{MIX}	$\bar{t}$
1	0.525	0.095	$4.7k^{-1}$
3	0.287	0.174	$6.98k^{-1}$

- **Key Point(s). Flow recycle arrangements can be employed to overcome some of the disadvantages of single PFRs with respect to such problems as shock loading while still reducing volumetric requirements below those of single CMFRs without incurring all of the costs of multiple CMFRs in series.**

10.4.4 CMFRs with Flow Recycle

A steady-state material balance on a fluid phase component of the CMFR with flow recycle represented schematically in Figure 10.6 yields

$$Q_{IN}C_{IN} + Q_{REC}C_{OUT} - (Q_{IN} + Q_{REC})C_{OUT} + rV_R = 0 \qquad (10.26)$$

Because the recycle terms in Equation 10.26 cancel out , and because $Q_{OUT} = Q_{IN}$, the MBE reduces to that given earlier in Equation 9.5 for a CMFR without

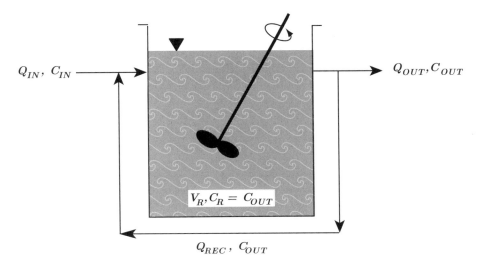

Figure 10.6 A CMFR with Flow Recycle

recycle, and thus the corresponding HRT design equation is the same as that given in Equation 9.8.

Recycle does not change the required volume of the reactor, which, from the definition of $\bar{t}$, is calculated from the feed flow rate, Q_{IN}. Instead, the effect of recycle is to decrease the detention time per pass (t_p) through the CMFR

Steady-State Per-Pass HRT for a CMFR with Flow Recycle	$\bar{t}_p = \dfrac{V_R}{Q_{IN} + Q_{REC}}$	(10.27)

Although $\bar{t}_p$ becomes smaller with increasing Q_{REC}, the number of passes increases, such that each fluid element still spends time a mean overall HRT of $\bar{t}$ in the reactor and the extent of reaction is the same as that without recycle. Thus, the principal values of this type of recycle system are to either: 1) level periodic concentration spikes in reactant(s) or reaction-inhibiting substances in the feed; 2) return dissolved products that "auto catalyze" the reaction; or, 3) advantageously control temperature in either endothermic or exothermic reactions.

10.4.5 CMFRs with Solids Recycle

Solids recycle is commonly practiced to enhance rates of solids-catalyzed reactions in CMFRs. Precipitation processes, for example have rate relationships described by $r = -k(C - C_S)C_{ps}$, where

$(C - C_S)$ *is the dissolved-phase concentration of precipitant in excess of the saturation concentration* C_S, *and* C_{ps} *is the dispersed-phase concentration of preformed (existing) solids.*

A solids separation operation following the CMFR is generally incorporated in the design of solids recycle systems to concentrate the solids for recycle. This is often a simple settling tank, such as that illustrated in Figure 10.7, but other techniques such as cross-flow filtration may also be employed. The choice usually depends upon the difficulty of separation involved and the degree of solids recovery desired. The solids are often the by-products of designed treatment processes. For example, chemical precipitates are produced in phosphorus removal and lime softening processes, and biomass is produced in biological treatment processes. These solids must be "wasted" (treated, reused, disposed of) at a rate equal to their production rate in order to maintain constant steady-state concentrations in designed treatment processes.

With reference to Figure 10.7, the solids concentration entering the CMFR is obtained from a material balance

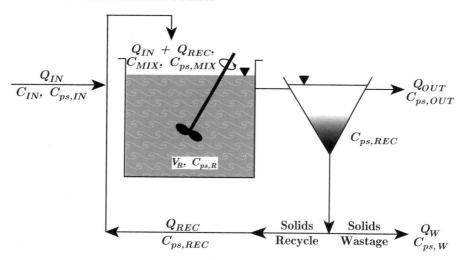

Figure 10.7 A CMFR with Solids Recycle

written after blending the feed and recycle rates

$$Q_{IN}C_{ps,IN} + Q_{REC}C_{ps,REC} - (Q_{IN} + Q_{REC})C_{ps,MIX} = 0 \qquad (10.28)$$

from which $C_{ps,MIX}$ can be calculated as

$$C_{ps,MIX} = \frac{Q_{IN}C_{ps,IN} + Q_{REC}C_{ps,REC}}{Q_{IN} + Q_{REC}} = \frac{C_{ps,IN} + R_Q C_{ps,REC}}{1 + R_Q} \qquad (10.29)$$

Usually, $C_{ps,IN}$ is so much smaller than $R_Q C_{ps,REC}$ that it can be neglected.

The mean solids residence time (SRT) or "age," $\bar{t}_S$, for systems such as that shown in Figure 10.7 is given by

$$
\boxed{
\begin{array}{l}
\textbf{Steady-State} \\
\textbf{Design SRT} \\
\textbf{for a CMFR} \\
\textbf{with Solids Recycle}
\end{array}
\qquad
\bar{t}_S = \frac{C_{ps,R} V_R}{M_W}
}
\qquad (10.30)
$$

where $C_{ps,R} V_R$ is the average mass of solids in the CMFR and M_W is the mass wastage rate (i.e., $M_W = Q_W C_{ps,W} + Q_{OUT} C_{ps,OUT}$, where $Q_{OUT} = Q_{IN} - Q_W$). If the rate of solids build-up is small, $C_{ps,R} \sim C_{ps,MIX}$. As evident from Equation 10.30, the age of the solids can be controlled by the recycle rate. The control of solids age can have important implications for reactor performance.

Example 10.4 describes a solids-recycle system in which an ancillary solids treatment process is incorporated in the recycle loop. Schemes of this type are sometimes used to "select" microorganisms with good settling characteristics (i.e., to eliminate poor settling characteristics) for return to the aeration tank.

Example 10.4. Solids Recycle in a Municipal Activated-Sludge Wastewater Treatment Plant with Solids Treatment to Control Sludge Bulking. (An example of the interplay of different unit operations comprising complex process operations.)

- *Situation. An activated sludge treatment system is used to treat 7500 m^3/day of an industrial wastewater. The success of the process depends in large measure on maintaining a steady-state biomass concentration of 1500 mg/L in the aeration tank, which has an HRT of 10 h. Biomass is settled, the excess growth is wasted, and the remainder is recycled to the head of the aeration tank. The recycle ratio, R_Q, is 0.4. It has been discovered that a steady-state concentration cannot be maintained because a significant fraction of the bacteria present in the recycle flow are species of the genus Nocardia. These filamentous bacteria form a low-density, poorly-settling floc which allows biomass to escape the final clarifier in the effluent; moreover, the suspended solids concentration is in excess of the discharge permit. The net growth rate of Nocardia is first order with respect to the microorganism concentration, C_N, and the growth rate constant, k_G, is $0.006\,h^{-1}$. Hydrogen peroxide is known to inactivate Nocardia. The rate of inactivation is also first order with respect to Nocardia and the reaction rate constant, k_R, is $4\,h^{-1}$. A well-mixed tank (i.e., a CMFR) having an HRT of 0.5 h is constructed on the solids recycle line to accommodate the hydrogen peroxide process, as indicated below.*

- *Question(s). Data from other treatment plants indicate that good settling will result if the Nocardia can be kept below 400 mg/L in the effluent*

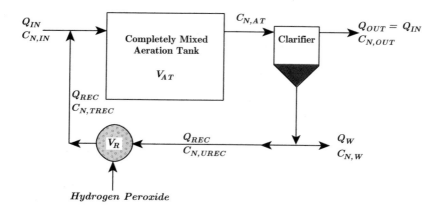

from the aeration tank. The active Nocardia concentration in the untreated recycled solids entering the hydrogen peroxide reactor, $C_{N,UREC}$, is
1200 mg/L. Will the Nocardia concentration in the treated recycled solids,
$C_{N,TREC}$, be low enough to meet the stated $C_{N,AT}$ objective?

- **Logic and Answer(s).**

    1. The steady-state material balance for active Nocardia species written
       around the aeration tank is

    $$Q_{IN}C_{N,IN}+Q_{REC}C_{N,TREC}-(Q_{IN}+Q_{REC})C_{N,AT}+k_G C_{N,AT}V_{AT} = 0$$

       where $C_{N,IN} = 0$. (Note: To use a steady-state analysis, we assume
       that the growth rate of Nocardia is similar to that of all other mi-
       croorganisms, for which case the wastage rate is exactly equal to the
       growth rate.)

    2. Solving for the concentration of Nocardia leaving the aeration tank
       gives

    $$C_{N,AT} = \frac{R_Q C_{N,TREC}}{1 + R_Q - k_G(V_{AT}/Q_{IN})}$$

       where $R_Q = Q_{REC}/Q_{IN}$.

    3. The material balance on Nocardia around the hydrogen peroxide re-
       actor is

    $$C_{N,TREC} = \frac{C_{N,UREC}}{1 + k_R \bar{t}_R}$$

       where $\bar{t}_R$ is the HRT of the recycle reactor.

    4. Returning the expression above to the material balance around the
       aeration tank (step 2) gives

    $$C_{N,AT} = \frac{R_Q C_{N,UREC}}{[1 + R_Q - k_G(V_{AT}/Q_{IN})]\,(1 + k_R \bar{t}_R)}$$

5. *Substitution of all the known parameters gives*

$$C_{N,AT} = \frac{0.4(1200)}{[1 + 0.4 - (0.006)(14)][1 + (0.4)(0.5)]} = 122\text{mg/L}$$

6. *The proposed treatment will therefore meet the objective of maintaining active Nocardia concentrations in the effluent of the aeration basin below 400 mg/L.*

- *Key Point(s). Solids recycle systems are used in a variety of ways to enhance the performance of engineered reactors. Because the solids involved are themselves reactive, recycle in precipitation, adsorption, and suspended-growth biological systems acts to increase reaction rates. In certain cases, such as that illustrated above, the solids to be recycled can be modified during the recycle process to make them even more reactive in the treatment process.*

10.5 CHAPTER SUMMARY

Several variations of the CMBR, CMFR and PFR ideal reactor configurations have been introduced. The first of these, the SBR, extends the concepts and enlarges the applications flexibility of the CMBR by incorporating a series of sequential process stages. It is conceivable that an entire complex sequence of species transformations and phase separations might be carried out in a single SBR. Such a scenario might call for adding all feed streams to be treated to the tank at the same time, and for removing all of the treated products after some predetermined residence/reaction time. Alternatively, sequential additions of feed streams and removal of products may be designed for, with intermediate stages involving appropriate combinations of reactants and products.

A more realistic scenario for SBR design and operation is a relatively straightforward three-stage process involving: 1) conditioning or homogenization (i.e., mass equalization) of a time-variable feed stream or streams during the filling of the SBR, with appropriate reagent addition taking place either during or at the end of the filling stage; 2) an essentially CMBR type reaction stage with an adjustable residence time to ensure that the desired level of treatment is accomplished; 3) a quiescent period to allow for any separation of phases that might be needed (this is commonly the case because it is generally a principal motivation for selection of an SBR; and, 4) a decanting and/or emptying stage in which the entire reactor contents may be removed or some part thereof retained for the next cycle of operation.

The SBR is particularly suitable for treatment of low and variable flow rate (possible even intermittent) streams that require variable composition, variable reaction times and reagent dosages that are difficult to predict in advance. If necessary or desired, several SBRs can be arranged on a header manifold and operated in parallel stages to produce essentially continuous treatment of an influent stream.

The second type of ideal reactor hybridization involves the operation of CMFRs in series. One of the major disadvantages of the CMFR is that its effluent concentration is also essentially the concentration that drives the reaction. Because effluent concentrations are low by intent and design in most engineered environmental systems, the associated CMFR reaction rates are also lower than those involved in CMBR and PFR systems. For CMFRs operated in series it is only the reaction that occurs in the last reactor that is driven by the low ultimate effluent concentration. Overall process efficiencies are thus increased, and total reactor volumes decreased, relative to those for single CMFR systems designed to yield equivalent treatment results. The performance characteristics of CMFRs-in-series systems fall somewhere between those of single ideal PFRs and CMFRs, depending upon the number of in-series reactors involved. In the conceptual limit, an infinite number of CMFRs operated in series should yield the same performance as a PFR having the same overall reactor volume.

Lastly, CMFRs and PFRs can be modified in a variety of ways by applying different types of recycle schemes. Effluent recycle can even be done in a way that allows the overall reactor scheme to approach the behavior of a CMBR; this type of recycle system we refer to as a CMET-recycle or batch-recycle reactor. Applications of this type of recycle reactor are limited for the most part to laboratory bench or pilot scale experimental systems.

In most full-scale CMFR and PFR recycle operations the end result is to produce behavior lying somewhere between these two ideal "frame of reference" parent systems, much as do CMFRs in series. In each case the recycle arrangement is designed, or at least intended, to yield more effective overall operation and treatment than either of the parent systems. In certain cases, such as for attached growth FBR bioreactors, effluent recycling helps to dilute feed concentrations to prevent overloading. Conversely, recycling of solids is generally used to increase reactive mass concentrations and rates of reaction in CMFR and PFR processes such as chemical precipitation, adsorption by powdered forms of activated carbon, and suspended-growth biotreatment processes.

10.6   CITATIONS AND SOURCES

Weber, W.J., Jr., and F.A. DiGiano, 1996, *Process Dynamics in Environmental Systems*, John Wiley & Sons, Inc., New York. (PDES is the source of most of the material presented in Chapter 10. Chapter 9 of PDES covers and expands upon the material presented in Chapter 10 of this text. It also identifies additional related background reading sources).

10.7 PROBLEM ASSIGNMENTS

10.1 An enzyme treatment process is proposed for partial oxidation of o-cresol using a sequencing batch reactor (SBR) configuration. The Michaelis-Menten equation describes the rate

$$-\frac{dC_{SU}}{dt} = \frac{k_3 C_{EN,0} C_{SU}}{\mathcal{K}_M + C_{SU}}$$

The enzyme is assumed to remain in the reactor after the treated wastewater has been decanted. The enzyme concentration at the beginning of each fill cycle is 2 μM, the o-cresol concentration is 2 μM, and the volume is 1000 L. The SBR is filled at a rate of 500 L/min for 18 min and the feed o-cresol concentration is 10 μM. The half-saturation constant, $\mathcal{K}_M$, is 50 μM, and thus it is assumed that the reaction rate can be approximated by a first-order expression. If the value of k_3 in the Michaelis-Menten kinetic expression is 1min^{-1}, find the time required in the react cycle to reach 2 μM. [*Hint:* The rate expression in the material balance must include dilution of the initial enzyme concentration as the tank fills. This leads to a different solution than given by Equation 10.8 and can be solved easily in terms of concentration rather than mass of reactant.]

Answers:

$$C_F = \frac{\kappa_2}{\kappa_1} \left\{ 1 - \frac{[V_R(0)]^{\kappa_1/Q}}{[V_R(0) + Qt]^{\kappa_1/Q}} \right\} + \frac{C(0)[V_R(0)]^{\kappa_1/Q}}{[V_R(0) + Qt]^{\kappa_1/Q}}$$

$$\kappa_1 = Q + \frac{k_3 C_{EN,0}(0)}{\mathcal{K}_M} V_R(0)$$

$$\kappa_2 = Q C_{IN}$$

$$t_{reacted} = 25.1 \text{min}$$

10.2 A water storage tank in a distribution system is filled at a rate of 300 m^3/h. The chlorine concentration of the water entering the tank from the treatment plant is 6 mg/L. Chlorine reactions with organic and inorganic constituents are first order with respect to chlorine and the average rate constant is 0.004 h^{-1}. Find the chlorine concentrations at: (a) the end of filling the storage tank if the volume at the beginning of the fill period is 2000 m^3, the chlorine concentration in that volume is 3 mg/L (due to chlorine demand exerted during previous storage), and the total storage volume is 4000 m^3; (b) the end of the next storage period of 10 h (assume no withdrawal); and (c) as a function of time during withdrawal from the storage tank if the rate of withdrawal is 500 m^3/h.

Answers: (a) 4.44 mg/L; (b) 4.27 mg/L.

10.3 A process used to treat a specific chemical waste is packaged in prefabricated reactor modules of fixed volume. The performance of each reactor module is close to that of an ideal CMFR. The reaction is first order and the existing treatment facility, which consists of one such module, achieves 90removal. by how much can the volumetric treatment capacity be increased and still achieve 90% removal if a second unit is installed (a) in parallel to the first unit; (b) in series with the first unit? Do a similar comparison for modules having behavior close to that of ideal PFRs.

10.4 A fluid containing a radioactive element having a very short half-life of 20 h is passed through two CMFRs in series. If the flow rate is 100 L/h and the volume of each reactor 40,000 L, what is the decay in activity?

10.5 An enzyme (with a molecular weight of 40,000 g/mol) is proposed for oxidation of creosote in a hazardous waste treatment facility. A series of CMFR experiments are conducted at a feed enzyme concentration of 4 mg/L. The following Michaelis-Menten rate expression is to be tested

$$-\frac{dC_{SU}}{dt} = \frac{k_3 C_{EN,0} C_{SU}}{\mathcal{K}_M + C_{SU}}$$

The steady-state exit concentration of substrate (creosote) is measured for four different combinations of HRT and substrate feed concentration, with the following results

$\bar{t}$	C_{IN}	C_{OUT}
(min)	(mmol/L)	(mmol/L $\times 10^2$)
2	1.0	8.44
8	1.0	1.41
2	2.0	40.0
6	2.0	4.82

Find the values of k_3 and $\mathcal{K}_M$.

Answers: $k_3 = 1^{-4}$ mmol substrate/mmol enzyme-min; $\mathcal{K}_M = 0.1$ mmol/L.

10.6 Hexachlorocyclohexanes (HCHs) are organochlorine pesticides frequently found in lakes and oceans. HCH compounds have been shown in laboratory tests to undergo a first-order base hydrolysis reaction. Measurements of HCHs in a small impoundment with a hydraulic retention time of 20 days indicate 30% removal. This impoundment behaves like two CMFRs in series. What would be the expected removal in another impoundment of the same pH which has a hydraulic retention time of 90 days and behaves like three CMFRs in series?

Answer: 83%.

10.7 A plug flow reactor with a recycle ratio of 1.0 is currently used to reduce the concentration of a contaminant to one third of its original value. The reaction, 2A $\Longrightarrow$ 2B, follows an elementary, second-order rate law. What will be the final concentration of the contaminant relative to its initial concentration if the recycle stream is shut off?

Answer: 14% of $C_{A,0}$.

10.8 In an irreversible first-order reaction the influent concentration of a 1000μM-phenol side stream to a catalytic plug flow reactor is reduced by 95%. Determine the exiting phenol concentration for a new operational configuration in which 75% of the effluent is recycled to the reactor entrance and the overall throughput of the entire system is the same.

Answer: 112 μM.

10.9 A differential FBR was used to determine the external mass transfer resistance for the photo oxidation of an atrazine waste stream over a TiO_2 catalyst bed. The initial reaction rate (r_0) was measured (observed in the equilization tank) as a function of superficial liquid velocity (v_s) across the FBR. The equalization tank had a volume of 1000 mL and the FBR was cylindrical with a radius of 1 cm and a height of 1.5 cm.

v_s [cm/s]	r_0 [mg atrazine/mg TiO_2/s]
0.001	0.056
0.004	0.054
0.007	0.051
0.022	0.056
0.035	0.082
0.054	0.087
0.069	0.108
0.075	0.117
0.088	0.120
0.096	0.118
0.11	0.119

(a) What volumetric flow rate do you suggest using to maximize the initial reaction rate? At that flow rate, what is the actual initial reaction rate in the FBR?

(b) Comment on the behavior of the initial reaction rate at low and high superficial velocities.

10.10 Plug flow reactors with recycle are particularly useful for autocatalytic reactions in which the accumulation of reaction products increases the reaction rate (as discussed in Chapter 8). An autocatalytic reaction, A $\Longrightarrow$ B, of interest in a particular pollution prevention scheme has a rate expression like that shown in Equation 8.33, where the rate of production of B can be described by

$$\frac{dC_B}{dt} = k_1(C_{A,0} - C_B) + k_2(C_{A,0} - C_B)C_B$$

Consider $C_{A,0} = 10\text{mol/L}$, $k_1 = 0.01\text{s}^{-1}$, and $k_2 = 0.1L \cdot \text{mol}^{-1} \cdot \text{s}^{-1}$.

(a) If $R_Q = 2$, determine the residence time of a recycle reactor required to treat 95% of the reactant A [*Hint:* See Equation 8.34 for integration].

(b) For the same treatment objective, what is the residence time if k_2 increases to $0.5 \ L \cdot \text{mol}^{-1} \cdot \text{s}^{-1}$?

(c) Plot the residence times required for 95% treatment of A for a variety of recycle ratios ranging from 0 to 10 and comment on your results.

Answers: a) 7.1 s, b) 1.4 s.

Chapter 11

Nonideal System Modeling and Design

Contents

11.0   CHAPTER OBJECTIVES

To learn how to describe the behavior of reactors that do not adhere to the assumptions of ideal reactor behavior discussed in Chapters 9 and 10. This will be done by constructing a conceptual model that accounts for a range of hypothetical "dispersion" conditions lying between the limiting cases of the PFR (zero dispersion) and the CMFR (infinite dispersion).

11.1   NONIDEAL REACTOR BEHAVIOR

Ideal CMFR and PFR conditions and characteristics, while usually the intent of design practice are often closely approximated but rarely achieved in most full-scale process applications. Deviations in flow patterns, and thus in residence times and extents of reaction can be caused by short-circuiting, by recycle, or by the presence of stagnant zones within reactors, as illustrated in Figure 11.1. To determine how reactor performance deviates from ideal conditions in such cases it is usually necessary to measure reactor flow and mixing characteristics experimentally.

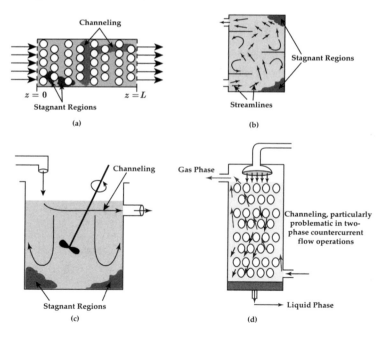

Figure 11.1 Some Causes of Nonideal Reactor Behavior

11.2 CHARACTERIZING REACTOR BEHAVIOR

The basic approach to treatment of nonideal reactor behavior is to obtain and analyze information on how long individual fluid elements reside in a particular reactor. This information can be expressed in terms of the distribution of "ages" of fluid elements within the reactor at any time, or of the ages of fluid elements contained in specific volumes exiting the reactor per unit of time. The ages of these fluid elements are referred to terms of either internal or exit age distribution functions, respectively. These functions are determined by a procedure termed residence time distribution (RTD) analysis. An RTD is usually obtained by application of stimulus-response analyses involving introduction to reactors of readily detectable tracers, as either pulse or step inputs, followed by observation and characterization of reactor responses to these stimuli. A pulse or delta input results from virtually instantaneous injection of a fixed mass of tracer to the influent of a reactor. A step input is achieved by suddenly introducing and subsequently maintaining a constant concentration of tracer in the reactor influent.

The design of a tracer test begins with selection of the tracer and the type of input (pulse or step) to be used. The tracer must be environmentally acceptable, nonreactive, and measurable at low concentrations. A nonreactive dye or a salt such as sodium chloride is often used in waste treatment systems, whereas sodium fluoride, a typical additive to drinking water, is often convenient for tracer tests in water treatment and distribution systems. *Reactive substances are inappropriate as tracers because the response curves they produce are attributable not only to reactor flow characteristics but to reaction phenomena as well.* Special care is needed in the design of pulse input tests to ensure that a sufficient amount of tracer is injected to give a measurable response in the exit stream.

11.2.1 Characteristic C and E Curves

When a pulse or delta input is used, the response of the reactor is given by a pattern of increasing and subsequently decreasing tracer concentration in the effluent stream as a function of time. The effluent tracer concentration profile for this type of stimulus-response relationship is known as the C curve. The dimensionless form of a C curve is shown in Figure 11.2a for a reactor of arbitrary flow characteristics. The ordinate in part a of Figure 11.2 is a dimensionless concentration, obtained by normalizing the effluent concentration, C_{OUT}, to a hypothetical concentration, C_Δ, representing an instantaneous dispersal of the tracer mass, M_T, throughout the reactor volume, V_R (i.e., $C_\Delta = M_T/V_R$). The C curve, with or without normalization of concentration, provides a visual impression of how fluid elements are distributed in time as they pass through the reactor. Some elements will

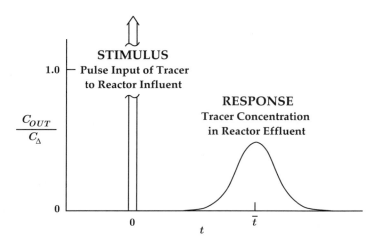

a. The C Curve, an Effluent Response to a Pulse Influent Stimulus

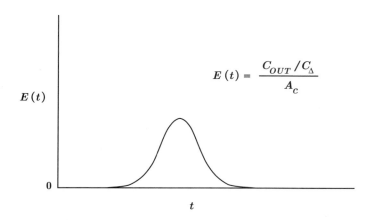

b. The E Curve, the Exit Age Distribution of a Fluid Element

Figure 11.2 Stimulus-Response   Relationships   for   Pulse   Inputs   of
Tracers   of   Arbitrary   Flow   Characteristics

exit in a time shorter than the HRT, while others will require periods greater than $\bar{t}$ to move through and out of the reactor.

When multiplied by the flow rate through the reactor, the area under a C curve that is not normalized by C_Δ yields the total mass of tracer, M_T, introduced in the pulse input

$$M_T = Q \int_0^\infty C_{OUT}(t)dt \qquad (11.1)$$

This simple mass balance provides a good check on the efficiency of tracer recovery and the assumption of nonreactivity.

The E curve, the exit age or Residence Time Distribution (RTD) curve, is represented in Figure 11.2b. This curve is a further normalization of the C curve obtained by dividing each value of C_{OUT}/C_Δ by the total area, A_C, under the C curve. From the normalized C curve shown in Figure 11.2a, the area under the C curve is

$$A_C = \frac{1}{C_\Delta} \int_O^\infty C_{OUT}(t)dt \qquad (11.2)$$

The **E** curve is thus defined as

$$\boldsymbol{E}(t) = \frac{C_{OUT}(t)}{C_\Delta} \left[\int_O^\infty \frac{C_{OUT}(t)}{C_\Delta} dt \right]^{-1} = \frac{C_{OUT}(t)/C_\Delta}{A_C} \qquad (11.3)$$

11.2.1.1 Mean Residence Time and Variance

Fluid elements are essentially carriers of dissolved solutes and suspended solids. From a transporting fluid quantity (fluid flow) perspective, one fluid element is the same as any other and the mean hydraulic residence time of the carrier fluid is simply the reactor volume divided by the flow rate (i.e., $\bar{t} = V_R/Q$). *From the dissolved solute or suspended solids fluid quality perspective, however, fluid elements differ in the amounts of materials contained within them. Thus it is not necessarily intuitive that the mean dissolved solute or suspended solids residence time distribution, t_m (i.e., the mean constituent residence time, CRT), should be the same as the mean hydraulic or fluid residence time, $\bar{t}$.*

The mean value of the constituent residence time of a material dissolved or suspended in a fluid is given by the first moment of the centroid of the RTD curve about the origin (zero-time axis) of the distribution

$$\boxed{\begin{array}{l} \textbf{\textit{CRT, First}} \\ \textbf{\textit{Moment of RTD}} \qquad t_m = \int_0^\infty t\,\boldsymbol{E}(t)dt \\ \textbf{\textit{About t = 0}} \end{array}} \qquad (11.4)$$

This integral is approximated from experimental measurements of tracer concentration at the reactor exit as a function of time.

The standard deviation, σ_1, of a distribution is the square root of the variance of the distribution about its mean value. Variance quantifies the extent of spreading of the tracer "cloud" produced by a pulse input (e.g., see Figure 4.4) and is thus a measure of the variation in residence times of fluid elements about t_m. Variance is given by the second moment of the centroid of the RTD about the mean of the distribution

$$
\begin{array}{ll}
\textbf{Variance, Second} & \\
\textbf{Moment of RTD} & \sigma_t^2 = \int\limits_0^\infty t^2 \, \boldsymbol{E}(t)dt - t_m^2 \qquad (11.5)\\
\textbf{About } t = t_m &
\end{array}
$$

The integral above is calculated from tracer data in a manner analogous to that for mean residence time. Standard deviation is often a more convenient measure of variation in the sense that it has the same units of measurement as the data. An illustration of the application of RTD analysis for determination of the performance characteristics of a system of sand filters in a water treatment plant is given in Example 11.1.

Example 11.1.   Evaluation of the Exposure of Giardia cysts to Applied Chlorine in a Sand Filter. (An application of RTD analysis to the characterization of exposure times for disinfection.)

- **Situation.** *A parallel arrangement of six sand filters at a water treatment plant operate at a total flow rate of 52,920 m³/day (14 mgd). The HRT in the filter box (volume above the filters), the filter media, and the underdrain is 50 min. Chlorine is added just ahead of these filters to prevent microbial growth on the media, which would otherwise cause premature clogging and reduce the time between required backwashings. The municipality is interested in determining the residence time distribution characteristics of water in the filters because this information can be used to estimate the disinfection of Giardia cysts occurring as a result of chlorine dosing. The most convenient point of addition of a tracer is in the pipeline leading to a common header for all six filters. A pulse input (2.9 kg) of sodium chloride is introduced. Following the pulse input, the sodium concentration is measured in the manifold, which collects the water from all six filters. The resulting data for time and sodium chloride concentration (after subtracting the background concentration), relating to a measurement time, t, are given in the first two columns of the spreadsheet developed below.*

- **Question(s).** *Characterize the residence time distribution (RTD) for the filters.*

- *Logic and Answer(s).*

    1. *The response data for this pulse input can be used to analyze only the average RTD for the six filters operating in parallel. If significant differences are expected in the RTDs of individual filters, a tracer test should be conducted for each filter.*

    2. *A spreadsheet is set up as illustrated below to summarize the time [Column (1)] and concentration [Column (2)] data and to determine the parameters required for the RTD analysis, namely the E curve [Column (3)], $tE(t)$ to determine the mean constituent residence time [Column (4)], and $t^2 E(t)$ to determine the variance [Column (5)]. The calculations given in this table and their use in RTD analysis are outlined in steps 3 through 8.*

	Data		RTD Calculations		
(1)	*(2)*	*(3)*	*(4)*	*(5)*
t	*C(t)*	*$E(t)$*	*$tE(t)$*	*$t^2 E(t)$*
(min)	*(mg/L)*	*(min^1)*	*(-)*	*(min)*
0	*0*	*0.00000*	*0.000*	*0.000*
10	*0.1*	*0.00134*	*0.013*	*0.134*
20	*1.4*	*0.01879*	*0.376*	*7.517*
30	*1.7*	*0.02282*	*0.685*	*20.537*
40	*1.5*	*0.02013*	*0.805*	*32.315*
50	*1.2*	*0.01611*	*0.805*	*40.268*
60	*0.7*	*0.00940*	*0.564*	*33.826*
70	*0.4*	*0.00537*	*0.376*	*26.309*
80	*0.2*	*0.00268*	*0.215*	*17.181*
90	*0.1*	*0.00134*	*0.121*	*10.872*
100	*0.1*	*0.00134*	*0.134*	*13.423*
110	*0.05*	*0.00067*	*0.074*	*8.121*
120	*0*	*0.00000*	*0.000*	*0.000*
130	*0*	*0.00000*	*0.000*	*0.0000*
Integrals*	*74.5 min · mg/L*	*1*	*42 min*	*2104 min^2*

*integrals calculated using trapezoid rule for each time segment, see step 3

    3. *For this analysis, the numerical evaluation of several integrals is required. There are several techniques that can be used to do this. The two-point trapezoidal rule is one of the simplest, and very appropriate here in that it uses the integrand evaluated at the limits of integration to evaluate the integral; i.e.,*

$$\int_{u_0}^{u_1} \phi(u)du = \frac{\Delta u}{2} \left[\phi(u_0) + \phi(u_1)\right]$$

when $\Delta u = u_1 - u_0$.

4. *Column (2)*

$$Q = \int_0^{130} C(t)dt = total\ tracer\ mass\ recovered$$

$$Q = \frac{52,920\ m^3/day}{1440\ min/day} \times \frac{10^3\ L}{m^3} = 36,750\ L/min$$

$$\int_0^{130} C(t)dt = 74.5\ min \cdot mg/L$$

$$Q = \int_0^{130} C(t)dt = 36,750\ L/min\cdot74.5\ min\cdot mg/L = 2.74\times10^6\ mg = 2.74\ kg$$

Of the 2.9 kg added, 2.74 kg was recovered, a 94.4% recovery, indicating that the tracer behaved conservatively.

5. *Column (3), from Equation 11.3*

$$\boldsymbol{E}(t) = \frac{C(t)}{\int_0^{130} C(t)dt} = \frac{C(t)}{74.5\ min \cdot mg/L}$$

We also note from the last row in Column (3) that the integral of $\boldsymbol{E}(t)$ is equal to 1, which must hold by definition of the $\boldsymbol{E}$ curve. The $\boldsymbol{C}(t)$ and $\boldsymbol{E}(t)$ curves shown indicate that the behavior deviates considerably from plug flow. This behavior can be explained by mixing that occurs in the filter box above the filter, and in channeling and dispersion that occur in flow through the porous media.

6. *Column(4), from Equation 11.4*

$$t_m = \int_0^{130} \boldsymbol{E}(t)dt = 42\ min$$

The mean CRT is somewhat shorter than the HRT (50 min), indicating the possibility of dead space in the reactor (i.e., volume through which flow does not pass).

7. *Column (5), from Equation 11.5*

$$\sigma_t^2 = \int_0^{130} t^2 \boldsymbol{E}(t)dt - t_m^2 = (2104 - 1764)min^2 = 340\ min^2$$

$$\sigma_t = 18.4\ min$$

indicating that 68% of fluid elements spend between 23.6 and 60.4 min in the reactor (i.e., $t_m \pm \sigma_t$).

- *Key Point(s). The RTD analysis tells us that deviations in flow from ideal PFR conditions in this filter plant will shorten the exposure time of many Giardia cysts to chlorine, and thus reduce the effectiveness of disinfection. Alternative solutions include modification of flow conditions (which in this case would be difficult) or increasing the chlorine dosage to shorten the time required for achieving the desired level of disinfection (see Example 11.2 for follow-up).*

11.2.1.2 Dimensionless E Curve

The numerical value of E depends on both the flow characteristics and the mean HRT of a reactor. Because the time required to observe a given tracer concentration at the exit of any reactor will depend on the value of t_m for that reactor, it follows from inspection of Equation 11.9 that reactors of identical flow characteristics but different sizes will have numerically different values for their respective variances. To make it possible to compare flow characteristics directly, the RTD is normalized for the effect of hydraulic residence time. That is, the E curve in Equation 11.3, which has units of time^{-1}, can be made dimensionless for scaling purposes by expressing time as the ratio of real fluid element time, t, to the HRT, $\bar{t}$, to yield the variable $\theta^\circ = t/\bar{t}$. Then, if $\bar{t} = t_m$,

$$E(\theta^\circ) = \frac{C_{OUT}(t)}{\int_0^\infty C_{OUT}(t)d\left(\frac{t}{t_m}\right)} = t_m E(t) \qquad (11.6)$$

We conclude that two reactors of different size that produce identical dimensionless plots of $E(\theta^\circ)$ against θ° have identical flow characteristics. Once again, the importance of dimensionless variables for process scaleup is evident.

A dimensionless form of the variance is obtained by dividing Equation 11.5 through by the square of the mean constituent residence time, t_m,

$$\sigma_{\theta^\circ}^2 = \int_0^\infty (\theta^\circ)^2 E(\theta^\circ)d\theta^\circ - 1 \qquad (11.7)$$

where

$$\sigma_{\theta^\circ}^2 = \frac{\sigma_t^2}{t_m^2} \qquad (11.8)$$

11.2.2 Characteristic F Curves

F curves, like C curves, are obtained from the response of reactors to influent tracers. In the case of the F curve, the tracer is introduced as a step-function stimulus. Because the tracer is fed continuously to the reactor after the step input is initiated, the exit concentration, C_{OUT}, must approach the feed concentration, C_{IN}, as time increases, as illustrated in Figure 11.3a. Figure 11.3b illustrates the $\boldsymbol{F}$ curve, which normalizes the effluent tracer concentration, C_{OUT}, by the feed concentration, C_{IN}. The value of $\boldsymbol{F}$ at any time, t, thus represents the fraction of tracer molecules having an exit age younger than t. This provides an important conceptual linkage between the $\boldsymbol{F}$ and $\boldsymbol{E}$ curves. Recalling that exit ages younger than t are also defined by the $\boldsymbol{E}$ curve (Equation 11.6), it follows that the $\boldsymbol{F}$ and $\boldsymbol{E}$ curves are related by

$$\boldsymbol{F}(t) = \int_0^t \boldsymbol{E}(t)dt \qquad (11.9)$$

or

$$\frac{d\boldsymbol{F}(t)}{dt} = \boldsymbol{E}(t) \qquad (11.10)$$

Tracer curve relationships thus reveal that the derivative of the experimentally determined $\boldsymbol{F}$ curve should be the expected $\boldsymbol{E}$ curve and, conversely, that the integral of the experimentally determined $\boldsymbol{E}$ curve should be the expected $\boldsymbol{F}$ curve.

Because the $\boldsymbol{F}$ and $\boldsymbol{E}$ curves are related mathematically, the $\boldsymbol{F}$ curve can be made dimensionless in the same manner discussed in Section 11.2.1.2 for the $\boldsymbol{E}$ curve. The statistical properties and analyses described in Section 11.2.1.1 for the $\boldsymbol{E}$ curve apply as well for the $\boldsymbol{F}$ curve. The mean residence time and variance of a reactor, for example, can be determined from its $\boldsymbol{F}$ curve as well as from its $\boldsymbol{E}$ curve. The mathematical relationship between the $\boldsymbol{F}$ and $\boldsymbol{E}$ curves, given by Equation 11.9, provides a convenient substitution into the expressions for t_m and σ_t^2 derived from the experimental $\boldsymbol{E}$ curve (Equations 11.4 and 11.5, respectively); that is,

$$t_m = \int_0^\infty t\boldsymbol{E}(t)dt = \int_0^1 td\boldsymbol{F}(t) \qquad (11.11)$$

and,

$$\sigma_t^2 = \int_0^1 t^2 d\boldsymbol{F}(t) - t_m^2 \qquad (11.12)$$

The values of t_m and σ_t^2 are determined readily from calculations related to the area above the $\boldsymbol{F}$ curve.

11.3   RESIDENCE TIME DISTRIBUTION ANALYSIS

RTD data can be used to compare the performances of real reactors to those of ideal reactors. We need first to develop the RTD patterns theoretically

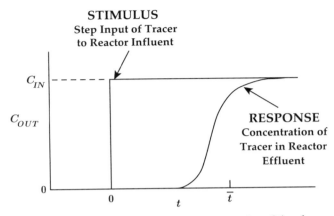

STIMULUS
Step Input of Tracer
to Reactor Influent

a. The C Curve, Reactor Effluent Response to a Step Stimulus

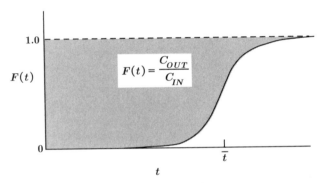

$$F(t) = \frac{C_{OUT}}{C_{IN}}$$

b. The F Curve, A Feed-Normalized C Curve

Figure 11.3 Stimulus-Response Relationships for Step Inputs of Tracers to Reactors of Arbitrary Flow Characteristics

expected for ideal reactor configurations (e.g., CMFRs, PFRs, and CMFRs in series), and then to analyze mathematically the responses of these reactors to either step or pulse inputs of nonreactive tracers. The response to either type of stimulus is inherently transient (i.e., unsteady state) because exit concentrations vary with time. This can be seen from inspection of the C, E, and F curves presented in Figures 11.2 and 11.3. In contrast to earlier applications of the material balance principle for steady-state conditions, we must here analyze unsteady conditions.

11.3.1   RTDs for Ideal CMFRs

The response of a CMFR to a pulse input of a nonreactive tracer follows from its material balance relationship

$$-QC_{OUT} = V_R \frac{dC_{OUT}}{dt} \tag{11.13}$$

In contrast to a general material balance for a CMFR (Equation 9.4), Equation 11.13 includes a mass rate term only for the tracer leaving the reactor because the tracer is injected into the reactor instantaneously. Further, because the tracer is nonreactive, the reaction rate term is zero. Integration of Equation 11.13 yields the C curve.

The initial condition must be specified to find the appropriate solution to Equation 11.13. For a pulse input, instantaneous injection of tracer mass, M_T, into a completely mixed reactor at $t = 0$ produces an initial concentration of tracer in the reactor, C_Δ, which is also the exit concentration at $t = 0$. Thus,

$$\frac{M_T}{V_R} = C_\Delta = C_{OUT}\mid_{t=0} \tag{11.14}$$

Equation 11.13 can be integrated by separation of variables

$$-\int_{C_\Delta}^{C_{OUT}} \frac{dC_{OUT}}{C_{OUT}} = \int_0^t \frac{dt}{\bar{t}} \tag{11.15}$$

to give

$$-\ln \frac{C_{OUT}}{C_\Delta} = \frac{t}{\bar{t}} \tag{11.16}$$

or

$$\frac{C_{OUT}}{C_\Delta} = e^{-t/\bar{t}} \tag{11.17}$$

The C curve described by Equation 11.17 and illustrated in Figure 11.4 is characterized by an exponential decay of tracer concentration (i.e., a washout of the tracer initially injected into the reactor).

A convenient way to test whether a real reactor behaves as an ideal CMFR is to compare the experimentally determined C curve with that predicted for an ideal CMFR. According to Equation 11.16, a plot of experimental data in terms of $\ln(C_{OUT}/C_\Delta)$ versus t for a reactor that behaves as an ideal CMFR should yield a straight line, the slope of which is the inverse of the HRT ($\bar{t} = V_R/Q$). If the predicted HRT is smaller than the experimentally determined value, some fraction of the reactor volume is most likely not fully active; that is, there is unused volume, or dead space, in the reactor.

The $E(t)$ curve is then generated from the C curve by

$$E(t) = \frac{C \; curve}{area \; under \; the \; C \; curve} = \frac{C_{OUT}}{C_\Delta \bar{t}} = \frac{e^{-t/\bar{t}}}{\bar{t}} \tag{11.18}$$

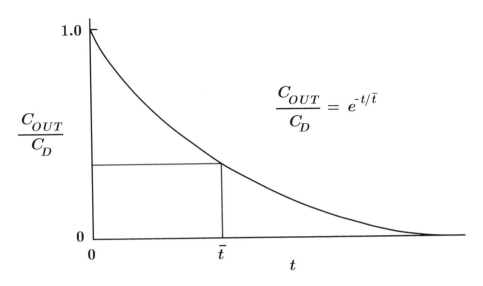

$$\frac{C_{OUT}}{C_D} = e^{-t/\bar{t}}$$

Figure 11.4 C Curve for an Ideal CMFR

Equation 11.18 can be expressed in dimensionless form by introducing Equation 11.6 and assuming that $\bar{t} = t_m$ to give

$$E(\theta^\circ) = e^{-\theta^\circ} \qquad (11.19)$$

Here again we see the value of dimensionless expressions of reactor properties and characteristics; namely, while different $E(t)$ versus t curves will result for CMFRs of different size (Equation 11.18), all will produce the same dimensionless E curve (Equation 11.19).

An important concept made clear by RTD analysis is that the mean constituent residence time, t_m, for an ideal CMFR is exactly equal to its hydraulic residence time, $\bar{t}$. The proof follows from the definition of mean residence time given in Equation 11.4 and substitution of $E(t)$ for an ideal CMFR from Equation 11.18

$$t_m = \int_0^\infty t \frac{e^{-t/\bar{t}}}{\bar{t}} dt = \bar{t} \qquad (11.20)$$

Thus, the HRT for an ideal CMFR, which we calculate from two known physical quantities, V_R and Q, is also the CRT.

The F curve for a CMFR follows from the material balance relationship

$$QC_{IN} - QC_{OUT} = V_R \frac{dC_{OUT}}{dt} \qquad (11.21)$$

The stimulus is now an instantaneous step input up to a new constant feed concentration, C_{IN}, of tracer; this is the origin of the first term on the left-hand side of Equation 11.21. The initial condition corresponds to the absence of tracer in the reactor. Integration by separation of variables yields

$$\int_0^{C_{OUT}} \frac{dC_{OUT}}{C_{IN} - C_{OUT}} = \int_0^t \frac{dt}{\bar{t}} \tag{11.22}$$

and

$$-\ln \frac{C_{IN} - C_{OUT}}{C_{IN}} = \frac{t}{\bar{t}} \tag{11.23}$$

or,

$$\boldsymbol{F}(t) = \frac{C_{OUT}}{C_{IN}} = 1 - e^{-t/\bar{t}} \tag{11.24}$$

The resulting $\boldsymbol{F}$ curve for an ideal CMFR is depicted in Figure 11.5. Note from Equation 11.11 that the shaded area above the $\boldsymbol{F}$ curve in Figure 11.5 is the mean constituent residence time. This expression can also be used to prove that the CRT and HRT are equal for an ideal CMFR.

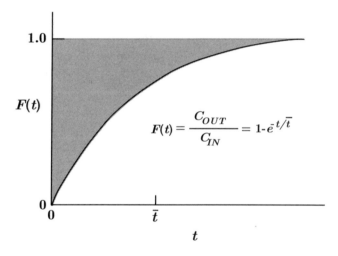

Figure 11.5 F Curve for an Ideal CMFR

An experimentally measured $\boldsymbol{F}$ curve can be tested to determine whether the behavior of a reactor conforms to that of an ideal CMFR by plotting the data according to the logarithmic form of Equation 11.24. Behavior similar to that of a CMFR is indicated if the data fit a straight line; the HRT is then given by the inverse slope of that line.

11.3.2   RTDs for Ideal PFRs

The responses of an ideal PFR to pulse and step inputs of tracer can be reasoned intuitively. Fluid elements do not intermix as they travel down the length of an ideal PFR. The expected response of such a reactor to a pulse input of tracer is thus a spike in concentration at a response time equal to the hydraulic residence time, $\bar{t}$, of the reactor. This **C** curve is depicted in Figure

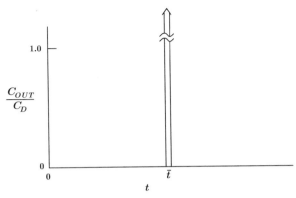

a. **The Dimensionless C Curve for a PFR**

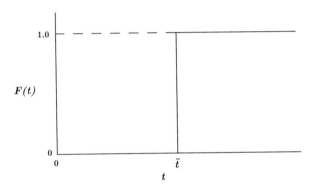

b. **The F Curve for a PRF**

Figure 11.6 C and F Curves for an Ideal PFR

11.6a as a spike of infinite height and zero width, with a unit enclosed area. The expected response of an ideal PFR to a step input is an instantaneous step increase in the exit concentration from zero to a value equal to the feed concentration at time $\bar{t}$. For the **F** curve depicted in Figure 11.6b this step increase is from 0 to 1 at $\bar{t}$. A more rigorous mathematical approach utilizing the Dirac delta function to describe a pulse input of tracer leads to the same result.

    RTD analyses for reactor configurations other than those of the CMFR and PFR systems are described in PDES. These include conditions of laminar flow in tubular reactors and CMFRs in series.

11.4   PFR-WITH-DISPERSION REACTOR (PFDR) MODEL

11.4.1   An Ideal Model for Nonideal Behavior

Most real reactors have RTDs that differ somewhat from those of ideal CMFR or PFR systems of seemingly similar volume, configuration, and flow. The performance of such real reactors thus cannot be determined directly from the design equations presented in Chapters 9 and 10. The most common method used to arrive at alternative design equations by utilizing the experimental information gained from RTD analyses is the application of a modified PFR model that can account quantitatively for observed deviations from true plug flow behavior. This is the method we will describe here. Additional procedures are given in PDES.

A plug flow reactor model that incorporates a hypothetical but empirically (experimentally) quantified dispersion term to account for deviation from ideal PFR behavior provides a conceptually satisfying and general way to quantify the fluid mixing characteristics of real reactors. As discussed in Chapter 4, dispersive mass transport is due to intermixing of fluid elements by large-scale eddies. The total flux in one-dimensional transport is the n sum of advective and dispersive transport processes. In Equation 4.26 we introduced the one-dimensional (x) form of the advection-dispersion-reaction or ADR equation as

$$\boxed{\quad \begin{matrix} \textbf{\textit{ADR}} \\ \textbf{\textit{Equation}} \end{matrix} \qquad -v_x \frac{\partial C}{\partial x} + \mathcal{D}_d \frac{\partial C^2}{\partial x^2} + \boldsymbol{r} = \frac{\partial C}{\partial t} \quad} \qquad (4.26)$$

We can apply this modification of the ideal PFR MBE (Equation 3.28) to characterize the hydraulic response of a nonideal reactor to a pulse input of tracer and then use the characterization to quantify the performance of that reactor with respect to anticipated process efficiency. In the first instance the component of interest is the nonreactive tracer, and its flux is affected only by advective and dispersive mass transport.

In the context of RTD analyses, we refer to Equation 4.26 as an ideal model for a plug-flow-with-dispersion reactor (PFDR) because the dispersion component, $\mathcal{D}_d(\partial^2 C/\partial x^2)$, is simply a hypothetical term having the form of Ficks second law added to the ideal PFR model as a means for phenomenologically incorporating observed deviations from ideal PFR behavior. As discussed in Chapter 3, Equation 3-26 has no particular mechanistic significance because its use requires empirical evaluation of the so-called hydrodynamic or mechanical dispersion term. In other words, the dispersion characteristics of a reactor may be measured and correlated with other system *properties, but they cannot be related in a rigorous mechanistic way to those other properties.* Equation 4.26 can be made dimensionless by introducing the variables

$$\zeta^\circ = \frac{x}{L} \quad and \quad \theta^\circ = \frac{v_x t}{L} = \frac{t}{\bar{t}}$$

to give, for a conservative (i.e., nonreacting, $r = 0$) tracer

Dimensionless PFDR Equation for a Conservative Tracer	$\dfrac{\partial C}{\partial \theta^\circ} = -\dfrac{\partial C}{\partial \zeta^\circ} = \mathcal{N}_d \dfrac{\partial^2 C}{\partial (\zeta)^2}$	(11.25)

where $\mathcal{N}_d$, the dispersion number, was defined in Chapter 4 as

$$Dispersion \ Number \ = \mathcal{N}_d = \frac{\mathcal{D}_d}{v_x L} \qquad (4.27)$$

11.4.2 The Dispersion Number

The dispersion number is essentially a dimensionless ratio of dispersive mass transport to advective mass transport. As this number increases, transport by dispersion increases relative to transport by advection. It is possible to show that the solution to Equation 11.25 for infinite dispersion results in a C curve identical to that for a CMFR. As the dispersion number decreases and approaches zero, the flow characteristics and resulting C curve approach those of a PFR.

The solution of Equation 11.25 yields a description of the concentration of a tracer as a function of time and distance in a hypothetical reactor having specific advective and dispersive transport characteristics. Several solutions are possible, depending on the extent of dispersion and the assumed boundary conditions at the inlet and outlet of the reactor. The unsteady-state condition of most interest is the response of a reactor to a pulse input of tracer.

For small amounts of dispersion (i.e., dispersion numbers smaller than 0.01) a response such as that shown in Figure 11.7 can be envisioned for a pulse input. The mass of tracer begins to spread gradually due to dispersion as it is transported down the reactor by advection. As the mass spreads and travel time, t_i, increases, concentrations produced by the pulse become lower as indicated by the lighter shading in Figure 11.7. If the dispersion number is sufficiently low, the spreading of the tracer curve is small enough that its shape can be considered essentially constant over the measurement interval at the exit end of the reactor, and the tracer curve thus considered essentially symmetrical.

Equation 11.25 can be solved assuming the so-called "open condition" at the boundaries of the reactor; that is, there is neither a transition from plug flow

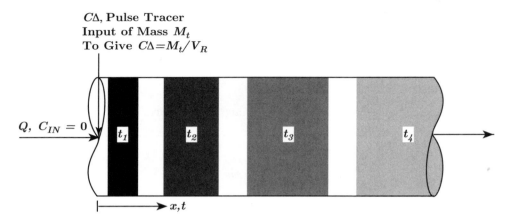

Figure 11.7 *Time-Series Transport of a Tracer Pulse Through a Nonideal Reactor*

superimposed by dispersion at the inlet nor a return to plug flow at the exit. Instead, the following boundary conditions are imposed over an infinite length of reactor

$$C = 0 \qquad \text{at } x = -\infty \qquad \text{for } t \geq 0$$
$$C = 0 \qquad \text{at } x = \infty \qquad \text{for } t \geq 0$$

For small amounts of dispersion, the analytical solution to Equation 11.25 for dimensionless tracer concentration at position L, corresponding to the end of the reactor, is expressed as a function of dimensionless time by

$$
\boxed{
\begin{array}{l}
\textbf{\textit{PFDR C}} \\
\textbf{\textit{Curve for}} \\
\textbf{\textit{Low}} \; \mathcal{N}_d \, \textbf{\textit{Values}}
\end{array}
\quad
\dfrac{C_{OUT}}{C_\Delta} = \dfrac{1}{(4\pi\mathcal{N}_d)^{0.5}} \exp\left[-\dfrac{(1 - \theta^\circ)^2}{4\mathcal{N}_d} \right]
}
\qquad (11.26)
$$

where C_Δ is given by the ratio of M_T, the mass of tracer injected as a pulse, to V_R, the volume of the reactor.

11.4.3   Variance-Dispersion Relationships

The dimensionless C curve given in Equation 11.26 has the same form as the Gauss-Laplace distribution functions presented in Appendix A.8.1 of PDES, and for this special case the variance is ex-

actly two times the dispersion number

$$
\boxed{
\begin{array}{l}
\textbf{\textit{Variance-Dispersion}} \\
\textbf{\textit{Relationship for}} \qquad \sigma_{\theta^\circ}^2 = 2\mathcal{N}_d \\
\textbf{\textit{Low }} \mathcal{N}_d \textbf{\textit{ Values}}
\end{array}
} \qquad (11.27)
$$

This demonstrates that dimensionless variance is in fact a measure of dispersion. In other words, having once determined the first and second moments of the RTD from tracer response data, values of σ_t^2 and t_m^2 can be used to calculate the dispersion number. However, as noted earlier, this procedure is valid only if the amount of dispersion is small and the C curve is reasonably close to symmetrical, as illustrated in Figure 11.8 for different values of $\mathcal{N}_d$. Note that all of these C curves are Gaussian in shape and symmetrical about $\theta^\circ = 1$. This is true, however, only for small amounts of dispersion. The extent of spreading of the C curves is seen to increase with increasing values of $\mathcal{D}_d$, which is intuitively reasonable.

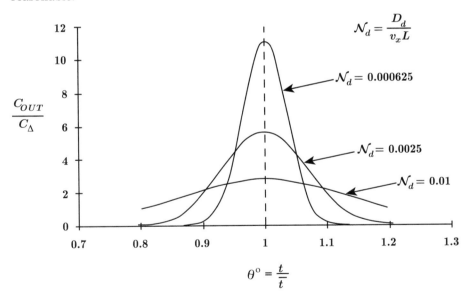

Figure 11.8 Symmetrical Form of Dimensionless C Curves for PFDRs Having Low Dispersion Numbers

For large amounts of dispersion, the RTD is no longer Gaussian and alternative approaches to Equation 11.26 are needed for determining the dispersion number from the variance of the tracer response data. A wider range of dispersion numbers can be described by using different boundary conditions to solve the PFDR model.

One such solution is obtained for a finite-length reactor, considered to conform to the open condition at the inlet but to be described at the outlet by closed condition; e.g., a Type 3 boundary condition such as that given in Equation 3.37

$$\left[v_x C - \mathcal{D}_d \left(\frac{\partial C}{\partial x} \right) \right]_{x=L} = v_x C_{OUT} \tag{3.37}$$

where C represents the concentration of tracer just inside the reactor at the exit. By further assuming that $C = C_{OUT}$, the boundary condition becomes simply

$$\frac{\partial C}{\partial x} = 0 \qquad \text{at } x = L \qquad \text{for } t > 0$$

The solution, provided over 50 years ago to describe mixing in aeration tanks, is

$$
\boxed{
\begin{array}{l}
\textbf{\textit{PFDR C}} \\
\textbf{\textit{Curve For}} \\
\textbf{\textit{High }} \mathcal{N}_d \\
\textbf{\textit{Values}}
\end{array}
\qquad
\frac{C_{OUT}}{C_\Delta} = 2 \sum_{n=1}^{\infty} u_n \frac{\alpha_D \sin u_n + u_n \cos u_n}{\alpha_D^2 + 2\alpha_D + u_n^2} \exp \Phi
}
\tag{11.28}
$$

where

$$\alpha_D = 0.5 \mathcal{N}_d^{-1}, \ u_n = \cot^{-1} \left[0.5 \left(\frac{u_n}{\alpha_D} - \frac{\alpha_D}{u_n} \right) \right], \ and \ \Phi = \left[\alpha_D - \frac{(\alpha_D^2 + u_n^2)\theta^\circ}{2\alpha_D} \right]$$

Such series solutions are typical when the transport equation being solved includes the derivative of the concentration gradient (i.e., the dispersive transport term). In this instance, the series is formed by the trigonometric roots, u_n, in the expression above.

The **C** curves predicted by Equation 11.28 are illustrated in Figure 11.9. When the dispersion number begins to exceed 0.25, the **C** curve begins to skew significantly from the typically symmetrical shape of a Gaussian distribution. The maximum skewness is reached when the dispersion number approaches infinity. This condition, in fact, yields the **C** curve for a CMFR, emphasizing again that our use of the terminology "completely mixed" implies the specific condition of infinite solute dispersion.

As discussed in more detail in PDES several approaches can be used to calculate and determine the dispersion number from an experimentally determined **C** curve. The approach we will employ here utilizes available relationships between $\sigma_{\theta^\circ}^2$ and the dispersion number derived for different reactor entry and exit conditions. We recall from Equation 11.8 that $\sigma_{\theta^\circ}^2$ is calculated from the variance and mean residence time obtained from tracer data. As discussed earlier in this section with regard to analysis and interpretation of C curves, two types of reactor entry and exit conditions are commonly used as boundary conditions to solve the PFDR model given in Equation 11.25. These lead to description of

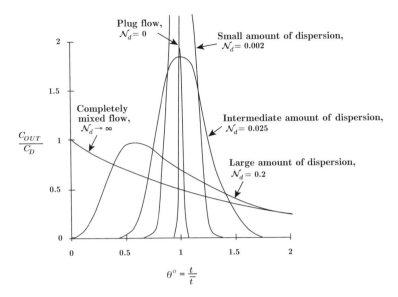

Figure 11.9 Deviations of Dimensionless C Curves from Symmetry as PFDR Dispersion Numbers Increase

the reactor as either closed or open with respect to the conditions existing at its entry and exit.

A closed vessel is one in which plug flow conditions are assumed to exist immediately before and after the vessel entrance and exit sections, respectively. This circumstance can be described by applying the Type 3 boundary condition (Robin condition) given by Equation 3.37 at both the inlet and outlet rather than just at the outlet as done in deriving Equation 11.28. This situation might occur if flow enters and leaves by a small pipe. An exact analytical solution to Equation 11.25 for these boundary conditions is not possible. A numerical solution of the equation gives the following approximate expression for relating experimentally measured values for $\sigma_{\theta^\circ}^2$ to the dispersion number, $\mathcal{D}_d/v_x L$,

$$
\begin{array}{ll}
\textit{Variance-Dispersion} & \\
\textit{Relationship for a} & \sigma_{\theta^\circ}^2 \simeq 2\mathcal{N}_d - 2\mathcal{N}_d^2 \left[1 - \exp(-\mathcal{N}_d^{-1})\right] \qquad (11.29) \\
\textit{Closed Vessel} &
\end{array}
$$

In contrast to a closed vessel, an open vessel is not characterized by plug flow at either end; it represents a section of a larger vessel in which dispersion is measured. The analytical solution to Equation

11.25 for these boundary conditions, as given by

$$\frac{C_{OUT}}{C_\Delta} = \frac{1}{(4\pi\theta°\mathcal{N}_d)^{0.5}} \exp\left[-\frac{(1-\theta°)^2}{4\theta°\mathcal{N}_d}\right]$$ (11.30)

The corresponding relationship between $\sigma^2_{\theta°}$ and the dispersion number is

Variance-Dispersion		
Relationship for an	$\sigma^2_{\theta°} = 2\mathcal{N}_d + 8\mathcal{N}_d^2$	(11.31)
Open Vessel		

In solutions to the advection-dispersion equation the dispersion number shown in Equations 11.29 and 11.31 is an implicit function of $\sigma^2_{\theta°}$. Thus, a trial-and-error solution is needed once has been calculated from an experimental tracer response curve.

11.4.4   Design Relationships

A design equation to predict the performance of a PFDR under steady-state operating conditions follows after determination of the dispersion coefficient as described above. Because there is no net change in constituent concentration(s) under steady-state conditions, the ADR Equation given in Equation 4.26 becomes

Steady-State		
MBE for	$\dfrac{\partial C}{\partial t} = -v_x \dfrac{\partial C}{\partial x} + \mathcal{D}_d \dfrac{\partial^2 C}{\partial x^2} - \boldsymbol{r} = 0$	(11.32)
a PFDR		

Various solutions to Equation 11.32 can be found for different assumptions concerning the inlet and outlet conditions of the reactor, of infinite or finite length. It has been demonstrated, however, that the following analytical solution is a very reasonable approximation regardless of inlet and outlet conditions

PFDR Design Equation
$\dfrac{C_{OUT}}{C_{IN}} = \dfrac{4\beta_D \exp \propto_D}{(1+\beta_D)^2 \exp \propto_D \beta_D - (1-\beta_D)^2 \exp - \propto_D \beta_D}$

(11.33)

where α_D is again $0.5\mathcal{N}_d^{-1}$, and $\beta_D = [1 + 4k\bar{t}\mathcal{N}_d]^{0.5}$ for a first-order reaction.

The design relationship given in Equation 11.33 reveals the dependence of the influent-normalized or fractional concentration remaining on two dimensionless groups, $\mathcal{D}_d/v_x$ *L and* $k\bar{t}$*. We recognize the* *former group as the dispersion number, $\mathcal{N}_d$. The latter group is the Damkohler group I number, $\mathcal{N}_{Da(I)}$ for a first-order reaction. More generally, for bulk flow by advection only, $\mathcal{N}_{Da(I)}$ is given by*

$$
\boxed{
\begin{array}{c}
\textbf{\textit{Damkohler Group I Number}} \\[2mm]
\mathcal{N}_{Da(I)} = \dfrac{chemical\ reaction\ rate}{advective\ flow\ rate} = \dfrac{r\,L}{v_x C} = k\bar{t}C^{n-1}
\end{array}
}
\tag{11.34}
$$

Expanding on the situation described earlier in Example 11.1, Example 11.2 provides an illustration of the PFDR modeling approach to nonideal reactor analysis.

Example 11.2. Estimation of the Effectiveness of Chlorine Dosing on Giardia Cyst Disinfection in a Sand Filtration System. (A comparison of analyses based on modifications to reactor and reaction models to account for nonideal behavior.)

- *Situation. An RTD analysis was performed in Example 11.1 on a set of filters in a water treatment plant to assess the potential for disinfection of Giardia cysts by addition of chlorine ahead of the filters. It is of interest now to evaluate the disinfection process itself in more detail. Disinfection rates are often described by the Chick-Watson equation*

$$
-\frac{dC_N}{dt} = kC_{Cl_2}C_N
$$

where in this case C_N is the remaining cyst concentration (number/L) and C_{Cl_2} the chlorine concentration (mg/L). This equation, together with the results of a step input tracer test, can be used in an empirical way to estimate the disinfection efficiency of the filters, which behave as nonideal reactors. Suppose, for example, that t_{10} is the time at which the concentration in the tracer response reaches 0.1 of the step concentration. We can then write the integrated form of the Chick-Watson equation as

$$
\frac{C_{N,OUT}}{C_{N,IN}} = e^{-(kC_{Cl_2}t_{10})}
$$

The equation above would "adjust" the HRT for nonideal behavior by effectively reducing its value to the t_{10} value while still using the PFR design equation. As the RTD of the actual reactor approaches that of an ideal PFR, t_{10} approaches the HRT and the maximum possible disinfection efficiency is achieved. Results of batch disinfection experiments found in the technical literature provide the value of k, which for the pH and temperature of the filter operation is 0.08 L/mg-min. The chlorine concentration applied to the filters is 2 mg/L.

- **Question(s).** *Use the pulse input tracer data developed in Example 11.1 to compare the disinfection efficiency predicted from the empirical relationship above and a step tracer test to that predicted by the more rigorous PFDR engineering approach to nonideal reactor behavior we discussed above.*

- **Logic and Answer(s).**

   1. *The empirical method for calculating Giardia inactivation requires measuring the response to a step input [i.e., generation of the $F(t)$ curve]. However, pulse input data and the resulting $E(t)$ curve (Example 11.1) can be used to generate this $F(t)$ curve. From Equation 11.9*

$$F(t_n) = \int\limits_{0}^{t_n} E(t)dt$$

   This integral can once again be evaluated using the trapezoid rule for each time step.

   2. *The spreadsheet from Example 11.1 is extended below [Column (3)] to obtain the $F(t)$ curve.*

(1)	(3)	(4)
t	$E(t)$	$F(t)$
(min)	(min^{-1})	(-)
0	0.0	0.0
10	0.0013	0.0067
20	0.019	0.11
30	0.023	0.32
40	0.020	0.53
50	0.016	0.71
60	0.0094	0.84
70	0.0054	0.91
80	0.0027	0.95
90	0.0013	0.97
100	0.0013	0.99
110	0.00067	1.0
120	0.0	1.0
130	0.0	1.0

   A plot of the $F(t)$ curve shows the expected behavior of the nonideal reactor described in Example 11.1.

   3. *The value of kC_{Cl_2} is assumed to remain constant at 0.08×2 or $0.16\ min^{-1}$ even though parallel oxidation reactions probably cause depletion of the chlorine concentration and a lowering of the*

observed pseudo-first-order rate constant, kC_{Cl_2} as the fluid packets travel through the filter. With this simplification, it is possible to proceed with three alternative calculations of disinfection efficiency.

4. *PFDR model. Assume for application of this model that the closed vessel condition describes the inlet and outlet to the filters (i.e., there is a transition from advective pipe flow to advection with dispersion within the filter box and again a transition back to advective pipe flow upon leaving the bottom of the filter). The dispersion number is calculated from Equation 11.29*

$$\sigma_{\theta\circ}^2 = 2\mathcal{N}_d - 2\mathcal{N}_d^2 \left[1 - \exp(-\mathcal{N}_d^{-1})\right]$$

where

$$\sigma_{\theta\circ}^2 = \frac{\sigma_t^2}{(\bar{t}_n)^2} = \frac{(19)^2}{(42)^2} = 0.21$$

A trial-and-error procedure gives $\mathcal{N}_d = 0.12$. The effluent to influent concentration ratio for a PFDR in which a first order reaction occurs is described by Equation 11.33

$$\frac{C_{N,OUT}}{C_{N,IN}} = \frac{4\beta_D \exp\alpha_D}{(1+\beta_D)^2 \exp\alpha_D\beta_D - (1-\beta_D)^2 \exp-\alpha_D\beta_D}$$

$$\beta_D = [1 + 4k\bar{t}\mathcal{N}_d]^{0.5} \quad and \quad \alpha_D = 0.5\mathcal{N}_D^{-1}$$

After substitution for $\mathcal{N}_d(0.12)$, $k(0.16\ min^{-1})$, and $\bar{t}\ (42\ min)$, we find

$$\frac{C_{N,OUT}}{C_{N,IN}} = 0.011$$

and

$$log\ inactivation\ = log\ \frac{C_{N,IN}}{C_{N,OUT}} = 1.95$$

5. *Empirical Model. From the **F** curve plot, the t_{10} value is 20 min; thus*

$$\frac{C_{N,OUT}}{C_{N,IN}} = e^{-k(C_{Cl_2})t_{10}} = e^{-0.16(20)} = 0.041$$

$$log\ inactivation\ = log\ \frac{C_{N,IN}}{C_{N,OUT}} = 1.39$$

6. *We conclude that the empirical approach provides a more conservative estimate of Giardia inactivation than the PFDR reactor model. These results, however, are dependent upon the nonideality of the reactor (e.g., the n value), the observed disinfection rate constant, and the hydraulic detention time. At some higher n and $k\bar{t}$ value, the empirical model gives more inactivation than predicted by nonideal-reactor-based models (Lawler and Singer, 1993).*

- **Key Point(s).** *Process efficiency under non-ideal flow conditions can often be estimated empirically by adjustment of associated rate models applied to standard ideal reactor models. In the example given above this approach provides a more conservative estimate. As noted, however, the estimates made by these two methods will vary relative to one another with the conditions of the system in question.*

A convenient graphical representation of Equation 11.33 for a first-order reaction is given in Figure 11.10. This figure allows comparison of the required volume of a "real" reactor simulated by a PFDR model to that of an ideal PFR to achieve the same extent of reaction (i.e., the same fractional solute concentration leaving the reactor). An equivalent way to express the ordinate scale is

$$\frac{k\bar{t}_{PFDR}}{k\bar{t}_{PFR}} = \frac{V_{PFDR}}{V_{PFR}} \qquad (11.35)$$

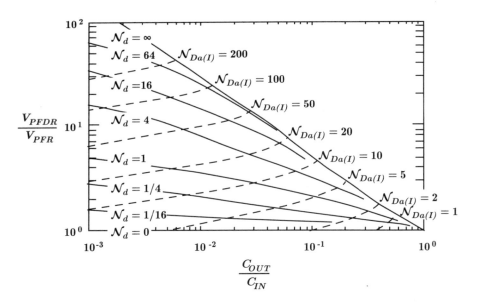

Figure 11.10 *Relative Performance Characteristics of PFDRs for First-Order Reactions*

The value of C_{OUT}/C_{IN} for each value of the Damkohler Group I number $(k\bar{t}_{PFDR})$ is determined from Equation 11.33 for a constant dispersion number. The $k\bar{t}$ values for these same C_{OUT}/C_{IN} values in a PFR are then calculated from the first-order relationship given for $\bar{t}_{PFR}$ in Table 9.1. Taking the ratio of the Damkohler numbers leads to the ordinate-scale values in Figure 11.10

and to the resulting plots (solid lines) for each dispersion number. The dashed lines derive from holding $k\bar{t}_{PFDR}$ constant while determining the relationship between C_{OUT}/C_{IN} and the dispersion number from Equation 11.33. A similar plot generated for second-order reactions is shown in Figure 11.11.

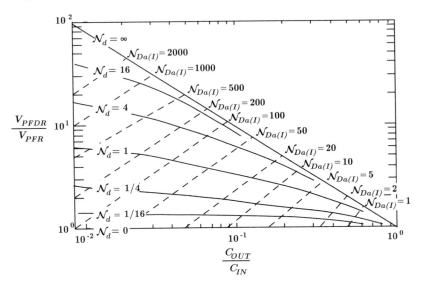

Figure 11.11 *Relative Performance Characteristics of PFDRs for Second-Order Reactions*

The solid lines in Figures 11.10 and 11.11 illustrate that for any specific fractional concentration remaining after reaction, the volume of a real reactor having a specified set of ideal PFDR-simulated properties increases relative to that of an ideal PFR as the dispersion number increases. The performance of a reactor characterized by a specific dispersion number can also be determined. Each intersection of a dashed line on the plot with a solid line gives the conversion obtained in a PFDR for a unique combination of dispersion number (solid line) and Damkohler number (dashed line). For any dispersion number corresponding to a particular solid line, therefore, the extent of conversion increases as the Damkohler number increases (i.e., as the reaction rate increases relative to advective velocity).

Figures 11.10 and 11.11 emphasize the relative importance of dispersion and reaction rate in determining the effectiveness of engineered reactors for water and waste treatment. In some processes, dispersion is neither necessary nor desirable. For instance, reactor systems for inactivation of microorganisms (disinfection processes) should be designed to minimize dispersion so that inactivation is maximized. In other instances complex mixing may be a necessity, even though the reactor will perform less efficiently; this is true, for example, in air sparging to maintain aerobic biological treatment. A stimulus-response tracer test and a related residence time distribution analysis is essential for determining the phenomenological extent of dispersion in any reactor and for making modifications to reduce the observed dispersion (e.g., by addition of baffles) in cases where it is not desired. An illustration of the sensitivity of process performance to reactor dispersion characteristics is given in Example 11.3 for a set of treatment conditions typical of drinking waters and wastewaters.

Example 11.3. Analysis of Increasing Reactor Size Requirements for Specified Process Efficiencies under Conditions of Increasingly Nonideal Reactor Behavior. (An exercise in the application of generalized relationships between reaction and reactor characteristics.)

- **Situation.** *An enzymatically induced partial oxidation of the pesticide diazinon has been shown in laboratory batch studies to reduce its aquatic toxicity. The reaction can be approximated as first order with respect to diazinon concentration over the range of interest. This process is to be applied for treatment of wastewater from a pesticide production operation. A full-scale demonstration study (flow rate of 10,000 m^3/day and hydraulic detention time of 25 min) is then conducted in which the enzyme is added to an existing unbaffled rectangular reactor and 90% removal of diazinon is observed. A tracer study is performed and the dispersion number for the reactor is found to be 1.*

- **Question(s).** *Regulatory requirements demand 95% removal of diazinon. How can this goal be met with the existing reactor?*

- **Logic and Answer(s).**

  1. *The rate constant for the reaction is not specified, but it can be found from the ideal PFDR model or, more conveniently, from the graphical representation of this model given in Figure 11.10.*

  2. *The intersection of $C_{OUT}/C_{IN} = 0.1$ and $\mathcal{N}_d = 1$ in Figure 11.10 corresponds to $\mathcal{N}_{Da(I)} = 5$, from which*

$$k = \frac{5}{\bar{t}} = \frac{5}{25} = 0.2 \ min^{-1}$$

  Note that the ordinate value corresponding to the intersection between C_{OUT}/C_{IN} and $\mathcal{N}_d$ is 2.2. Thus the real reactor is 2.2 times as large as an ideal PFR capable of achieving the same degree of treatment.

  3. *To increase diazinon removal to 95% without increasing the volume of the existing reactor will require reducing the dispersion. It is possible to calculate the required dispersion number, $\mathcal{N}_d$, for 95% removal by entering the graph on the abscissa at $C_{OUT}/C_{IN} = 0.05$ and finding the intersection with $\mathcal{N}_{Da(I)} = 5$. This intersection yields a dispersion number of 0.25.*

4. *A logical approach to decreasing the dispersion number from 1 to 0.25 is to install baffles. The success of different baffling arrangements in reducing the dispersion number may be explored on a pilot-plant scale. The dimensions of the existing reactor and flow rate must be properly scaled down in the pilot plant (i.e., dimensional scaling of flow conditions). Tracer tests will then determine the extent to which dispersion is reduced by different baffling schemes.*

- *Key Point(s). In this case an RTD analysis is used not only to develop a dispersion number for a potentially usable existing reactor, but, by comparison of performance to ideal PFRs, an effective rate coefficient for the reaction itself. While the performance of the reactor does not meet treatment requirements, identification of the reason for its failure to do so suggests ways in which the reactor can be relatively easily and inexpensively modified in order to enhance performance and meet treatment requirements.*

Although the PFDR model is most often employed for analysis of engineered systems, it may be used also to describe fate and transport of contaminants in natural systems. Caution must be exercised, however, when using a simple one-dimensional steady-state model such as that given by Equations 11.32 and 11.33. Dispersive transport in natural environment systems is often multidimensional; this applies to both surface and subsurface systems. In addition, steady state is established only if the contaminant source term remains constant over time. If these cautions are properly observed, the dispersion and Damkohler numbers can be important and useful dimensionless groups in the modeling and assessment of contaminant fate and transport in natural environmental systems.

11.5   CHAPTER SUMMARY

Real reactors and natural environmental systems seldom behave exactly as any one of the ideal reactors discussed in Chapters 9 and 10, although the models for those ideal reactor are very useful for first approximations. They can, moreover, be physically replicated in carefully designed bench-scale laboratory reactors to allow accurate identification and measurement of important process variables. We have learned in Chapter 11 that to quantify deviations in the behaviors of real reactors from those of ideal reactors requires that we be able to characterize the residence time distributions (RTDs) of the real reactors, which can be done experimentally by means of tracer tests. RTD analysis is a powerful tool for performance predictions. It leads directly to structured descriptions of nonideal reactor behavior using ideal reactor models, including those that we can use to mimic non-ideal behavior (e.g., PFDRs).

In a way, the reliance on the experimental analysis of macroscale transport behavior in a reactor (i.e., the RTD) is analogous to reliance on experimental analysis of transformation behavior (i.e., the development of reaction rate expressions). In both instances, theory can provide the framework required to develop a working understanding of an observed process, but the experimental observations that can be made usually do not allow direct theoretical interpretations of process.

11.6   CITATIONS AND SOURCES

Lawler, D.F., and P.C. Singer, 1993, "Analyzing Disinfection Kinetics and Reactor Design: A Conceptual Approach Versus the SWTR," Journal of the American Water Works Association, 85(11), 611.76. (Example 11.2)

Levenspiel, O., and K.B. Bischoff, 1959, "Backmixing in the Design of Chemical Reactors" Industrial Engineering Chemistry, 51, 1431. (Figures 11.11 and 11.12)

Levenspiel, O., and K.B. Bischoff, 1961, "Reaction Rate Constants May Modify the Effects of Backmixing" Industrial Engineering Chemistry, 53, 313. (Figures 11.11 and 11.12)

Levenspiel, O., and K.B. Bischoff, 1963, Advances in Chemical Engineering, 4, 95. (Equations 11.26, 11.29 and 11.30)

Thomas, H.A., Jr., and J.E. McKee, 1944, "Longitudinal Mixing in Aeration Tanks," Water and Sewage Works, 16(1), 42. (Equation 11.28)

Weber, W.J., Jr., and F.A. DiGiano, 1996, *Process Dynamics in Environmental Systems*, John Wiley & Sons, Inc., New York. (PDES is the source of most of the material presented in Chapter 11. Chapter 9 of PDES covers and expands upon the material presented in Chapter 11 of this text. It also identifies additional related background reading sources).

Wehner, J.F, and R.H. Wilhelm, 1956, "Boundary Conditions for Flow Reactors," *Chemical Engineering Science, 7*, 187. (Equation 11.26)

11.7   PROBLEM ASSIGNMENTS

11.1 Determine the residence time distribution (RTD) that results when a CMFR with an HRT of $\bar{t}_1$ is followed by a PFR with an HRT of $\bar{t}_2$. Reverse the order of the two reactors and again determine the RTD. Based on these results, can RTD analysis be used to distinguish between early and late mixing in a nonideal reactor?

11.2 Find the effluent concentration for each of the two reactor combinations in Problem 11.1 if the feed concentration is 10 mg/L, $\bar{t}_1$ is 2 min, $\bar{t}_2$ is 4 min, and the reaction is first order with a rate constant of 0.2 min^{-1}. Repeat the determination of effluent concentrations for a second-order reaction with a rate constant of 0.2 L/mg-min. What do you conclude about the importance of early versus late mixing and reaction order?

11.3 A step input of fluoride to the clear well of a water treatment plant produces the following results:

Time After Step Input (h)	C_{OUT}/C_{IN}	Time After Step Input (h)	C_{OUT}/C_{IN}
0	0.000	3.00	0.551
0.5	0.000	3.33	0.700
1.00	0.000	3.67	0.800
1.33	0.017	4.00	0.876
1.67	0.106	4.33	0.915
2.00	0.220	4.67	0.957
2.33	0.313	5.00	0.987
2.67	0.431	5.50	1.00

The volume of the clear well is $37{,}500$ m^3 (9.9 mg) and the flow rate during the tracer test was $285{,}000$ m^3/d (75 mgd).

(a) Compare constituent residence time (t_m) values obtained from the $\boldsymbol{F}$ and $\boldsymbol{E}$ curves.

(b) Compare constituent residence time with the HRT.

(c) Calculate the dispersion number assuming a closed vessel configuration.

11.4 Chlorine is usually added ahead of the clear well described in Problem 11.3 to provide for disinfection. Chlorine is also consumed in various oxidation reactions such that the chlorine concentration is reduced from 4.6 mg/L entering the clear well to 2.6 mg/L in the exit stream.

(a) Assume that the rate of chlorine demand is first order and estimate the rate constant, k, using the dispersion model.

(b) The so-called $C-t_{10}$ rule for adequate disinfection in U.S. drinking water regulations requires that the product of the exit disinfectant concentration (C) and the time (t_{10}) for 10% of the tracer to exit after a step input exceed 60 (mg/L) (min) (for the pH of this water). Will this regulation be met given the current feed chlorine concentration and the chlorine demand kinetics at flow rates of $285{,}000$ m^3/d and $570{,}000$ m^3/d MGD? State any assumptions you need to make to adjust the estimate of t_{10} for the higher flow rate.

11.5 A regulated organic compound is treated by chemical oxidation in an existing industrial waste treatment facility. The oxidation process is first order with respect to the organic compound, with $k = 0.5\text{min}^{-1}$. The reactor in which the process is carried out is characterized by a dispersion number of 0.25 and an HRT of 10 min. Expansion of plant operations are planned which will generate an additional waste stream that must be sent to the same reactor. Through waste minimization, the flow rate of the additional waste stream is 25% of the existing waste stream and the compound concentration is 50% of that in the existing waste stream. In anticipation of this expansion, a tracer test is conducted at the increased flow rate ($1.25Q$), with the following results

$$\sigma_t = 5.3 \text{ min} \qquad t_m = 7 \text{ min}$$

Find the fractional change in the effluent concentration [i.e., $(C_{OUT})_{new}/(C_{OUT})_{exist}$], when the new waste stream is added to the existing waste stream.

11.6 A synthetic organic chemical, A, is found in a river section having a length of 3000 m, a velocity of 0.05 m/s, and a dispersion coefficient of 9.4 m^2/s. This chemical is susceptible to rapid photochemical degradation. The reaction rate at a given light intensity is thought to be first order with respect to the concentration of A, but the rate constant has never been measured. If the concentration is reduced by 98% in this stretch of river, how much decomposition can be expected in a more turbulent reach (with similar photochemical reaction characteristics) which has a length of 1500 m, a flow velocity of 0.08 m/s, and a dispersion coefficient of 30 m^2/s?

11.7 Effluent disinfection by chlorine is to be abandoned in favor of UV irradiation at a wastewater treatment plant to eliminate aquatic toxicity problems related to chlorinated organics. Banks of ultraviolet lamps are installed directly in the existing chlorine contact chamber, which has an HRT of 30 min. After startup, it is found that only a two-log reduction (i.e., log (C_{IN}/C_{OUT}) = 2) in fecal coliform could be obtained, whereas a three-log reduction is needed. A tracer test reveals that $\sigma_t = 19$ min and the constituent residence time (t_m) is 26 min. What is the maximum improvement in disinfection efficiency that can be expected if the UV disinfection rate is first order with respect to fecal coliform concentration and the reactor can be modified with baffles to more closely approach plug flow behavior?

11.8 A state regulatory agency requires that all water treatment plants conduct a step input tracer test on clear wells to determine the t_{10} (i.e., the time for the tracer concentration to reach 10% of the input concentration). The value of t_{10} is multiplied by the exit disinfectant concentration to determine if adequate disinfection is being achieved. Personnel at a particular water treatment plant decided that it is more convenient to use a "negative step tracer input," whereby they interrupted the feed of fluoride to the clear well instead of increasing the feed rate to produce a positive step tracer input. The state regulatory agency is concerned that the test procedure will not yield the same t_{10} as by the conventional procedure. Are the results equivalent?

11.9 The Hanford Site, a former plutonium production facility located on the Columbia River in southeastern Washington State, is managed by the U.S. Department of Energy and currently engaged in the world's largest environmental cleanup project. On site, large tanks of radioactive mixed wastes are stored for eventual disposal. Consider a hypothetical situation in which Cesium-137, a radioactive compound with a half-life much longer than 10 years, is accidentally released to the Columbia River (approximate flow 4000 m³/s), with the concentration profile drawn below being observed at Bonneville Dam, approximately 400 km downstream.

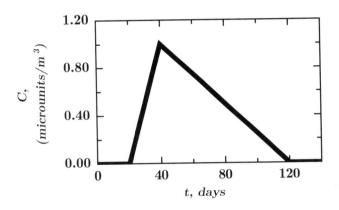

(a) Determine for this hypothetical how many radioactive units of this tracer would have been accidentally released.

(b) Determine the volume of the Columbia River between Bonneville Dam and the Hanford Site.

Answers: (a) 50 radioactive microunits/m³; (b) 9.1 × 10⁷ m³

11.10 The $E(t)$ profile for two CMFRs in series having different volumes is

$$E(t) = \frac{1}{\tau(2m-1)}\left\{ exp\left(\frac{-t}{\tau m}\right) - exp\left[\frac{-t}{(1-m)\tau}\right]\right\}$$

where

$$\tau = \frac{V_1 + V_2}{Q} = \frac{V_T}{Q}$$

and

$$m = \frac{V_1}{V_1 + V_2} = \frac{V_1}{V_T}$$

(a) Plot $E(t)$ as a function of t for different values of m (e.g., $m = 0.01$, 0.1, etc.) and comment on what you observe.

(b) Plot $E(t)$ as a function of t for different values of τ and comment on what you observe.

Chapter 12

Multiphase Process Equilibria

Contents

12.0   CHAPTER OBJECTIVES

To extend general thermodynamic relationships developed for homogeneous systems to multiphase systems, making appropriate additional considerations for chemical species that change phase or that migrate from one phase to another.

12.1   PHASE TRANSFORMATIONS

12.1.1   Types

Distinctions between different types of phase changes are important in extending our considerations of thermodynamic principles to heterogeneous systems. The most elementary type of phase change involves conversion of pure chemical substances from one physical state to another. Simple examples are the freezing and boiling of water to form ice and water vapor, respectively. Water and waste treatment processes that rely on such phase changes include: 1) the freezing or distillation of water to separate inorganic impurities; 2) the use of supercritical fluids to facilitate the dissolution or oxidative destruction of organic impurities; and, 3) the condensation of organic vapors to allow their removal from gas streams. A similar but more complex phase change occurs when two dissolved or aqueous-phase chemical species combine to form a precipitate, a solid phase. Precipitation equilibria were illustrated for selected metal ions and inorganic ligands in Figure 5.2, Table 5.3 and Example 5.3. The formation of a solid phase is caused by input of chemical energy in the form of increased masses of reactants, or from inputs or extraction of thermal energy that change the solubility relationships between reacting species. This type of phase change occurs in a broad range of environmental processes, particularly those involving reactions of metal ions with organic and inorganic ligands to form solid precipitates.

Another frequent type of phase transformation is one in which a relatively minor component of one phase migrates or is transferred to another phase without significant change in the temperature or pressure of either phase. Some common examples include: 1) the dissolution of oxygen from air into water; 2) the volatilization of an organic contaminant, such as benzene, from water to air; and, 3) the sorption of a hydrophobic contaminant, such as a polychlorinated biphenyl (PCB), by lake sediments or by activated carbon in an engineered waste treatment system. When minor components of one phase migrate to another, their chemical structure may or may not change. The motivation for migration in these cases is to achieve a greater degree of compatibility between the chemical structure of the migrating component and the phase into or onto which it migrates.

12.1.2 Chemical Character and Phase Transfer

Phase transformations cause temporary phase instability. For example, molecular oxygen has a limited solubility in water, as discussed in Chapter 2. If amounts of oxygen exceeding this limit at a given temperature and pressure are forced into water, local pressures increase momentarily and an unstable condition results. This instability eventually causes the excess dissolved oxygen to escape to the air phase until a balanced distribution between the water and air is achieved. Oxygen is in a zero-oxidation state in both phases, a state that is more thermodynamically compatible with air than with water. As its oxidation state is reduced to (-II) by reactions in the water, the reduced oxygen becomes much more compatible with the polar solvent water than with air.

Because of their particular forms, certain chemical substances are not compatible with any phase to which they have access in a given system. Instead, these substances gather at interfaces between phases, sometimes forming their own interfacial "phases." Interfacial accumulation is typified by surface-active agents, such as detergents, which are only marginally compatible with water and even less so with air. Such substances thus tend to form foams at air-water interfaces.

As the foregoing discussion illustrates, chemical character not only affects reactivity within individual phases, but also the distribution of species among and between phases and phase interfaces. This explains why large proportions of chemicals such as benzene and trichloroethylene that are discharged to water eventually find their way to the atmosphere, while polychlorinated biphenyls (PCBs) and polynuclear aromatic hydrocarbons (PAHs) eventually concentrate primarily in sediments. The tendency for species to distribute differently among phases forms the basis for separation technologies employed in engineered systems. Two examples of such separation technologies are: 1) air stripping for removal of benzene and trichloroethylene from contaminated groundwater; and, 2) adsorption by activated carbon for removal of PCBs and PAHs from contaminated waste streams.

12.2 PHASE EQUILIBRIA

12.2.1 Concepts

We are concerned in this chapter with several aspects of the interactions of species among multiple phases in complex environmental systems. Chemical species ranging from molecular level to particle level are discussed. We must consider such a wide span of entities because contaminants and other chemical species exist in various forms in environmental systems. This in turn leads to the existence of various phases and associated phase transfer and separation processes. For instance, molecules of certain soluble species can interact with one another to form polymolecular (or polynuclear) entities (i.e., polymers) of sufficient size to transform them from the dissolved state to the macromolecular or colloidal state; proteins behave in this manner. Alternatively, soluble, well-defined molecular species may associated with what are often poorly defined macromolecules or colloids, such as humic and fulvic acids, clays, bacteria, or algae. In such cases the fate and behavior of the molecular species of concern may change markedly, and thermodynamic "stability" in a given environmental system may be controlled entirely by parameters and features that are unique to that system. A good example of species that undergo shifts in thermodynamic stability is high molecular-weight PCBs. As dissolved species PCBs are unstable in aquatic environments. When attached to a macromolecule or colloid, however, a PCB may remain in a stable or metastable suspended state. Its transport with the flow of water may thus be facilitated.

We begin our considerations of energy relationships in heterogeneous systems with relatively simple systems in which substances are transferred directly from a "dissolved" state in one phase to a "dissolved" state in another phase. For these cases we can use thermodynamic considerations directly to determine distributions of different species in different phases, or environmental "compartments." The logical starting point for our discussions lies in thermodynamic criteria that govern phase behavior. These criteria are rooted in principles that translate into familiar constants and properties of different substances with respect to different phases, such as: 1) Henry's constant, $\mathcal{K}_H$; 2) the octanol-water partitioning coefficient, $\mathcal{K}_{OW}$; 3) aqueous phase solubility, C_S; 4) vapor pressure, P^v; and, 5) melting and boiling points, T_m and T_b, respectively. Table 12.1 provides a tabulation of these constants and properties for selected carbon compounds of environmental significance.

12.2.2 Thermodynamic Criteria

Certain thermodynamic requirements exist for establishment of equilibrium conditions between components in different phases of heterogeneous systems. First and most simply, for systems that are closed and for which the phases are each of constant volume and composition, the zeroth law stipulates that these phases must be equal in temperature for thermal equilibrium to exist; that is, there can be no net interphase heat flow at equilibrium. Thus, for two phases j and k, $T_j = T_k$.

Second, and more importantly for our considerations of phase equilibria, if the pressures and temperatures of the two phases are constant, then $\mu_j = \mu_k$. Thus, for constant temperature and pressure, the thermodynamic requirement for a stable chemical equilibrium is that the chemical potential of each component must be the same in each phase.

12.2.3 Phase Exchange Laws

Two ideal-solution laws govern the equilibrium behavior of chemical species distributed between adjacent gas and liquid phases. The first of these, Raoult's law, governs the behavior of pure or nearly pure solid or liquid substances with respect to pure vapor phases. The

Table 12.1 Thermodynamic Properties of Selected Organic Compounds

Formula	Compound	$\left(\dfrac{atm - m^3}{mol} \times 10^3\right)$	$log\ \mathcal{K}_{OW}$
CH_4	Methane	639	1.09
CH_3OH	Methanol	0.14	-0.74
CH_3Cl	Chloromethane (methyl chloride)	9.6	0.91
CH_2Cl_2	Dichloromethane	2.6	1.15
$CHCl_3$	Trichloromethane (chloroform)	3.3	1.97
CCl_3F	Trichlorofluoromethane	113.3	2.53
CCl_4	Tetrachloromethane (carbon tetrachloride)	24.0	2.73
C_2H_6	Ethane	490	1.81
C_2H_5OH	Ethanol	0.0063	-0.30
$C_2H_4Cl_2$	1,1-Dichloroethane (1,1-DCA)	6.0	1.79
$C_2H_4Cl_2$	1,2-Dichloroethane (1,2-DCA)	1.1	1.47
C_2H_3Cl	Chloroethane (vinyl chloride)	22.4	0.60
$C_2H_3Cl_3$	1,1,1-Trichloroethane (1,1,1-TCA)	23.2	2.47
$C_2H_3Cl_3$	1,1,2-Trichloroethane (1,1,2-TCA)	0.9	1.89
$C_2H_2Cl_2$	1,1-Dichloroethylene (1,1-DCE)	154.5	2.13
C_2HCl_3	Trichloroethylene (TCE)	11.7	2.29
C_2Cl_4	Tetra(per)chloroethylene (PCE)	27.5	2.88
C_4H_9OH	t-butyl alcohol (TBA or tBA)	0.0118	0.35
$C_5H_{12}O$	Methy t-butyl ether (MTBE or MtBE)	1.8	1.12
C_6H_{14}	n-Hexane	768	4.0
C_6H_6	Benzene	5.49	2.13
C_6H_5OH	Phenol	0.0004	1.50
C_6H_5Cl	Chlorobenzene	3.71	2.84
$C_6H_5NO_2$	Nitrobenzene	0.024	1.85
$C_6H_4Cl_2$	1,4-Dichlorobenzene	2.24	3.38
$C_6H_3Cl_3$	1,2,4-Trichlorobenzene	2.75	4.26
C_6Cl_6	Hexachlorobenzene	412.4	5.47
C_7H_8	Toluene	6.66	2.73
C_8H_{18}	n-Octane	2,960	5.15
$C_8H_{18}O$	1-Octanol	0.0159	3.07
C_8H_{10}	Ethylbenzene	7.94	3.15
C_8H_{10}	o-Xylene	5.27	3.12
$C_{10}H_{22}$	n-Decane	6,900	6.25
$C_{10}H_8$	Naphthalene	0.42	3.35
$C_{12}H_{26}$	n-Dodecane	7,400	6.80
$C_{12}H_{10}$	Acenaphthene	0.24	3.92
$C_{14}H_{10}$	Anthracene	0.06	4.50
$C_{14}H_{10}$	Phenanthrene	0.04	4.52
$C_{16}H_{22}O_4$	n-Butyl phthalate	0.0018	4.72
$C_{16}H_{10}$	Pyrene	0.0089	5.22
$C_{20}H_{12}$	Benzo[a]pyrene	0.0005	6.04

Table 12.1 (continued)

Formula	C_S (mg/L)	P^v ($atm \times 10^3$)	T_m ($^\circ C$)	T_b ($^\circ C$)
CH_4	22.7	275.4×10^3	-182.5	-161.5
CH_3OH	misc	131.6	-97.8	64
CH_3Cl	5,287	5.65×10^3	-97.7	-24.2
CH_2Cl_2	19,442	588.8	-95.1	39.7
$CHCl_3$	7,709	228.5	-63.5	61.7
CCl_3F	1,100	1.05×10^3	-111.0	23.8
CCl_4	969	151.4	-22.9	76.5
C_2H_6	61.4	39.8×10^3	-183.3	-88.6
C_2H_5OH	misc	65.8	-114.1	78.5
$C_2H_4Cl_2$	4,960	301.9	-97.0	57.5
$C_2H_4Cl_2$	8,425	91.2	-35.4	83.5
C_2H_3Cl	2,790	3.89×10^3	-153.8	-13.4
$C_2H_3Cl_3$	730	126.7	-32.0	113.0
$C_2H_3Cl_3$	4,500	29.1	-36.5	113.8
$C_2H_2Cl_2$	400	791.2	-122.1	37.0
C_2HCl_3	1,100	97.7	-73.0	87.0
C_2Cl_4	151.2	25.1	-19.0	121.0
C_4H_9OH	misc	52.6	25.6	82.4
$C_5H_{12}O$	48,000	326.4	-109.0	55.2
C_6H_{14}	11	199.9	-95.4	68.7
C_6H_6	1,770	125.7	5.5	80.1
C_6H_5OH	80,200	0.70	40.6	181.9
C_6H_5Cl	472	15.6	-46.5	132.0
$C_6H_5NO_2$	1,900	0.20	5.7	210.6
$C_6H_4Cl_2$	83.1	0.89	53.1	174.0
$C_6H_3Cl_3$	40.6	0.60	17.0	213.5
C_6Cl_6	0.005	2.3×10^{-5}	230.0	322.0
C_7H_8	534	37.6	-94.9	110.6
C_8H_{18}	0.71	18.6	-56.8	125.0
$C_8H_{18}O$	540	6.6×10^{-2}	-15.4	195.2
C_8H_{10}	160	12.6	-94.9	136.2
C_8H_{10}	175	8.68	-25.2	144.4
$C_{10}H_{22}$	0.015	1.74	-29.6	174.1
$C_{10}H_8$	31	0.10	80.2	217.9
$C_{12}H_{26}$	0.0037	0.16	-9.6	216.2
$C_{12}H_{10}$	3.8	7.9×10^{-3}	95	277.5
$C_{14}H_{10}$	0.062	7.9×10^{-6}	217.5	342.0
$C_{14}H_{10}$	1.1	1.6×10^{-4}	99.5	340.2
$C_{16}H_{22}O_4$	3.2	1.3×10^{-2}	135.0	340.0
$C_{16}H_{10}$	0.135	5.9×10^{-6}	156.0	360.0
$C_{20}H_{12}$	0.004	6.9×10^{-9}	175.0	—

Note : The numerical values given are for 25° unless otherwise stated. They derive from a variety of sources and are presented only by way of illustration and are not represented as absolute. See Appendix A.6.1 in PDES for additional values.

second, Henry's law, governs events at the opposite end of the con-
centration spectrum, namely the behavior of extremely dilute aqueous
solutions of dissolved solutes with respect to air.

Figure 12.1 depicts a closed-two-phase system comprised initially by pure water and pure air. We know intuitively that, with time, some water will enter the air in vapor form and some of each component of air (i.e., carbon dioxide, nitrogen, and any trace constituents) will dissolve in the water. But why? What thermodynamic relationships govern this phenomenon and eventually determine the equilibrium concentrations of the water in the air and of oxygen, for example, in the water?

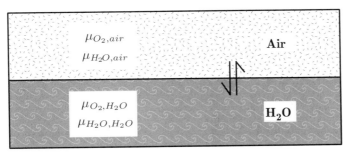

Equilibrium Condition	Governing Law
$\mu_{O_2,air}$ / μ_{O_2,H_2O}	**Henry's Law**
$\mu_{H_2O,air}$ / μ_{H_2O,H_2O}	**Raoult's Law**

Figure 12.1 Application of Raoult's and Henry's Laws for a Closed Air-Water System

Driven by the vapor pressure of nearly pure water (i.e., its tendency to vaporize), a net evolution of water vapor into the nearly pure air occurs until a phase equilibrium is attained. The primary determinant of the concentration (actually chemical potential) of water in the air is thus its vapor pressure. The equilibrium distribution of water between the two phases is therefore governed by Raoult's law. Oxygen, which has a mole fraction of $X_{O_2} = 0.21$ in air (i.e., pure air is 21% oxygen) and a much lower saturation (solubility limit) mole fraction (i.e., $X_{O_2} \sim 10^{-5}$) in water, is dissolved in the water until an equilibrium determined largely by the aqueous-phase activity of oxygen is achieved. Because the oxygen has limited solubility and is thus very dilute in the solvent water, the equilibrium distribution of oxygen between the two phases is governed by Henry's law.

Several Henry's law expressions having different units and dimensions are variously used in the literature; i.e., the units and associated values of the Henry's constant differ with the units used to describe component concentrations in the gas and liquid phases. The most common expressions and the relationships among them are presented in Table 12.2. For gas-phase concentrations in atmospheres and solution phase concentrations in moles per cubic meter, the units of $\mathcal{K}_H$ are atm $-$ m^3/mol. For concentrations expressed as dimensionless mass or molar ratios (e.g., partial pressures, p, and mole fractions, X), Henry's constant is dimensionless and designated as $\mathcal{K}_H^o$. Values of $\mathcal{K}_H$ in atm $-$ m^3/mol can be converted to dimensionless values of $\mathcal{K}_H^o$ (see the last entry in Table 12.2) by dividing by $\mathcal{R}T$, where $\mathcal{R}$ is the universal gas constant and T is absolute temperature. The value of $\mathcal{R}$ is 8.314 J/mol-K = 8.314 Pa $-$ m^3/mol-K, = 1.987 cal/mol-K = 8.21×10^{-5}atm $-$ m^3/mol $-$ K. Thus at 20°C (293 K), $\mathcal{K}_H^o$ (dimensionless) = $\mathcal{K}_H$(atm $-$ m^3/mol) $\times$ 41.57. One of these expressions may in any given instance be more convenient to use than another, depending on the situation at hand.

Table 12.2 Common Expressions for Henry's Law

Expression	Definition of Terms		Units for $\mathcal{K}_H$
$P = \mathcal{K}_H X_a$	$X_a =$	mole fraction of constituent in aqueous phase	*atm (per mole fraction)*
	$P =$	pressure exerted by constituent in vapor phase (atm)	
$P = \mathcal{K}_H C_a$	$C_a =$	molar concentration of constituent in aqueous phase	atm $-$ m^3/mol

Note : $\mathcal{K}_H(atm - m^3/mol) = \mathcal{K}_H(atm)X_a/C_a$
$= \mathcal{K}_H(atm)/55.6 \times 10^3 = \mathcal{K}_H(atm) \times 18 \times 10^{-6}$

$p = \mathcal{K}_H X_a$	$p =$	partial pressure of constituent in vapor phase, P/P_T	dimensionless *(partial pressure)*
	$P_T =$	total pressure of vapor phase (atm)	
$C_v = \mathcal{K}_H^o C_a$	$C_v =$	molar concentration of constituent in vapor phase, where $C_v = P/\mathcal{R}T$	dimensionless *(molar concentration ratio)*

Note : $\mathcal{K}_H^o(\textit{partial pressure}) = \mathcal{K}_H(atm)/P_T$
$\mathcal{K}_H^o(\textit{conc.ratio}) = \mathcal{K}_H\ (atm)X/\mathcal{R}TC_a = \mathcal{K}_H(atm - m^3/mol)/\mathcal{R}T$

Henry's constant, introduced and discussed briefly in Chapter 2, can be further explored using the fugacity equilibrium principle. The fugacities of any solute in the aqueous (f_a) and vapor (f_v) phases of Figure 12.1 are equal at equilibrium, such that

$$
\boxed{\begin{array}{ll} \textbf{\textit{Fugacity}} \\ \textbf{\textit{Equilibrium}} & f_a = X\alpha_a P^v = f_v = \alpha_v P \\ \textbf{\textit{Principle}} \end{array}}
\qquad (12.1)
$$

in which X is the mole fraction of the solute in the aqueous phase, P^v is the vapor pressure of the pure solute, P is the pressure exerted by the solute in the vapor phase, and α_a and α_v are the activity coefficients in the aqueous and vapor phases, respectively. The activity coefficient in the vapor phase is assumed to be one, but the activity coefficient in a liquid phase is one only for a liquid comprised by a pure solute. The Henry's law relationship for a dissolved component of water (e.g., O_2) is thus written

$$
P = (\alpha_a P^v)X \qquad (12.2)
$$

from which we conclude that the Henry's constant, $\mathcal{K}_H$, for a solute, stated in terms of the vapor pressure and aqueous phase activity coefficient for that solute, is

$$
\boxed{\begin{array}{ll} \textbf{\textit{Henry's Constant}} \\ \textbf{\textit{Vapor Pressure}} & \mathcal{K}_H = \alpha_a P^v \quad \text{(in atm)} \\ \textbf{\textit{Relationship}} \end{array}}
\qquad (12.3)
$$

A closed three-phase system represented by "pure" air, "pure" water, and "pure" xylene is illustrated in Figure 12.2. Here the concentration of xylene in the air is driven by the vapor pressure of xylene, whereas its concentration in the water is determined by its activity in the aqueous phase.

If, as depicted in Figure 12.3, the pure xylene phase is removed from the system, then the equilibrium condition for xylene between the two remaining "dilute" phases is driven by its partial pressure in the air and its activity in the aqueous phase; for this situation Henry's law governs the phase distribution.

Example 12.1 illustrates how equilibrium phase distributions of substances driven by absorption phenomena can be quantified by application of the simple "linear free energy" phase equilibrium relationships given by Henry's and Raoult's laws.

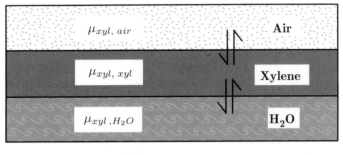

Equilibrium Condition	Governing Law
$\mu_{xyl,\,air}$ / $\mu_{xyl,\,xyl}$ / $\mu_{xyl,\,H_2O}$	Raoult's Law

Figure 12.2 Application of Raoult's and Henry's Laws for a Closed Air-Water-Xylene System

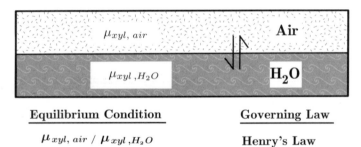

Equilibrium Condition	Governing Law
$\mu_{xyl,\,air}$ / $\mu_{xyl,\,H_2O}$	Henry's Law

Figure 12.3 Application of Raoult's and Henry's Laws for a Closed System of Air and Xylene Dissolved in Water

---

Example 12.1. Local Air and Water Contamination Caused by a Spill of a Volatile NAPL. (An illustration of the applications of Henry's and Raoult's phase equilibrium laws.)

- *Situation.* During a particularly heavy and prolonged rainstorm, the air brakes on a tanker truck containing 10 tons of o-xylene (2-xylene) fail as it turns off a highway into a fueling station. The truck jumps a curb, crashes through one wall of a glass enclosure over a heated (25° C) swimming pool at an adjacent motel, and plunges into the 250 m³ of water in the pool. It then overturns, dumping its contents as it does so. The xylene dissolves to the extent of its solubility limit throughout the water column, and the remaining excess floats as a "free product" on the pool surface. The accident occurs at 6:00 a.m. on a Monday morning. The emergency response authorities have the truck removed by 9:00 a.m. the following morning, and at that time begin cleaning up the spill. The cleanup operation involves *two stages; first, removal of the free (floating) xylene and, second, treatment of the water with activated carbon to remove the dissolved xylene. It is imperative from a worker safety point of view for the cleanup crews to know both the water and local air (immediately above pool) concentrations of xylene at both stages of operation.*

- **Question(s).** *Determine the initial concentrations of o-xylene in the water of the swimming pool and in the air within the glass enclosure above the pool. After the free xylene has been removed, the water remains saturated with xylene. Determine the equilibrium vapor phase concentration of o-xylene at the initiation of the second stage of cleanup.*

- **Logic and Answer(s).** *It can be assumed that the vigorous initial mixing caused by the truck's indelicate entry to the pool, coupled with the time elapsed until initiation of the cleanup, allowed the xylene and water phases to equilibrate with each other and subsequently separate. The resulting three-phase system condition is essentially that depicted in Figure 12.2.*

    1. *As indicated below Figure 12.2, the governing law is Raoult's law, and according to Raoult's law at equilibrium*

$$X_{xyl,v} = (P^v_{xyl}/P_T)X_{xyl,l}$$

    where $X_{xyl,v}$ is the mole fraction of xylene in the vapor phase, $X_{xyl,v}$ is the mole fraction of xylene in the liquid (pure xylene) phase, P^v_{xyl} is the vapor pressure of xylene, and P_T is the total pressure of the system.

    2. *Because the water is saturated with xylene at equilibrium, the aqueous-phase concentration (Table 12.1) is 175 mg/L, which translates into*

$$(0.175g/L)(1mol/106g) = 0.00165 \ mol/L$$

    3. *The xylene floating on the surface (comprising an approximately 5-cm deep layer of free product) constitutes the liquid phase for Raoult's law; thus*
$$X_{xyl,l} = 1.0.$$

    4. *The vapor pressure of pure xylene is given in Table 12.1 as 8.68×10^{-3} atm at $25°C$. Thus, since the total pressure, P_T, is 1 atm*

$$X_{xyl,v} = 8.68 \times 10^{-3}$$

    and the dimensionless vapor-phase concentration, c°_v, for the first stage of cleanup, is
$$
\begin{aligned}
c^\circ_v &= (8.68 \times 10^{-3})(106 \ g \ xylene/mol/28.8g \ air/mol) \\
&= 31.95 \times 10^{-3} \ g \ xylene/g \ air
\end{aligned}
$$

5. *After removal of the free xylene the system condition is essentially that given in Figure 12.3, a two-phase condition for which Henry's law is the governing law. In concept, however, no xylene has been removed from either the air or the water, and it seems intuitive that these phases would remain in equilibrium with each other even after the pure xylene phase has been removed. Let's do some calculations to see if our "common sense" is on target.*

6. *The aqueous-phase concentration remains at the saturation limit of 175 mg/L (0.00165 mol/L). It is now this concentration, and Henry's law, which together determine the air-phase concentration.*

7. *One statement or form of Henry's law (Table 12.2) is given by*

$$\mathcal{K}_H = P_{xyl}/C_{xyl,a}$$

where $\mathcal{K}_H$ is the Henry's law constant (atm-m^3/mol), P_{xyl} is the pressure of xylene in the vapor phase (atm), and $C_{xyl,a}$ is the aqueous-phase concentration of xylene (mol/L).

8. *From Table 12.1, $\mathcal{K}_H$ for xylene can be taken as 5.27×10^{-3} atm-m^3/mol (5.27 atm-L/mol) at 25° C. It follows that*

$$P_{xyl} = \mathcal{K}_H \times C_{xyl,a} = (5.27)(0.00165) = 8.68 \times 10^{-3} \ atm$$

9. *The total pressure is 1.0 atm, thus*

$$X_{xyl,v} = \frac{P_{xyl}}{P_T} = \frac{8.68 \times 10^{-3}}{1.0} = 8.68 \times 10^{-3}$$

Viva l'intuition et l'ordinaire bon sens!

- **Key Point(s). Even for the relatively simple situation described above the different governing conditions and associated reference states relating chemical potentials (or chemical activities) of substances involved in multiple phase exchange relationships can make calculations cumbersome. We shall see shortly that fugacity calculations are more convenient for description of equilibrium conditions in multiphase systems.**

12.2.4   Absorption, Dissolution, and Partitioning

The term sorption is a general descriptor for two distinctly different classes of processes (i.e., absorption and adsorption) that may occasionally exhibit similar behaviors. From mechanistic and thermodynamic points of view, substances that are distributed throughout

a phase and intermixed with that phase on a molecular basis, as de-
picted in Figures 12.1 through 12.3 and discussed in the immediately
preceding example, should be thought of as being absorbed by those
phases. The associated process is therefore customarily referred to
as absorption. The equilibria of absorption processes are generally
controlled by the linear free energy chemical potential relationships
discussed in Chapters 5 and 6. This type of intraphase solute distribution,
illustrated schematically by the sketch in part a of Figure 12.4, can occur between gas and liquid phases, different gas phases, different liquid phases, and
may even involve some highly amorphous "solid" phases.

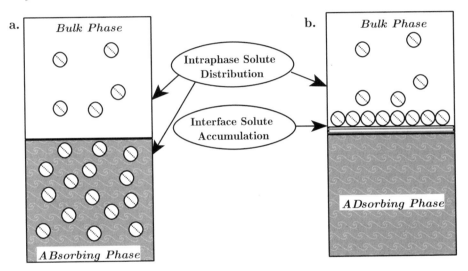

Figure 12.4 Schematic Characterizations of Absorption and
Adsorption Processes

   The strict definition of absorption as a "dissolution process" is generally
restricted to exchanges involving pure phases of a substance and/or very dilute
concentrations of a substance in otherwise nearly pure phases. The term has
fallen into common usage, however, to describe many non-ideal environmental
separations that manifest similar phenomenological behavior.

   There is a different class of sorption processes involving gases,
solids, and liquids that results in the accumulation of a constituent
of one phase at an interface between that phase and another. This
type of sorption process, depicted schematically in parts b and c of
Figure 12.4, is customarily referred to as adsorption. As suggested
Figure 12.5, the energetics of adsorption processes can become much
more complex than those of absorption processes when the interfaces
within or surfaces upon which adsorption occurs are heterogeneous
in character.

   In this Chapter we focus our discussions principally upon the interphase

a.   b.

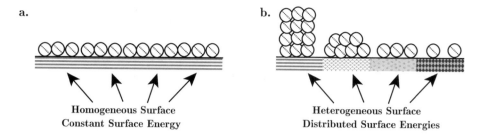

Figure 12.5 Schematic Characterizations of Homogeneous and
Heterogeneous Surfaces for Adsorption

equilibrium considerations associated with absorption processes. The interfacial
equilibrium considerations of adsorption processes are dealt with in Chapter 13.

Absorption phenomena underlie a number of processes referenced previously,
notably: 1) the dissolution of gaseous oxygen from air into water; 2) the dissolution of xylene from its pure liquid state into water; 3) the vaporization of
water and xylene from their respective pure liquid states into air; and, 4) the
volatilization of xylene from a dissolved aqueous state into air.

As depicted in Figure 12.1 through 12.3 and again in part a of Figure 12.4,
the interphase equilibrium condition for absorption processes mandates a uniform intraphase (internal) distribution of a chemical species in each of the phases
involved. The distribution will in all likelihood be different between the phases,
but conceptually it should be uniform throughout each phase. With specific reference to the phases depicted in Figures 12.1 through 12.3, dissolved oxygen and
xylene molecules are each theoretically distributed uniformly throughout the water and air phases at equilibrium, and xylene molecules uniformly throughout
the pure liquid xylene. Because these substances are considered as being dissolved, their absorption in each phase can be related to their solubility in that
phase. The liquid xylene, for example, dissolves to a greater extent in organic
liquids such as hexane than it does in water because nonpolar and slightly polar
organic liquids are more compatible with each other than they are with water, a
highly polar liquid. In other words, the hydrocarbon character of xylene is one
that makes this substance more compatible with the hydrogen-carbon structure
of hexane than with the hydrogen-oxygen structure of water. Xylene, like many
organic compounds, is thus more organophilic than it is hydrophilic. In fact,
many organic compounds are distinctly water-disliking, or hydrophobic.

The partitioning of a chemical species between different phases in a multiphase system depends on its relative thermodynamic compatibility in those
phase. In that the extent of dissolution of a substance in a given phase can
be thought of as one measure of its thermodynamic compatability with that
phase (see Chapter 5), it can be categorized as a partitioning process. In most
situations, particularly with inorganic precipitates but also with non-aqueous
phase liquids (NAPLs), once the solubility limit of a substance in a given phase
(e.g., an aqueous phase) is reached, any further addition of that substance to the

system remains in its own relatively "pure" phase. We must be aware, however, that the thermodynamics of systems in which water is one of two or more phases differ significantly from simple homogeneous aqueous solutions. Aqueous phase solubility or saturation implies a fixed and identifiable limiting concentration that may not occur as such in multiphase systems. Instead, the solubility of a component in any one phase is dependent on its concentration in the other(s), if there are two or more alternative phases with which it can associate in "dissolved" states. The term phase partitioning is thus used most properly in the sense of the relative dissolution of a solute in each of two or more different phases.

12.2.5 The Linear Distribution Model

The equilibrium partitioning of a solute between two phases is controlled by a linear free energy relationship equating the chemical potentials (and thus the activities, or approximately the chemical concentrations) of that solute in each of the two phases (e.g., Henry's Law). We can surmise intuitively that the same linear relationship will not hold for the heterogeneous adsorption processes depicted in Figure 12.5. Moreover, for reasons that will become evident in our discussion of interfacial phenomena in Chapter 13, the equilibrium phase relationship even for the homogeneous surface in part a of that figure is also generally nonlinear over wide ranges of residual solute concentrations in the phase from which adsorption occurs. The exception to this latter situation for which linear adsorption occurs is a special condition involving a sufficiently dilute bulk phase solute concentration to cause only a sparse accumulation of solute at the surface of the adsorbing phase (a so-called "Henry's type adsorption" condition).

Nonetheless, for the dilute concentration ranges of many environmental systems, and most particularly over small concentration ranges of observation that may highlight a part of the overall sorption process that involves only a relatively homogeneous fraction of a heterogeneous sorbent, it is possible for absorption and adsorption to manifest phenomenologically similar linear phase distributions of the type depicted in Figure 12.6. The term C_e in Figure 12.6 represents the solute concentration in one phase (e.g., water) at equilibrium, and q_e the corresponding solute concentration in a second phase (e.g., a NAPL, or a soil or sediment).

It can be argued that any process yielding experimental data that can be fit by a linear trace such as that given in Figure 12.5 can be described by the simple Linear Distribution Model (LDM)

$$\boxed{\textit{\textbf{Linear Distribution Model}} \quad q_e = \mathcal{K}_D C_e} \tag{12.4}$$

The parameter $\mathcal{K}_D$ in Equation 12.4 is assigned the generic term distribution coefficient unless there is other specific evidence (other

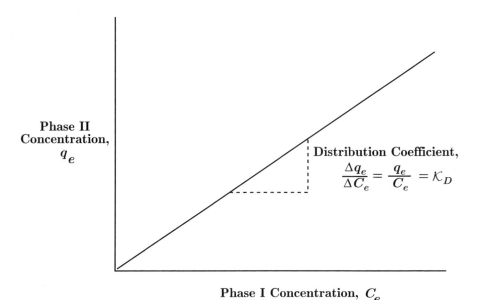

Figure 12.6 A Linear Equilibrium Phase Distribution

than just an apparent linear fit) to support referencing it as a partitioning coefficient. One must be cautious about extending any such arguments and/or derivative models beyond actual ranges of observed data, particularly from one system to another. The "slippery slope" associated with model projections or extrapolations beyond ranges of actual calibration data even for single specific systems lies in the widely recognized fact that many (if not most) phenomena in natural and engineered environmental systems are log-linear rather than linear in character.

An illustration of a system that involves both a case of sorption that is known to be of a strictly phase-partitioning (between air and water) character and a case of sorption (between solid particles and water) that is only assumed for convenience to be linear is given in Example 12.2.

Example 12.2. Volatilization and Sorption of An Organic Contaminant From Aqueous Phase in a Closed Vessel. (Two examples of linear phase distribution modeling, one rigorously correct and the other convenient but questionable.)

- *Situation.* A closed vessel having a volume of 12 m^3 is used to collect 10 m^3 of an intermittently generated aqueous industrial waste containing 4.2 mg/L (0.023 mol/m^3) of 1,2,4-trichlorobenzene (MW = 181.45

g/mol) and 100 mg/L (100 g/m^3) of suspended particulate matter. The suspended matter settles and forms a sludge that is withdrawn for landfilling. The supernatant is decanted and diluted with other waste streams for further treatment. Sorption of the tricholorobenzene (TCB) onto the suspended matter is suspected because of the hydrophobicity of this compound (log $K_{OW} = 4.26$, see Table 12.1). If significant sorption occurs, further treatment of the sludge may be necessary (e.g., by thermal desorption of TCB and return of the liquid stream to the wastewater treatment plant) before the solids can be landfilled. No simple and direct way is available to measure the sorbed-phase concentration. The presence of suspended matter also interferes with determination of the liquid-phase concentration. However, a small air vent in the vessel provides a convenient location for vapor-phase measurements. The vapor-phase concentration is found to be $1.91 \times 10^{-3} mol/m^3$ at a temperature of 25° C and pressure of 1 atm.

- **Question(s).** *Determine the solid- and liquid-phase concentrations of TCB in the vessel.*

- **Logic and Answer(s).**

  1. *We assume first that equilibrium exists between the suspended solids (ss), aqueous (a) and vapor (v) phases. The appropriate material balance relationship is then written as*

$$M_T = C_v V_v + C_a V_a + C_{ss} M_{ss}$$

where M_T is the total mass of TCB, M_{ss} is the mass of suspended solids, and the subscripted C values are the concentrations of TCB in the respective phases. At equilibrium, Henrys law applies to relate liquid- and vapor-phase concentrations, so that

$$M_T = C_v V_v + \frac{\mathcal{R}T}{\mathcal{K}_H} C_v V_a + C_{ss} M_{ss}$$

Solving for the solid-phase concentration gives

$$C_{ss} = \left(M_T - C_v V_v - \frac{\mathcal{R}T}{\mathcal{K}_H} C_v V_a \right) \div M_{ss}$$

  2. *The $\mathcal{K}_H$ value for 1,2,4-TCB is 2.75×10^{-3} atm − m^3/mol (see Table 12.1). The other data needed are*

$$M_T = 10 \ m^3 \times 0.023 \ mol/m^3 = 0.23 \ mol$$
$$M_{ss} = 10 \ m^3 \times 100 \ g/m^3 = 1000 \ g$$
$$\mathcal{R} = 8.21 \times 10^{-5} \ atm - m^3/mol - K$$
$$T = 298 \ K$$
$$V_a = 10 \ m^3$$
$$V_v = 2 \ m^3$$
$$C_v = 1.91 \times 10^{-3} \ mol/m^3$$

We determine from the material balance that

$$C_{ss} = 5.63 \times 10^{-5} \ mol/g = 10.2 \ mg/g$$

The aqueous-phase concentration is then calculated from Henry's law

$$C_a = \frac{\mathcal{R}T}{\mathcal{K}_H}C_v = 16.99 \times 10^{-3} \ mol/m^3 = 3.1 \ mg/L$$

3. *Equilibration with the vapor and solid phases has thus reduced the aqueous-phase concentration only slightly, from 4.2 mg/L in the feed to 3.1 mg/L in the discharge from the vessel. The small amount of TCB on these particles (0.005 g/g) may suggest absorption into an amorphous organic carbon phase surrounding the particle surfaces. If a linear sorption is assumed from this single set of measurements, the corresponding distribution coefficient is calculated as*

$$\mathcal{K}_D = \frac{C_{ss}}{C_a} = \frac{5.63 \times 10^{-5} \ mol/g}{16.99 \times 10^{-3} \ mol/m^3} = 3.31 \times 10^{-3} \ m^3/g$$

- **Key Point(s). It has been assumed from the single data point for the distribution of the TCB between solution and solid phases that the general distribution relationship is of the simple linear form given in Equation 12.4. This is a risky assumption. More data should be obtained at different solids concentrations and/or TCB concentrations in the vessel to validate the assumption and to confirm that the sorption relationship is in fact linear. Even if linearity is confirmed, however, the relationship should not be extrapolated beyond the range of the experimentally observed C_a values. Such relationships are examined in more detail in the next section of this chapter.**

One of the most widely argued generalizations regarding the partitioning of organic solutes between water and alternative environmental phases is that direct correlations exist between the "sorption capacities" of these alternative phases and the hydrophobicity of the sorbing solute. This argument has been extended in the case of natural sorbents such as soils and sediments to those parts of such solids comprised by natural organic matter, the logic being that hydrophobic organic solutes will prefer "hydrophobic" organic matter over the more "hydrophilic" mineral components of such natural sorbents. By additional analogies between natural organic matter and "pure" organic phases such arguments have led to the common usage of linear models and casual application of the term "partitioning" to describe soil and sediment sorption processes.

Two seductive aspects of linear partitioning analogies or approximations are that they: 1) "justify" the sorts of risky assumptions illustrated in Example 12.2;

and, 2) appear to reduce the information required to predict sorption behavior to two readily obtained parameters. *That is, it ostensibly becomes possible in such circumstances to normalize the distribution coefficient, $\mathcal{K}_D$, to the organic content, or mass fraction of organic carbon, ϕ°_{OC}, for a particular solid. This normalized $\mathcal{K}_D$ can then be related directly to some convenient measure of solute hydrophobicity, such as the octanol-water partition coefficient, $\mathcal{K}_{OW}$. Thus,*

$$\begin{array}{l} General \\ \mathcal{K}_{OC} - \mathcal{K}_{OW} \\ Correlation \end{array} \qquad \log \frac{\mathcal{K}_D}{\phi^\circ_{OC}} = \log \mathcal{K}_{OC} = \alpha_P \log \mathcal{K}_{OW} + \beta_P \qquad (12.5)$$

The coefficients, α_P and β_P in correlations of this type have been related to the sorbent properties and to the sorption efficiency of the organic carbon fraction of the sorbent for the solute, respectively. The general utility of such correlations is constrained, however, by the system specificity of the calibration coefficients, α_P and β_P.

A further constraint on the conceptual correctness and general utility of correlations based on Equation 12.5 is that they assume and accommodate only linear equilibria. Even modest sorption nonlinearity is generally evidence of the contributions and potential dominance of sorption processes other than simple partitioning. Nonlinearity can be expected for adsorption of solutes to surfaces over wide solution concentration ranges. Nonlinear behavior may be exhibited also for sorption into quasi-solid organic matrices if there are specific interactions leading to increases or decreases in the affinity of sorbed solute molecules for those organic matrices. *If appropriate consideration is given the limitations discussed above, and corresponding cautions exercised, relationships of the type given in Equation 12.5 can be useful for making first-cut approximations to the anticipated environmental behavior of contaminants, as illustrated in Example 12.3. At the same time, this example illustrates the system specificity and non-general character of such approximation methods.*

Example 12.3. Estimating the Sorption of an Organic Contaminant Using the Linear Distribution Model and Correlations of $\mathcal{K}_D$ with $\mathcal{K}_{OW}$. (An example of the ranges and magnitudes of potential error associated with tenuous assumptions.)

- *Situation. Example 12.1 dealt with prediction of aqueous and gas-phase xylene concentrations after a spill into a motel swimming pool occurred. After cleaning up the spill, the response team notes that in the course of its erstwhile flight to the pool, the truck had hit and ruptured a 55-gallon drum of pesticide that had been sitting on a concrete pad next to a shed alongside the motel. The contents of this drum, since identified as lindane, have been washed by the heavy rainfall into a shallow depression in the ground next to the pad, and have seeped with the runoff water into the temporarily saturated soil.*

- *Question(s).* *As leader of the response team, you decide to implement an immediate pumping scheme to remove the lindane-contaminated water from the subsurface before it can migrate any farther. What initial determinations must you make to establish reasonable locations for the emergency pumping wells?*

- *Logic and Answer(s).*

    1. *An estimate of the distances to which the lindane has migrated from the point of its entry into the soil column will allow reasonable approximations for locating the emergency pumping wells. The extent of migration relates in part to the water flow that carries the lindane into and within the subsurface, and in part to the extent to which the soil is able to retain the lindane and thus "retard" its migration. The former estimate can be made from knowledge of the surface and subsurface hydrology involved. The latter estimate, of most interest for this particular illustration, involves a projection of the distribution of the lindane between the dissolved aqueous phase and the soil (solid) phase. This can be approached as outlined below.*

    2. *You are compelled in this case to act quickly and thus do not have time to conduct a full sorption isotherm study. You can, however, order a quick determination of the organic carbon content of the soil, and within 2 hours you have results that indicate that the value of the soil ϕ_{OC}° is 0.02.*

    3. *In consulting a handbook of environmental "data and facts," you find that a relationship similar to that given in Equation 12.5 may be useful for relating a modified soil partitioning coefficient, $\mathcal{K}_{OC}$, to the octanol-water partitioning coefficient, $\mathcal{K}_{OW}$, of the organic contaminant. In this case, for units of L/kg for $\mathcal{K}_{OC}$, the values of α_P and β_P are given as 0.72 and 0.49, respectively, so that*

    $$\log \mathcal{K}_{OC} = \log \frac{\mathcal{K}_D}{\phi_{OC}^{\circ}} = 0.72 \ \log \ \mathcal{K}_{OW} + 0.49$$

    4. *The distribution coefficient of the soil for lindane sorption can be estimated from the octanol-water partitioning coefficient for lindane ($\log \mathcal{K}_{OW} = 3.72$) given in Table 2.2; i.e.*

    $$\log \mathcal{K}_{OC} = 0.72(3.72) + 0.49 = 3.17$$

    $$\mathcal{K}_{OC} = 10^{3.17} = 1.48 \times 10^3$$

    $$\phi_{OC}^{\circ} = 0.02 \ for \ this \ soil, \ thus$$

    $$\mathcal{K}_D = (1.48 \times 10^3)(0.02) = 29.6 \ L/kg$$

5. *Before making estimates of the retention of lindane by the soil you decide to check several other references, in which two alternative correlations between $\mathcal{K}_{OC}$ and $\mathcal{K}_{OW}$ are found; namely*

$$\log \mathcal{K}_{OC} = \log \mathcal{K}_{OW} - 0.21$$

$$\log \mathcal{K}_{OC} = 0.38 \log \mathcal{K}_{OW} + 0.19$$

(Note: All three of the above correlations are in fact drawn from experimental results reported in technical peer-reviewed publications.)

6. *You decide to use these relationships to check your earlier estimates of $\mathcal{K}_D$ values.*

   (a) *For the first alternative correlation*

   $$\log \mathcal{K}_{OC} = 3.7 - 0.21 = 3.49 \quad and, \quad \mathcal{K}_{OC} = 30.9 \times 10^2$$

   Thus, $\mathcal{K}_D = 61.8$ L/kg.

   (b) *For the second alternative correlation*

   $$\log \mathcal{K}_{OC} = (0.38)(3.7) + 0.19 = 1.60 \quad and, \quad \mathcal{K}_{OC} = 39.8$$

   Thus, $\mathcal{K}_D = 0.80$ L/kg.

- *Key Point(s). Correlations between soil "partitioning" and the organic content of soil developed in different investigations may give markedly (i.e., orders of magnitude) different estimates, with little if any clear guidance for choosing an appropriate value for the soil in question. This underscores the need for caution in generalizing relationships or observations that, because of their empirical character, are inherently system (or at least "system type") specific.*

12.3   PHASE DISTRIBUTIONS

12.3.1   Equilibrium Criteria

Chemical species released to multiphase environmental systems eventually attain different equilibrium concentrations in the phases comprising those systems. Their concentrations in each phase should in theory be quantifiable in terms of the thermodynamic parameters discussed previously. In cases of air-water partitioning, for example, phase concentration ratios can be expressed in terms of the Henry's law constant, $\mathcal{K}_H$ (Equation 12.3 and Table 12.2). For sediment-water partitioning, the parameter $\mathcal{K}_D$ (Equation 12.4) is commonly used, at least as a "first-cut" estimator of the distribution of solute between two phases. Other examples of parameters employed to describe phase distributions include bioconcentration factors, $\mathcal{K}_B$, and, as reference values, octanol-water partition coefficients, $\mathcal{K}_{OW}$. For each solute, a partitioning coefficient can be defined for each pair of environmental phases. While such partitioning coefficients are useful, it is conceptually more satisfying, and eventually more practical in complex systems, to express equilibrium phase distributions in terms of fundamental quantities that control concentration distributions.

Gibbs demonstrated that an equilibrium in the distribution of a solute between two phases occurs when the chemical potentials of the solute are equal in each of the phases. Partitioning can, however, be generalized in terms of a more convenient criterion for equilibrium between phases than chemical potential: namely, in terms of solute fugacity. We noted in Chapter 6 and earlier in this chapter that the fugacity of a solute can be viewed as its tendency to escape from (or its escaping pressure within) a particular phase. Equilibrium conditions for the distribution of a solute between two phases occurs when the escaping pressure of that solute in one phase is equal to that in the other.

12.3.2   The Thermal Equilibrium Analogy

As pictured schematically in Figure 12.7, an analogous and very familiar situation exists for definition of thermal equilibrium between two phases. The criterion for thermal equilibrium between two phases is that they have equal temperatures even though their respective thermal concentrations are different. Like chemical potential, heat is a form of energy (ML^2T^{-2}), an extensive property of a system. Like fugacity, temperature is an intensive parameter that determines the relative state of each of two or more phases, and their respective equilibria among the phases of a system similarly reflect equilibration of their respective thermodynamic potentials.

The "concentration" and the temperature of heat in any given phase are interrelated by the heat capacity of that phase

$$\boxed{\textbf{Heat Capacity} \qquad Q^{\circ}_{H,V} = \frac{C_H}{T}} \qquad (12.6)$$

where C_H is the "concentration" of heat ($ML^{-1}t^{-2}$), T is the absolute or Kelvin temperature (K), and $Q^{\circ}_{H,V}$ is a volumetric heat capacity ($ML^{-1}t^{-2}T^{-1}$) given by the product of the mass heat capacity and the phase density. The volumetric heat capacity is essentially the thermal energy acquired or released by a unit volume of a phase per unit temperature change. Like the relationship of heat concentration and temperature to heat capacity, the concentration and fugacity of a solute in any given phase are related linearly at low concentrations by the

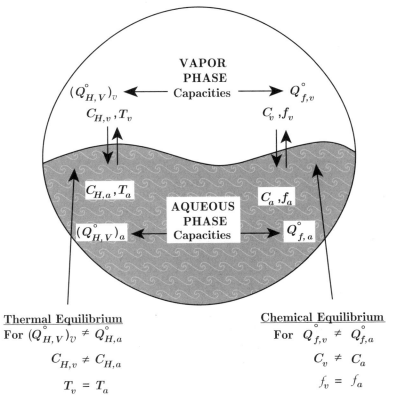

VAPOR PHASE Capacities

$(Q^{\circ}_{H,V})_v$

$C_{H,v}, T_v$

$Q^{\circ}_{f,v}$

C_v, f_v

$C_{H,a}, T_a$

C_a, f_a

AQUEOUS PHASE Capacities

$(Q^{\circ}_{H,V})_a$

$Q^{\circ}_{f,a}$

Thermal Equilibrium

For $(Q^{\circ}_{H,V})_v \neq Q^{\circ}_{H,a}$

$C_{H,v} \neq C_{H,a}$

$T_v = T_a$

Chemical Equilibrium

For $Q^{\circ}_{f,v} \neq Q^{\circ}_{f,a}$

$C_v \neq C_a$

$f_v = f_a$

Figure 12.7 A Two-Phase Analogy Between Heat and Fugacity Capacities

fugacity capacity of that phase

$$\text{Fugacity Capacity} \qquad Q^{\circ}_f = \frac{C}{f} \tag{12.7}$$

where Q°_f is expressed in terms of concentration per unit escaping pressure ($\text{ML}^{-3}/\text{pressure} = \text{L}^{-2}\text{t}^2$).

Heat accumulates in phases having high heat capacity, mass accumulates in phases having high fugacity capacity. For example, a copper rod suspended in air in a closed system accumulates much more of the available system heat per unit of its volume than does the air. By analogy, hydrophobic organic compounds partition from aqueous phases into lipid phases because the latter have higher Q°_f values for such compounds.

The equilibrium distribution of a substance between two phases, 1 and 2, is reached when its fugacities in those two phases are equal

$$f_1 = f_2 \tag{12.8}$$

or, from Equation 12.7,

$$\frac{C_1}{Q^{\circ}_{f,1}} = \frac{C_2}{Q^{\circ}_{f,2}} \tag{12.9}$$

and

$$\frac{C_1}{C_2} = \frac{Q^{\circ}_{f,1}}{Q^{\circ}_{f,2}} = \mathcal{K}_{1,2} \tag{12.10}$$

where $\mathcal{K}_{1,2}$ is the partitioning coefficient controlling the distribution of a solute between two phases i.e., the ratio of the fugacity capacities of the two phases for that solute. To characterize and quantify phase distributions, it is therefore necessary to characterize and quantify the respective fugacity capacities of different phases for each solute.

12.3.3　Prevailing System Fugacity

Environmentally relevant phases generally include: (1) vapors; (2) aqueous solutions; (3) sorbed phases; (4) biota; and, (5) pure solids and liquids, including the common organic reference phase, octanol. The fugacity condition that must be met for the equilibrium distribution of a solute in a system comprised by these several phases is given by

$$\boxed{\begin{array}{l} \textit{Equilibrium} \\ \textit{Fugacity} \qquad f_v = f_a = f_s = f_b = f_p = f_o = f_{system} \\ \textit{Condition} \end{array}} \tag{12.11}$$

This condition is pictured schematically in Figure 12.8.

From Equation 12.7, the prevailing system fugacity f_{system}, is given by the overall system value of C/Q°_f. Thus, for a system of k phases

$$\boxed{\begin{array}{l} \textit{Prevailing} \\ \textit{System} \qquad f_{system} = \left(\sum_{j=1}^{k} \frac{M_j}{V_j} \right) \left(\sum_{j=1}^{k} \frac{1}{Q^{\circ}_{f,l}} \right) = \frac{M_T}{\sum_{j=1}^{k} Q^{\circ}_{f,l} V_j} \\ \textit{Fugacity} \end{array}} \tag{12.12}$$

where M_j is the number of moles or the mass of solute in phase j, V_j is the volume of that phase, and M_T is the total number of moles or the mass of solute in the system. We can draw upon our previous discussions of phase relationships and chemical thermodynamics to define the fugacity of a solute in each of these phases, some more rigorously than others. The most straightforward

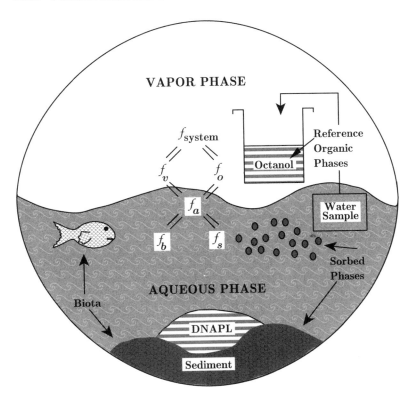

Figure 12.8 Equilibrium Partitioning in a Multiphase Environmental System

considerations apply to vapor phases, aqueous phases, and pure-solute phases, as we shall see shortly. Once the fugacity of a substance in a given phase is defined, it is then a straightforward matter to apply Equation 12.7 to define the fugacity capacity of that phase.

12.3.4 Phase Fugacity Capacities

12.3.4.1 Vapor Phase

The fugacity of a component of a mixed vapor phase is given by

$$f_v = \alpha_f X_v P_T \approx P \tag{12.13}$$

where X_v is the mole fraction of the solute in the vapor phase, P_T and P are the total and component pressures, respectively, and a_f is a dimensionless fugacity coefficient introduced to account for nonideal behavior. Except for solutes that associate with one another in vapor phases, the coefficient α_f has a value close to 1 at atmospheric pressure.

For the conditions stipulated, and pursuant to the ideal gas law, the concentration of a solute in a vapor phase is given by its partial pressure

$$C_v = f_v Q^\circ_{f,v} = n/V = p/\mathcal{R}T = f_v/\mathcal{R}T \tag{12.14}$$

The fugacity capacity of the vapor phase for that solute is simply

$$\boxed{\begin{array}{ll} \textbf{Vapor Phase} & Q^\circ_{f,v} = \dfrac{1}{\mathcal{R}T} \\ \textbf{Fugacity Capacity} & \end{array}} \tag{12.15}$$

and thus independent of the nature of the solute or the composition of the vapor for the conditions stated.

12.3.4.2   Aqueous Phase

The aqueous phase fugacity of a solute is given by

$$f_a = X_a \alpha_a f_p \approx X_a \alpha_p P^v \tag{12.16}$$

where X_a is the aqueous phase mole fraction; α_a and α_p are the aqueous phase and pure solute phase activity coefficients, respectively; f_p is a reference fugacity relating to the pure liquid solute at the temperature of the system; and P^v is the vapor pressure of the pure liquid solute at the same temperature. In the standard state defined by Raoult's law, when X_a is unity, α_p is also unity, and f_p is given by the pure liquid state component vapor pressure, P^v. Generally, for nonionizing substances, α_a increases to infinite dilution values as X_a decreases to zero. This is problematic for pure solid phases, which are not liquid at the common temperatures of natural systems (i.e., $T < 25°C$). In such cases, the Henry's law reference state in which $\alpha_a \to 1$ as $X_a \to 0$, can be invoked, and an infinite dilution value of $\alpha_a f_p$ specified so that

$$Q^\circ_{f,a} = \frac{1}{V_{m,a} \alpha_a P^v} \approx \frac{1}{V_{m,w} \alpha_a P^v} \tag{12.17}$$

where $V_{m,a}$ is the molar volume ($L^3 mole^{-1}$) of the aqueous phase, which is essentially the same as that for pure water, $V_{m,w}$.

According to Equation 12.10, the vapor-aqueous phase partition coefficient, $\mathcal{K}_{v,a}$, is defined by the ratio of the vapor and aqueous phase fugacity capacities. Recalling that $\mathcal{K}_{v,a} = Q^\circ_{f,v}/Q^\circ_{f,a} = C_v/C_a = P/\mathcal{R}TC_a = \mathcal{K}_H/\mathcal{R}T$ (see Table 12.2) we can define $Q^\circ_{f,a}$ as

$$\boxed{\begin{array}{ll} \textit{Aqueous Phase} & Q^\circ_{f,a} = \dfrac{Q^\circ_{f,v}}{\mathcal{K}_{v,a}} = \dfrac{Q^\circ_{f,v}\mathcal{R}T}{\mathcal{K}_H} = \dfrac{1}{\mathcal{K}_H} \\ \textit{Fugacity Capacity} & \end{array}} \tag{12.18}$$

The aqueous phase fugacity capacity for a substance is thus the reciprocal of the Henry's constant for that substance. This agrees with our earlier definition of fugacity in terms of partial pressure, and with the relationship between Henry's constant and partial pressure.

Hydrophobic compounds are often sorbed to colloidal or suspended materials, or may even be present as colloidal entities themselves at concentration levels in excess of their solubility limits. In such cases, these solutes are associated with a phase other than water, and thus do not contribute to solution fugacity. Equation 12.18 thus applies only to those solutes, or fractions of solutes, which exist as dissolved species in the aqueous phase.

12.3.4.3 Pure Solids and Liquids

According to Raoult's law the activity coefficient, a_p, for pure solids or liquids is unity. The fugacity of the pure phase is thus given by the vapor pressure, P^v. At the same time, concentrations are defined by the inverse of molar volumes, $V_{M,p}(L^3 mole^{-1})$. Fugacity capacity for such pure phases is thus determined by the relationship

$$\boxed{\textbf{\textit{Pure-Solute Phase Fugacity Capacity}} \qquad Q_{f,p}^{\circ} = \frac{C_p}{f_p} = \frac{1}{P^v V_{m,p}}} \tag{12.19}$$

Pure liquid or solid phases occur environmentally only when the solubility of a solute in another phase is exceeded and "precipitation" occurs. This is a common circumstance in water-saturated subsurface contamination scenarios, in which non-aqueous phase liquids (NAPLs) or submerged organic solids are often found. Combining Equations 12.10, 12.15, and 12.19 reveals that the partitioning coefficient of a solute between air and its pure state is dictated essentially by the vapor pressure of that solute; that is

$$\mathcal{K}_{v,p} = \frac{Q_{f,v}^{\circ}}{Q_{f,p}^{\circ}} = \frac{P^v V_{m,p}}{\mathcal{R}T} \tag{12.20}$$

where $V_{m,p}/\mathcal{R}T$ is constant for any given temperature.

Similarly, the water solubility, or aqueous phase saturation concentration, C_s, of an organic compound, essentially dictates the partition coefficient for water and the pure solute

$$\mathcal{K}_{a,p} = \frac{Q_{f,a}^{\circ}}{Q_{f,p}^{\circ}} = \frac{P^v V_{m,p}}{\mathcal{K}_H} = C_s V_{m,p} \tag{12.21}$$

The aqueous-phase solubility for liquid solutes is

$$(C_S)_{liquid\ solutes} = C_{S(l)} = \frac{1}{V_{m,a}\alpha_a} \tag{12.22}$$

whereas for solid solutes, $C_{s(s)}$

$$(C_S)_{solid\ solutes} = C_{S(s)} = \frac{P^v_{(s)}}{P^v_{(l)} V_{m,a} \alpha_a} \tag{12.23}$$

where $P^v_{(s)}$ and $P^v_{(l)}$ are the solid and liquid vapor pressures of the solute, respectively.

12.3.4.4   Sorbent Phases

The fugacity of a solute taken up from a fluid by a sorbing phase (e.g., the amorphous organic matter associated with soils and sediments must be equal to the fugacity of that solute existing as a residual in the fluid phase when the two phases are at equilibrium. Thus, if $Q^\circ_{f,s}$ is the sorbed-phase fugacity capacity, and C_e and q_e are, respectively, the solution (or gas) phase and solid organic phase concentrations of the solute at equilibrium

$$f_a = \frac{C_e}{Q^\circ_{f,a}} = f_s = \frac{q_e}{Q^\circ_{f,s}} \tag{12.24}$$

The linear phase distribution relationship is the simplest of sorption models and will be used here because of its simplicity to illustrate how fugacity capacities can be defined for sorbing phases. As noted previously, the LDM given in Equation 12.4 is adequate for describing the "partitioning" type sorption phenomena, but has serious potential limitations for description of non-partitioning sorption processes.

To apply the LDM to determination of fugacity capacities for soils and sediments in natural systems, the parameters of Equations 12.4 and 12.8 must be expressed in mass and volume units that are consistent. The sorbed phase concentration, q_e, can be expressed as moles of solute per 106 grams of sorbent (mol/106g), $\mathcal{K}_D$, as cubic meters of water per 106 grams of sorbent (m^3/10^6 g), and the sorbent concentration or dosage, D_o, as the product of its volume fraction (dimensionless), and its density ρ_s(g/cm^3). The sorbed-phase concentration expressed in terms of the volume of sorbent is then given by $q_e \rho_s$(moles/m^3). Putting these units together with Equations 12.24 and 12.18 gives

$$\boxed{\textbf{\textit{Sorbent Phase}} \atop \textbf{\textit{Fugacity Capacity}}} \quad Q^\circ_{f,s} = \frac{\rho_s q_e}{\mathcal{K}_H C_e} = \frac{\rho_s \mathcal{K}_D}{\mathcal{K}_H} \tag{12.25}$$

The dimensionless product, $\rho_s \mathcal{K}_D$, in the above equation is actually the partition coefficient expressed on a mole-per-unit-volume basis. The concentration of dissolved material is $Q^\circ_{f,a} f_s$, or $(f_s/\mathcal{K}_H)$ moles of solute per m^3 of solution; that is, $f_s/\mathcal{K}_H$ moles are dissolved in the one cubic meter. The sorbed phase concentration is $f_s Q^\circ_{f,s}$, or $\rho_s q_e$ moles of solute per m^3 of sorbent, or a total of

$f_s Q_{f,s}^\circ C_s$ moles, or $f_s \rho_s \mathcal{K}_D C_s / \mathcal{K}_H$. A mass balance on the solute then yields

$$\begin{matrix} \text{Total} \\ \text{Solute} \end{matrix} = \frac{f_s}{\mathcal{K}_H} + \frac{f_s \rho_s \mathcal{K}_D C_s}{\mathcal{K}_H} = \frac{f_s(1 + \rho_s \mathcal{K}_D C_s)}{\mathcal{K}_H} \qquad (12.26)$$

where

$$\begin{matrix} \text{Dissolved} \\ \text{Fraction} \end{matrix} = \frac{f_s}{\mathcal{K}_H} \left(\frac{f_s(1 + \rho_s \mathcal{K}_D C_s)}{\mathcal{K}_H} \right)^{-1} = \frac{1}{(1 + \rho_s \mathcal{K}_D C_s)} \qquad (12.27)$$

and

$$\begin{matrix} \text{Sorbed} \\ \text{Fraction} \end{matrix} = \frac{f_s \rho_s \mathcal{K}_D C_s}{\mathcal{K}_H} + \left(\frac{f_s(1 + \rho_s \mathcal{K}_D C_s)}{\mathcal{K}_H} \right)^{-1} = \frac{\rho_s \mathcal{K}_D C_s}{(1 + \rho_s \mathcal{K}_D C_s)} \qquad (12.28)$$

The distribution coefficient, $\mathcal{K}_D$, can be estimated for organic solute uptake by the amorphous organic phases of sediments and soils from correlations with the octanol-water partition coefficient, $\mathcal{K}_{OW}$ (see Equation 12.5), again with appropriate cautions kept in mind.

12.3.4.5 Biota

A bioconcentration factor, $\mathcal{K}_B$, is commonly used in the same manner as the linear distribution coefficient for expression of the uptake of solute by biotic phases. When expressed as a ratio of solute concentration in biotic tissue (basically an organic phase) measured on a wet-weight basis to that in water on a volumetric basis, $\mathcal{K}_B$ is identical to $\mathcal{K}_D$. It is also analogous to the group $\rho_s \mathcal{K}_D$, with ρ_s being replaced by the density of the biota, ρ_b; because ρ_b commonly has a numerical value near unity, between $\mathcal{K}_D$ and $\rho_b \mathcal{K}_D$ the difference is generally only dimensional.

12.3.4.6 Octanol

We have demonstrated that the octanol-water partition coefficient, $\mathcal{K}_{OW}$, is a useful indicator of hydrophobicity. It is thus a useful reference for fugacity calculations as well. *A value for $Q_{f,o}^\circ$ for a solute in octanol can be specified by analogy to that for a solute in the aqueous phase, as set forth in Equation 12.17*

$$\boxed{\begin{matrix} \textit{Octanol Phase} \\ \textit{Fugacity Capacity} \end{matrix} \quad Q_{f,o}^\circ = \frac{1}{V_{m,o} \alpha_o P^v}} \qquad (12.29)$$

where α_o is the activity coefficient of the solute in octanol; P^v is the vapor pressure of the liquid solute at the system temperature; and $V_{m,o}$ is the molar volume of octanol saturated with water. At equilibrium, the fugacities of a solute distributed between octanol and *water phases must be equal in the two phases. The vapor pressures cancel to give*

| Octanol-Water Partitioning Coefficient | $\mathcal{K}_{OW} = \dfrac{C_{e,o}}{C_{e,w}} = \dfrac{Q^{\circ}_{f,o}}{Q^{\circ}_{f,a}} = \dfrac{V_{m,a}\alpha_a}{V_{m,o}\alpha_o}$ | (12.30) |

where $\mathcal{K}_{OW}$ is expressed as a concentration ratio. For most hydrophobic organic compounds, the value of $\mathcal{K}_{OW}$ is dominated by α_a. Because α_a controls aqueous solubility, it follows that solubility and $\mathcal{K}_{OW}$ are closely related.

An illustration of the use of fugacity concepts to estimate the distribution of an organic contaminant among various phases or compartments of an environmental system under equilibrium conditions is given in Example 12.4.

Example 12.4. Distribution of a Volatile Organic Contaminant Among the Local Environmental Compartments of an Airplane Repair Hanger. (An application of fugacity concepts and relationships to ascertain thermodynamically driven equilibrium phase distributions.)

- **Situation.** *The waste from a parts cleaning solvent bath at an airplane repair hanger is to be treated by sedimentation for removal of solids prior to discharge to an airport collection system. The waste contains a low-molecular-weight (100 g/mol) volatile halogenated organic solvent at a concentration of 100 mg/L. The waste is otherwise low in dissolved organic content, but the colloidal and settleable solids are comprised partially by insoluble organic matter. The treatment will be carried out in a modified sump under a steel grating in the hanger floor. The sump is to be operated in a fill-and-draw (sequencing batch reactor) mode to a filled depth of 2 m above sludge level. All of the settleable solids are removed in this operation. The surface dimensions of the sump are 5 × 10 m, yielding a water volume of 100 m^3. The waste flows into the sump from a submerged discharge pipe. One cubic meter of sludge having a solids concentration of 5% is collected on each cycle of settling, and the residual concentration of colloidal organic matter in the tank effluent is 10 mg/L.*

- **Question(s).** *You are asked to estimate anticipated concentrations of halogenated solvent in the effluent and in the sludge from the stump in order to prescribe additional treatment requirements.*

- **Logic and Answer(s).**

  1. *The fugacity relationships discussed in this chapter provide a means for making such an estimate, but further information is required to facilitate their application.*

2. *Further information required includes*

   (a) *the volume of air into which the halogenated solvent may volatilize from the sump;*

   (b) *the volatility of that solvent; and,*

   (c) *the partitioning relationships of the solvent with respect to the settleable solids and residual colloids in the sump effluent*

3. *Development of the information required is as follows*

   (a) *the hanger building is measured to be 20×50 m^2 in area with a uniform overhead height of 10 m, giving an air (vapor) volume of 10,000 m^3;*

   (b) *Henry's constant for the solvent is determined from an appropriate reference to be $\mathcal{K}_H = 10^{-4}$ atm-m^3/mol; and,*

   (c) *Adsorption isotherms are measured for sorption of the solvent on settleable and colloidal solids. The following results are obtained;*

      (a) *Settleable solids, linear isotherm, $\mathcal{K}_D = 10^{-2}$ m^3/g; and,*

      (b) *Colloidal solids, linear isotherm, $\mathcal{K}_D = 2 \times 10^{-2}$ m^3/g.*

4. *Approach: Equation 12.11 tells us that the fugacities of the compound in the vapor, aqueous, settleable solids, and colloidal phases are equal at equilibrium; that is*

$$f_{system} = f_v = f_a = (f_s)_{ss} = (f_s)_c$$

If we assume that the fill-and-draw time of the tank allows for establishment of an equilibrium or near-equilibrium condition, the concentration of the compound in each phase is given by the product of the fugacity capacity, Q_f°, for that phase and the prevailing fugacity of the system.

5. *Calculations:*

   (a) *Tabulate volumes of phases involved.*

Air in building	=	*10,000 m^3*
Water in tank	=	*100 m^3*
Sludge in tank	=	*1 m^3*
Colloids (in water)	=	*100 m^3*

   (b) *Determine the fugacity capacities of each phase. From Equation 12.15*

$$Q_{f,v}^\circ = 1/\mathcal{R}T; \qquad \mathcal{R}T = 0.0244 \ m^3-atm/mol \ (at \ 25°C)$$

$$Q_{f,v}^\circ = \frac{1}{0.0244} = 40.9 \ mol/m^3 - atm$$

From Equation 12.18

$$Q_{f,a}^\circ = 1/\mathcal{K}_H; \qquad \mathcal{K}_H = 10^{-4} \ m^3-atm/mol$$

$$Q^{\circ}_{f,a} = 10^4 \ mol/m^3 - atm$$

From Equation 12.25

$$Q^{\circ}_{f,c} = \rho_s \mathcal{K}_D / \mathcal{K}_H; \qquad \mathcal{K}_D = 2 \times 10^{-2} \ m^3/g$$

$$\rho_s = 10 \ mg/L = 10 \ g/m^3; \quad Q^{\circ}_{f,c} = 2 \times 10^3 \ mol/m^3 - atm$$

From Equation 12.25

$$Q^{\circ}_{f,ss} = \rho_s \mathcal{K}_D / \mathcal{K}_H; \qquad \mathcal{K}_D = 10^{-2} \ m^3/g$$

$$\rho_s = 50 \times 10^3 \ g/m^3$$

$$Q^{\circ}_{f,ss} = (10^{-2})(50 \times 10^3)/10^{-4} = 50 \times 10^5 \ mol/m^3 - atm$$

(c) *Calculate the prevailing system fugacity. The total amount, M_T, of the compound involved in each fill-and-draw operation is, by specification*

$$M_T = 100 \ mg/L \times 10^5 \ L = 10^4 \ g = 100 \ mol$$

From Equation 12.12 the prevailing system fugacity can then be determined to be

$$f_{system} = \frac{M_T}{\sum_{j=1}^{k} Q^{\circ}_{f,j} V_j}$$

$$= \frac{100}{(40.9)(10^4)(10^4)(10^2)} + (2 \times 10^3)(10^2) + (50 \times 10^5)(1)$$

$$= 1.52 \times 10^{-5} \ atm$$

Compartment	$C = f Q^{\circ}_{fj} (mol/m^3)$	Total Amount in Each Phase (mol)
Air	6.2×10^{-4}	6.0
Water	1.5×10^{-1}	15.0
Sludge	7.6×10^{1}	76.0
Colloids	3.0×10^{-2}	3.0
	Total amount in all phases =	100.0

- **Key Point(s).** *The fugacity/fugacity-capacity approach provides a relatively simple and intuitive basis for evaluation of equilibrium phase distributions of solutes in complex multiphase environmental systems. The calculation of appropriate fugacity capacities for simple homogeneous phases such as air, water, and pure liquid or solid solutes is straightforward and thermodynamically rigorous. For heterogeneous and less well-defined phases such as soils, sediments, and biota it is necessary to invoke empirically derived relationships to estimate fugacity capacities.*

12.4 CHAPTER SUMMARY

A fundamental engineering analysis of any environmental system, whether to predict the fate and transport of anthropogenic chemicals in natural systems or to design separation processes for such chemicals in engineered systems, must begin with a rigorous development of relevant thermodynamic equilibrium relationships. Multiphase compositions and heterogeneities are the rule rather than the exception for most environmental systems, and must be adequately addressed in the energy relationships used to characterize those systems.

Throughout this chapter we have emphasized the thermodynamic roots of various phase partitioning relationships; for example, the thermodynamic basis of solubility constants and of octanol-water partition coefficients. Fugacity is one thermodynamic parameter having particularly general practical significance for quantification of multiphase partitioning predictions. Fugacity describes the tendency of a species to escape or flee from one particular phase to another, and thus can be used to estimate equilibrium concentrations of species in each of several adjacent phases. Fugacity relationships for different species, and the corresponding fugacity capacities of various phases for those species, necessarily incorporate partitioning relationships and relevant thermodynamics.

The term phase partitioning is often used without due regard for the particular mechanism(s) affecting the distribution of a compound between two phases. This is problematic when any of the phases involved is a complex heterogeneous solid phase, such as a soil or sediment. In such cases the adsorption forces discussed in Chapter 13 and their associated thermodynamic considerations may be at least as important as are those of absorption. We differentiate in this book between adsorption and absorption phenomena, and we use the term partitioning only for description of absorption processes. The term sorption is used largely when we cannot clearly distinguish between processes; i.e., when both absorption and adsorption may be inextricably involved.

12.5 CITATIONS AND SOURCES

Weber, W.J., Jr., and F.A. DiGiano, 1996, *Process Dynamics in Environmental Systems*, John Wiley & Sons, Inc., New York. (PDES is the source of most of the material presented in Chapter 12. Chapter 6 of PDES covers and expands upon the material presented in this text. It also identifies additional related background reading sources).

12.6 PROBLEM ASSIGNMENTS

12.1 A 0.05-mL volume of carbon tetrachloride (CCl_4) and 0.02 g of *p*-dichlorobenzene (*p*-DCB, $C_6H_4Cl_2$) are added to a 500-mL separatory funnel containing 300 mL of water and 200 mL of octanol. Calculate the concentrations of both compounds in the octanol and water phases after mixing.

12.2 A wash-water waste containing a dominant volatile organic solvent is generated at a volumetric rate of Q_l from an automobile paint booth operation. The waste drain from this operation passes through a closed collection chamber en route to the plant's central treatment facility. The chamber is vented by air passing over the wastewater at a flow rate of Q_g. The wastewater volume (V_l) and air volume (V_g) can each be considered uniformly mixed. Interphase mass transfer of each solvent is given by

$$N_l = k_{f,l}(C_{S,l} - C_l)$$

where $C_{S,l}$ is the equilibrium liquid-phase solubility of solvent based on its partial pressure in the air above the vessel and C_l is its liquid-phase concentration within the chamber. Derive a process model to predict the concentrations of the solvent in the air and water leaving the vessel as functions of Q_l, Q_g, $t(= V_l/Q_l)$, $k_{f,l}(a_s^\circ)$, the Henry's constant for the solvent, $\mathcal{K}_H$, and the feed concentration of solvent, C_{IN}. *Hint:* Material balances are needed for the water and air streams. The concentration in the airstream is obtained from the ideal gas law $(PV = n\mathcal{R}T)$, and the specific interfacial area for mass transfer, (a_s°), is the area of interface per volume of wastewater in the vessel; remember, the vessel is closed, so that the solvent partial pressure is not zero.

Answer: $C_{l,OUT} = C_{IN}\left(1 + \dfrac{1}{1/\bar{t}k_{f,l} + Q_l\mathcal{R}T/Q_g\mathcal{K}_H}\right)^{-1}$

12.3 Consider a modification of Problem 12.2 in which the wastewater stream is generated and discharged to the drain in batches, but the airstream still passes continuously through the collection chamber. Set up the appropriate material balances and derive the model to predict the concentration of solvent remaining in the wastewater and that leaving in the airstream with time.

12.4 Volatilization of chlorine gas from waters of elevated temperatures is of concern in cooling towers because it reduces the effectiveness of disinfection. To assess the extent to which such volatilization occurs, it is necessary to know Henry's constant for various temperatures. To this end a laboratory stripping column of the type shown below is devised to measure the Henry's constant.

Associated with the measurements are assumptions that: (1) the only loss of solute is by volatilization; (2) the stripping column is well mixed; (3) the gas-phase solute concentration, C_g, in the bubbles at the liquid-atmosphere interface (top of the column) is in equilibrium with the liquid-phase solute concentration, C_l; (4) Henrys law describes equilibrium; and (5) the liquid volume remains constant.

The water volume, V_l, in the stripping column is 5 L and the flow rate of air is 4 L/min. An experiment is performed at 20°C and at pH 5 (to minimize dissociation of HOCl to OCl$^-$). The data collected for residual

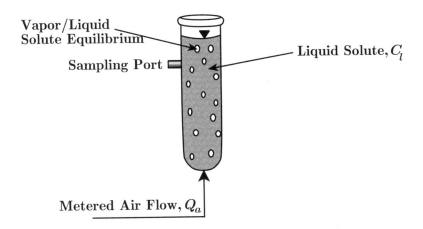

chlorine concentration (as Cl_2) in the stripping column as a function of time are given below.

Time (min)	Cl_2 (mg/L)
0	5.0
1200	4.75
2400	4.6
4800	4.2
6000	4.0
7200	3.8
9600	3.5

Determine the Henry's constant at 20°C in atm. *Hint:* Start with the following material balance

$$-V_l \frac{dC_l}{dt} = Q_g C_g$$

Remember that the gas-phase and liquid-phase concentrations are in equilibrium as bubbles exit the stripping column. See Table 12.2 for an appropriate expression of Henry's law.

Answer: $\mathcal{K}_H = 0.06$ *atm.*

12.5 A chemical manufacturing company produces a variety of polynuclear aromatic hydrocarbons (PAHs), including fluorine. In a trucking accident involving a shipment of fluorine across the Deep Gorge Bridge, an 800-kg quantity of product is spilled into a seep-fed wetlands at the bottom of the Gorge. The deep and narrow conditions of the gorge inhibit air circulation above the relatively well-mixed waters of the small wetlands. The seep that feeds the wetlands is near its center, and outflow occurs only by seepage return to the subsurface along its perimeters. You are asked to perform an analysis to assess the potential distribution of fluorine in this system if equilibrium conditions are attained. The following issues are of specific interest

(a) The acute aqueous-phase toxicity limit of the rare Deep Gorge fresh-water fiddler toad for fluorine is 100 mg/L. Is the fiddler in immediate danger of chemical poisoning?

(b) Discounting degradation and wash-out, determine what percentage of the total mass spilled into the lake will eventually be taken up by its sediments.

Your staff has compiled the system data given below

Estimated phase volumes:

$\quad$ Water $= 25{,}000$ m^3

$\quad$ Sediment $= 1200$ m^3; $\rho_{sediment} = 1200$ kg/m^3

$\quad$ Biota $= 10$ m^3

$\quad$ Air in the gorge above the wetlands $= 125{,}000$ m^3

Temperature: $T = 25°$C

From appropriate references you are able to determine the following correlations:

$\log \mathcal{K}_D$ (m^3 water/kg soil) $= 0.904 \log \mathcal{K}_{OW} - 4{,}779$

$\log \mathcal{K}_B$ (m^3 water/kg biota) $= 3.04 - 0.568 \log C_S$

12.6 A new pesticide, MCTP, is added to a closed ecosystem containing air, water, and fish, all at 25°C. Given the information below, compute the approximate distribution of MCTP in the system if:

(a) 0.1 mol of MCTP is added to the system.

(b) 75.0 mol of MCTP is added to the system.

(c) after removing some of the MCTP from the system in part (b), the equilibrium concentration of MCTP in the ecosystem air is 5×10^{-4}mol/m^3.

Estimated phase volumes:

$\quad$ Ecosystem $= 200$ m^3

$\quad$ Water $= 18$ m^3

$\quad$ Fish $= 0.001$ m^3

MCTP properties:

$\quad \mathcal{K}_{OW} = 3200$

$\quad \mathcal{K}_B = \mathcal{K}_{OW}/0.7$

$\quad$ Molecular weight $= 150$ g/mol

$\quad$ Aqueous solubility $= 200$ mg/L

Vapor pressure $= 400$ Pa

Density $= 1.4$ g/mL

12.7 (a) Assuming for simplicity that octane is used as a pure organic substance for fuel in automobiles, calculate the amount of octane in grams ($C_8H - 8$, MW $- 118$, $P^v = 0.015$ atm) that is lost to the gas phase from a 25% full 70-liter fuel tank of an automobile on a nice summer day (temperature 70° F, 21° C).

(b) Since octane is not used as a pure substance to fuel automobiles, calculate the actual mass of octane lost if the molar fraction of octane in the gasoline used as a fuel is 0.002.

Answers: a) 7.45 mg; b) 3.73 grams.

12.8 Small fish taken from a contaminated lake are found to have acquired a chlorobenzene concentration of 0.1 ppm in their fatty tissues. From an appropriate reference you are able to find a relevant correlation for $\mathcal{K}_B$ having the form $log\mathcal{K}_B = 0.885 \ log\mathcal{K}_{OW} - 0.70$. Estimate the aqueous-phase concentration of chlorobenzene in the lake from which the fish were taken.

12.9 The spill of a large volume of toluene that occurred as a result of a tanker truck accident on a roadway next to a small pond in December becomes of some concern to local fishermen the following Spring. Specifically, they would like to know how contaminated the fish they might catch will be. It was determined at the time of the accident that the total mass of toluene spilled was about 100 kg, and that most of this drained directly to the pond. The concentration of toluene in the water phase was measured in April to be 0.5 moles/m³. The volume of fish in the pond is estimated at about 2×10^{-3}m³. The fish-water partition coefficient is 130 cm³/g and the density of a fish is 1.5 g/cm³. Estimate expected upper limits for: a) the concentration of toluene in the fish (in mg/g); and, b) the percentage of the spilled toluene that eventually ended up in the fish. State all assumptions involved in your estimates.

12.10 The benzene hold on an oil tanker transiting a lock in the Panama Canal is ruptured by a spar that breaks loose from an on-board derrick. As a result of the spill, a 1-cm thick benzene film forms over the entire water surface of the lock. The volume of affected biota (i.e., aquatic organisms) is estimated as 0.2 m³. The biota-water partition coefficient is 15 cm³/g and the density of the biota is approximately 1.1 g/cm³. Determine the anticipated effect of this accident on: a) the concentration of benzene in the air in the immediate vicinity of the lock; and, b) the mass of benzene in the biota. State all assumptions.

Chapter 13

Interfacial Process Equilibria

Contents

13.0 CHAPTER OBJECTIVES

*To characterize the energetics and equilibria of processes that oc-
cur at surfaces and in phase interfaces, and to develop from these
characterizations corresponding functional relationships that can be
incorporated in models for simulation of interfacial phenomena in
natural systems and for design of interfacial separation processes.*

13.1 ADSORPTION PROCESSES

13.1.1 Concepts

*Adsorption involves the attraction of substances from fluid phases
and their accumulation at the surfaces of an adjacent phase or in
interfaces between phases. Certain adsorption phenomena can be
related to the expulsion of solute from one phase and its indifferent accumulation at the interface of that phase. Accumulation may
occur because the solute has no other compatible phase into which
it can partition; the formation and accumulation of foams at air-
water interfaces is an example. Alternatively, adsorption may occur strictly as the result of an attraction of a surface or interface
for a constituent of some other phase; an example is the adsorption of phenol from water by activated carbon. These two distinctly
different types of adsorption are referred to respectively as solvent-
motivated (entropy-driven) and sorbent-motivated (enthalpy-driven)
adsorptions. Most adsorption phenomena are comprised by the actions on a solute of some combination of solvent rejection and adsorbent attraction forces.*

13.1.2 Solvent-Motivated Adsorption

Dissolved substances that are hydrophobic (i.e., water-disliking) in character
can effectively reduce the surface tension of water by migrating from bulk aqueous phases to surfaces or interfaces with other phases. Surface tension is that
particular case of interfacial tension for which the second phase is air. Air exerts
virtually no effect on the behavior of nonvolatile hydrophobic molecules. The
air-water interface is consequently one of the most "indifferent" interfaces found
in environmental systems. Detergents and other "surface-active" agents readily
migrate from water to its interfaces with air to reduce its surface tension. They
also migrate readily to interfaces of water with other phases, such as water-solids
interfaces, to reduce interfacial tension. The energy driving such molecules out
of aqueous phases can be explained in the context of the structure of water. The
concept discussed in Chapter 5 of water behaving more like a "polymer" than
as a single discrete molecule relates to the fact that each molecule is linked by
tetrahedral coordination to four other water molecules *via* hydrogen bonding,
yielding a structure similar to that of a liquid "ice." A nonpolar solute molecule

can thus be held in solution by an arrangement of the ice-like polymers that encapsulate it in a molecular "cage." The favorable enthalpy associated with these ice-like polymers is countered, however, by an unfavorable entropy of solution resulting from the increased ordering of solvent molecules.

Solute molecules may be driven from solution at concentrations below their maximum solubility if the system in which the solution exists (including all of its interfaces) achieves a thermodynamically more favorable state than that in which actual precipitation of solute would eventually occur. Large polymeric aromatic hydrocarbons such as PAHs and PCBs, for example, are "expelled" from water to other phases or interfaces at aqueous-phase concentrations well below those that would normally result in their precipitation if no other phase were present. They adsorb to virtually any surface because the adsorbed state is energetically preferable to the aqueous state. The reactions in such cases are predominantly entropic in character; that is, the solutes are driven from the solution phase by energies associated with the ordering of solvent molecules rather than being specifically attracted by the surfaces or phase interfaces at or in which they accumulate.

Thermodynamically rigorous adsorption relationships can be defined for conditions in which equilibrium surface or interfacial tensions are reduced with increasing concentrations of solute at an interface. These relationships are rooted in an expression developed by J. Willard Gibbs for expressing changes in interfacial tension as functions of the extent of adsorption of solutes at interfaces. For dilute solutions of one solute at an equilibrium molar concentration of C_e and in contact with air, the Gibbs model relating changes in surface tension to changes in solute concentration is given by

$$\text{The Gibbs Adsorption Model} \qquad d\sigma^\circ \bigg|_{T,P} = -\mathcal{R}T\Gamma \frac{dC_e}{C_e} \tag{13.1}$$

According to Equation 13.1, any solute that reduces the surface tension $(d\sigma^\circ/dC_e < 0)$ of a liquid results in an increase in Γ, the surface excess. If $\Gamma > 0$, the solute is present at the surface in higher concentration than in bulk solution (i.e., it is in "excess"), and the larger is the magnitude of Γ the greater is the extent of adsorption.

The Gibbs adsorption model derives from fundamental energy relationships discussed earlier in Section 6.1. It is thus more general than suggested by Equation 13.1 in terms of relating characteristic adsorbed phase variables to solution or gas phase variables for the adsorbing substance; e.g., chemical potential, activity, pressure, or concentration. The same functional form describes the adsorbed phase chemical potential (μ_s) or the spreading pressure (π_s) as functions of any gas or solution phase intensive variable relating to the adsorbing substance. Spreading pressure is in fact the most appropriate intensive variable with which to describe adsorbed phases on indifferent (i.e., "chemically inert") surfaces. It is a key variable in advanced models for describing competition for sites among several adsorbing substances, as discussed in Chapter 6 of PDES.

Example 13.1 provides an illustration of how such information can be put to practical use, in this case as a first-cut means for selecting a polyelectrolyte to study for destabilizing a suspension of dredge spoil solids.

Example 13.1. Selection of a Potential Destabilizing Agent for a Dredge Spoil. *(An illustration of how certain properties of chemical substances, in this case their relative tendencies to depress surface tension, can be used to make first-cut estimates of their potential for use in specific process operations.)*

- **Situation.** *Unpolluted dredge spoil from a navigational channel is to be discharged at a rate of $4m^3/h$ from a scow to a deep-water area in a lake, where the ambient water temperature is $10°C$. To minimize turbidity impacts on biota in the dump area, the spoil will be mixed with an organic polyelectrolyte prior to discharge in order to destabilize its colloidal fractions and thus enhance sedimentation. Three cationic polyelectrolytes (A, B, and C) of equivalent cost and molar charge density are being considered for feasibility testing and process optimization.*

- **Question(s).** *You are asked to make a first-cut estimate as to which of the polyelectrolytes is likely to be most useful so that further tests on that material can be conducted. Although destabilization data are not available, the surface reduction tendencies of the compounds for water are known and readily available to you. Based on such information, make a first-cut prediction of which of the three polyelectrolytes is likely to function best for the intended purpose.*

- **Logic and Answer(s).**

  1. *Because the molar charge densities (charges per mole) of the three polyelectrolytes are the same, it is likely that the one that adsorbs in amounts over and above those associated with electrostatic forces of attraction will be most effective in accomplishing total charge neutralization and destabilization of the colloidal particles. This assumes that the extent of adsorption is not great enough in any case to lead to charge reversal and restabilization. The relative adsorption tendencies of the three materials can be roughly estimated from their comparative effects on surface tension, which are presented below in graphical form. The greater the effect on surface tension, the larger will be the surface excess, that is, the greater will be the concentration of polyelectrolyte present at the surface of the colloids relative to that in the bulk solution. As a first cut, then, the polyelectrolyte with the largest surface excess, Γ, is likely to be the most effective.*

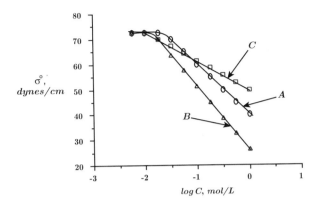

2. *An expression for calculating Γ from the information presented in the figure above develops as follows from Equation 13.1*

$$d\sigma^\circ = -\mathcal{R}T\Gamma dC_e/C_e = -\mathcal{R}T\Gamma d\ln C_e$$

and

$$\Gamma = \frac{-d\sigma^\circ}{\mathcal{R}Td\ln C_e} = \frac{-d\sigma^\circ}{2.3\ \mathcal{R}Td\ \log\ C_e}$$

3. *The slope of each line given in the figure above is an expression of $d\sigma^\circ/d(\log C_e)$ for that particular polyelectrolyte. The surface tension, σ°, is expressed in dyn/cm, and d log C_e is dimensionless. Thus the surface excess in mol/cm² can be calculated from the figure as follows*

$\Gamma \quad = -d\sigma^\circ/2.3\mathcal{R}Td\ \log\ C_e$
$\quad\quad = -d\sigma^\circ/(8.314 \times 10^7 dyn - cm/mol - K)(283K)(2.3)d\ \log\ C_e$
$\quad\quad = -1.85 \times 10^{-11} \times slope\ (mol/cm^2)$

4. *The surface excess for each polyelectrolyte may now be calculated.*

   (a) *For polyelectrolyte A*
      $d\sigma^\circ/d\log C_e = -20 \quad and \quad \Gamma = 3.7 \times 10^{-10} mol/cm^2$

   (b) *For polyelectrolyte B*
      $d\sigma^\circ/d\log C_e = -25 \quad and \quad \Gamma = 4.63 \times 10^{-10} mol/cm^2$

   (c) *For polyelectrolyte C*
      $d\sigma^\circ/d\log C_e = -11.4 \quad and \quad \Gamma = 2.11 \times 10^{-10} mol/cm^2$

5. *Polyelectrolyte B is chosen for further testing because it has the highest surface excess, Γ, and its effect per unit of concentration added on colloid destabilization is thus most likely to be the greatest of the three compounds.*

- *Key Point(s). For strictly solvent-motivated solute accumulations at "indifferent" surfaces we can use readily available measures of surface tension reduction potential, $d\sigma^\circ/d\log C_e$, to* *forecast adsorption from solution. Compare this measure conceptually and operationally to that of the octanol-water partitioning coefficient, K_{OW}, referenced in Equation 12.5 and in Example 12.3.*

13.1.3 Sorbent-Motivated Adsorption

Various types of attractive forces exist between solute molecules or ions and those of adsorbing surfaces. All of these have their origins in electromagnetic interactions of nuclei and electrons. Three loosely defined categories are traditionally distinguished: 1) chemical; 2) electrostatic; and, 3) physical. The energies associated with the attraction of solute molecules by surfaces are largely enthalpic in character, in contradistinction to the entropic energies we have discussed relative to the repulsion of solute molecules by solvent phases.

Chemical adsorption, or chemisorption, involves solute-sorbent interactions having the characteristics of true chemical bonds. Such sorptive phenomena are thus characterized by large heats of adsorption, typically 100 to 400 kJ/mol, although they may be even larger in some cases. Substantial activation energies may be involved in chemisorption reactions, in which cases they can be induced to occur at greater rates, and thus to greater extents within fixed time intervals, at elevated temperatures.

Electrostatic adsorption resulting from Coulombic attraction between oppositely charged species also involves high-energy forces and bonds, just as do electrostatic interactions between charged chemical species in solution phase (see Chapter 5). Such forces have differential heats of adsorption as large as 200 kJ/mol. They are particularly strong in ion-exchange processes, in both natural processes (e.g., cation exchange by soils) and in engineered processes (e.g., ion-exchange systems for water softening, demineralization, and metal ion removal and recovery). They are significant also with respect to the stability of particles suspended in aqueous systems, as discussed in some detail in Chapter 6 of PDES.

Physical adsorption results from the action of van der Waals forces, comprised by a combination of London dispersion forces and classical electrostatic forces, the latter of which are generally negligible for non-polar hydrophobic compounds. London dispersion forces involve interactions among rapidly fluctuating temporary dipole and quadrupole moments associated with the motion of electrons in their molecular orbitals. As a molecule from bulk solution approaches the surface of an adsorbent, electron distributions interact to induce additional dipole and quadrupole moments. The result is a net attraction attributable to dipole-dipole, dipole-quadrupole, and quadrupole-quadrupole interactions. Dipole-dipole interactions are generally the most important, varying as they do inversely with the sixth power of the distance between molecules (dipole-quadrupole and quadrupole-quadrupole interactions are proportional to the eighth and tenth powers of intermolecular separation distances, respectively). Repulsive forces vary with the twelfth power of distance, and are therefore negligible except at the extremely small intermolecular distances characterized by the van der Waals radius.

Differential heats of adsorption for interactions of the van der Waals type are generally on the order of 5 to 10 kJ/mol for small molecules. This relatively small bonding force is amplified in the case of hydrophobic molecules by the solvent-motivated entropy gradient that functions to drive them from solution. *The combined effect is often referred to simply as hydrophobic bonding. Because the hydrophobic effects themselves generally contribute differential heats of adsorption of 5 to 10 kJ/mol, combinations of hydrophobic and van der Waals sorptions may have associated heats of adsorption of 10 to 20 kJ/mol.*

Adsorption processes in environmental systems involve various combinations of forces and interactions, and this makes it difficult to assess directly the relative importance of each. The heterogeneous nature of natural surfaces and engineered adsorbents, such as activated carbon, necessarily precludes any thorough evaluation of surface chemistry, and potential sorbent-sorbate chemical interactions thus remain largely speculative. Nonetheless, it is possible to draw some inferences by the extent to which observed data can be described by different types of conceptual adsorption models. Such models must be developed in any event for describing data observations and trends in the context of system simulation and design models. Thus, the extent to which they can inform and elucidate our understandings of process mechanisms in particular situations provides a source of "low hanging" intellectual fruit.

13.2 EQUILIBRIUM MODELS

Several thermodynamically based equilibrium models for describing adsorption phenomena are considered and their applications discussed in this section. It is essential to recognize in practice however that, in the absence of independent confirmation of sorption mechanism(s), these models can be considered no more than fitting tools.

Equilibrium studies of adsorption relationships are conducted by equilibrating known quantities of adsorbent(s) with solutions of solute(s). Plots of the resulting data relating solid-phase concentrations (amounts of solute adsorbed per unit mass of solid) to solution-phase concentrations are termed adsorption isotherms. They are referred to as isotherms because the data are collected at constant temperature. Figure 13.1 provides graphical representations of several different forms that such isotherms may take. In the context of Figure 13.1, favorable adsorption processes are those in which capacities for uptake by the solid phase increase sharply at low residual solution-phase concentrations to generate convex isotherms. Such adsorptions are favorable because the amount adsorbed per unit mass of adsorbent (q_e) decreases only gradually as the residual concentration (C_e) of a contaminant decreases; thus efficient use of the adsorbent occurs when reducing any process influent value, C_{IN}, to a lower targeted process effluent level, C_{OUT}. When such isotherms approach a limiting value at some value of q_e while C_e continues to increase, they are referred to as *Type I* isotherms and described by the Langmuir model. In the same context, concave isotherms, can be thought of as reflecting unfavorable sorption processes because sorption decreases sharply with lower concentrations; i.e., the sorbent loses efficiency as the influent concentration is reduced to the effluent concentration. Isotherms shaped like the unfavorable isotherm depicted in Figure 13.1 are termed *Type III* isotherms. *Type II* isotherms are shaped like *Type I* isotherms at low solution phase concentrations, but do not approach a plateau in q_e at high residual solution phase concentrations.

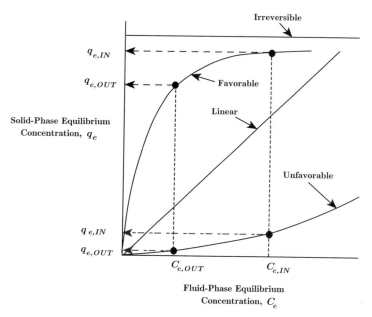

Figure 13.1 Graphical Representations of Isotherm Models

A variety of models have been developed to characterize the relationships shown in Figure 13.1. Any particular model may be found to describe experimental data reasonably under one set of conditions, but not under different conditions. No single model has been found to be generally applicable. This is not unexpected, given the restrictive assumptions associated with the developments of such models and the complexity and variability of environmental systems and surfaces. The first of these factors is considered in the ensuing discussion of various conceptual models, and the second in the subsequent section on nonclassical environmental sorption processes.

13.2.1 The Linear Model

We presented the linear distribution model (LDM, Equation 12.4) in the context of absorption, dissolution, and partitioning processes in the previous chapter. As noted in that discussion, processes involving adsorption phenomena may also in some cases and under certain conditions manifest, or appear to manifest, linear behavior. Figure 13.2, for example, represents a set of q_e vs C_e data collected for the sorption of tetra(per)chloroethylene (PCE) by a typical natural soil. The trace drawn through the data in Figure 13.2 is the statistically best linear regression of that data and appears to describe the data quite well.

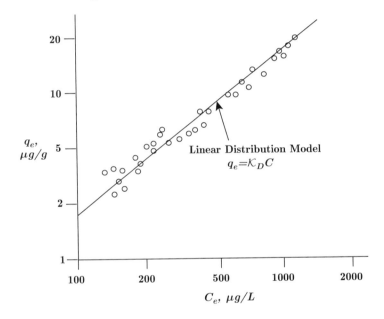

Figure 13.2 PCE Isotherm Data Fit by a Linear Model

True linear behavior may be observed when residual solute concentrations are very low and unoccupied adsorption sites are readily available. This relatively limited region of adsorption, which we will note exists in the Langmuir model to be considered shortly, is often referred to as the "Henry's region" because of its apparent linearity and the limited applicability of Henry's law to very dilute solution conditions. While it is accepted jargon and expressive of observed behavior, the Henry's "partitioning" analogy does not strictly apply to adsorption phenomena.

Apparent linear behavior sometimes results from inadequate measurements. Inadequate measurements may mean simply too few observations to reveal nonlinear behavior over the relevant residual concentration (C_e) range, or the use of data and observations for model calibration that are too limited (e.g., too narrow a range of residual concentrations) with respect to the expected ranges of application of the model being developed from the data.

     Linear models may be involved inappropriately if one is incautious about the implications of assuming, either explicitly or implicitly, that a linear model is "close enough for all practical purposes." This is a tempting assumption to make in that it imparts simplicity to the modeling and calibration efforts required. It is an assumption that is often relatively easy to rationalize qualitatively, particularly if model sensitivity analyses are not performed to assess the potential implications of the assumption. To illustrate this point, let's consider Figure 13.2 again. The data in that figure is both substantial and covers a significant range of C_e values, extending well above those corresponding to the "Henry's" region. It is not difficult then on the basis of this plot to make an argument for the adequacy of an LDM fit to this data. Would you be tempted to do so for the purpose of formulating a transport model designed to predict the time and extent of PCE appearance in a down-gradient well?

13.2.2 The Langmuir Model

     The Langmuir adsorption isotherm model is usually written

$$\boxed{\textbf{Langmuir Model} \qquad q_e = \frac{Q_a^\circ \ell C_e}{1 + \ell C_e}} \qquad (13.2)$$

where $Q_a^\circ (MM^{-1})$ is the solid-phase concentration corresponding to a condition in which all available sites are filled (i.e., the limiting or maximum adsorption capacity), and the coefficient, ℓ, is related to the net enthalpy of adsorption, dH_a

$$\ell = \beta_{a,h} \exp\left(\frac{-dH_a}{\mathcal{R}T}\right) \qquad (13.3)$$

Equation 13.2 can be linearized in a variety of forms for purposes of assessing adsorption data and determining the parameters Q_a° and ℓ. Three such forms are presented in Equations 13.4 through 13.6.

$$\frac{C_e}{q_e} = \frac{1}{Q_a^\circ \ell} + \frac{C_e}{Q_a^\circ} \qquad (13.4)$$

$$\frac{1}{q_e} = \frac{1}{Q_a^\circ} + \frac{1}{\ell Q_a^\circ C_e} \qquad (13.5)$$

$$q_e = Q_a^\circ - \frac{q_e}{bC_e} \qquad (13.6)$$

While all are equivalent, one form may give a more reliable fit to a particular set of data than the others, depending on the range and spread of the data to be described. Alternatively, a nonlinear regression of the data using Equation 13.2 may be preferred.

Inspection of Equation 13.2 reveals that b is in fact the reciprocal of that value of the residual solution-phase concentration at which $q_e = 0.5Q_a^\circ$ (i.e., at which "half saturation" occurs). As such, it is easily recognized as a measure of the "energy" of adsorption. That is, the greater the energy for adsorption the steeper is the approach to "saturation" (Q_a°) as residual concentration in solution (C_e) increases. Values of b obtained from sets of isotherm tests conducted at different temperatures allows calculation of dH_a by plotting $\ln b$ vs T^{-1} pursuant to a linearization of Equation 13.3; i.e.,

$$\ln b = \ln \beta_{a,h} - \frac{dH_a}{\mathcal{R}} \frac{1}{T} \tag{13.7}$$

Division of the slope of such a plot by the Universal Gas Constant R thus yields a value of the net enthalpy of adsorption. This quantity is usually termed the isoteric heat of adsorption, given that b is found by measuring the solution concentration for the same fractional surface coverage (0.5) at different temperatures.

13.2.3   The BET Model

The Langmuir model was extended by Brunauer and co-workers to include the adsorption of multiple layers of molecules. The resulting Brunauer-Emmett-Teller (BET) model assumes that the first molecules to adhere to a surface do so with an energy comparable to the heat of adsorption for monolayer development, while deposition of subsequent layers is treated essentially as a condensation reaction. If all layers beyond the first have equal energies of adsorption, the BET equation takes the form

$$\boxed{\textbf{\textit{BET Model}} \qquad q_e = \frac{\beta C_e Q_a^\circ}{(C_S - C_e)[1 + (\beta - 1)(C_e/C_S)]}} \tag{13.8}$$

where C_S is the solution saturation concentration (solubility limit) of the solute. The parameter β in the BET model, like b in the Langmuir model, is expressive of the energy of adsorption, such that

$$\beta \approx \exp\left(\frac{-dH_a}{\mathcal{R}T}\right) \tag{13.9}$$

where dH_a is again the net enthalpy of adsorption of the first layer of adsorbate. Equation 13.8 can be linearized to facilitate fitting or calibration to a set of empirical adsorption data

$$\frac{C_e}{(C_S - C_e)q_e} = \frac{1}{\beta Q_a^\circ} + \frac{\beta - 1}{\beta Q_a^\circ} \frac{C_e}{C_S} \tag{13.10}$$

It may be noted that Equation 13.8 reduces to Equation 13.2 if $b = \beta/C_S$, $C_e << C_S$, and $\beta >> 1$.

13.2.4   The Freundlich Model

Despite the sound theoretical bases of the Langmuir and BET models, they often fail to describe environmental sorption data adequately. Data for environmental sorption processes, especially for sorption from aqueous solutions, are frequently best described by an exponentially concentration-dependent relationship for q_e termed the Freundlich model

$$\boxed{\textbf{\textit{Freundlich Model}} \qquad q_e = \mathcal{K}_F C_e^{\mathit{n}}} \qquad (13.11)$$

where $\mathcal{K}_F$ and n are characteristic constants. The Freundlich equation can be linearized by logarithmic transform to give

$$\log q_e = \log \mathcal{K}_F + \mathit{n} \log C_e \qquad (13.12)$$

Both Freundlich parameters can be determined by plotting the experimental data according to Equation 13.12, or by performing a non-linear regression of data using Equation 13.11.

The parameter $\mathcal{K}_F$ in the Freundlich model is indicative of sorption capacity at a specific solution-phase concentration; i.e., it is a measure of specific capacity. The exponent n can be shown to be a joint measure of the cumulative magnitude and distribution of energies associated with an adsorption process in which adsorption site energies vary from one type of site to another. Indeed, it is the deviation of n from a value of 1.0 that distinguishes the Freundlich model from the LDM. The LDM, like the partitioning model on which it is predicated, assumes that all sites (or at least all occupied sites) are of the same type and the same energy. For this limited condition, the value of n is in fact 1.0.

One can argue a theoretical basis for the Freundlich equation as a special case of the Gibbs relationship. If the Gibbs surface excess, Γ, is assumed to equal the amount adsorbed, q_e, for dilute solutions, the Gibbs relationship presented in Equation 13.1 can be rearranged to give

$$\Gamma_a = q_e = -\frac{C_e}{\mathcal{R}T}\frac{d\sigma^\circ}{dC_e} = \frac{C_e}{\mathcal{R}T}\frac{\sigma_o^\circ - \sigma_s^\circ}{Q_a^\circ}\frac{dq_e}{dC_e} \qquad (13.13)$$

where σ_o° is the initial surface tension of the pure solvent and σ_s° is that of the surface covered with a complete monolayer of solute. The surface tension, σ_f°, for fractional surface coverage ϕ_m° is then given by

$$\sigma_f^\circ = \sigma_o^\circ (1 - \phi_m^\circ) + \sigma_s^\circ \phi_m^\circ \qquad (13.14)$$

Integration of Equation 13.13 yields the indefinite integral

$$\ln q_e = \frac{\mathcal{R}TQ_a^\circ}{\sigma_o^\circ - \sigma_s^\circ}\ln C_e + \ln \kappa \qquad (13.15)$$

which reduces to the Freundlich equation if the constant of integration, κ, is taken as $\mathcal{K}_F$ and if n is given by

$$n = \frac{\mathcal{R}TQ_a^\circ}{\sigma_o^\circ - \sigma_s^\circ} \tag{13.16}$$

While the above argument reveals one potential theoretical justification of the Freundlich model, it does not serve as a satisfactory means for the general development of that model. This is so because the primary assumption associated with the approach, namely that $\Gamma_a = q_e$, is valid only for relatively high surface concentrations and low residual concentrations of solute in solutions.

13.2.5 Competitive Adsorption Models

Materials to be adsorbed from environmental fluids are commonly mixtures of more than one compound. As will be shown shortly, the compounds comprising such mixtures should not interfere with each other in true absorption processes, and solute competition is thus not a factor in such processes. In adsorption, however, compounds in mixtures may mutually enhance their respective adsorptions, may act relatively independently, or may interfere with one another. Mutual inhibition of adsorption capacity can be predicted if: (1) adsorption is confined to a single or a few molecular layers; (2) the adsorption affinities of the solutes do not differ by several orders of magnitude; and, (3) there are no specific interactions between solutes to enhance adsorption. The degree of mutual inhibition of competing sorbates is related to the comparative sizes of the molecules being adsorbed, to their relative adsorptive affinities, and to their respective concentrations.

An isotherm model designed to incorporate the effects of competition should be able to describe the sorption of each of the compounds involved over wide ranges in their respective concentrations. Competitive equilibrium interactions are subject to exact and systematic description, at least theoretically.

Competition among solutes that each exhibit Langmuir-type isotherms may often be predicted from a simple extension of the Langmuir monolayer adsorption model (see PDES for development). This competitive model expresses the extent of adsorption, $q_{e,i}$ of the ith solute from an n-solute mixture as

$$\boxed{\textbf{\textit{Langmuir}} \atop \textbf{\textit{Competitive}} \atop \textbf{\textit{Model}} \qquad q_{e,i} = Q_{a,i}^\circ \, b_i C_{e,i} \left(1 + \sum_{j=1}^{n} b_j C_{e,j} \right)^{-1}} \tag{13.17}$$

For a two-solute mixture of substances A and B, for example, Equation 13.17 written for solute A becomes

$$q_{e,A} = \frac{Q_{a,A}^\circ \, b_A C_{e,A}}{1 + b_A C_{e,A} + b_B C_{e,B}} \tag{13.18}$$

where $Q_{a,A}^\circ$, b_A, and b_B are Langmuir constants determined from adsorption measurements in solutions containing each single solute, and $C_{e,A}$ and $C_{e,B}$ are equilibrium concentrations in the mixture of the two solutes. When the concentrations of the two solutes are sufficiently large that surface coverage is substantially complete, the first term in the denominator of Equation 13.18 may be neglected, allowing the equation to be linearized in the form

$$\frac{1}{q_{e,A}} \left(\frac{C_{e,A}}{C_{e,B}} \right) = \left(\frac{1}{Q_{a,A}^\circ} \right) \frac{b_B}{b_A} + \frac{1}{Q_{a,A}^\circ} \left(\frac{C_{e,A}}{C_{e,B}} \right) \tag{13.19}$$

Similarly, if written in terms of $q_{e,B}$, the corresponding linear form of Equation 13.18 is

$$\frac{1}{q_{e,B}} \left(\frac{C_{e,B}}{C_{e,A}} \right) = \left(\frac{1}{Q_{a,A}^\circ} \right) \frac{b_A}{b_B} + \frac{1}{Q_{a,B}^\circ} \left(\frac{C_{e,B}}{C_{e,A}} \right) \tag{13.20}$$

If the Langmuir competitive model is appropriate for describing experimental observations, plots of data reworked in terms of the left hand sides of Equations 13.19 and 13.20 versus the corresponding ratios of concentration in the furthest right hand terms of these equations should be linear, with intercepts of $b_B/b_A Q_{a,A}^\circ$ and slopes of $1/Q_{a,A}^\circ$ and $1/Q_{o,B}^\circ$, respectively.

For a thermodynamically more rigorous approach to the description of competitive sorption phenomena the reader is referred to the ideal adsorbed solution theory (IAST) described in PDES. The IAST model affords predictions of sorption in multisolute systems based on measurements of single-solute isotherms for each of the components of a mixture.

13.2.6   Model Applications

The treatment and analysis of equilibrium sorption data generally begins with selection of an appropriate isotherm model and an evaluation of the constants for that model. The first step is often influenced by the intended use of the data and model parameters. For example, mathematical simplicity may be the most important consideration if description of the sorption process comprises only a submodel in a larger system model. In this case, any model that adequately describes the data over the concentration range of interest may suffice. Plots of the amount sorbed as a function of the equilibrium solution concentration for the several models described above are shown in Figure 13.3. A comparison of similar plots for data from a particular system of interest indicates which of the models is most appropriate for simulation of the sorption process for that system.

The choice of a model may be based in part upon the usefulness of model parameters. For example, the Freundlich $\mathcal{K}_F$ term has been used widely to quantify the extent of sorption at a specific residual solution phase concentration and provides an easy way to compare different sorbents or conditions for a particular system. Conversely, if an indication of ultimate sorptive capacity is desired and the Langmuir model appears to adequately describe the experimental data, the monolayer saturation term, Q_a°, of that model may be of

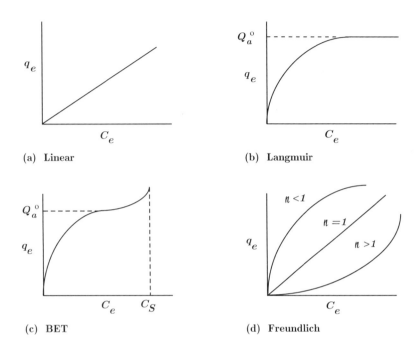

Figure 13.3 Graphical Representations of Isotherm Models

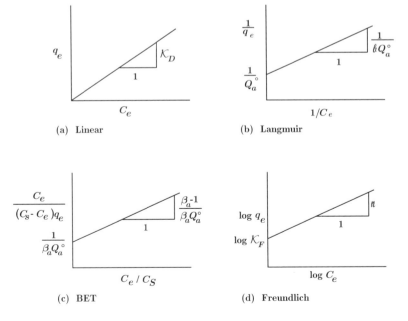

Figure 13.4 Graphical Evaluations of Isotherm Parameters

more interest. Figure 13.4 depicts graphical methods for evaluating isotherm parameters for the linear, Langmuir, BET, and Freundlich models. Example 13.2 provides an illustration of how such parameters might be interpreted in the context of practical applications of adsorption isotherms.

Example 13.2. Isotherm-Based Screening of Activated Carbons. (An illustration of important characteristics of adsorption isotherms to consider relative to the needs and objectives of specific applications.)

- *Situation. A municipal authority responsible for both water and waste treatment is confronted by a multifaceted organic contamination problem. A halogenated solvent used in the spray cleaning of bus wheels in a municipal terminal has in the past been discharged from a floor drain to the municipal wastewater treatment plant. New pretreatment regulations require that the concentration of this solvent in the discharge be reduced from its current level of 1.0 mg/L to a level of 50 µg/L. Some environmental damage has already been done, however, in that losses of the solvent from the municipal sewer system have contaminated both the shallow and deep aquifers of the region, the latter of which is used as a source of raw water supply for the municipality. The shallow aquifer has an average level of 20 µg/L of contaminant and the deep aquifer a level of 5 µg/L. The municipality is required by a consent decree to remediate the shallow aquifer to a level of no more than 5 µg/L, and drinking water regulations require no more than 1 µg/L in the treated water supply. The engineering staff of the municipality determine that the best approach to each of these problems is to treat with activated carbon.*

- *Question(s). Samples of activated carbon from three major suppliers are obtained, and adsorption isotherm tests are conducted on each of the three aqueous streams to be treated. Apart from the concentrations of solvent present, the three streams are very similar. The measured isotherms for the three carbons are shown below, and all three are found to be described reasonably well by the Langmuir isotherm model. If their costs per pound are equal, which of the three carbons would you choose?*

- *Logic and Answer(s).*

    1. *On first consideration, Carbon 1 would appear to have the highest capacity for the solvent. The adsorption isotherm data agree with manufacturer's data that document this carbon as having a high surface area, and the suppliers claim it has the highest "capacity" for chlorinated solvent adsorption of the carbons being considered.*

    2. *The high "capacity" of Carbon 1 must, however, be put into proper context for each of the three applications.*

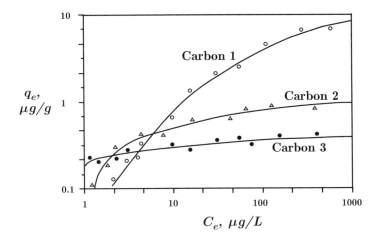

3. *For the drinking water application, for example, the ultimate capac-*
ity as measured by Q_a° has little significance, because it is based on
a concentration range that does not apply for this use. Carbon 3 is
reported to have the lowest surface area and is measured to have the
lowest isotherm capacity for the solvent. However, it shows a signif-
icantly higher effective capacity than carbon over the concentration
range (5 $\mu g/L \rightarrow 1 \mu g/L$) of concern for the drinking water applica-
tion because of its higher energy of adsorption, as reflected by a larger
value of the Langmuir energy constant, b.

• *Key Point(s). Isotherm constants and manufacturer specifica-*
tions for adsorbents such as activated carbon must be assessed
carefully in the context of specific applications. In the situa-
tion considered here, each of the several different applications
would seem to be best addressed by a different carbon among
the three tested. Considerations of supply, handling, regener-
ation, and unit costs being equivalent, Carbon 3 would be the
best choice for the drinking water treatment, Carbon 2 for the
shallow aquifer remediation, and Carbon 1 for pretreatment of
the bus-cleaning rinse waters. Note that there are further con-
siderations that must be made with respect to relative rates of
sorption, as we shall discuss in Chapter 15.

You were asked at the end of section 13.2.1 if you would be tempted to employ
the linear fit to the PCE isotherm data presented in Figure 13.2 as the adsorption
component of a predictive transport model to forecast the temporal profile of
contaminant concentration at a down-gradient well. Figure 13.5 presents the
same plot and linear trace, along with a nonlinear statistically best-fit trace of

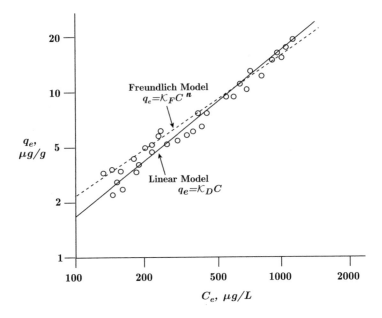

Figure 13.5 PCE Isotherm Data with Linear and Freundlich Model Fits

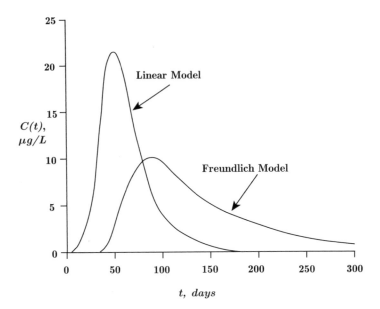

Figure 13.6 ADR Model Projections of PCE Concentration Profiles at a Down-Gradient Well as a Function of Time after an Up-Gradient Spill

the data; the linear trace is equivalent to that for a Freundlich model having an n value of 1.0 while the nonlinear trace has an n value of 0.78. In Figure 13.6 we see the different results obtained for two ADR transport models (e.g., Equation 4.26) calibrated with field-representative parameters that are identical in every regard except for the values of n used in the reaction (adsorption) component; these values correspond respectively to the linear ($n = 1$) and nonlinear ($n = 0.78$) isotherm fits given in Figure 13.5.

For the field conditions employed, and an assumption of instantaneous local adsorption equilibrium, Figure 13.6 reveals that use of the linear isotherm model forecasts: 1) the initial arrival (i.e., $(t) > 0$) of the contaminant plume at the downgradient well only a few days after the upgradient spill; 2) occurrence of the peak contaminant concentration after about 50 days; and, 3) complete passage of the plume in approximately 175 days. Conversely, the nonlinear isotherm model projects: 1) the initial arrival of contaminant at about 30 days; 2) a peak concentration at between 75 to 100 days; and, 3) continued plume tailing for more than 300 days.

It should be readily apparent from the above exercise that one cannot be cavalier about assuming linear sorption behavior by organic contaminants for purposes of modeling their fate and transport in environmental systems. Imagine, for example, the ineffectiveness and cost inefficiencies of a pump-and-treat remediation effort put in place to capture the plume at the downgradient well based on the output of the linear-isotherm version of the ADR transport model.

13.3 PRACTICAL INTERFACES AND PROCESSES

Each of the classical models described above is based on some implicit or explicit assumption(s) about the energetics and distributions of sorption sites on or within a sorbent. In the linear model, for example, all of the sorption reactions of a specific solute with a specific sorbent are assumed to have the same energy associated with them, and the number of sites available for such reactions is assumed to be unlimited. In the Langmuir model, the reaction energy is assumed constant, but the number of sites is limited. Finally, in the Freundlich model, a continuum of limited sites of different reaction energies is assumed (see the development of the Freundlich model as a series of Langmuir models given in Chapter 6 of PDES).

Most environmental sorption processes are inherently heterogeneous; i.e., they involve multiple reaction phenomena. Explanations of observed solute uptake and release derived from models predicated on single sorption reactions may thus be highly system and event specific. This specificity effectively limits their use for predicting sorption behavior in different systems or under different conditions within a given system.

Particles of different environmental solids typically contain different types, amounts, and distributions of surfaces and associated amorphous, condensed, or microcrystalline organic matrices. Different classes of reactions associated with different types of surfaces differ widely with respect to magnitude and mechanism. It is therefore reasonable to expect the reactivities of environmental solids that have widely varying constituent compositions and surface types to be distributed in character, thus yielding typically nonlinear overall sorption behavior.

Most environmental sorption processes are energetically less straightforward than those suggested by either the linear-free-energy partitioning model discussed in Chapter 12 or the constant-energy, limited-surface Langmuir model discussed in this Chapter. Sorption equilibrium data for environmental systems are often best described by the Freundlich model given in Equation 13.11, which essentially assumes an infinite number of different site energies with a limited number of sites at each energy level. Unlike the Q_a° term in the Langmuir model, the Freundlich $\mathcal{K}_F$ is not a limiting capacity, but rather a capacity that corresponds to a specific solution phase concentration.

The interpretation of the Freundlich model as a summation of component Langmuir isotherms given in Chapter 6 of PDES reveals that non-linearity may result also from particularly high-affinity interactions of solute molecules with small specific fractions of a sorbent's total available surface. The greater is the solute affinity for any particular surface, the lower will be the concentration required to establish high sorbent loadings at that surface. This is reflected by sorbent "saturation," being approached at lower solute concentrations, an initially steeper isotherm, a lower value of n, and a more non-linear overall equilibrium relationship; in other words, a highly favorable isotherm. The lower the affinity of the solute for the sorbent or the lower the variability of site energies, the more closely will the value of n approach unity. Accordingly, the sorption process will come closer to a partitioning or to a low surface-coverage Langmuir process. Adsorptions that are of very low affinity require an even greater solution concentration (i.e., "pressure") to force solute onto a surface, thus yielding unfavorable or concave isotherms. Observed degrees of non-linear behavior for sorption of organic compounds of environmental interest by different types of adsorbents range broadly. Freundlich n values as low as 0.3 and greater than 1.0 have been reported for single-solute isotherms.

Example 13.3 illustrates comparative applications of the Langmuir and Freundlich isotherm models for determination and interpretation of associated model parameters for assessment of typical CMBR equilibrium adsorption data.

Example 13.3. Evaluation of the Effects of Prechlorination on the Performance of Activated Carbon in a Water Treatment Plant. (An exercise in the use of the Langmuir and Freundlich isotherm models and the interpretation of measured model parameters.)

- *Situation. It is proposed that activated carbon beds be added to a water* treatment plant for removal of a targeted synthetic organic contaminant (SOC). Chlorine is currently dosed ahead of the point where the carbon beds would be added. The adsorptive characteristics of surface sites on activated carbon can be affected by contact with oxidants such as chlorine due to formation of surface oxides. CMBR adsorption equilibrium tests are required to assess the change in adsorbability of the SOC that might occur after long-term exposure of the activated carbon to chlorine.

- **Question(s).** How can the adsorption data be obtained and interpreted?

- **Logic and Answer(s).**

    1. The suggested experiment is as follows. Prior to the equilibrium adsorption tests, a specified mass of activated carbon is exposed to a solution containing a specified mass of chlorine. Different dosages of this carbon are then added to flasks containing a 100 $\mu g/L$ solution of the SOC. An identical series of dosages of activated carbon particles that have not been exposed to chlorine is then added to another series of flasks having the same initial SOC concentration. Equilibrium is assumed in each flask when there is no further change in SOC concentration with time of contact. The solid-phase concentration, q_e, is calculated from

    $$q_e = \frac{C_0 - C_e}{D_0}$$

    where $C_0 = 100 \mu g/L$ and D_0 is the dosage (mg/L) of activated carbon added.

    2. The results of the experiment described above are as follows

Carbon Dosage	Test 1 No Exposure to Chlorine		Test 2 After Exposure to Chlorine	
$D_0 (mg/L)$	$C_e (\mu g/L)$	$q_e (\mu g/mg)$	$C_e (\mu g/L)$	$q_e (\mu g/mg)$
1	4.8	95.1	13.8	86.3
2	2.3	48.1	6.6	46.7
3	1.5	32.8	4.3	31.9
6	0.7	16.5	2.1	16.3
12	0.4	8.4	1.1	8.2

    The increase in C_e values at each dosage in Test 2 indicates a significant loss in sorptive capacity due to exposure of activated carbon to chlorine.

    3. A Langmuir isotherm can be fit to the data from Tests 1 and 2 (e.g., by linearization according to Equation 13.5) to determine the corresponding Langmuir parameters, which are found to have the following values

	Test 1	Test 2
$Q_a^\circ (\mu g/mg)$	343	400
$b (L/\mu g)$	0.07	0.02

*These results suggest a significant change in the adsorptive charac-
teristics of the carbon as a result of surface oxidation and/or surface
oxide deposition. This change is reflected by an increase in the capacity, but a lower energy of adsorption.*

4. *Suppose we assume that the surface oxidation/deposition process
causes the complete loss of certain sites of some specific sorptive energy. The b and Q_a° values for those lost sites (subscript LS) can be
found by a two-parameter search, subject to the constraint that at any
given C_e value,*

$$q_{e,RS} + q_{e,LS} = q_{e,T}$$

*where the subscript RS refers to the remaining sites, for which Lang-
muir isotherm constants are given from Test 2, and the subscript T
to the total sites, for which Langmuir isotherm constants are given
by Test 1. The resulting values for Langmuir constants for the lost
sites that fit the data from Tests 1 and 2 are*

$$Q_{a,LS}^\circ = 500 \mu g/mg$$

$$b_{LS} = 0.03 L/\mu g$$

*A total isotherm is obtained by adding together the q_e values for the
lost sites and the remaining sites at the same C_e, as illustrated below.*

$C_e(\mu g/L)$	$q_{e,LS}(\mu g/mg)$, Best Fit	$q_{e,RS}(\mu g/mg)$, From Test 2	$q_{e,T}(\mu g/mg)$, Calculated
0.5	7.4	4.0	11.3
1	14.6	7.8	22.4
3	41.3	22.6	63.9
5	65.2	36.4	101.6
10	115.4	66.7	182.1

5. *All of the isotherms above are shown below on a ln q_e-ln C_e plot to
illustrate that (a) the experimental data for Tests 1 and 2 in step 2
can also be fairly well described by a Freundlich isotherm (Equation
13.15), and (b) the hypothesis of the total isotherm consisting of two
Langmuir isotherms (for remaining and lost sites) as determined in
step 4 is fairly well described by a Freundlich isotherm; this should be
expected, given that the Freundlich isotherm represents a patchwork
of Langmuir isotherms for each site energy (see Chapter 6 in PDES).
The corresponding Freundlich parameters are listed below.*

Freundlich Parameter	Test 1 Data	Best-Fit Lost Sites	Test 2 Data
n	0.93	0.92	0.92
$K_F(\mu g/mg)(L/\mu g)^n$	22.3	14.4	8.1

- *Key Point(s). Materials that are "regenerated" and reused in engineered environmental systems are often modified either by other processes to which they are exposed in complex treatment systems or to processes used to regenerate them. This is true, for example, for adsorbents such as activated carbons and synthetic resin adsorbents. It is true as well for membranes in such processes as microfiltration, ultrafiltration, nanofiltration and reverse osmosis. Indeed it is even true for such relatively primitive recycled solids as chemical precipitates and bio-solids. This reality should be factored into process design because, as illustrated above, it can profoundly affect the nature of the materials involved, and thus their performance in the processes into which they have been designed.*

13.4 CHAPTER SUMMARY

In this Chapter we have discussed thermodynamic approaches for understanding and quantifying the accumulation of species at interfaces between phases. The thermodynamic concepts associated with interfacial equilibria and the engineering goals of processes involving interfacial phenomena are connected in at least two important ways. First, reliable predictions of phase separations and distributions in natural systems are important because they affect regulatory policy concerning discharges of chemicals to environmental systems; i.e., they identify those compartments (phases) of the environment in which contaminants are expected to accumulate. Second, our ability to predict the efficiency of separation technologies affects the development of new approaches for control of environmental contaminants in a host of engineered-system settings.

The approaches presented for characterizing and modeling adsorption processes in this Chapter are rigorous. Their applications in practice are confounded, however, by the facts that: 1) they are each predicated on certain assumptions of "ideality;" and, 2) surfaces involved in environmental systems (e.g., soils and other natural and synthetic adsorbents) are neither ideal nor easily quantified.

Classical adsorption models, such as those of Langmuir and Freundlich can be very useful for describing and interpreting the phenomenological characteristics of experimental data and observations. However, the necessarily empirical nature of the ways in which they must commonly be applied should be made clear. These models, and others not specifically discussed, can seldom be used in truly predictive ways because thermodynamically embedded sorbate and sorbent properties are generally not sufficiently well known. Moreover, as useful as isotherm models can be in helping to understand and describe equilibrium adsorption phenomena and processes, they are not of and by themselves sufficient for this purpose. As made evident in Chapters 14 and 15, knowledge of accompanying rate processes is equally important.

13.5 CITATIONS AND SOURCES

Weber, W.J., Jr., P.M. McGinley, and L.E. Katz, 1991, "Sorption Phenomena in Subsurface Systems: Concepts, Models, and Effects on Contaminant Transport," *Water Research, 25*(5), 499-528. (Figures 13.2, 13.5 and 13.6)

Weber, W.J., Jr., and F.A. DiGiano, 1996, *Process Dynamics in Environmental Systems*, John Wiley & Sons, Inc., New York. (PDES is the source of most of the material presented in Chapter 13. Chapter 6 of PDES covers and expands upon the material presented here. It also identifies additional related background reading sources).

13.6 PROBLEM ASSIGNMENTS

13.1 The adsorption of carbon dioxide from a gaseous process stream on a solid adsorbent is found to follow a Langmuir-type adsorption equilibrium distribution, with the following equilibrium values for p_{CO_2} and q_e,

p_{CO_2} (mm)	q_e (mg CO_2/mg adsorbent)
25	0.75
200	2.00
330	2.20
460	2.30

If the area occupied by a single CO_2 molecule is $1.2 \times 10^{-15} cm^2$, determine the specific active surface area of the adsorbent.

13.2 100 mL of a solution with a trichloroethylene (TCE) concentration of 200 mg/L is placed in four small bottles containing variable doses of activated carbon. The samples are then placed on a shaker table and allowed to equilibrate for one week. After this time period, the samples are filtered and the aqueous concentration of TCE is measured. The following data is obtained

Carbon dose (g)	TCE conc. (mg/L)
1	124.8
5	37.2
7	17.4
10	7.2

Determine the Freundlich isotherm parameters, $\mathcal{K}_F$ and $\textbf{\textit{n}}$, and plot the isotherm.

13.3 Individual isotherms for uptake of solutes A and B from solution on activated carbon are found to conform to the Langmuir model for adsorption. The following data are obtained from such measurements:

$$Q_{a,A}^\circ = 5 \times 10^{-4} \text{ moles/g}$$
$$Q_{a,B}^\circ = 10^{-3} \text{ moles/g}$$
$$\ell_A = 5 \times 10^6 \text{ liters/mole}$$
$$\ell_B = 1 \times 10^5 \text{ liters/mole}$$

A 25-mg quantity of the carbon is mixed with 1 liter of a mixture of A and B until equilibrium is attained, and the equilibrium concentrations of A and B are found to be 0.9×10^{-5} and 1.4×10^{-5} moles/liter, respectively. Determine the initial concentrations of A and B in the mixture.

13.4 Toptree Inc., a wood processing company, uses an activated sludge system to treat process water. Pentachlorophenol is, however, being left untreated by this system. In order to remedy this problem, a process engineer proposes adding powdered activated carbon (PAC) directly to the activated sludge aeration basin. A portion of the wastewater will be diverted to a 12 L reactor with a hydraulic retention time of 3 hours. Assuming that the contact time is sufficient for equilibrium to be attained in the reactor, calculate the carbon dose (g/hr) that should be added to the reactor to reduce the $750\mu g/L$ influent concentration to $10\mu g/L$.

Additional information: Freundlich parameters for pentachlorophenol are $K_F = 150 \ mg/g(L/mg)^\mathfrak{n}$ *and* $\mathfrak{n} = 0.45$.

13.5 Ozonation is used in a variety of water and waste treatment operations for oxidation of organic matter. By-products formed in ozonation processes may influence the efficiencies of subsequent treatment processes. In the situation considered here, it is desired to evaluate the impact of pre-ozonation on the efficiency of activated carbon for removing dissolved organic matter in the "tertiary" treatment of an effluent from an activated sludge wastewater treatment plant. After filtration through a 0.45-micron filter, samples of the "secondary" effluent are found to contain an average of 20 mg/L of total organic carbon (TOC). Adsorption isotherms (expressed in terms of TOC) are measured for the filtered effluent before and after pre-ozonation.

(a) Based on the isotherm data presented, write calibrated Freundlich isotherm models for the two sets of data.

(b) Using the appropriate Freundlich isotherm parameter for each set of data, determine which isotherm is more "favorable." Describe the basis for your response.

Values of q_e and C_e are tabulated below.

C_e (mg TOC/L)	q_e (mg TOC/g) After O_3	q_e (mg TOC/g) Before O_3
1.0	2.0	5.0
3.0	4.8	7.0
5.0	7.3	8.1
7.0	9.5	9.0
9.0	11.6	9.7
11.0	13.6	10.3
13.0	15.6	10.8
15.0	17.5	11.3
17.0	19.3	11.7
19.0	21.1	12.1

13.6 Two major components of a small, intermittently generated, aqueous waste stream are to be adsorbed by activated carbon. Batch treatment with a holding time sufficient for adsorption to reach equilibrium is proposed. The initial concentrations of the two components are $C_{0,1} = 2$ mmol/L and $C_{0,2} = 1$ mmol/L; the corresponding discharge permit limits are 1 mmol/L and 0.1 mmol/L, respectively. Determine the carbon dosage, D_0 (mg/L), required to satisfy both of these limits. The Langmuir isotherm constants are $Q^\circ_{a,1} = 100$ mmol/g, $\boldsymbol{\ell}_1 = 1$ L/mmol, $Q^\circ_{a,2} = 500$ mmol/g, and $\boldsymbol{\ell}_1 = 2$ L/mmol. [*Hint:* The possible combinations of equilibrium concentrations, $C_{e,1}$ and $C_{e,2}$, can be obtained by solving the Langmuir competitive model together with the material balance for each component; for example, for component 1

$$q_{e,1} = \frac{C_{0,1} - C_{e,1}}{D_o} = \frac{Q^\circ_{a,1}\boldsymbol{\ell}_1 C_{e,1}}{1 + \boldsymbol{\ell}_1 C_{e,1} + \boldsymbol{\ell}_2 C_{e,2}}$$

where D_0 is the dosage of activated carbon. Solving each material balance expression and equating them (D_0 is the same) provides a way to relate $C_{e,1}$ to $C_{e,2}$. Meeting the permit limit for one of the components will control the dosage required.]

Answers: $D_0 = 21.8$ mg/L; $C_{e,1} = 1$ mmol/L; $C_{e,2} = 0.09$ mmol/L.

13.7 In Section 13.1.2 we stated that the Gibbs adsorption model (Equation 13.1) can be extended in functional form from one describing changes in surface tension ($d\sigma^\circ$) to one describing changes in spreading pressure ($d\pi_s$). Assume that the equation of state for an adsorbed gas can be treated as analogous to the ideal gas law for a three-dimensional gas phase (i.e., $PV = n\mathcal{R}T$).

(a) Develop an isothermal expression for q_e as a function of C_e for adsorption of a gas on a nonporous solid having an indifferent surface.

(b) Compare and discuss the form of the adsorption isotherm you have developed with those of other models presented in Section 13.2.

(c) Discuss any limitations of the model associated with your derivation.

13.8 An algal metabolite, 2-Methylisoborneol (MIB), is a common taste- and odor-causing compound in surface waters. Adsorption on activated carbon is one treatment option. A series of batch adsorption equilibrium tests were performed using powdered activated carbon (PAC) as the sorbent. It was of interest to measure the adsorbability over a wide range of MIB concentrations because MIB production varies in surface waters, and the concentration needed after treatment may vary depending on the intensity of the taste and odor problem. The following data were obtained

C_0 (mg/L)	C_e (mg/L)	D_0 (mg/L)
1.0	0.01	20
1.0	0.05	10
1.0	0.10	7
1.0	0.50	2
5.0	1.0	10
5.0	2.0	6
5.0	3.0	3

where C_0 is the initial MIB concentration, C_e is the equilibrium MIB concentration, and D_0 is the PAC dosage. Discuss the goodness of fit of the Freundlich and Langmuir adsorption models to these data and determine the corresponding constants for each model.

13.9 A preliminary adsorption isotherm study is performed to assess the feasibility of activated carbon treatment of a waste stream having a TOC concentration of 250 mg/L. Six flasks containing 200 mL of waste and different amounts of activated carbon are used for the CMBR tests. An additional flask containing 200 mL of waste but no carbon is run as a control. The following data are obtained from these experiments.

C_e (mg/L)	D_o (mg/L)
4.1	790
5.7	604
9	468
15	335
27	257
52	189
74	145
111	91
250	0

Determine the Langmuir and BET model parameters using this isotherm data and discuss the implications of the results.

13.10 The following adsorption isotherm data were obtained from an experiment using two types of activated carbon (A and B) for the removal of synthetic organic chemicals (SOCs) from 10^6 liters of a spent resin elutriation bath used in a polymer production pilot study. The same amounts of activated carbon (1.0 g) and volume of liquid (1.0 L) were used in each CMBR experiment.

Initial SOC Concentration, (mg/L)	Equilibrium SOC Concentrations, (mg/L)	
	Carbon A	Carbon B
1	0.01	0.053
2	0.02	0.124
4	0.04	0.29
8	0.08	0.677
16	0.165	1.58
32	0.344	3.67
64	0.751	8.52
128	1.843	19.66

(a) Determine the most appropriate model for describing each set of isotherm data.

(b) Two existing fill-and-draw CMBRs of equal size are to be used to reduce the SOC of this water from 12 mg/L to a level of less than 1 mg/L prior to discharge to a municipal sewer system. One 50-kg bag of each carbon is available for this purpose. If a bag of carbon B costs twice as much as a bag of Carbon A, and only one type of carbon is used in each reactor, what is the least costly approach to achieving the treatment objective?

Chapter 14

Passive Interphase Mass Transfer

Contents

14.0   CHAPTER OBJECTIVES

To understand and learn to model processes that cause and control the rates at which nonreacting species undergo transfer from one phase to another under thermodynamically favorable non-equilibrium conditions and associated gradients in chemical potential and concentration.

14.1   DIFFUSIVE MASS TRANSPORT

14.1.1   Concentration-Dependent Transport Processes

In any system that contains a component that is not homogeneously distributed throughout that system (i.e., if one or more spatial concentration gradients and thus spatial chemical potential gradients exist) natural thermodynamic forces will act to transfer the mass of that component to reduce the spatial concentration differences. These forces will continue to exert themselves until they eventually reduce the gradient to zero at a condition of thermodynamic equilibrium. The diffusion of oxygen from bubbles in an aeration basin, the removal of water from chemical and biological sludges, and the air stripping of dissolved gases from wastewaters are typical examples of transport processes effected by concentration gradients. These examples involve gradients and mass transport across phase boundaries; that is, interphase mass transport processes. Spatially variable distributions of mass within a given phase can similarly lead to intraphase mass transport processes, which are important considerations in many water quality systems. Examples of intraphase mass transfer processes include diffusion in the interstitial waters of soils and other porous media, diffusion of adsorbed substances within the pores of activated carbon, the diffusive mass transport of salt in estuarine systems, and diffusion of oxygen through the water column of a stream or lake after it has crossed the air-water interface during reaeration.

The time required for a substance to distribute homogeneously within a system can vary widely. In a totally quiescent system, the mechanism of intraphase mass transport leading to reduction of concentration gradients is the random molecular motion of individual molecules. If the system is not quiescent, the dynamic characteristics of fluid movement affect groups or clusters of molecules and thus tend to diminish concentration gradients more rapidly. These two distinctly different modes of transport of dissolved substances within and among the fluid elements of a water system are distinguished by the terms diffusive mass transport and dispersive mass transport, respectively. On a fundamental level, both processes involve the exchange of momentum but at different scales. Diffusion occurs at the microscale (the molecular level) whereas dispersion oc-

curs at the macroscale and involves the mixing of fluid elements, as described in detail in Chapter 3 of PDES.

14.1.2 Molecular Diffusion

The behavior of the individual molecules of a substance dissolved in a dilute solution contained in a sealed and totally quiescent vessel provides a convenient model to illustrate natural diffusive processes. Because of their respective kinetic energies, the solute and solvent molecules comprising this system continuously undergo Brownian motion, and frequent collisions occur among them. As a result of these collisions, each solute molecule travels a course that changes direction continuously and randomly. The resulting path may carry an individual molecule away from a region of high concentration, or away from a region of low concentration.

The movement of a particular molecule in the system described above is random, and the process is frequently referred to as a random-walk process. The fact that there are greater numbers of molecules moving about in regions of higher concentration, however, means that there must be a net random movement of molecules out of these regions into regions of lower concentration. The magnitude of such net diffusive transport of a substance is thus functionally dependent upon spatial differences in its concentration, C. While this description of diffusive transport is probabilistic in character, the early development of diffusion relationships was largely empirical, and ostensibly deterministic.

14.1.3 Fick's First Law

In 1855 Adolf Fick proposed the empirical relationship

$$\text{\textit{Fick's First Law}} \qquad J_x = \mathcal{D}_l \frac{dC}{dx} \qquad (14.1)$$

to describe one-dimensional (x), steady-state diffusion of a component in a dilute solution. This relationship, referred to as Ficks first law of diffusion, states that the diffusive flux, J_x, is directly proportional to the component's observed spatial concentration gradient, dC/dx. The coefficient of proportionality, $\mathcal{D}_l$, termed the free-liquid diffusion coefficient, has dimensions of $L^2 t^{-1}$. Equation 14.1 includes a negative sign to reflect the fact that the flux is positive when the concentration is decreasing in the positive x-direction.

Strictly speaking, the term J_x in Equation 14.1 defines the flux of one component relative to that of the molar average flux of a mixture of two components and is therefore a flux measured relative to a moving coordinate system. For most applications of interest, the second component is water, the solvent in which a component of interest is dissolved. The notation N is used to describe flux relative to a fixed coordinate system, and can be thought of as the sum of the diffusional flux, J, and that caused by bulk motion. In a quiescent system the latter flux is significant only if the concentration of the component of interest is very large. Thus, J and N are used interchangeably when diffusion occurs in dilute solutions, the most common situation for aqueous environmental systems.

Example 14.1. Performance Characteristics of a Passive Dosimeter. (Analysis of a gas-phase mass transfer diffusion process.)

- **Situation.** *Passive dosimetry is often an effective and inexpensive method for detecting the presence of volatile organic chemicals in the vapor phase above the groundwater table in the vicinity of underground storage tanks. Passive dosimetry has been used for years in the field of industrial hygiene to measure the exposure of workers to airborne contaminants in the workplace. A schematic diagram of a dosimeter is shown below*

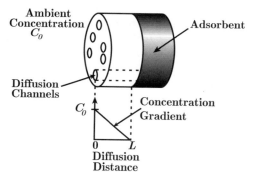

Passive dosimeters often take the form of "badges" worn by workers on their outer garments. If we assume that the ambient contaminant concentration, C_o, remains constant over the dosimeter exposure period, and that the concentration remains at zero at the far end of the diffusion channel in the badge due to the presence of the large mass of adsorbent, this diffusion process can be assumed to occur under steady-state conditions. At the end of the exposure period, the adsorbent is removed from the badge and extracted to measure the total mass of contaminant collected during the exposure period.

- **Question(s).** *Analyze the performance characteristics of a passive dosimeter of the type described above and discuss its applicability to this problem.*

- **Logic and Answer(s).**

    1. *If the contaminant is adsorbable, and can be desorbed for measurement of the mass collected, a passive dosimeter could be lowered into*

a sampling well, the walls of which are perforated above the ground-water table to allow equilibration with the surrounding vapor phase.

2. In such a case, Fick's first law would apply if the ambient concentration remains relatively constant over the sampling time and the adsorbent mass is sufficiently large to insure that the concentration at the end of the diffusion channel nearest the adsorbent is approximately zero.

3. The total molar flux, N, of contaminant with respect to the fixed-coordinate system represented by the normal plane of the dosimeter face is, according to Fick's first law (Equation 14.1), given by

$$N = -\mathcal{D}_g \frac{(C_o - 0)}{(0 - L)}$$

where $\mathcal{D}_g$ is the free gas-phase diffusion coefficient for the component.

4. The total mass of contaminant collected by the dosimeter in time t is

$$M(t) = NAt = \mathcal{D}_g \frac{C_o At}{L}$$

where A is the total cross-sectional area of the diffusion channels exposed to the ambient vapor-phase. The mass of contaminant collected by the dosimeter is measured by extracting the adsorbent material. The critical dosimeter dimensions, A and L, and the sampling time, t, can be selected to achieve the desired sensitivity once the minimum detectable mass, M_{min}, is known.

5. The concentration, C_o, is, therefore, given by

$$C_o = \frac{M(t)L}{\mathcal{D}_g At}$$

- *Key Point(s). The same concept may be applicable to long-term monitoring of the ambient concentrations of contaminants in rivers and lakes, in which case a dosimeter of selected critical dimensions can be submerged at a particular location for a prescribed length of time. The important diffusion process is in this case free liquid-phase diffusion, and the appropriate diffusion coefficient is $\mathcal{D}_l$ [see DiGiano et al. (1988)].*

14.1.4   Fick's Second Law

Fick's first law does not relate changes of concentration at a particular point in a system to changes in time, and thus defines only the

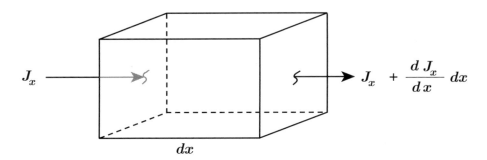

Figure 14.1 One-Dimensional Diffusion Through a Differential Control Volume

steady-state condition for diffusion. An expression to describe time-varying (transient) conditions is obtained by writing a mass balance equation for a differential control volume of unit cross-section, A, and of length dx along the diffusion path, as shown in Figure 14.1. This balance yields

$$\left[J_x - \left(J_x + \frac{dJ_x}{dx} dx \right) \right] A = \frac{dC}{dt} A dx \qquad (14.2)$$

Dividing Equation 14.2 by the volume, Adx, and dropping the directional subscript, x, for convenience, gives

$$-\frac{dJ}{dx} = \frac{dC}{dt} \qquad (14.3)$$

The flux, J, is given by Fick's first law (Equation 14.1). Assuming that $\mathcal{D}_l$ is not a function of x, Equation 14.3 can be rewritten to give Fick's second law of diffusion

$$\boxed{ \begin{array}{ll} \textbf{Fick's} \\ \textbf{Second Law} \end{array} \quad \mathcal{D}_l \frac{d^2 C}{dx^2} = \frac{dC}{dt} } \qquad (14.4)$$

For many environmental systems the boundary conditions are such that solution of the partial differential equation specified by Fick's second law results in

$$\frac{C(x,t)}{C_o} = erfc \left(\frac{x}{2(\mathcal{D}_l t)^{0.5}} \right) C_o \qquad (14.5)$$

where C_o is the concentration at $x = 0$ and *erfc(z)* is a standard mathematical function known as the complementary error function $[erfc(z) = 1 - erf(z)]$. Recall that this function appeared in the solution to the non-steady-state transport equation discussed in Example 3.4 of Chapter 3. The error function, which is described in detail in Chapter 8 of PDES, defines the cumulative probability distribution, again supporting the description of diffusion as a random process. A variety of environmental process applications involving steady-state or unsteady-state diffusion as an overall rate-limiting condition are discussed in PDES, as are cases of diffusion accompanied by chemical reaction, partitioning, and adsorption phenomena in various types of diffusion domains.

14.2   INTERPHASE MASS TRANSFER

Rarely are environmental transformations restricted to single homogeneous phases. Interphase mass transfer is therefore a frequently encountered microtransport process. Interphase mass transfer is defined as the transfer of a species from one phase to another (or to or from an interface between phases) in response to thermodynamically favorable spatial concentration gradients. Not unexpectedly, we find that characterizations of this mode of transport are structured upon concepts of molecular diffusion. Interphase mass transfer can be either passive or reactive. In passive mass transfer the diffusing species retains its chemical identity. In reactive mass transfer the diffusion process is accompanied by one or more transformations in the chemical form(s) of the diffusing species.

Mass transport considerations relating to the interphase movement of material between boundary surfaces and moving fluids or between two immiscible fluids are extremely important in many treatment processes. The resistance to mass transfer at an interface may limit the supply of reactants reaching the phase in which reaction occurs, therefore limiting the rate of reaction and thus controlling reactor design. Typical examples of mass transfer-controlled processes include transport of gases and volatile organic compounds across interfaces between air and water; organic solutes across interfaces between water and solid adsorbents such as activated carbon; ionic species across interfaces between water and solid-ion exchange materials, such as clays and synthetic resins; and particles and molecule across interfaces between water and filter materials such as sands, screens, and porous membranes.

14.2.1   Transport Across Boundaries and Interfaces

Bulk flow in most natural environmental systems is turbulent, and in treatment operations an appropriate degree of mixing is provided to insure that high rates of mass transfer obtain. In heterogeneous phase systems, however, such bulk turbulence is commonly dampened in the regions of boundaries and phase interfaces, as it is at the boundaries of homogeneous systems. The movement of a fluid past a surface or past another fluid brings about the development of a boundary layer wherein mass transport occurs through a combination of molecular and turbulent diffusion. Molecular diffusion occurs close to the surface, where a viscous sublayer exists, while further away from the surface, eddies move randomly and transfer reactant by turbulent diffusion.

Turbulence can be dampened at interfaces between water and air phases and a second phase suspended by cocurrent local movement of the two phases if the second phase travels advectively at essentially the same velocity as the fluid element in which it is suspended. This is characteristic of highly dispersed two-phase systems such as small oxygen bubbles and/or clay particles dispersed in advection-driven water columns, or in rapidly stirred but not well-mixed reactors. Thus, although bulk mixing and macroturbulence may be great in such systems, the microturbulence at phase interfaces is low. Systems in which the second phase is fixed in space with respect to the fluid phase are at the opposite end of the physical spectrum but subject to the same net result. In a fixed bed of adsorbent or a sand filter, for example, boundary conditions dictate zero relative velocity at the immediate interface between the fluid and solid phases, and, thus no interfacial microturbulence.

For multiphase systems such as those described above, the transport of mass at relatively quiescent interfaces between phases reduces to a process similar to that of molecular diffusion. Transport of material from one phase to the other is controlled by the gradient in concentration (rigorously, chemical potential) of the material across the interface, in a manner analogous to that described by Equation 14.1. It differs, however, from homogeneous-phase molecular diffusion in the sense that the impedances of the domains through which diffusion occurs, and thus resistances to diffusion are not those of a well-defined single fluid but rather those of system-specific interfacial conditions. The coefficient of the concentration gradient thus becomes a lumped parameter which must account for more than molecular resistance. For example, it must also account for relative fluid velocities in the interface and, potentially, for differences in the standard states of the diffusing substance(s) in different phases.

The description of a concentration gradient, and hence of a driving force for a material being transferred from one phase to another, must relate to differences between its respective values of chemical potential, μ, in the two phases. Unlike molecular diffusion in homogeneous phases, this difference in chemical potential is not simply given by the concentration difference because the standard-state potential, μ°, of the substance may differ from one phase to another. As discussed in Chapter 12, one phase is likely to have a higher or lower thermodynamic affinity for the substance being transferred. Indeed, such differences in thermodynamic potential and affinity comprise the basis for phase separation processes such as gas transfer, adsorption, ion exchange, membrane separations, and solvent extractions. By way of simple analogy, differences in the chemical potential of a substance between two different phases can be compared to differences between the heat capacity of a homogeneous metal rod suspended in a fluid and that of the fluid itself. Expanding on this analogy, diffusive mass transfer from one phase to another can be likened to the conductance of heat between the rod and the fluid in which it is suspended.

The nature of microturbulence at interfaces cannot be characterized precisely. Interfacial turbulence relates to relative phase velocities, roughnesses of surfaces at the interface, frictional and adhesive forces, surface tensions, and several other parameters. Description of each of these parameters is difficult and tedious at best; characterization of their interactions in terms of microturbulence is impossible. From an engineering perspective, it is therefore necessary to conceptualize the interface in one of two ways: 1) a finite domain with properties that can be correlated to the hydrodynamic properties of the bulk phases it partitions; or, 2) a molecular layer to which mass is transported advectively by infinitesimally small fluid elements circulating in the bulk phase. The first of these conceptual micro-models, termed the stagnant film model or more simply the film model, involves a steady-state description of interphase mass transport. The second, the penetration or surface-renewal model, describes convective mass transport in non-steady-state terms (see PDES). Both models facilitate quantification of mass flux by correlating microturbulence at interfaces to overall bulk-phase turbulence. We will focus our discussions here on the film model.

14.2.2 The Film Model

Mass transfer from one phase to another is generally driven by a concentration (chemical potential) gradient existing across a boundary layer that separates the two phases. The film theory is used to describe this boundary layer in a simplistic way as illustrated in Figure 14.2.

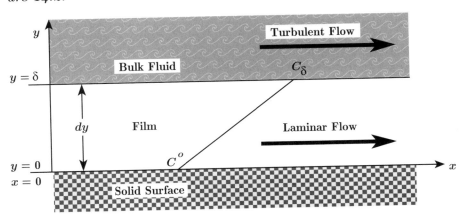

Figure 14.2 The Film Model for Interphase Mass Transfer

The concentration of a component in solution immediately adjacent to the solid surface depicted in Figure 14.2 is designated by C^o. The thickness of the boundary layer or film is δ and the concentration, C_δ, is the same as that in bulk solution. A variety of surfaces are possible. For instance, the surface may be a precipitated form of solute such that C° is given by its solubility limit. Alternatively, it may be the liquid form of an organic solvent which then evaporates into a flowing air stream; C° would then be given by the vapor pressure of the solvent.

Mass transfer through the film shown in Figure 14.2 occurs by diffusion. The diffusional flux in the y-direction for the usual case of dilute mass transfer is described by

$$N = \mathcal{D}_l \frac{dC}{dy} \tag{14.6}$$

which has the same form as Fick's first law (Equation 14.1).

The concentration gradient, dC/dy is not known because the thickness of the concentration boundary layer, δ, is not measurable. Equation 14.6 is therefore reduced to

Film Mass Transfer Model $$N = N^\circ = \mathcal{D}_l \frac{\Delta C}{\delta} = k_f \Delta C \tag{14.7}$$

where N° is the flux measured at the interface; ΔC is the difference in concentration between the surface and the bulk fluid $(C^\circ - C_\delta)$; and, k_f is a mass transfer coefficient that quantifies the relationship between the flux of the diffusing species and the driving force. This coefficient has the dimensions of length per unit time and is defined by

Film-Model Mass Transfer Coefficient $$k_f = \frac{\mathcal{D}_l}{\delta} \tag{14.8}$$

Several distinctions between the diffusion coefficient and the mass transfer coefficient are noteworthy. First, the dimensions of $\mathcal{D}_l$ are $L^2 t^{-1}$, whereas those for k_f are Lt^{-1}. Phenomenologically, k_f depends upon relative velocities in the vicinity of the interface and upon the thickness, δ, of the film. Although it is not possible to measure film thickness, we can reason that it is an inverse function of microturbulence at the phase interface, which, in turn, is directly dependent on bulk fluid-phase turbulence. Thus δ decreases and k_f increases with bulk turbulence, at least to certain limiting values. If bulk flow is reasonably steady, then δ is essentially constant. Further, if the bulk solution is well mixed, the bulk concentration of the component of interest in the phase from which net transport occurs is essentially constant in time.

Film transfer plays an important role in a large number of environmental systems and processes, often in conjunction with other transfer processes. As such, it may control overall process rate only under certain conditions, while the other transfer process(es) may control under other conditions. A sense of this is given in Example 14.2, in which the adsorption of a contaminant from solution by activated carbon in a fixed-bed adsorber is considered.

Example 14.2. Water Treatment in a Fixed Bed of Activated Carbon. (Assumption of a film mass transfer rate model and estimation of an associated rate coefficient.)

- **Situation.** *A fixed bed of activated carbon is to be used to adsorb a contaminant from water. A small adsorption column is set up in the laboratory for a preliminary test. The column has a diameter of 2.5 cm (cross-sectional area of 4.9 cm^2) and length of 5 cm. It is packed with activated carbon granules having an equivalent spherical diameter of 0.8 mm and a particle density (i.e., including internal pore volume) of 1.4 g/cm^3. The resulting bed porosity is 0.4. The feed concentration is 100 µg/L and the superficial velocity of flow is 0.5 cm/s. It is noted that the exit concentration remains constant and equal to 50 µg/L for the first several hours of operation, and then begins to increase. Other data indicates that the effective capacity of the adsorbent for the contaminant under the test conditions is 10% on a weight basis.*

- **Question(s).** *How can the data obtained from the preliminary test be used to develop and calibrate an appropriate mass transfer rate model for the first few hours of adsorber operation?*

- **Logic and Answer(s).**

  1. *The macroscopic and microscopic aspects of fixed-bed adsorbers were depicted in Figure 1.5a. Analysis of adsorption rate processes at the microscopic scale (i.e., particle level) leads to mathematical models that can be used to predict concentrations of contaminants as functions of time and spatial position at the macroscopic scale. It is generally assumed that adsorption processes occurring immediately at the surfaces of an adsorbent are virtually instantaneous. Overall rates of solute uptake are therefore generally controlled by rates of transport across external films surrounding adsorbent particles (see Figure 1.5a) and/or by rates of transport to adsorption sites within the porous structure of an adsorbent.*

  2. *Let's first analyze what is known about this system and then make a rational decision about which of the two microscopic transport processes to employ in a macroscopic reactor model.*

  3. *In this experiment, the detention time of water in the bed is very short; i.e.*
  $$detention\ time = \frac{0.4(5\ cm)}{0.5\ cm/sec} = 4\ sec$$

This limits the amount of mass transfer that can occur from a finite volume of the aqueous phase to the adsorbent. In addition, the hourly rate at which contaminant is being introduced is very low: (0.5 cm/s) (3600s/hr) (4.9 cm^2) (100 mg/L) (10^{-3} L/cm^3) or 882 μg/hr. If the carbon in the bed reaches its expected effective capacity, it will equilibrate with about 2 g of contaminant; i.e., (1-0.4) (4.9 cm^2) (5 cm) (1.4 g/cm^3) (0.1 g/g). Thus, the amount of contaminant introduced during the first few hours is an extremely small fraction of the adsorptive capacity. Given the excess of adsorptive capacity during this time, the local concentration in the fluid adjacent to the adsorbent surface, $C°$ should be nearly equal to zero.

4. *If external mass transfer is a very fast process, the exit concentration of the column at start up would also have been zero because the bulk fluid concentration, C, would be equal to the concentration adjacent to the surface, $C°$. However, the data show that the exit concentration is large at startup. This can be explained only if external diffusion is a relatively slow process; i.e., one that limits the amount of contaminant being transferred to the adsorptive surface. We can also reason that the exit concentration will remain constant temporarily because $C°$ will remain very close to zero due to rapid adsorption of each molecule that passes through the external film.*

5. *The mass transfer rate is thus apparently controlled by external film diffusion, which initially occurs under essentially steady-state conditions. Gradually the adsorption sites at the immediate film/surface boundary become occupied by contaminant molecules, which diffuse slowly along these surfaces to inner parts of the carbon particles. As this happens, $C°$ must rise and the concentration gradient across the external film must decrease, which steadily lowers the overall mass transfer rate to the level of that controlled by the intraparticle diffusion process. This produces an increase in the exit concentration and an unsteady-state condition.*

6. *The steady-state material balance can be written over an elemental control volume of the adsorber unit as*

$$-v_s \frac{dC}{dx} \epsilon_B A dx + N(a_s°)_R \epsilon_B A dx = 0$$

in which ϵ_B is the bed porosity or void ratio, v_s the superficial or Darcy velocity (flow rate/cross-sectional area), A the cross-sectional area of the bed, and N for the steady-state process of film diffusion is, from Equation 14.7

$$N = k_f(C - C°) = k_f(C - 0)$$

and $(a_s°)_R$ is the specific surface area available for mass transfer per *unit volume of reactor, or*

$$(a_s^\circ)_R = \left(\frac{surface\ area\ of\ sphere}{volume\ of\ sphere}\right)\left(\frac{volume\ of\ spheres}{volume\ of\ bed}\right)$$

$$(a_s^\circ)_R = \frac{6}{d_p}(1-\epsilon_B) = \frac{6}{0.08\ cm}(0.6) = 45cm^{-1}$$

7. *Dividing the material balance relationship given in step 6 above by* $\epsilon_B A dx$ *and substituting the flux relationship above yields*

$$-v_s\frac{dC}{dx} - k_f(a_s^\circ)_R C = 0$$

8. *To solve for the mass transfer coefficient,* k_f, *we must integrate the equation above, which in turn requires that we specify the boundary condition (i.e., at* $x = 0$, $C = 100\mu g/L$). *The result is*

$$\frac{C}{100} = \exp\left(-\frac{k_f(a_s^\circ)_R}{v_s}x\right)$$

from which we find that

$$k_f = -\frac{v_s}{x(a_s^\circ)_R}\ln\left(\frac{C}{100}\right)$$

$$= -\frac{0.5\ cm/sec}{(45\ cm^{-1})(5\ cm)}\ln\left(\frac{50}{100}\right)$$

$$= 1.54 \times 10^{-3}\ cm/sec$$

9. *We find upon observation of the complete set of adsorber data that the model we have assumed and the coefficient we have calculated fail to adequately describe the data beyond the first four hours.*

- *Key Point(s). Mass transfer coefficients for single-film interface boundaries between two fluids or between a fluid and a solid are typically in the range of 10^{-2} to 10^{-3} cm/sec, and our calculated coefficient falls in this range. However, our assumed model and its calibration coefficient have been justified by logical arguments only for the first few hours of steady-state operation of the adsorber. Does this mean that the film mass transfer coefficient we have calculated is in fact not constant and that it will change as the overall rate process in the adsorber gradually shifts over to intraparticle diffusion control? If you do not think the coefficient changes, what other reason would you argue for the model failure?*

14.2.3   Solubility-Driven Mass Transfer

Common treatments of interphase mass transfer describe C in Equation 14.7 as the difference between the concentration in one phase and the limiting concentration in that phase were it in equilibrium with the second phase. For instance, suppose that mass transfer controls the rate of dissolution of precipitated solids. The dissolution rate will be determined by the difference between the saturation concentration and the actual concentration of the soluble ions in the bulk liquid. Similarly, consider subsurface contamination by a relatively immiscible organic solvent that becomes entrapped in some fraction of the pore space and exists there as ganglia (or "blobs") of non-aqueous-phase liquid (NAPL). This NAPL subsequently undergoes dissolution into the groundwater (see Example 14.4) until, according to equilibrium principles, a maximum dissolved concentration in the water is determined by the aqueous-phase solubility of the organic solvent. For this case the mass transfer expression given by Equation 14.7 is $k_f(C_S - C_b)$ where C_S is the solubility limit of the solvent and C_b is the bulk concentration of that material dissolved in the water.

14.2.4   Volumetric Mass Transfer Coefficient

An important feature of the film model is the interfacial area of the phase into which mass transfer is occurring. When this parameter is specified, mass transfer can be expressed in a manner analogous to a rate of reaction, namely

$$\boxed{\textbf{\textit{Overall Mass Transfer Rate}} \qquad \boldsymbol{r}_{mt} = N(a_s^\circ)_R} \qquad (14.9)$$

where $\boldsymbol{r}_{mt}$ is the overall rate of mass transfer with dimensions of $ML^{-3}t^{-1}$, and $(a_s^\circ)_R$ is the specific interfacial area per unit volume of reactor, with dimensions of L^{-1}. This overall mass transfer rate depends upon two system constants, k_f and $(a_s^\circ)_R$. It may be possible to determine k_f experimentally if $(a_s^\circ)_R$ can be specified (see Example 14.2). The difficulty, however, is that in many instances $(a_s^\circ)_R$ cannot be easily determined. For example, it is difficult to quantify the total interfacial surface area formed by bubbles of air rising through a column of water. This will depend on, among other factors, the distribution of bubble sizes produced by the sparger apparatus and on the depth of the overlying water column. It is even more difficult to determine the interfacial area of blobs of NAPL entrapped between soil grains and in contact with groundwater. Moreover, to varying degrees in both cases, the interfacial areas will change as constituents of the gas and NAPL phases dissolve into the water.

The difficulty in specification of $(a_s^\circ)_R$ is usually overcome by assessing a lumped system-specific constant, referred to as the volumet-

ric mass transfer coefficient (t^{-1}); i.e.,

$$
\boxed{
\begin{array}{l}
\text{Volumetric} \\
\text{Mass Transfer} \qquad k_v = k_f(a_s^\circ)_R \\
\text{Coefficient}
\end{array}
}
\qquad (14.10)
$$

Because k_v is system specific, its value must be evaluated separately for each system of interest (e.g., see Examples 14.2 and 14.3).

The Sherwood number provides a useful means for quantifying mass transfer relationships in a way that allows extrapolation of information regarding these relationships from one system to another. This dimensionless number, like the Reynolds number, Dispersion number and other dimensionless groups introduced earlier, is a ratio of relevant forces contributing to a process in a given system. The Sherwood number for a given system comprised by the elements of mass transfer depicted in Figure 14.2 can be obtained by writing a flux balance relationship between the mass transport across δ and the diffusion at the surface of that system as in Equation 14.11.

$$
\boxed{
\begin{array}{l}
\text{Mass Transfer} \\
\text{and Diffusive} \qquad k_f(C^\circ - C_\delta) = -\mathcal{D}_l \left.\dfrac{dC}{dy}\right|_{y=0} \\
\text{Flux Balance}
\end{array}
}
\qquad (14.11)
$$

For a constant surface concentration, C°, the diffusive flux term on the right-hand side of Equation 14.11 can be written

$$
-\mathcal{D}_l \left.\frac{dC}{dy}\right|_{y=0} = \mathcal{D}_l \left.\frac{d(C^\circ - C)}{dy}\right|_{y=0}
\qquad (14.12)
$$

Combining Equations 14.11 and 14.12 and multiplying both sides of the resulting equation by the thickness of the film then yields a dimensionless term in which δ is the characteristic length (L_c)

$$
\frac{k_f \delta}{\mathcal{D}_l} = \left(\left.\frac{d(C^\circ - C)}{dy}\right|_{y=0} \right) \left(\frac{\delta}{(C^\circ - C_\delta)} \right)
\qquad (14.13)
$$

The numerator of the term on the right hand side of Equation 14.13 represents the driving force for molecular diffusion and the denominator of that term is the driving force for interfacial transport. The inverse of the numerator is the impedance or resistance to diffusion and the inverse of the denominator is the impedance to interfacial mass transfer.

The dimensionless group on the left hand side of Equation 14.13 is a form of the Sherwood number which, upon substitution of L_c for *δ as a general characteristics length, is defined as*

$$
\boxed{
\begin{array}{l}
\textbf{Sherwood} \\
\textbf{Number}
\end{array}
\quad
\mathcal{N}_{Sh} = \frac{interfacial\ mass\ transfer\ impedance}{molecular\ diffusion\ impedance} = \frac{k_f L_c}{\mathcal{D}_l}
}
\qquad (14.14)
$$

The impedance to interfacial mass transfer depends upon system hydrodynamics and upon the diffusion properties of the component undergoing transfer. As we will show later, development of appropriate relationships between the Sherwood number for a system and the dimensionless parameters that describe the hydrodynamics (the Reynolds number) and diffusion properties (the Schmidt number) of that system is possible from boundary layer theory. However, only simple boundary layer conditions are easily analyzed with mass and momentum balances (e.g., laminar flow over a flat plate). Other boundary layers, such as those created by fluid flow around irregularly shaped grains of sand or adsorbent media in packed beds, are more difficult to describe from first principles. Consequently, experimental correlations between the Sherwood number and other dimensionless parameters must be developed for each type of boundary layer.

The utility of correlations between the Sherwood number and other definable dimensionless groups of similar systems is that they allow estimation of the corresponding mass transfer coefficient for any system of a given type once its hydrodynamic and interfacial conditions have been specified.

Direct use of relationships between the free-liquid diffusion coefficient and mass transfer coefficients derived from film theories to calculate the mass transfer coefficient is difficult for two reasons. First, these models include a "system" constant, δ, that is not measurable directly. Accordingly, mass transfer coefficients must be obtained from experimental measurements or from experimental correlations with certain system variables (e.g., intensity of mixing). The development of mass transfer correlations will be explored in ensuing sections of this chapter.

From a practical point of view, if the proper dependence on free-liquid diffusivity is known, the k_f (or more commonly the k_v) of an easily measured reference solute (designated by the subscript r), can be used to predict the mass transfer coefficient of any other solute, i; i.e.

$$
\boxed{
\begin{array}{l}
\textbf{Mass Transfer} \\
\textbf{Coefficient} \\
\textbf{Referencing}
\end{array}
\quad
(k_f(a_s^\circ)_R)_i = (k_f(a_s^\circ)_R)_r \left(\frac{\mathcal{D}_{l,i}}{\mathcal{D}_{l,r}}\right)^{\psi}
}
\qquad (14.15)
$$

where the exponent ψ is a system-specific empirical factor, the magnitude of which depends on reactor configuration and mixing conditions.

The notion of using a reference component is particularly appealing when the component of interest is difficult or expensive to analyze. However, it is essential that the reference component have a Henry's constant that is similar to the component of interest in order to assure that the overall mass transfer coefficient of both components is determined by similar contributions of gas- and liquid-phase impedance (see Chapter 4 of PDES for details on limitations).

14.3 MASS TRANSFER CORRELATIONS

The film model provides a way to determine mass transfer coefficients from measurements of flux and concentration in any system, regardless of its hydrodynamic and geometric complexity. It does not, however, relate the mass transfer process either to a measurable characteristic dimension or to the hydrodynamics of the system. Operational correlations among these parameters and processes are therefore needed, and dimensional analysis plays an important role in the development of such relationships. In this approach, the general form of a mass transfer relationship is formulated through dimensional analysis. Experiments are then designed to obtain empirical information that is specific for a given type of system.

14.3.1 Buckingham Pi Theorem

The dimensional analysis of any process or system must begin with a reasonably good understanding of the variables that influence that process or system. Once the appropriate variables have been identified, they are then organized or arranged into the smallest number of dimensionless groups possible. The Buckingham Pi theorem, developed in 1915, states that once the number of dimensionless groups is reduced to the smallest number, each then may be related functionally to the other groups in a discrete manner. Thus, if each dimensionless group is designated as Π_i° (hence, the name Pi theorem), any one of them (e.g., Π_i°) can be expressed as some function of the others as

$$\boxed{\begin{array}{ll} Pi \\ Theorem \end{array} \quad \Pi_1^\circ = \phi(\Pi_2^\circ, \Pi_3^\circ, \ldots, \Pi_{n-m}^\circ)} \tag{14.16}$$

where n is the number of variables and m is the number of basic dimensions included in the variables. We can use the results from boundary layer theory to gain an appreciation for the fundamental variables that affect mass transport. We found that k_f is a function of fluid velocity, fluid density, fluid viscosity, molecular diffusivity, and a characteristic mass transfer length. Given that the basic dimensions are length (L), mass (M) and time (t), we conclude that the minimum number of dimensionless groups is 5 - 3 = 2.

The so-called exponent method of dimensional analysis will be used here. We begin by proposing a relationship between k_f and all other significant system variables of the general form

$$k_f = \phi(v^a, \rho^b, \mu_v^c, \mathcal{D}_1^d, L_c^e) \tag{14.17}$$

Because k_f has the dimensions Lt^{-1}, each of the terms making up the final dimensionless groups must also have dimensions of Lt^{-1}. Thus the exponent to which each variable is raised must yield the final dimensions of length per time, or

$$\frac{L}{T} = \left(\frac{L}{T}\right)^a \left(\frac{M}{L^3}\right)^b \left(\frac{M}{LT}\right)^c \left(\frac{L^2}{T}\right)^d (L)^e \tag{14.18}$$

Thus,

$$\sum M = 0 = b + c$$

$$\sum L = 1 = a - 3b - c + 2d + e$$

$$\sum T = -1 = -a - c - d$$

With three equations and five unknowns, we need to select two exponents and thus two dimensionless groups with which to express k_f. Choosing k_1 and k_3 gives

$$k_f = \phi \left[v^a \rho^{-c} \mu_v^c \mathcal{D}_l^{(1-a-c)} L_c^{(-1+a)} \right] \tag{14.19}$$

The smallest number of dimensionless groups comprising all significant variables is then formed by grouping those variables having the same exponents, leading to a functional relationship among those dimensionless groups that is characteristic of the system or process of interest.

Characteristic Dimensionless Group Relationship $\dfrac{k_f L_c}{\mathcal{D}_l} = \phi \left[\left(\dfrac{v L_c}{\mathcal{D}_L}\right)^a \left(\dfrac{\mu_v}{\rho \mathcal{D}_l}\right)^c \right]$	(14.20)

Each of the dimensionless groups given in the characteristic dimensionless group relationship expressed by Equation 14.20 has a distinct physical significance for the particular type of system or process to which the dimensional analysis is applied. For the case at hand, the term on the left side of Equation 14.20 is recognized from Equation 14.14 as the Sherwood number, while the second term in the brackets on the right side is the Schmidt number. The first term in the brackets on the right side is the product of the Reynolds and Schmidt numbers. This product constitutes another dimensionless group known as the Peclet number, a ratio relating advective to diffusive transport

Peclet Number $\mathcal{N}_{Pe} = (\mathcal{N}_{Re})(\mathcal{N}_{Sc}) = \left(\dfrac{v L \rho}{\mu_v}\right)\left(\dfrac{\mu_v}{\rho \mathcal{D}_l}\right) = \dfrac{v L_c}{\mathcal{D}_l}$	(14.21)

14.3.2   General and System-Specific Correlations

Because the Schmidt number appears in both dimensionless groupings in Equation 14.20, we can combine them to obtain

$$\mathcal{N}_{Sh} = \phi \left[(\mathcal{N}_{Re})^a (\mathcal{N}_{Sc})^{c-a} \right] \tag{14.22}$$

or, the form of this functional relationship commonly referred to as the general mass transfer correlation

$$\boxed{\begin{array}{l} \textbf{General Mass} \\ \textbf{Transfer Correlation} \end{array} \quad \mathcal{N}_{Sh} = \psi_1 (\mathcal{N}_{Re})^{\psi_2} (\mathcal{N}_{Sc})^{\psi_3}} \tag{14.23}$$

where ψ_1, ψ_2, and ψ_3 are empirical constants for description of a particular experimental data set. Experimental measurements of k_f for a wide range of values of the important system variables allow empirical determination of the exponents of the Reynolds and Schmidt numbers and the value of the constant, ψ_1. Fluid velocity, type of solute, temperature, and characteristic length of the mass transfer surface (e.g., the diameter of spheres in a packed bed) are typical experimental variables.

An illustration of the use of a mass transfer correlation for evaluating rates of dissolution of a NAPL in a subsurface system is given in Example 14.3.

Example 14.3.   Contaminant Release from Subsurface Non-Aqueous Phase Liquids. (An illustration of the use of dimensional analysis to assess rate controlling factors.)

- *Situation. The release of immiscible liquids to the subsurface is a common cause of groundwater contamination problems. These non-aqueous-phase liquids (NAPLs) are retained in the interstitial spaces between the particles. Interphase mass transfer from such "residual sources" of contaminant to the aqueous phase, the solid phase and the vapor phase are possible.*

- *Question(s). Using dimensional analysis, explore the system parameters that affect interphase mass transfer of solute between an immobile NAPL and the aqueous phase and design an experiment to measure an appropriate mass transfer coefficient.*

- *Logic and Answer(s).*

  1. *The dimensionless parameters of interest are porosity, the percent NAPL saturation of the soil, and the contact angle between the solid phase and the NAPL $\cos \theta_c$. In addition,*

  $$k_f (a_s^\circ)_{N,a} = \phi \left(\mu_{v,a}, \mu_{v,n}, \rho_a, \rho_n, d_p, v_a, \mathcal{D}_l, \sigma_{n,a}^\circ, g \right)$$

where $k_f(a_s^\circ)_{N,a}$ is the product of the mass transfer coefficient and the specific interfacial surface area per unit volume of NAPL, lumped together as such because of the difficulty of experimentally measuring $(a_s^\circ)_{N,a}$ independently. The other terms in the above expression are: μ_v = viscosity; ρ = density; d_p = particle diameter of the porous media; v_a = mean aqueous-phase pore velocity; $\mathcal{D}_l$ = diffusivity of the solute in water; $\sigma_{n,a}^\circ$ = interfacial tension; g = acceleration of gravity; and the subscripts a and n refer to the aqueous and nonaqueous phases, respectively.

2. Dimensional analysis using the Buckingham Pi theorem yields seven dimensionless groups. In addition to $\mathcal{N}_{Re}$, $\mathcal{N}_{Sc}$, and $\mathcal{N}_{Sh}$, these are: $\mathcal{N}_{Ca}$, the capillary number; $\mathcal{N}_{Bo}$, the Bond number; ϕ_{VM}°, the viscosity mobility ratio; and $\mathcal{N}_{Go}$, the Goucher number.

$$\mathcal{N}_{Ca} = \frac{v_a \mu_a}{\sigma_{n,a}^\circ}; \quad \mathcal{N}_{Bo} = \frac{(\rho_a - \rho_n)g d_p^2}{\sigma_{n,a}^\circ}; \quad \phi_{VM}^\circ = \frac{\mu_n}{\mu_a}; \quad \mathcal{N}_{Go} = \frac{d_p^2 \rho_a g}{\sigma_{n,a}^\circ}$$

Although 10 dimensionless groups are possible, not all need be included in the initial testing of a correlation. NAPL saturation and porosity can be combined to form the volumetric fraction, $\phi_{V,N}^\circ$.

3. The correlation to be tested is that suggested by Miller et al. (1990), which has the form

$$\mathcal{N}_{Sh} = \beta_o \mathcal{N}_{Re}^{\beta_1} (\phi_{V,N}^\circ)^{\beta_2} \mathcal{N}_{Sc}^{0.5}$$

where the modified Sherwood number is given by

$$\mathcal{N}_{Sh} = \frac{(k_f(a_s^\circ)_{N,a}) \, d_p^2}{\mathcal{D}_l}$$

The exponent of $\mathcal{N}_{Sc}$ is assumed from the literature.

4. The mass transfer experiment consists of a laboratory-scale column of glass beads to which a specific volume of NAPL is added. The beads are mixed to give a uniform initial distribution of the NAPL and the degree of saturation is determined by the amount of NAPL added. Distilled, deionized water is pumped through the column until a steady-state concentration of the solute in the aqueous phase is reached in the effluent. The point form of the material balance on solute in the water phase leads to

$$\mathcal{D}_d \frac{\partial^2 C}{\partial x^2} - v_a \frac{dC}{dx} + k_f(a_s^\circ)_{N,a}(C_S - C) = 0$$

where $\mathcal{D}_d$ is the dispersion coefficient in the x direction (along the column length), v_p is the pore velocity of the aqueous phase and C_S is the aqueous solubility of the solute. The analytical solution is

$$\frac{C(x)}{C_s} = 1 - \exp\left[\left(\frac{x}{2\mathcal{D}_d}\right)\left(v_a - (v_a^2 + 4\mathcal{D}_d k_f(a_s^\circ)_{N,a})^{0.5}\right)\right]$$

5. *The dispersion coefficient, $\mathcal{D}_d$, is measured independently (see Chapter 11 for test procedures using tracers). For any experiment, v_a is known and $C(x)$ is measured at the end of the column; thus, $k_f(a_s^\circ)_{N,a}$ can be calculated directly by running a series of experiments in which v_a and d_p are varied and with different initial amounts of NAPL (this determines $\phi_{V,N}^\circ$). The coefficients ψ_o, ψ_1, and ψ_2 of the correlation given in step 3 are then determined.*

6. *Given a typical $\mathcal{N}_{Re}$ number (based on d_p), $\phi_{V,N}^\circ$ and $\mathcal{N}_{Sc}$ number, $k_f(a_s^\circ)_{N,a}$ is on the order of 2,000 day^{-1}. With typical velocity and dispersivity values, the equation given in step 4 predicts that the solute reaches saturation in the groundwater in a time of travel of less than 0.1 day.*

- ***Key Point(s). Dimensional analyses provide means for the development of insights to the process-governing variables of complex environmental systems, and to the interrelationships between and interplay among these variables under different system conditions. At a minimum, such analyses stimulate thought processes that can lead to such insights.***

A few common mass transfer correlations for flow of liquids past flat plates and spheres as well as gases and liquids in packed and fluidized beds are given in Table 14.1.

Numerical values of coefficients associated with mass transfer correlations are determined from experimental data, and are therefore subject to experimental error. The mass transfer coefficients calculated from these correlations should thus be considered as average values with associated confidence intervals. Further, the range of conditions (e.g., Reynolds number, Schmidt number, type of fluids and type of solutes), as well as the amount of data collected to develop the coefficients, are correlation specific. These are all reasons to proceed cautiously when selecting a correlation for use for any particular situation. At the very least, a mass transfer correlation must be restricted to the range of Reynolds and Schmidt numbers for which it has been calibrated by rigorous and extensive experimental data.

Correlations such as those given in Table 14.1 have a variety of applications in engineered and natural systems. Mass transfer coefficients are important, for example, in the design of packed beds of activated carbon and ion-exchange materials, and in the design of air stripping towers for removal of volatile organic chemicals from water. Familiar correlations for the former case are the Williamson et al. (1963) and Wilson and Geankopolos (1966) mass transfer

Table 14.1 Common Mass Transfer Correlations

Application	Equation	Limits
Liquid flow past parallel flat plates	$\mathcal{N}_{Sh} = 0.99\mathcal{N}_{Re}^{0.5}\mathcal{N}_{Sc}^{0.33}$	$600 < \mathcal{N}_{Re} < 50,000$
Liquid flow past single spheres	$\mathcal{N}_{Sh} = 2 + 0.95\mathcal{N}_{Re}^{0.5}\mathcal{N}_{Sc}^{0.33}$	$2 < \mathcal{N}_{Re} < 2,000$
	$\mathcal{N}_{Sh} = 0.347\mathcal{N}_{Re}^{0.62}\mathcal{N}_{Sc}^{0.33}$	$2,000 < \mathcal{N}_{Re} < 17,000$
	$\mathcal{N}_{Re} = \dfrac{vd_p\rho_l}{\mu_{v,1}};\ \mathcal{N}_{Sh} = \dfrac{k_f d_p}{\mathcal{D}_l}$	
	d_p = particle diameter	
Liquids in packed beds of spheres	$\mathcal{N}_{Sh} = (0.25/\epsilon_B)\mathcal{N}_{Re}^{0.69}\mathcal{N}_{Sc}^{0.33}$	$55 < \mathcal{N}_{Re} < 1,500$
	ϵ_B = bed porosity	$165 < \mathcal{N}_{Sc} < 10,690$
		$0.35 < \epsilon_B < 0.75$

*Adapted from Geankoplis (1978).

correlations given in Equations 14.24 and 14.25, respectively.

Williamson et al. Correlation
$$\mathcal{N}_{Sh} = 2.4\epsilon_B\mathcal{N}_{Re}^{0.34}\mathcal{N}_{Sc}^{0.42}$$
$$0.08 < \mathcal{N}_{Re} < 125,\ 150 < \mathcal{N}_{Sc} < 1300$$
(14.24)

Wilson and Geankoplis Correlation
$$\mathcal{N}_{Sh} = \frac{1.09}{\epsilon_B}\mathcal{N}_{Re}^{0.33}\mathcal{N}_{Sc}^{0.33}$$
$$0.0016 < \mathcal{N}_{Re} < 55,\ 165 < \mathcal{N}_{Sc} < 70,600$$
(14.25)

Similar correlations are available for assessing the fate of volatile organic chemicals in surface waters and the fate of immiscible organic liquids (e.g., originating from leaking underground storage tanks) in subsurface systems. Familiar correlations for surface waters are the O'Connor and Dobbins and Churchill et al. correlations, given in Equations 14.26 and 14.27, respectively.

O'Connor and **Dobbins** **Correlation**	$k_v = \left(\dfrac{\mathcal{D}_l v}{H_D^3}\right)^{0.5}$	**Based on** **Surface** **Renewal Theory**	(14.26)

Churchill **et al.** **Correlation**	$k_v = 11.6 v^{0.97} H_D^{-1.67}$	**Based on** **Data from** **Natural Streams**	(14.27)

The term k_v is the volumetric mass transfer coefficient introduced in Equation 14.10; $\mathcal{D}_l$ and v are again the free liquid diffusivity and flow velocity (cm^2/s and cm/s), respectively, and H_D is the water depth (cm).

It is clear in comparing Equation 14.24 to Equation 14.25, and Equation 14.26 to Equation 14.27, that it is common to find more than one correlation that might address the needs and conditions of a particular application. The comparison provided in Example 14.4 illustrates the general magnitude of differences that might be expected for widely used correlations having overlapping application domains.

Example 14.4. Trichloroethylene Removal in a Fixed-Bed Adsorber. (An example of the application of transfer correlations.)

- *Situation.* A fixed bed of activated carbon is employed to remove trichloroethylene (TCE) from a contaminated groundwater. While the physical characteristics of the packed bed and its operation are known, there is presently no quantitative means to estimate its performance under different operation conditions. Mass transfer to the adsorption sites on the activated carbon particles is limited in part due to transport of TCE across the laminar liquid layer surrounding the particles.

- *Question(s).* You are asked to examine available mass transfer correlations in order to calculate the mass transfer coefficient. You are given the system properties listed below.

    - *Flow velocity, v = 0.6 cm/s.*
    - *Characteristic diameter of activated carbon particles, d_p = 0.5 cm.*
    - *Bed porosity ϵ_B = 0.5.*

- *Logic and Answer(s).*

1. *Compare k_f using the Williamson et al. and Wilson and Geanko-plis mass transfer correlations and verify that the system meets the Reynolds and Schmidt numbers constraints.*

2. *From Equation 14.24 we determine that the Williamson et al. correlation is*

$$\mathcal{N}_{Sh} = 2.4\epsilon_B \mathcal{N}_{Re}^{0.34} \mathcal{N}_{Sc}^{0.42}$$

   which is valid for $0.08 < \mathcal{N}_{Re} < 125$ and $150 < \mathcal{N}_{Sc} < 1300$; and that the Wilson and Geankoplis correlation from Equation 14.25 is

$$\mathcal{N}_{Sh} = (1.09/\epsilon_B)\, \mathcal{N}_{Re}^{0.33} \mathcal{N}_{Sc}^{0.33}$$

   which is valid for $0.0016 < \mathcal{N}_{Re} < 55$ and $165 < \mathcal{N}_{Sc} < 70,600$.

3. *Other data required for using these correlations are identified below.*
   - *Fluid viscosity, $\mu_v = 1.5 \times 10^{-2}$ g/cm-s.*
   - *Fluid density, $\rho = 1.0 g/cm^3$.*
   - *Free-liquid diffusivity of TCE, $\mathcal{D}_l = 1.02 \times 10^{-5} cm^2/s$.*

4. *From the definitions of the Reynolds and Schmidt number we can then calculate numerical values of*

$$\mathcal{N}_{Re} = \frac{vd\rho}{\mu_v} = 20$$

   and

$$\mathcal{N}_{Sc} = \frac{\mu_v}{\rho \mathcal{D}_l} = 1471$$

   The applicability range criteria are thus met for both correlations.

5. *The Williamson correlation gives $\mathcal{N}_{Sh} = 71.1$ and so*

$$k_f = 71.1 = \frac{\mathcal{D}_l}{d_p} = 1.45 \times 10^{-3} cm/sec$$

   The Wilson and Geankoplis correlation gives $\mathcal{N}_{Sh} = 65.1$ and so

$$k_f = 65.1 = 1.33 \times 10^{-3} cm/sec$$

6. *We thus see that the correlations vary by approximately 9% (lowest to highest values). This is a reasonably good agreement, and not un-typical of the relative range of coefficient values estimated by different correlations meeting the same basic applications criteria.*

- **Key Point(s). Mass transfer correlations derived from dimensional analyses of carefully controlled and reproducible experiments can prove to be extremely valuable tools for the straightforward estimation of mass transfer coefficients for systems having conditions similar to those for which the correlations** *were originally developed. The latter phrase presumes an important caveat, however. As stated in the text, the application of a given correlation must be restricted to the conditions under which it was experimentally calibrated and verified. This restriction pertains most specifically to the ranges of Reynolds and Schmidt numbers involved. As evident in the foregoing example, more than one mass transfer correlation may be found to meet those conditions. The design engineer thus has to exercise some latitude of discretionary choice. Calculations such as those shown in the Example can be made to determine degrees of differences involved between such estimates, and sensitivity analyses then done over the range of coefficient values involved.*

14.4   CHAPTER SUMMARY

Relationships to describe microtransport processes draw upon a broad array of principles from the fields of fluid mechanics, chemical kinetics and thermodynamics, and probability theory. We have seen that diffusion of molecules can be explained using empirical, statistical or chemical potential approaches. Similarly, mass transport across interfaces can be explained either in terms of molecular diffusion or in terms of hydrodynamic interactions at and within those interfaces (e.g., surface residual theory, the basis of Equation 14.26). While the theoretical foundations upon which these relationships are structured is sound, the outcome of such an analysis is generally not a set of immutable physical constants governing molecular diffusion and interphase mass transport. Our knowledge of hydrodynamics and molecular movement at the microscale is imperfect, and so we must depend ultimately upon empirical observations and experimental data. The Sherwood, Reynolds, and Schmidt number correlations for mass transfer coefficients illustrate clearly this dependence on experimental data. These engineering-oriented equations and constants are very useful in process analysis, but the nature and limitations of the data bases upon which they have been developed must be recognized and deemed suitable before they are applied to a specific system or process. To ensure their suitability for any system to which they are to be applied, the chemical and hydrodynamic properties of that system must of course themselves be thoroughly characterized.

14.5   CITATIONS AND SOURCES

Churchill, M.A., H.C. Elmore, and R.A. Buckingham, 1962, "Prediction of Stream Reaeration Rates," *Journal of the Sanitary Engineering Division, Amer Society of Civil Engineers, 88,* SH4, 1. (Equation 14.27)

DiGiano, F.A., D. Elliot, and D. Leith, 1988, "Application of Passive Dosimetry for Detection of Trace Organic Contaminants," *Environmental Science and Technology, 22*, 1365-67. (Example 14.1 and Problem 14.1)

Geankoplis, C.J., 1978, *Transport Processes and Unit Operations*, Allyn and Bacon, Inc., Boston. (Table 14.1)

Miller, C.T., M.M. Poirier-McNeill, and A.S. Mayer, 1990, "Dissolution of Trapped Nonaqueous Phase Liquids: Mass Transfer Characteristics," *Water Resources Research, 26*, 11, 2783-2796. (Example 14.3 and Problem 14.7)

O'Connor, D.J. and W. Dobbins, 1956, "The Mechanism of Reaeration in Natural Streams," *Journal of Sanitary Engineering Division, American Society of Civil Engineers, 82*, SA6, 1115. (Equation 14.26)

Taffinder, G.G. and B. Batchelor, 1993, "Measurement of Effective Diffusivities in Solidified Wastes," *Journal of the Environmental Engineering Division, American Society of Civil Engineers, 119*, 17-33. (Problem 14.2)

Weber, W.J., Jr., and F.A. DiGiano, 1996, *Process Dynamics in Environmental Systems*, John Wiley & Sons, Inc., New York. PDES is the source of most of the material presented in Chapter 14. Chapter 8 of PDES provides more thorough discussions of the topics covered herein. Microscale mass transfer processes, alternative mass transfer models, the development of mass transfer concepts from boundary layer theory, an extensive table of additional mass transfer correlations, and additional readings.

Williamson, J.E., K.E. Bazaire, and C.J. Geankoplis, 1963, "Liquid-Phase Mass Transfer at Low Reynolds Numbers," *Industrial and Engineering Chemistry, Fundamentals, 2*(2), 126-129. (Equation 14.24)

Wilson, E.J. and C. J. Geankoplis, 1966, "Liquid Mass Transfer at Very Low Reynolds Numbers," *Industrial and Engineering Chemistry, Fundamentals, 5*(1), 14.12. (Equation 14.25)

14.6 PROBLEM ASSIGNMENTS

14.1 A passive dosimeter is to be designed for use in obtaining monthly average concentrations of atrazine in a stretch of river. Typical concentrations range from 10 to 50 μg/L. Atrazine, a herbicide commonly found in runoff from agricultural lands, has the structure

$(CH_3)_2CHNH$ ... Cl ... $NHCH_2CH_3$

The dosimeter (see the sketch in Example 14.1) will use activated carbon as the adsorbent (DiGiano et al., 1988). To maximize diffusion rate, the diffusion barrier adjacent to the activated carbon is to be a polycarbonate membrane filter that has pores with a nominal diameter of 1 mm and a total surface area of pores that is estimated as 0.635 cm^2. The length of the diffusion channels is the thickness of the membrane (10 μm). Tests have shown that atrazine adsorbs very strongly on activated carbon such that 2 g of activated carbon should be sufficient to ensure that the concentration remained close to zero at the surface of the activated carbon. Given the percent recovery of adsorbed atrazine (using a solvent extraction), the volume of solvent and the sensitivity of the analytical method (a gas chromatographic procedure), the minimum mass of atrazine accumulated by the activated carbon that is capable of detection is 10 μg.

(a) Determine whether this dosimeter design will be adequate to detect atrazine given the sampling time and the typical concentration range mentioned above.

(b) Discuss the limitations of this monitoring approach.

14.2 One widely accepted treatment technique for hazardous inorganic chemicals (e.g., heavy metals) involves stabilization by cementation. However, consideration must be given to the possibility of diffusion of ions through the porous structure of cement under the worst case scenario of the cement slab being buried below the groundwater table. Taffinder and Batchelor (1993) describe experimental methods they used to determine the effectiveness of solidification/stabilization as a function of the water-to-cement ratio, the curing time and the thickness of cement. They calculated a Mac-Mullin number, $\mathcal{N}_M$, defined as

$$\mathcal{N}_M = \frac{\mathcal{D}_l}{\mathcal{D}_e}$$

where $\mathcal{D}_l$ is the free-liquid diffusivity that would be observed in the pore water of the cement and $\mathcal{D}_e$ is the effective diffusivity that accounts for a tortuous path (i.e., pores are not lined up horizontally through the slab) and adsorption of ions to the cement itself. A "classic diffusion cell," shown schematically below, was used for the measurements

Molar solutions of potassium bromide and lithium chloride were placed in chambers 1 and 2, respectively, on opposite sides of the cement test slab and the concentration of Br and Li were measured with time. The results for bromide in chamber 2 are shown below

$t, (d)$	$C_{Br}(mg/L)$
0	0
6	11,155
8	13,321
9	14,225
11	17,996
31	30,479
34	32,061

The diffusion cell has $V_1 = 1,000\text{cm}^3$; $V_2 = 1,000\text{cm}^3$; area (A) of cement slab normal to diffusion direction $= 127.5\text{cm}^2$; and diffusion length (L) of cement slab $= 0.44$ cm. The molar volume of Br can be estimated as 50 cm^3/mol.

(a) Find an expression for C_2 as a function of t, V_1, V_2, $\mathcal{D}_e$, A, its initial concentration, $C_{1,0}$ in chamber 1 and L, assuming quasi-steady-state diffusion (i.e., concentration changes slowly in each chamber such that Fick's first law is appropriate to describe flux through the distance, L).

(b) Find the MacMullin number and discuss its implications.

[*Hint:* Material balances can be written to express (1) the loss of Br from V_1 due to steady-state diffusion through the cement ($V_1 dC_1/dt = NA$); (2) the gain of Br in V_2 due to steady-state diffusion through the cement; and (3) $C_1V_1 + C_2V_2 = C_{1,0}V_1$.]

14.3 A schematic of a hollow fiber membrane used for water purification is shown below.

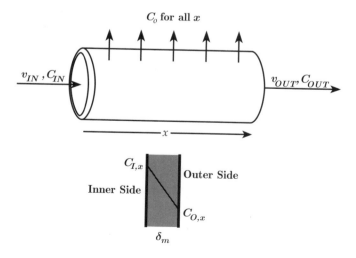

The flow of water is laminar along the length of the tube (no dispersion). In response to the applied pressure, product water flows radially through the walls of the tube, thus producing purified water. Most of the contaminant is rejected by the membrane, but the membrane is not completely impervious to contaminant molecules. For membranes containing very small pores (nanometers or less in diameter), contaminant transport through the membrane can be modeled simplistically as a diffusion-driven process (see the cross section of the wall). In this model, the pressure-driven, advective transport of pure water is an independent process and does not account for transport of contaminant. The steady-state diffusion flux is given by

$$N_m = \mathcal{D}_m \frac{C_{l,x} - C_{O,x}}{\delta_m}$$

in which N_m is the flux ($ML^{-2}t^{-1}$) through the membrane, $\mathcal{D}_m$ is the diffusion constant within the membrane material, $C_{l,x}$ is the contaminant concentration on the inner side of the membrane at distance x, $C_{O,x}$ is the contaminant concentration on the outer side of the membrane, and δ_m is the thickness of the membrane (see the note below). Assume that $C_{O,x}$ is the same down the entire length of the membrane tube. Develop a mathematical model and show the general shape of the function describing the contaminant concentration on the inner side of the membrane as a function of membrane length, x. Do this first by assuming that v_x is a constant. Repeat by assuming that the loss of water through the membrane is linear with length such that

$$v_x = V_{IN} - \kappa x$$

Note: The assumption that flux is independent of radial position within the membrane wall is often justifiable. That is, for a thin wall, the radial flux at steady state is $R_I N_I = R_O N_O$, where the subscripts refer to the inside and outside radius of the tube wall. We can express the outside flux as $N_O = N_I(R_I/R_O)$. However, for thin walls, $R_I \approx R_O$ and we see that the flux can be approximated as independent of radius.

14.4 Another aspect of membrane treatment is the development of a concentration polarization layer on the inner edge of the membrane wall as depicted below.

The concentration is higher at the wall due to the rejection of contaminant by the membrane. The concentration is thus higher at the inner edge of the wall than in the bulk water inside the membrane. This concept is used to estimate the velocity, v_y, of the water moving toward the membrane. There is an advective flux of contaminant within the concentration polarization layer in the direction of the wall given by $v_y C_y$. In addition, we have a contaminant backflux into the tube that can be described by Fick's law as

$$N = -\mathcal{D}_l \frac{dC_y}{dy}$$

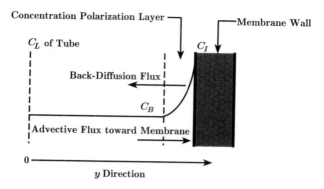

where $\mathcal{D}_l$ is the diffusivity of the contaminant in the water. Set up a differential equation to describe the net flux toward the wall and find the contaminant concentration as a function of distance, y, in the concentration polarization layer. If we know the value of C_I (based on an estimated molecule packing near the wall) and C_b, show how the model can be used to calculate the water flux. State all assumptions and discuss what you think the profile of C_y may look like.

14.5 Spherical-shaped "blobs" of a non-aqueous-phase liquid (NAPL) have contaminated a saturated subsurface system. This NAPL can dissolve into the groundwater. At the microscale of the interstitial pore volume, dissolution is a diffusion process, as shown below.

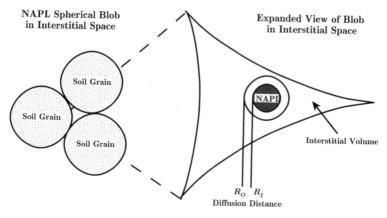

The following assumptions are made: (1) the volume of the NAPL sphere is very small relative to the interstitial volume, V_I; (2) the solubility limit, C_S, of the NAPL in water is reached in the water just at the outer-edge surface of NAPL sphere ($r = R_I$); (3) the NAPL diffuses through the distance between $r = R_I$ and $r = R_O$ and then becomes well mixed into the interstitial water; and (4) the initial diffusion flux can be approximated as steady state (this is known as the quasi-steady-state assumption) because C_S is constant, the concentration in the bulk interstitial water is close to zero, and R_I does not change rapidly (so the diffusion distance does not change significantly over the period of concern).

(a) Find the initial-rate of change in concentration $(mg/cm^3 - s)$ in the interstitial volume, V_I, caused by diffusion of the NAPL if $C_S = 10$ mg/L, $\mathcal{D}_l = 1 \times 10^{-5} cm^2/s$ (typical value), $R_I = 0.01$ cm, $R_O = 0.015$ cm, and $V_I = 0.01 cm^3$.

(b) Estimate the initial-rate of change of NAPL radius, dR_I, if the density of the NAPL is $0.8 g/cm^3$.

(c) Assuming that the flux remains constant (i.e., that the NAPL radius is changing very slowly and that the change in concentration of NAPL at R_O is small enough to ignore), find the concentration in the interstitial volume after 10 min.

(d) Discuss how you may still use the quasi-steady-state model to estimate flux and account for the effect of an increasing concentration in the interstitial volume (C_I) and decreasing sphere radius (R_I).

[*Hint:* The beginning point for this problem is to show that steady-state radial flux at the surface of the sphere can be related to flux at any other location between R_I and R_O by

$$N_{R_I} R_I^2 = N_r(r)^2$$

Since N_r is given by the diffusion equation, N_{R_I} can be expressed after integration in terms of R_I, R_O, C_S, C_I, and $\mathcal{D}_l$.]

Answers: (a) $3.77 \times 10^{-6} mg/cm^3 - s$; (b) $3.75 \times 10^{-8} cm/s$; (c) 2.27 mg/L.

14.6 The mass transfer correlation for liquid flow past a single sphere at low Reynolds number $(2 < \mathcal{N}_{Re} < 2000)$ is given in Table 14.1 as

$$\mathcal{N}_{Sh} = 2 + 0.95 \mathcal{N}_{Re}^{0.5} \mathcal{N}_{Sc}^{0.333}$$

(a) Apply steady-state analysis of radial diffusion from a sphere into a surrounding quiescent medium, as was used in Problem 14.5, to show that the limiting lower value of the Sherwood number in the correlation above is fundamentally correct. [*Hint:* Assume that the radial diffusion distance is much greater than the radius of the sphere and refer to Chapter 3 Section 3.2.3.2 for guidance in writing the material balance.]

(b) Reconsider the "blob" of NAPL in the interstitial volume of subsurface shown in Problem 14.5 and determine its dissolution rate (g/h) if the groundwater velocity is 1 m/day, the diffusivity of the NAPL is $1 \times 10^{-5} cm^2/s$, the NAPL density is $0.8 g/cm^3$, the diameter of the NAPL blob is 100 μm and the temperature of groundwater is 10°C. Assume that the volume of water is very large compared to the volume of NAPL and the solubility limit is low such that the concentration in the bulk liquid is close to zero.

14.7 The solubilization of non-aqueous phase liquids (NAPLs) into groundwater provides an excellent example of the importance of interphase mass transfer. Suppose that toluene is the NAPL of interest. The volume fraction of NAPL held within the porous media, θ_n, is 0.008, the average diameter of the porous media particles or grains is 0.400 mm, the aqueous phase pore velocity, v_p, is 1 m/d. Assume that viscosity is 0.01 g/cm/s and free-liquid diffusivity of toluene is 1.1×10^{-5} cm^2/s. Use the Miller et al. (1990) correlation provided in Example 14.3 to determine the mass transfer coefficient.

(a) Show the fraction of the toluene saturation in the groundwater, C/C_s, as a function of distance if the dispersion coefficient is 0.1 m^2/day.

(b) Suppose dispersion is absent. Derive the material balance to describe advection and interphase mass transfer and use it to obtain C/C_s as a function of distance. Compare the results from parts (a) and (b).

14.8 The dissolution of lead from Pb-soldered joints in household water piping is of concern. New drinking water regulations require that Pb not exceed 15 μg/L. The dissolution of Pb can be considered a mass-transfer-limited process. If the water is corrosive, Pb dissolves on the surface of the joint. Pb is then transported through a hydrodynamic boundary layer into the bulk water as shown below.

A mass transfer correlation given by Geankoplis (1978) for flow in pipes is appropriate here (see PDES)

$$\mathcal{N}_{Sh} = 0.023 \mathcal{N}_{Re}^{0.83} \mathcal{N}_{Sc}^{0.33}$$

where the characteristic length in the Sherwood and Reynolds numbers is pipe diameter, d_p.

(a) Find the steady-state concentration of Pb in μg/L in the bulk water downstream of the Pb-soldered joint if

   • Pb concentration at the surface of the joint = 10 μg/L;

- length of the Pb-soldered joint $= 5$ cm;
- velocity of water, $v = 20$ cm/s;
- diameter of pipe, $d_p = 2.5$ cm;
- free-liquid diffusivity of Pb, $\mathcal{D}_l = 1 \times 10^{-5} \text{cm}^2/\text{s}$;
- $\mu_v = 0.01$ g/cm-s
- $\rho = 1\text{g/cm}^3$.

(b) Suppose that an identical Pb-soldered joint exists some distance further along the pipe, say for example, 4m, and Pb is not removed by any mechanism between the two joints. Assuming that the same corrosive conditions exist, determine the concentration of Pb downstream of this second joint.

14.9 Trichloroethylene begins leaking from a 55 gallon drum of at a chemical production facility and enters the floor drain where it mixes with other process wastes to yield a constant concentration of 2 mg/L in the wastewater stream for a period of 6 h. This wastewater stream with a flow rate 80 m3/day then enters a well-mixed aerated tank (volume of 20 m³) in the industry's biological wastewater treatment plant. The presence of TCE raises concerns about toxicity to the microorganisms in the treatment plant and about violation of the discharge permit for TCE.

(a) Assuming that TCE is not in the waste stream before the leak, compare the peak concentration of TCE leaving the aerated tank with and without volatilization if the volumetric mass transfer coefficient is

$$k_f(a_s^\circ)_R = 1 \times 10^{-4} s^{-1}$$

(b) How long will it take for the effluent concentration of TCE to drop to 0.1 mg/L after the leak stops for each of two assumptions?

Answers: (a) without volatilization, 1.26 mg/L and with volatilization, 0.61 mg/L; (b) without volatilization, 15.2 h and with volatilization, 3.2 h.

14.10 Napthalene spheres (mothballs) have been buried below the water table at a disposal site, where they are being dissolved by the groundwater flowing past them. The conditions are: groundwater temperature, 10°C; groundwater velocity, 100 cm/day; aquifer porosity, 0.3; mothball diameter, 1.0 cm; free-liquid diffusivity of napthalene, $0.5 \times 10^{-5} \text{cm}^2/\text{s}$; and one-dimensional advective transport (ignore dispersion, although this is unrealistic). The Wilson and Geankoplis mass transfer correlation given in Equation 14.25 is appropriate for such cases of liquid flow in packed beds of spheres; i.e.,

$$\mathcal{N}_{Sh} = \frac{1.09}{\epsilon_B} \mathcal{N}_{Re}^{0.33} \mathcal{N}_{Sc}^{0.33} \text{ for } 0.0016 < \mathcal{N}_{Re} < 55$$

[*Note:* The appropriate velocity to use is the "superficial" velocity (i.e., the velocity as though entire cross-sectional area were available for flow when in actuality, flow can only pass through pore space) and the appropriate length scale is the particle diameter, d_p.] Given 160 mothballs per cubic meter of aquifer, determine the length of aquifer through which initially clean water must travel before the concentration of napthalene reaches 1% of napthalene solubility, C_s.

Answer: 3.1 m

Chapter 15

Reactive Interphase Mass Transfer

Contents

15.0   CHAPTER OBJECTIVES

To incorporate rates of transformation in models used for describing the transfer of species from one phase to another under conditions of simultaneous nonequilibrium mass transfer and reaction.

15.1   INTRODUCTION

15.1.1   Concepts

Many reactions of importance in natural and engineered environmental systems involve more than one phase. We refer to these as heterogeneous reactions. The equilibrium principles discussed in Chapters 12 and 13 determine the ultimate distributions of constituents between two or more phases (e.g., between water and air, between water, air and sediment, or between water and activated carbon). It is essential in the analysis and modeling of process and system dynamics that we also characterize the rates at which equilibrium conditions are approached. In many instances, reaction rates themselves (i.e., intrinsic rates) may be very fast, but associated microscale transport processes (e.g., interphase mass transfer from solution to reactive phases or intraphase mass transfer within reactive phases) may be slow, and therefore rate determining. The adsorption of organic solutes onto activated carbon surfaces, for example, is a very fast reaction, but the overall rates of processes involving the uptake of organic compounds from solution by carbon are much slower because the solutes must diffuse through the internal pores of this material to reach interior adsorption sites before reacting.

Heterogeneous reactions may involve mass transfer from gases or liquids to the external surfaces of solids, and if the solids are porous (e.g., activated carbon), internal mass transport as well. We refer to these as microscale transport processes because they occur over spatial scales that are small relative to the spatial scales of mass transport through the reactor systems in which they take place. Three microtransport conditions are shown in Figure 15.1. In Figure 15.1a, reactants are first transported across a laminar fluid layer or film before reactions occur at the external surfaces of the solid. The laminar fluid layer is an external impedance or resistance to mass transfer. If as depicted in Figure 15.1b, the solid is porous and reaction sites are located internally, potential reactions encounter internal resistance to mass transfer as well, a transport process generally referred to as intraparticle diffusion. When reaction sites are located internally, both external and internal impedances in series often occur, as illustrated in Figure 15.1c.

If external and internal impedances are similar in magnitude in any system, both are included in the formulation of heterogeneous rate relationships. If one impedance is much less than the other, it generally can be ignored. For example, if the external resistance to diffusive mass transfer is much less than the internal resistance,

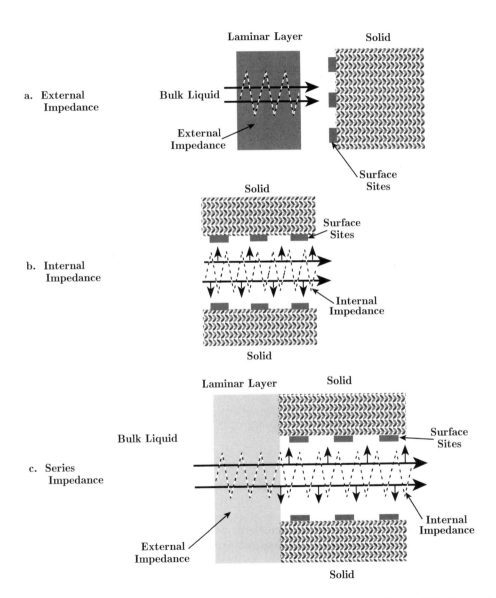

Figure 15.1 Microscale Transport Involving External and Internal Mass Transfer Impedances

the latter is said to be controlling and the rate analysis is simplified accordingly.

Both macroscale and microscale transport processes occur in reactors designed to accommodate heterogeneous reactions. This is illustrated for solid-liquid and gas-liquid reactions respectively in parts a and b of Figure 15.2. Macroscale transport is responsible for the movement of reactants in the axial direction through the reactor, either by advection alone or by a combination of advection and dispersion. Within any elemental volume, microscale transport occurs in a radial direction and, in these examples, is responsible for mass transfer from the liquid to the external solid surfaces and within the solid in Figure 15.2a, and mass transfer from the gas bubbles to the liquid in Figure 15.2b. *The microscale transport processes are incorporated into an "overall rate expression" for use in the material balance equation for an elemental volume of the reactor, in much the same way as is the appropriate rate relationship for a homogeneous reaction. This chapter deals with the development of overall rate expressions for heterogeneous processes. Their applications to reactor design for fluid-solid and fluid-fluid contact systems are addressed in Chapter 16.*

15.1.2   Interphase Boundary Conditions

As illustrated in Figure 15.1, diffusional flux through a hydrodynamic boundary layer or film of some thickness, $x = \delta$, between two phases is a common rate control on interphase mass transfer. Systems of greatest interest for the present discussion involve interfaces between aqueous phases and either solid surfaces or gas phases. As discussed in Chapter 14, diffusional flux through a boundary layer or film is generally defined by a mass transfer relationship lumping the diffusion coefficient and the boundary layer thickness into a mass transfer coefficient. From Equations 14.7 and 14.8 we can describe the flux for systems involving mass transfer between water and a solid surface as

$$N = -\mathcal{D}_l \frac{C_\delta - C_0}{\delta} = \frac{\mathcal{D}_l}{\delta}(C_0 - C_\delta) \qquad (15.1)$$

or

$$N = k_f(C_0 - C_\delta) \qquad (15.2)$$

where k_f is the mass transfer coefficient, and C_0 and C_δ are the concentrations at the up-gradient and down-gradient boundaries of the diffusion domain (boundary layer or film), respectively.

For systems involving mass transfer between water and a gas, a two-film model for flux is sometimes employed

$$N = \hat{k}_{f,l}(C_S - C_b) \qquad (15.3)$$

where C_S is the saturation concentration of the gas in the liquid as calculated by Henrys law for a specified set of temperature and partial pressure conditions,

a. Liquid-Solid Phase System

Packed Bed of Reactive Media

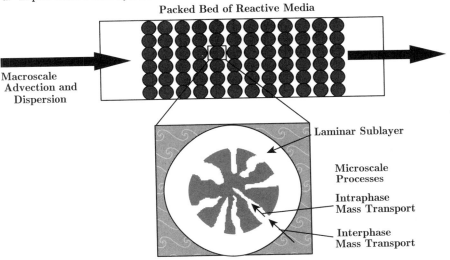

Macroscale
Advection and
Dispersion

Laminar Sublayer

Microscale
Processes

Intraphase
Mass Transport

Interphase
Mass Transport

b. Gas-Liquid System

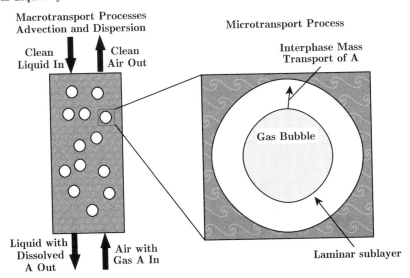

Macrotransport Processes
Advection and Dispersion

Microtransport Process

Clean
Liquid In

Clean
Air Out

Interphase Mass
Transport of A

Gas Bubble

Liquid with
Dissolved
A Out

Air with
Gas A In

Laminar sublayer

Figure 15.2 Macroscale and Microscale Transport Processes
in Heterogeneous Systems

C_b is the concentration in the bulk liquid, and $\hat{k}_{f,l}$ is the overall mass transfer coefficient relative to the liquid form of the diffusing solute, defined by

$$\hat{k}_{f,l} = \frac{1}{\mathcal{R}T/\hat{k}_{f,g}\mathcal{K}_H + 1/\hat{k}_{f,l}} \tag{15.4}$$

If the resistance to mass transfer on the gas side of the film is negligible, $\hat{k}_{f,g}$ is very large, and we can approximate the overall mass transfer coefficient as

$$\hat{k}_{f,l} \approx k_{f,l} \tag{15.5}$$

Chapter 4 in PDES provides a detailed discussion of two-film mass transfer phenomena and models.

The termination point of a diffusion film or domain may also be a reactive solid surface (e.g., a catalyst) or a reactive fluid (e.g., the bulk aqueous solution). These physical boundary conditions determine the nature of the rate expression for reactions that are preceded by the microtransport step; that is, for processes in which mass transfer and reaction take place in series.

15.2   FLUID-SOLID SURFACE REACTIONS

Our analysis of various boundary conditions at the end of a simple diffusion domain begins with that of transformation reactions that occur on contact with surfaces. The rates of such reactions must be expressed in terms of moles reacted per unit area of surface per unit time because they occur on surfaces instead of in bulk liquids.

Consider, for example, a first-order surface reaction

$$-\boldsymbol{r}^\circ = k^\circ C^\circ \tag{15.6}$$

where $\boldsymbol{r}^\circ$ represents the rate of surface reaction in the dimensions specified above ($\text{mol L}^{-2}\text{t}^{-1}$), and C° is the concentration of solute immediately adjacent to the surface (moles L^{-3}). To be consistent with this definition of reaction rate, the first-order rate constant, k°, has the dimensions of length per unit time (Lt^{-1}) instead of time^{-1} (t^{-1}) for a first-order homogeneous reaction (i.e., the same dimensions as a simple linear-driving free mass transfer coefficient). Continuity of flux requires that

$$k_f(C_b - C^\circ) = k^\circ C^\circ \tag{15.7}$$

The surface concentration usually cannot be determined, but this parameter can be eliminated from the rate relationship by expressing it in terms of C_b and the mass transfer and reaction coefficients; that is,

$$C^\circ = \frac{k_f C_b}{k_f + k^\circ} \tag{15.8}$$

Substitution of Equation 15.8 into Equation 15.6 gives

$$\boxed{\textit{First-Order} \quad\quad -\boldsymbol{r}^\circ = k_f k^\circ C_b k_f + k^\circ \atop \textit{Surface} \atop \textit{Reaction Rate}}$$
                                                                            (15.9)

15.2.1   Relative Rates of Mass Transfer and Reaction

Equation 15.9 can be used to examine the relative importance of the mass transfer and reaction rate coefficients for an in-series process. For very fast reactions, $k^\circ >> k_f$ and we obtain

$$\boldsymbol{r}^\circ = k_f C_b$$
                                                                            (15.10)

The overall process rate can be increased in such instances only by increasing the rate of mass transfer (i.e., increasing either the mass transfer coefficient or the fluid-phase concentration). This is termed a mass-transfer-limited process.

As discussed in Section 14.3 of Chapter 14, mass transfer correlations (see, for example, Table 14.1) are available for various conditions, and these provide insight into how increases in k_f can be effected. Correlations for spheres, for example, show that k_f is increased by an increase in fluid velocity (i.e., an increase in $\mathcal{N}_{Re}$) and/or by a decrease in particle diameter, d_p. The latter result is made apparent by inspection of the general form of the Sherwood, Reynolds, and Schmidt number interrelationships for mass transfer, i.e.,

$$\mathcal{N}_{Sh} = \psi_1 (\mathcal{N}_{Re})^{\psi_2} (\mathcal{N}_{Sc})^{\psi_3}$$
                                                                            (14.23)

Because the Sherwood and Reynolds numbers are both directly proportional to d_p, it follows that the mass transfer coefficient is proportional to $d_p^{\psi_2-1}$ and because $\psi_2 < 1$, the mass transfer coefficient (from the Sherwood number) must increase with decreasing d_p. For very slow reactions, $k^\circ << k_f$, and Equation 15.9 reduces to

$$-\boldsymbol{r}^\circ \approx k^\circ C_b$$
                                                                            (15.11)

In this instance, the overall process is said to be reaction-rate limited. Processes that are mass-transfer limited can become reaction-rate limited if fluid velocity is increased or particle diameter is decreased sufficiently to make k_f large relative to k°.

15.2.2   Effectiveness Factors and Damkohler Numbers

Effectiveness factors have been developed as practical engineering tools to quantify the effects of microtransport on observed rates of reaction. The external reaction effectiveness factor, $\eta_{R,E}$, defines the ratio of the observed rate of surface reaction to the intrinsic rate in the absence of mass transfer limitations

$$
\begin{array}{l}
\textit{\textbf{External}}\\
\textit{\textbf{Reaction}}\\
\textit{\textbf{Effectiveness}}\\
\textit{\textbf{Factor}}
\end{array}
\qquad
\eta_{R,E} = \frac{observed\ rate\ of\ surface\ reaction}{intrinsic\ rate\ of\ surface\ reaction}
\qquad (15.12)
$$

The external reaction effectiveness thus lies between zero (severe mass transfer limitations) and 1 (no mass transfer limitations). For the first-order surface reaction described above, Equation 15.9 represents the observed rate and Equation 15.11 the intrinsic rate. The dimensionless external effectiveness factor is thus expressed as

$$
\begin{array}{l}
\textit{\textbf{External Effectiveness}}\\
\textit{\textbf{Factor for First Order}}\\
\textit{\textbf{Surface Reactions}}
\end{array}
\qquad
\eta_{R,E} = \frac{k_f}{k^\circ + k_f}
\qquad (15.13)
$$

Another important pair of dimensionless parameters is comprised by the group I and group II Damkohler numbers, $\mathcal{N}_{Da(I)}$ and $\mathcal{N}_{Da(II)}$. For surface reactions limited by external mass transfer or internal mass transfer, the Damkohler number is classified by standard nomenclature as being in the Group II category. More specifically, for this application the Damkohler number is defined as

$$
\begin{array}{l}
\textit{\textbf{Group II}}\\
\textit{\textbf{Damkohler}}\\
\textit{\textbf{Number}}
\end{array}
\qquad
\mathcal{N}_{Da(II)} = \frac{rate\ of\ reaction}{rate\ of\ diffusional\ mass\ transfer}
\qquad (15.14)
$$

and for a **first-order surface reaction and film diffusion model** is given by

$$
\begin{array}{l}
\textit{\textbf{Damkohler II}}\\
\textit{\textbf{for First Order}}\\
\textit{\textbf{Surface Reaction}}
\end{array}
\qquad
\mathcal{N}_{Da(II)} = \frac{k^\circ C_b}{k_f C_b} = \frac{k^\circ}{k_f}
\qquad (15.15)
$$

Combining Equations 15.13 and 15.15 yields the following relationship between the external reaction effectiveness factor and the Group II Damkohler number

$$
\begin{array}{l}
\eta_{R,E} - \mathcal{N}_{Da(II)}\\
\textit{\textbf{Relationship for}}\\
\textit{\textbf{First-Order}}\\
\textit{\textbf{Surface Reactions}}
\end{array}
\qquad
\eta_{R,E} = \frac{1}{1 + \mathcal{N}_{Da(II)}}
\qquad (15.16)
$$

We observe that when a process is mass-transfer limited (i.e., $k° >> k_f$), $\mathcal{N}_{Da(II)}$ is large and the effectiveness factor approaches zero. At the opposite extreme, when a process is reaction-rate limited (i.e., $k° << k_f$), $\mathcal{N}_{Da(II)}$ is small and the effectiveness factor approaches 1.

An approach to the analysis of potential rate-controlling steps in processes involving in-series transport and surface reaction phenomena in fluid-solids systems is illustrated in Example 15.1.

Example 15.1. Industrial Waste Treatment by Catalytic Oxidation/Reduction. (An analysis of the dependence of a surface catalysis reaction rate on diffusional film mass transfer.)

- **Situation.** *A catalytic chemical oxidation/reduction treatment process is being evaluated for potential application to an industrial waste containing chromium (VI) and several recalcitrant synthetic organic chemicals. The process is based on UV-light-catalyzed reactions at the surface of titanium dioxide (TiO_2) and is expected in this application to reduce Cr(VI) to a less toxic and more readily removed form, Cr(III), and to partially oxidize the organic compounds to increase the effectiveness of downstream biological treatment. Although finely divided TiO_2 particles have been shown to be effective, gravity separation of these particles after treatment has proven difficult. A new technique has been developed to attach finely divided TiO2 particles to larger inert particles which settle more readily, yielding a catalyst surface area of 10,000 cm^2/g. A series of rate tests is conducted using one concentration of catalyst particles (1 g/L) and different impeller speeds, ranging from 400 to 2000 rpm, in a CMBR. Measurements of the fractional remaining concentration of Cr(VI) with time $C(t)/C_0$ are shown below (Prairie et al., 1993).*

Time (min)	400 rpm	1000 rpm	1500 rpm	2000 rpm
0	1	1	1	1
2	0.55	0.38	0.34	0.32
4	0.30	0.15	0.11	0.10
6	0.17	0.06	0.04	0.03
8	0.09	0.02	0.01	0.01

- **Question(s).** *A first-order surface reaction is proposed to account for the reduction of Cr(VI) on TiO_2. Determine whether the data above support this hypothesis.*

- **Logic and Answer(s).**

1. *The bulk-phase concentration, C_b, of a substance undergoing reaction in a CMBR decreases with time such that*

$$V_R \frac{dC_b}{dt} = -k_f(C_b - C^\circ)A_P^\circ = -k^\circ C^\circ A_P^\circ$$

where V_R is the volume of the solution in the reactor, A_P° is the total external surface area of the particles, and C° is the concentration of solute at the surface of the catalyst.

2. *The right-hand side of the above equality can be solved for C° (see Equation 15.8) to give*

$$\frac{dC_b}{dt} = -\frac{k^\circ k_f(a_s^\circ)_R}{k_f + k^\circ} C_b$$

where $(a_s^\circ)_R$ is the specific external surface area of particles per unit volume of solution in the CMBR. Letting $\hat{k}$ be the overall or lumped reaction rate coefficient

$$\hat{k} = \frac{k^\circ k_f(a_s^\circ)_R}{k_f + k^\circ}$$

and integrating the CMBR rate expression gives

$$-\ln \frac{C_b}{C_{b,0}} = \hat{k}t$$

where $C_{b,0}$ is the initial ($t = 0$) concentration of $Cr(VI)$.

3. *If this model is applicable to the process, each set of rate data should give a straight line when plotted according to the expression above. As shown below, such plots indicate good agreement with the proposed model.*

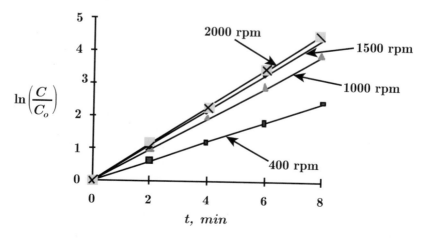

4. The CMBR data show that the rate of Cr(VI) reduction is nearly the same at stirring speeds of 1500 and 2000 rpm. This suggests that the surface reaction becomes almost entirely rate controlling ($k^\circ \ll k_f$) at 2000 rpm and thus that $\hat{k} \approx k^\circ (a_s^\circ)_R$. The slope of the line for the data collected at 2000 rpm determines the value of $\hat{k}$, and it follows that

$$k^\circ = \frac{\hat{k}}{(a_s^\circ)_R} = \frac{0.6(min^{-1}) \cdot (min/60s)}{10,000(cm^2/g) \cdot 0.001(g/cm^3)} = 0.001cm/s$$

5. Knowing $k^\circ (a_s^\circ)_R$, the rate data at the other stirring speeds can be used to determine k_f from the relationship

$$k_f = \frac{\hat{k}k^\circ}{k^\circ (a_s^\circ)_R - \hat{k}}$$

6. The Damkohler numbers and external effectiveness factors calculated from Equations 15.15 and 15.16, respectively, and summarized below indicate that mass transfer controls overall process rate to a significant extent unless the stirring speed is kept above 1500 rpm.

Stirring Speed (rpm)	k_f (cm/s)	k° (cm/s)	$\mathcal{N}_{Da(II)}$	$\eta_{R,E}$
400	0.001	–	1	0.5
1000	0.004	–	0.25	0.8
1500	0.01	–	0.1	0.9
2000	–	0.001	–	–

- **Key Point(s).** The external reaction effectiveness factor and the Group II Damkohler number provide excellent insight to the relative roles of mass transfer and reaction rates with respect to controlling overall process rate in complex reactive interphase mass transfer processes. Such insights reveal which system conditions must be modified to enhance overall process rates.

15.3 GAS-LIQUID BULK-PHASE REACTIONS

15.3.1 The Two-Film Model

Unlike fluid-solid surface interfaces, fluid-fluid interfaces are comprised by two fluids through which diffusional mass transfer occurs.

Thus, pursuant to the two-film theory introduced briefly in Section 15.1.2, gas-liquid mass transfer occurs in a domain that corresponds to a combination of gas and liquid "sides" of an interface.

If the reaction of the gas is limited to the bulk liquid phase, another form of boundary condition is produced. Although in this case the reaction of the diffusing gas takes place entirely in the bulk liquid phase, the rate of gas transfer into the liquid is important because it limits the rate of reaction in that phase. Diffusion occurs in series with the reaction, and the rate of gas transfer into the solution must therefore equal the rate of reaction in solution, i.e.,

$$NA_F^\circ = rV_R \tag{15.17}$$

where A_F° is the interfacial surface area of the liquid film and V_R is the volume of the bulk solution contained in the reactor.

If we assume that gas flux is controlled by the liquid side of the film, and that the reaction rate is first order, we have

$$\hat{k}_{f,l}(a_s^\circ)_R(C_S - C_b) = kC_b \tag{15.18}$$

where, according to Equation 15.5, $\hat{k}_{f,l} = k_{f,l}$ and $(a_s^\circ)_R$ is the interfacial area per bulk volume of liquid in the reactor. This equation can be rearranged to give the bulk phase concentration, C_b; that is,

$$C_b = \frac{\hat{k}_{f,l}(a_s^\circ)_R C_S}{k + \hat{k}_{f,l}(a_s^\circ)_R} \tag{15.19}$$

The smaller the reaction rate constant, k, the higher the bulk concentration for any specific value of the overall volumetric mass transfer coefficient, $\hat{k}_{v,l} = \hat{k}_{f,l}(a_s^\circ)_R$. Thus, as can be reasoned intuitively, for very slow reactions the bulk concentration approaches the saturation concentration, and mass transfer resistance is no longer important.

The general rate expression for a bulk-phase first-order reaction that is controlled (i.e., limited) by an external film mass transfer process is given by

$$-r = kC_b \tag{15.20}$$

and, after substituting for C_b from above, we obtain

First-Order Reaction Rate for Liquid-Film Mass Transfer Control	$-r = \dfrac{\hat{k}_{f,l}(a_s^\circ)_R k}{k + \hat{k}_{f,l}(a_s^\circ)_R}C_S = \dfrac{C_S}{1/\hat{k}_{f,l}(a_s^\circ)_R + 1/k}$	(15.21)

We can see from the expression given in Equation 15.21 that the effect of mass transfer resistance is to lower observed reaction rate. If resistance to mass transfer is negligible $\hat{k}_{f,l}(a_s^\circ)_R$ is large and Equation 15.21 reduces to

$$r = -kC_S \qquad (15.22)$$

In other words, the rate of reaction in the absence of mass transfer is determined by the intrinsic kinetics, for which the bulk concentration, C_b, is equal to the saturation concentration, C_S, in the bulk phase.

Example 15.2 applies the procedures given above for rate analysis to the decomposition of ozone in a CMFR treating a fluid mixture of discrete gas and liquid phases.

Example 15.2. *Aqueous-Phase Decomposition of Ozone in a CMFR Bubble Contactor. (An analysis of the effect of mass transfer from gas phase to liquid phase on the rate of a liquid-phase reaction.)*

- **Situation.** *When dissolved in water, ozone decomposes to oxygen through a complex chain reaction in which hydroxyl radicals are produced. This chain reaction is initiated (catalyzed) by hydroxide ions; the rate of decomposition thus increases with increasing pH. Rates of ozone decomposition are important because the oxidizing powers of molecular ozone and the hydroxyl radical are different. Molecular ozone reacts more slowly and is more specific than highly reactive than the hydroxyl radical.*

  The CMFR shown below is set up in the laboratory and operated at $20°\,C$ to investigate the rate of molecular ozone decomposition.

  Three experiments are conducted in which the percent of O_3 in the feed air is varied from 1 to 3% while the pH is buffered at 8.0. The ozone concentration in solution and the percent ozone in the air leaving the reactor in each experiment at steady state are shown below.

Ozone in Air Mixture Entering Reaction (%)	Ozone in Air Mixture Leaving Reactor(%)	Aqueous-Phase Ozone Leaving Reactor C_{OUT} (mmol/L)
1	0.8	0.08
2	1.6	0.16
3	2.4	0.24

  The overall volumetric mass transfer coefficient, $\hat{k}_{v,l} = \hat{k}_{f,l}(a_s^\circ)_R$, was determined in separate experiments at pH 2, where ozone decomposition can be ignored because of the low OH- concentration. The material balance at steady state is

$$-QC_{OUT} + \hat{k}_{f,l}(a_s^\circ)_R(C_S - C_{OUT})V_R = 0$$

  where C_S is the saturation concentration, C_{OUT} is the exit concentration, Q_l is the flow rate, and V_R is the volume of the reactor. Knowing C_S from

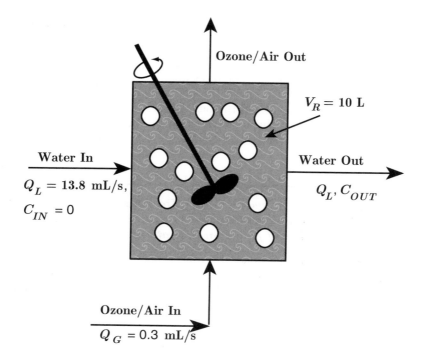

Henry's law and Q_l, V_R, and C_{OUT} from each experiment, the value of $\hat{k}_{f,l}(a_s^\circ)_R$ is found to be $40 h^{-1} (0.011 s^{-1})$.

- **Question(s).** Use the data collected at pH 8 to characterize ozone decomposition rates in these systems.

- **Logic and Answer(s).**

  1. A search of the literature reveals that ozone decomposition is frequently described empirically as a first-order reaction. Other orders (e.g., 1.5 and 2.0) have also used empirically. We use the data from pH 8 to determine whether a first-order reaction rate formulation is reasonable. Moreover, we assume that the reaction is slow enough to be limited to the bulk solution.

  2. For sparingly soluble gases such as ozone it is reasonable to assume that the liquid side of the gas-liquid film controls the rate of mass transfer.

  3. If ozone decomposes slowly, the appropriate rate expression for the observed rate of ozone decomposition is given by Equation 15.21

$$-r = \frac{C_S}{1/\hat{k}_{f,l}(a_s^\circ)_R + 1/k}$$

  According to this model the rate of ozone decomposition is proportional to the saturation concentration of ozone.

4. *The observed steady-state rate of ozone decomposition must equal the rate of ozone transfer, or*

$$-r = \frac{Q_g}{V_R} \left(\frac{P_{IN}}{\mathcal{R}T} - \frac{P_{OUT}}{\mathcal{R}T} \right) - \frac{Q_l C_{OUT}}{V_R}$$

where $\mathcal{R} = 8.21 \times 10^{-5} atm - m^3/mol - K$ *and* $T = 293\ K$.

5. *The saturation concentration is determined from Henry's law*

$$C_S = \frac{P_{OUT}(atm)}{\mathcal{K}_H(atm - m^3/mol)}$$

The $\mathcal{K}_H$ *value for ozone from Table 2.1 is* $67.7 \times 10^{-3} atm - m^3/mol$. *The partial pressure of ozone is that in the exit gas stream, assuming that the gas bubbles are completely mixed within the reactor. If the air is at 1 atm, the pressure of ozone in atm is given by the percent* O_3 *in the exit gas stream divided by 100.*

6. *Values for the rate of decomposition (calculated from step 4) and the ozone saturation (calculated from step 5) are tabulated below*

$-r(mmol/L - s \times 10^4)$	$C_S\ (mmol/L)$
4.0	0.12
8.0	0.24
12.0	0.36

7. *The figure below shows a linear relationship between decomposition rate and the saturation concentration, as predicted by Equation 15.21, with a slope of*

$$slope = \frac{-r}{C_S} = (1/\hat{k}_{f,l}(a_s^\circ)R + 1/k)^{-1} = 3.45 \times 10^{-3} s^{-1}$$

The value of k computed from the slope is $5 \times 10^{-3} s^{-1}$.

8. *The effect of mass transfer on the observed rate of decomposition is given by Equation 15.20*

$$-r = kC_b = (1/\hat{k}_{f,l}(a_s^\circ)R + 1/k)^{-1} C_S = 3.45 \times 10^{-3} C_S$$

In the absence of mass transfer limitations, the rate would be higher; that is

$$-r = kC_S = 5 \times 10^{-3} C_S$$

• *Key Point(s). Reagents for reactions in bulk aqueous phases are often introduced to reactors either as pure gas phases or as admixtures with air. This is particularly true for biochemical reactions, in which the gas-phase reactant is commonly oxygen. It is also true for many chemical oxidation and disinfection reactions such as that for ozone in this particular example. In*

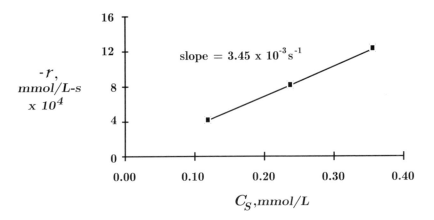

such cases, be the systems involved natural or engineered, overall reaction rates are commonly controlled by the rates of mass
transfer through fluid/fluid interfacial films. By recognizing the
nature of such films and writing appropriate mass transfer expressions, we can usually quantify the mass influence on overall
rate by comparing that rate to the intrinsic reaction rate. The
intrinsic reaction rate is the rate that would occur if the gas and
liquid phases were in equilibrium (i.e., if C_b were equal to C_S).

15.4   ADSORPTION IN POROUS SOLIDS

There are many important examples in which rates of transformation or
separation in natural and engineered environmental processes involve simultaneous diffusion and adsorption. In subsurface systems, for example, hydrophobic organic molecules diffusing within aggregates and microporous soil particles
associate simultaneously with soil organic matter. Water quality specialists
concerned with transport and fate predictions for contaminants in such systems must develop quantitative descriptions of these combined rate phenomena.
In engineered systems, microporous granules of activated carbon or polymeric
resins are used to adsorb contaminants from water flowing past them in a variety of different reactor configurations, again requiring an understanding of
heterogeneous rate phenomena to optimize reactor configuration.

15.4.1   Diffusion and Adsorption in Micropores

Adsorbent media of environmental interest are typically solid
structures containing labyrinths of pores. From a transport point

*of view, movement of solute can occur by diffusion of solute in flu-
ids contained in the pores, pore diffusion, and by migration of sorbate
along the wall surfaces of the internal pores, surface diffusion. When
sorbed-phase concentrations are sufficiently high, transport of solute
by the latter mechanism can be a significant, even dominant, part
of the overall intraparticle or intra-aggregate solute flux. In contrast
to the catalytic reactions discussed to this point, rates of sorption
reactions are inherently unsteady because surface sites are depleted
continually. This complicates mathematical analysis of diffusion with
reaction because two dependent variables, diffusion and time, must
be considered.*

In this chapter we provide an overview of adsorption rate phenomena and relationships, but we limit mathematical developments to simple, one-dimensional
diffusion in rectangular coordinates, as illustrated schematically in Figure 15.3.
Other important physical descriptions of diffusion domains are dealt with in
greater detail in PDES, including simultaneous pore and surface diffusion, external and internal impedances in series, and spherical coordinate systems.

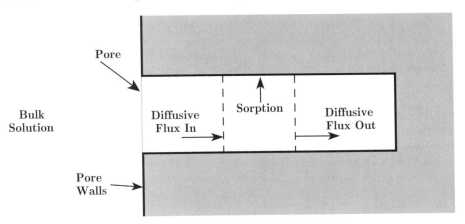

*Figure 15.3 One-Dimensional Diffusion with Surface Adsorption in
an Elemental Pore Volume*

Microscale transport by internal diffusion accounts for flux through the pore
spaces of microporous particles and other porous domains. Diffusion in such
domains is influenced by both the porosity of the domain or particle, ϵ_p, and
the tortuosity, τ, of the diffusion path with respect to the primary direction x
in Figure 15.3) of the overall diffusion flux. Flux is generally measured external
to the diffusion domain, with the coefficient of diffusion being an "effective"
diffusivity that accounts phenomenologically for the effects of both porosity and
tortuosity; i.e., $\mathcal{D}_e = \epsilon_p \mathcal{D}_l/\tau$. Incorporating this definition of effective diffusivity,
we obtain

$$\epsilon_p \frac{\partial C}{\partial t} = \mathcal{D}_e \frac{\partial^2 C}{\partial x^2} - (1 - \epsilon_p)\rho_s \frac{\partial q}{\partial t} \qquad (15.23)$$

An alternative definition of effective diffusivity is the effective pore diffusivity, $\mathcal{D}_{p,e} = \mathcal{D}_l/\tau$, obtained by dividing both sides of Equation 15.23 by the porosity of the particle, to give

$$
\boxed{\begin{array}{ll} \textbf{\textit{Uptake Rate}} \\ \textbf{\textit{for a Porous}} \\ \textbf{\textit{Adsorbent}} \end{array} \qquad \frac{\partial C}{\partial t} = \mathcal{D}_{p,e}\frac{\partial^2 C}{\partial x^2} - \frac{(1-\epsilon_p)\rho_s}{\epsilon_p}\frac{\partial q}{\partial t}} \qquad (15.24)
$$

The two dependent variables, C and q, must be related before applying Equation 15.24. The chain rule for derivatives can be used for this purpose, yielding

$$
\boxed{\begin{array}{ll} \textbf{\textit{Uptake Rate}} \\ \textbf{\textit{Coupling}} \\ \textbf{\textit{q and C}} \end{array} \qquad \frac{\partial C}{\partial t} = \mathcal{D}_{p,e}\frac{\partial^2 C}{\partial x^2} - \frac{(1-\epsilon_p)\rho_s}{\epsilon_p}\frac{\partial q}{\partial C}\frac{\partial C}{\partial t}} \qquad (15.25)
$$

Solution of Equation 15.25 requires that the relationship between the liquid and solid phase concentrations, $\partial q/\partial C$, be known at all locations along the pore length. One convenient assumption that remarkably simplifies the "arithmetic" is that equilibrium exists between the two phases at each local point; i.e., although microscale transport processes may control arrival of solute at sorption sites, the sorption reaction itself is very fast at each specific site. However, the validity of this assumption, referred to as the local equilibrium assumption, is generally questionable. Its validity decreases sharply as the scale of the term "local" increases. While probably valid for microscopic points along the path of an individual pore, the assumption is rarely valid for the scale of the particle, and even less so for that of the reactor.

As discussed in Chapter 13, equilibrium sorption relationships between q_e and C_e may be linear or nonlinear in environmental systems. Most are in fact nonlinear, and analytical solutions to Equation 15.25 are possible only for cases of linear sorption. It is possible in some situations to approximate a weakly nonlinear sorption by a linear relationship, or a strongly nonlinear sorption by an irreversible isotherm expression, over narrow concentration ranges. When valid, these assumptions permit cautious use of analytical solution techniques, but only over limited ranges of C_e. Examples are presented in PDES.

To simplify our discussion of sorption rates by avoiding the potential mire of complex mathematical manipulations, we make two highly "convenient" assumptions. Specifically, we assume that both linear and local equilibrium conditions exist as soon as a solute reaches a specific reactive site; that is, a linear equilibrium is attained instantaneously. We emphasize that these compound assumptions are made only for convenience of illustrating the relative effects of sorption rates, and caution that they each have only limited validity for either natural or engineered environmental processes and systems.

In order to apply to Equation 15.25, the derivative, $\partial q / \partial C_e$, is needed. The linear equilibrium sorption model, presented in Chapter 12, has the form

$$q_e = \mathcal{K}_D C_e \qquad (12.4)$$

Thus, the required derivative is obtained for the case of local linear equilibrium (LLE) by differentiating Equation 12.4 to obtain a single constant; i.e.,

$$\frac{\partial q}{\partial C} = \frac{\partial q_e}{\partial C_e} = \mathcal{K}_D \qquad (15.26)$$

Substitution into Equation 15.26 and simplification yields

$$\mathcal{D}_a \frac{\partial_2 C}{\partial x^2} = \frac{\partial C}{\partial t} \qquad (15.27)$$

in which the apparent diffusivity, $\mathcal{D}_a$, is given by

$$\boxed{\textit{\textbf{Apparent Diffusivity}} \qquad \mathcal{D}_a = \frac{\mathcal{D}_{p,e}}{1 + (1 - \epsilon_p)\rho_s \mathcal{K}_D / \epsilon_p}} \qquad (15.28)$$

Equation 15.27 has the same mathematical form as Fick's second law (Equation 14.4) for unsteady-state free diffusion in a liquid. The difference between the two lies in the definition of the diffusion coefficient; that is, the free-liquid diffusivity in Fick's law is replaced by an apparent diffusivity in Equation 15.27. Apparent diffusivity accounts for impedances to microscale transport caused by three factors: (1) free-liquid diffusion; (2) sorption to solid phases; and, (3) restrictions in diffusion pathways through a solid.

15.4.2 Concentration Profiles and Error Functions

Many different solutions to Equation 15.27 are possible for different initial and boundary conditions. For illustrative purposes, consider a diffusion domain that begins at $x = 0$ and is of infinite length in the x-direction. The concentration of solute is initially zero in both liquid and solid phases throughout the domain. A constant concentration, C_0, is then applied at $x = 0$ for all time. The initial and boundary conditions required to solve Equation 15.27 for this situation are

the initial condition,
$$C(x > 0), t = 0) = 0 \qquad (15.29)$$

the first boundary condition,
$$C(x = 0, t > 0) = C_0 \qquad (15.30)$$

and the second boundary condition,

$$C(x \to \infty, t > 0) = 0 \tag{15.31}$$

The following solution is obtained by Laplace transforms to give $C(x,t)/C_0$, the spatial-temporal concentration distribution or concentration profile

$$\text{Concentration Profile} \quad \frac{C(x,t)}{C_0} = erfc\left[\frac{x}{2(\mathcal{D}_a t)^{0.5}}\right] \tag{15.32}$$

where *erfc* is the error function complement. The shape of the concentration profile produced by simultaneous diffusion and sorption is important to understand because it determines the flux of solute at the up-gradient boundary or entrance to the diffusion domain (i.e., at $x = 0$).

To appreciate the solution given by Equation 15.32, we must consider the nature of the error function complement (erfc) of an arbitrary variable z. The error function (erf), a standard mathematical function having broad applications in mathematics and physics, is defined by

$$\text{Error Function} \quad erf(z) = \frac{2}{\pi^{0.5}} \int_0^z \exp(-z^2)dz \tag{15.33}$$

The error function complement is related to the error function by

$$\text{Error Function Complement} \quad erfc(z) = 1 - erf(z) \tag{15.34}$$

The error function and the error function complement are further discussed and tabulated in Chapter 8 of PDES. The error function is encountered frequently in statistical analysis, where it constitutes the standardized normal cumulative distribution (i.e., the integral of the standardized normal distribution). This reinforces the notion of diffusion as the resultant of a random movement of solute molecules through a fluid, and thus as a probability predictable by a probability function. Detailed discussion of the use of the error function for describing diffusion processes is presented in Chapter 11 of PDES.

Concentration profiles within the diffusion domain described above, and calculated with Equation 15.32, are shown in Figure 15.4 for two different values of apparent diffusivity and a fixed time (three years) after diffusion begins. We observe that the larger value of apparent diffusivity produces greater penetration into the porous sorbent. Larger apparent diffusivities correspond to smaller $\mathcal{K}_D$ values and thus less sorption (see Equation 15.28). In other words, and as one should expect intuitively, strongly adsorbed solutes migrate more slowly than do solutes that are either not adsorbed or that adsorb less strongly. Diffusion is in any case a slow process, as indicated by the fact that it takes three years for concentrations to rise to the values shown in Figure 15.4 over a distance of only 10 cm.

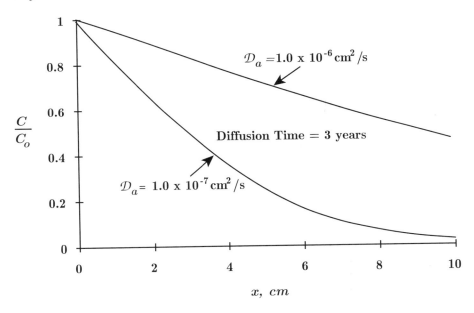

Figure 15.4 Dimensionless Concentration Profiles for Two Different Apparent Diffusivities

The restrictions under which Equation 15.32 applies must be noted carefully. In reality, no sorption domain has infinite length. However, analytical solutions based on this assumption are reasonably accurate up to the times when the concentration rises significantly above zero at the end of a finite diffusion length, L. More complex analytical and numerical solutions are available to handle the general case of finite-length media, for which concentration at L cannot be assumed to be zero. Some of these solutions are discussed in Chapter 11 of PDES.

From a process engineering standpoint, the sorption rate at $x = 0$ may be of as much or more interest as the concentration profile within the diffusion domain. This boundary flux might represent, for example, the net rate at which solute is removed from bulk solution as it flows past a sorbent surface. Diffusional flux at the $x = 0$ boundary *is given by*

$$\boxed{\begin{array}{l}\textbf{\textit{Diffusional}}\\ \textbf{\textit{Boundary}}\\ \textbf{\textit{Flux}}\end{array} \qquad N = -\mathcal{D}_a \frac{\partial C}{\partial x}\Big|_{x=0}}$$ (15.35)

The derivative, $\partial C/\partial x$, is determined by first writing Equation 15.32 as

$$\frac{C(x,t)}{C_0} = c^\circ = 1 - \frac{2}{\pi^{0.5}} \int_0^\zeta \exp(-\zeta^\circ)^2 d\zeta^\circ$$ (15.36)

in which it is assumed that the concentration at the beginning of the diffusion domain is the same as the bulk-phase concentration (i.e., $C_0 = C_b$) and where ζ°, a dimensionless diffusional length ratio, is

$$\zeta^\circ = \frac{x}{2(\mathcal{D}_a t)^{0.5}}$$ (15.37)

The derivative of interest is obtained by the chain rule

$$\frac{\partial c^\circ}{\partial x} = \frac{\partial c^\circ}{\partial \zeta^\circ} \frac{\partial \zeta^\circ}{\partial x}$$ (15.38)

It can be shown that

$$\frac{\partial c^\circ}{\partial \zeta^\circ}\Big|_{\zeta^\circ=0} = -\frac{2}{\pi^{0.5}}$$ (15.39)

and thus we have

$$\frac{\partial c^\circ}{\partial x}\Big|_{x=0} = -\frac{1}{(\pi \mathcal{D}_a t)^{0.5}}$$ (15.40)

Finally, substitution of C/C_0 for c° gives the desired derivative in Equation 15.35, from which the flux is calculated as

$$N\Big|_{x=0} = \mathcal{D}_a C_0 \frac{1}{(\pi \mathcal{D}_a t)^{0.5}} = C_0 \left(\frac{\mathcal{D}_a}{\pi t}\right)^{0.5}$$ (15.41)

15.4.3   Mass Uptake Rates

The mass of solute, $M(t)$, sorbed as a function of time is calculated by integrating the foregoing flux expression over time

$$\frac{M(t)}{A_N^\circ} = \int_0^t n\big|_{x=0}\, dt = C_0 \left(\frac{\mathcal{D}_a}{\pi}\right)^{0.5} \int_o^t t^{-0.5} dt$$ (15.42)

The result after integration is

$$\boxed{\begin{array}{l}\textbf{\textit{Solute Mass}}\\ \textbf{\textit{Uptake Rate}}\end{array} \qquad \frac{M(t)}{A_N^\circ} = 2C_0 \left(\frac{\mathcal{D}_a t}{\pi}\right)^{0.5}}$$ (15.43)

where A_N° is the sorbent surface area normal to the direction of diffusion.

Unsteady-state diffusion accompanied by sorption thus causes the uptake of mass to be proportional to the square root of time. Adherence of experimental data to this relationship is frequently cited as evidence of a diffusion controlled sorption process. The relationship is valid, however, only if (1) the concentration of solute at the beginning of the diffusion domain remains constant, and (2) the diffusion domain can be approximated as having an infinite length. These conditions may hold reasonably well for microporous sorbent particles, but only during the initial stages of solute uptake.

An unusual practical illustration of the application of the foregoing concepts regarding adsorption processes in microporous media with accompanying transport and reaction phenomena is given in Example 15.3. This illustration is put in the context of an operating and maintenance issue in a water treatment plant for a relatively simple circumstance in which adsorption might logically be described in terms of a local linear equilibrium relationship.

Example 15.3. Decontamination of Porous Stone Aerator Heads in a Water Treatment Plant. (An exercise in the application of coupled microscale diffusional transport and adsorption process relationships.)

- *Situation. After performing routine maintenance on two off-line aeration tanks used for taste and odor control at a water treatment plant, an inexperienced assistant operator introduces a solvent to a flow of water used to flush the tanks for removal of accumulated residues. He realizes too late that the solvent is a chlorinated compound, dichloroethylene (DCE), which may be sorbed from the flush water and retained by the porous-stone aerators in the tank. The sorbed solvent might then be released to the drinking water when the aeration units are put back on line. After realizing the error, the assistant stops the flow, drains the solvent containing the flush water from the tanks, and refills them with clean rinse water. The two tanks were not flushed simultaneously and so the exposure time of their aerators to DCE were different; 10 min in one case and 1 h in the other. The chief operator instructs the assistant to repeat the draining and filling process several times until the DCE is desorbed from the diffusers completely. The assistant is further instructed to measure DCE concentrations in the rinse water each time and to do a mass balance to ensure complete desorption.*

- *Question(s). How can the assistant operator determine that all of the DCE has been removed from the diffusers?*

- *Logic and Answer(s).*

1. The amount to be removed must equal the amount sorbed, which can be estimated if the following information is known.

2. The diffusers are configured as flat circular plates having a wall thickness of 10 cm. They are known also to have a porosity of 0.4, a pore tortuosity factor of 2.0, and a domain density (exclusive of pores) of $\rho_d = 1.30 g/cm^3$. The free-liquid diffusivity of the DCE is estimated as $10^{-5} cm^2/s$, and the sorption of this material by the diffuser stone material is taken as a linear process having an estimated $\mathcal{K}_D$ value of 10 L/g. The DCE concentration to which the diffusers were exposed is estimated as 100 mg/L.

3. Each diffuser had a surface area of 100 cm^2 and the total number in each tank is 1000.

4. Equation 15.43 can be used to determine uptake, provided that Equation 15.32 is the appropriate solution to the transient diffusion problem. Equation 15.43 is appropriate if the concentration at a distance of 10 cm remains close to zero after 1 h. $\mathcal{D}_a$ is

$$\mathcal{D}_a = \frac{\mathcal{D}_{p,e}}{1 + (1 - \epsilon_d)\rho_s \mathcal{K}_D/\epsilon_d}$$

$$= \frac{(1 \times 10^{-5} cm^2/s)/2}{1 + \left[(0.6/0.4)\left(1.3\frac{g}{cm^3}\right)\left(10,000\frac{cm^3}{g}\right)\right]} = 0.26 \times 10^{-10} cm^2/s$$

Substitution into Equation 15.32 gives

$$\frac{C(at\ 10\ cm, 1\ h)}{C_0} = erfc\frac{x}{2(\mathcal{D}_a t)^{0.5}}$$

$$= erf\frac{10\ cm}{2\left[\left(0.26 \times 10^{-10}\frac{cm^2}{s}\right)(3600\ s)\right]^{0.5}}$$

$$\approx erfc(\infty) = 0$$

The concentration at 10 cm is thus still approximately zero, so Equation 15.43 can be accepted as a valid predictor of uptake. For the tank that was flushed for 10 min, the prediction is

$$\frac{M(t)}{A_N^\circ} = 2C_0\left(\frac{\mathcal{D}_a t}{\pi}\right)^{0.5} = 2\left(0.1\frac{mg}{cm^3}\right)\cdot\left[\frac{(0.26 \times 10^{-10}\ cm^2/s)(600\ s)}{\pi}\right]^{0.5}$$

$$M(t) = \left(1.4 \times 10^{-5}\frac{mg}{cm^2}\right)(10^5\ cm^2) = 1.4\ mg$$

and for 1 h,

$$M(t) = \left(3.43 \times 10^{--5}\frac{mg}{cm^2}\right)(10^5\ cm^2) = 3.43\ mg$$

• **Key Point(s).** **This example, like many others in the text, illustrates the advantage of understanding process dynamics from** *a fundamental point of view. As mentioned at the beginning of our discussions in Chapter 1, many seemingly unique problems in natural and engineered systems have their solution roots in similar fundamental sciences. Knowing this, and knowing the fundamental sciences, no problem is beyond our ability to solve.*

The mathematical relationships that develop from Equation 15.25 become more complex when sorption equilibria cannot be described by linear isotherms. The Freundlich equation is one of the most frequently used nonlinear equilibrium adsorption models. As presented in Chapter 13, this model has the form

$$q_e = \mathcal{K}_F C_e^n \tag{13.11}$$

If local equilibrium conditions ($q(t) = q_e$) are assumed, we can write the associated derivative required for Equation 15.25 as

$$\frac{\partial q}{\partial C} = \frac{\partial q_e}{\partial C_e} = n\mathcal{K}_F C_e^{n-1} \tag{15.44}$$

which for microporous particle domains leads to

$$\mathcal{D}_{p,e}\frac{\partial^2 C}{\partial x^2} = \left[1 + \frac{(1 - \epsilon_p)\rho_s}{\epsilon_p}(n\mathcal{K}_F C_e^{n-1})\right]\frac{\partial C}{\partial t} \tag{15.45}$$

Unlike Equation 15.27, which resulted from the assumption of linear equilibrium, the expression above cannot be solved analytically, and numerical techniques (e.g., finite difference, orthogonal collocation, or finite element methods) are required.

15.5   CHAPTER SUMMARY

In Chapter 14 we have examined the overall rate characteristics of several types of coupled mass transfer and reaction process commonly operative in heterogeneous natural and engineered environmental systems. We have illustrated in each instance how useful rate formulations can be developed to account for the combined effects of microscale transport and reaction phenomena on overall process behavior. Our purpose has been two fold. First, we have demonstrated that fundamental understandings of mass transport, chemical reaction, and material balance principles together comprise the basic tools for tackling environmental process problems of any type and/or complexity. Second, we have developed appropriate formulations based on these tools that are essential for the application of reactor design principles to several important environmental processes involving heterogeneous systems. In the next, and final, chapter of the book we will illustrate applications of these process formulations for articulation of reactor designs.

15.6   CITATIONS AND SOURCES

Beltran, F.J., V. Gomez-Serranno, and A. Duran, 1992, "Degradation Kinetics of *p*-Nitrophenol by Ozonation in Water," *Water Research, 26*(1), 9-17. (Problem 15.5)

Gould, J.P. and G.V. Ulirsch, 1992, "Kinetics of the Heterogeneous Ozonation of Nitrated Phenols," *Water Science and Technology, 26*(1-2), 169-180. (Problems 15.6 and 15.7)

Weber, W.J., Jr., and F.A. DiGiano, 1996, *Process Dynamics in Environmental Systems,* John Wiley & Sons, Inc., New York. PDES is the source of most of the material presented in Chapters 14 and 15. Chapter 8 of PDES provides thorough discussions of microscale mass transfer processes, alternative mass transfer models, the development of mass transfer concepts from boundary layer theory, an extensive table of additional mass transfer correlations, and additional readings.

15.7   PROBLEM ASSIGNMENTS

15.1 Powdered titanium dioxide is added as a catalyst to solutions of different concentrations of dichloroethane (DCA) in a series of CMBR experiments in which UV irradiation is used to oxidize the DCA. Prior isotherm measurements have indicated that the Langmuir monolayer capacity of the TiO_2 for adsorption of DCA is $Q_a^\circ = 0.5$ mmol/g. Data from oxidation experiments yields the following information regarding initial-rates of DCA removal

Initial DCA Concentration (mmol/L)	Initial-Rate (mmol/g TiO_2-min)
500	0.66
100	0.35
56	0.25
47	0.20

Determine the surface reaction rate coefficient, $k^\circ(s^{-1})$ and the Langmuir adsorption energy parameter, b (L/mol), from these data, assuming that the surface reaction is rate controlling and that the oxidation products do not compete with DCA for adsorption on the TiO_2.

15.2 The photolytic reduction of Cr^{6+} to Cr^{3+} on a solid catalyst is thought to involve a direct surface reaction (i.e., adsorption does not have to occur first). The external surface area of the catalyst is 2000 cm^2/g. The following CMBR rate data are collected using a catalyst dosage of 1 g/L and a stirring speed sufficient to eliminate any potential mass transfer limitations

Time	Cr^{6+} Concentration
(s)	(mg/L)
0	60.0
60	41.9
120	29.2
180	20.4
240	14.2

Another CMBR test is then conducted at a much lower stirring speed, with the following results

Time	Cr^{6+} Concentration
(s)	(mg/L)
0	40
60	34.6
120	30.0
180	26.0
240	22.4

Determine: (a) the surface reaction rate constant k° (cm/s); (b) the mass transfer coefficient k_f (cm/s); (c) the Group II Damkohler number, $\mathcal{N}_{Da(II)}$; and, (d) the effectiveness factor, $\eta_{R,E}$.

Answers: $k^\circ = 0.003$ cm/s; $k_f = 0.002$ cm/s; $\mathcal{N}_{Da(II)} = 1.5$; $\eta_{R,E} = 0.4$

15.3 Chlorine is reduced to chloride by reaction with the surface of activated carbon. A model in which chlorine first adsorbs and then reacts with the surface, and in which no sorption competition with intermediates occurs, is proposed for description of this process. Equilibrium adsorption experiments give the following Langmuir model constants: $b = 5$ L/mmol and $Q_a^\circ = 0.1$ mmol/g. A series of CMBR rate tests are conducted to determine the value of the surface reaction rate constant, k°. The same dose of activated carbon ($D_0 = 0.5$ g/L) is added in each batch. The diameter and density of these particles is 0.01 cm and 1.5 g/cm^3, respectively. Each solution is agitated with an impeller at a rate that yields a mass transfer coefficient for the uptake of chlorine from solution of 0.005 cm/s. The initial-rate of surface reaction can be determined from the data given below.

Initial Cl_2 Concentration (mmol/L)	Cl_2 Remaining After 5 min (mmol/L)
0.1	0.08
0.2	0.17
0.3	0.26
0.5	0.43

(a) Determine $k°(s^{-1})$, assuming that both mass transfer and surface reaction contribute to rate control. Tabulate the Damkohler numbers and solute concentrations at the surface of the particle, ignoring the effects of internal diffusion.

(b) Use $k°$ to calculate the surface reaction rate, $r°$ (mmol/g-s), corresponding to reaction rate control. Discuss the difference between this rate and the rate actually measured.

(c) Test the model for rate control by surface reaction using the experimental data. Compare the $k°$ value obtained to that determined in part (a).

Answers: (a) Average $k° = 0.023s^{-1}$; (b) e.g., at $C_0 = 0.5$ mmol/L, $r° = 1.64 \times 10^{-3}$ mmol/g-s compared to 7.8×10^{-4} mmol/g-s, which was measured; (c) the $k° = 0.0035s^{-1}$ obtained from the best fit to the "linearized" plot is much lower than that in part (a) because the concentration at the surface is less than in the bulk solution due to mass transfer limitations, and the bulk concentration was used in calculating the surface rate constant in part (c); this is an example of disguised kinetics.

15.4 Flue gas (sulfur dioxide) is to be used in an industrial wastewater treatment operation for pH adjustment. SO_2 undergoes hydrolysis at pH 8 to produce sulfuric acid (H_2SO_3), which in turn dissociates. The hydrolysis reaction is pseudo first order with respect to SO_2, with a rate constant of $3.4 \times 10^6 s^{-1}$. To what extent can this reaction be expected to enhance the absorption of SO_2 into the waste stream?

15.5 Example 15.2 described a situation involving the decomposition of ozone to oxygen in water. That situation can be approached by writing a material balance for ozone gas transfer and reaction in a CMBR; i.e.,

$$-QC_{OUT} + \hat{k}_{f,l}(a_s°)_R(C_S - C_{OUT})V_R - kC_{OUT}V_R = 0$$

where C_{OUT} is the exit concentration of ozone in solution. Use this material balance equation and the data provided in the example to obtain the value of k. Discuss why this approach is reasonable.

15.6 A semibatch reactor is set up to measure initial-rates of oxidation of p-nitrophenol (PNP) by ozone at a number of different partial pressures and a temperature of 20°C. The Henry's constant for ozone is 67.7×10^{-3}atm $-$ m^3/mol. The results of the measurements are summarized below.

Initial-Rate of PNP Oxidation (mmol/L-min $\times 10^2$)	Pressure of O_3 in Feed Gas (atm $\times 10^3$)
0.38	5.0
0.54	7.0
0.77	10.0
1.15	15.0

Assume that (1) the oxidation reaction is very slow (which is true at low pH), (2) the stoichiometric ratio of ozone to PNP is 3:1, and (3) the amount of ozone reacted is small compared to the amount fed. PNP is added in excess so that the initial-rate of reaction is pseudo first order with respect to ozone concentration. Because PNP is in excess, it is also reasonable to assume that the bulk ozone concentration is zero. Develop and test a model to determine the volumetric mass transfer coefficient for ozone. [*Hint:* See Beltran et al. (1992).]

Answer: $0.0156 min^{-1}$

15.7 Studies on the ozonation of 2,6-dimethyl-4-nitrophenol (2,6-Me-4-NP) have been reported by Gould and Ulirsch (1992). The pressure of ozone in the feed gas to a semibatch reactor was 0.033 atm. Two different initial concentrations of 2,6-Me-4-NP were used to obtain the following results

	2,6-Me-4-NP Concentration (mmol/L)	
t (min)	$C_{0,1}$	$C_{0,2}$
0	0.164	0.116
0.5	0.146	0.098
1.0	0.128	0.080
1.5	0.110	0.062
2.0	0.092	0.044
2.5	0.074	0.026
3.0	0.056	0.008

The reaction was thought to be fast enough to assume instantaneous reaction. Independent measurements of the volumetric mass transfer coefficient produced a value of about 20 h^{-1}. The stoichiometric ratio of ozone to 2,6-Me-4-NP is 4:1. Determine whether (and discuss why or why not) the rate data support the use of an instantaneous reaction model.

15.8 A zero-order reaction model was proposed by Gould and Ulirsch (1992) to provide a better explanation of the data given in Problem 15.7. The reaction is restricted to the bulk solution phase and fast enough that the ozone concentration is zero at the film-bulk solution interface throughout the rate experiment. The oxidation rate (r_{ox}) for 2,6-Me-4-NP is

$$r_{ox} = -\frac{\hat{k}_{v,l}}{\gamma} C_{S,O_3}$$

Justify the form of this model and use it to reexamine the rate data given in Problem 15.7. Compare the predicted and measured values of the volumetric mass transfer coefficient, $\hat{k}_{v,l}$. [*Hint:* The integral form of the rate expression should be used.]

15.9 A deep lake becomes stratified during the summer months. Oxygen concentrations near the sediment surface drop to zero due to lack of mixing with oxygen-rich water above. The onset of cooler weather in the fall causes the lake to destratify. The dissolved oxygen concentration in the near sediment water suddenly increases from zero to 5 mg/L and remains at this concentration for a protracted period. To what depth of sediment will oxygen reach a level of 1 mg/L at the end of 30 days if the free-liquid diffusion coefficient is $1 \times 10^{-5} \text{cm}^2/\text{s}$, sediment pore tortuosity is 2.0, porosity is 0.5, and there is no reaction within the sediment?

Answer: 6.48 cm.

15.10 A thick layer of sorptive soil lines an artificially created lagoon used for storage of an industrial waste prior to treatment. A question has been raised regarding potential penetration of trichlorophenol (TCP) and trichloroethylene (TCE) through this soil layer into an underlying aquifer over the 10-year period since construction of the lagoon. Batch experiments with soil particles and water containing these two contaminants show that partitioning between the water and soil is linear, with $\mathcal{K}_D = 30\text{cm}^3/\text{g}$ for TCP and $0.3\text{cm}^3/\text{g}$ for TCE.

(a) Determine the concentration profiles for each contaminant in the soil pore water after 10 years if the concentration of each is constant at 10 mg/L at the surface of the soil, the porosity and tortuosity of the soil are 0.4 and 2, respectively, the soil particle density is 2g/cm^3, and the free-liquid diffusivities of TCP and TCE are 8.4×10^{-6} and $7.2 \times 10^{-6}\text{cm}^2/\text{s}$, respectively.

(b) Determine the total mass of each contaminant that has penetrated the soil at the bottom of the lagoon if the surface area of the bottom is 5000 m^2.

Answer: (b) 12 kg of TCP and 13 kg of TCE.

Chapter 16

Multiphase System Modeling and Design

Contents

16.0 CHAPTER OBJECTIVES

To integrate interphase mass transfer rates, reaction rates, re-action energetics, and reactor dynamics in the development of sim-ulation and design models for heterogeneous natural and engineered systems involving two or more phases and associated interphase mass transfer processes.

16.1 INTRODUCTION

This chapter deals with the development of process models to describe hetero-geneous natural systems and design engineered reactors in which components are removed or produced by reactions involving interphase mass transfer processes. These models are developed in much the same way as are those for homogeneous systems in the sense that they include characterization of transport processes that affect the movement and distribution of reactive components. Transport phenomena and their effects on reaction processes in homogeneous systems are usually described at the macroscale (reactor scale). For heterogeneous systems, however, it is necessary also to consider transport between and within reacting phases; i.e., transport processes at the microscale.

Descriptions and designs of natural and engineered environmental systems commonly require application of heterogeneous process reac-tor models. The behavior of contaminants in atmospheric systems and in surface and subsurface aquatic systems is typically affected by both interphase and intraphase mass transfer, and in such cases both processes must be modeled accurately to provide reliable predictions of species fate and transport. Heterogeneous-phase process modeling has a somewhat different goal in its applications to engineered reactor systems. Here we wish to model interphase and intraphase transport processes to determine reactor designs that maximize rates of mass transfer, and thus maximize process rates.

Various reactor configurations can be applied for the design and implemen-tation of engineered systems for two-phase processes, each having specific mass transfer properties. The amounts of surface area available for interphase mass transfer and the path lengths for intraphase transport within reacting media are features that contribute to determination of rates of mass transfer. Fluid velocity is also important because it influences the thickness of boundary layers between phases, and thus associated impedances to mass transfer. Examples of certain types of contactor configurations were given in Figure 15.2 of the previous chapter. Simple illustrations involving these and several other con-figurations are provided in this chapter to demonstrate applications of reactor principles to heterogeneous systems.

16.2 FLUID-SOLID PROCESSES

Fluid-solid reactions require contact of liquids or gases with reactive surfaces. The rate relationships developed in Chapter 15 emphasize that observed rates of reaction incorporate the effects of microscale transport processes. External resistances to mass transfer encountered in boundary layers between fluids and solid surfaces may limit rates at which components arrive at reactive surfaces. Similarly, for microporous and aggregated solids, internal resistances to mass transfer may limit the arrival of components at reactive surface sites incorporated within the solids.

16.2.1 Fixed-Bed Reactor (FBR) Systems

Fluid-solid mass transfer and reaction processes are common in natural environmental systems, and in such engineered separation operations as filtration, ion exchange, adsorption, heterogeneous catalysis, and attached film bioreactors. In most such systems the life-cycle or useful lifetime of the solid phase is very long with respect to its contact time with a specific volume of fluid; i.e., with respect to the HRT of the reactor or system in question. For this reason, the most common reactor configuration is one in which the solid phase is retained within the reactor during its operation. Such a reactor is referred to as a fixed-bed reactor (FBR), several different operating configurations of which are depicted schematically in Figure 16.1.

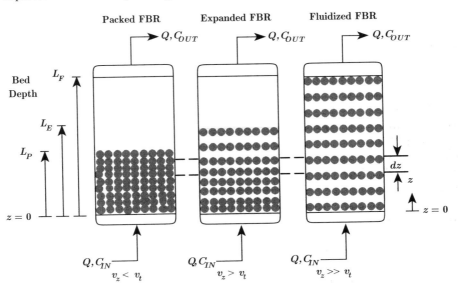

Figure 16.1 Fixed-Bed Reactor Configurations

The operating configurations illustrated in Figure 16.1 all involve upward fluid flow, during which the solid materials or "packings" in *the FBR may: (1) remain packed (i.e., a packed-bed FBR) if the superficial face velocity (v_z) of the fluid phase is less than the terminal settling velocity (v_t) of the solid phase; (2) be expanded (i.e., an expanded-bed FBR) if $v_z > v_t$; or, (3) be fluidized by the flow through the bed (i.e., a fluidized-bed FBR) if $v_z >> v_t$.*

The terms L_P, L_E, and L_F in Figure 16.1 represent the respective heights of the packed, expanded, and fluidized beds of solids during operation.

16.2.2 Film Mass Transfer (FMT) in FBRs

Regardless of which of the operating conditions illustrated in Figure 16.1 applies, the one-dimensional steady-state material balance equation for a differential control volume defined by $A_R dz$ is

---

Steady-State MBE for External Film Mass Transfer within a Differential Control Volume of an FBR

$$dN_z \varepsilon_B A_R + N^\circ (a_s^\circ)_{E,R} A_R dz = 0$$

(16.1)

---

where N_z is the macrotransport flux along the length of the reactor, ε_B is the bed porosity, N° is the microscale transport flux at and normal to the surfaces of the particles of packing material, $(a_s^\circ)_{E,R}$ is the specific external surface area of the solid phase available for reaction per volume of reactor, and A_R is the cross-sectional area (assumed constant along z) of the reactor. For spherical particles of diameter, d_p, $(a_s^\circ)_{E,R}$ is given by

$$(a_s^\circ)_{E,R} = \frac{6(1 - \varepsilon_B)}{d_p}$$

(16.2)

We note that Equation 16.1 is predicated on an assumption of steady-state conditions. These conditions of operation will in fact be assumed for all reactor MBEs developed in this Chapter. Parallel cases of non-steady state reactor operation are developed in Chapter 11 of PDES. The assumption of steady-state has to be carefully assessed for validity in the case of heterogeneous phase reactors. For example, steady-state exists in an FBR only if the net rate of the accompanying surface reaction does not change with time. This is the case, for example, for gas-phase or dissolved contaminants undergoing transformation upon contact with catalyst particles such as titanium dioxide, enzymes immobilized on a support medium, or biocatalysts; i.e., microorganisms attached to support media, but neither accumulating upon nor otherwise altering these catalysts. The assumption is not valid if the surface of the catalyst is in any way depleted or inactivated by the reaction or, as in FBR adsorbers, by accumulation of adsorbed materials.

The longitudinal flux when macroscale transport is limited to advection (i.e., a PFR flow condition) is given by $N_z = v_{p,z}C$, where $v_{p,z}$ is the interstitial or "pore" velocity. Interstitial velocity, $v_{p,z}$, is related to the superficial ("Darcy" or approach) velocity, v_z, by

$$v_{p,z} = \frac{v_z}{\varepsilon_B} \tag{16.3}$$

Substitution of this relationship into Equation 16.1 and division of the resulting equation by the differential volume, $A_R dz$, yields the one-dimensional point form of the continuity equation for an FBR operating at steady-state conditions

$$-v_z\frac{dC}{dz} + N^\circ(a_s^\circ)_{E,R} = 0 \tag{16.4}$$

The flux normal and immediately adjacent to the surface of the sphere, N° can then be described by the linear driving force film model for interphase mass transfer

$$N^\circ = k_f(C_b - C^\circ) \tag{16.5}$$

where C_b and C° are the concentrations in the bulk and immediately adjacent to the surface, respectively. Substituting the above expression into the material balance relationship given in Equation 16.4 for steady-state operation yields

---

**PFR Steady-State MBE for an
FBR with Film Mass Transfer**

$$-v_z\frac{dC}{dz} + k_f(a_s^\circ)_{E,R}(C_b - C^\circ) = 0$$

(16.6)

16.2.3 FMT and Surface Reaction in FBRs

It is necessary to relate C° to C_b in order to solve Equation 16.6. At steady state, the flux at (and normal to) the surface must equal the rate of surface reaction. It was shown in Chapter 15 for a first-order surface reaction ($r^\circ = -k^\circ C^\circ$), for example that

$$C^\circ = \frac{k_f C_b}{k_f + k^\circ} \tag{15.8}$$

When external film mass transfer (FMT) controls (i.e., $k_f \ll k^\circ$ and $C^\circ \ll C_b$) we can approximate $(C_b - C^\circ)$ in Equation 16.6 by C_b. This allows separation of variables and integration to yield

$$\frac{C_b}{C_{IN}} = exp\left(-\frac{k_f(a_s^\circ)_{E,R}}{v_z}\right)z \tag{16.7}$$

where C_{IN} is the bulk concentration entering the reactor and C_b is the bulk concentration at any distance, z, along the length of the reactor. For a reactor of length, L, we note that

$$\frac{L}{v_z} = \bar{t} \tag{16.8}$$

where $\bar{t}$ is the mean hydraulic residence time (HRT). In the case of reactors containing solids, such as fixed-bed reactors, the mean HRT for the reactor if it were empty of solids is referred to as the empty bed contact time (EBCT). The overall extent of reaction for the FBR as given by Equation 16.7 for $z = L$ and $C_b = C_{OUT}$ can then be expressed as

> **PFR Design Equation for an FBR**
> **with FMT Rate Control**
>
> $$\frac{C_{OUT}}{C_{IN}} = exp\left[-k_f(a_s^\circ)_{E,R}\bar{t}\right]$$

$$\tag{16.9}$$

A similar analysis can be made even when external resistance to flux at the surface is not entirely rate controlling, as long as the value of k_f for FMT and k° for the surface reaction are of similar magnitude. Equation 15.8 shows that the surface concentration, C°, would then be a significant fraction of the bulk concentration, C_b. Substitution for C° from Equation 15.8 into Equation 16.6 leads to

> **PFR Design Equation for an FBR with FMT**
> **and Surface Reaction Rate Control**
>
> $$\frac{C_{OUT}}{C_{IN}} = exp\left[-\frac{k_f k^\circ(a_s^\circ)_{E,R}\bar{t}}{k_f + k^\circ}\right]$$

$$\tag{16.10}$$

The foregoing analysis can be extended to nonideal reactors, wherein macroscale transport along the length of the reactor occurs by both advection and dispersion. The material balance relationship given by Equation 16.1 still holds, but the flux, N_x, along the length of the reactor is now the sum of advection and dispersion, yielding the steady-state plug flow with dispersion and reaction model described in Chapters 3 and 11 modified to account for the presence of a reactive solid packing material; i.e.

> **PFDR Steady-State MBE for an**
> **FBR with Film Mass Transfer**
>
> $$-v_z\frac{dC}{dz} + \varepsilon_B \mathcal{D}_d\frac{d^2C}{dz^2} + k_f(a_s^\circ)_{E,R}(C_b - C^\circ) = 0$$

$$\tag{16.11}$$

Substituting for C° for a first-order surface reaction and defining a dimensionless length $(\zeta^\circ = z/L)$ yields

$$-\frac{dC}{d\zeta^\circ} + \frac{\varepsilon_B \mathcal{D}_d}{v_z L} \frac{d^2 C_b}{d(\zeta^\circ)^2} + \frac{k_f(a_s^\circ)_{E,R} k^\circ}{k_f + k^\circ} \frac{L}{v_z} C_b = 0 \qquad (16.12)$$

Two dimensionless groups emerge; the FBR dispersion number, $\mathcal{N}_d = \varepsilon_B \mathcal{D}_d / v_z L$, and the product of the observed rate constant and the empty-bed hydraulic residence time, L/v_z. The solution to this ordinary differential equation has a form similar to that given in Equation 11.33 for a first-order homogeneous reaction

---

**PFDR Design Equation for an FBR
with FMT and Surface Reaction**

$$\frac{C_{OUT}}{C_{IN}} = \frac{4\beta_D exp\ \alpha_D}{(1 + \beta_D)^2 exp\ \alpha_D \beta_D - (1 - \beta_D)^2 exp - \alpha_D \beta_D} \qquad (16.13)$$

The differences between the two lie in the definitions of: 1) the dispersion number, which for an FBR incorporates the bed porosity, ε_B (i.e., $\mathcal{N}_d = \varepsilon_B \mathcal{D}_d / v_z L$); and, 2) the rate coefficients and the HRTs in the dimensionless groups that appear in β_D. For a reaction that is completely controlled by external film mass transfer

---

**FMT
Rate
Control**
$$\beta_D = \left[1 + 4k_f(a_s^\circ)_{E,R} \bar{t} \left(\frac{\varepsilon_B \mathcal{D}_d}{v_z L} \right) \right]^{0.5} \qquad (16.14)$$

---

and for a reaction in which external mass transfer is significant but not entirely rate controlling

---

Coupled FMT and Surface Reaction Rate Control

$$\beta_D = \left[1 + 4 \left(\frac{k_f(a_s^\circ)_{E,R} k^\circ}{k_f + k^\circ} \right) \bar{t} \left(\frac{\varepsilon_B \mathcal{D}_d}{v_z L} \right) \right]^{0.5} \qquad (16.15)$$

The models above are based on steady-state conditions, that, as noted earlier, can exist for catalytic surface reactions as long as the surface concentration remains constant over time at every location in the reactor. This circumstance is illustrated in the model applications described in Example 16.1 for a catalytic oxidation process. Conversely, for sorption processes in FBRs, steady state is not attained because sorption results in continuous accumulation of sorbate, and thus surface concentrations that change over time. For FBR adsorbers the exit concentration of the reactor increases over time, eventually reaching the feed concentration as the surfaces of the adsorbent become saturated. Analyses of FBRs under nonsteady conditions of this type are discussed in Chapter 11 of PDES.

Example 16.1. An Advanced Oxidation Process for Treatment of an Herbicide Contaminated Water Supply. (Determination of reactor specifications for a heterogeneous catalytic process in an FBR.)

- **Situation.** A UV-light-activated catalyst material is being developed for oxidation of atrazine, a pre-emergent herbicide occasionally found in raw water supply sources. The surface reaction rate $(mol/cm^2 - s)$ has been found in CMBR experiments to follow a first-order model with a rate constant, k°, of 0.01 cm/s. The presence of certain other constituents in the water, however, can cause catalyst poisoning, which reduces k° to 0.001 cm/s. Although the catalyst material is available only as very fine powder, it can be coated onto an inert support medium comprised by spherical particles having diameters in the range of 0.8 to 1.5 mm. The proposed design is a fixed-bed reactor. A first-cut analysis of reactor design is needed to determine the effect of reactor hydrodynamics, support-medium size, and catalyst poisoning on the empty-bed contact time (EBCT) required to achieve 95 percent removal of atrazine.

- **Question(s).** Develop a general approach for analysis of the proposed reactor system.

- **Logic and Answer(s).**

    1. An ideal plug flow reactor assumption would yield the lowest estimate of the required EBCT, but attainment of ideal plug flow under these circumstances is not realistic. Reactor hydrodynamics will be influenced by the size of the support media and by the interstitial velocity. A PFDR model would thus appear more reasonable for description of the proposed FBR. To assess the differences between PFR model predictions and those given by incorporation of dispersion effects (i.e., a PFDR model), we will perform both analyses.

    2. The PFR model is considered first. To begin the analysis, we need to determine the external mass transfer coefficient, k_f, by way of a mass transfer correlation. A number of such correlations exist for a variety of different conditions (Chapter 4, PDES) one of which is the Gnielinski correlation

$$\mathcal{N}_{Sh} = (2 + 0.644\mathcal{N}_{Re}^{0.5}\mathcal{N}_{Sc}^{0.33})[1 + 1.5(1 - \varepsilon_B)]$$

3. *We assume or determine the following values for this application of the Gnielinski correlation*

$\varepsilon_B = 0.4$ *(typical value)*

$d_p = 0.8$ *mm (measured)*

$v_z = 4$ *m/h (typical value)*

$\mathcal{D}_l = 6.3 \times 10^{-6} cm^2/s$ *(obtained from Wilke-Chang correlation)*

$\nu_v = 8.96 \times 10^{-3} cm^2/s$ *(given).*

4. *For these conditions, the Reynolds number is*

$$\mathcal{N}_{Re} = \frac{d_p v_{p,z}}{\nu_v} = \frac{d_p(v_z/\varepsilon_B)}{\nu_v} = 2.5$$

the Schmidt number is

$$\mathcal{N}_{Sc} = \frac{\nu_v}{\mathcal{D}_l} = 1422$$

and, the Sherwood number is determined from the Gnielinski correlation to be

$$\mathcal{N}_{Sh} = 25.4$$

5. *The mass transfer coefficient is then calculated as*

$$k_f = \frac{\mathcal{N}_{Sh}\mathcal{D}_l}{d_p} = 2 \times 10^{-3} cm/s$$

6. *The steady-state PFR effluent concentration relationship for an FBR with first-order reaction at the surface of the solid is given by Equation 16.10*

$$\frac{C_{OUT}}{C_{IN}} = exp\left[-\frac{k_f k^\circ (a_s^\circ)_{E,R}\bar{t}}{k_f + k^\circ}\right]$$

Rearranging to solve for the required EBCT gives

$$\bar{t} = \left[\frac{k_f + k^\circ}{k_f k^\circ (a_s^\circ)_{E,R}}\right] ln\frac{C_{IN}}{C_{OUT}}$$

where $(a_s^\circ)_{E,R} = 6(1 - \varepsilon_b)/dp = 45$. Thus, the EBCT required for 95% removal is

$$\bar{t} = \frac{0.002 + 0.01}{0.002 \times 0.01 \times 45} ln\ 20 = 40s$$

Changing the approach velocity and particle diameter will change k_f and $(a_s^\circ)_{E,R}$.

7. *If dispersion is now included, Equation 16.13 provides the solution for Equation 16.11*

$$\frac{C_{OUT}}{C_{IN}} = \frac{4\beta_D exp\ \alpha_D}{(1 + \beta_D)^2 exp\ \alpha_D\beta_D - (1 - \beta_D)^2 exp - \alpha_D\beta_D}$$

and, Equation 16.15 defines β_D

$$\beta_D = \left(1 + 4\left(\frac{k_f(a_s^\circ)_{E,R}k^\circ}{k_f + k^\circ}\right)\bar{t}\left(\frac{\varepsilon_B \mathcal{D}_d}{v_z L}\right)\right)^{0.5}$$

An implicit solution technique is needed to find the EBCT for a given percentage removal. Alternatively, a convenient graphical form of the solution of the very similar PFDR relationship given in Equation 11.33 for a first order reaction is provided in Figure 11.10. The lumped "rate constant" in the above term β_D required to use the graph is given by

$$k = \frac{k_f k^\circ (a_s^\circ)_{E,R}}{k_f + k^\circ} = 0.075 s^{-1}$$

8. *It would be necessary in practice to determine the dispersion number experimentally for the packed reactor at different flow rates. To illustrate the effect of dispersion, we assume that the dispersion number is 1 in which case $\beta_D = (1 + 4k\bar{t})^{0.5}$. For a residual fractional concentration of 0.05, Figure 11.10 shows that $k\bar{t} \approx 8$, and then*

$$\bar{t} = \frac{8}{0.075} = 107s$$

The effect of dispersion is thus to increase the EBCT from 40s to 107s.

9. *The effect of superficial velocity, particle diameter, and catalyst poisoning (i.e., a decrease in k°) on the EBCT can be explored for both the PFR and PFDR models using the approach shown above. For simplicity, we assume that bed porosity, ε_B, does not change with particle diameter. The results are shown in the table below, in which the entries are EBCTs in seconds.*

Velocity and Particle Diameter	PFR Model		PFDR Model	
	Normal Catalyst, $k^\circ =$ 0.01 cm/s	Poisoned Catalyst, $k^\circ =$ 0.001 cm/s	Normal Catalyst, $k^\circ =$ 0.01 cm/s	Poisoned Catalyst, $k^\circ =$ 0.001 cm/s
$v_x = 4$ m/h				
$d_p = 0.8$ mm	40	100	107	258
$d_p = 1.5$ mm	55	115	141	297
$v_x = 8$ m/h				
$d_p = 0.8$ mm	32	92	82	236
$d_p = 1.5$ mm	42	102	109	264

10. *The effect of superficial velocity is to increase the Reynolds number, and the mass transfer coefficient, k_f, is thus increased. An increase in k_f decreases the required EBCT, but the amount is determined by the extent of rate control offered by external resistance. When the catalyst is not poisoned, the external resistance is almost entirely rate*

controlling ($k_f << k^\circ$) and a doubling of superficial velocity reduces the EBCT by 20 to 24% (depending on particle diameter and type of reactor). The lower rate constant associated with the poisoned catalyst causes rate control to shift to the surface reaction. Thus, doubling the superficial velocity reduces the EBCT by only about 8 to 11%. Particle size affects the magnitude of the Reynolds number and the specific external surface area available for reaction $(a_s^\circ)_{E,R}$. The net effect is that increasing the particle diameter increases the EBCT for all situations examined in the table. The effect of catalyst poisoning is to increase the EBCT. The increase in EBCT is greater at the higher superficial velocity, because k_f has increased and rate control has shifted more toward the surface reaction.

- *Key Point(s). Reactor models that properly account for each of the transport, mass transfer, and reaction processes involved in complex systems facilitate the identification of design and operating parameters and conditions that can be adjusted and controlled to meet overall process objectives in cost-effective manners.*

16.2.4   Intraparticle Mass Transfer (IMT) in FBRs

Most of the reactive surfaces of microporous sorbents, ion-exchange media, and heterogeneous catalysts are contained within individual particles. The internal surface areas of such materials are typically 300 to 1000 m^2/g, while their external surface areas are generally small by comparison. For a particle having a diameter of 0.2 cm and a density of 1.5 g/cm^3, for example, the external surface area is only 30 cm^2/g. The extent of reaction per unit volume of particle, and thus per unit volume of a fixed-bed reactor, can therefore be much greater for porous materials than for nonporous materials.

Porous catalysts have been used for years in a variety of industrial processes, and a number of porous materials that catalyze specific oxidation or reduction reactions are commercially available for water and wastewater treatment applications. Many important fixed-bed reactor applications of microporous media that inherently involve catalysis-type reactions are found in water and wastewater treatment processes. Activated carbon adsorbents with microorganisms attached to their external surfaces, for example, comprise biological catalysts. In this case substrates adsorbing from solution undergo biodegradation while diffusing through the assemblage of attached microorganisms. The adsorption and oxidation of free and combined chlorine on the surfaces of activated carbon provides another example. Strictly speaking, chlorine reduction by carbon is not a true catalytic process because surface reaction sites are slowly depleted;

nonetheless, the general notion of this being a diffusion-with-reaction process is valid. The diffusive intraparticle transport of solutes that simply adsorb on surfaces within the micropore structures of noncatalytic adsorbents and ion-exchange materials is similarly a diffusion-with-reaction process, although it is one that involves a much more complex, nonsteady, equilibrium-approaching reaction between solid and liquid phases. Unsteady-state FBRs of this type, including many natural systems involving microporous adsorption or ion-exchange media (e.g., zeolites, clays, shales), configured in a way that allows them to be modeled as FBRs, are treated in detail in Chapter 11 of PDES.

The steady-state material balance over an element of an FBR in which a surface reaction occurs internal to particles of the packing material is given by

> **Steady-State MBE for Internal Surface Reaction in a Differential Control Volume of an FBR**
>
> $$dN_x \varepsilon_B A_R + \boldsymbol{r}^\circ_{obs}(a^\circ_s)_{I,P}(1 - \varepsilon_B)A_R dx = 0$$

(16.16)

where $\boldsymbol{r}^\circ_{obs}$ is the specific surface reaction rate in mass or moles per unit time per unit area, $(a^\circ_s)_{I,P}$ is the specific internal surface area per unit particle volume, and

$$1 - \varepsilon_B = \frac{total\ particle\ volume}{volume\ of\ bed}$$

(16.17)

If advection is the only significant mechanism for macrotransport in the FBR, the resulting point form of Equation 16.16 is

> **PFR Steady-State MBE for an FBR with Internal Surface Reaction**
>
> $$-v_z \frac{dC}{dz} + \boldsymbol{r}^\circ_{obs}(a^\circ_s)_{I,P}(1 - \varepsilon_B) = 0$$

(16.18)

For first-order internal surface reactions (ISR) accompanied by strong intraparticle mass transfer (IMT) limitations in spherical particles of radius R, Equation 16.18 can be closely approximated as

> **PFR Steady State MBE for an FBR with IMT and First-Order ISR**
>
> $$-v_z \frac{dC}{dz} - (1 - \varepsilon_B)\frac{3}{R}\left[\mathcal{D}_e k^\circ (a^\circ_s)_{I,P}\right]^{0.5} C = 0$$

(16.19)

A more compact expression can be written by recognizing that the product of $(1 - \varepsilon_B)$ and $3/R$ is $(a^\circ_s)_{E,R}$ the external surface area of a sphere per volume of reactor (see Equation 16.2).

Integration of Equation 16.19 by separation of variables gives

$$\frac{C_{OUT}}{C_{IN}} = exp\left\{-(a_s^\circ)_{E,R}\left[\mathcal{D}_e k^\circ(a_s^\circ)_{I,P}\right]^{0.5}\bar{t}\right\} \qquad (16.20)$$

This solution is analogous to the PFR model for external impedance with simultaneous reaction in packed FBRs (see Equation 16.9). The effects of important process design parameters on reactor performance are clear. For a given reactant, increased removal may be accomplished by increasing (1) the surface area per unit volume of bed $(a_s^\circ)_{E,R}$, (2) the internal surface area per unit volume of particle $(a_s^\circ)_{I,P}$, or (3) the empty-bed mean residence time $(\bar{t})$. External surface area can be increased by employing particles of smaller diameter, but internal surface area can be increased only by changing the physical character of the catalyst material. Equation 16.20 also indicates that removal is *reactant dependent*; that is, for a given reaction energy, reactants that diffuse more rapidly are removed more effectively. The dependence on diffusion rate is expected because the process model assumes that internal mass transport impedance is dominated by intraparticle diffusion control.

Reactor analysis when macrotransport includes advection, dispersion, and internal impedance control parallels that presented earlier for external impedance control. For a reaction that is intrinsically first-order and for which the internal process is strongly diffusion controlled the appropriate FBR-PFDR model is given by

$$\boxed{\begin{array}{c} \textbf{\textit{PFDR Steady State MBE for an FBR}} \\ \textbf{\textit{with IMT and First-Order ISR}} \\[4pt] -v_z\dfrac{dC}{dz} + \varepsilon_B\mathcal{D}_d\dfrac{d^2C}{dz^2} - (a_s^\circ)_{E,R}\left(\mathcal{D}_e k^\circ(a_s^\circ)_{I,P}\right)^{0.5}C = 0 \end{array}} \qquad (16.21)$$

This equation is of the same form as Equation 16.11, and its solution thus has the same general form as given in Equations 16.13 through 16.15, the only difference relating to definition of the rate constant, which in Equation 16.21 is given by the expression $(a_s^\circ)_{E,R}\left(\mathcal{D}_e k^\circ(a_s^\circ)_{I,P}\right)^{0.5}$.

A practical application of the foregoing relationships to the characterization and quantification of coupled diffusion and reaction in microporous media for a typical water and waste treatment process is given in Example 16.2.

Example 16.2. Activated Carbon Catalysis of Ammonia Oxidation by Chlorine. (Analysis of a chemical reaction accompanied by intraparticle transport in a microporous solid.)

- **Situation.** One means for removing ammonia from waters and wastewaters involves reacting it with chlorine to form monochloramine in a homogeneous substitutive oxidation reaction, with subsequent complete oxidation *of nitrogen to N_2 by heterogeneous catalysis on the surfaces of activated carbon. The second reaction can be envisioned as a two-step process in which monochloramine reacts with active surface sites, S_{AC}, on the carbon in one step to produce surface oxide sites, $S_{AC}O$*

$$NH_2Cl + H_2O + S_{AC} \rightarrow NH_3 + H^+ + Cl^- + S_{AC}O$$

The surface oxide sites in turn react with more monochloramine to produce N_2 and regenerated active sites

$$2NH_2Cl + S_{AC}O \rightarrow N_2 + H_2O + 2Cl^- + S_{AC}$$

These reactions take place at sites internal to the activated carbon. Pore diffusion thus often dominates overall transformation rates. Rate experiments have shown that the surface reaction is first order with respect to monochloramine and that the surface reaction rate constant, k°, is 1.6×10^{-9} cm/s.

- **Question(s).** *To evaluate the feasibility of this process for a particular application you decide to build a small pilot-scale reactor with materials that are readily available in the plant laboratory. These include a bag of fairly uniform activated carbon having a mean particle diameter of 0.15 cm and a specific internal surface area per unit weight $(a^\circ_{s,w})_P$, of 1000 m^2/g, and a fixed-speed pump and a column of specific capacity and size, which together provide a superficial velocity of 4 m/h and an empty-bed contact time (EBCT) of 8 min. Estimate the removal of monochloramine that might be expected at steady state in the pilot plant. What would the anticipated monochloramine removal have been had you employed a similar grade of activated carbon having a particle diameter of 0.05 cm?*

- **Logic and Answer(s).**

  1. *For the purpose of simplicity, assume that the pilot column behaves as an ideal PFR.*

  2. *The following information is available*
     - *Bed porosity (ε_B) = 0.4 (measured)*
     - *Solid phase density (ρ_s) = 2.1 g/cm^3 (measured)*
     - *Particle porosity (ε_P) = 0.66 (measured)*
     - *Effective diffusivity $(\mathcal{D}_e)$ of monochloramine = 5.5×10^{-6} cm^2/s (assumes a tortuousity factor of 2)*

  3. *The specific-internal surface area per unit volume of particle is calculated as*

  $$(a^\circ_s)_{I,P} = (a^\circ_{s,w})_{I,P}(1-\varepsilon_B)\rho_s = 10^7 \times (1-0.66) \times 2.1 = 7.14 \times 106 \ cm^{-1}$$

  and for a particle diameter of 0.15 cm $(R = 0.075$ cm$)$, the external surface area of spherical (assumed) particles per unit volume of *reactor is given by*

$$(a_s^\circ)_{E,R} = (1 - \varepsilon_B)\frac{3}{R} = (1 - 0.4)\frac{3}{0.075} = 24 \; cm^{-1}$$

4. From Equation 16.20 we can calculate C_{OUT}/C_{IN} as

$$\frac{C_{OUT}}{C_{IN}} = exp\left\{-(a_s^\circ)_{E,R}\left[\mathcal{D}_e k^\circ (a_s^\circ)_{I,P}\right]^{0.5}\bar{t}\right\}$$

$$= exp\left\{-24 \; cm^{-1}\left[5.5 \times 10^{-6} \; cm^2 s^{-1}\left(1.6 \times 10^{-9} \; cms^{-1}\right)\right.\right.$$
$$\left.\left. \times \left(7.14 \times 10^6 \; cm^{-1}\right)\right]^{0.5}(8)(60) \; s\right\}$$

$$= exp\left\{-24 \; cm^{-1}\left[2.51 \times 10^{-4} \; cms\right] 480s\right\}$$

$$= exp\left\{-2.89\right\} = 0.06$$

or, an expected removal of 94%.

- **Key Point(s).** *You will note that Equations 16.20 and 16.21 have been specifically identified as being applicable to first order reactions accompanied by strong intraparticle limitations on reaction rate. In the particular situation given above the parameters involved actually result in only modest intraparticle transport limitations and the percentage removal calculated is an overestimate of what will actually be achieved.*

    In order to achieve 95% removal for the given reaction and diffusion rates and contact time the particle size of the carbon would have to be reduced by approximately a factor of three from 0.15 cm to about 0.05 cm. Methods to assess the relative significance of simultaneous reaction and diffusion processes in porous solids in terms of a parameter referred to as the Thiele modulus, and alternative design equations for different circumstances are given in Chapter 10 of PDES.

Design equations for processes involving intrinsic first-order reactions coupled with various types of external and internal impedances are presented and application of these relationships in the interpretation of rate limitations and formulation of design equations for a water and waste treatment processes are given in Chapter 10 of PDES.

16.3 GAS-LIQUID PROCESSES

16.3.1 Alternative Reactor Configurations

Reactors involving gas-liquid exchanges and reactions are frequently employed in water and wastewater treatment, and commonly found in natural systems. In engineered systems, for example, gaseous reagents such as ozone, chlorine dioxide, and chlorine are dissolved into water to serve as oxidants and disinfectants. Stripping operations using air for removal of unwanted dissolved gases such as carbon dioxide, ammonia, hydrogen sulfide, and volatile organic chemicals, either by sparging air through water or by dispersing water droplets into air, are standard treatment procedures.

We confine our discussion in this chapter to the general principles of reactor analysis and draw upon a few salient illustrations, focusing on dissolution of gases accompanied by reaction. Ozone is an especially interesting example because it undergoes auto-decomposition while simultaneously oxidizing other species. The intrinsic rates of such reactions may range from very slow to very fast, with interphase mass transfer being important in both cases. Reactions that are slow occur in bulk solution but are controlled by interphase mass transfer. Fast reactions occur simultaneously with diffusion through interfacial regions. The rate relationships developed in Chapter 9 are applied here for different reactor configurations.

A variety of different devices and reactor configurations can be used for absorption and stripping of gases and volatile inorganic and organic chemicals. Some of the more common reactor schemes are illustrated in Figure 16.2. The choice of reactor configuration is usually driven by economic considerations. A CMFR (Figure 16.2a) is commonly used to sparge gas into water. Referred to as a bubble sparger, this type of reactor is used to transfer gaseous forms of oxidants (e.g., ozone) into solution for oxidation and disinfection reactions, or to transfer volatile organic chemicals from solution into air bubbles. Mechanical surface aeration (Figure 16.2b) may be used to transfer oxygen from the atmosphere into solution to accommodate chemical oxidations of such inorganic species as iron (II), biochemical oxidations of various organic chemicals, or to strip volatile organic chemicals from solution. A bubble contactor (Figure 16.2c) involving either co-current or countercurrent flow of water and gas bubbles in a tower configuration can be used for the same purposes. Advection and dispersion may be important in both water and gas phases in this type of reactor. The packed-tower contactor shown in Figure 16.2d is often used for gas absorption or stripping of volatile contaminants. Again, flow of water and air can be either co-current or countercurrent. A variety of commercial packing materials is available to create surface area and promote mass transfer. While often modeled as PFRs, dispersion may be important in both the gas and liquid phases in packed FBR systems of this type.

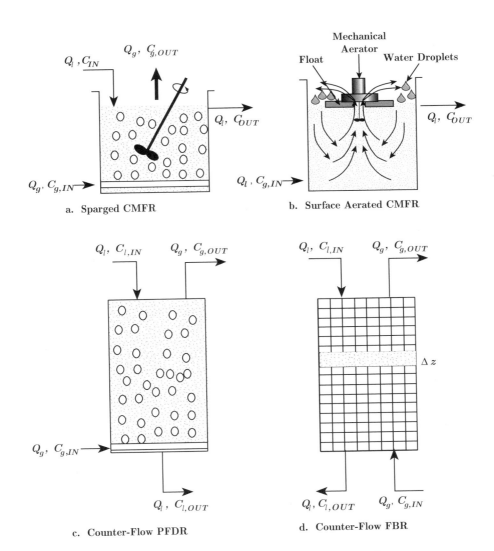

Figure 16.2 *Typical Gas-Liquid Contact Systems*

16.3.2   Mass Transfer and Reaction in CMFRs

The general liquid-phase material balance for gas sparging of a liquid in a CMFR, as depicted in Figure 16.2a, is

$$
\boxed{
\begin{array}{c}
\textbf{\textit{Steady-State Liquid-Phase MBE}} \\
\textbf{\textit{for Gas Sparging in a CMFR}} \\[6pt]
Q_l C_{l,IN} - Q_l C_{l,OUT} + N_l (a_s^\circ)_R V_R + r V_R = 0
\end{array}
}
\qquad (16.22)
$$

in which N_l is the flux of a constituent into or out of the liquid phase, V_R the volume of the reactor, and $(a_s^\circ)_R$ the specific mass transfer surface area (i.e., of bubbles) per unit volume of reactor. If N_l is positive, one or more constituents of the sparging gas phase are transferred into solution (i.e., absorbed); conversely, if N_l is negative, one or more constituents of the liquid phase are transferred out of solution (i.e., stripped).

A common example of a gas-liquid absorption process is the oxygenation of water by the sparging of air into a CMFR. The subsequent liquid phase reaction in such cases often involves the oxidation of iron (II) to iron (III) or of sulfur (-II) to elemental sulfur (0). In both cases the oxidation products can then be removed by sedimentation and/or filtration. Gas absorption phenomena accompanied by very fast liquid-phase reactions require consideration of simultaneous diffusion and reaction in liquid interfacial films. This approach to reactor modeling is described and illustrated for first-order interfacial film reactions in Chapter 10 of PDES. For the present discussion we will assume that no significant reaction occurs within liquid interfacial films, in which case, for a first-order bulk liquid phase reaction (LPR), Equation 16.22 becomes

$$
\boxed{
\begin{array}{c}
\textbf{\textit{Liquid-Phase MBE for Gas Sparging in a CMFR}} \\
\textbf{\textit{with FMT and First-Order LPR}} \\[6pt]
Q_l C_{l,IN} - Q_l C_{l,OUT} + k_f (a_s^\circ)_R (C_{l,e} - C_{l,OUT}) V_R - \\
k C_{l,OUT} V_R = 0
\end{array}
}
\qquad (16.23)
$$

Note that in this case the flux into the liquid phase is positive while the liquid-phase reaction leads to depletion of the constituent, and thus carries a negative sign.

If we assume further that the feed stream does not contain the dissolved gas, Equation 16.23 can be written as

$$
C_{l,OUT} = \frac{k_f (a_s^\circ)_R C_{l,e} \bar{t}}{1 + k \bar{t} + k_f (a_s^\circ)_R \bar{t}}
\qquad (16.24)
$$

or, more conveniently

$$
\boxed{
\begin{array}{ll}
\textbf{\textit{Design Equation}} \\
\textbf{\textit{for a Gas-Sparged}} \quad C_{l,OUT} = \dfrac{C_{l,e}}{\dfrac{1}{k_f(a_s^\circ)_R \bar{t}} + \dfrac{k}{k_f(a_s^\circ)_R} + 1} \\
\textbf{\textit{CMFR Absorber}}
\end{array}
}
\qquad (16.25)
$$

Inspection of Equation 16.25 reveals that as $k_f(a_s^\circ)_R$ increases, the equilibrium concentration, $(C_{l,e})$, of the constituent of interest in the liquid-phase reactor effluent approaches the saturation or solubility limit corresponding to the partial pressure of the gas in the system, as given by Henrys law. Substituting $C_{l,e}$ for $C_{l,OUT}$ in Equation 16.23 shows clearly that the rate of reaction is no longer limited by mass transfer, and that the reaction rate within the CMFR is thus simply $kC_{l,e}$. We note also that the exit concentration is increased by increasing the hydraulic detention time for a given mass transfer system [i.e., for a given $k_f(a_s^\circ)_R$]. Because reaction occurs in the bulk solution, however, $C_{l,e}$ can never be achieved. Increasing the reaction rate constant for a given $k_f(a_s^\circ)_R$ and $\bar{t}$ causes the exit concentration to decrease.

The stripping or release of gases or volatile organic chemicals from solution phase to gas phase is analyzed in a manner similar to the absorption of gases from vapor phase into solution, except that the concentration in solution phase now decreases as a result of the mass transfer process. The appropriate steady-state liquid-phase material balance relationship for mass transfer in the absence of reaction is then

$$
QC_{l,IN} - QC_{l,OUT} + k_f(a_s^\circ)_R(C_{l,e} - C_{l,OUT})V_R = 0 \qquad (16.26)
$$

the same as that given by Equation 16.23 if the reaction term is neglected. However, for a stripping operation to be effective the condition $C_{l,e} < C_{l,OUT}$ is necessary (i.e., for the direction of flux to be into the gas phase) and so the mass transfer term of Equation 16.26 automatically becomes negative (i.e., $C_{l,e} - C_{l,OUT} < 0$).

If a surface aerator is used to bring droplets of water into contact with the open atmosphere for purposes of stripping a volatile dissolved compound into the air, as illustrated in Figure 16.2b, the gas phase concentration of the volatile chemical is assumed to remain at zero due to its large dilution in the atmosphere; thus, $C_{l,e}$ in Equation 16.26 must also be zero. The resulting design equation is

$$
\boxed{
\begin{array}{ll}
\textbf{\textit{Design Equation}} \\
\textbf{\textit{for a Surface-Aerated}} \quad \dfrac{C_{l,OUT}}{C_{l,IN}} = \dfrac{1}{1 + k_f(a_s^\circ)_R \bar{t}} \\
\textbf{\textit{CMFR Stripper}}
\end{array}
}
\qquad (16.27)
$$

Conversely, as discussed in the next session, if a bubble contactor (Figure 16.2c) is used for stripping, the gas phase concentration of the volatile compound is zero only at the bubble inlet position. As the air bubbles rise, their gas-phase concentrations increase, and $C_{l,e}$ increases correspondingly. The specific surface area, $(a_s^\circ)_R$, involved in the case of surface aeration is the surface area of the water droplets generated per unit volume of the reactor. This of course differs from that involved in the cases of both sparging systems and bubble contact reactors.

16.3.3   Mass Transfer in Counter-Flow PFDRs

The mass transfer rate of a dissolved gas or volatile chemical from solution into a single rising bubble in a counter-flow PFDR such as that shown in Figure 16.2c is

$$\textbf{\textit{Rate of Mass Transfer from a Rising Bubble}} \quad V_B \frac{dC_g}{dt_b} = -k_f A_B^\circ (C_g - C_{g,e}) \tag{16.28}$$

where t_b is the travel time of the rising bubble, C_g is the concentration of the volatile compound in the gas phase (mol/L^3), $C_{g,e}$ its concentration in the gas phase were it in equilibrium with the liquid-phase concentration at that instant in time, V_B the volume of the bubble, and A_B° the surface area of the bubble, and k_f the film mass transfer coefficient. Note that by following the change in gas-phase concentration as the bubble rises, we adopt a Lagrangian analytical perspective.

If a more sophisticated two-film model is used, as briefly referenced in Chapter 15 (Section 15.3.1) and described in detail in Chapters 4 and 10 of PDES, then the k_f in Equation 16.28 becomes the gas side mass transfer coefficient, which is given by dividing the liquid side mass transfer coefficient.

The projected surface area of all the bubbles in the reactor is

$$(A_B^\circ)_T = \frac{Q_g \bar{t}_b}{V_B} A_B^\circ \tag{16.29}$$

in which Q_g is the gas flow rate ($L^3 t^{-1}$) and $\bar{t}_b$ is the average residence time of the rising bubbles, assuming that they rise in a manner simulating plug flow.

The latter point raises a question about use of the term PFDR to describe this type of reactor. While the bubble field is assumed to be rising in a "plug-flow" pattern, the reality is that these bubbles will generate some mixing of fluid elements in the aqueous phase. The dispersion caused by mixing of fluid elements in the aqueous phase will depend on the size, total volume, and velocity of the rising bubbles. Under some conditions such dispersion may approach that associated with the liquid phase in a CMFR. This point will momentarily surface again in the context of modeling flow in the liquid phase.

Substitution of Equation 16.29 into Equation 16.28 gives

$$\frac{dC_g}{dt_b} = -k_f \frac{(A_B^\circ)_T}{Q_g \bar{t}_b}(C_g - C_{g,e}) \tag{16.30}$$

The change in C_g as a function of vertical position in the contact reactor rather than as a function of time is obtained from

$$t_b = \frac{z}{v_t} \tag{16.31}$$

where v_t is the terminal rise velocity of the bubble and z is the vertical distance traveled. If it is assumed that the bubble attains terminal velocity almost immediately after introduction to the reactor, the bubble velocity can in turn be expressed as

$$v_t = \frac{Z_B Q_g}{(V_B)_T} = \frac{Z_B}{\bar{t}_b} \tag{16.32}$$

where $(V_B)_T$ is the total volume of bubbles in a contactor providing a total bubble travel length of Z_B. Substitution of v_t from Equation 16.32 into Equation 16.31, taking the derivative with respect to time, and substituting this result into Equation 16.30 yields the following expression for the spatial gradient in gas-phase concentration of the volatile substance being stripped from or absorbed into the aqueous phase

> **Spatial Gradient in Gas-Phase Concentration**
> $$\frac{d(C_g)}{dz} = k_f \frac{(A_B^\circ)_T}{Z_B Q_g}(C_{g,e} - C_g) \tag{16.33}$$

A more general definition of the interfacial area available for mass transfer is given by $(a_s^\circ)_R$, the specific area per unit volume of the reactor. If V_R is the volume of the contact reactor, then $(a_s^\circ)_R = (A_B^\circ)_T/V_R$, and

$$\frac{d(C_g)}{dz} = k_f(a_s^\circ)_R \frac{V_R}{Z_B Q_g}(C_{g,e} - C_g) \tag{16.34}$$

The concentration in the gas phase depends on the local pressure on the gas bubble, which in this case is simply the hydrostatic pressure. The ideal gas law dictates that

$$C_g = \frac{P_H}{\mathcal{R}T}X_g \tag{16.35}$$

where P_H is the hydrostatic pressure and X_g is the mole fraction of the volatile substance in the gas phase. Substituting the foregoing definition for C_g (and likewise for $C_{g,e}$) into Equation 16.34, we have

$$\frac{X_g}{P_H}\frac{dP_H}{dz} + \frac{dX_g}{dz} = k_f(a_s^\circ)_R \frac{V_R}{Z_B Q_g}(X_{g,e} - X_g) \tag{16.36}$$

To simplify the mathematical solution to Equation 16.36 we can ignore the change in hydrostatic pressure with depth (i.e., $dP_H/dz = 0$). If $X_{g,e}$ is taken as a constant mole fraction of the volatile compound in the gas phase in equilibrium with the average liquid-phase concentration across the depth of the contactor. This ordinary differential equation then simplifies to

$$\boxed{\begin{array}{ll} \textbf{\textit{Spatial Gradient}} \\ \textbf{\textit{in Gas-Phase}} \\ \textbf{\textit{Mole Fraction}} \end{array} \qquad \dfrac{dX_g}{dz} = \beta_Z(X_{g,e} - X_g)} \qquad (16.37)$$

to give an expression of the spatial rate of change of the mole fraction of the volatile substance in rising bubbles. The term β_Z in Equation 16.37 has the form

$$\beta_Z = \frac{k_f(a_s^\circ)_R V_R}{Z_B Q_g} \qquad (16.38)$$

which includes the same basic parameters as the pre-ΔC term in Equation 16.33, with $(A_B^\circ)_T$ now being expressed as $(a_s^\circ)_R V_R$.

The general solution to Equation 16.37 can be obtained by separation of variables, yielding

$$X_g = X_{g,e} + \kappa \, \exp(z\beta_Z) \qquad (16.39)$$

where κ is a constant of integration. The particular solution for either gas absorption or stripping is then obtained by an appropriate mathematical statement of the gas-phase concentration in the bubble at the inlet to the reactor. The solution for stripping of a volatile compound into a gas bubble is determined by the condition

$$X_g = 0 \qquad\qquad \text{at } z = 0 \qquad (16.40)$$

For this condition, Equation 16.39 becomes

$$X_g = X_{g,e}[1 - \exp(z\beta_Z)] \qquad (16.41)$$

The mole fraction of the volatile compound in the gas bubble when it reaches the top of the contactor ($z = Z_B$) is more conveniently expressed through the ideal gas law as

$$X_g = C_{g,OUT}\frac{\mathcal{R}T}{P_H} \qquad (16.42)$$

where $C_{g,OUT}$ is the gas-phase concentration of the compound in the bubbles leaving the contactor. Substitution of this relationship for X_g in Equation 16.41 gives

$$\boxed{\begin{array}{l} \textbf{\textit{Counter-Flow PFDR Exit Gas Phase Concentration}} \\[6pt] C_{g,OUT} = C_{g,e}\left[1 - \exp(Z_B\beta_Z)\right] = C_{g,e}\left[1 - \exp\left(\dfrac{k_f(a_s^\circ)_R V_R}{Q_g}\right)\right] \end{array}} \qquad (16.43)$$

A design equation to determine the loss of the compound from the liquid phase follows directly from the development above if we assume that the dispersive mixing in the counter-flow PFDR caused by the rising bubble field is sufficiently large to cause the reactor to behave as a CMFR with respect to its liquid phase. The material balance for the liquid phase can then be written

> **Liquid Phase**
> **MBE for Complete** $\quad Q_l C_{l,IN} - Q_l C_{l,OUT} - Q_g C_{g,OUT} = 0$ (16.44)
> **Mixing Assumption**

It should be noted that this CMFR assumption is a tenuous one for most circumstances, and that the derivative design equations should be treated accordingly as only approximations.

For the assumed conditions the concentration $C_{g,OUT}$ in Equation 16.44 is given by Equation 16.43. We note further from Equation 16.43 that $C_{g,e}$ is the gas-phase concentration that exists in equilibrium with the liquid-phase concentration within the contactor, which for a CMFR is equal to $C_{l,OUT}$. The appropriate Henrys law relationship is

$$C_{g,e} = \frac{\mathcal{K}_H}{RT} C_{l,OUT} = \mathcal{K}_H^\circ C_{l,OUT} \tag{16.45}$$

where, as noted in Table 8-2, $\mathcal{K}_H^\circ$ is the dimensionless Henrys constant, $\mathcal{K}_H/RT$, obtained when concentrations are expressed in terms of molar ratios.

Accordingly, Equation 16.44 can be written for a gas stripper as

> **Counter-Flow PFDR Design Equation for Stripping**
>
> $$\frac{C_{l,OUT}}{C_{l,IN}} = \left[1 + \frac{Q_g \mathcal{K}_H^\circ}{Q_l} \left(1 - \exp\left(-\frac{k_f(a_s^\circ)_R V_R}{Q_g \mathcal{K}_H^\circ} \right) \right) \right]^{-1}$$

(16.46)

The two dimensionless parameter groups that appear in Equation 16.46 are

> **Stripping** $\quad R_S = \dfrac{Q_g \mathcal{K}_H^\circ}{Q_l}$ (16.47)
> **Factor**

the so-called stripping factor, and

> **Stripping** $\quad \beta_S = \dfrac{k_f(a_s^\circ)_R V_R}{Q_g \mathcal{K}_H^\circ}$ (16.48)
> **Parameter**

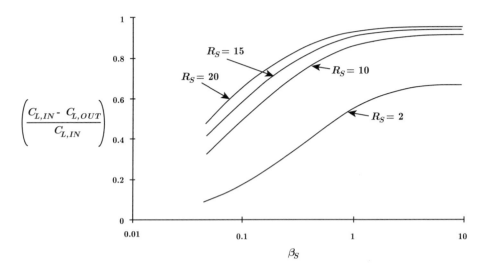

Figure 16.3 Stripping of Volatile Compounds in a Counter-Flow PFDR

a stripping parameter that incorporates the mass transfer rate.

Stripping efficiency $(C_{l,IN} - C_{l,OUT})/C_{l,IN}$ as a function of β_S is shown for various values of R_S in Figure 16.3. The stripping factor term characterizes the equilibrium partitioning properties of the compound of interest, $\mathcal{K}_H^\circ$, and the ratio of gas to liquid flow rates. The parameter β_S accounts for the rate of mass transfer in the contactor, incorporating as it does the overall volumetric mass transfer coefficient, $k_v = k_f(a_s^\circ)_R$. Increasing β_S while holding R_S constant causes stripping efficiency to increase, asymptotically, approaching a limiting value determined by R_S. Increasing R_S values, accomplished by increasing either the gas-liquid flow ratio or the Henrys constant, yield higher limiting stripping efficiencies. The effects of each of these major design parameters on stripping are logical and intuitive. The overall mass transfer coefficient or the volume of the contactor (and thus the liquid holdup time) must be increased to increase β_S without changing R_S. An increase in these parameters might be expected to improve stripping. It is an oversimplification, however, to discuss the impacts of the overall mass transfer and the gas and liquid flow rates as if they are independent parameters. In fact, as evidenced in Appendix A.4.1 of PDES, experimental correlations show that the overall mass transfer coefficient depends on the gas and liquid flow rates.

Example 16.3 provides a detailed illustration of how the principles and derivative relationships above can be applied, in this particular case to analysis of the performance characteristics to be expected for two different air stripper design configurations being considered for a groundwater decontamination application.

Example 16.3. Air Stripping of a Volatile Organic Groundwater Contaminant. (Design of a counter-flow PFDR for removal of TCE in a pump-and-treat remediation scheme.)

- **Situation.** *Air stripping of groundwater pumped from a contaminated aquifer is selected for removal of trichloroethylene (TCE). A counter-flow PFDR is being considered for this application. The sparging device selected for use in the reactor is specified as generating bubbles having an average diameter of 0.1 cm. The TCE concentration must be reduced from 50 $\mu g/L$ to 5 $\mu g/L$. The groundwater pumping rate is 0.0438 m^3/s (1 mgd) and the temperature is 15° C.*

- **Question(s).** *Compare the relative performance characteristics of single- and three-stage counter-flow PFDRs for this application.*

- **Logic and Answer(s).**

  1. *The appropriate design relationship is given in Equation 16.46 as*

  $$\frac{C_{l,OUT}}{C_{l,IN}} = \left[1 + \frac{Q_g \mathcal{K}_H^\circ}{Q_l}\left(1 - \exp\left(-\frac{k_f(a_s^\circ)_R V_R}{Q_g \mathcal{K}_H^\circ}\right)\right)\right]^{-1}$$

  2. *As a first-cut analysis, we can determine the ratio of gas-liquid flow rates required if the mass transfer rate is fast enough to allow the TCE to reach equilibrium between the air bubbles and water leaving the reactor. For large values of $k_f(a_s^\circ)_R V_R$, Equation 16.46 reduces to*

  $$\frac{C_{l,OUT}}{C_{l,IN}} = \left(1 + \frac{Q_g \mathcal{K}_H^\circ}{Q_l}\right)^{-1}$$

  Note that this relationship can also be obtained by writing the following material balance for the equilibrium situation

  $$Q_l C_{l,IN} - Q_l C_{l,OUT} = Q_g \mathcal{K}_H^\circ C_{l,OUT}$$

  3. *A value of $\mathcal{K}_H = 11.7 \times 10^{-3} \mathrm{atm} - m^3/\mathrm{mol}$ is known for TCE for a temperature of 25° C (see Table 8-2), while the groundwater of interest is at 15° C. The temperature dependence of equilibrium constants was discussed in Chapter 4, and the associated vant Hoff equation relating the equilibrium constant for a reaction to the enthalpy of that reaction was given in Equation 6.35. Montgomery (1985) has reported enthalpy values (ΔH_r°) (expressed in kcal/mol) and constants of integration (κ) for Henrys constant (expressed in units of atmospheres) for several organic compounds of common environmental interest, as listed below.*

Compound	ΔH_r° (kcal/mol)	κ
$CHCl_3$	4.00	9.10
CCL_4	4.05	15.06
$CCHCl_3$	3.41	8.59
C_2Cl_4	4.29	15.38
C_6H_6	3.68	8.68

Thus, we can estimate that $\mathcal{K}_H$ for TCE at 15° C is

$$\log \mathcal{K}_H = -\frac{\Delta H_r^\circ}{\mathcal{R}T} + \kappa = \frac{-3.41}{1.987 \times 10^{-3}(288)} + 8.59 = 2.63$$

$$\mathcal{K}_H = 426.6 \text{ atm, or } 426.6 \times 18 \times 10^{-6} = 7.7 \times 10^{-3} \text{atm} - \text{m}^3/\text{mol}$$

4. *The dimensionless form of Henrys constant needed above is*

$$\mathcal{K}_H^\circ (\text{dimensionless}) = \frac{\mathcal{K}_H (\text{atm} - \text{m}^3/\text{mol})}{\mathcal{R}T}$$

$$= \frac{7.7 \times 10^{-3}}{0.0821 \times 10^{-3} \times 288} = 0.326$$

5. *Solving for the gas-liquid flow ratio for a single-stage contactor gives*

$$\frac{Q_g}{Q_l} = \frac{1 - \dfrac{C_{l,OUT}}{C_{l,IN}}}{\mathcal{K}_H^\circ \dfrac{C_{l,OUT}}{C_{l,IN}}} = 28$$

6. *From Equation 16.47, the stripping factor for the one-stage system is*

$$R_S = \frac{Q_g \mathcal{K}_H^\circ}{Q_l} = 9$$

7. *The gas-liquid flow ratio and stripping factor for a three-stage system can be found in a similar way. If the same Q_g/Q_l is used in each stage, and equilibrium between gas and liquid is reached in each, the fractional removal of TCE must be the same in each stage. The overall fractional removal is then given by*

$$\frac{C_{l,OUT}}{C_{l,IN}} = \left(\frac{C_{l,i+1}}{C_{l,i}}\right)^3 = 0.1$$

Thus, the fractional removal per stage is 0.46.

8. *The relationship given in step 5 can be used to find the gas-liquid flow ratio required for each stage*

$$\frac{Q_g}{Q_l} = \frac{1 - \dfrac{C_{l,OUT}}{C_{l,IN}}}{\mathcal{K}_H^\circ \dfrac{C_{l,OUT}}{C_{l,IN}}} = 3.5$$

9. *The total gas-liquid flow ratio is thus $3 \times 3.5 = 15.6$, which is considerably less than the value of 28.0 for a single-stage bubble contact reactor. Similarly, the stripping factor is reduced from 9.0 to 3.5. The reason for the improvement in efficiency is analogous to that found when comparing a single CMFR to several CMFRs in series. Here, the fractional concentration in the exit liquid stream of each contactor is made larger by staging, and less is stripped into the gas flow in each stage, so that a lower Q_g/Q_l is required. Note that as more stages are added, a minimum Q_g/Q_l is approached.*

10. *We can also determine the depth of contactor needed to approach equilibrium. First, we write Equation 16.46 in a form that includes the depth of the contactor by making the following substitutions*

$$(a_s^\circ)_R = \frac{(A_B^\circ)_T}{V_R} = \frac{[Q_g \bar{t}_b/(\pi d_b^3/6)]\pi d_b^2}{V_R}$$

and

$$\bar{t}_b = \frac{z}{v_t}$$

leading to

$$\frac{C_{l,OUT}}{C_{l,IN}} = \left[1 + \frac{Q_g \mathcal{K}_H^\circ}{Q_l}\left(1 - \exp\left(-\frac{6k_f z}{v_t d_b \mathcal{K}_H^\circ}\right)\right)\right]^{-1}$$

11. *The mass transfer coefficient is obtained from an appropriate correlation provided in Appendix A.4.1 of PDES*

$$\frac{k_f}{\mathcal{D}_l} = \frac{2.0}{d_b} + 0.31\left[\frac{(\rho_l - \rho_g)g}{\mu_{v,l}\mathcal{D}_l}\right]^{0.333}$$

Given that $\mathcal{D}_l = 8.37 \times 10^{-10}\text{m}^2/\text{s}$ for TCE, $\rho_g = 1.205\text{kg/m}^3$, $\rho_l = 1000\text{kg/m}^3$, $\mu_{v,l} = 10^{-3}$ kg/m-s, and $g = 9.8\text{m/s}^2$, we can calculate

$$k_f = 6 \times 10^{-5}\text{m/s} = 6 \times 10^{-3}\text{cm/s}$$

12. *The bubble rise velocity, which can be calculated from Stokes law, depends upon the flow condition (laminar, transitional, or turbulent), which is in turn determined by the size of the rising bubbles. For a bubble diameter of 0.1 cm, transition region flow occurs and the appropriate expression is (Weber, 1972)*

$$v_t = \left[0.072g(\rho_l - \rho_g)d_b^{1.6}\rho_l^{-0.4}\mu_{v,l}^{-0.6}\right]^{0.714} = 15.8\text{cm/s}$$

13. *The depth required to obtain equilibrium between the exit gas and liquid to obtain is approached when the exponential term in the expression for $C_{l,OUT}/C_{l,IN}$ (step 10) becomes very small. All of the parameters within the exponential term are known except z. If we let*

$$\exp\left(-\frac{6zk_f}{v_t d_b \mathcal{K}_H^\circ}\right) = 0.01$$

then

$$\frac{6zk_f}{v_t d_b \mathcal{K}_H^\circ} = 4.6$$

and

$$z = \frac{4.6 v_t d_b \mathcal{K}_H^\circ}{6k_f} = 44.0\text{cm}$$

- **Key Point(s).** *The above calculation shows that equilibrium is reached in a very short bubble travel distance. Design of a bubble contact reactor of any depth greater than that required is pointless. However, the depth to equilibrium increases with bubble diameter as noted in the equation for Z_B given above. According to Stokes law, rise velocity is proportional to d_b^2 for laminar flow, $d_b^{1.6}$ for transition flow, and $d_b^{0.5}$ for turbulent flow (Weber, 1972). The mass transfer coefficient may also increase somewhat, but the net effect is that coarser bubbles require greater depths for equilibrium to obtain.*

16.3.4   Mass Transfer in Counter-Flow FBRs

The essential features for analysis of countercurrent operations of packed FBRs are shown in Figure 16.2d. The material balance for a component in the liquid phase taken over a differential control volume accounts for mass transfer into (absorption by) or out of (stripping from) the liquid

> **PFR Steady-State MBE for a
> Differential Control Volume of an FBR**
>
> $$dN_{l,z}A_R + N^\circ(a_s^\circ)_R A_R dz = 0$$

(16.49)

where $N_{l,z}$ is the macroscopic longitudinal flux of the component in the liquid phase, A_R is the cross-sectional area of the reactor, N° is the flux of the component into or out of the liquid phase due to mass transfer, and $(a_s^\circ)_R$ is the interfacial (gas-liquid) mass transfer area per unit volume of reactor. For simplicity, we assume that advection is the only form of macroscopic transport through the tower (i.e., PFR behavior), and that the component being absorbed from the gas stream or stripped from the liquid stream does not undergo reaction. Substituting the appropriate definitions for these fluxes, the resulting point form of the material balance equation is

$$
\boxed{
\begin{array}{c}
\textbf{PFR Steady-State MBE for} \\
\textbf{Absorption or Stripping in an FBR} \\[2mm]
-v_z \dfrac{dC_l}{dz} + k_f(a_s^\circ)_R(C_{l,e} - C_l) = 0
\end{array}
}
\qquad (16.50)
$$

Separation of variables and arrangement for integration leads to

$$
\int_0^z dz = \frac{v_z}{k_f(a_s^\circ)_R} \int_{C_{l,IN}}^{C_{l,OUT}} \frac{dC_l}{C_{l,e} - C_l}
\qquad (16.51)
$$

The pre-integral term on the right side of Equation 16.51 is defined as the height of a transfer unit (HTU)

$$
\boxed{
\begin{array}{cc}
\textbf{Height of a} & \\
\textbf{Transfer Unit} & HTU = \dfrac{v_z}{k_f(a_s^\circ)_R}
\end{array}
}
\qquad (16.52)
$$

HTU has the dimension of length. It incorporates $k_f(a_s^\circ)_R$ and is thus a function of the mass transfer capacity of the packing material in the tower. Two of the most commonly used mass transfer correlations for packed towers, the Onda and the Sherwood-Holloway correlations, are given in Appendix A.4.1 of PDES. Key parameters in these correlations are the gas and liquid velocities in the tower, often referred to as the gas and liquid loading rates, respectively, because they derive from ratios of flow rates to reactor unit cross-sectional area. Other parameters to be specified in the correlation relate to the characteristics of the packing material.

The quantity within the right-hand integral of Equation 16.51 is termed the number of transfer units (NTU); that is

$$
\boxed{
\begin{array}{cc}
\textbf{Number of} & \\
\textbf{Transfer Units} & NTU = \displaystyle\int_{C_{l,IN}}^{C_{l,OUT}} \dfrac{dC_l}{C_{l,e} - C_l}
\end{array}
}
\qquad (16.53)
$$

NTU is a dimensionless quantity, the magnitude of which depends on the difference between the equilibrium $(C_{l,e})$ and actual (C_l) liquid-phase concentrations at each position in the tower. Adopting the definitions above for HTU and NTU, the design height, Z_T, of a *tower required for a given stripping or absorption process is given by Equation 16.51 as*

$$\boxed{\begin{array}{l} \textbf{\textit{Design}} \\ \textbf{\textit{Tower}} \qquad Z_T = HTU \cdot NTU \\ \textbf{\textit{Height}} \end{array}} \qquad (16.54)$$

It is necessary to determine $C_{l,e}$ as a function of tower height to find the value of NTU. This is analogous to the mass transfer situation in counter-flow PFDRs, where $C_{l,e}$ depends on the local gas-phase concentration, C_g, at any height. As discussed in Section 12.2.3 of Chapter 12, the molar gas-phase concentration of a component is in turn given as a function of its pressure contribution, P, by the ideal gas law

$$C_g = \frac{P}{\mathcal{R}T} \qquad (16.55)$$

or, as a function of the liquid-phase concentration, by Henrys law

$$C_g = \frac{\mathcal{K}_H}{\mathcal{R}T} C_{l,e} = \mathcal{K}_H^\circ C_{l,e} \qquad (16.56)$$

The relationship between gas- and liquid-phase concentrations within the packed tower is determined by an overall or macroscopic material balance which accounts for the gain or loss of component in each phase

$$\boxed{\begin{array}{l} \textbf{\textit{Macroscopic}} \\ \textbf{\textit{Gas-Liquid}} \qquad Q_g C_{g,IN} - Q_g C_{g,OUT} = Q_l C_{l,OUT} - Q_l C_{l,IN} \\ \textbf{\textit{FBR MBE}} \end{array}} \quad (16.57)$$

In countercurrent operation, $C_{g,OUT}$ refers to the gas-phase concentration at the point of entrance of the liquid phase to the tower and $C_{g,IN}$ to the gas-phase concentration at the point of exit of the liquid phase from the tower (see Figure 16.2d).

Both gas absorption and stripping operations in FBRs can be analyzed using the above material balance relationship. The stripper design equation is developed here because it has such wide utility for removal of volatile organic chemicals from contaminated waters, wastewaters, and liquid hazardous waste streams. The reader is encouraged as an exercise to develop an analogous equation for the design of a gas absorption system.

Stripping in an FBR is generally accomplished by air flowing upward through a tower of packing material while water flows downward (i.e., a countercurrent operation), although other configurations are possible. A common and reasonable assumption by which the analysis can be simplified is that the concentration of the compound of interest entering with the airstream is zero. This is in fact an operating condition that would be normally selected for the design of a single-stage stripper. For $C_{g,IN} = 0$, the macroscopic or "end-to-end" FBR material balance can be written as

$$\frac{Q_g}{Q_l} = \frac{C_{l,IN} - C_{l,OUT}}{C_{g,OUT}} \tag{16.58}$$

The gas-phase exit concentration is then given by rearranging Equation 16.58 to obtain

$$C_{g,OUT} = \frac{Q_l}{Q_g}(C_{l,IN} - C_{l,OUT}) \tag{16.59}$$

When plotted as in Figure 16.4, the relationship given in Equation 16.59 defines the operating line. Any point (C_g, C_l) on the operating line is defined by

$$C_g = \frac{Q_l}{Q_g}(C_l - C_{l,OUT}) + C_{g,IN} \tag{16.60}$$

where for stripping it is common to assume that $C_{g,IN} = 0$ (see Problem 16.10 for exceptions). The maximum liquid-phase concentration that could exist in equilibrium with the gas-phase concentration at any point on the operating line is determined from Henry's law

$$C_{l,e} = \frac{\mathcal{R}T}{\mathcal{K}_H}C_g = \frac{C_g}{\mathcal{K}_H^\circ} \tag{16.61}$$

The relationship given in Equation 16.61 determines the equilibrium line shown in Figure 16.4. The horizontal distance between the equilibrium and operating lines at any gas-phase concentration is $(C_{l,e} - C_l)$ the driving force for stripping. The inherently negative value of $(C_{l,e} - C_l)$ indicates loss from the liquid phase. This driving force expression is needed to solve Equation 16.51. A similar definition of the driving force exists for absorption, in which case, as shown in Figure 16.4, the operating line obtained from Equation 16.59 is above and to the left of the equilibrium line; accordingly, $(C_{l,e} - C_l)$ is positive.

Combining Equations 16.60 and 16.61 gives

$$C_{l,e} = \frac{Q_l}{\mathcal{K}_H^\circ Q_g}(C_l - C_{l,OUT}) \tag{16.62}$$

Substituting Equation 16.62 and Equation 16.51 yields

$$\int_0^z dz = \frac{v_z}{k_f(a_s^\circ)R} \int_{C_{l,IN}}^{C_{l,OUT}} \frac{dC_l}{\frac{Q_l}{\mathcal{K}_H^\circ Q_G}(C_l - C_{l,OUT}) - C_l} \tag{16.63}$$

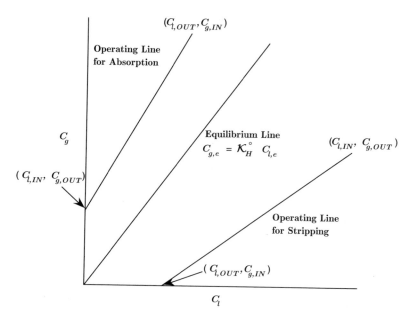

Figure 16.4 Equilibrium and Operating Lines for FBR Gas Strippers and Absorbers

We observe that the value of the integral on the right-hand side of this equation (i.e., the NTU value) depends on the value of Henry's constant and on the ratio of gas to liquid flow rates selected. This integral can be simplified by combining the two terms in the denominator containing the variable, C_l, after which the integral is of the general form and solution

$$\int \frac{dC_l}{\kappa_1 + \kappa_2 C_l} = \frac{1}{\kappa_2} \ln(\kappa_1 + \kappa_2 C_l) \tag{16.64}$$

where the constants κ_1 and κ_2 are given by

$$\kappa_1 = -\frac{Q_l C_{l,PIT}}{\mathcal{K}_H^\circ Q_g} \quad \text{and} \quad \kappa_2 = \frac{Q_l}{\mathcal{K}_H^\circ Q_g} - 1 \tag{16.65}$$

The integral on the right side of Equation 16.63 is then

> ### Transfer Unit Stripping Factor Relationship
>
> $$NTU = \frac{R_S}{R_S - 1} \ln \left(\frac{\dfrac{C_{l,IN}}{C_{l,OUT}} (R_S - 1) + 1}{R_S} \right) \tag{16.66}$$

where R_S is the stripping factor defined in Equation 16.47.

Strictly speaking, the relationship given in Equation 16.66 holds only for situations in which the influent gas to the FBR is free of the contaminant to be stripped from the liquid. The reader is asked in Problem 16.10 to develop an equation of similar form for the more general case; i.e., for a non-zero contaminant level in the influent gas. The latter situation is normally of concern only for multistage stripping operations. The relationships given by Equation 16.66 between the fraction of a contaminant remaining in the liquid effluent of an FBR ($C_{L,OUT}/C_{L,IN}$) for a specific stripping factor (R_S), and number of transfer units (NTU) provide important insights to the design of stripping towers. These relationships are represented conveniently in Figure 16.5.

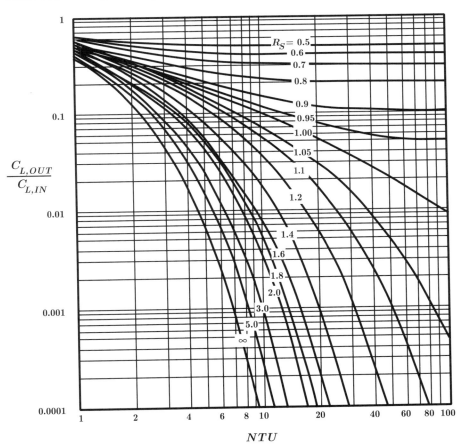

Figure 16.5 Relationships Between Removal Efficiency and Number of Transfer Units for FBR Gas Strippers

There are many ways in which Figure 16.5 can be used with Equation 16.54 to design and analyze FBR stripping and absorption tower performance. For example, the relationship of tower height, Z_T, to removal of a particular compound at a fixed gas-liquid flow rate, and thus a fixed R_S, is determined by first finding the NTU value corresponding to the fractional removal targeted in a particular application. Given Equation 16.54, and assuming that the HTU value is fixed by the packing material and the gas-liquid flow ratio, the value of Z_T can be calculated. According to Figure 16.5, NTU must increase as the desired fractional removal increases; this means that a tower of greater depth or height is needed. Tower height is influenced also by compound volatility. A more volatile compound gives a larger R_S for a given gas-liquid flow rate ratio. Thus, the tower height needed to achieve the same fractional removal as a less volatile compound is smaller because NTU is smaller. Gas-liquid flow rate ratio affects both the NTU and HTU values. A higher ratio will give a higher R_S value and, therefore, the same fractional removal can be achieved at a lower NTU value, with a resulting savings in tower height. Increasing the gas-liquid flow ratio also affects the boundary layer between the two phases, usually leading to an increase in the mass transfer coefficient, as illustrated by the correlations presented earlier in this chapter. The HTU value is thus decreased, allowing a further reduction in tower height. There are economic and practical limits to changing gas flow rates, however. For instance, when the gas pressure drop becomes so large at high gas flow rates that it impedes the downward flow of water, tower flooding occurs, a condition in which the tower is literally flooded with water.

An application of the above principles and relationships to the design of an FBR stripping column is given in Example 16.4. The conditions specified in this example are the same as those given earlier in Example 16.3, thus affording a direct comparison between the performance of counter-flow PFDR and FBR reactors.

Example 16.4. Air Stripping of a Volatile Organic Groundwater Contaminant. (Design of a countercurrent fixed bed packed reactor for removal of TCE in a pump-and-treat remediation scheme.)

- **Situation.** *The influent conditions and treatment objectives for removal of trichloroethylene (TCE) discussed in Example 16.3 are to be met using a counter-flow FBR employing 25-mm Intalox saddles, a widely used commercial packing material. The volumetric liquid loading rate, $Q_l/A_R = v_z$, to the FBR is specified as $0.035 m^3/m^{-2}/s^{-1} (51.5 gal/min^{-1}/ft^{-2})$, and P_H is 1 atm.*

- **Question(s).** *Develop a design procedure for the stripping tower.*

- **Logic and Answer(s).**

    1. *Alternative designs can be obtained for different stripping factors, R_S, and for different volumetric liquid loading rates. For this analysis, Q_l/A_R is specified as $0.035 m^3/m^{-2}/s^{-1}$. Assume $R_S = 3$. The*

dimensionless form of the Henrys constant for TCE at $15°C$ was determined in Example 16.4 to have a value of 0.326.

2. *Using Equation 16.47, the gas-liquid flow ratio is determined to be*

$$\frac{Q_g}{Q_l} = \frac{R_S}{\mathcal{K}_H^\circ} = \frac{3}{0.326} = 9.2$$

and the required volumetric flow of air is

$$Q_g = 9.2 \times 0.438 \mathrm{m}^3/\mathrm{s}^{-1} = 0.40 \mathrm{m}^3/\mathrm{s}^{-1}$$

3. *The number of transfer units is obtained from Equation 16.66*

$$NTU = \frac{R_S}{R_S - 1} \ln \left(\frac{\frac{C_{l,IN}}{C_{l,PIT}}(R_S - 1) + 1}{R_S} \right) = 2.92$$

4. *The height of a mass transfer unit (HTU) requires selection of a mass transfer correlation to determine the overall volumetric mass transfer coefficient, $k_f(a_s^\circ)_R$. The Sherwood-Holloway correlation (Appendix A.4.1 of PDES) is used (Note: This is one of those correlations noted as having dimensional terms and as being dimensionally inconsistent)*

$$\frac{k_f(a_s^\circ)_R}{\mathcal{D}_l} = 10.76 \psi_1 \left(\frac{0.3048 N_l}{\mu_{v,l}} \right)^{1-\psi_2} \left(\frac{\mu_{v,l}}{\rho_l \mathcal{D}_l} \right)^{0.5}$$

in which the mass liquid flux or loading rate, N_l, is $(0.035 \mathrm{m}^3/\mathrm{m}^2 - \mathrm{s})$ $\times 1000 \mathrm{kg/m}^3$. The other parameters needed are $\mu_{v,l} = 10^{-3}$ $\mathrm{kg/m} - \mathrm{s}$, $\rho_l = 103 \mathrm{kg/m}^3$, and $\mathcal{D}_l = 8.37 \times 10^{-10} \mathrm{m}^2/\mathrm{s}$. Typical values of ψ_1 and ψ_2 for the 25-mm Intalox saddles are 63 and 0.28, respectively. The value of calculated from this correlation and the parameter values given is 0.016 s-1.

5. *Then, from Equation 16.52*

$$HTU = \frac{v_z}{k_f(a_s^\circ)_R} = \frac{0.035 \mathrm{m}^3/\mathrm{m}^2 - \mathrm{s}}{0.016 \mathrm{s}^{-1}} = 2/2 \mathrm{m}$$

6. *The height of the tower can now be determined from Equation 16.54 as*

$$Z_T = HTU \cdot NTU = 2.2 \times 2.92 = 6.5 \mathrm{m}$$

and the reactor cross-sectional area as

$$A_R = \frac{Q_l}{v_z} = \frac{0.0438 \mathrm{m}^3/\mathrm{s}}{0.035 \mathrm{m}^3/\mathrm{m}^2 - \mathrm{s}} = 1.25 \mathrm{m}^2$$

- *Key Point(s). For different assumed values of the stripping factor, the liquid loading rate will yield different values for HTU and NTU, different tower heights, and different cross-sectional areas. Other important aspects of tower type designs are the power requirements to lift the water to the top of the tower and to force air through the tower. The gas pressure drop for a given packing material and temperature (referred to as the packing factor) has been shown by experiment to increase with the liquid-to-gas flow ratio (i.e., the inverse of the R_S value) and with the liquid loading rate.*

16.4   MASS TRANSFER COEFFICIENTS

Mass transfer coefficients must be specified for every heterogeneous reactor discussed in this chapter. These coefficients depend on reactor configuration, specific operating conditions, physical characteristics of interfaces between the phases involved, and the physical-chemical properties of the component(s) being transferred. Mass transfer correlations such as those discussed in Chapter 14 are used extensively. Table 14.1 in this book and Appendix A.4.1 in PDES provide useful compendia of correlations applicable to a variety of natural and engineered environmental systems.

16.5   CHAPTER SUMMARY

In this Chapter and in several previous chapters we have discussed and designed a wide range of reactor engineering applications under steady-state conditions. A general categorization of such applications is presented in Table 16.1.

The material we have covered enables a performance or design equation to be obtained for each application listed in this table. The same general framework for process analysis can be used for more complex, steady-state situations [e.g., for the analysis of combined advective and dispersive transport with reaction in fluid-fluid systems (PFDR systems)]. The resulting design equations may not be as straightforward as those discussed above, and numerical methods may be needed to solve the corresponding material balance equations. Such model extensions are discussed in Chapter 12 of PDES. The analysis of unsteady-state situations, which is inherently more involved because concentrations of reactants are functions of both space and time, is addressed in Chapter 11 of PDES.

Table 16.1 Summary of Reactor Engineering Applications Addressed for Homogeneous and Heterogeneous Systems Operated at Steady State

Reactor Type	System Type		
	Homogeneous	Fluid-Solid	Fluid-Fluid
CMFR	Zero-, first-, and second-order rates	Zero-, first-, and second-order rates. External and internal mass transfer	Slow-to-fast first-order rates.
PFR and PFDR	Zero-, first-, and second-order rates	Zero-, first-, and second-order rates. External and internal mass transfer	Mass transfer in counter-flow PFDRs and FBRs

16.6 CITATIONS AND SOURCES

M.D. Gurol and P.C. Singer, "Kinetics of Ozone Decomposition: A Dynamic Approach," *Environmental Science and Technology, 16*(7), 377-383 (1982). (Problem 16.7)

R.D. Letterman, M. Haddad, and C.T. Driscoll, "Limestone Contactors: Steady-State Design Relationships," *Journal of Environmental Engineering, 117*, 339-358 (1991). (Problem 16.5)

J.M. Montgomery, *Water Treatment Principles and Design*, John Wiley & Sons, Inc., New York, 1985. (Example 16.6)

R.E. Treybal, *Mass Transfer Operations*, 3rd Edition, McGraw-Hill Book Company, New York, 139-145, 1980. (Example 16.4, Figure 16.3)

W.J. Weber, Jr., *Physicochemical Processes for Water Quality Control*, Wiley-Interscience, New York, 111-115, 1972. (Example 16.5)

W.J. Weber, Jr. and F.A. DiGiano, *Process Dynamics in Environmental Systems*, John Wiley & Sons, Inc., New York, 1996. (Source of most of the material presented here. See Chapter 10 of PDES for more details on phase transfer processes).

16.7 PROBLEM ASSIGNMENTS

16.1 Oxidation of zero-valent iron by trichloroethane (TCE), essentially a corrosion reaction, has been shown to cause reductive dechlorination of this organic compound. The intrinsic rate of the surface reaction is first order, with a rate constant of 1.8×10^{-7} cm/s. As an application of this technology, it is proposed to excavate a trench in the path of a contaminated groundwater plume at the site of a TCE spill, and backfill it with iron filings as a permeable barrier to provide *in-situ* dechlorination of the TCE. The filings have a mean diameter of 5 mm and their porosity in the trench is 0.4. The longitudinal dispersion coefficient has been estimated as 1 m^2/d and the pore velocity as 0.3 m/s. A published mass transfer correlation yields an estimate of 1×10^{-3} cm/s for the mass transfer coefficient between the groundwater and the surfaces of the iron filings. Determine the width of barrier (in the flow direction) required to achieve 95 percent dechlorination of the TCE.

Answer: 1.5 m.

16.2 The uppermost 1 cm of sediment in a small impoundment contains organic matter that is biodegrading aerobically. Oxygen diffusing through this sediment layer is consumed in the biodegradation reaction. If the impoundment behaves as a CMFR, find the steady-state oxygen concentration in the impoundment effluent given the following data

> flow rate = 40 m^3/day
>
> volume of impoundment = 1000 m^3
>
> inlet oxygen concentration = 6 mg/L
>
> first-order biodegradation reaction rate constant, $k = 0.64 \times 10^{-4} s^{-1}$
>
> diffusion coefficient for oxygen in sediment = $1 \times 10^{-5} cm^2/s$
>
> sediment surface area to impoundment volume ratio = $0.5 m^{-1}$

16.3 Bacteria are known to regrow in water distribution systems. They form biofilms on pipeline walls even in the presence of disinfectant residuals. Once established, such biofilms may be responsible for chemical reduction of disinfectants. The process may be conceptualized as one of diffusion into the biofilm accompanied by reaction within that film. Find the fraction of disinfectant remaining at the first tap in a distribution system for the following circumstances: (1) flow in the pipeline is essentially plug flow; (2) external resistance to mass transport in the laminar boundary layer adjacent to the biofilm is negligible; (3) the biofilm thickness is steady at 0.01 cm; (4) reduction of the chemical disinfectant within the biofilm is a first-order surface reaction ($k^\circ = 2.25 \times 10^{-3}$ cm/s); (5) the internal area of reactive sites per volume of biofilm is $(a_s^\circ)_{I,B} = 10 cm^2/cm^3$; (6) the effective diffusivity within the biofilm is $\mathcal{D}_e = 1 \times 10^{-6} cm^2/s$; (7) the pipe diameter is 50 cm; and (8) the HRT in the pipeline between the treatment plant and the first tap is 720 min. [*Hint:* Consider that the biofilm is very thin in comparison to the pipe radius such that the change in diffusional flux in the radial direction can be ignored. The diffusional flux (and the effectiveness factor) is written in one-dimensional rectangular coordinates rather than in radial coordinates. See Chapter 2 for a discussion of the material balance when accounting for wall diffusion normal to advective flow in conduits].

Answer: Fraction remaining = 0.626.

16.4 In the absence of prechlorination, a thin biological film has grown around anthracite particles used as a filter medium in a water treatment plant. Chlorine is applied to oxidize and inactivate the biofilm. During an initial period immediately following application of chlorine, the inactivation rate is pseudo first order with respect to chlorine because the number of cells in the biomass is large and thus changes slowly. Determine the concentration of chlorine remaining in the exit stream of the filter if: (1) the chlorine concentration in the feed is 2 mg/L; (2) k_f is 0.03 cm/min; (3) the empty-bed contact time is 5 min; (4) the diameter of the filter media particles is 0.15 cm; (5) the bed porosity is 0.4; and (6) the inactivation reaction is limited to the surface of the biofilm and is sufficiently fast that external mass transfer is entirely rate controlling.

16.5 FBR limestone contactors may be used to treat acidic waters for pH adjustment and corrosion control. The rate of $CaCO_3$ dissolution in slightly acidic-to-alkaline solutions is controlled by interfacial calcium mass transfer and first-order surface reaction in series. The rate of mass transfer is modeled as

$$r = \hat{k}(a_s^\circ)_L(C_e - C)$$

where mass transfer and reaction are included in the overall rate coefficient $\hat{k} = \left(\dfrac{1}{k_f} + \dfrac{1}{k^\circ} \right)^{-1}$, $(a_s^\circ)_L$ is the specific surface area per unit volume of interstitial fluid, and C_e is the equilibrium calcium concentration. The surface reaction rate has been correlated with pH as follows

$$k^\circ(\text{cm/s}) = 1.6 \times 10^{14}[\text{H}^+]_e^{1.7}$$

where $[\text{H}^+]_e$ is the equilibrium hydronium ion concentration.

(a) Size a contactor of length L to treat a mildly acidic water having a pH of 4.4 to a desired effluent pH of 8.3. The design flow and loading rates are 0.001 m^3/s and 1.2 cm/s, respectively. The equilibrium concentration of calcium is 4.13 mg/L, and the equilibrium pH is 9.65. The effluent calcium concentration corresponds to an effluent pH of 8.3 and is equal to 1.68 mg/L. For this design, assume a calcium particle diameter, d_p, of 1 cm, a bed porosity, ε_B of 0.4, a calcium free-liquid diffusivity of 1.2×10^{-5}cm^2/s, and neglect axial dispersion. Assume an influent calcium concentration, $C_{Ca,0}$, of zero. Estimate the mass transfer coefficient from an appropriate correlation for liquids in packed beds from Chapter 4.

(b) Compare your design with the following design equation given by Letterman et al. (1991), which includes the effects of dispersion

$$(C_{Ca})_{z=L} = C_{Ca,e}$$

$$+ \left\{ \exp \left[\frac{\hat{k}(a_s^o)_{I,L} L \varepsilon_B}{v_p} + \left(\frac{\hat{k}(a_s^o)_{I,L} L \varepsilon_B}{v_p} \right)^2 \mathcal{N}_d \right] (C_{Ca,0} - C_{Ca,e}) \right\}$$

where v_p is the interstitial velocity and $\mathcal{N}_d$ is the dispersion number, approximated by $2d_p/L$.

Discuss qualitatively the effects of dispersion on process performance.

16.6 A groundwater containing dissolved Fe(II) is to be aerated to form Fe(III), which can then be precipitated and removed as $Fe(OH)_3(s)$. Studies of Fe(II) oxidation rates at different pH and oxygen gas-phase pressures indicate the following rate relationship

$$- \frac{d[Fe(II)]}{dt} = k[Fe(II)]P_{O_2}[OH^-]^2$$

in which $k = 1.5 \times 10^{13} L^2/mol^2 - min - atm$. The aeration tank is described as a CMFR, pH is 7.5, and oxygen is to be maintained at 80

(a) Determine the HRT required to achieve a reduction in Fe(II) concentration from $6.25 \times 10^{-5} M$ (3.5 mg/L) to $3.6 \times 10^{-6} M$ (0.2 mg/L).

(b) Determine the overall volumetric mass transfer coefficient $k_f = k_f(a_s^o)_R$, needed to maintain the stated oxygen concentration if the Henry's constant for oxygen at the water temperature of interest is 0.73 atm-m^3/mol and the incoming water is devoid of oxygen.

16.7 A CMFR is used to transfer ozone to water to accommodate oxidations that will occur in a downstream reactor. Assume that the only reaction of importance in the upstream CMFR is ozone decomposition, rate expressions for which have been given in a model proposed by Gurol and Singer (1982)

$$-\boldsymbol{r} = k[OH]^{0.55}[O_3]^2$$

where $k = 1.4 \times 10^4 s^{-1} M^{-1.55}$. Determine the ozone concentration in the effluent from the CMFR, with and without consideration of ozone decomposition, if the pH is 8; the overall volumetric mass transfer coefficient, $k_v = k_f(a_s^o)_R$, is 0.5 min^{-1}; and the HRT is 4 min. Use a Henry's constant for ozone of 0.0677 atm-m^3/mol and assume that the average ozone composition of the gas bubbles in the tank is 3%.

16.8 A field test of an ozone bubble contact reactor is made to determine the overall volumetric mass transfer coefficient, $k_v = k_f(a_s^o)_R$. The incoming water has been stripped of all ozone-demanding substances, and the pH is sufficiently low that ozone decomposition is not significant. The resulting ozone concentration in the effluent water is 0.18 mol/m^3 (8.64 mg/L) at steady state. Determine $k_f(a_s^o)_R$ and the efficiency of ozone transfer, $(C_{g,IN} - C_{g,OUT})/C_{g,IN}$, given the following information

bubble contactor volume = 100m^3

contactor depth $= 3$ m

water flow rate $= 1200$ m^3/h

percentage ozone in the gas feed $= 4\%$

gas flow rate $= 178$ m^3/h

temperature $= 20°$C

Universal gas constant, $\mathcal{R} = 8.314 \times 10^{-5}$ J/mol-K

Henry's constant for ozone is $\mathcal{K}_H = 0.0677$atm $-$ m^3/mol

[*Hint:* Do all calculations of concentrations in both gas and liquid phases in mol/m^3 to avoid conversion factors. Calculate the unitless Henry's constant from the $\mathcal{K}_H$ value that is given. Calculate the inlet concentration of ozone in the gas stream using the mid-depth for determination of P_H; i.e., P_H will be greater than 1 atm due to hydrostatic pressure on the gas bubble.]

Answers: $k_f(a_s^\circ)_R = 10h^{-1}$ *and efficiency = 0.64.*

16.9 A countercurrent flow air stripping tower is to be designed to reduce trichloroethylene in a groundwater supply from 100 μg/L to 5μg/L. The water flow rate is 0.044 m^3/s (1 mgd) and the temperature is 15°C. The air-to-water flow ratio (m^3*air*/m^3 water) has been set at 11.4/1 and the water loading rate (velocity) at 0.05 m^3/m^2 $-$ s in order to have a pressure drop of 10 kg/m^2 per meter of tower height.

(a) Determine the tower height and diameter and justify your selection of an overall volumetric mass transfer coefficient.

(b) What would the TCE exit concentration be if the feed concentration increases to 200 μg/L?

16.10 The design relationship given in Equation 16.66 for the number of transfer units required to obtain a given stripping efficiency was predicated on an influent gas stream free of the contaminant to be stripped from a given water. This will not always be the case, and certainly not for gas streams entering downstream strippers in multistage operations. Develop an appropriate expression for *NTU* for cases in which $C_{g,IN} > 0$.

Answer: $NTU = \dfrac{R_S}{R_S - 1} \ln\left\{\left[\dfrac{C_{l,IN} - (C_{g,IN}/\mathcal{K}_H^\circ)}{C_{l,OUT} - (C_{g,IN}/\mathcal{K}_H^\circ)}\right]\dfrac{R_S - 1}{R_S} + \dfrac{1}{R_S}\right\}.$

Notation

Contents

1.0   ENGLISH ALPHABET

a =   chemical activity
         subscript:
            i =   component i

a_s° =   specific surface area, per unit volume basis (L^{-1})
         subscripts:
            B =   biofilm
            E =   external
            I =   internal
            L =   per liquid volume
            N =   NAPL (nonaqueous phase liquid)
            P =   per particle or bubble volume
            R =   per reactor volume
            T =   total
            W =   wetted

A =   area(L^2)
         subscripts:
            E =   effective
            C =   under curve
            N =   normal to flux
            P =   particle
            R =   reactor

A_f =   Arrhenius collision frequency factor ($L^3M^{-1}t^{-1}$)

A° =   surface or interstitial area (L^2)
         subscripts:
            B =   of bubble(s)
            F =   of film
            N =   normal to flux
            P =   of particle(s)

b =   coefficient, constant, general variable (arbitrary dimensions)

b =   Langmuir energy-related isotherm parameter
         (L^3M^{-1} or $L^3\ mol^{-1}$)

β_a =   BET energy-related isotherm parameter (dimensionless)

C =   concentration, mass (ML^{-3}), molar $(mol\ L^{-3})$, or number (L^{-3})
subscripts:

     a =   aqueous phase
     b =   bulk phase
     $BM=$ biomass
     $EN=$ enzyme
     $ES=$ enzyme/substrate complex
     H =   heat $(ML^{-1}t^{-2})$
     δ =   at distance δ from a specified point of reference
     g =   gas phase
     $IN=$ influent
     l =   liquid phase
     L =   at distance $x=L$ from $x=0$
     N =   number concentration
     o =   octanol phase
     $OUT=$ effluent
     p =   pure phase
     $PR=$ product
     ps =   preformed or precipitated solids
     r =   at a radial distance r from $r=0$
     R =   concentration reacted or in a reactor, as specified
     s =   sorbed or solid
     ss =   suspended solids
     S =   saturation (equilibrium) or solubility limited
     $SU=$ substrate
     T =   total
     v =   vapor phase
     W =   water
     0 =   initial (spatially or temporally)
     δ =   film or boundary layer
     Δ =   hypothetical initial value from pulse input M_T/V_R

$C(t)$ =   concentration as a function of time $(ML^{-3},\ mol\ L^{-3}\ or,\ L^{-3})$
subscripts: see concentration, C

C° =   concentration adjacent to a surface (ML^{-3})
subscripts: see concentration, C

$\boldsymbol{C}(t)$ = $\boldsymbol{C}$ curve $= C_{OUT}/C_{\Delta}$ as a function of time for a *pulse* or *delta* input of nonreactive tracer to a reactor of arbitrary flow characteristics

d =   diameter (L)

         subscripts:

             b =   bubble

             d =   droplet

             p =   particle

             P =   pipe

D_o =   dosage (ML^{-3})

$\mathcal{D}$ =   diffusion or dispersion coefficient L^2t^-)

         subscripts:

             a =   apparent diffusion

             d =   mechanical or hydrodynamic dispersion

             e =   effective diffusion

             g =   gas-phase free molecular diffusion

             l =   liquid-phase free molecular diffusion

             p =   pore diffusion

$\mathcal{D}°$ =   diffusivity to a surface or into an interface (L^2t^{-1})

e =   base of Napierian logarithms = 2.71828. . .

$e°$ =   elementary electric charge, $1.602 \times 10^{19}C$

e_m =   energy per unit mass L^2t^{-2})

E =   energy (ML^2t^{-2})

         subscripts:

             a =   activation energy

             r =   reaction

E_H =   electrode potential ($MQ^{-1}L^2t^{-2}$)

$E_H°$ =   standard state electrode potential ($MQ^{-1}L^2t^{-2}$)

$\boldsymbol{E}(t)$ = $\boldsymbol{E}$ curve, an exit age or residence time (t) distribution function for a reactor of arbitrary flow characteristics = $(C_{OUT}/C_\Delta)A_c^{-1}$

$\boldsymbol{E}(\theta)$ =   dimensionless $\boldsymbol{E}$ curve, a dimensionless exit age or residence time ($\theta°$) for a reactor of arbitrary flow characteristics = $(C_{OUT}/C_A)t_m A_c^{-1}$

f =   fugacity ($ML^{-1}t^{-2}$)

         subscripts:

             a =   aqueous phase

             b =   biotic phase

             c =   colloidal phase

             cs =   crystalline solid state

             l =   liquid state

             o =   octanol phase

             p =   pure phase (liquid or solid)

             s =   sorbed phase

             v =   vapor phase

$f°$ =   standard fugacity ($ML^{-1}t^{-2}$)

         subscripts: see fugacity, f

F =   force (MLt^{-2})
            subscripts:
               C =   coulombic (Q^2L^{-2})

$\boldsymbol{F}(t)$ = $\boldsymbol{F}$ curve $= C_{OUT}/C_{IN}$ as a function of time (t) for a *step* input of nonreactive tracer to a reactor of arbitrary flow characteristics

$\boldsymbol{F}(\theta)$ =   dimensionless $\boldsymbol{F}$ curve $= C_{OUT}/C_{IN}$ as a function of dimensionless time ($\theta°$) for a *step* input of nonreactive tracer to a reactor of arbitrary flow characteristics

$\mathcal{F}$ =   Faraday constant: given by the product of Avogadro's number ($\mathcal{N}_{Av} = 6.022 \times 10^{23}$ mol^{-1}) and the elementary charge ($e° = 1.602 \times 10^{-19}$ coulombs); i.e., 96,485 C/mol; 96,485 Joules (23,060 calories) per volt-equivalent

G =   Gibbs free energy (ML^2t^{-2})
            subscripts:
               a =   adsorption
               f =   formation
               l =   liquid phase
               r =   reaction
               v =   vapor phase

$G°$ =   standard-state Gibbs free energy (ML^2t^{-2})
            subscripts: see Gibbs free energy, G

$\mathcal{G}$ =   gravitational acceleration constant (Lt^{-2}) 32.2 ft/s^2; 760 cm/s^2; 6.67×10^{-8} (dyn $-$ cm)^2/g^2

$\boldsymbol{\mathcal{G}}$ =   gravity vector

h =   hydraulic head (L)
            subscripts:
               l =   head loss
               se =   specific energy head

H =   enthalpy (ML^2t^{-2})
            subscripts:
               a =   adsorption
               f =   formation
               l =   liquid phase
               r =   reaction
               v =   vapor phase

H_D =   height or depth (L)
            subscript:
               c =   critical depth

$H°$ =   standard-state enthalpy (ML^2t^{-2})
            subscripts: see enthalpy, H

I =   Helmholtz free energy (ML^2t^{-2})

J =   diffusive flux ($ML^{-2}t^{-1}$)

k =   reaction or mass transfer rate coefficient; if not specifically sub-scripted, k denotes a reaction rate coefficient; its dimensions are dependent on the corresponding reaction order

             subscripts:

a	=	adsorption
d	=	desorption
e	=	effective
f	=	mass transfer (Lt^{-1})
F	=	forward reaction rate coefficient
obs	=	observed
ps	=	pseudo-order rate coefficient
R	=	reverse reaction rate coefficient
v	=	volumetric mass transfer (t^{-1})

$\hat{k}$ =   overall (lumped) reaction rate coefficient (arbitrary dimensions)

$\hat{k}_f$ =   overall two-film mass transfer coefficient (Lt^{-1})

             subscripts:

g	=	relative to the gas-side concentration of a component
l	=	relative to the liquid-side concentration of a component

k° =   first-order surface reaction rate coefficient (Lt^{-1})

             subscripts:

obs	=	observed
ps	=	pseudo first order

K =   equilibrium constant (arbitrary dimensions)

             subscripts:

a	=	acidity or protolysis
f	=	formation

$\mathcal{K}$ =   equilibrium-related constant (arbitrary dimensions)

             subscripts:

B	=	biota or bioconcentration
BM	=	half saturation constant (Monod)
D	=	distribution
F	=	Freundlich
H	=	Henry's (for dimensions, see Table 12.2)
i,j	=	generic $i-j$ phase partition
M	=	Michaelis-Menten
OW	=	octanol-water partition
P	=	partition
s	=	half-saturation
S	=	solubility
v,a	=	$\mathcal{K}_H/\mathcal{R}T$ = vapor-aqueous phase partition coefficient

$\mathcal{K}_H^\circ$ =   dimensionless Henry's constant

L   =   a length dimension (L)

L =   length (L)

    subscripts:

     c =   characteristic

     E =   expanded bed

     F =   fluidized bed

     P =   packed bed

     R =   reactor

     x =   distance from $x = 0$ along x co-ordinate

m =   general variable (arbitrary dimensions); integer number (dimensionless)

M   =   a mass dimension (M)

M =   mass or number of moles of a substance (M or mol)

    subscripts:

     i =   in phase i

     j =   in phase j

     ss =   suspended solids

     T =   total and/or tracer

M_W =   mass wastage rate (MT^{-1})

$M(t)$ =   mass accumulated in time t(M)

n =   general variable (arbitrary dimensions); integer number (dimensionless)

$\boldsymbol{n_v}$ =   normal vector (dimensions associated with vector quantity involved)

$\mathfrak{n}$ =   Freundlich isotherm parameter (MM^{-1} or $molM^{-1}$)

N =   flux ($ML^{-2}t^{-1}$ for mass flux; Mt^{-3} for heat or energy flux)

$N°$ =   flux *to* or *into* a surface or interface ($ML^{-2}t^{-1}$ for mass flux)

$\boldsymbol{N}$ =   flux vector ($ML^{-2}t^{-1}$ for mass flux)

$\mathcal{N}_{Av}$ = 6.022×10^{23} mol^{-1}

$\mathcal{N}_{Bo}$ =   bond number (dimensionless)

$\mathcal{N}_{Ca}$ =   capillary number (dimensionless)

$\mathcal{N}_d$ =   dispersion number (dimensionless)

$\mathcal{N}_{Da,I}$ =   Damkohler number I (dimensionless)

$\mathcal{N}_{Da,II}$ =   Damkohler number II (dimensionless)

$\mathcal{N}_{Eu}$ =   Euler number (dimensionless)

$\mathcal{N}_{Fr}$ =   Froude number (dimensionless)

$\mathcal{N}_{Pe}$ =   Peclet number (dimensionless)

$\mathcal{N}_{Re}$ =   Reynolds number (dimensionless)

$\mathcal{N}_{Sc}$ =   Schmidt number (dimensionless)

$\mathcal{N}_{Sh}$ =   Sherwood number (dimensionless)

p =   partial pressure (dimensionless; see definition of P)

    subscripts:

     i =   component i

p^v	$=$	partial vapor pressure (dimensionless; see definition of P^v)
P	$=$	pressure ($ML^{-1}t^{-2}$)
$\boldsymbol{P}$	$=$	pressure vector
P°	$=$	dimensionless pressure
P^v	$=$	vapor pressure ($ML^{-1}t^{-2}$)
q	$=$	amount of solute sorbed per unit weight of sorbent (MM^{-1} or mol M^{-1})
q_e	$=$	equilibrium value of q
Q	$=$	a measure of the quantity of electricity (Q)
Q	$=$	volumetric flow rate (L^3t^{-1})

subscripts:

g	$=$	gas
l	$=$	liquid
T	$=$	total

Q_H	$=$	heat (ML^2t^{-2} or mol L^2t^{-2}, per mole or unit mass)

subscripts:

m	$=$	melting (fusion)
v	$=$	vaporization

Q_r	$=$	reaction quotient (arbitrary dimensions)
Q°	$=$	capacity

subscripts:

a	$=$	Langmuir isotherm parameter MM^{-1} or mol M^{-1})
f	$=$	fugacity ($L^{-2}t^2$)
H	$=$	specific heat or heat capacity ($ML^2t^{-2}T^{-1}$ or mol $L^2t^{-2}T^{-1}$; per mole or unit mass)
H, V=		volumetric heat ($ML^{-1}t^{-2}T^{-1}$)

r	$=$	characteristic radial distance (L) or direction (dimensionless)

subscripts:

c	$=$	cylindrical coordinates
s	$=$	spherical coordinates

$\boldsymbol{r}$	$=$	reaction rate (arbitrary dimensions; e.g., $ML^{-3}t^{-1}$, Mt^{-1}, mol $L^{-3}t^{-1}$, etc.)

subscripts:

a	$=$	adsorption
BM=		biomass growth rate
d	$=$	desorption
F	$=$	forward reaction
max=		maximum (Michaelis-Menten)
mt	$=$	overall mass transfer rate
obs	$=$	observed
ox	$=$	oxidation
R	$=$	reverse reaction
v	$=$	volatilization

$r°$	=	surface reaction rate (arbitrary dimensions; e.g., $ML^{-2}t^{-1}$, mol $L^{-2}t^{-1}$, etc.)
		subscripts: see reaction rate, r
R	=	radius (L)
		subscripts:

H	=	hydraulic
I	=	inner
N	=	nozzle
O	=	outer
p	=	particle
P	=	pipe

R_L	=	length scaling factor (dimensionless)
R_Q	=	recycle ratio (dimensionless)
R_S	=	stripping factor (dimensionless)
$\mathcal{R}$	=	universal gas constant $(ML^2t^{-2}T^{-1})$ 8.314 J/mol K, 8.314 Pa-m^3/mol-K, 8.21×10^{-5} atm-m^3/mol-K
S	=	entropy (ML^2t^{-2})
$S°$	=	standard-state entropy (ML^2t^{-2})
S_C	=	control surface $(L)^2$
t	=	a time dimension (t)
t	=	time (t)
		subscripts:

c	=	contact
L	=	lag
m	=	mean constituent residence
p	=	residence per pass (recycle reactors)
r	=	mean hydraulic residence
R	=	reaction stage (SBR)
S	=	solids residence

$\bar{t}$	=	average residence time, mean hydraulic residence time, HRT (t)
		subscripts: see time, t
$\bar{t}_n$	=	total mean HRT for n reactors (t)
T	=	temperature
		subscripts:

b	=	boiling
m	=	melting

u	=	general variable (arbitrary dimensions)
		subscripts:

n	=	root of a trigonometric function
0	=	initial value

U	=	internal energy (ML^2t^{-2})

v =   velocity (Lt^{-1})
               subscripts:

a	=	aqueous phase
b	=	bulk
c	=	characteristic
d	=	droplet
f	=	fluidization
l	=	liquid
m	=	mixture
mo	=	molar
p	=	pore or interstitial
r	=	in radial direction r
s	=	superficial or "Darcy"
t	=	terminal settling or rise (e.g., particles or bubbles)
x	=	in direction x

$\boldsymbol{v}$ =   velocity vector
V =   volume (L^3)
               subscripts:

a	=	aqueous phase
B	=	bubble
C	=	control
g	=	gas phase
H	=	head space
I	=	interstitial
m	=	molar $(L^3 mol^{-2})$
p	=	pure phase
P	=	particle
R	=	reactor (generally, the volume of liquid in a reactor)
T	=	total
v	=	vapor phase
V	=	pore or void volume
W	=	water

$V(t)$ =   volume as a function of time (L^3)
               subscripts: see volume, V
W_g =   weight (MLt^{-2})
               subscripts:

e	=	equivalent $(M\ eq^{-1})$
mo	=	molecular $M\ mol^{-1})$
s	=	specific, (weight per unit volume)(ML^{-3})

x =   general variable, characteristic distance (L) or directional coordinate (dimensionless)

X $=$ mole fraction (dimensionless)
subscripts:

a $=$ aqueous phase

g $=$ gas phase

l $=$ liquid phase

m $=$ mass fraction

o $=$ octanol phase

p $=$ pure phase

r $=$ reacted

s $=$ sorbed or solid phase

S $=$ at saturation or solubility limit

v $=$ vapor phase

$X(t)$ $=$ mole fraction as a function of time (dimensionless)
subscripts: see mole fraction, X

y $=$ general variable, characteristic distance (L) or directional coordinate (dimensionless)

Y $=$ finite length in the y direction (L)
subscripts:

W $=$ width in y direction

z $=$ general variable, characteristic distance (L) or directional coordinate (dimensionless)

z° $=$ electronic charge (Q)

Z $=$ finite length in the z direction (L)
subscripts:

B $=$ bubble travel distance

T $=$ tower height $=$ HTU $\times$ NTU

W $=$ width in z direction

2.0   GREEK ALPHABET

α =   coefficient, constant, general variable (arbitrary dimensions)
subscripts:

$\quad$ a =   aqueous-phase solute activity coefficient

$\quad$ D = $0.5\mathcal{N}_d^{-1}$

$\quad$ f =   fugacity coefficient (dimensionless)

$\quad$ o =   octanol-phase solute activity coefficient

$\quad$ p =   pure solute-phase activity coefficient

$\quad$ r =   reaction-characteristic rate coefficient

β =   coefficient, constant, general variable (arbitrary dimensions)
subscripts:

$\quad$ A = $0.4343 E_a / \mathcal{R} T_1 T_2$

$\quad$ a =   Langmuir adsorption-energy parameter

$\quad$ D = $[1 + 4\dfrac{kL}{v_x}\mathcal{N}_d]^{0.5}$ for a first-order homogeneous reaction

$\quad$ P =   empirical parameter relating the partition constant of a solute to its octanol-water partition constant

$\quad$ r =   reaction-characteristic rate coefficient

$\quad$ S =   stripping parameter relating mass transfer rate to gas flow rate (dimensionless)

$\quad$ T = 10^{β_A}

γ =   stoichiometric coefficient (dimensionless)
Γ =   surface excess (mol L^{-2})
δ =   depth, thickness, incremental distance (L)
subscripts:

$\quad$ L =   laminar boundary layer
$\quad$ L, s =   laminar boundary sublayer
$\quad$ m =   medium or membrane
$\quad$ p =   incremental particle movement
$\quad$ T =   turbulent boundary layer

ϵ = porosity or void ratio (dimensionless)
  subscripts:
  B = bed
  d = domain
  p = particle
ζ = arbitrary space variable or coordinate position
ζ° = length ratio or $x/2(\mathcal{D}_a t)^{0.5}$ (dimensionless)
η = efficiency, effectiveness, efficiency factor (dimensionless)
  subscripts:
  R, E= external reaction efficiency factor
θ° = ratio of specific time to average time $t/\bar{t}$ (dimensionless)
κ = arbitrary constant (arbitrary dimensions)
μ = chemical potential (ML^2t^{-2})
μ° = standard chemical potential (ML^2t^{-2})
μ_m = arithmetic mean value, first moment of the centroid of an empirical frequency distribution about its origin (arbitrary dimensions)
μ_v = dynamic viscosity $(ML^{-1}t^{-1})$
ν_v = kinematic viscosity (L^2t^{-1})
ξ = permeability (L^2)
π = 3.14159...
Π° = parameter group in the Buckingham Pi theorem (dimensionless)
ρ = density (ML^{-3})
  subscripts:
  a = aqueous phase
  b = biota (apparent)
  B = bulk (bed)
  bm = biomass (apparent)
  d = droplet or bubble
  g = gas
  l = liquid
  m = suspending medium
  mo = molar
  n = nonaqueous phase
  p = particle or object (apparent)
  s = solid phase (apparent)
  W = water
σ = standard deviation, root-mean-square value of the deviations of a set of observations from the mean value of those observations, the square root of the second moment of the centroid of an empirical frequency distribution about its mean (arbitrary dimensions)

σ^2 =   variance, the second moment of the centroid of an empirical frequency distribution about its mean (arbitrary dimensions)

subscripts:

     t =   second moment about $t = t_m$

     θ° =   second moment about $t = \bar{t}$

σ° =   surface tension Mt^{-2})

subscripts:

     a =   aqueous phase

     f =   of surface with fractional monolayer coverage

     n =   nonaqueous phase

     o =   of original pure solvent

     s =   of surface covered with a complete monolayer (saturated)

ϕ =   angle (degrees or radians)

ϕ° =   fraction, ratio, or coefficient (dimensionless)

subscripts:

     d =   diameter ratio

     D =   solute distribution parameter

     f =   fugacity coefficient

     g =   fractional gas hold-up

     m =   of monolayer adsorbed or surface covered

     V, N=   nonaqueous phase volumetric fraction

     OC =   organic carbon

     r =   reacted

     R =   remaining

     V =   volume ratio or fraction

     VM=   viscosity mobility

$\phi(\cdot)$ =   function of $(\cdot)$

Φ = $\left[\alpha_D - \dfrac{(\alpha_D^2 + u_n^2)\theta^\circ}{2\alpha_o} \right]$

ψ =   system specific coefficient (arbitrary dimensions)

3.0 MATHEMATICAL NOTATION

$\dfrac{dx}{dy}$ = ordinary derivative of x with respect to y

$\dfrac{\partial x}{\partial y}$ = partial derivative of x with respect to y

erf $(\cdot)$ = error function of $(\cdot)$

erfc $(\cdot)$ = error function complement of $(\cdot)$

Δ = finite increment of change in a variable (dimensions related to the variable)

$\sum(\cdot)$ = sum of quantities $i \ldots n$

$\prod(\cdot)$ = product of quantities $i \ldots n$

∇ = del operator, three-dimensional gradient of a variable (dimensions associated with variable)

4.0   COMMONLY ABBREVIATED TERMS

ADR   =   Advection-dispersion-reaction equation/model
CMBR =   Completely mixed batch reactor
CMFR =   Completely mixed flow reactor
CRT   =   Constituent residence time
erf(·)   =   Error function (·)
erfc(·) =   Error function complement (·)
FBR   =   Fixed bed reactor
FMT   =   Film mass transfer
HRT   =   Hydraulic residence time
HTU   =   Height of a transfer unit
IMT   =   Intraparticle mass transfer
ISR   =   Internal surface reaction
LDM   =   Linear distribution model
MBE   =   Material (or mass) balance equation
NTU   =   Number of transfer units
PDES =   *Process Dynamics in Environmental Systems*
PFR   =   Plug flow reactor
PFDR =   PFR with dispersion
RTD   =   Residence time distribution
RTI   =   Reaction time interval
SBR   =   Sequencing batch reactor
SRT   =   Solids residence time

Indices

Contents

1.0 INTRODUCTION TO ENVIRONMENTAL PROCESSES AND SYSTEMS

2.0 PROCESS ENERGETICS AND EQUILIBRIA

3.0 PROCESS RATES AND MASS TRANSFER

5.0 EXAMPLES

6.0 SELECTED SUBJECTS